# Audubon
# Wildlife Report
# 1987

# Audubon
# Wildlife Report
# 1987

Roger L. Di Silvestro
*Editor*

William J. Chandler
*Research Director*

Katherine Barton
*Assistant Research Director*

Lillian Labate
*Editorial Assistant*

## The National Audubon Society
New York, New York

1987

ACADEMIC PRESS, INC.
**Harcourt Brace Jovanovich, Publishers**
Orlando   San Diego   New York   Austin
Boston   London   Sydney   Tokyo   Toronto

*18h NAS*

Academic Press Rapid Manuscript Reproduction

COVER PHOTO: G. C. Kelley/Photo Researchers, Inc.

ACADEMIC PRESS, INC.
Orlando, Florida 32887

*United Kingdom Edition published by*
ACADEMIC PRESS INC. (LONDON) LTD.
24–28 Oval Road, London NW1 7DX

LIBRARY OF CONGRESS CATALOG CARD NUMBER: 86 — 643440

ISSN 0885—6044
ISBN 0—12—041000—1

PRINTED IN THE UNITED STATES OF AMERICA

87 88 89 90      9 8 7 6 5 4 3 2 1

# Contents

Foreword    ix
*Donal C. O'Brien, Jr.*

Preface    xi
*Roger L. Di Silvestro*

Acknowledgments    xv

Contents of Previous Volumes    xvii

## Part One. The Featured Agency

Bureau of Land Management    3
*Katherine Barton*

## Part Two. Federal Agencies and Programs

Federal Grants for State Wildlife Conservation    63
*William J. Chandler*
Migratory Bird Protection and Management    83
*William J. Chandler*
Federal Inland Fisheries Management    107
*William J. Chandler and Richard Magder*
Federal Marine Fisheries Management    131
*Michael Weber*
The Federal Endangered Species Program    147
*Michael J. Bean*
Marine Mammal Protection    163
*Michael Weber*
Federal Wetlands Protection Programs    179
*Katherine Barton*
Water Projects and Wildlife    201
*Ruth Norris*
The Federal Animal Damage Control Program    223
*Ruth Norris*

The National Wildlife Refuge System    239
  *Ruth Norris and Cynthia Lenhart*
Wildlife and the U.S. Forest Service    265
  *Katherine Barton*
Wildlife and the National Park Service    291
  *Richard C. Curry*
International Wildlife Conservation    307
  *Michael J. Bean*
Federal Fish and Wildlife Agency Budgets    321
  *Katherine Barton*

## Part Three. Species Accounts

The Walrus    357
  *John L. Sease and Francis H. Fay*
The Mission Blue Butterfly    371
  *Richard A. Arnold*
The Wood Duck    381
  *Frank C. Bellrose and Robert A. Heister*
The Bobcat    399
  *Gary Koehler*
The Lynx    411
  *Stephen DeStefano*
The Cui-ui    425
  *Chester C. Buchanan and Mark E. Coleman*
The Running Buffalo Clover    439
  *Judy F. Jacobs and Rodney L. Bartgis*
The Black-Footed Ferret    447
  *Max Schroeder*
The Southern Sea Otter    457
  *Wilbur N. Ladd, Jr., and Marianne L. Riedman*
The Red-Cockaded Woodpecker    479
  *Jerome A. Jackson*
The Elk    495
  *Jack Ward Thomas and Larry D. Bryant*
The Piping Plover    509
  *Susan M. Haig and Lewis W. Oring*
The Black Bear    521
  *Michael Pelton*
The Rough-Leaved Loosestrife    531
  *Nora Murdock*
The Paiute Trout    539
  *Bob Behnke*

# Part Four. Appendices

Appendix A.  Forest Service Directory    549
Appendix B.  U.S. Fish and Wildlife Service Directory    553
Appendix C.  National Park Service Directory    558
Appendix D.  Bureau of Land Management Directory    561
Appendix E.  Wetlands Management Directory    563
Appendix F.  National Marine Fisheries Service
    Directory    568
Appendix G.  Budget Information Contacts on Federal Fish
    and Wildlife Programs    570
Appendix H.  Congressional Contacts and Addresses    572
Appendix I.  The Federal Endangered and Threatened
    Species List    576
Appendix J.  The National Wildlife Refuge System
    Directory    604
Appendix K.  Land and Water Conservation Fund:
    Appropriations by Agency, 1981–1987    615
Appendix L.  The National Forest Plan Status Report and
    Appeals    628
Appendix M.  Budget Histories of Agencies with Fish and
    Wildlife Habitat Management Responsibilities: FWS,
    BLM, USFS, NPS, NMFS    652

Index    675

# Foreword

Since its inception more than 80 years ago, the National Audubon Society has maintained a firm commitment to the wise use and conservation of wildlife resources, to promoting an understanding of wildlife issues, and to encouraging biological research and the dissemination of its results. All of these goals so central to the Audubon Society come together in the *Audubon Wildlife Report* series.

The first volume of the series reached readers less than two years ago. Yet already the report has earned a reputation among conservationists as the definitive text on wildlife management in the United States. It contains a rich body of facts and data, much of it never before compiled within the pages of a single book.

The *Wildlife Report* series has sought to maintain a high level of objectivity, letting facts speak for themselves. The reports are not a forum for opinions on various wildlife issues. They are instead sourcebooks of hard facts that should be a boon to any conservationist who has attempted to labor over the mountain of data and documents that overshadows federal and state wildlife management work.

This volume attempts to cover the many important events that highlighted wildlife conservation last year. Among these may be found much cause for optimism. Last year, for example, major changes were made in the plan for the Garrison Diversion Unit, a massive federal water development project that for years threatened to inundate a vital waterfowl habitat in North Dakota. The modifications of the Garrison plan may be a harbinger for a whole new approach to the construction and development of federal water projects, an approach that seeks to balance the needs of wildlife, people, and economic growth.

Headway also was made in a plan to establish a new sea otter population off the coast of California. This move would help ensure against the possibility that a major oil spill within the range of the California sea otter would wipe out the whole subspecies, now composed of a single population found along some 200 miles of California coast. Opposition to establishing the second population is strong, but the groundwork for negotiating an agreement on the plan is in place.

Similarly, plans are in the making to reintroduce wolves to Yellowstone National Park. It is encouraging that such a plan is being discussed, even if fruition is still many months away. Not many years have passed, after all, since federal agencies were in the frontline of efforts to extirpate, rather than repatriate, the wolf.

Progress of this type is founded upon an informed citizenry. Information placed in the right hands is the key to garnering support for better management of the nation's grasslands and old-growth forests, for better monitoring of migratory birds, for better protection of endangered, threatened, and nongame species. The *Audubon Wildlife Report* represents a massive effort to provide that vital information for the many active conservationists who are making wildlife management successful in the United States. In this connection, I would like to recognize Amos S. Eno, who first conceived the *Audubon Wildlife Report* and who led the effort that has resulted in its publication.

I hope that you, too, will find cause for optimism in the vast body of information before you. I hope, also, that that optimism will generate the energy and enthusiasm required for the continued success of wildlife conservation in America.

Donal C. O'Brien, Jr.
*Chairman of the Board*
*National Audubon Society*

# Preface

Wildlife management and its attendant science, wildlife biology, are among the youngest of the life sciences. Indeed, it was not until Aldo Leopold, who started his career as a federal forester, published the classic *Wildlife Management* in 1933 that the field took on the trappings of a formal profession.

Because of its youth, wildlife management is still changing. For example, the study and management of wildlife has become increasingly politicized in the brunt of recent human population pressures. Consequently, wildlife managers often have to place politics before biology, something their immediate professional forebears might never have thought necessary. The wildlife manager cannot presume, for example, to reintroduce red wolves, now extinct in the wild, into their ancestral home range without first considering the interests and concerns of hunters. Grizzly bear biologists cannot hope to properly protect the last of the Lower-48 grizzlies without attending to the opinions and positions of hikers and campers, logging companies, ski-lodge developers, livestockmen, and a host of others. Those who wish to save endangered fishes, insects, and mollusks from water impoundment projects cannot do so without encountering, understanding, and negotiating with power-plant developers, irrigators, and the vast and often forbidding federal bureaucracy that encompasses both endangered species conservation and the building of dams and power plants.

To work successfully with these various special interest groups requires a clear understanding of the political and bureaucratic ramifications of many conservation issues. It also requires a thorough comprehension of how the federal government conducts conservation policy. Unfortunately, the many federal agencies that direct the nation's wildlife-policy administration can seem monolithic and impenetrable to the biologist, the student, the attorney, the conservationist, the educator, and even the legislator. Yet understanding how the federal bureaucracy works is so essential to successful wildlife conservation that it cannot be ignored.

The *Audubon Wildlife Report* is an attempt by the National Audubon Society to gather together much of the diverse data about federal wildlife-policy administration and make it easily accessible to anyone interested in the conservation of wildlife resources. It does this by providing, much of it for the first time anywhere, a vast array of data on federal wildlife management, including comparative tables on the budgeting process. It examines many federal wildlife programs, from the migratory bird protection program, which in a sense gave birth to the federal role in wildlife conservation, to the endangered species program, called the most important wildlife conservation effort in the world. It features discussions of the many important wildlife issues that were highlighted the past year.

This third volume of the *Audubon Wildlife Report* features the Bureau of Land Management in an opening chapter that surveys the vast range of wildlife issues in which the Bureau is involved. In presenting this major chapter, the *Audubon Wildlife Report 1987* follows a tradition set by the two previous volumes. The 1985 book featured the U.S. Fish and Wildlife Service, and the 1986 book featured the U.S. Forest Service.

Much of the historical and administrative background of the agencies and programs covered in the report series was included in the first two volumes. This information is vital to a full understanding of the issues and agendas of wildlife conservation in the United States. However, these historical data are repeated here only where necessary for illumination of a particular issue.

With some exceptions, the agency chapters are organized as follows:

*Overview* — a brief discussion of salient historical points
*Current Developments* — an examination of significant problems and concerns confronted by conservationists in 1986
*Legislative Developments* — bills enacted during the 99th Congress (1985–1986) and how they affect wildlife programs
*Legal Developments* — a discussion of significant court cases decided in 1986

The species account chapters, all written by biologists expert in the particular species, follow this outline:

*Species Description and Natural History* — what the species looks like, where and how it lives
*Significance of the Species* — a discussion of its biological importance and its value to man
*Historical Perspective* — an examination of the developments that led to the species' current status
*Current Trends* — a discussion of the problems and successes presently affecting the species

*Management*—a description of what wildlife professionals are doing to protect and preserve the species

*Prognosis*—a prediction about what could happen to the species within the near future

*Recommendations*—a discussion of what should be done to ensure the species' survival

As did previous volumes, this edition closes with numerous appendices that include lists of personnel contacts, budget data, and other material useful to conservation activists and professionals.

Thanks go to the many readers who last year returned to Audubon the questionnaire sent out with each book. The responses were helpful in determining how well the book is meeting reader needs and in setting the agenda for future volumes. Any new suggestions or comments would be welcome and should be sent to Wildlife Report, National Audubon Society, 950 Third Avenue, New York, New York 10022.

Roger L. Di Silvestro
*Editor*

# Acknowledgments

The *Audubon Wildlife Report* has now reached its third year, an accomplishment that would not have been possible without the generosity and support of the following individuals and foundations to whom we owe a deep and great debt:

Avatar Holdings, Inc.; Bowater Incorporated; James A. Buss; Peter Coors–Adolph Coors Company; Forbes Foundation; Merrill G. and Emita E. Hastings Foundation; Henry J. and Drue E. Heinz Foundation; W. Alton Jones Foundation; Robert H. Kanzler; Lakeside Foundation; Mr. and Mrs. Patrick F. Noonan; Mary Norris Preyer Oglesby; Nathaniel P. Reed; Peter Sharp; L. A. Shelton; H. R. Slack; Peter Stroh; The Stroh Foundation; Tides Foundation; Union Camp Corporation; Charlotte C. Weber; Frederick and Margaret L. Weyerhaeuser Foundation; the Williams Companies; Robert Winthrop Charitable Trust.

Special recognition goes to Amos S. Eno, who has left the National Audubon Society to work for the Department of the Interior. While at Audubon, he made many positive and lasting contributions to wildlife conservation in America. He was the inspiration and driving force behind this series, the *Audubon Wildlife Report*.

For their help in the preparation and review of material for this volume, thanks are due to the Marine Mammal Commission, U.S. Fish and Wildlife Service, National Marine Fisheries Service, National Park Service, Department of State, Department of the Interior, U.S. Army Corps of Engineers, Environmental Protection Agency, Bureau of Land Management, Department of Agriculture, U.S. Forest Service, Department of Agriculture Extension Service, House Merchant Marine and Fisheries Committee, Senate Environment and Public Works Committee, House Interior and Insular Affairs Committee, Canadian Wildlife Service, Columbia River Intertribal Fish Commission, North Atlantic Salmon Treaty Organization, International Union for the Conservation of Nature and Natural Resources, International Association of Fish and Wildlife Agencies, Defenders of Wildlife, National Parks and Conservation Association, National Wildlife Federation, Izaak Walton League of America, Natural Resources Defense Council, Sierra Club Legal Defense Fund, Environmental Defense Fund, Sport Fishing Institute,

Wildlife Management Institute, Friends of the Earth, the American Fisheries Society, the Environmental Policy Institute, and the Center for Environmental Education. Special thanks goes to the Wilderness Society for help in producing the forest plans table in the appendices.

Thanks also are extended to the National Audubon Society's Mary McCarthy, for her vigorous and accurate production of the many graphs that appear in this volume; Mercedes Lee, for her efforts in the final days of editorial production; Chris Wille, for continued guidance; and Charlene Dougherty, Maureen Hinkle, Cynthia Lenhart, and Whit Tilt for their advice and review.

# Contents of
# Previous Volumes

## Audubon Wildlife Report 1985

**Part One. The Featured Agency**

The U.S. Fish and Wildlife Service
  *William J. Chandler*

**Part Two. Federal Agencies and Programs**

Migratory Bird Protection and Management
  *William J. Chandler*
The Endangered Species Program
  *Dennis Drabelle*
Inland Fisheries Management
  *William J. Chandler*
The Federal Animal Damage Control Program
  *Roger L. Di Silvestro*
The National Wildlife Refuge System
  *Dennis Drabelle*
Marine Mammal Protection
  *Michael Weber*
Wetlands Preservation
  *Katherine Barton*
Federal Funding for Wildlife Conservation
  *Dennis Drabelle*
Wildlife and the National Park Service
  *Chris Elfring*
Wildlife and the U.S. Forest Service
  *Whit Fosburgh*
Wildlife and the Bureau of Land Management
  *Katherine Barton*

**Part Three. Species Accounts**

The California Condor
  *John C. Ogden*
The Grizzly Bear
  *Chris Servheen*
The Striped Bass
  *Whit Fosburgh*
Arctic Geese
  Introduction
    *David Cline*
  The Cackling Canada Goose
    *William Butler*
  The Dusky Canada Goose
    *David Cline and Cynthia Lenhart*
  The Aleutian Canada Goose
    *Michael J. Amaral*
  The Black Brant
    *Christian P. Dau and Mary E. Hogan*
  The Pacific White-Fronted Goose
    *Calvin J. Lensink*
  The Emperor Goose
    *Margaret R. Petersen*
The Wood Stork
  *John C. Ogden*
The Desert Bighorn
  *Allen Cooperrider*
The Puerto Rican Parrot
  *Kirk M. Horn*
The Woodland Caribou
  *Michael Scott*
The Bald Eagle
  *Nancy Green*

The Green Pitcher Plant
  *E. LaVerne Smith*
The West Indian Manatee
  *Patrick M. Rose*
Hawaiian Birds
  *J. Michael Scott and John L. Sincock*

**Part Four. Appendices**

Directory of Key Personnel
U.S. Fish and Wildlife Service
National Park Service Regional Offices
  and Contacts
U.S. Forest Service
Fishery Assistance Offices

Cooperative Fish and Wildlife Research
  Units
FWS Research Laboratories and Centers
Regional Species of Special Emphasis
National Species and Species Groups of
  Special Emphasis
Types of Permits Issued by the FWS
Origin, Size, and Cost of National
  Wildlife Refuges
Endangered and Threatened Wildlife and
  Plants

Index

# Audubon Wildlife Report 1986

**Part One. The Featured Agency**

The U.S. Forest Service
  *Katherine Barton*
Wildlife Issues in the National
Forest System
  *Whit Fosburgh*

**Part Two. Federal Agencies and
Programs**

Federal Grants for State Wildlife
Conservation
  *William J. Chandler*
Migratory Bird Protection and
Management
  *William J. Chandler*
Federal Marine Fisheries Management
  *Michael Weber*
The Endangered Species Program
  *Michael J. Bean*
Federal Wetlands Protection
Programs
  *Katherine Barton*
The National Wildlife Refuge
System
  *Wendy Smith Lee*
Wildlife and the National Park
Service
  *Chris Elfring*
Wildlife and the Bureau of Land
Management
  *Katherine Barton*
International Wildlife Conservation
  *Michael J. Bean*

**Part Three. Conservation and the States**

State Wildlife Conservation: An
Overview
  *William J. Chandler*
State Wildlife Law Enforcement
  *William J. Chandler*
State Nongame Wildlife Programs
  *Susan Cerulean and Whit Fosburgh*

**Part Four. Species Accounts**

The Whooping Crane
  *James C. Lewis*
The Common Loon
  *Judy McIntyre*
The Atlantic Salmon
  *Lawrence W. Stolte*
Chinook Salmon of the Columbia
River Basin
  *Lloyd A. Phinney*
The Spotted Owl
  *Eric Forsman and E. Charles
  Meslow*
Sage Grouse
  *Robert Autenrieth*
The Small Whorled Pogonia
  *Richard W. Dyer*
The Polar Bear
  *Steven C. Amstrup*
The Peregrine Falcon
  *Gerald Craig*
The Hooded Warbler
  *George V. N. Powell and
  John H. Rappole*

The Black Duck
  *Howard E. Spencer, Jr.*
The Red Knot
  *Brian Harrington*
The Osprey
  *Mark A. Westall*
Lange's Metalmark Butterfly
  *Paul A. Opler and Lee Robinson*
Kemp's Ridley Sea Turtle
  *Jack B. Woody*
The Loggerhead Shrike
  *James D.Fraser and*
  *David R. Luukkonen*
The Knowlton Cactus
  *Peggy Olwell*
The Gray Wolf
  *Rolf O. Peterson*

**Part Five. Appendices**

Forest Service Directory
U.S. Fish and Wildlife Service Directory
National Park Service Directory
Bureau of Land Management Directory

Wetlands Management Directory
Federal Offices Involved in the
  Management of Marine Fisheries and
  the Conservation of Marine Mammals
Budget Information Contacts on Federal
  Fish and Wildlife Programs
Congressional Contacts and Addresses
Major Population Objectives, Status and
  Trends of Migratory Bird Species of
  Special Management Emphasis
The Development of Annual Waterfowl
  Hunting Regulations
Permit Requirements for Federally
  Protected Fish and Wildlife Species
Species and Special Groups for Which
  National Resource Plans Are Prepared
  by FWS
Fish and Wildlife Species for Which
  Regional Resource Plans are Prepared
National Forest System Acreage by State
  as of September 30, 1984

Index

# Part One

# The Featured Agency

An ancient giant falls in a Bureau of Land Management forest near Mill City, Oregon. Cutting of old-growth timber on Bureau lands in the Northwest Pacific is one of the most controversial of BLM wildlife issues. *Bureau of Land Management*

# Bureau of Land Management

Katherine Barton

## OVERVIEW

The Bureau of Land Management (BLM) manages more land than any other federal agency. It oversees more than 270 million acres, which comprise approximately an eighth of the land in the United States and about 60 percent of all land under federal jurisdiction. BLM also has jurisdiction over mineral resources that underlie an additional 300 million acres of land administered by state or other federal agencies or in private ownership.

The public lands provide a permanent or seasonal home for some 3,000 species of mammals, birds, reptiles, fish, and amphibians. BLM lands include virtually every major type of ecosystem found west of the Mississippi, including the Sonoran and Mojave deserts of the Southwest; the glaciers, arctic plains, and forests of Alaska; the rich old-growth stands of Douglas fir in the Pacific Northwest; and the canyon-carved plateaus of the Rocky Mountains. No other agency manages land with as much visual and ecological variety.

The public lands protect essential and rare fish and wildlife habitats. Eighty-five percent of desert bighorn sheep in the United States reside on the public lands. The 25-million-acre California

Audubon Wildlife Report 1987

3

Desert Conservation Area is home to more than 700 species of flowering plants, including 217 species found nowhere else in the world. The Snake River Birds of Prey Natural Area in Idaho harbors the densest nesting population of birds of prey in the world. BLM lands support 122 federally listed endangered and threatened species of plants and animals, as well as hundreds of species under consideration for future listing. The bureau also manages vital remnants of riparian and aquatic ecosystems on which a majority of wildlife species depend.

Fish and wildlife, however, are just one of many natural resources managed by BLM. The major law covering the management of the public lands, the Federal Land Policy and Management Act (43 U.S.C. 1701 *et seq.*), requires BLM to manage for multiple uses. In addition to fish and wildlife habitat, BLM manages the public lands for energy-resource development, hardrock mining, timber production, livestock grazing, utility rights-of-way, recreation, and protection of cultural resources and natural scenic and scientific values, and as range for wild horses and burros. Thus the management of wildlife habitat on the public lands is a balancing act, a matter of trade-offs among competing uses.

## BLM History and Politics

BLM is criticized frequently and heavily by conservation organizations. They charge that the bureau defers to the wishes of the livestock industry at the expense of wildlife and other resources, gives preference to commodity uses of BLM lands, does not manage for balanced multiple use, and has not restored its largely deteriorated lands to a satisfactory condition. While these charges are true in part, political pressures and the circumstances surrounding the bureau's establishment can make it difficult for BLM to do otherwise, as discussed below.[1]

*Location and Type of Lands.* BLM manages lands leftover after the homesteaders, states, railroads, and other federal land systems took what they wanted from the public domain. Large forested tracts and spectacular scenic areas were reserved from the public domain as national forests and national parts. Lands with the highest productivity and best water sources were claimed by homesteaders. Railroads were granted alternating, "checkerboard" sections of land along their rights-of-way. States were granted substantial amounts of land, usually in small scattered parcels, to provide revenues for public roads and schools.

1. The roots of BLM's current problems are discussed in more detail in an article by Sally Fairfax (Fairfax 1984), from which part of this discussion is drawn.

BLM therefore is left with lands that generally have low productive potential and that frequently form no logical management units. Much of this property is scattered among lands in state, local, or private ownership. BLM land-management decisions thus frequently influence management on surrounding nonfederal lands and may be highly controversial. On the other hand, BLM has substantial opportunities for consolidating the ownership of lands containing important resources by making land exchanges — an approach the bureau has used to gain management control over critical environmental resources in certain areas.

***Poor Range Condition.***  Almost all the acreage under BLM management in the lower 48 states had been degraded seriously by heavy overgrazing of livestock at the time it came under federal management. With the enactment of the Taylor Grazing Act in 1934, the federal government was directed to manage the public lands for livestock grazing and at the same time to improve range condition. In 1936, the first range-condition study found 84 percent of the range in unsatisfactory (poor to fair) condition. Most experts agree that range condition has improved somewhat under federal management, although to what degree is uncertain.[2] Regardless, the majority of the public range clearly is still seriously deteriorated and producing far below its potential.

Recent reports on desertification in the United States indicate that much of the western range is in poor condition, including lands managed by BLM. According to a 1981 report by the President's Council on Environmental Quality, approximately 225 million acres in the United States — an area roughly the size of the 13 original states — is undergoing severe or very severe desertification, and almost twice this area is threatened with desertification (Sheridan 1981). A study on desertification in North America estimated that approximately 10,500 square miles has undergone "very severe" desertification, an amount almost double that on the African continent. A significant portion of two[3] of the three large areas of very severe desertification, all of which have been subjected to heavy livestock grazing, are under BLM management (Sheridan 1981).

This legacy leaves BLM with a difficult job. As one range scientist explained, "It is obvious that BLM has the responsibility for managing

2. In 1984, BLM — using inventories on 98 million acres and "professional judgment" on 70 million acres — reported that only 60 percent of the range was in unsatisfactory condition, nearly a 30 percent improvement since 1934 (Department of Interior 1984a). In 1984, two conservation groups, using BLM data on 118 million acres, reported that 81 percent of the range was still in unsatisfactory condition (Wald and Albersworth 1985). Neither study was based on comprehensive inventory or monitoring data.

3. In New Mexico and Idaho.

most of the land lowest in productive potential in the U.S. In addition, the land it received to manage in 1934 was already seriously depleted. Those are difficult conditions to overcome" (Box *et al.* 1979).

***Range Politics.*** These problems are compounded by BLM's political legacy. The agency has a history of domination by the livestock industry, arising out of the early implementation of the Taylor Grazing Act (43 U.S.C. 315 *et seq.*). The first two stated purposes of the law were to halt overgrazing and soil deterioration on the public lands and to provide for range improvement. But the law was implemented primarily to accomplish the third purpose: to stabilize the western livestock industry, which was suffering as a result of the uncontrolled use and overgrazing of the public-domain range.

The first director of the agency—which was first called the Division of Grazing and was later renamed the Grazing Service—was a livestock operator who established and relied largely on grazing advisory boards, composed of livestock operators, to help administer the range. A 1936 amendment to the Taylor Grazing Act required all senior Grazing Service officials to be residents of the states they served and to have practical range experience. This provision favored personnel with ranching backgrounds over those with scientific training and made it likely that the agency's staff would be sympathetic to the needs of those they were regulating. Grazing permits were allocated to individuals with private "base" property—essentially tying the permits to that property—and permits were issued for periods of 10 years with almost certain renewal. The Taylor Grazing Act specified that the administration of grazing was an interim measure pending the public domain's final disposal, and it was not until 1976 that Congress declared that the public lands would remain in public ownership. All these factors encouraged livestock operators to view grazing on the public lands as a right, rather than as a privilege granted to them by the public.

The livestock industry's political power is wielded in several ways. The industry intimidates BLM into transferring, demoting, or firing field staff that rile local interests by exerting what is seen as too strong a management hand. And it uses pressure from allies in Congress, state legislatures or agencies, and the Interior Department to have decisions by BLM field staff overturned at upper levels. Such tactics not only result in the specific policy changes sought, but can cause BLM personnel to second-guess agency politics and to be wary of going out on a limb to make tough management decisions. Congress at times also has stifled BLM management and control of its lands by slashing funding and personnel.[4]

4. Various examples of such political manipulation of BLM are described in *Public Land Politics* by Philip Foss (1960).

The most extreme tactic, used several times since the beginning of federal range management, has been the threat by states and local private interests to wrest BLM lands from federal control. Such land grabs have never progressed very far, but the firestorm of criticism and intimidation they bring with them inhibits the agency's ability to exert control. The most recent example is the so-called Sagebrush Rebellion of the late 1970s, which had the stated goal of privatizing the public lands but the implicit, more practical goal of reducing federal interference in and control of the land's management.

The livestock industry's political clout has been aided by the general lack of public and congressional interest in the public domain. Westerners traditionally have dominated the public land subcommittees in Congress and continue to do so today, while eastern legislators have placed their priorities elsewhere. Conservation and environmental groups began to show interest in these lands only in the 1970s, and even now most environmental organizations only sporadically focus on BLM issues.

***Internal History.*** Finally, BLM is still partly a captive of its bureaucratic roots. The bureau was created in 1946 out of two beleaguered agencies: the Grazing Service and the General Land Office. The Grazing Service had been consistently under funded and understaffed. This was largely the result of Interior Secretary Harold Ickes' promise that the administration of the public lands would be cheap and the bureaucracy small, a promise made in order to convince Congress to place administration of the lands under the Department of the Interior rather than under the Forest Service in the Department of Agriculture. The bureau's limited budget and staff remain a problem today.

Also important are the missions of the BLM precursor agencies. The Grazing Service was staffed by range personnel with the mission of supporting the livestock industry. The General Land Office, a paper-shuffling agency with a reputation for corruption, was responsible for disposing of the public lands, administering the hardrock mining laws, and issuing industry energy and mineral leases. More recently, a merger of some Minerals Management Service activities into BLM brought additional minerals responsibilities and personnel into the agency. Although BLM added a substantial number of staff from other professions in the 1970s, some critics maintain that BLM is still — by virtue of the types of staff in top positions and its historical mandates — dominated by grazing and minerals concerns. In addition, the BLM director is by law a political appointee — a factor frequently blamed for some of BLM's lack of independence, highly political nature, and wide swings in management philosophies.

While politics outside and inside the Interior Department often are blamed for impeding sound management of BLM lands, observers of the agency have consistent praise for its staff. A frequent critic of the agency has said that harsh words about BLM "must be tempered by praise for individuals within it" (Coggins 1984). Another public land expert has called BLM personnel "its major asset. Far from being servile captives of industry, they have bent without breaking and have stood for something. The resilience and dedication of Bureau personnel is the BLM's major resource for future development" (Fairfax 1984).

**BLM Today**

A recent study of federal natural-resource agencies called BLM a "shooting star" — an agency that burned brightly for a short period of time, rising quickly only to face a relatively precarious future (Clarke and McCool 1985). This characterization is certainly true of BLM treatment of noncommodity resources in recent years.

In the mid-1970s, several events combined to increase sharply BLM's focus on wildlife and other noncommodity resources. As a result of a court order directing BLM to prepare more than 100 separate environmental impact statements on its grazing program, BLM hired numerous renewable-resources specialists and began detailed inventories of much of its lands. With the passage of the Federal Land Policy and Management Act in 1976, BLM received permanent authority to retain the public lands and to manage them for multiple uses. And under the aggressive implementation of the act by the Carter administration, BLM received badly needed increases in budget and staff — particularly for noncommodity resource management — and moved fairly quickly to reduce livestock grazing to the carrying capacity of the range. BLM was still criticized by fish and wildlife interests for favoring commodity resources and moving too slowly to achieve true multiple-use management, but most critics thought the bureau was moving in the right direction.

Then, just as BLM began to make progress, the Sagebrush Rebellion, fueled in part by BLM actions, called for less federal intervention in western land management and ultimately a return of these lands to the states. With the election of self-proclaimed sagebrush rebel Ronald Reagan — and the appointment of a BLM grazing permittee, Robert Burford, as BLM director — the bureau's multiple-use mission has suffered. The administration proposed sharp cuts in budget and staff, particularly in renewable-resource programs, and revamped regulations and policies on grazing, land-use planning, water rights, forest management in western Oregon, and energy and minerals development. BLM generally describes these changes as providing needed regulatory reform, promoting the more efficient management necessary to reduce federal spending, and improving coordination and cooperation with the states and with local users of the public lands.

Conservation organizations maintain that the changes are intended to and in fact have had the effect of giving priority to commodity uses, reducing the federal management control and initiatives necessary to ensure protection of noncommodity resources, and deferring to the wishes of livestock permittees on matters of range management.

Proposed budget cuts have been repudiated partially by Congress, and some of the regulatory changes have been blocked in court by conservation organizations. At the field level, many of BLM's professional and highly committed personnel still have been able to undertake some significant initiatives for fish and wildlife conservation. BLM has given greater attention to riparian area management and in some areas to using range-improvement funds for fish- and wildlife-habitat enhancement, after these issues were raised by conservationists in draft range legislation. But in general, progress toward balanced multiple-use management on the public lands has substantially slowed under the revamped priorities.

These changes come at a time when population growth in the West is placing increasing demands on the noncommodity resources of the public lands. A recent governor's task force on recreation in Arizona, for example, reported that "recreation has become the single most important use of our federal lands in Arizona" (Babbit 1986). The report concluded: "The Task Force believes that federal policies for land management in Arizona are inappropriately biased toward traditional 'commodity' uses of the federal lands, such as timber, mining, and grazing." Whether BLM will be able to meet these future challenges remains to be seen. The authors of the shooting star theory of BLM management say that "perhaps more than any agency, BLM has undergone rapid changes to its mission and priorities" under the Reagan administration and warn that "its future is in doubt" (Clarke and McCool 1985).

## ORGANIZATION AND RESPONSIBILITIES

### Land Base

BLM manages approximately 272 million acres. Approximately 177 million acres is in the 10 western states: Arizona, California, Colorado, Idaho, Montana, Nevada, New Mexico, Oregon, Utah, and Wyoming. BLM also administers roughly 95 million acres in Alaska. BLM acreage in Alaska has declined steadily as it has transferred lands into state and Alaska Native ownership in order to comply with land-settlement agreements. When these transfers are complete, BLM will be left to manage approximately 65 million acres in Alaska. Outside of these 11 states, BLM manages only a few hundred-thousand acres scattered in 17 other states. In some states, BLM lands account for a substantial share of the state's acreage: 30 percent in Wyoming, 42 percent in Utah, and 68 percent in Nevada (see Figure 1 and Table 1).

## PUBLIC LANDS IN THE WESTERN STATES

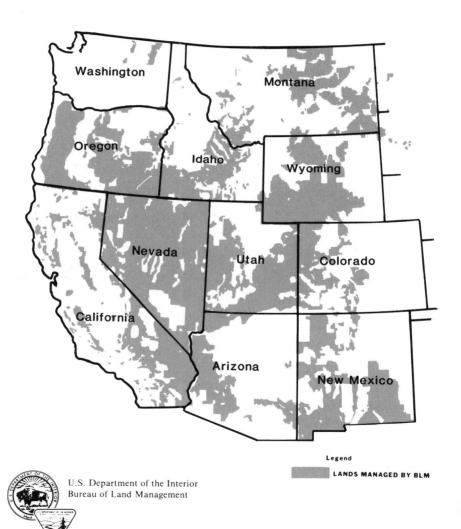

Legend

▓ LANDS MANAGED BY BLM

U.S. Department of the Interior
Bureau of Land Management

Figure 1

**TABLE 1**
**Acreage under BLM Management by State**
**as of Fiscal Year 1985**

| State | Acres |
|---|---|
| Arizona | 12,232,171 |
| California | 17,151,663 |
| Colorado | 8,362,137 |
| Idaho | 11,906,460 |
| Montana | 8,087,071 |
| Nevada | 47,812,525 |
| New Mexico | 12,899,533 |
| Oregon | 15,697,724 |
| Utah | 18,091,649 |
| Eastern States | 748,235 |
| Subtotal, lower 48 | 176,443,905 |
| Alaska (BLM estimate)[a] | 95,000,000 |
| TOTAL (estimate) | 271,443,905 |

[a] Acreage in Alaska is constantly changing as BLM completes required land transfers to the state and Alaska Natives.

Source: *Public Land Statistics 1985.* Bureau of Land Management, U.S. Department of the Interior. Washington, D.C.

BLM also is responsible for administering the energy and mining laws for federal mineral resources underlying an additional 300 million acres. These include lands managed by other federal agencies as well as private lands where the federal government owns the subsurface mineral resources. Prior to 1983, BLM also was responsible for issuing offshore oil and gas leases, but this responsibility has since been transferred to the Minerals Management Service.

Approximately 170 million acres of BLM lands in the lower 48 states, including almost all BLM lands in the 10 western states, are classified as rangeland. It is on these lands that most public attention and this chapter focus. These are the lands with the most extensive and generally most serious resource conflicts. BLM also manages five million acres of commercial forest in the lower 48 states, including two million acres of highly profitable timberlands in western Oregon generally called the Oregon and California Grant Lands. BLM management of old-growth forest and habitat for the northern spotted owl in the O and C lands is highly controversial and is covered in the spotted owl discussion in the Forest Service chapter.[5]

5. See the *Audubon Wildlife Report 1985* for more detailed discussion of the management of the Oregon and California Grant Lands and background on the spotted owl controversy.

**Agency Structure and Function**

The Bureau of Land Management is an agency within the Department of the Interior, supervised by the assistant secretary for Land and Minerals Management, who also oversees three other agencies with mineral responsibilities: the Bureau of Mines, the Minerals Management Service, and the Office of Surface Mining. BLM is headed by a director who is a political appointee.

BLM headquarters staff operations were reorganized in 1986, essentially removing one layer of managers. Most of the programs discussed in this chapter fall under the assistant director for Lands and Renewable Resources, who oversees the Division of Wildlife and Fisheries, the Division of Rangeland Resources, and the Division of Recreation, Cultural, and Wilderness Resources, among others. The Office of Planning and Environmental Coordination, formerly attached to the Deputy Director for Lands and Renewable Resources, is now under the assistant director for Support Services. The reorganization was accompanied by personnel changes at the top levels in the agency, and together these actions have concentrated authority in political appointees. Long-time BLM employees say there are more political appointees in the agency now than at any time in recent history.

BLM operations in the field are overseen by 12 state offices: one in Alaska, one in Virginia to carry out BLM responsibilities east of Kansas City, and one in each of the 10 western states. Each office is headed by a state director, who is assisted by the state office staff and who reports directly to the BLM director. The area within the jurisdiction of each state office is divided into districts. BLM has 59 district offices, each headed by a district manager. Districts are further divided into resource areas, the basic field component of BLM. Each of the 146 resource areas is headed by an area manager responsible for day-to-day management activities and on-the-ground implementation of BLM programs. BLM has at least one wildlife biologist in each state and district office, but not in all resource areas.

BLM is highly decentralized, and major land-management decisions are made by the field staff. The divisions at BLM headquarters establish program policies and priorities, but may have little ability to oversee or enforce them. The state offices are required to report only to BLM headquarters, and cumulative data on the status or progress of BLM programs frequently are unobtainable. This also makes public assessment of the effectiveness of BLM management difficult.

BLM has a number of responsibilities that are not discussed in the rest of this chapter. These include issuing permits for rights-of-way across BLM lands; overseeing land exchanges, transfers, and disposals; and authorizing various uses of its lands. BLM also has responsibility for protecting and managing wild horses and burros on the public lands, a frequently controversial program discussed in previous *Audubon Wildlife Reports*. Although wild burros cause some conflicts with desert bighorn sheep, wild-burro management generally does not have major fish and wildlife impacts.[6] BLM conducts a limited amount of research, although it has no research program *per se*. BLM research focuses heavily on applied research and development, and roughly half of its research is funded through other agencies. The research program runs about $10 million, about two percent of the total BLM budget.

**Energy and Minerals Management.** One major BLM responsibility not covered in detail in this chapter is energy and minerals management. BLM is responsible for administering exploration and development of energy and mineral resources on approximately 570 million acres, including lands managed by other federal agencies such as the Forest Service and the Fish and Wildlife Service, and lands in state and private ownership where the federal government owns the mineral resources. These lands hold a variety of important energy and minerals resources, including a third of the nation's coal, 35 percent of the uranium reserves, 60 percent of known or prospective geothermal-resource areas, and 75 to 80 percent of the nation's oil-shale and tar-sands reserves. BLM says it also has "world class" deposits of molybdenum, phosphate, sodium, lead, zinc, and potash.[7]

Energy and mineral activities may have numerous impacts on fish and wildlife. The extent of these impacts depends on the species involved, type and location of the development, size of the area disturbed, types and extent of facilities required, timing and duration of operations, types of mitigation measures employed, and adequacy of mining reclamation. Most current controversy has focused on oil and gas leasing and development and on coal leasing.

Oil and gas leasing has been most controversial on the National Forest System, particularly in the greater Yellowstone ecosystem.[8] Although BLM under law has final responsibility for issuing oil and gas leases and drilling permits on the national forests, in practice the Forest Service largely determines where and how oil and gas leasing will occur on its lands. Oil and gas leasing on the National Forest System is discussed in the *Audubon Wildlife Report 1986* in the Forest Service chapter.

The coal leasing program has been in almost constant turmoil

6. See *Wild and Free-Roaming Horses and Burros, Final Report*, by the National Research Council, for an interesting discussion of the impacts and management of wild horses and burros on the public lands (National Research Council 1982).

7. All statistics are from BLM annual reports or budget submissions to Congress.

8. See *Yellowstone Under Siege: Oil and Gas Leasing in the Greater Yellowstone Region*. (Sierra Club, 1986).

since 1971, when a moratorium was placed on regional coal leasing.[9] Leasing resumed briefly in 1981 but was halted by Congress in 1983 in response to federal coal sales, conducted under Interior Secretary James Watt, that were sold for far less than their fair market value. Congress directed the establishment of a commission to study fair-market-value policy. Congress also directed the congressional Office of Technology Assessment to study and make recommendations for improving the program's environmental-protection requirements, which conservation organizations believed had been weakened substantially by regulatory revisions made under Watt.

The federal coal program was reestablished in February 1986, when the Interior Department adopted most of the recommendations made by the commission and the Office of Technology Assessment. Several program elements related to environmental protection are still being revised or developed, including revisions of regulations for identifying lands unsuitable for coal leasing and increasing the consideration given to protecting riparian and wetland resources. The new program is a compromise, in part criticized and in part praised by conservation organizations. In general, the changes are intended to slow and stabilize leasing. Conservationists believe this should permit better environmental planning. A number of steps remain before regional coal leasing can resume, although with energy demand currently low it is uncertain when leasing will revive.

In general, conservation organizations believe that the Interior Department in recent years has given energy and mineral development priority over other uses. BLM minerals policy, for example, directs land-use plans and multiple-use management decisions to "recognize that mineral exploration and development can occur concurrently or sequentially with other resource uses," and a 1984 policy on oil and gas leasing specifies that "in virtually all cases, unless lands are excluded from leasing by law, regulation, or are formally withdrawn, [lease] applicants should at least be offered a lease with a NSO [no surface occupancy] stipulation." BLM minerals staff also have been shielded from personnel cuts, while renewable-resource staffs have been reduced substantially. Federal minerals officials say that the increased emphasis on energy and minerals comes from pressures outside the agency and largely is due to the OPEC oil embargoes of the 1970s.

**Budget and Personnel**

BLM administers more land than other federal land-managing agencies, but it has one of the smallest budgets and lowest levels of staffing.

9. Some coal leasing has proceeded under mechanisms other than regional coal sales. In 1985, for example, six leases were issued on 1,473 acres.

**TABLE 2**
**Comparison of Land-Managing Agency Budgets, 1985**

|  | Acreage managed (in millions of acres) | Appropriations (in $000s) | Full-time equivalents |
|---|---|---|---|
| National Park Service | 75 | $ 918,834 | 16,155 |
| Fish and Wildlife Service | 90 | 419,565 | 5,790 |
| Forest Service | 191 | 1,610,750 | 33,196 |
| Bureau of Land Management | 270 | 631,939 | 9,727 |

Furthermore, BLM is the only agency that received the majority of its lands in an already seriously degraded condition and that is required by law to improve the land it manages (see Table 2).

***Current Budget and Staff Levels.*** In 1986, the total BLM budget was approximately $646 million,[10] and its staffing level was 9,700 full-time equivalents.[11] This included about $14 million in permanent and trust funds, consisting primarily of payments to states and counties of their share of the receipts from activities conducted on BLM lands.[12] It also included approximately $100 million in appropriated funds for payments to states and countries in lieu of taxes. Subtracting these various payments to other parties, BLM had an operating budget of approximately $530 million in 1986 (see Table 3).

Almost all BLM land-management activities are funded through the Management of Lands and Resources account, which totaled $461 million in 1986. Programs discussed in this chapter are funded under two activities in this account: Energy and Minerals Management, funded at $80 million or about 17 percent of the total account; and Renewable Resources Management, funded at $113 million or 25 percent of the account. The largest subactivity or program under Renewable Resources is Range Management, which includes $29 million for grazing and $16 million for wild-horse and burro

10. This includes an estimated $86 million in firefighting and rehabilitation costs. BLM initially covers firefighting expenses by borrowing funds from other agencies; Congress then appropriates the necessary funds to reimburse these agencies in the following fiscal year. Final costs may differ from this estimate, and thus totals used in this chapter may not exactly match actual budget totals. The $86 million estimate is used throughout this chapter. All budget numbers are from the BLM budget office.

11. Full-time equivalents are the total number of hours worked by an individual divided by the total number of compensable hours in a year. Work of part-time and intermittent employers is converted to full-time equivalents and, when added to the number of full-time employees, gives a measure of total employment.

12. This number usually averages around $75 million. Payments were unusually low in 1986 because an early payment to Oregon and California grant-land counties caused funds that normally would be reflected in the 1986 budget to be reflected in 1985 levels instead.

**TABLE 3**
**BLM Appropriations, Fiscal Year 1986**

| | (in $000s) | Full-time equivalents (estimated) |
|---|---|---|
| Management of Lands and Resources | | |
| Energy and Minerals Management | | |
| Energy Resources | $ 65,783 | 1,626 |
| Nonenergy Minerals | 14,512 | 366 |
| Subtotal, Energy and Minerals Management | 80,295 | 1,992 |
| Lands and Realty Management | 39,923 | 1,098 |
| Renewable Resources Management | | |
| Forest Management | 7,396 | 150 |
| Range Management | 45,553 | 905 |
| [Wild Horse and Burro Management] | [16,234] | [130] |
| [Grazing Management] | [29,319] | [775] |
| Soil, Water, and Air Management[1] | 15,686 | 290 |
| [Hazardous Waste Management] | [1,705] | [n/a] |
| [Soil, Water, and Air] | [13,981] | [n/a] |
| Wildlife Habitat Management | 15,364 | 320 |
| Recreation Management | 20,477 | 465 |
| Fire Management | 8,444 | 140 |
| Subtotal, Renewable Resources Management | 112,920 | 2,270 |
| Planning and Data Management | 22,153 | 435 |
| Cadastral Survey | 25,605 | 430 |
| Firefighting and Rehabilitation | 86,000[2] | 868 |
| Technical Services | 14,814 | 232 |
| General Administration | 79,528 | 1,195 |
| Total, Management of Lands and Resources | 461,238[3] | 8,520 |
| Construction and Access | 1,335 | 25 |
| Payments in Lieu of Taxes | 99,882 | 1 |
| Land Acquisition | 2,188 | 7 |
| Oregon and California Grant Lands | 53,379 | 998 |
| Range Improvement Fund | 9,570 | 119 |
| Service Charges, Deposits, and Forfeitures | 4,247 | 57 |
| Miscellaneous Trust Funds | 100 | 0 |
| TOTAL, Appropriations | $631,939[3] | 9,727 |
| Permanent and Trust Funds | 13,663[4] | 127 |
| Other FTEs | — | 203 |
| TOTAL, BLM | $645,602[3] | 10,057 |

1 Since 1983, hazardous waste management funds have been appropriated as part of soil, water, and air, although the hazardous waste program is managed under Energy and Minerals.

2 Firefighting and Rehabilitation expenditures are estimated. BLM traditionally has funded this activity by borrowing funds from other agencies; actual costs are reimbursed in the following year by a congressional appropriation.

3 Totals may not match actual appropriations because firefighting and rehabilitation expenditures are estimated.

4 This account consists almost entirely of payments to states and counties of their share of receipts from various activities on the public lands.

Numbers may not total due to rounding.

**TABLE 4**
**BLM Wildlife Habitat Management Appropriations**
**Fiscal Year 1981–1986 (in $000s)**

| Year | Budget requested | Congressional appropriations | Appropriations in 1982 constant dollars |
|------|------------------|------------------------------|------------------------------------------|
| 1981 | n/a | $16,017 | $17,196 |
| 1982 | 12,594 | 14,918 | 14,918 |
| 1983 | 13,642 | 15,150 | 14,550 |
| 1984 | 10,515 | 13,604 | 12,555 |
| 1985 | 11,705 | 15,833 | 14,109 |
| 1986 | 13,485 | 15,364 | 13,333 |

management.[13] Wildlife habitat management at $15 million gets about half the funding of grazing management and even slightly less than wild horses and burros. Soil, water, and air management is funded at $14 million,[14] and recreation management at $20 million. Other accounts with some significance for fish and wildlife that are not included under Management of Lands and Resources are the Oregon and California Grant Lands account at $53 million; Land Acquisition at $2.2 million; and the Range Improvement Fund at $9.6 million (see Figure 2)

BLM uses an accounting method based on what it calls "benefitting subactivities," in which activities are funded by the program they primarily are intended to benefit. For example, time spent by wildlife biologists evaluating the impacts of a proposed mining operation and developing mitigation measures is paid for from the energy and minerals account. This accounting method means that all the work conducted for the protection of fish and wildlife and all the efforts of the fish and wildlife biologists and botanists are not accounted for in the wildlife-habitat-management appropriation and full-time equivalents. It also means that the wildlife program sometimes has to negotiate with other programs for funds to conduct necessary assessment work.

***Budget and Personnel Trends.*** In fiscal year 1977, when the Federal Land Policy and Management Act was enacted, BLM land-management programs in the Management of Lands and Resources account were funded at about $214 million,[15] and expenditures on

13. Prior to 1985, wild-horse and burro management was funded at levels of $4 million to $6 million. Congress has provided a substantially higher level of funding since 1985 to allow an accelerated round-up of excess animals.

14. Does not include about $1.8 million appropriated to this program for hazardous-waste management.

15. Includes only onshore energy and minerals management. Prior to 1983, BLM also had responsibility for leasing of offshore oil and gas, but this responsibility was transferred to the Minerals Management Service and is omitted from budget figures throughout this discussion for purposes of comparison.

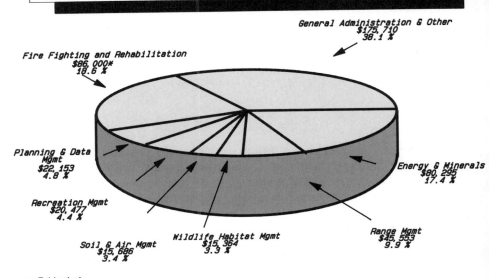

Management of Lands and Resources, Fiscal Year 1986
Distribution of Appropriations (In Millions)
Total = $461,238

General Administration & Other
$175,710
38.1 %

Fire Fighting and Rehabilitation
$86,000*
18.6 %

Planning & Data Mgmt
$22,153
4.8 %

Recreation Mgmt
$20,477
4.4 %

Soil & Air Mgmt
$15,686
3.4 %

Wildlife Habitat Mgmt
$15,364
3.3 %

Range Mgmt
$45,553
9.9 %

Energy & Minerals
$80,295
17.4 %

\* Estimated

Figure 2

renewable-resources management, with the exception of range management, were low. While energy and minerals management was
funded at $32 million and range management at $27 million, recreation was at $7 million, and wildlife at $6 million. After the
enactment of the Federal Land Policy and Management Act, the
Carter administration requested and Congress approved rapid increases
in the bureau's budget and approved larger proportional increases in
wildlife and recreation as part of an effort to bring more balanced
multiple-use management to BLM lands. By 1981, total
land-management funding had increased about 75 percent, to $377
million, and funding for wildlife and recreation had more than tripled.
Wildlife funding was at $16 million, soil, water, and air at $18 million,
and recreation at almost $20 million. Range and minerals funding also
increased, but to a lesser degree, with range at $42 million and energy
and minerals at $53 million.[16]

Beginning with the 1982 budget, however, the Reagan Administration repeatedly proposed sharp cuts in the bureau's renewable-

16. The 1977 and 1981 budget numbers are not strictly comparable, since the 1977
numbers include general-administration costs in each account while the 1981 numbers
do not include administrative costs. This only means, however, that the budget increases
between 1977 and 1981 were even greater than is revealed by these numbers.

resources programs. The renewable-resource cuts were moderated somewhat by Congress, particularly for wildlife-habitat management, but the thrust of the administration's budget has been retained. Recreation-management appropriations rose at first in order to fund a wilderness study, but by 1986 had declined back to about the 1981 level of $20 million. Funding in 1986 for all other renewable resources was below 1981 levels. Wildlife funding was down four percent, grazing management 19 percent, and soil, water, and air funding 22 percent. When converted into fiscal year 1982 constant dollars to reflect changes in spending power, the severity of the cuts is more apparent: recreation was down 10 percent, wildlife-habitat management 22 percent, grazing management 34 percent, and soil, water, and air management 37 percent. If Congress had approved the president's requested budget for the bureau in 1986, purchasing power would have been even more dramatically reduced: by 19 percent for recreation management, 32 percent for wildlife, 35 percent for grazing, and 45 percent for soil, water, and air (see Figures 3 and 4 and Table 4).

Staffing levels, measured in full-time equivalents, have followed a pattern similar to that of the budget levels. From 1982, the first year BLM measured staff levels using full-time equivalents, to 1986, full-time equivalents remained about level in recreation and dropped in the

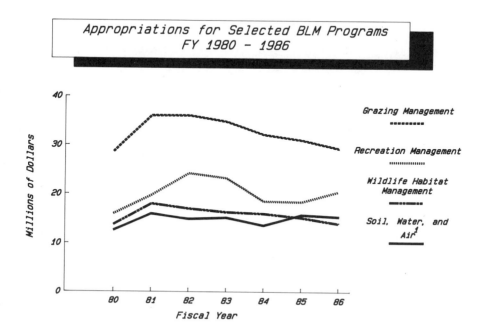

Appropriations for Selected BLM Programs
FY 1980 – 1986

[1] Does not include funds for hazardous waste management.

Figure 3

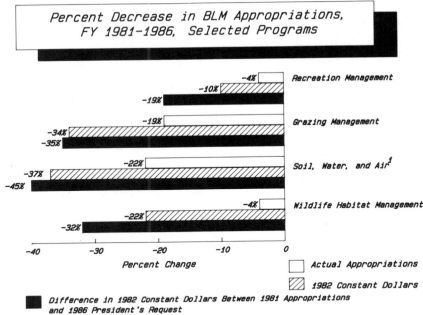

*Percent Decrease in BLM Appropriations, FY 1981-1986, Selected Programs*

Recreation Management: -4%, -10%, -19%

Grazing Management: -19%, -34%, -35%

Soil, Water, and Air[1]: -22%, -37%, -45%

Wildlife Habitat Management: -4%, -22%, -32%

Percent Change (-40, -30, -20, -10, 0)

☐ Actual Appropriations
▨ 1982 Constant Dollars
■ Difference in 1982 Constant Dollars Between 1981 Appropriations and 1986 President's Request

[1] *Does not include funds allocated to hazardous waste management.*

Figure 4

other renewable-resource programs: by 22 percent for grazing, 11 percent for soil, water, and air, and six percent for wildlife.

More serious than the decline in full-time equivalents is the decline in professionals and specialists in the renewable-resources accounts. For example, since 1981, fish and wildlife biologists and botanists have been cut 26 percent, from 366 to 270. Since 1980, soil scientists have been cut 39 percent, from 122 to 74, and hydrologists by 32 percent, from 81 to 55. With such low numbers of scientists, a single specialist may be responsible for planning, assessment, or management of activities on millions of acres of BLM land. Some states and districts simply lack certain types of professionals. In Nevada, for example, as of August 1986, 19 wildlife biologists were responsible for land-use planning, inventory and monitoring, improvement projects, and assessment and mitigation of impacts of mining, grazing, and other activities on 48 million acres. Two fishery biologists were responsible for 1,100 miles of streams, and the state had no BLM botanists. BLM says it has access to necessary specialists through state agencies, local universities, and other private organizations. It also points out that BLM personnel with one title may be trained in other areas. For example, range conservationists usually have taken botany courses, and some are professionally trained biologists. Nevertheless, at the staff level substantial concern exists about inadequate numbers of staff, poor distribution of existing staff, or lack of certain types of expertise in some states or districts.

The one program that has received funding increases over this time period is energy and minerals management. Most if not all of this increase, however, is from new minerals-management responsibilities assumed by BLM in 1983 and 1984 in a merger with the Minerals Management Service, so that funding for energy and minerals management appears to have remained about even or suffered a small cut since 1981. Since 1984, the most recent year with which accurate comparisons can be made, energy and minerals management funding has increased four percent, actually a two percent decline in constant dollars.

Energy- and minerals-management full-time equivalents have increased from 1,270 in 1982 to 1,992 in 1986. Almost all of this increase is accounted for by the merger, meaning that in effect, energy and minerals staffing has remained level while renewable-resource programs staff has been cut substantially. Some BLM staff also say that the greater numbers of minerals personnel have contributed to the higher priority given minerals development in BLM in recent years.

## LAND-USE PLANNING

BLM is required by the Federal Land Policy and Management Act to make decisions about public-land management in accordance with comprehensive, multiple-use plans developed with public participation. Important decisions on fish- and wildlife-habitat management are to be made in the plans, including identification of areas where site-specific habitat-management plans will be developed for individual species or groups of species, designation of areas of critical environmental concern, determination of areas unsuitable for coal leasing because of wildlife or other environmental considerations, establishment of long-term goals for livestock grazing levels, and identification of priority fish and wildlife species and establishment of objectives for maintaining and improving their habitat.

BLM began developing land-use plans in the 1960s, when the agency began to move toward multiple-use management. At the time of Federal Land Policy and Management Act passage in 1976, BLM had developed land-use plans, then called management framework plans, for 80 to 85 percent of the public lands in the lower 48 states. The remaining acreage was primarily in scattered parcels that did not readily form manageable units.

With enactment of the Federal Land Policy and Management Act, Congress made land-use planning mandatory and set forth key principles to guide BLM planning. The new plans, called resource management plans and prepared under the act's planning regulations, are improved in a number of ways from the older management framework plans: development, display, and assessment of alternatives is improved; coordination with state and local governments is stronger; planning and environmental impact analyses are integrated so that impact assessment findings are available before the preferred management alternative is selected; a single planning document that can be reproduced and distributed to interested parties is prepared for each planning area; and public participation is substantially increased, with the required participation standards specified in BLM regulations.

In consideration of the limited level of funding and staffing traditionally afforded BLM, the bureau was not required to replace all its existing plans at one time. Thus BLM provided for a phased transition to the use of resource management plans. Those management framework plans that were determined to comply with the basic Federal Land Policy and Management Act planning requirements are allowed to continue to serve as valid land-use plans until issues arise that are not covered by existing plans or until the plans otherwise become inadequate.

### Planning Process and Public Participation

The planning process provides several key opportunities for public participation, including the identification of significant resource-management problems and conflicts that set the tone and scope for the rest of the planning effort.[17] Once major resource issues are identified, BLM provides for public review of the proposed planning criteria that establish standards, rules, and measures to guide subsequent actions in the planning process. BLM then collects necessary data, formulates management alternatives, evaluates their effects, and selects a preferred alternative. Formal participation is not required at these stages, although relevant documents are available to the public.

The most important public participation step is review of the draft resource management plan and draft environmental impact statement during a 90-day public comment period. After review of public comment on the draft plan, the district manager makes his final recommendation and the state director publishes the proposed resource management plan. Those who have participated in the planning process have 30 days to file a protest with the director of BLM objecting

17. The resource-management planning process is described in more detail in the *Audubon Wildlife Report 1985* and is covered comprehensively in a BLM pamphlet, "BLM Planning: A Guide to Resource Management Planning on the Public Lands."

to all or any part of the plan that may affect their interests adversely. If a protest results in significant changes to the proposed plan, an additional public comment period is provided.

Once a plan is approved, all BLM management actions must conform with it. When considering new proposals, district managers make written conformance determinations which find that an action either does or does not conform with the plan. If a proposed action does not conform, it may either be rejected or considered further in a plan amendment procedure. Plan amendments must be prepared with opportunity for public participation, interagency coordination, and environmental impact analysis, although the level of participation and analysis varies depending on the significance and potential impact of the change being considered.

The plans also are to contain standards for monitoring and evaluating the implementation of the plan in order to determine whether plan goals and objectives are being met. As BLM has focused on plan development, the Washington office has provided only minimal guidance for implementing plan monitoring requirements. As more resource management plans are completed, plan monitoring will become an increasingly important and potentially controversial issue.

## Planning Controversies

Conservationists have leveled a number of complaints at the planning process. One major criticism is the slow pace at which BLM is replacing the older management framework plans with the resource management plans required by the Federal Land Policy and Management Act. At the end of fiscal year 1986, 10 years after the passage of the act, only 32 resource management plans had received final approval. Another 14 plans had been proposed for approval, and six plans had been issued in draft form. BLM expects to complete 61 resource management plans covering 43 percent of the public lands outside of Alaska by the end of fiscal year 1988 — roughly half the number of resource management plans, covering about half the acreage, that BLM ultimately expects to prepare. BLM planning regulations do not require management framework plans to be converted to resource management plans by any particular time. BLM says it expects to have the staff and funding to start new plans at the rate of one per state per year. In this case, it would be roughly 1994 before all management framework plans would be replaced by resource management plans — nearly 20 years after the passage of the Federal Land Policy and Management Act.

Fish and wildlife interests are concerned about the slow rate of plan preparation because many of the management framework plans are getting very old. Even though BLM may amend these plans to address specific conflicts, conservationists think 15 to 20 years is simply too long before the overall management of an area is reviewed to determine if it is meeting current needs.[18]

Another key concern among conservationists has been the quality and content of the plans. Conservation organizations charge that the plans have been highly inconsistent in their treatment of wildlife and other resources—a problem that BLM also recognized after a review of early plans. To address this problem, BLM has developed and released for public review draft guidance for each resource program, outlining what should be included in the land-use plan. This guidance is called "supplemental program guidance for resource management planning." It does not give any assurance that wildlife or other resources will be treated favorably in the plans, but it does help the public ensure that certain aspects of resource management are addressed. The guidance does not apply to plans completed or near completion at the time of its issuance. Conservationists have had a number of specific criticisms of the guidance, but generally have applauded its issuance, which they consider long overdue.

Conservation groups also have charged that the plans are too general, that they postpone decisions and do not control future management, particularly with regard to livestock grazing. This controversy is in part the result of policy changes made under the Reagan administration to delay grazing level reductions or implemention of new grazing systems (discussed later under "Grazing Management"). BLM maintains that the purpose of resource management plans is to develop broad management goals and objectives and general strategies to achieve them. The bureau says that more specific and detailed management prescriptions should be made in the activity plans—such as allotment management plans—developed pursuant to the resource management plan. Since activity plans far outnumber land-use plans, and since public participation in activity-plan development is far less formal than in the land-use planning process or is nonexistent, wildlife interests outside BLM find it difficult to influence the agency at this level. A district court decision in 1985 supported the BLM position (*Natural Resources Defense Council v. Hodel*, 624 F.Supp. 1045, D.Nev. 1985), but the case has been appealed.

## WILDLIFE AND FISH HABITAT MANAGEMENT

Fish and wildlife management on the public lands is a cooperative effort between the state and federal governments. Technically, the

18. A lawsuit pending in federal district court eventually may force BLM to step up its development of resource management plans (*National Wildlife Federation v. Burford*, Civil Action No.85-2238). See the *Audubon Wildlife Report 1986*, p.522, for further discussion.

states are responsible for managing fish and wildlife populations, including regulation of hunting and fishing, while BLM is responsible for managing fish and wildlife habitat. In practice, however, the state fish and game agencies and the BLM wildlife staff work closely together to develop plans and management approaches for fish and wildlife on the public lands.

BLM conducts a wide variety of habitat projects and in a number of cases has made innovative use of its authorities, funding, and cooperative arrangements. In Arizona, BLM used its authority to exchange public and private lands to negotiate a land trade with Tenneco Corporation that gave BLM ownership of a unique riparian area on the San Pedro River, subsequently designated for protection by Congress as the San Pedro Riparian Area. In Idaho, BLM is taking advantage of scattered, isolated tracts of public land to provide patches of upland-game-bird habitat in the middle of intensively farmed private cropland. In California, wildlife personnel have compiled a list of habitat-protection land acquisition needs and are working with The Nature Conservancy, the Trust for Public Lands, and the state wildlife conservation board to gain protection for these areas. BLM in New Mexico exchanged a 280-acre parcel adjacent to Santa Fe for 8,000 acres of elk winter range. Elsewhere, primarily in the Rocky Mountain states, BLM has worked with the Fish and Wildlife Service on a highly successful program of peregrine falcon reintroductions.

Big-game populations throughout the West are far below their original, pre-settlement levels. Overall populations are at less than 15 to 20 percent of original size and bison, bighorn sheep, and pronghorn populations are at less than five percent of their original levels, according to one speculative estimate (Wagner 1978). According to BLM wildlife officials and statistics collected by the states, big-game populations on the public lands appear to be stable or to have increased in recent years. Almost all western states report increases in antelope, bear, bighorn sheep, and elk populations over the past 10 years. Information on the status of small-game and nongame species is limited, except for those that have reached dangerously low levels.

## Activities and Priorities

The BLM wildlife and fish habitat management program is coordinated at BLM headquarters under the Division of Wildlife and Fisheries. In recent years, the program's top priority has been to provide wildlife data and expertise in the planning of other bureau programs and initiatives—such as energy and minerals development, grazing, forestry, and realty activities—primarily through the land-use plans and grazing environmental impact statements.[19] This includes conducting inventories to determine the type and condition of resources in an area and, after implementation of the plans, monitoring to ensure that management objectives are being met. The manner in which these nonwildlife activities are conducted generally is the major factor limiting wildlife populations or determining the quality of fish and wildlife habitat on BLM lands. The Wildlife Management Institute, for example, has said that the most important plans for wildlife are the grazing allotment management plans (Wildlife Management Institute 1981).

The second major element of the wildlife and fisheries program is habitat maintenance, management, and improvement. Habitat management is carried out primarily through habitat management plans, site-specific activity plans prepared after the need for them is identified in a land-use plan. BLM has developed approximately 400 habitat management plans, although slightly more than 100 plans have been implemented to completion. Current emphasis is on implementing existing plans and on-the-ground management actions. Historically, wildlife management in BLM, as in other federal agencies, focused largely on game species. In recent years, however, the Wildlife and Fisheries Division has directed BLM state offices to give priority to the most vulnerable and critical habitats — those for endangered and threatened species and riparian and wetland habitats — and secondarily to aquatic and fisheries habitats.

The wildlife and fisheries program gives special emphasis to protection and management of endangered and threatened species and devotes about 25 percent of its budget to this purpose. At the end of fiscal year 1986, BLM had some management responsibility for 122 listed species located on public lands managed by BLM or on private lands where BLM manages federal subsurface mineral rights.[20] These include 46 animal species, 31 fish species, and 45 plant species. Another 11 animal species and 13 plant species affected by BLM management are proposed for listing, and some 170 animal species and more than 600 plant species on the public lands are candidates for listing.[21]

At the end of fiscal year 1986, 60 recovery plans had been

19. BLM wildlife and fisheries staff also coordinate with other BLM programs and activities on a more site-specific basis to ensure that wildlife is considered in their planning and management. This type of work is considered to support the primary program and is not budgeted or planned for in the wildlife program itself.

20. The Fish and Wildlife Service has lead responsibility for implementing the Endangered Species Act, but other federal agencies assume various levels of management responsibility for listed species on their lands.

21. Candidate species are species that the Fish and Wildlife Service believes warrant listing but have not been proposed formally for listing because other species are higher priority or because additional information is needed.

completed for endangered and threatened species on BLM lands and BLM was implementing at least a portion of its responsibilities for 47 of these plans. The Division of Wildlife and Fisheries also is developing a policy that will require positive efforts to manage candidate species in order to eliminate the need to list them. In 1985, BLM began to develop regulations for the protection of rare plants on its lands— including more than 600 candidates currently unprotected from collection and other abuse—but this effort has been delayed pending completion of a new long-range plan for the wildlife and fisheries program.

The Division of Wildlife and Fisheries came under a new chief in 1986 and currently is developing a long-range plan to guide fish and wildlife habitat management over the next 10 years. Under that plan, not yet finalized, the bureau's wildlife and fish program would be divided into three major components: wildlife-habitat management, fisheries-habitat management, and threatened- and endangered-species management. Specific goals and objectives are being formulated for each component.

## Budget and Staffing

Like the other multiple-use programs in BLM, the wildlife habitat management program is relatively new. BLM started hiring wildlife biologists in the 1950s, but placed them under other programs, such as range, forestry, and lands. The first practicing wildlife biologist was hired in the Nevada BLM state office in 1961 and the Division of Wildlife was established in 1965. In the mid-1970s, prompted by the court order to prepare grazing environmental impact statements and by the enactment of the Federal Land Policy and Management Act, the program grew and diversified. The program's budget and staff increased rapidly from $3 million and 95 wildlife scientists in 1974 to a high of $16 million and 366 wildlife professionals in 1981. In addition, a variety of specialists, such as limnologists, zoologists, and botanists, were hired.

Since 1981, however, the Reagan administration consistently has requested substantially lower funding levels for the wildlife program, as it has for most other programs except energy and minerals. Congress repeatedly has appropriated levels above the administration request, but the program still is funded at levels lower than in 1981 (see Table 4, p. 17). In constant-dollar spending power, funding for the program declined 22 percent between 1981 and 1986.

While the effective budget decline is a problem in wildlife habitat management, staffing is the more limiting factor because the work needed to coordinate with other program activities has not slowed as the wildlife staff has declined. The number of fish and wildlife

**TABLE 5**
**BLM Wildlife-Related Scientists, August 1986**

| State | Wildlife Biologists | Wildlife/ Fishery Biologists | Fishery Biologists | Botanists | Other[a] | Total |
|---|---|---|---|---|---|---|
| Alaska | 8 | 1 | 2 | — | 1 | 12 |
| Arizona | 18 | — | — | 1 | — | 19 |
| California | 21 | — | 1 | 1 | 4 | 27 |
| Colorado | 16 | — | 3 | — | 3 | 22 |
| Idaho | 22 | 1 | 3 | 1 | 2 | 29 |
| Montana | 18 | — | 2 | — | 1 | 21 |
| Nevada | 19 | — | 2 | — | — | 21 |
| New Mexico | 15 | — | — | — | — | 15 |
| Oregon | 27 | — | 12 | 5 | 1 | 45 |
| Utah | 19 | — | 2 | — | 1 | 22 |
| Wyoming | 18 | — | 2 | — | — | 20 |
| Eastern States | 2 | — | — | — | 2 | 4 |
| Washington Office[b] | 7 | 1 | 2 | — | 3 | 13 |
| TOTAL[c] | 210 (16) | 3 | 31 (2) | 8 (1) | 18 (2) | 270 (21) |

[a] Includes natural resource specialists, statisticians, analytical wildlife research biologists, supervisory raptor research biologists, and an economist.
[b] Includes Denver Service Center and Phoenix Training Center.
[c] Numbers in parentheses indicate number of positions shown that were vacant at the time of the survey.

biologists and botanists was cut from 366 in 1981 to 270 by August 1986, a 26 percent drop. The cut has been particularly severe on fisheries biologists, whose numbers have declined from 58 in 1981 to 31 in 1986, a period during which riparian and aquatic habitat were supposed to be top priorities. Fisheries biologists also are unevenly distributed among the states: In 1986, Oregon had 12 fisheries biologists, five other states had two each, California had one, and New Mexico and Arizona had none.

The largest proportional cut has been in the number of BLM botanists. This is particularly serious because of BLM's extensive plant-protection responsibilities, including the more than 600 species of candidate plants. Botanist numbers have been cut in half, from 16 in 1981 to eight in August 1986. Their distribution also is uneven. Five of the eight are in Oregon, one is in Arizona, one in California, and one in Idaho. The remaining seven states have no botanists, even though Colorado and Nevada each have six endangered or threatened plant species, New Mexico has 10, and Utah has 11 (see Table 5).

## Volunteers and Private Contributions

One way that BLM has coped with the reduced wildlife program budget and staff is to seek the donation of private funds and labor to assist in a variety of wildlife efforts. The Division of Wildlife and Fisheries estimates that some $1.5 million are contributed yearly, mostly in volunteer labor, and has assembled a task force to identify ways to increase contributions. Congress has aided this effort by providing a small portion of the wildlife program's appropriations in the form of challenge grants to encourage contribution of matching funds from nonfederal sources. Challenge grants of approximately $300,000 a year since 1984 have supported substantial recovery efforts for the desert bighorn sheep.

## Riparian Area Management

Aquatic areas on BLM lands and their adjacent wetlands, floodplains, and border vegetation — generally referred to as riparian areas — are used by wildlife disproportionately more than any other habitat and have been called "the most critical wildlife habitats in managed rangelands" (Thomas 1979). Many aquatic and semi-aquatic species, such as waterfowl, otters, beavers, fish, reptiles, and amphibians, are found only in riparian areas. In some areas, as much as 80 percent of terrestrial wildlife species are directly dependent on riparian habitat or use it more than any other habitat type (Thomas 1979, Luoma 1986).

This most vital wildlife habitat also is among the most scarce. Riparian zones along waterways encompass some 900,000 acres of BLM lands in the lower 48 states, about half a percent of the total acreage (Department of the Interior 1985). This limited area is especially important since riparian zones on surrounding private lands, which originally contained the richest water sources, largely have been settled and developed.

Furthermore, most riparian areas on BLM lands are in seriously degraded condition. Although BLM has not completed an inventory of the condition of these valuable riparian areas or compiled the results of various riparian studies, limited surveys and professional observations indicate that riparian-area degradation is extensive. For example, one report found that livestock grazing was damaging 883 miles of the roughly 1,100 miles of stream-bank riparian habitat on BLM lands in Nevada (Department of Interior 1974). In 1977, BLM determined that more than 80 percent of riparian-area acreage was in need of management (Almand and Krohn 1978).

A variety of uses is responsible for this degradation. However, road construction along streams and rivers may have a more critical and long-lasting adverse impact on riparian habitat than any other activity (Thomas 1979).

Oil and gas development, particularly in the Overthrust Belt, is causing serious erosion and water-quality problems for riparian areas (Elder and Moore 1985). Heavy recreation, timber harvesting, agriculture, rock and gravel mining, urbanization, and water development and irrigation also can have adverse impacts on riparian areas.

The most widespread impact on riparian areas, however, has been from livestock grazing. Left uncontrolled, cattle—attracted by water, forage, and shade—concentrate in riparian areas and cause a number of serious impacts. Improper grazing can reduce water quality, eliminate streamside shrubs, compact soils, and accelerate erosion. As stream banks collapse, streams become wider and shallower, causing water temperatures to rise. Streams that used to flow year-round may flow only intermittently. Stream channels may erode and cut deep gullies, lowering water tables and eliminating wet meadows adjacent to the waterway. Impacts on fish can be particularly severe: Warmer water temperatures eliminate trout and other cool water fisheries, and sediments destroy the essential mix of riffles and holes required by some game fish.

Effective management of livestock grazing is a key ingredient for restoring riparian areas to a productive and healthy condition. Recent studies and BLM experience have shown that eliminating livestock from degraded riparian areas can restore year-round water flows to intermittent streams, double and triple trout production, restore fish and beaver populations eliminated by livestock grazing, and dramatically increase wildlife use. In Oregon, BLM staff have demonstrated that riparian restoration efforts also can sharply increase grazing forage. Although most research to date has focused on the impacts of eliminating livestock from riparian areas, in some cases livestock may have to be removed only temporarily or perhaps not at all. Some riparian areas may be improved by reducing livestock numbers, establishing special grazing systems to improve livestock distribution, changing the season of use, switching from cattle grazing to sheep, and conducting rehabilitation projects such as planting vegetation or adding artificial stream structures.

As awareness of the importance of riparian areas has grown, BLM's wildlife division has assigned high priority to their management, and wildlife programs in the states have conducted a variety of riparian-habitat projects. In mid-1985, as conservation organizations sought amendments to the Federal Land Policy and Management Act establishing a comprehensive riparian-area program,[22] BLM began developing a riparian-area policy that would have required all relevant BLM programs to work to maintain, restore, or improve these areas. BLM has a strong existing riparian policy developed under the Carter administration. This policy, however, largely has not been implemented because it has been perceived, incorrectly, as applying only to

22. Efforts to develop draft legislation are discussed in *Audubon Wildlife Report 1986.*

the wildlife program. Many believed the adoption of a new policy by the current administration would signal all divisions to give priority to riparian management. However, when Congress dropped the range legislation at the end of 1985, the pressure on BLM to adopt the new policy was relaxed. The policy still had not been issued by the end of fiscal year 1986.

Nevertheless, BLM has increased its attention to riparian area management. General directives on budget priorities have emphasized riparian-area management, and in mid-1986, BLM directed each state office to select riparian areas to serve as demonstration management projects. The goal is to evaluate the effectiveness of various management techniques while building awareness of and support for riparian-area values and restoration among BLM employees, ranchers and other range users, and the public in general. Each district is to establish at least one project by the end of fiscal year 1987.

## GRAZING MANAGEMENT

Livestock grazing is authorized on almost all of the 177 million acres of BLM land in the lower 48 states and is the major activity on the public lands affecting fish and wildlife habitat. BLM issues permits or leases to almost 20,000 livestock operators for about 2.2 million cattle and 2.1 million sheep and goats on the public lands. In 1985, livestock on the public lands used approximately 11.2 million animal unit months (AUMs) of forage.[23] Based on 1982 data, livestock operators using BLM lands account for slightly more than one percent of cattle operators in the nation, and public-land forage accounts for two percent of the total feed consumed by cattle in the United States. On a local or regional scale, public-land grazing can take on more significance. About a third of the beef cattle in the western states graze at least part of the year on BLM or Forest Service public rangelands[24] (Department of Agriculture and Department of the Interior 1986). In 1982, about 10 percent of BLM permittees used 47 percent of the forage on BLM lands, while about half of BLM permittees were small operators with fewer than 100 head. Such small operations generally show negative returns and depend on other sources of income for a large proportion of their livelihood (Department of Agriculture and Department of the Interior 1986).

Grazing management on the public lands is coordinated at BLM headquarters by the Division of Rangeland Resources. Grazing is

23. An animal unit month is the amount of forage consumed by one cow or five sheep in a month.
24. Separate numbers for BLM alone not available.

authorized through permits and leases, which generally are issued for a period of 10 years and are required by the Federal Land Policy and Management Act to specify the numbers of livestock that may be grazed and the allowable seasons of use. BLM categorizes grazing allotments into three management categories—improve, maintain, or custodial—with improve allotments to receive the most intensive management and custodial the least. For allotments requiring more intensive management, BLM may prepare an allotment management plan, which may describe a grazing-management system to be used on the allotment and range improvements to be made.

Decisions about grazing determine whether sufficient wildlife forage is available, whether critical wintering, nesting, breeding, and other habitats are protected, and whether valuable streams and streamside habitat can be maintained or restored. A 1977 Department of the Interior seminar concluded that livestock grazing "is the single most important factor limiting wildlife production in the West" (Department of Interior 1977). And livestock grazing—especially prior to federal management—largely has been responsible for the generally poor condition of the range: According to the Council on Environmental Quality, overgrazing is "the most potent desertification force, in terms of total acreage affected, within the United States" (Sheridan 1981).

Livestock grazing often can coexist with fish and wildlife if the grazing is managed to prevent overgrazing, to exclude livestock from critical habitat areas or remove them at appropriate times, and to prevent destruction of streamside habitat and other vital riparian areas. In the many areas where the range is degraded, range improvements for livestock need to be planned carefully so as not to harm wildlife and to benefit it where possible, and range improvements intended specifically to benefit wildlife should be implemented where needed.

In principle, range interests agree that these are the types of steps that need to be taken. In practice, controversy over when, where, how, and how quickly to apply such management actions can be intense. This chapter focuses on three major and controversial aspects of the grazing program: the development and implementation of specific grazing plans and adjustments through BLM land-use plans and grazing environmental impact statements; grazing fees; and grazing advisory boards and the use of range improvement funds.

## Grazing Plans and Adjustments

Throughout the 50 years of federal management of the public lands, Interior has made three major attempts to reduce livestock grazing levels. Although grazing levels have been reduced significantly since the early 1900s, overall grazing levels still have not been reduced to the land's carrying capacity.

The first attempt to reduce grazing levels, completed in 1942 when the Grazing Service issued the first 10-year leases under the Taylor Grazing Act, left range forage "wildly overallocated" because of political pressures (Fairfax 1984). When these permits came due for renewal, the newly established BLM attempted to bring livestock numbers into line with the carrying capacity of the range and to allocate forage between livestock and wildlife. However, almost all BLM state offices subsequently reported that numerous political compromises resulted in the failure to reduce stocking rates effectively and suggested that insufficient forage was allocated to wildlife (Box *et al.* 1979). The third and current effort began in the mid-1960s when BLM, in an internal push for more balanced multiple-use management, began developing its first multiple-use land-use plans as well as more specific grazing-allotment management plans. This effort initially was attacked by livestock interests. Since changes were made to address the industry's concerns, it has been attacked by conservationists.

Two events in the mid-1970s forced dramatic changes in BLM's approach to the grazing-allotment planning begun in the 1960s. In 1974, the Nevada BLM office issued a report highly critical of BLM range management in the state. It found uncontrolled and unplanned livestock use was occurring in approximately 85 percent of the state and reported that "damage to wildlife habitat can be expressed only as extreme destruction" (Department of Interior 1974). In-house reports prepared in other states indicated similar problems.

That same year, several environmental groups represented by the Natural Resources Defense Council successfully sued BLM for failing to conduct an adequate environmental assessment of its grazing program. The court agreed that BLM preparation of a single environmental impact statement to cover the entire grazing program on all 170 million acres did not comply with the National Environmental Policy Act and ordered the bureau to prepare site-specific impact statements for the program.

BLM decided to use the impact statements, in coordination with land-use plans, as vehicles for addressing the types of grazing problems identified in the Nevada report. Based on intensive range inventories, the initial grazing environmental impact statements determined the carrying capacity of the range and allocated the available forage among various uses, including livestock, wildlife, wild horses and burros, and watershed protection.

The first grazing impact statements and plans began to come out under the Carter administration. According to BLM, the first 22 environmental impact statements recommended grazing reductions on about half the allotments covered. The average reduction recommended for these areas was 10 percent below actual livestock use. However, some individual allotments had cuts as high as 80 percent

(U.S. Congress 1980).[25] Livestock permittees could appeal, but BLM required that the cuts begin to be phased in during the grazing year following approval of the plan even if the appeals were not completed.

The livestock industry raised a storm of protest and with the help of its supporters raked BLM over the coals for its proposals. BLM was blasted in congressional field hearings, lawsuits were filed against the bureau and others were threatened, and Congress prohibited BLM from reducing grazing levels by more than 10 percent yearly. In addition, the Sagebrush Rebellion, fueled in part by BLM's more aggressive range management, called for removal of the public lands from federal control.

Critics of BLM made two key charges: that the bureau failed to consult with permittees and that it incorrectly based its grazing decisions on one-point-in-time inventory data, which the critics said could misrepresent general range condition if there had been unusual weather conditions or range use in the year the data was collected. This criticism was supported by the Society for Range Management, a professional association of range scientists, which recommended that BLM conduct utilization studies[26] and monitor the range trend over several years before establishing proper livestock numbers (Society for Range Management 1984).

BLM range officials today maintain that this approach also was endorsed by a National Research Council workshop on range-science issues, a workshop initiated at BLM's request under the Carter administration. In fact, recommendations made by participants in the workshop varied widely. One panel, for example, recommended that grazing adjustments be made over five to 10 years based on monitoring data, while another recommended that BLM continue to use current data and adopt even more conservative grazing levels than it had[27] (National Research Council 1984). Current BLM range officials say the agency's use of inventory data would have been overturned in court. However, this was never tested, and conservationists point out that BLM has used inventory data to make grazing decisions throughout its history.

Many political scientists familiar with BLM believe that scientific methodology was never the real issue in this debate. Public-land expert Sally Fairfax called the data issue "simply a front for the real issues regarding who is going to decide range policy issues and on what basis . . . the conflict is overallocations and outcomes, not data" (Fairfax

25. The reductions were greater when compared with grazing "preference," the maximum level of grazing assigned to the base property. Reductions in preference cause reductions in permit value and therefore reductions in property value.
26. "Utilization" is the amount of forage removed by animals grazing on a particular plant species.
27. Funding for the council's workshop review was terminated by the Reagan administration before it completed a unified set of recommendations or a final report.

1984a). Even BLM's range division chief said that differences on what level of inventory was necessary were more philosophical than scientific, not only in terms of scientific methodology, but also in terms of management objectives (U.S. Congress 1979).

BLM responded to the political heat. In the last days of the Carter administration, BLM issued regulations requiring extensive participation of grazing permittees and other interests throughout the grazing impact statement and adjustment process. Grazing levels still were to be determined using inventory data and still would begin to be phased in within a year after they were approved. However, reductions would be phased in over a five-year rather than three-year period and could be changed if revisions were indicated by monitoring data.

In 1981, the election of President Reagan, a self-proclaimed "sagebrush rebel," brought into office those who had been opposing BLM efforts to reduce grazing levels. James Watt, whose legal foundation had taken BLM to court on the issue, became Secretary of the Interior. Robert Burford, a rancher who held a public-land grazing permit in Colorado, became director of the Bureau of Land Management.

By September 1982, BLM had substantially revamped how grazing is dealt with in the land-use plans and environmental impact statements, largely eliminating the use of inventory data in making decisions and thus delaying grazing reductions while multi-year monitoring data is collected. Because inventory data is no longer considered sufficient for decisions, grazing impact statements are no longer required to set grazing carrying capacity, although some statements still include estimates. Likewise, without an estimate of total available forage, BLM no longer determines levels of various resource uses by allocating forage among them. Instead, BLM sets population goals for wildlife species and wild horses and burros and sets management objectives for range condition and utilization of key plant species. Livestock grazing is to be adjusted as necessary to meet the range objectives. If implemented correctly, this approach gives wildlife and horses and burros first priority to the vegetation, since any overutilization of the range would be addressed by adjusting livestock use.

A key criticism of the new policy, however, is that it directs field staff, if they feel that adequate data to support a grazing adjustment do not exist, to delay the adjustment until it is supported by monitoring data. Up to five years of monitoring data may be collected before a decision is made or agreement with the permittee is reached. Decisions or agreements on grazing adjustments are to be issued within five years of the publication of the *Range Program Summary*, a document that summarizes the grazing-management decisions embodied in BLM land-use plans. Once a decision or agreement is made, the adjustment may be phased in over an additional five years, so that grazing adjustments may not take full effect for 10 years.

***Monitoring.*** With grazing decisions dependent on monitoring data, BLM is under a heavy burden to ensure that adequate monitoring studies are completed. Conservationists are concerned that adequate monitoring is not being done and that this may result in further delays in grazing adjustments. It is difficult to assess the adequacy of BLM's overall monitoring efforts since the bureau has no agency-wide prescriptions for monitoring requirements and no compilation of what is being accomplished.

The limited information available raises serious questions about both the quantity and quality of BLM monitoring.[28] For example, an evaluation of monitoring in Utah—a state that says it has placed high priority on monitoring—outlined numerous problems with the program, some of which could mean that "the agency will not have sufficient data on which to base management decisions in the future" (Department of Interior 1984b). The evaluation also found that Utah BLM staff generally are doubtful that the monitoring data being gathered can or will be used by managers to make resource-management decisions. In 1986, BLM conducted an agency-wide evaluation of on-the-ground monitoring studies, but had not released the results by the end of the fiscal year.

***Progress and Outlook.*** BLM has no data with which to assess progress in making grazing adjustments under the new policy.[29] The range division says that adjustments required in plans completed prior to 1982, when BLM still operated largely under the Carter administration policy, should be fully implemented. The bureau lacks data on grazing adjustments that were completed or scheduled as a result of plans and impact statements completed since the 1982 policy changes, although BLM says it is gathering such information.

Because BLM collects no more than five years of monitoring data before it makes grazing decisions, grazing adjustments to implement plans developed since 1982 begin coming due in 1987. In May 1986, BLM issued instructions to the field clarifying and emphasizing this policy, and the Range Division began to compile data to determine if appropriate allotments were being monitored adequately to support decisions due in 1987 and 1988. The need to ensure that at least some adjustments are made was supported by a federal district judge in a suit brought against BLM's land-use plan and grazing environmental impact statement for the Reno resource area (*Natural Resources*

---

28. This topic is discussed in more detail in the *Audubon Wildlife Report 1986.*

29. BLM says 1,200 to 1,500 grazing decisions or agreements have been made each year but cannot identify what the decisions were or where they were made.

*Defense Council v. Hodel*, 624 F. Supp. 1045, D. Nev. 1985). The judge ruled against the Natural Resources Defense Council, among other things maintaining that BLM did not have to allocate forage in the plans and did not have to make grazing adjustments based on available inventory data.[30] However, the judge did state that if BLM had still failed to take steps to implement the plan and move toward achieving its objectives within five years, the plaintiffs might be able to sue BLM to enforce the plan.

Conservationists have been sharply critical of BLM's policy of delaying grazing adjustments, especially since various reports, such as the 1974 Nevada report, have shown that overgrazing is occurring in numerous areas and is causing serious range damage. They also are skeptical that adjustments, or adequate adjustments, will be made as decisions come due. In the long term, BLM range managers argue that a continual program of monitoring will end BLM's historical pattern of trying to adjust stocking rates only in a massive reform effort every 10 to 20 years. They say that under the new management approach, BLM will make grazing adjustments whenever monitoring data indicate they are needed as a result of changes in climate, wildlife use, or other factors. Such a program, however, will require an expanded and long-term commitment to providing the funds and personnel to conduct the necessary monitoring and a willingness to make the decisions that the data call for.

### Additional Grazing Management Issues.

Conservationists charge that the decision to delay grazing reductions was motivated primarily by the administration's intent to grant the wishes of the sagebrush rebels to return control to the ranchers. They maintain that several other policy changes, including the changes in water rights policy (discussed under soil and water) and a variety of revisions to the grazing regulations indicate a similar approach. One of the most controversial of these changes was BLM's issuance of regulations in 1984 to implement a "cooperative management agreement program," which allowed certain livestock operators wide latitude to manage livestock grazing. The program was overturned in 1985 by a federal district court, which called it a "naked violation" of the law and found that "the apparent goal and inevitable result of the CMA [Cooperative Management Agreement] program is to allow ranchers . . . to rule the range as they see fit with little or no governmental interference." (*Natural Resources Defense Council v. Hodel*, Civil Suit 84–616, August 30, 1985.) Conservation organizations believe these policy changes convey a message to field personnel that they are not to pursue BLM's multiple-use mandate aggressively. In fact, a report by Interior's

---

30. The Natural Resources Defense Council has appealed the decision on a number of counts.

inspector general found a perception by field personnel "that BLM must acquiesce to permittees in order to obtain their cooperation" (U.S. Congress 1986a).

One additional factor that has limited BLM's ability to manage livestock grazing has been budget and staff cuts in the grazing management program since 1981. Grazing-management appropriations have dropped from $36.1 million in 1981 to $29.3 million in 1986, a 19 percent cut in current dollars and a 34 percent cut in 1982 constant dollars. Personnel levels have been reduced from 994 full-time equivalents in 1982, the first year for which full-time equivalents numbers are available, to 775 in 1986, a 22 percent cut. According to the inspector general's 1985 audit, BLM field personnel cite a lack of adequate staff resources as a factor in their inability to fully implement and accomplish grazing and range-improvement objective (U.S. Congress 1986a).

### Grazing Fees

Over the past several years, grazing fees have been one of the most hotly debated aspects of grazing management. BLM says that grazing decisions are based solely on range-management needs, but conservationists maintain that the fees are artificially low and thus encourage overgrazing. Also, conservationists maintain that the low fees increase political pressure from ranchers against grazing reductions because the low fees create or add to "permit value." Permit value is the result of the difference between the fee paid for grazing on public lands and the market rental value of the grazing over time. Because public-land grazing permits generally are tied to a rancher's private "base" property and are generally transferred to the new owner when the land is sold, the permit value is commonly considered part of the permittee's property and is included in the market price and loan value of the property. Permit value can be substantial and maybe larger than the sales value of the land itself[31] (U.S. Congress 1986a).

Conservationists also charge that the low fees do not provide adequate returns to the range improvement fund, from which money is taken to repair damage caused to the public lands by livestock grazing in the past. Supporters of fee increases further argue that the low fees are unfair to the vast majority of ranchers and farmers in the United

31. Permit value is a market phenomenon and is not formally recognized by the federal government. Public-land grazing permittees have tried to sue the government for reimbursement of the lost permit value when grazing reductions are made, but the courts have agreed with the federal government that public land grazing is a privilege, not a right.

States who do not graze on the public lands, that they do not provide fair return to the public for consumption of public forage, that they do not cover even the direct costs of administering public-land grazing, and that they have not helped to stabilize the livestock industry.

Public-land permittees argue that grazing fees on public lands cannot be compared with fees on private lands because permittees incur higher costs, in part to satisfy other multiple-use objectives, and receive fewer services than lessees on private lands. They also maintain that grazing-fee receipts should not be expected to cover the cost of the grazing-management budget because portions of that budget are spent on range-management activities associated with maintaining other resource uses.

Federal grazing fees have a long history of controversy. In fact, BLM was created after the Grazing Service was essentially dismantled in a congressional battle over grazing fees.[32] The current controversy dates from 1969, when BLM and the Forest Service began to phase in fee increases with the goal of charging a fair market fee within 10 years. The fee increases were blocked several times by Congress. And although Congress specified in the Federal Land Policy and Management Act that it is government policy to receive fair market value for the use of public-land resources, Congress froze grazing fees in the Federal Land Policy and Management Act at their below-market levels and required a government study to devise a fee that would be equitable both to the United States and to the holders of grazing permits.

Two years later, in the Public Rangelands Improvement Act of 1978 (43 U.S.C. 1901 *et seq.*), Congress for the first time legislatively set the fee formula, which was based not on fair market value but on beef prices and production costs and hence the livestock operator's ability to pay. Under this new formula, the fee rose for two years to a high of $2.36 per AUM in 1980 and then steadily declined to $1.35 in 1985. During this same period, the range improvement fund, composed primarily of 50 percent of grazing fee receipts, dropped from $13.5 million to $10 million and was prevented from falling lower only by appropriations from general revenues to maintain the $10 million floor imposed by the Public Rangelands Improvement Act.

In 1986, a grazing-fee study conducted by the departments of the Interior and Agriculture found that the public-land grazing fee was substantially lower than grazing fees charged elsewhere and was far below fair market value. In 1983, for example, the public-land grazing fee was $1.40. That same year the average grazing fee on western

---

32. See *Politics and Grass* by Philip Foss for a discussion of this struggle (Foss 1960).

private lands was $6.87, and the appraised market value of cattle grazing on public rangelands ranged from $4.05 to $8.55 (Department of Agriculture and Department of Interior 1986). Grazing fees charged by other federal agencies during the early 1980s ranged from $1.58 to $18.05 (U.S. Congress 1984). The clearest proof that the fee is far below market value is that in 1983, while BLM permittees paid the government $1.40 for the privilege of grazing, 860 of them subleased their public-grazing privileges at rates ranging from $4 to $12 (U.S. Congress 1984).

The fee formula established by the Public Rangelands Improvement Act was set to expire at the end of 1985. As the expiration date drew near, key committee leaders in Congress tried to develop compromise legislation to address the fee issue as well as range improvement issues raised by conservationists (see the *Audubon Wildlife Report 1986* for details). But the effort fell apart without a bill ever being introduced, and authority to set the fee reverted to the administration. The president's Office of Management and Budget pressed for fee increases and this, combined with the administration's strong support for user fees and concern for reducing the federal deficit, seemed to indicate the fees would be raised. In the meantime, however, 28 western senators asked President Reagan not to change the grazing-fee formula. In February 1986, President Reagan issued an executive order indefinitely extending the existing Public Rangelands Improvements Act fee formula, although the order did set a minimum fee of $1.35 (E.O. 12518, Feb. 14, 1986). The Economic Research Service projects the fee will remain at $1.35 through 1991 (U.S. Congress 1986).

Environmental groups, including the Natural Resources Defense Council, the National Audubon Society, and the National Wildlife Federation among others, have filed suit in the U.S. District Court for the Eastern District of California, challenging the fee formula. The suit, *National Resources Defense Council v. Hodel* (Civ. No. 86-0548) argues that the fee was adopted without required public participation, that it violates the Federal Land Policy and Management Act's statutory requirement that fair market value be obtained for the use of public resources, and that because the fee formula will have significant environmental consequences, the government violated the National Environmental Policy Act by failing to assess its environmental impacts.

## Grazing Advisory Boards and Range Improvements

The grazing advisory boards, made up solely of livestock permittees, advise BLM on the development of allotment management plans and expenditure of range improvement funds. Conservationists object to the boards as inappropriate, single-interest advisors and as a key element in perpetuating rancher dominance of BLM resource-management policy. In a partial effort to address these concerns, the Federal Land Policy and Management Act extended the boards only through 1985 and authorized the establishment of multiple-use advisory councils, made up of 10 to 15 people "who are representative of the various major citizens' interests" in public-land management, to advise BLM on a broad spectrum of land-use planning, disposal, and management issues.

Conservationists, however, have criticized BLM use of the councils on the grounds that the councils do not fairly or adequately represent the various multiple uses of the public lands, especially the noncommodity uses. According to a review of the councils' 1984 membership lists by the Natural Resources Defense Council, the livestock industry was the largest single interest represented, holding 100 of the approximately 500 to 700 seats. Livestock interests held 56 of the 81 renewable-resource seats and on a majority of councils represented one to four additional interests as well, including the wildlife, environmental-protection, and recreation interests.

Conservationists urged that the boards be allowed to expire on the 1985 termination date. They recommended that the boards' functions be turned over to the multiple-use councils and that the councils be revamped to represent truly the various public-land interests. When Congress failed to take up range legislation in 1985, the Federal Land Policy and Management Act authority for the grazing advisory boards expired. However, the grazing boards were reinstated in May 1986 by an administrative directive issued by the BLM director.

***Range Improvements.*** One criticism of the grazing advisory boards is that they have ensured that range improvement funds are used solely for projects intended to benefit livestock, even though the Federal Land Policy Management Act specifies that the use of these funds is to include fish- and wildlife-habitat enhancement. In fiscal year 1985, BLM officials said that not a single project funded with range improvement funds was conducted primarily for the benefit of wildlife. However, BLM range officials maintain that many if not most range improvements have some benefits for wildlife. For example, ranchers are required to provide for wildlife use at water developments. Conservationists counter that ranchers do not always comply with these requirements and that livestock improvements are sometimes harmful to wildlife. For example, water developments intended to distribute cattle more evenly will bring grazing into areas that previously were undisturbed wildlife habitat.

Within the past year, however, some significant movement has occurred in BLM to use range improvement funds for wildlife projects.

In New Mexico, roughly nine percent of range improvement funds were used for wildlife projects in fiscal year 1986, and the state director instructed each district to allocate 25 percent of range improvement funds to wildlife-habitat improvement projects beginning in fiscal year 1987. In Utah, the state director has emphasized that these funds may be used for wildlife projects and asked each district to submit a list of such projects for implementation in fiscal year 1988. Idaho is emphasizing the use of these funds for riparian-area improvements, and BLM staff say that in some of the state's districts, 20 to 25 percent of the funds were used on riparian projects in fiscal year 1986. BLM's Division of Wildlife and Fisheries asked other state directors to consider similar efforts.

## SOIL, WATER, AND AIR

Soil, water, and air are the basic resources on which most other public-land resources and activities—such as vegetation and wildlife, grazing and recreation—depend. BLM conducts two types of general activities with respect to these resources. It conducts projects to protect and improve the condition of the resources themselves, and it collects information on these resources that is needed for the planning and management of other public-land resources and activities. These programs are critical for good wildlife-habitat management. Deteriorated soils and watersheds can have severe impacts on fish and wildlife habitat, and information on soil and water resources often determines whether and what types of habitat management will be successful in a given area. The Soil, Water, and Air Branch of the Division of Rangeland Resources coordinates activities related to these resources.[33]

BLM has no comprehensive assessment of erosion, sedimentation, or water quality on the public lands. But the Society for Range Management has termed erosion in the West "spectacular" (Branson *et al.* 1972). Studies have shown that runoff increases as ranges deteriorate in condition, and in spite of some improvements under federal management, the majority of the BLM range is in deteriorated condition. Stream courses throughout the West also are suffering. Many western waterways have been plagued with severe erosion and greatly

33. The air program is not covered in this chapter. The basic activity of this program is monitoring climatic conditions and air quality to assist in BLM planning efforts and to provide necessary information for activities such as grazing, prescribed burning, fire rehabilitation, and energy and minerals development. BLM also operates a number of acid-rain monitoring stations as part of an interagency effort to gather data on acid deposition.

**TABLE 6**
**BLM Soil Scientists and Hyrologists, 1980-1986**

| Year | Soil scientists | Hydrologists |
|------|-----------------|--------------|
| 1980 | 122 | 81 |
| 1981 | 115 | 76 |
| 1982 | 103 | 73 |
| 1983 | 89 | 67 |
| 1984 | 83 | 65 |
| 1985 | 77 | 60 |
| 1986 | 74 | 55 |

reduced water yields as water tables are lowered and as streams lose their capacity to store water (see section on riparian-area management).

## Soils Management

The major activity of the soils program is a comprehensive soil survey of BLM lands in the lower 48 states. By the end of fiscal year 1986, BLM had completed inventories on 131 million acres. BLM is scheduled to complete its inventory of 157 million acres by 1989, although two states are expected to fail to meet this deadline.[34] Survey information on soil can be used for numerous purposes related to fish and wildlife, such as determining the susceptibility of soils to erosion in order to minimize stream sedimentation, determining whether and what types of habitat-management manipulations will succeed in an area, and identifying deficiencies in wildlife-forage nutrients and quality.

As BLM completes the soil surveys, the emphasis of the soils program should shift to using the data collected.[35] Yet, as the soil surveys have been completed, soil-scientist positions have been rapidly terminated. The number of soil scientists decreased from 122 in 1980 to 74 in 1986, a 39 percent cut (see Table 6). On most of the public lands this cut is even more severe, because during this period the number of soil scientists increased from 14 to 17 in the Oregon and California Grant Lands, where road building and timber harvesting have relatively high potential for increasing erosion. Thus on the remainder of the public lands, soil-scientist numbers have decreased from 108 to 46, nearly a 50 percent cut.

Despite the reductions, BLM could still make the expertise of its 74 soil scientists available in all management areas by placing one soil

34. The survey falls short of the 177 million acres of BLM lands in the lower 48 states because soils in the California Desert Conservation Area and in scattered tracts of public lands will not be surveyed.

35. BLM soil scientists say that, aside from conducting some more intensive site-specific surveys as needed, the current inventory should be relevant for 25 to 30 years.

**TABLE 7**
**BLM Soil Scientists and Hydrologists by State, Fiscal Year 1986**

| State | Soil scientists | Hydrologists |
|---|---|---|
| Alaska | 0 | 1 |
| Arizona | 1 | 3 |
| California | 2 | 4 |
| Colorado | 4 | 8 |
| Idaho | 5 | 4 |
| Montana | 8 | 5 |
| Nevada | 13 | 5 |
| New Mexico | 4 | 2 |
| Oregon | 22 | 5 |
| Utah | 4 | 5 |
| Wyoming | 9 | 6 |
| Eastern States | 0 | 1 |
| Denver Service Center | 1 | 4 |
| Washington Office | 1 | 2 |
| TOTAL | 74 | 55 |

scientist in each state and district office. But currently their distribution is highly uneven. For example, Arizona—with 12 million acres of public lands and some of the bureau's most deteriorated range—has one soil scientist. California, with 17 million acres of public land, including the fragile California Desert Conservation Area, has only two soil scientists, neither of which serves the conservation area. Oregon, on the other hand, has 22 (see Table 7).

With the loss of trained soil scientists, BLM is losing the expertise it needs to interpret and make use of the soil-survey data it has spent so much time and money to collect. BLM officials say wildlife and range personnel manage and monitor vegetation as basic soil protection and that the agency has access to soil expertise in other federal agencies. But some BLM soil specialists say that for the most part, neither BLM managers nor other bureau scientists are trained in how to interpret and use the soil information themselves and that the data are not being used to full potential. This situation is aggravated because to date most research in the interpretation of soil data has been oriented toward agriculture, and little work has been done on how to interpret soil data for application to fish- and wildlife-habitat management.

## Watershed Management

BLM conducts two main types of activities in watershed management. It collects data on the four basic elements that determine the condition of the watershed—soil erosion, stream sedimentation, water yield or quantity, and water quality. It also implements projects to improve watershed condition, such as seedings to stabilize soil, construction of dikes or check dams to stabilize streambanks, and construction of other projects to rehabilitate watershed damaged by overgrazing or mining activities.

The focus of watershed management has changed. When it was established in 1965, the Division of Watershed focused on construction of improvement structures. Concern that the focus on structures was treating the symptoms rather than the real problems led to a de-emphasis on construction in the mid-1970s. With the budget squeeze of the 1980s, BLM has focused on maintenance of existing improve-ments and on treating the source of erosion problems through vegeta-tive manipulation, grazing systems, and smaller improvement projects.

For the past four years, BLM has been working with other agencies to develop a new approach to watershed-condition analysis. This effort may help establish more consistency among BLM state offices in addressing watershed condition and should clarify the program's objectives. Using the data gathered in the watershed-condition inven-tories, watershed units would be classified in one of four categories based on their condition, their vulnerability, and their likely respon-siveness to treatment. Priorities for funding would be based on these determinations, with the most money going to units that are in unsatisfactory condition but that would be highly responsive to treatment. This approach to analysis should make hydrological data and information more useful to BLM managers.

Like the soils program, the water resources program has suffered sharp personnel cuts. The number of hydrologists has been reduced from 81 in 1980 to 55 in 1986, a 32 percent cut (see Table 6). BLM has only 49 hydrologists in the field, not even enough to place one in each district. Alaska has only one hydrologist, New Mexico two, and Arizona three (see Table 7). This reduction comes at a time when BLM is supposed to give increasing attention to riparian-area management, a key component of which is hydrologic considerations. It raises questions as to whether the riparian-area demonstration program — under which each district is to establish a model riparian area man-agement project — can be carried out adequately.

One problem in both the soil and water resources programs is their lack of clear identity within the bureau. Both are relatively new programs. BLM's soils program began in the mid-1970s, when it hired soil scientists to collect information for the court-ordered grazing environmental impact statements. The Division of Watershed was established in 1965, but initially focused largely on supporting the grazing program. Hydrologists were not hired in significant numbers until the 1970s as well. Thus both programs had been in existence a relatively short time before sharp cuts were initiated in their staffs and budgets. The soil, water, and air budget has been cut 22 percent since 1981, a 37 percent cut in 1982 constant-dollar spending power.[36]

This lack of identity has been aggravated by organizational shifts. The Division of Watershed was abolished in 1979 and was replaced by a Water Policy staff. In 1982, this staff was abolished and a Soil, Water, and Air Branch was placed under the Range Division. This latter move has been criticized as reinforcing a tendency in the bureau to view the soils and water-resources programs largely as support for grazing management rather than as programs responsible for resources that are vitally important in and of themselves.

## Water Rights

Water is scarce in much of the West, including on most BLM lands, and who controls the water is a critical question. In most of the western states, water rights are determined by appropriation systems established by state law. Each state's system varies, but in general, water rights are granted to whoever first puts the water to a beneficial use — regardless of who owns the land — and only in the amount that is actually used. The earlier a beneficial use was established, the higher priority that user has to a water right.

Because the right to use the water generally is not related to land ownership, even the federal government for the most part must apply to the states for the rights to water on the public lands. However, some water rights are considered reserved to the United States. These are primarily on lands reserved from the public domain by Congress such as national forests, wilderness areas, and wild and scenic rivers.

In 1984, BLM began a comprehensive inventory of existing types, locations, and amounts of water uses on the public lands in preparation for filing for water rights as the states begin their water-rights adjudications. BLM has completed the inventory in several states and expects to complete inventories by 1988 in all states except California, Utah, and Wyoming. Once current water uses are inventoried, BLM still will need to maintain the inventory as new water sources or uses arise or as uses change.

Over the past 10 years or so, the question of what water rights are retained by the federal government and what rights it will file for with the states has been highly controversial. Until the late 1970s, the Interior Department had no formal policy regarding water rights. BLM staff say there was a general notion that the federal government had the right to water on its lands, but that BLM staff in each state dealt with the question differently.

36. Not including funds budgeted under the soil, water, and air activity for hazardous waste management.

In 1979, as a result of President Carter's water policy initiative, the Interior Department's solicitor issued the department's first comprehensive opinion on federal water rights. The opinion generally claimed for the federal government broad rights to the water necessary to manage its lands. The assertion of strong federal rights, which often conflicted with state law, caused a firestorm of protest from the western states, where the anti-federal government, sagebrush-rebellion sentiment already was brewing.

With the election of President Reagan and confirmation of James Watt as Interior Secretary, the Interior Department made a philosophical about-face from trying to assert federal rights and control to trying to defer as much as possible to state law. In a series of solicitor opinions and policy statements, Interior made important changes in three areas: reserved water rights, nonreserved water rights, and rights to water for livestock on public lands. These changes have raised questions about whether BLM will retain sufficient control over water on its lands to meet its multiple-use management responsibilities, including management of fish and wildlife habitat.

***Reserved Water Rights.*** In 1926, in order to prevent individuals from monopolizing or controlling large areas of the public lands surrounding water sources, President Coolidge issued Public Water Reserve No. 107, withdrawing small, unsettled parcels of land surrounding springs and waterholes. Under the Carter administration, the Interior Department said that these withdrawals were intended to preserve sufficient water to support such uses as growing crops and to sustain fish and wildlife as food for settlers and their families. Interior maintained that all the water at each site was reserved to BLM, although BLM would make available to other users, through permits and licenses, any water not needed to fulfill the purposes of the withdrawal. In 1983, however, under the Reagan administration the Interior Department substantially revised this option and asserted reserved rights at springs and waterholes only to the amount of water necessary for human and livestock consumption.

Under current policy, then, BLM field staff theoretically must identify each withdrawn spring and waterhole, must quantify the amount of water necessary for human and livestock consumption, and must notify the state that it is asserting a reserved right. To obtain rights to water from these sources for any other uses, BLM must apply to the state for an appropriative right. In addition, BLM policy specifies that the reservation applies only where private control of the water source would monopolize the resources, giving its field staff yet another difficult determination to make.

Under current Interior Department policy, BLM also has limited reserved water rights for wild and scenic rivers and wilderness. It is current BLM policy to assert a federal reserved right only where doing so would be more effective than applying for a right under state law. BLM wilderness officials say no federally reserved rights have been asserted yet for BLM's 369,000 acres of wilderness. Reserved rights have been asserted on two of 13 BLM wild and scenic rivers.

**Federal Non-Reserved Water Rights.** The assertion of federal non-reserved water rights was the most controversial aspect of the Carter administration's policy. The Interior solicitor's opinion said the federal government had rights to whatever water was necessary to carry out programs specifically authorized by Congress, even if the lands had not been reserved or withdrawn. This opinion maintained that it was implicit that Congress intended federal agencies to have the water necessary to comply with the laws it passed. This determination was significant for BLM lands, because most of them are not withdrawn or reserved and thus are not eligible for federal reserved rights. The opinion maintained that BLM had a non-reserved right to water for its various multiple-use management needs, including for instream flows and fish and wildlife.

Interior began to back away from this position under the Carter administration, and under the Reagan administration the department issued a new opinion asserting that there is no such thing as federal non-reserved water rights. Under this policy, federal agencies must apply to the states to obtain water rights for congressionally recognized and mandated purposes on unreserved lands. This can be a problem since some states do not recognize water rights for uses such as wild-life and instream flows to maintain fisheries or protect riparian habitat.

**Stock Watering Water Use.** Under the Carter administration's non-reserved water-rights policy, BLM theoretically had an automatic right to water for livestock grazing. When this policy was overturned in 1981, BLM could obtain such rights only by applying to the states. The bureau subsequently issued a controversial policy encouraging private permittees, rather than BLM, to file in many cases for the rights to water at stock-watering developments on the public lands. The policy states that if the permittee pays for construction of the stock-watering facility, he may apply for the right; if BLM pays for the development, BLM will apply for the right. If BLM and the permittee share the cost of the development, who files for the right depends on when the development was constructed. For projects constructed after October 1, 1981, BLM and the permittee will file jointly as coholders of the right. If the improvement were made prior to that date, the permittee may apply for the right if BLM does not already hold it.[37]

This policy was vigorously protested within and outside of BLM. In most states, a water right is similar to a property right: It can be sold, applied to a different use, and in some cases transferred to a new location. A majority of the state directors warned that BLM would not be able to carry out multiple-use management responsibilities if the permittee obtained the water right and that the permittee would become insulated from management and land-use changes, although he would be able to change those uses himself (U.S. Congress 1986a). BLM and Interior officials, however, say BLM has a number of ways to prevent permittees from transferring waters to other uses, owners, or locations. For example, BLM could refuse a right-of-way permit to anyone seeking to divert the water to a different location. And in most, if not all, states, the permittee would have to get state approval to change the use or location of the water, an action that BLM could protest in what Interior officials say is a relatively *pro forma* proceeding.

Philosophically, the changes in water rights have been extreme, swinging from a strong assertion of federal rights to an overwhelming deference to state law. But the practical effect is difficult to determine. Because each state law is different, few generalizations about BLM progress on water rights can be made. In addition, as with many BLM programs, the Washington headquarters has little useful data on state-office activities. It even lacks data on what water rights the livestock permittees or other users have applied for on public lands.

Some wildlife interests say the water-rights policy changes may have the most far-reaching, detrimental effects of any of the Reagan administration policy changes, ultimately preventing BLM from properly managing the public lands for multiple use in some areas. Others say that regardless of the policy changes, the fact that BLM has a coherent policy and is quantifying and applying for water rights in a comprehensive manner is a substantial improvement over the haphazard approach to water rights prior to the late 1970s. Some say that the practical effect of these changes, although they could have some negative impacts, is likely to be small. They maintain that most sensitive or fragile resources requiring water on BLM lands are in headwater areas, where upstream diversion under private water rights is not a problem, and that because the states are becoming more sensitive to environmental requirements, ultimately they will ensure that water is available for fish, wildlife, and recreational uses.

37. BLM officials can give no rational explanation for this difference in policy. Sources say that BLM initially wanted to allow permittees to file for sole rights where projects were cost-shared, but that the solicitor's office maintained that where BLM put up some of the money it must file for the right. BLM applied this requirement only from the date of its new policy forward.

# SPECIAL MANAGEMENT AREAS

BLM has a variety of special designations that can be used to highlight an area's management needs or to provide an additional measure of protection to various resources, including wildlife. Some of these are designations that can be made only by Congress, such as lands designated for inclusion in the National Wilderness System and the Wild and Scenic Rivers System. Other designations may be made by BLM through its planning process, such as outstanding natural areas, research natural areas, and areas of critical environmental concern.

For the most part, these special-management designations have not been used extensively on the public lands. BLM has three million acres designated as some type of natural area, but almost half of this acreage is in just two areas in California. BLM has three national conservation areas and 13 wild and scenic rivers. These designations generally have not been controversial (see Table 8).

In contrast, wilderness and areas of critical environmental concern have been quite controversial in recent years. BLM has only 368,000 acres of designated wilderness and is conducting a comprehensive wilderness study that has been sharply criticized by conservationists. BLM also has been criticized for failure to give priority to designating areas of critical environmental concern. This failure is in violation of the mandates of the Federal Land Policy and Management Act, and BLM is moving to correct it. This chapter focuses on these two areas.

## Areas of Critical Environmental Concern

The Federal Land Policy and Management Act established a new type of special management designation for BLM lands: areas of critical environmental concern. The act defines these as areas within the public lands "where special management attention is required . . . to protect and prevent irreparable damage to important historic, cultural, or scenic values, fish and wildlife resources, or other natural systems or processes, or to protect life and safety from natural hazards." Congress directed BLM to give priority to identifying these areas while conducting inventories of public-land resources, to give priority to their designation and protection in developing or revising land-use plans, and to promptly develop regulations and plans for the protection of designated areas. The designation of areas of critical environmental concern is the only explicit planning priority named in the law.

Areas of critical environmental concern differ from designations such as wilderness. They can be nominated by any member of the public or by BLM and are designated by BLM through the planning process without any congressional action. Furthermore, since Congress set no particular standards or management requirements for areas

**TABLE 8**

**Established Bureau of Land Management Natural Areas as of September 30, 1985**

| Administrative state | Research natural areas | | Outstanding natural areas | | Other natural areas | | Primitive areas | | Recreation lands | | National natural landmarks | | Total | |
|---|---|---|---|---|---|---|---|---|---|---|---|---|---|---|
| | # | acres | # | acres | # | acres | # | acres | # | acres | # | acres[a] | # | acres[b] |
| Alaska | 1 | 120 | — | — | — | — | — | — | — | — | — | — | 1 | 120 |
| Arizona | 2 | 314 | 1 | 8,400 | — | — | — | — | 1 | 23,070 | 2 | 5,678 | 6 | 37,462 |
| California | 6 | 38,395 | 1 | 1,500 | 2 | 1,412,763 | 1 | 3,941 | 1 | 6,065 | 11 | 167,490 | 22 | 1,632,154 |
| Colorado | 6 | 2,158 | 1 | 3,200 | — | — | 1 | 40,400 | 1 | 30,135 | 2 | 1,160 | 11 | 77,053 |
| Idaho | 2 | 26,480 | 1 | 3,500 | — | — | — | — | — | — | 7 | 76,695 | 10 | 106,675 |
| Montana | — | — | 1 | 1,947 | — | — | 2 | 31,206 | — | — | 4 | 38,050 | 7 | 71,203 |
| Nevada | 6 | 1,759 | 12 | 75,645 | 3 | 35,944 | — | — | 2 | 70,881 | 1 | 400 | 24 | 184,629 |
| New Mexico | 5 | 35,437 | 3 | 89,503 | — | — | — | — | 2 | 27,167 | 1 | 65,874 | 16 | 217,981 |
| Oregon | 33 | 69,895 | 9 | 18,625 | 1 | 1,620 | — | — | 3 | 180,247 | 7 | 600 | 47 | 270,987 |
| Utah | 4 | 2,520 | 6 | 174,545 | — | — | 2 | 81,328 | — | — | 3 | 33,720 | 15 | 292,113 |
| Washington | — | — | — | — | — | — | — | — | — | — | 2 | 7,095 | 2 | 7,095 |
| Wyoming | — | — | — | — | — | — | 1 | 6,680 | — | — | 6 | 44,640 | 7 | 51,320 |
| TOTAL | 58 | 160,016 | 32 | 413,026 | 4 | 1,439,663 | 7 | 163,555 | 9 | 337,565 | 41 | 407,052 | 128 | 2,915,447 |

[a]Includes Bureau of Land Management and other ownerships.
[b]Includes duplication of acreage where designations overlap.

*Research natural areas* are established and maintained for the primary purpose of research and education.

*Outstanding natural areas* are established to preserve scenic values and areas of natural wonder.

*"Other natural areas"* are acreage in California, Nevada, and Oregon that has been set-aside for a variety of natural area and scenic protection purposes.

*Primitive areas* are established to remove lands from the effects of civilization and are being studied to determine their status for wilderness designation by Congress.

*Recreation lands* are natural areas, usually several thousand acres in size, where recreation is, or is expected to be, the major use.

*National natural landmarks* are selected areas throughout the United States that are nationally significant representatives of the country's natural heritage (on public or private land) under the National Park Service's National Natural Landmarks Program to identify and encourage their protection.

**TABLE 9**
**Areas of Critical Environmental Concern, October 1, 1986**

| State | ACECS added in FY 86 # | Acres | Total ACES # | Acres | Percent of total BLM state acreage in ACECs[a] |
|---|---|---|---|---|---|
| Alaska | 16 | 2,767,861 | 16 | 2,767,861 | 4.3 percent |
| Arizona | 0 | 0 | 0 | 0 | 0 |
| California | 3 | 14,318 | 90 | 780,344 | 4.5 |
| Colorado | 3 | 159,640 | 15 | 346,442 | 4.1 |
| Idaho | 3 | 43,300 | 8 | 271,645 | 2.3 |
| Montana | 0 | 0 | 1 | 12,048 | .1 |
| Nevada | 0 | 0 | 4 | 1,479 | negligible |
| New Mexico | 10 | 40,794 | 17 | 60,186 | .5 |
| Oregon | 6 | 7,938 | 70 | 247,999 | 1.5 |
| Utah | 3 | 11,495 | 10 | 100,726 | .6 |
| Wyoming | 0 | 0 | 13 | 208,385 | 1.1 |
| Eastern States | 0 | 0 | 0 | 0 | 0 |
| TOTAL | 44 | 3,045,346 | 244 | 4,797,115 | 2.0 |

[a] Calculated using 65 million acres for Alaska and 242 million acres total to omit lands scheduled for transfer to the state of Alaska and Alaska Natives.

of critical environmental concern, designation does not automatically prohibit any particular activities. Management prescriptions for designated areas are set forth in the land-use plan. Activities inconsistent with the purposes of the designated areas of critical environmental concern and associated management prescriptions are prohibited unless the plan is formally amended to allow them.

The BLM record in designating areas of critical environmental concern has varied widely among the states, and wildlife and other conservation interests have charged that BLM has failed to follow the Federal Land Policy and Management Act's mandate to give priority to their identification, designation, and protection.[38] At the end of fiscal year 1986, BLM had designated 244 areas of critical environmental concern, encompassing 4.8 million acres, just 1.8 percent of the public lands. And the distribution of these areas and acreage was highly uneven: Alaska alone accounted for 58 percent of the designated acreage; California and Oregon accounted for 66 percent of the total number of areas. Arizona had no designated areas and Montana had only one (see Table 9).

Several factors contribute to BLM's failure to designate areas of critical environmental concern. BLM guidance, particularly since 1981, has been infrequent, sometimes unclear, and has not conveyed

38. See "Areas of Critical Environmental Concern on the Public Lands: Part II," published by the Natural Resources Defense Council, for an in depth discussion (Callison 1986). BLM's failure to designate areas of critical environmental concern also is discussed in more detail in previous *Audubon Wildlife Reports*.

the Federal Land Policy and Management Act directive that the designation is to receive priority. This has created confusion and uncertainty—and a wide array of interpretations—about how to apply the designation. Some field managers have considered the areas of critical environmental concern designation as unnecessary for proper management of an area and in some cases even as a hindrance to proper management. In addition, designations frequently have been opposed by livestock and mining interests, and most states lack counterbalancing public pressure in support of designations.[39] The resulting inconsistent and uncertain treatment of areas of critical environmental concern in the development of land-use plans, and BLM's failure to designate the areas in a number of its plans, have made this issue the most frequent subject of protests against proposed plans.

In 1986, BLM headquarters began to respond to the confusion and criticism surrounding areas of critical environmental concern by proposing new guidance. The draft guidance, issued for public review, reiterates the Federal Land Policy and Management Act's mandate that BLM give priority to designation and protection of areas of critical environmental concern in the planning process and expands substantially on existing guidance regarding the purpose of the designations, the circumstances in which an area should qualify for the designation, and procedures for ensuring that potential areas of critical environmental concern are identified and given full consideration and priority in the planning process. The draft guidance also proposes that all natural areas—such as research natural areas and outstanding natural areas—be designated through the areas of critical environmental concern process. The final guidance, expected in fiscal year 1987, will be issued as a directive to the field and will be incorporated into the BLM manual.

## Wilderness

***Wilderness Study.***   When Congress passed the Wilderness Act in 1964 (16 U.S.C. 1131-1136), the public lands under BLM, although they constitute the largest category of federal lands, were omitted from the law's study provisions. Not until 1976, with the passage of the Federal Land Policy and Management Act, was BLM directed to study its lands for their wilderness potential. As of the end of fiscal year 1986, BLM lands contained only 369,000 acres of designated wilderness, and final wilderness recommendations for most BLM lands were several years off.

BLM has two sources of authority for conducting wilderness studies. Section 603 of the Federal Land Policy and Management Act

39. Described in *Audubon Wildlife Report 1986*.

directs the bureau to conduct a comprehensive wilderness study on all roadless areas of 5,000 acres that are identified as having wilderness characteristics. The act requires the secretary of the Interior to make wilderness recommendations to the president by 1991, and the president is required to send his recommendations to Congress within two years. Section 603 also required an accelerated study of areas classified as primitive or natural areas prior to November 1, 1975, referred to as "instant study areas." In addition, under Section 202 of the Federal Land Policy and Management Act, BLM can consider wilderness recommendations in its land-use planning process, including recommending designation of areas smaller than 5,000 acres.

The wilderness study is proceeding on schedule. BLM has identified for study approximately 25 million acres in almost 900 tracts. BLM has completed draft environmental impact statements and made preliminary recommendations on almost 23 million acres, and has recommended nine million acres, or 39 percent, as suitable for wilderness designation (see Table 10). After BLM completes the final impact statements, the U.S. Geological Survey studies the areas recommended as suitable for wilderness in order to determine their mineral potential. BLM state directors evaluate the mineral reports to determine if changes in the wilderness-suitability recommendations should be considered and may prepare a supplemental environmental impact statement if significant changes are proposed. The Interior Department will then package its wilderness recommendations on a statewide basis and submit them to the president. Recommendations for most states are scheduled for submission by September 1990. In the meantime, recommendations have been made for almost all of the instant study areas, and some areas have been designated.

BLM lands in Alaska were exempted from the Section 603 wilderness-study requirements of the Federal Land Policy and Management Act by the Alaska National Interest Lands Act of 1980. BLM still retains its authority to make wilderness recommendations in Alaska as part of the land-use planning process, but in 1981 Secretary of the Interior James Watt directed that no further wilderness study was to be undertaken in Alaska. This policy continues today.

Wilderness and other conservation interests charge that BLM's wilderness inventory, which identified 25 million acres for wilderness study, was inadequate and that BLM may have studied as little as half of the acreage that actually qualifies. They also charge that the studies themselves have been inadequate and that BLM is recommending insufficient acreage as suitable for wilderness. One of the most controversial studies has been in Utah. Of the 22 million acres of public land in the state, BLM studied about three million acres and made a preliminary recommendation of 1.89 million acres as suitable for wilderness. The Utah Wilderness Coalition is proposing five

**TABLE 10**
**Status of BLM Wilderness Study, April 1986**

| State | Draft environmental impact statement | | Percentage of area studied and recommended as suitable | Percentage of BLM lands in state recommended as suitable | Estimated completion date of last final environmental impact statement | Final recommendation to President |
|---|---|---|---|---|---|---|
| | Suitable | Unsuitable | | | | |
| Arizona | 559,061 | 1,108,355 | 34 | 5 | 3/89 | 9/90 |
| California | 2,372,125 | 4,485,201 | 35 | 14 | 3/89 | 9/89 |
| Colorado | 301,591 | 412,767 | 42 | 4 | 9/88 | 9/90 |
| Idaho | 846,442 | 691,594 | 55 | 7 | 3/89 | 9/90 |
| Montana | 129,888 | 265,350 | 33 | 2 | 9/89 | 9/90 |
| Nevada | 1,667,782 | 2,683,832 | 38 | 3 | 3/89 | 9/90 |
| New Mexico | 407,919 | 385,035 | 51 | 3 | 3/88 | 9/90 |
| Oregon | 949,989 | 1,359,671 | 41 | 6 | 3/88 | 9/89 |
| Utah | 1,892,402 | 1,338,925 | 59 | 9 | 9/87 | 9/90 |
| Wyoming | 84,155 | 388,252 | 21 | .04 | 3/89 | 9/90 |
| Instant Study Areas | 424,946 | 142,930 | 75 | — | | |
| TOTAL | 9,636,300 | 13,261,912 | 42 | 5 | | |

million acres for wilderness designation. BLM found 407,919 acres as suitable in New Mexico, about three percent of the 12.9 million acres of public lands in the state and less than a third of the 1.3 million acres of wilderness favored by a coalition of New Mexico conservationists. In Oregon, BLM recommended less than a million acres of wilderness, compared with the environmentalists' proposal for 2.5 million acres.

***Study Area Management.*** The Federal Land Policy and Management Act requires that wilderness study areas be managed during the study process so as not to impair their suitability for wilderness designation, except that the law authorizes the continuance of certain grazing and mining activities that existed at the time of the act's passage "in the manner and degree" in which they were being conducted at that time. Over the past several years, wilderness interests have charged that BLM has protected wilderness inadequately from unauthorized, destructive uses, such as road construction and illegal mining, and at the same time has authorized numerous activities that are damaging the wilderness character of the areas and that could jeopardize their potential for eventual wilderness designation. After Congress took BLM and the administration to task on this issue at several hearings, secretary of the Interior Donald Hodel took several steps to address these criticisms. BLM wilderness officials say that as a result of the public scrutiny and controversy, as well as the secretarial directives, personnel and field staff throughout the bureau have developed a heightened sensitivity to the need to protect wilderness study areas. Wilderness groups say BLM has made only marginal changes in its pattern of decisions and that the bureau still allows incompatible uses under the premise that the impacts are only temporary or affect only a small area.

***Wilderness Management.*** To date, BLM has 23 designated wilderness areas totalling 368,739 acres. Four of the areas are contiguous to national forest lands designated as wilderness, three of which are administered by the Forest Service. Most areas designated so far either were BLM instant study areas or were designated in legislation concerned primarily with national-forest wilderness.

Like other units of the wilderness system, BLM wilderness areas are managed under the authority of the 1964 Wilderness Act. Unless Congress specifies otherwise, the following activities are prohibited in wilderness areas: permanent or temporary roads; use of motorized vehicles, equipment, or motorboats; landing of aircraft; and structures. Commercial uses also are prohibited, except livestock grazing and certain ongoing mining and mineral leasing. Fishing, hunting, and trapping are allowed in wilderness subject to state and federal regulations and laws.

In 1986, BLM, the Forest Service, and the state fish and wildlife agencies agreed on guidelines for consistent management of fish and wildlife populations and habitat in wilderness areas. The guidelines, which have been incorporated into BLM manuals, describe when and how various management activities may take place, including research and management surveys, habitat alteration, actions to protect and recover threatened and endangered species, fish stocking, transplanting of wildlife, and wildlife damage control. The guidelines specify that wilderness management should ensure that natural ecological succession operates as freely as possible with only minimum influence by humans.

With so little wilderness designated, BLM wilderness management generally has not been controversial. In 1986, however, BLM began to issue wilderness management plans for designated areas. The Wilderness Society was highly critical of some elements of the initial plans, in general expressing concern that the plans were incomplete, provided insufficient protection for wilderness resources, and failed to assess fully the environmental impacts of the actions proposed in the plans. Wilderness management may be a subject of substantial debate in the near future.

# REFERENCES

Almand, D. and W.B. Krohn. 1978. "Position Paper: The Position of the Bureau of Land Management on the Protection of Riparian Ecosystems," in *Strategies for Protection and Management of Floodplain Wetlands and Other Riparian Ecosystems, Proceedings of the Symposium, Dec. 11-13, 1978, Callaway Gardens, Georgia.* General Technical Report WO-12. U.S. Department of Agriculture, Washington, D.C.

Babbitt, B. 1986. *Arizonans' Recreation Needs on Federal Lands: The Governor's Task Force on Recreation on Federal Lands.* State of Arizona, Phoenix.

Box, T.W., Don D. Dwyer, and F.W. Wagner. 1979. "The Public Range and Its Management," in U.S. Congress, Senate, Committee on Energy and Natural Resources, Subcommittee on Parks, Recreation, and Renewable Resources. *Hearings on Bureau of Land Management Grazing Program, First Session on Livestock Grazing on Public Lands, Las Cruces, New Mexico, Aug. 6, 1979.* Government Printing Office. Washington, D.C.

Branson, F.A., G.F. Gifford, and J.R. Owen. 1972. *Rangeland Hydrology.* Society for Range Management. Denver, Colorado.

Callison, C. 1986. *Areas of Critical Environmental Concern on the Public Lands, Part II: Record of Performance by the Bureau of Land Management.* Wild Wings Foundation and Public Lands Institute. New York.

Clarke, J.N. and D. McCool. 1985. *Staking Out the Terrain: Power Differentials among Natural Resource Management Agencies.* State University of New York Press. Albany, New York.

Coggins, G. 1984. "Public Rangeland Management Law: FLPMA and PRIA" in National Research Council/National Academy of Sciences, Commission on Natural Resources, Board of Agriculture and Renewable Resources, *Developing Strategies for Rangeland Management: A Report Prepared by the Committee on Developing Strategies for Rangeland Management.* Westview Press. Boulder and London.

Elder, R.G., and R.C. Moore. 1985. "Impacts of Oil and Gas Development on Riparian Zones in the Overthrust Belt: The Role of Industrial Siting" in *Riparian Ecosystems and Their Management: Reconciling Conflicting Uses, First North American Riparian Conference, April 16-18, 1985. Tucson, Arizona.* U.S. Department of Agriculture. General Technical Report RM-120. Government Printing Office. Washington, D.C.

Fairfax, S. 1984. "Coming of age in the Bureau of Land Management: Range management in search of a gospel," *in* National Research Council/National Academy of Sciences, Commission on Natural Resources, Board on Agriculture and Renewable Resources, *Developing Strategies for Rangeland Management: A Report Prepared by the Committee on Developing Strategies for Rangeland Management.* Westview Press. Boulder and London.

Foss, P. 1960. *Politics and Grass.* University of Washington Press. Seattle.

National Research Council/National Academy of Sciences, Commission on Natural Resources, Board on Agriculture and Renewable Resources. 1984. *Developing Strategies for Rangeland Management: A Report Prepared by the Committee on Developing Strategies for Rangeland Management.* Westview Press. Boulder and London.

National Research Council, Board on Agriculture and Renewable Resources, Committee on Wild and Free-Roaming Horses and Burros. 1982. *Wild and Free-Roaming Horses and Burros.* Final Report. National Academy Press. Washington, D.C.

Sheridan, D. 1981. *Desertification of the United States.* Council on Environmental Quality. U.S. Government Printing Office. Washington, D.C.

Sierra Club. 1986. *Yellowstone Under Siege: Oil and Gas Leasing in the Greater Yellowstone Region.* Sierra Club. San Francisco, California.

Society for Range Management, Range Inventory Standardization Committee. 1983. *Guidelines and Terminology for Range Inventories and Monitoring.* Society for Range Management. Albuquerque, New Mexico.

Thomas, J.W., C. Maser, and J.E. Rodick. 1979. *Wildlife Habitats in Managed Rangelands — the Great Basin of Southeast Oregon, Riparian Zones.* General Technical Report PNW-80. U.S. Department of Agriculture, Forest Service, Pacific Northwest Forest and Range Experiment Station. Washington, D.C.

U.S. Congress, House of Representatives, Committee on Government Operations. 1986a. *Hearings on Management of Livestock Grazing on Federal Lands by the Bureau of Land Management and the Forest Service, December 13, 1985.* Government Printing Office. Washington, D.C.

U.S. Congress, House of Representatives, Committee on Government Operations. 1986b. *Federal Grazing Program: All Is Not Well on the Range.* House Report 99-593. Government Printing Office. Washington, D.C.

U.S. Congress, House of Representatives, Committee on Appropriations, Surveys and Investigation Staff. 1984. "A Report to the Committee on Appropriations, U.S. House of Representatives, on the BLM Grazing Management and Rangeland Improvement Program," in *Hearings on Department of the Interior and Related Agencies Appropriations for 1985, Part 11.* Government Printing Office. Washington, D.C.

U.S. Congress, Senate, Committee on Energy and Natural Resources, Subcommittee on Parks, Recreation, and Renewable Resources. 1980. *Hearings on BLM Wilderness Review and Rangeland Management Programs, February 22 and March 11, 1980.* Pub. No. 96-105. Government Printing Office. Washington, D.C.

U.S. Congress, Senate, Committee on Energy and Natural Resources, Subcommittee on Parks, Recreation, and Renewable Resources. 1979. *Hearings on Bureau of Land Management Grazing Program, First Session on Livestock Grazing on Public Lands, Las Cruces, New Mexico, Aug.6, 1979.* Government Printing Office. Washington, D.C.

U.S. Department of Agriculture, Forest Service, and U.S. Department of the Interior, Bureau of Land Management. 1986. *Grazing Fee Review and Evaluation: Final Report, 1979-1985.* Government Printing Office. Washington, D.C.

U.S. Department of the Interior, Bureau of Land Management. 1986. *Public Land Statistics 1985*. Government Printing Office. Washington, D.C.

U.S. Department of the Interior, Bureau of Land Management. 1984a. *50 Years of Public Land Management*. Washington, D.C.

U.S. Department of the Interior, Bureau of Land Management, Utah State Office. 1984b. *Special Evaluation Report: Utah Statewide Rangeland Monitoring Evaluation.*

U.S. Department of the Interior, Fish and Wildlife Service, Office of Biological Services. 1977. *Improving Fish and Wildlife Benefits in Range Management, Proceedings of a 41st North American Wildlife and Natural Resources Conference, March 20, 1976.* Washington, D.C.

U.S. Department of the Interior, Bureau of Land Management. 1975. *Effects of Livestock Grazing on Wildlife, Watershed, Recreation, and Other Resource Values in Nevada.* Washington, D.C.

Wagner, F.H. 1978. "Livestock Grazing and the Livestock Industry," *in* Howard Brokaw ed., Council on Environmental Quality, *Wildlife and America: Contributions to an Understanding of American Wildlife and Its Conservation.* Government Printing Office. Washington, D.C.

Wald, J. and D. Alberswerth. 1985. *Our Ailing Public Rangelands: Condition Report — 1985.* National Wildlife Federation and Natural Resources Defense Council. Washington, D.C.

Wildlife Management Institute. 1981. *Evaluation of Bureau of Land Management Program Interactions with Rangeland Management.* Washington, D.C.

# Part Two

◇

# Federal Agencies and Programs

Recreational fishing programs are among many state fisheries activities funded by the federal Dingell-Johnson Program. *Oklahoma Department of Wildlife Conservation*

# Federal Grants for State Wildlife Conservation

William J. Chandler

## OVERVIEW

The federal government makes annual matching grants to states and territories[1] for the conservation and management of birds, mammals, and sport fish and for promoting public recreational use of these biological resources. The legal authorities for such assistance are:

- the Federal Aid in Wildlife Restoration Act, also referred to as the Pittman-Robertson Act;
- the Federal Aid in Fish Restoration Act, also known as the Dingell-Johnson Act; and
- the Fish and Wildlife Conservation Act, also called the Forsythe-Chafee Act or the Nongame Act.

All three laws are administered by the Division of Federal Aid in the Interior Department's Fish and Wildlife Service (FWS).

The federal-aid budget for fiscal year 1987, $250.7 million, makes up 37 percent of the total FWS budget authority ($674 million) for fish and wildlife management. All of this $250 million, less a small amount for program administration, is apportioned to the states. Federal-aid

1. Referred to hereafter as the states for brevity.

Audubon Wildlife Report 1987

funds are derived from federal excise taxes on firearms, ammunition, archery equipment, handguns, and sport-fishing equipment; import duties on yachts and fishing equipment; and a portion of the federal tax on gasoline to cover the amount sold for motorboat fuel.

Federal-aid funds make up a significant proportion of state fish- and wildlife-agency budgets. On average, 17.8 percent of state wildlife agency budgets in the late 1970s were financed by federal assistance of one kind or another. Federal assistance totaled $107 million at that time. Of this amount, most was provided through the federal-aid program (The Wildlife Conservation Fund of America 1980).

Federal grants under the Pittman-Robertson Act are used by the states principally to benefit game animals, including migratory waterfowl, such as ducks, geese, and swans; big game, such as deer, elk, bears, and moose; small game, such as squirrels, rabbits, and foxes; and nonmigratory birds, such as quail and pheasants. Projects eligible for funding include research, land acquisition, development of wildlife areas and access to them, administrative coordination, planning, technical assistance, and hunter education, including the construction and operation of public shooting ranges.

Dingell-Johnson Act grants are used to benefit 30 to 40 species of sport fish. Projects eligible for funding include research; land and water acquisition, development of fishing areas, fish restoration facilities, and access to them; administrative coordination; planning; technical assistance; development of recreational boating facilities; and aquatic-education programs.

According to FWS officials, an estimated 10 to 12 percent of the Pittman-Robertson funds spent help benefit nongame. Although conservation actions taken on behalf of game species and sport fish have provided benefits for nongame species, such benefits largely are serendipitous. Some states do apply a portion of their federal-aid funds to projects directly benefitting nongame species, but the lion's share of their money still goes to conserve and manage game species. The Forsythe-Chafee Act or Nongame Act was passed in 1980 to encourage state conservation actions for hundreds of nongame fish and wildlife species, but no appropriations ever have been made to implement that law.

## CURRENT DEVELOPMENTS

### 50th Anniversary of the Pittman-Robertson Act

1987 marks the fiftieth anniversary of the Federal Aid in Wildlife Restoration Program, launched by the Pittman-Robertson Act (16

U.S.C.A. *669 et seq.*). FWS has published a book commemorating the program and its accomplishments (Department of Interior, In press).

The Pittman-Robertson program, according to federal and state wildlife-management professionals, has been a resounding success. The Pittman-Robertson Act is credited with impelling the professionalization of wildlife management in the United States. The guarantee of a more or less predictable yearly sum of federal financial assistance enabled the states to establish and progressively develop fish and wildlife programs. The states have substantially increased populations of game animals such as elk, deer, and turkey; protected or improved millions of acres of wildlife habitat; expanded the distribution of many game species; and significantly improved state wildlife-management efforts through surveys, inventories, and research. In addition, all states have established hunter-education programs.

Clearly one of the most impressive achievements of the program is the amount of wildlife habitat protected with federal assistance. Through fiscal 1984, the states had acquired with Pittman-Robertson funds a total of 3,806,213 acres of land and water at a cost of $224.9 million. But when other public and privately owned lands managed for wildlife under the Pittman-Robertson program are counted, the program has placed 38,232,858 acres either in refuges or under some type of wildlife management (Department of Interior 1984; see Table 1 and Table 2).

***Biological Achievements.*** While the accomplishments of the Pittman-Robertson program are universally acclaimed, a quantifiable assessment of its biological achievements is not available. Even though the original purpose of the Pittman-Robertson Act was to achieve "the continent-wide restoration for all species of wildlife"—a clear resource objective—the Division of Federal Aid does not keep records at the national level to show precisely how the many species eligible for federal-aid assistance are faring (U.S. Congress, Senate 1937).

A major reason such quantitative biological data has not been collected is FWS' perception of its role in the federal-aid program. FWS views its role as helping the states to achieve wildlife goals. FWS officials emphasize that they do not try to guide the states in setting conservation priorities. Their major duty, say FWS officials, is to ensure that federal grant funds are used for the types of conservation activities specified by the law and that the states follow sound procedure in selecting projects and use effective tools, methods, and strategies in their conservation work.

FWS' inactive role in setting guidelines for species-conservation priorities is not compelled by law. The purpose of the Pittman-Robertson Act, according to its legislative history, is to restore and maintain all wildlife species, a term defined by FWS to include all birds

**TABLE 1**
**Lands Acquired in Fee Title Fiscal Years 1938–1984**

| State | Wildlife | | Fish | | Combination Fish and Wildlife | | Total | |
|---|---|---|---|---|---|---|---|---|
| | Acreage | Cost | Acreage | Cost | Acreage | Cost | Acreage | Cost |
| Alabama | 29,773 | $ 1,454,269 | 325 | $ 68,249 | 5 | $ 13,000 | 30,103 | $ 1,535,518 |
| Alaska | 248 | 227,000 | 2 | 424 | – | – | 250 | 227,424 |
| Arizona | 13,758 | 550,803 | – | – | 526 | 556,013 | 14,284 | 1,106,816 |
| Arkansas | 199,137 | 11,192,412 | 5,937 | 2,043,814 | – | – | 205,074 | 13,236,226 |
| California | 67,154 | 964,344 | – | – | – | – | 67,154 | 964,344 |
| Colorado | 124,448 | 3,500,000 | 4,321 | 1,046,801 | 7,467 | 387,759 | 136,236 | 4,934,560 |
| Connecticut | 10,670 | 4,382,859 | 154 | 35,483 | 416 | 1,144,114 | 11,240 | 5,562,456 |
| Delaware | 7,150 | 466,449 | 236 | 87,320 | 617 | 820,584 | 8,003 | 1,374,353 |
| Florida | 113,246 | 4,198,737 | – | – | – | – | 113,246 | 4,198,737 |
| Georgia | 29,655 | 1,757,578 | 386 | 269,000 | – | – | 30,041 | 2,026,578 |
| Hawaii | – | – | – | – | – | – | – | – |
| Idaho | 55,934 | 2,240,738 | 1,412 | 137,303 | 634 | 16,072 | 57,980 | 2,394,113 |
| Illinois | 32,902 | 3,879,536 | 577 | 479,317 | – | – | 33,479 | 4,358,853 |
| Indiana | 20,955 | 3,390,737 | 552 | 169,804 | 35,317 | 8,604,842 | 56,824 | 12,165,383 |
| Iowa | 42,146 | 8,324,270 | 6,220 | 1,005,238 | 6,081 | 636,506 | 54,447 | 9,966,014 |
| Kansas | 47,570 | 3,114,874 | 757 | 79,943 | 2,138 | 300,000 | 50,465 | 3,494,817 |
| Kentucky | 36,935 | 7,025,792 | 44 | 13,700 | 2 | 10,875 | 36,981 | 7,050,367 |
| Louisiana | – | – | – | – | – | – | – | – |
| Maine | 15,099 | 218,387 | – | – | – | – | 15,099 | 218,387 |
| Maryland | 60,858 | 1,198,498 | 246 | 45,457 | – | – | 61,104 | 1,243,955 |
| Massachusetts | 12,382 | 982,263 | 1,954 | 424,546 | 1,867 | 477,917 | 16,203 | 1,884,726 |
| Michigan | 191,770 | 15,749,969 | 2,293 | 954,314 | – | – | 194,063 | 16,704,283 |
| Minnesota | 351,182 | 23,928,233 | 5,440 | 878,979 | 403 | 1,850,132 | 357,025 | 26,657,344 |
| Mississippi | 24,316 | 3,640,343 | 6 | 5,200 | 9,814 | 2,204,005 | 34,136 | 5,849,548 |
| Missouri | 107,711 | 19,626,751 | 5,888 | 501,905 | 10,463 | 5,835,590 | 124,062 | 25,964,246 |

|  | | | | | | | | |
|---|---|---|---|---|---|---|---|---|
| Montana | 92,803 | 4,533,729 | 4,218 | 164,814 | – | – | 97,021 | 4,698,543 |
| Nebraska | 22,576 | 3,341,566 | 707 | 77,180 | 7,528 | 1,718,934 | 30,811 | 5,137,680 |
| Nevada | 34,372 | 1,276,517 | 1,393 | 247,143 | – | – | 36,227 | 1,523,660 |
| New Hampshire | 6,348 | 914,397 | 149 | 110,625 | 462 | 157,701 | 8,788 | 1,182,723 |
| New Jersey | 26,873 | 506,815 | 763 | 255,973 | 2,291 | 1,333,333 | 34,329 | 2,096,121 |
| New Mexico | 211,917 | 3,926,139 | 355 | 305,900 | 6,693 | 3,472,761 | 246,731 | 7,704,800 |
| New York | 25,231 | 816,215 | – | – | 34,459 | – | 25,231 | 816,215 |
| North Carolina | 51,403 | 1,038,037 | 20 | 8,604 | 2,109 | – | 51,423 | 1,046,641 |
| North Dakota | 36,918 | 1,538,213 | 3,571 | 413,739 | 603 | 103,842 | 42,598 | 2,055,794 |
| Ohio | 58,359 | 10,293,686 | 2,921 | 624,236 | 2,766 | 147,970 | 61,883 | 11,065,892 |
| Oklahoma | 72,145 | 1,324,727 | 1,169 | 73,356 | 3,240 | 208,143 | 76,080 | 1,606,226 |
| Oregon | *86,362 | 6,137,641 | *3,456 | 674,845 | – | 1,713,000 | 93,058 | 8,525,486 |
| Pennsylvania | 175,396 | 3,733,578 | 6,185 | 883,161 | 1,819 | – | 181,581 | 4,616,739 |
| Rhode Island | 6,042 | 1,449,111 | 474 | 272,727 | 4,768 | 110,225 | 8,335 | 1,832,063 |
| SouthCarolina | 24,460 | 281,992 | – | – | 101 | 132,167 | 29,228 | 414,159 |
| South Dakota | 67,620 | 2,826,626 | 3,119 | 590,724 | – | 10,104 | 70,840 | 3,427,454 |
| Tennessee | 119,717 | 1,723,835 | 1,985 | 1,282,523 | – | – | 121,702 | 3,006,358 |
| Texas | 163,961 | 5,711,140 | 5 | 15,000 | 5,003 | – | 163,966 | 5,726,140 |
| Utah | 235,442 | 7,987,782 | 2,255 | 818,350 | 158 | 77,967 | 242,700 | 8,884,099 |
| Vermont | 20,553 | 1,561,417 | 486 | 217,876 | 15,940 | 4,938 | 21,197 | 1,784,231 |
| Virginia | 59,576 | 9,093,910 | 55 | 4,464 | – | 527,559 | 75,571 | 9,625,933 |
| Washington | *154,223 | 2,422,862 | *2,441 | 706,788 | 7,445 | – | 156,664 | 3,129,650 |
| West Virginia | 29,967 | 195,473 | 22 | 16,000 | 275 | 409,106 | 29,989 | 211,473 |
| Wisconsin | 252,781 | 24,194,516 | 45,876 | 10,225,321 | – | 10,582 | 306,102 | 34,828,943 |
| Wyoming | 176,169 | 6,144,555 | 2,135 | 159,732 | – | – | 178,579 | 6,314,869 |
| American Samoa | – | – | – | – | – | – | – | – |
| Guam | – | – | – | – | – | – | – | – |
| Puerto Rico | – | – | – | – | – | – | – | – |
| Virgin Islands | – | – | – | – | – | – | – | – |
| Totals | 3,806,213 | $224,989,321 | 120,510 | $26,395,878 | 171,410 | $32,995,741 | 4,098,133 | $284,380,940 |

* Acquired by exchange of land, only difference in acreage and value shown.

Source: FWS, Federal Aid in Fish and Wildlife Restoration 1984 (Department of Interior 1984).

## TABLE 2
## Wildlife Management Areas and Wildlife Refuges Acquired, Developed or Managed as of September 30, 1984 with Federal Aid Grants*

| State | Number Of Areas | Total Acreage | Hunting Acreage | | | Total Hunting Acreage | Total Refuge Acreage |
|---|---|---|---|---|---|---|---|
| | | | Water | Land | | | |
| Alabama | 30 | 701,155 | 12,287 | 681,748 | | 694,035 | 7,120 |
| Alaska | 2 | 249 | – | – | | – | 249 |
| Arizona | 19 | 68,313 | 440 | 67,873 | | 68,313 | – |
| Arkansas | 39 | 1,632,964 | 7,167 | 1,612,312 | | 1,619,479 | 13,485 |
| California | 12 | 109,987 | 26,254 | 75,967 | | 102,221 | 7,766 |
| Colorado | 55 | 204,143 | 2,559 | 200,584 | | 203,143 | 1,000 |
| Connecticut | 58 | 226,604 | 6,245 | 202,604 | | 208,849 | 17,755 |
| Delaware | 17 | 29,784 | 6,943 | 21,356 | | 28,299 | 1,485 |
| Florida | 53 | 4,885,191 | 151,158 | 4,722,033 | | 4,873,191 | 12,000 |
| Georgia | 52 | 979,989 | 12,000 | 967,989 | | 979,289 | 700 |
| Hawaii | 9 | 430,800 | – | 430,800 | | 480,800 | – |
| Idaho | 19 | 98,035 | 2,500 | 94,600 | | 97,100 | 935 |
| Illinois | 52 | 459,159 | 23,990 | 415,364 | | 439,354 | 20,811 |
| Indiana | 20 | 63,479 | 4,600 | 54,109 | | 58,709 | 4,770 |
| Iowa | 240 | 193,148 | 49,170 | 129,807 | | 178,977 | 14,171 |
| Kansas | 37 | 231,329 | 50,415 | 161,729 | | 212,144 | 19,185 |
| Kentucky | 28 | 645,489 | 106,268 | 418,049 | | 519,317 | 126,172 |
| Louisiana | 35 | 737,518 | 21,147 | 712,871 | | 734,018 | 3,500 |
| Maine | 63 | 6,036,497 | 19,373 | 6,015,855 | | 6,035,228 | 1,269 |
| Maryland | 45 | 199,908 | 4,300 | 192,262 | | 196,562 | 3,346 |
| Massachusetts | 44 | 51,461 | 7,976 | 43,485 | | 51,461 | – |
| Michigan | 89 | 349,053 | 63,148 | 276,608 | | 339,756 | 9,297 |
| Minnesota | 970 | 972,673 | 47,236 | 864,005 | | 911,241 | 61,432 |
| Mississippi | 31 | 1,025,192 | 80,045 | 930,447 | | 1,010,492 | 14,700 |
| Missouri | 76 | 1,570,482 | 1,779 | 1,559,435 | | 1,561,214 | 9,268 |

|  | | | | | | |
|---|---|---|---|---|---|---|
| Montana | 33 | 123,889 | 10,188 | 112,366 | 122,554 | 1,335 |
| Nebraska | 83 | 158,322 | 75,502 | 81,118 | 156,620 | 1,702 |
| Nevada | 11 | 248,879 | 43,879 | 205,000 | 248,879 | – |
| New Hampshire | 33 | 10,897 | 2,229 | 8,062 | 10,291 | 606 |
| New Jersey | 45 | 275,137 | 105,000 | 154,402 | 259,902 | 15,235 |
| New Mexico | 26 | 261,560 | 224 | 255,201 | 255,425 | 6,135 |
| New York | 658 | 269,698 | 29,019 | 218,055 | 247,104 | 22,594 |
| North Carolina | 79 | 2,012,865 | 7,235 | 2,002,630 | 2,009,865 | 3,000 |
| North Dakota | 112 | 117,492 | 34,204 | 79,472 | 113,676 | 3,816 |
| Ohio | 59 | 260,184 | 23,910 | 226,992 | 250,902 | 9,282 |
| Oklahoma | 42 | 403,002 | 5,907 | 304,408 | 346,315 | 56,687 |
| Oregon | 14 | 89,614 | 6,622 | 73,415 | 80,037 | 9,577 |
| Pennsylvania | 451 | 3,345,449 | 6,617 | 3,326,403 | 3,333,020 | 12,429 |
| Rhode Island | 20 | 33,008 | 1,586 | 29,207 | 30,793 | 2,215 |
| South Carolina | 9 | 1,522,534 | 90,591 | 1,431,067 | 1,521,658 | 876 |
| South Dakota | 89 | 905,511 | 92,688 | 802,038 | 894,726 | 10,785 |
| Tennessee | 46 | 1,081,755 | 32,291 | 1,037,654 | 1,069,945 | 11,810 |
| Texas | 23 | 320,955 | 11,960 | 304,664 | 316,624 | 4,331 |
| Utah | 60 | 453,951 | 44,082 | 406,303 | 450,385 | 3,566 |
| Vermont | 69 | 113,048 | 5,214 | 105,883 | 111,097 | 1,951 |
| Virginia | 52 | 2,195,147 | 549 | 2,178,519 | 2,179,078 | 16,069 |
| Washington | 27 | 606,229 | 1,547 | 604,362 | 605,909 | 320 |
| West Virginia | 32 | 773,672 | 3,469 | 770,089 | 773,558 | 144 |
| Wisconsin | 180 | 503,016 | 13,268 | 470,917 | 487,185 | 15,831 |
| Wyoming | 34 | 229,278 | 6,050 | 221,659 | 227,709 | 1,569 |
| American Samoa | – | – | – | – | – | – |
| Guam | – | – | – | – | – | – |
| Puerto Rico | 3 | 14,128 | 490 | 13,416 | 13,906 | 222 |
| Virgin Islands | – | – | – | – | – | – |
| Totals | 4,385 | 38,232,858 | 1,361,821 | 36,306,224 | 37,670,355 | 563,503 |

* Includes areas leased by the state and areas on state and federal lands managed for wildlife.
*Source:* FWS, *Federal Aid in Fish and Wildlife Restoration 1984* (Department of Interior 1984).

and mammals. The law gives the secretary of the Interior the power to reach *mutual agreements* with the states regarding the implementation of wildlife projects that conform with the act's purposes and objectives and with standards fixed by him. While the statute does not make clear the secretary's role in determining species priorities, neither does it require that he play absolutely no role in setting conservation goals. In fact, the law's requirement that the secretary and the states reach mutual agreement on projects that conform with the act's purposes could be construed as giving the secretary a strong voice in determining which species or categories of species—for example, endangered mammals, shorebirds, etc.—should benefit from federal grant funds.

Another factor compounding the difficulty of obtaining a precise assessment of the program's biological impact is the way federal-aid funds are distributed and used. The states have the option of requesting federal matching assistance for whatever types of projects they choose, and a project may benefit more than one species. One state may use its entire federal-aid allocation on just a few types of activities, such as land acquisition and research, and spend its own funds on planning, technical-assistance activities, and the like. Another state may do just the opposite.

Furthermore, a state may vary over time the amount of federal-aid funds it uses to conserve any particular species. For example, during the early stage of a restoration project, the state may match all of its work with federal funds. Later, the state may rely minimally on federal assistance to manage the restored species. Thus, it is difficult to determine whose dollar benefited which species and to what degree over time.

The bottom line is this: While the Pittman-Robertson program is rightly praised for its many contributions over the past 50 years, it is impossible for FWS to demonstrate how well all of the birds and mammals supposedly covered by the program are faring, or even whether the states are working on the most urgent wildlife-conservation priorities. In view of the federal deficit and continuing pressure to cut federal expenditures, FWS is in the awkward position of not being able to explain with adequate precision the efficacy of its largest program. According to FWS officials, FWS has attempted to devise ways to measure program accomplishments realistically and accurately, but such efforts have not been as successful as FWS would like.

**Status of State Planning Efforts**

In an effort to improve the efficiency and comprehensiveness of state fish- and wildlife-agency conservation programs, Congress amended the Pittman-Robertson and Dingell-Johnson acts in 1970 to allow use of federal-aid funds for the preparation of comprehensive fish- and wildlife-resource management plans (see Table 3). Comprehensive planning was needed, said the Senate report accompanying the legislation, to promote the efficient use of federal-aid funds and to enable the state fish and wildlife departments to protect fish and wildlife resources adequately from the impacts of development activities, such as urbanization, road-building, and timber harvest (U.S. Congress, Senate 1970).

When the Forsythe-Chafee Act (16 U.S.C.A. 2901 *et seq.*) was passed in 1980, Congress again emphasized the need for planning by state wildlife agencies. The Forsythe-Chafee Act called for the preparation of "conservation plans" that covered both game and nongame species and regular assessments of the state's effectiveness in conserving plan species.

Although no funds for implementation of the Forsythe-Chafee Act ever have been appropriated, FWS implemented the planning provisions of the act, integrating them with those of the Pittman-Robertson and Dingell-Johnson programs. The states now have the option of obtaining federal-aid funds to finance the development of either modular or comprehensive fish and wildlife plans. Modular plans address one or more of the agency's resource-management responsibilities, such as big game, warm-water fish, nongame, or hunter education. Comprehensive plans may cover all species of wildlife and all activities for which the agency has responsibility, but usually focus on a selected number of species that the state wants to manage. All state planning efforts financed with Pittman-Robertson or Dingell-Johnson funds must provide for public participation.

**TABLE 3**
**Percentage of State Pittman-Robertson Expenditures by Project Type for Selected Years**

| | 1949 | 1959 | 1969 | 1979 | 1984 | Percent of all expenditures during the period 1939–1984 |
|---|---|---|---|---|---|---|
| Surveys and Investigations | 19.3 | 21.7 | 28.7 | 29.5 | 25.3 | 27.6 |
| Land Acquisitions | 22.9 | 23.6 | 18.1 | 9.6 | 8.2 | 14.5 |
| Development | 51.9 | 50.3 | 47.3 | 45.8 | 49.6 | 46.5 |
| Coordination | 5.9 | 4.4 | 5.8 | 5.4 | 4.4 | 4.8 |
| Hunter Education* | 0 | 0 | 0 | 7 | 9 | 4.7 |
| Planning* | 0 | 0 | .0005 | .01 | 1.1 | .7 |
| Tech Guidance | 0 | 0 | .001 | .01 | 2.4 | 1.0 |

* Hunter education and planning uses authorized in 1970.
*Source:* Based on expenditure statistics supplied by FWS, Division of Federal Aid.

Progress toward better wildlife planning has been slow. Fifteen years after the comprehensive planning option was made available, only four states—Colorado, Tennessee, Kansas, and Wyoming—have approved comprehensive plans; only Maryland and Wisconsin have an approved modular plan. Altogether, 31 states and territories have initiated planning efforts of one type or another, but 23 still have no formal planning effort of any kind, federally funded or not, according to federal-aid officials.

The states have been slow to adopt a formal planning process for several reasons, say FWS officials. These include inertia, hostility to planning by state fish and wildlife agencies that do not appreciate the importance of planning, and the failure of university wildlife-management programs to teach administrative management skills. In addition, some states fear that adoption of a formal planning process would require the state wildlife agency to deal with certain wildlife organizations whose outlook on state goals and priorities may not be the same as those of the agency's traditional constituency groups, hunters and fishermen. In sum, say FWS officials, state planning efforts—even many of those now under way—have yet to measure up to the sound goals originally promulgated by Congress: promoting efficient use of federal-aid funds and protecting wildlife resources from the adverse impacts of development. However, this situation is changing. FWS officials say that in the past few years, state interest in planning has increased, largely because of promotional efforts by the Federal Aid Division staff and the Organization of Wildlife Planners (see Table 4).

**TABLE 4**
**Status of State Fish and Wildlife Planning Efforts**
**(with and without Federal Assistance)**

|  | Comprehensive Plan | One or More Modular Plans |
|---|---|---|
| Alabama | N | N |
| Alaska | N | YD |
| Arizona | YD | |
| Arkansas | YD | |
| California | N | YC |
| Colorado | YC(FA) | |
| Connecticut | N | YD |
| Delaware | N | YD |
| Florida | YD | |
| Georgia | N | N |
| Hawaii | N | N |
| Idaho | N | YC |
| Illinois | YD(FA) | |

*(continued)*

**TABLE 4** *(Continued)*

| | Comprehensive Plan | One or More Modular Plans |
|---|---|---|
| Illinois | YD(FA) | |
| Indiana | YD | |
| Iowa | N | N |
| Kansas | YC(FA) | |
| Kentucky | N | N |
| Louisiana | N | N |
| Maine | N | YC(FA) |
| Maryland | N | YC(FA) |
| Massachusetts | N | N |
| Michigan | N | YD |
| Minnesota | YD(FA) | |
| Mississippi | YD | |
| Missouri | N | YC |
| Montana | YD(FA) | |
| Nebraska | N | N |
| Nevada | N | YD |
| New Hampshire | N | N |
| New Jersey | N | YD |
| New Mexico | YC | |
| New York | N | N |
| North Carolina | N | N |
| North Dakota | N | N |
| Ohio | YD | |
| Oklahoma | N | N |
| Oregon | N | YD |
| Pennsylvania (Game) | N | N |
| Pennsylvania (Fish) | N | N |
| Rhode Island | N | N |
| South Carolina | N | N |
| South Dakota | N | N |
| Tennessee | YC(FA) | |
| Texas | N | YD |
| Utah | YD | |
| Vermont | N | N |
| Virginia | N | N |
| Washington | YC | |
| West Virginia | YD(FA) | |
| Wisconsin | N | YC(FA) |
| Wyoming | YC(FA) | |
| American Samoa | N | N |
| Guam | N | N |
| Puerto Rico | N | YD(FA) |
| Virgin Islands | N | N |

Legend:  N = No
Y = Yes
C = Complete
D = Developing
FA = Federal Aid Funds Used

*Source:* Division of Federal Aid, FWS, December 1986

**New Uses of Dingell-Johnson Funds**

Amendments attached to the Deficit Reduction Act of 1984 (P.L. 98-269) have changed the Dingell-Johnson program significantly. That law established an Aquatic Resources Trust Fund, known as the Wallop-Breaux Fund, consisting of two accounts: the Boating Safety Account and the Sport Fish Restoration Account, which contains the receipts from excise taxes and other sources that fund Dingell-Johnson activities. The 1984 amendments also expanded the sources and amounts of revenue for the sport-fish restoration program and authorized the expenditure of funds for several new activities. Total program funds jumped from $38 million in fiscal 1985 to $122 million in fiscal 1986 to $141 million in fiscal year 1987. Individual state share allocations have tripled.

This large increase in Dingell-Johnson funds was approved by Congress because state fish and wildlife agencies said they lacked the money to maintain adequate sport-fishery resources in the face of increased numbers of fishermen using more advanced fishing technology. A 1982 survey conducted by the American Fisheries Society reported unmet state fishery-management needs of $134 million yearly (U.S. Congress, House 1983).

In addition to increasing the amount of sport-fish restoration funds, Congress also made changes in ways the funds can be used. To ensure that excise-tax receipts collected on marine sport-fishing equipment are used to benefit marine sport fish, the Dingell-Johnson Act was amended to require coastal states to distribute their grant allocation equitably between saltwater and freshwater fish projects, such distribution to be proportional to the number of freshwater and saltwater fishermen in the state. The 1984 amendment also requires the states to use a minimum of 10 percent of their funds to develop recreational boating facilities. Finally, the law was amended to allow the states the option of spending up to 10 percent of their allocation on aquatic-resource education programs.

The states are expected to use their new funds in a variety of ways. Arizona, for example, intends to use its increase on hatchery renovation, dam repair and maintenance, and construction of boat access facilities. Florida will use its funds to build boat access ramps, to establish a permanent biological research team on Lake Okeechobee, to poll fishery users regarding their needs, to conduct an urban-fisheries program in coordination with metropolitan recreation departments, to increase the number of fish in several impoundments, and to develop an aquatic education program for public schools. More specific details on how each state plans to use its new funds may be found in the American League of Anglers and Boaters 1986 publication "State Fishing and Boating Statistics, Projected Plans for Wallop-Breaux Funds" (American League of Anglers and Boaters 1986).

**Incompatible Use of Areas Acquired with Federal Aid Funds**

Thousands of fish and wildlife areas have been acquired or leased since 1937. These include 4,385 wildlife areas and refuges, 361 constructed or restored fishing lakes, and 1,348 access sites to fish and wildlife resources.[2] When such land and waters are acquired or leased by the states with federal-aid funds, the property must be operated and maintained in accordance with the uses described in the state application for project assistance.

With increasing development pressures, the rapid growth in the number of people participating in all types of outdoor recreation, and the inherent difficulty of monitoring project lands—many of them small tracts—scattered throughout a state, some fish and wildlife areas inevitably have been converted to nonwildlife uses. Some examples:

- A private ski resort located on Forest Service property in Washington wants to expand its operations onto a Pittman-Robertson wildlife area that provides summer and winter range for elk.
- Areas purchased for hunting areas have been closed to hunting and used for purposes such as tree nurseries.
- Wildlife on project areas has been disturbed by the unauthorized use of the property by horseback riders and skimobilers.
- A large storage building was constructed on five acres of the Flat River State Management Area by the Michigan Waterways Division.
- Two hundred and forty-six acres of elk winter range in Baker County, Oregon, were sold by the state to an irrigation district for a reservoir site.

The Division of Federal Aid requires the states to "maintain adequate control of federally funded real property" and encourages the states to develop and use their own property-control systems provided they meet certain minimum requirements, including the "physical verification at reasonable intervals, that all real property serves its intended purpose and is properly maintained" (Interior 1982). If federal-aid properties are converted to nonprogram uses, either deliberately or unknowingly, the state is required either to correct the problem or replace the property with land of equal value and with equal wildlife benefits.[3]

According to FWS officials, only about half the states have systems adequate for monitoring the status of real property acquired with federal-aid funds. That theoretically leaves FWS regional offices with

2. Statistics are current through fiscal year 1984.

3. A state may dispose of federal-aid property that is no longer needed if it receives the approval of the FWS regional director and reimburses the program for the federal share of the current market value of the property.

the responsibility of directly monitoring hundreds of areas. FWS officials say that field offices simply do not have the personnel or travel budgets to allow them to inspect all previously acquired sites in addition to their more pressing duties of administering current projects. Hence, FWS depends on state wildlife agencies to notify it when a project area is used improperly.

The Division of Federal Aid does not keep nationally aggregated records on how often project areas are checked by its regional staff or the states themselves, how many cases of incompatible use come to light annually, or how such cases are resolved. Thus, no way exists to determine accurately the exact status of these areas or how serious the problem of incompatible use may be. FWS officials say that current procedures for monitoring federal-aid properties are sufficient to uncover most cases of incompatible use and that more intensive review of properties by FWS personnel is not warranted.

## Research Coordination

According to FWS officials, no mechanism exists at the national level for aggregating information on fish and wildlife research undertaken by federal, state, and private entities. The Division of Federal Aid has taken the lead in partially correcting this deficiency by establishing computerized data banks for all research studies undertaken and completed with federal-aid funds and by requesting other researchers to enter their data into the same banks.

The division's Current Federal Aid Research System became functional in 1980. It is a computerized data base that summarizes all current research being undertaken by the states with Pittman-Robertson and Dingell-Johnson funds. Each spring, the division also publishes two reports, one for fish and one for wildlife, that summarize and categorize current research studies.[4] Additional information can be found in the Fish and Wildlife Reference Service, a computer data base of all significant reports and publications completed under federal-aid projects. Both the Current Federal Aid Research System and the Fish and Wildlife Reference Service may be accessed by telephone or computer terminal to conduct information searches or to obtain copies of stored materials.

The Federal Aid Division has encouraged all FWS offices and other federal agencies to enter their fish and wildlife research studies intothe Current Federal Aid Research System. The various research divisions of FWS have entered their data. The National Marine Fisheries Service also has agreed to enter its research data, though there is no deadline as

4. See "Current Federal Aid Research Report, Wildlife" (Department of Interior 1986a) and "Current Federal Aid Research Report, Fish" (Department of Interior 1986b).

to when this will be achieved. As yet, no other federal wildlife-managing agencies, such as the Forest Service, BLM, or National Park Service, have agreed to enter their data. Also missing is information on research projects being funded by the states without federal-aid assistance and on projects conducted by independent academic researchers. The Federal Aid Division lacks the funds to centralize all completed fish and wildlife research in the Fish and Wildlife Reference Service.

The establishment of a comprehensive national data base on current and completed research obviously would increase the efficiency of fish and wildlife researchers everywhere, as well as avoid duplication of effort. However, the purely voluntary nature of the effort, combined with the lack of sufficient resources to get the job done, will retard the centralization project.

## LEGISLATION

### Reagan Initiative to Cut Federal Aid Staff

In its proposed fiscal 1986 budget for FWS, the Reagan administration surprised fishing, boating, and conservation organizations by requesting a drastic cutback in funds to be spent under the Sport Fish Restoration Account of the Wallop-Breaux Fund on Dingell-Johnson activities. Congress soundly rejected the cutback proposal, and the Reagan administration did not attempt to resurrect it in the fiscal 1987 budget. The administration did, however, recommend that the federal-aid-program staff be halved, from 100 to 48, and that the division's administrative budget be reduced by about $5 million. In addition, the administration proposed to eliminate funds for all of the special research projects conducted by the division, including the periodic national hunting and·fishing survey.

According to FWS officials, the proposed budget cuts would turn the federal-aid-program staff into a group of desk-bound paper shufflers who would have little interaction with state wildlife personnel. Yet, today the states are seeking an increase in assistance from the division.

Both House and Senate appropriations committees rejected the cutbacks as unjustifiable. However, they called for a workload analysis of the federal-aid program to be submitted to them before the fiscal 1988 budget is forwarded to Congress. This analysis will enable Congress to assess more competently any future proposals for increasing or decreasing the federal-aid administrative budget and staff.

### Nongame Act Funding Study and Reauthorization Legislation

When the Forsythe-Chafee Act was passed in 1980, Congress authorized up to $5 million yearly in general appropriations to fund the program through fiscal year 1985. However, because of the general policy of budget restraint pursued by President Reagan, no funds have ever been requested by FWS to implement the act, nor has Congress taken the initiative to appropriate funds.

Section 12 of the act requires FWS to prepare a study of various ways to finance state nongame-conservation projects. The report, *Potential Funding Sources to Implement the Fish and Wildlife Conservation Act of 1980* (Interior 1985) was submitted in February 1985, but lacked a Reagan administration recommendation for implementing any of the funding alternatives discussed.

A total of 25 potential funding methods, including general appropriations, fees, and excise taxes, were considered by FWS. The 18 deemed most appropriate and feasible were examined in detail.[5] Each potential funding method was evaluated for its revenue-raising potential, economic impact, benefits received by those paying a tax, and the ability of the public to pay a tax or fee. The pros and cons of each financing method were presented in detail, as were summaries of public comments on each alternative.

Only eight of the 18 funding methods studied would provide $10 million or more annually. A five to 10 percent excise tax at the manufacturer or importer level on bird seed, houses, and feeders would raise considerably less. At the recommended maximum 10-percent tax rate, a bird-seed tax would generate $7.3 million yearly; a bird-house tax, $0.9 million; a feeder tax, $2.5; and a tax on bird baths and other equipment, $1.2 million.

During the course of the study, FWS solicited written comments from manufacturers, trade associations, user groups, conservation organizations, wildlife agencies, and the general public. Only four funding methods received more favorable responses than negative ones: (1) use of general appropriations; (2) a tax on wildlife identification books; (3) a voluntary tax check-off; and (4) sale of semi-postal stamps (see Table 5).

Irrespective of the study results, the Reagan administration declined to promote any new funding proposal. In his letter transmitting the report to Congress, FWS Director Robert Jantzen cited the "present fiscal situation and Administration policies on Federal spending and taxation" as reasons for inaction. On the other hand, Jantzen hinted that the sale of semi-postal stamps was a voluntary financing method worthy of consideration, but that the U.S. Postal Service opposed it (Jantzen 1985).

---

5. In addition, the report includes an addendum that discusses the potential of levying developer fees for various economic uses of federal lands—including grazing, timber harvesting, mineral extraction, recreation and tourism, and use of lands for power generation sites—and for other development activities that involve the federal government.

**TABLE 5**
**Estimated Revenues from Potential**
**Nongame Act Funding Methods**

| Funding Method | Estimated Annual Revenue in Millions (1980 Dollars) |
|---|---|
| 5–10% tax on wild animal furs | $ 11.2–21.4 |
| 5–10% tax on hiking/camping items | $ 14.3–28.1 |
| 2–5% tax on off-road vehicles | $ 76.8–147.3 |
| Fees ($.50–$2.00) for use of federal lands | $103.1 |
| Voluntary contribution, income tax check-off | $ 40 |
| Sale of semi-postal stamps (25–50% of value) | $ 11.3–203.4 |
| 1–5% tax on photographic equipment and film | $ 25.2–124.0 |
| Mining claim renewal fee ($10–$15) | $ 12.1–30.2 |

*Source:* Potential Funding Sources to Implement the Fish and Wildlife Conservation Act of 1980 (Department of Interior 1985)

The House held one day of hearings on nongame-reauthorization legislation (H.R. 1406) and the financing study. At the House hearings, Eugene Hester, deputy director of FWS, speaking for the Reagan administration, opposed the reauthorization of appropriations for the act on four grounds:

1. no funds have yet been appropriated under this act;
2. the current emphasis on federal deficit reduction would not allow room in the budget for this program for several years into the future;
3. existing Pittman-Robertson funds can be used for certain nongame purposes at the discretion of the states; and
4. the states are moving ahead on their own to expand nongame-wildlife-management efforts.

In lieu of federal funding, Hester recommended that the states be encouraged to use their own funds to expand their nongame-conservation efforts, since they have primary jurisdiction over nongame wildlife species. The states, on the other hand, supported a combination of federal financing methods, including the sale of semi-postal stamps and the levying of excise taxes on selected photographic equipment, backpacking and camping equipment, binoculars, and wild-bird feed. A spokesman for the American Recreation Coalition opposed excise taxes on outdoor-recreation equipment and instead urged that monies be derived from development activities that destroy wildlife habitat.

Ultimately, the House approved a simple, three-year reauthorization of the Nongame Act through fiscal year 1988, with authority for annual appropriations set at $5 million. The Merchant Marine and Fisheries Committee, while interested in voluntary financing programs such as the sale of semi-postal stamps, declined to pursue this approach further. Other factors influencing the committee's action were the lack of overwhelming support for any one financing mechanism, as well as the Reagan administration's general opposition to new taxes and increases in federal spending. In addition, nonprofit conservation organizations demonstrated little visible support for a nongame fund, according to committee staff members.

The Senate Environment and Public Works Committee followed the House's lead, approving a three-year reauthorization of the Nongame Act (P.L. 99-375). No Senate hearings were held on financing mechanisms for a variety of reasons. According to Senate-committee staff members, many of the financing methods in Interior's report are not realistic. Product manufacturers, for example, uniformly oppose taxes on their products. Furthermore, once again no consensus existed among conservation organizations about which financing methods should be pursued, nor did any real political momentum exists to pro mote passage of financing legislation. Until these problems are overcome, chances are small that a special fund will be created to imple ment the Nongame Act. That leaves nongame species at risk and puts the burden on state wildlife agencies to take measures to conserve them.

## LEGAL DEVELOPMENTS

Very little litigation has ever occurred concerning the federal-aid program, a circumstance that wildlife-law specialist Michael J. Bean, of the Environmental Defense Fund, finds "striking," given the "duration and magnitude of the Pittman-Robertson program and the widely divergent views of those interested in its administration . . ." (Bean 1983). This dearth of legal activity continued in 1986. No court decisions were made in 1986 pertaining to either the Pittman-Robertson or Dingell-Johnson statutes, and no suits were filed or pending. A discussion of previous litigation regarding the Pittman-Robertson and Dingell-Johnson acts is found in *The Evolution of National Wildlife Law* (Bean 1983).

## REFERENCES

American League of Anglers and Boaters. 1986. "State Fishing and Boating Statistics, Projected Plans for Wallop-Breaux Funds." American League of Anglers and Boaters. Washington, D.C.

Bean, Michael J. 1983. *The Evolution of National Wildlife Law.* Praeger Publishers. New York, New York. 449 pp.

Jantzen, R. 1985. Letter to Senator Robert T. Stafford, Chairman, Senate Committee on Environment and Public Works, February 8, 1985.

The Wildlife Conservation Fund of America. 1980. "Fish and Wildlife Agency Funding." The Wildlife Conservation Fund of America. Columbus, Ohio.

U.S. Congress, Senate, Special Committee on Conservation of Wildlife Resources. 1937. United States Aid to States in Wildlife Restoration Projects. Report to Accompany S.2670, 75th Congress, 1st Session, Senate Report 868.

U.S. Congress, Senate, Committee on Commerce. 1970. Report to Accompany H.R. 12475, 91st Congress, 2nd Session, Senate Report 91-1289.

U.S. Department of the Interior, Fish and Wildlife Service. 1982. *Federal Aid Manual*. Washington, D.C.

U.S. Department of the Interior, Fish and Wildlife Service. 1984. *Federal Aid in Fish and Wildlife Restoration 1984*. Washington, D.C.

U.S. Department of the Interior, Fish and Wildlife Service. 1985. *Potential Funding Sources to Implement the Fish and Wildlife Conservation Act of 1980*. Washington, D.C.

U.S. Department of the Interior, Fish and Wildlife Service. 1986a. "Current Federal Aid Research Report, Wildlife, Spring, 1986." Division of Federal Aid, Fish and Wildlife Service. Washington, D.C.

U.S. Department of the Interior, Fish and Wildlife Service, 1986b. "Current Federal Aid Research Report, Fish, Spring, 1986." Division of Federal Aid, Fish and Wildlife Service. Washington, D.C.

U.S. Department of the Interior, Fish and Wildlife Service. In Press. *Restoring America's Wildlife 1937-1987*. Government Printing Office. Washington, D.C.

*William J. Chandler is president of W.J. Chandler Associates, a Washington D.C. environmental policy and government relations consulting firm.*

The Canada goose, one of the most readily recognized and popular of waterfowl, is one of 59 hunted species managed by the federal migratory bird program. *Leonard Lee Rue III*

# Migratory Bird Protection and Management

## William J. Chandler

## OVERVIEW

The federal government has treaty and legislative authority to protect, manage, and conserve 832 migratory-bird species[1] identified in bird-protection treaties between the United States and Canada, Mexico, Japan and the U.S.S.R.

Authority over migratory birds was assumed by the federal government when it became clear that the states were not protecting waterfowl or other migratory-bird species adequately. In 1916, the United States signed a bird-protection treaty with Canada that gave the U.S. government its first authority to regulate the hunting of migratory game birds and prohibited the hunting of all other migratory birds. The states, however, retain authority over nonmigratory birds, principally members of the order Galliformes (pheasants, quail, grouse) and over introduced, nonnative species such as the European starling.

1. Approximately 600 to 650 of these 832 species regularly occur within the United States. The total number of protected species fluctuates yearly depending upon various administrative, regulatory, and treaty charges. For example, the number will decrease in 1987 when the U.S. Pacific trusts, such as Guam, assume more independence, ending U.S. control over their species.

Migratory-bird conservation is the responsibility of the U.S. Fish and Wildlife Service (FWS), an agency of the Department of the Interior. Within FWS, the principal coordinating office is the Division of Migratory Bird Management. The major responsibilities of the division include the conduct of annual bird-population and hunter-kill surveys, promulgation of federal hunting regulations, and preparation of management plans for individual species and populations of species. The Division of Refuge Management provides policy guidance for the management of all national wildlife refuges, about 75 percent of which were established for migratory waterfowl. FWS regional directors supervise the refuges within their regions and refuge managers implement day-to-day management activities (see Table 1).

The management of wide-ranging birds is accomplished through a partnership between FWS and counterpart agencies in Canada and Mexico. State fish and wildlife agencies have established four flyway

**TABLE 1**
**Principal Offices Responsible for Migratory Bird Activities of the U.S. Fish and Wildlife Service**

| Activity | Office and Supervisor |
| --- | --- |
| 1. Annual population and harvest surveys | Division of Migratory Bird Management, Assistant Director – Refuges and Wildlife |
| 2. Bird banding program | Division of Migratory Bird Management, Assistant Director – Refuges and Wildlife |
| 3. Breeding bird survey | Division of Migratory Bird Management, Assistant Director – Refuges and Wildlife |
| 4. Basic and applied research | Division of Fish and Wildlife Research and Division of Cooperative Units, Assistant Director – Research and Development |
| 5. Annual hunting regulations | Division of Migratory Bird Management, Assistant Director – Refuges and Wildlife |
| 6. Land acquisition | Division of Realty, Director – Refuges and Wildlife |
| 7. Management of migratory bird refuges | Division of Refuges and Wildlife |
| 8. Enforcement of migratory laws | Division of Law Enforcement, Assistant Director – Refuges and Wildlife |
| 9. Review of federal actions and permits impacting migratory birds | Division of Ecological Services, Assistant Director – Fish and Wildlife Enhancement |
| 10. Provision of grants to states for migratory bird conservation projects | Division of Federal Aid, Assistant Director – Fish and Wildlife Enhancement |

Source: U.S. Fish and Wildlife Service 1986.

councils—Atlantic, Mississippi, Central, and Pacific—to provide advice and cooperative assistance to the federal government in the management of waterfowl species that pass through or occupy their territories. The states help establish hunting regulations, conduct research and banding programs, acquire and manage habitat, manage a few federally acquired waterfowl refuges, and assist in the enforcement of federal hunting regulations and bird protection laws.

Several private, nonprofit organizations conduct programs that complement FWS migratory-bird activities. Ducks Unlimited leases and manages habitat for migratory waterfowl, primarily in Canada. The Nature Conservancy acquires significant wetlands within the United States in order to protect them from development and either resells the land to federal or state conservation agencies or retains them as nature reserves. The National Audubon Society acquires and manages bird sanctuaries and conducts bird research.

FWS classifies migratory birds into two categories, game and nongame. Game includes 162 species that may be hunted, although only 59 are at present. Nongame (unhunted) birds include 670 species, some 80 percent of all migratory-bird species under federal authority. However, since 103 former game species no longer are hunted, the actual number of nongame birds is 773, 93 percent of all federally protected species.

Sixteen species of migratory birds under federal authority are listed as threatened or endangered throughout their entire range. Another 25 species are threatened or endangered in part of their range. These listed species are managed by the Office of Endangered Species.

Certain game birds have received intensive study and management over the years. FWS officials say this is because more information is needed about heavily hunted species to ensure that they are not overhunted and because federal wildlife laws tend to emphasize game species. Nongame species have received considerably less attention from FWS. Although nongame birds have been protected from hunting since 1916, relatively little has been done by the federal government to gather a comprehensive body of information on their biological status or habitat needs. In 1965, FWS took a step toward remedying this situation by establishing a breeding-bird survey to monitor yearly population trends for about 500 nongame species. However, the survey is capable of providing sufficiently precise trend data for only about 250 species.

Today, FWS focuses its management on coots; woodcocks; sandhill cranes; rails; gallinules, 44 species of ducks, geese, and swans; and six species of doves. While FWS conducts a few activities to benefit nongame species, the nongame budget is severely limited and only a tiny fraction of the amount devoted to game birds.

## CURRENT DEVELOPMENTS

### Nationwide Phase-out of Lead Shot

The long-standing controversy over how to effectively protect water-fowl and other migratory birds from toxic poisoning by spent lead shot finally was settled in 1986 when FWS announced a nationwide ban on lead-shot use for waterfowl hunting. The ban will be phased in over a five-year period commencing with the 1987-88 hunting season.

Since 1976, FWS has pursued a "hot-spot" strategy of identifying areas of the country where high accumulations of spent lead shot occurred and requiring that waterfowl hunting in those areas be conducted with steel shot, the only currently available, nontoxic lead substitute. After it was adopted, the hot-spot strategy came under increasing attack from various conservation organizations and many state fish and wildlife agencies as a totally inadequate approach to the lead-poisoning problem. The essence of the critics' argument was that too many birds still were dying from lead poisoning and that such deaths could be reduced significantly by using steel shot for waterfowl hunting throughout the nation.[2]

While the logic of the critics' argument was irrefutable, FWS was under pressure from a handful of hunting groups and a few state wildlife agencies who opposed conversion to steel shot. These parties argued that steel shot was more costly, more damaging to gun barrels, and crippled more waterfowl than did lead. In 1978, this minority opposition secured passage of the Stevens amendment to the Interior appropriations bill, by giving the states, not FWS, final authority to determine which and how many areas were to be designated as steel-shot zones. In states where opposition to steel shot was strong, the state wildlife agencies refused to allow FWS to ban lead in some areas. Nevertheless, FWS continued working with cooperative states to designate additional steel-shot zones.

In 1984, the National Wildlife Federation petitioned FWS to designate new steel-shot zones throughout the country in areas where bald eagles, listed as endangered in 43 states, had been lead poisoned after eating waterfowl crippled or killed by hunters. This initiative ultimately led to the collapse of the FWS hot-spot strategy.

FWS denied the federation petition, but in 1985 proposed its own list of 30 counties as steel-shot zones to protect the eagle. In its final rule, however, FWS in response to state opposition designated only 12 counties. At the same time, however, FWS warned the states that the other 18 areas would be designated for the 1987-88 hunting season and

2. It is estimated that approximately two to three percent of the fall/winter waterfowl population die yearly from lead poisoning. FWS estimates annual deaths to range between 1.6 to 2.4 million birds (Department of the Interior 1976).

that state failure to approve the designations would lead to a closure of those areas to waterfowl hunting.[3]

The federation protested the rule and won. In 1985, the federal district court for the Eastern District of California issued an order requiring the use of steel shot in the 30 counties (*National Wildlife Federation v. Hodel*, 23 ERC 1089). The court found that FWS failure to designate the 30 counties as steel-shot zones violated the Endangered Species Act prohibition against the taking of an endangered species as well as the act's mandate that all reasonable actions be taken to recover a species to a more sound biological status.

By the end of 1985, hunter organizations and state wildlife agencies that opposed additional steel-shot zones were clearly on the defensive. FWS, however, continued to pursue its incremental hot-spot strategy for dealing with the problem. In December 1985, it released a draft environmental impact statement reaffirming its intention to continue designating steel-shot zones only in areas where lead-shot poisoning is a proven problem (Department of the Interior 1985a). This, in turn, meant a continuing process of negotiations with states over the location and boundaries of the problem areas.

This limited approach was unacceptable to the federation, which filed suit in February 1986, seeking a nationwide ban on lead-shot use for waterfowl hunting in the 1987-88 hunting season. In its brief, the National Wildlife Federation noted that nontoxic steel shot has been available for 12 years and that the secretary of the Interior has complete authority to end the unnecessary deaths of waterfowl and bald eagles "almost overnight with one stroke of the pen but refuses to do so."

The possibility of another federation court victory prompted state wildlife agencies and the Interior Department into action. In March 1986, the International Association of Fish and Wildlife Agencies endorsed the phase-out by 1991 of lead-shot for migratory-bird hunting. The phase-out would take place first in counties with the highest waterfowl kills. Interior quickly embraced this proposal and asked the federation to drop its lawsuit in favor of a consensus solution. However, negotiations between the federation and Interior fell apart when Interior refused to give a written guarantee that the five-year phase-in proposal would in fact be adopted.

Interior then adopted the five-year phase-in as the preferred alternative in a supplement to the final environmental impact state-

---

3. Under the Migratory Bird Treaty Act (16 U.S.C.A. 703 *et. seq.*) the secretary of the Interior has authority to determine when, to what extent, and by what means migratory birds are hunted. In short, the secretary has the power *not* to open an area to waterfowl hunting if he so chooses, says FWS. Asserting this secretarial authority effectively negates the veto power over steel-shot-zone designations given to the states by the Stevens amendment.

ment it filed with the court the day of the hearing (Department of the Interior 1986a). As a result, the District Court for the Eastern District of California dismissed the federation's suit as premature, noting that Interior had acceded to the request for a nationwide ban. The court agreed with Interior that a five-year phase-in seemed reasonable given the need to balance protection of waterfowl with the need to educate the public about the ban and the need to minimize economic dislocations (*National Wildlife Federation v. Hodel.* CIVS-86-194-EJG, September 10, 1986).

The lead-shot phase-out plan will work as follows: Beginning in the 1987-88 hunting season, lead-shot use will be prohibited in all counties where waterfowl take levels are 20 or more birds per square mile. About 66 percent of the annual waterfowl kill occurs in those counties. In each succeeding year, lead shot will be banned in additional counties as shown in Table 2.

The Interior phase-out plan permits the states to delay the ban if state monitoring studies demonstrate that lead poisoning is not a problem in certain areas that otherwise would be affected by the conversion schedule.

Barring further court action by one of the states or hunting organizations that consistently has opposed a nationwide ban, the lead-shot issue finally has been put to rest. FWS officials estimate that a noticeable drop off in waterfowl poisonings from lead should occur within five years after lead is banned from an area.

Meanwhile, for the 1986-87 season, FWS banned lead shot in areas where about 49 percent of the annual U.S. waterfowl take occurs. FWS also banned lead-shot use in 173 counties, some of which overlap with waterfowl steel-shot zones, in 26 states in order to protect the bald eagle. Once the phase-in plan takes effect in 1987-88, special zones for eagles no longer will be designated.

## Duck Population Increases,
## But Hunting Restrictions Still Maintained

North American duck populations have been declining since 1979, primarily because of drought in key breeding areas and degradation or

**Table 2**
**Objectives for Lead-Shot Ban by Year and Harvest Level**

| Harvest Level (Waterfowl/mi$^2$) | Year Lead Shot Prohibited | Percentage of U.S. Waterfowl Take Occurring in Affected Zones |
|---|---|---|
| 15 or more | 1988-89 | 69 |
| 10 or more | 1989-90 | 75 |
| 5 or more | 1990-91 | 84 |
| Fewer than 5 | 1991-92 | 100 |

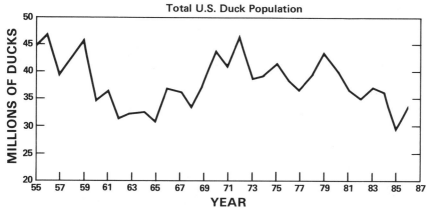

Source: U.S. Fish and Wildlife Service

Figure 1

destruction of breeding habitat by farmers. In 1986, North American ducks rebounded slightly from the extremely low population level recorded in 1985 (see Figure 1). FWS officials attributed the increase both to an improvement in climatic and habitat conditions on the breeding grounds and to restrictive hunting regulations for the 1985-86 season that reduced the total number of ducks killed by 27 percent from the previous season.[4]

Although the duck breeding population increased between 1985 and 1986, FWS determined that the situation was still precarious enough to warrant a continuation of the restrictive hunting regulations for the 1986-87 season. Unlike the first year, however, when the regulations were protested vigorously by some hunting organizations and states, the more recent FWS proposal was accepted with less controversy.

***Breeding Population.*** Each year, FWS, the Canadian Wildlife Service, and certain states conduct surveys of duck breeding grounds in the United States and Canada to assess environmental conditions and to estimate the number of breeding ducks and their reproductive success. These data in turn are used to estimate the fall-flight size of 14 duck species that breed in the survey areas.[5] Hunting regulations then are promulgated by FWS to achieve the desired level of take deemed

4. FWS estimates of total ducks killed by U.S. hunters within the United States are 12.1 million (1981-81 season); 11.8 million (1981-83); 12.9 million (1983-84); 12.5 million (1984-85); and 9.2 million (1985-86).

5. The FWS annual duck survey covers 50 areas surveyed by air and ground. The breeding-population and fall-flight sizes developed from these surveys are representative only of the survey areas and do not account for ducks that breed outside these areas. Hence the survey data should not be viewed as a comprehensive assessment of the total number of ducks in North America.

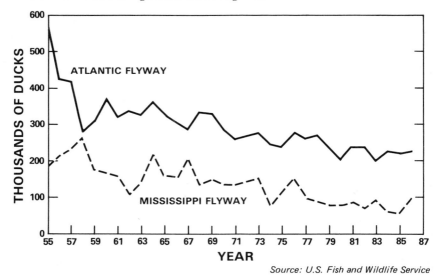

Figure 2

Source: U.S. Fish and Wildlife Service

consistent with maintaining sufficient breeding pairs of ducks for the following breeding season. The regulations may be designed so as to achieve species-specific kill levels as necessary.

The 1986 duck survey, "Status of Waterfowl and Fall Flight Forecast" (Department of the Interior 1986b), indicates that the duck breeding population in the surveyed areas increased from 30.8 million in 1985 to 35.1 million in 1986, a 14-percent increase. Nevertheless, the 1986 population still was 12 percent below the average annual breeding population of 1955-85 (see Figure 2).

All of the 10 most commonly hunted species showed breeding population increases over 1985 except the American wigeon (down two percent) and scaup (no change). However, the populations of six species were smaller than their average annual size during the 1955-85 period: mallard (-24 percent); American wigeon (-23 percent); blue-winged teal (-5 percent); northern pintail (-44 percent); canvasback (-22 percent); scaup (-10 percent) (see Table 3).

One species of particular concern is the black duck, which has been in a long-term decline since 1955. Population-trend estimates for the black duck are developed from special winter surveys and evaluations of breeding-ground habitat conditions and reproductive-success studies.[6] Winter survey results for 1986 indicate that black ducks increased 16 percent over 1985. The winter-survey black duck population now is only one percent smaller than the 10-year average. In the

6. FWS does not estimate the annual breeding-population or fall-flight sizes for black ducks because of a lack of valid survey methods.

**TABLE 3**

**Duck Breeding Population Estimates Adjusted for Birds Present That Were Not Seen by Aerial Survey Crews 1985–1986 (Excludes Scoters, Eiders, Oldsquaws, and Mergansers)**

| Survey area | 1985[a] | 1986[a] | Percentage Change |
|---|---|---|---|
| Alaska—Old Crow | 3,564 | 4,328 | +21 |
| N. Alberta—Northwest Territories | 6,852 | 7,498 | + 9 |
| N. Saskatchewan—N. Manitoba—W. Ontario[b] | 3,685 | 3,284 | −11 |
| S. Alberta | 3,406 | 2,685 | −21 |
| S. Saskatchewan | 6,060 | 6,244 | + 3 |
| S. Manitoba | 1,050 | 1,990 | +90 |
| Montana | 492 | 601 | +22 |
| Wyoming | 288 | 356 | +24 |
| Colorado | 110[c] | 105 | −5 |
| North Dakota | 2,456 | 3,138 | +28 |
| South Dakota | 1,765 | 3,771 | +114 |
| Nebraska | 75 | 69 | −8 |
| Minnesota | 644 | 597 | −7 |
| California | 170 | 124 | −27 |
| Wisconsin | 263 | 332 | +26 |
| Total | 30,883 | 35,122 | +14 |

[a] Estimates in thousands.

[b] Long-term average used in W. Ontario in 1985; in 1986 W. Ontario was surveyed and figure includes these results.

[c] No survey in 1985; figure represents 1984 survey results.

Atlantic Flyway, the population increased two percent from 1985 but is still five percent below the 10-year average. In the Mississippi Flyway, black ducks increased 67 percent from 1985 and are 11 percent above the 10-year average.[7] While the 1986 increases may indicate that the declining trend is bottoming out, FWS says it will take several more years of data to confirm that.

***Fall Flight.*** The 1986 estimated fall-flight size of ducks migrating south from the surveyed areas was 73 million. Although this represents a 17.7 percent increase over 1985's 62 million birds, it is still the second lowest fall flight estimate made by FWS since 1969, the year FWS began making the estimate.

***Hunting Regulations.*** According to FWS, the hunting regulations promulgated for the 1985-86 season helped reduce the total duck kill by 27 percent, from 12.5 million in 1984-85 to 9.2 million. The 1986-87 regulations were designed to continue the restoration of breeding-population numbers with special emphasis on the mallard and pintail,

7. This large increase in the survey does not necessarily mean that the actual Mississippi Flyway population has increased similarly. The number of birds seen in the winter survey may vary widely from one year to the next.

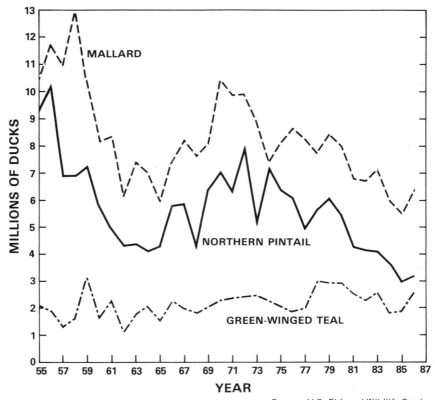

Source: U.S. Fish and Wildlife Service

Figure 3

the two most avidly hunted species. In addition, the hunting of canvasback ducks in the Atlantic, Central, and Mississippi flyways was prohibited. The 1986 eastern breeding population of canvasbacks is estimated at 303,000. FWS management plans halt hunting of the species when the breeding population drops below 360,000.

Black duck kill levels in some Atlantic and Mississippi flyway states also were reduced in an attempt to achieve a 25-percent reduction from the 1977-81 level in all states. However, the black duck kill rate in Canada remains high relative to the U.S. rate. A decrease in the Canadian take of black ducks is necessary, says FWS, to evaluate the overall kill-reduction program and its relationship to the population trend. Canada and the United States are developing a cooperative program to better manage black duck populations. Components of this effort include improved inventory methods, regular surveys, research, and other actions.

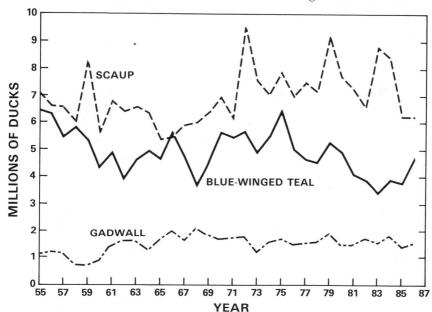

Figure 4

## North American Waterfowl Management Plan Adopted

The United States and Canada formally adopted a "North American Waterfowl Management Plan" in May 1986 (Interior 1986c). The plan is considered a good first step toward improved management of the waterfowl shared by the two countries because it recognizes the need

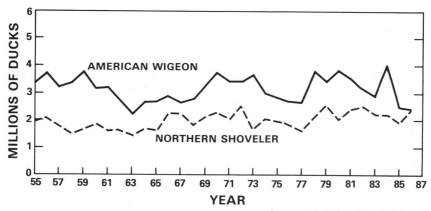

*Source: U.S. Fish and Wildlife Service*

Figure 5

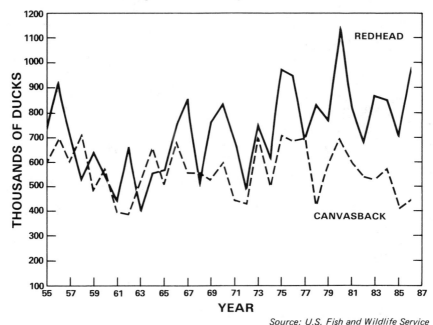

Source: U.S. Fish and Wildlife Service

Figure 6

for agressive, cooperative action. In agreeing to the plan, the United States and Canada have committed themselves to a highly ambitious program to produce by the year 2000 a breeding population of 62 million ducks annually and a yearly fall flight of 100 million ducks.[8] In addition, the plan calls for joint action to raise the populations of five goose species to acceptable levels and to maintain other goose populations at 1980-84 levels (see Table 4 and Table 5).

***Habitat Protection.*** According to the plan, the "loss and degradation of habitat is the major waterfowl management problem in North America" and the conservation of habitat is "the pressing imperative." In the far north of Canada, waterfowl habitats so far have escaped serious damage, but future land-use decisions could affect those areas adversely. Formerly secure waterfowl habitats interspersed in the boreal forests of Canada now are in jeopardy because of hydropower and recreational developments, forestry practices, and water and air pollution.

Waterfowl breeding habitat in the midcontinent prairie region already has been impacted severely. More than 50 percent of the

8. These goals are for the entire population of North American ducks, including those in FWS-surveyed areas plus ducks in unsurveyed areas. The numbers of ducks in unsurveyed areas are highly debatable since no accepted survey methods exist to measure them with any degree of precision.

**TABLE 4**
**Breeding Duck Population Status, Trends and Goals for the 10 Most Common Species in the Surveyed Area[a,b]**

| Species | Status (1985) United States | Canada | Total | Population Trend (1970–1985)[c] | Goals (year 2000)[d] |
|---------|------------|--------|-------|-------------------------|---------------------|
| Mallard | 1,597 | 3,878 | 5,475 | Decreasing | 8,700 |
| Pintail | 1,339 | 1,596 | 2,935 | Decreasing | 6,300 |
| Gadwall | 464 | 946 | 1,410 | No change | 1,600 |
| Wigeon | 969 | 1,537 | 2,506 | No change | 3,300 |
| Green-winged teal | 433 | 1,440 | 1,873 | No change | 2,300 |
| Blue-winged and cinnamon teal | 1,190 | 2,566 | 3,756 | Decreasing | 5,300 |
| Shoveler | 769 | 1,156 | 1,925 | No change | 2,100 |
| Redhead | 167 | 539 | 706 | No change | 760 |
| Canvasback | 126 | 285 | 411 | No change | 580 |
| Scaup | 1,339 | 4,893 | 6,232 | No change | 7,600 |

Source: North American Waterfowl Management Plan (Department of the Interior 1986c)

[a] In thousands of ducks

[b] The surveyed area includes Strata 1-50 and data from the six states that contribute information to the annual "Status of Waterfowl and Fall Flight Forecast."

[c] Status of several species declined significantly in 1985 from previous trends.

[d] The average of 1970-1979 for Strata 1-50 plus six cooperating states.

original wetlands of the United States have been lost to agriculture, urbanization, and industrial development, and the same forces are at work in Canada. Agriculture has been especially destructive of prairie wetlands and contiguous grasslands used by ducks for nesting cover. As a result, breeding ducks are concentrated in remaining patches of suitable habitat where they suffer high losses to predators such as skunks and foxes. In the past decade, a third of remaining prairie grasslands was converted to cropland and destruction of the rest continues at a rate of two percent yearly, according to FWS.

In eastern North America, wetlands used for breeding habitat in boreal forests and along coastal lowlands and estuaries are being lost or degraded. Migration and wintering habitats are similarly threatened.

To counteract these adverse trends, the plan calls for a coordinated effort by government and private conservation organizations to improve waterfowl habitats, primarily by changing private land-use practices across the continent. Specific goals include the following:

- Protect 3.6 million acres of habitat in Canada at an estimated cost of $1 billion over the next 15 years. Most of this acreage would be protected through agreements with private landowners to manage wetlands and grasslands for waterfowl. These waterfowl-management practices would benefit agriculture as well by conserving soil and maintaining water quality. Only 14 percent of the 3.6 million acres would be acquired.

**Table 5**
**Status of and Goals for North American Goose Populations[a]**

| Species and Populations | Winter Population Index (1984–1985) | Recent Trend (1980–1984) | Winter Index Goals (Year 2000) |
|---|---|---|---|
| Canada Goose | | | |
| Atlantic Flyway | 814,000 | Increasing | 850,000 |
| Tennessee Valley | 130,000 | Stable | 150,000 |
| Mississippi Valley | 477,000 | Increasing | 500,000 |
| Eastern prairie | 168,000 | Stable | 200,000 |
| Western prairie | 135,000 | Increasing | 200,000 |
| Great Plains | 17,000[b] | Increasing | 50,000[c] |
| Tallgrass prairie | 197,000 | Increasing | 250,000 |
| Shortgrass prairie | 194,000 | Stable | 150,000 |
| Hi-line | 93,000 | Stable | 80,000 |
| Rocky Mountain | 90,000 | Increasing | 50,000 |
| Pacific | 25,000[b] | Increasing | 29,000[c] |
| Lesser Pacific Flyway | 150,000 | Stable | 125,000 |
| Dusky | 7,500 | Decreasing | 20,000 |
| Cackling | 23,000 | Decreasing | 250,000 |
| Aleutian | 3,800 | Increasing | Delist[d] |
| Snow Goose | | | |
| Greater | 250,000[e] | Increasing | 185,000[c] |
| Midcontinent lesser | 1,974,000[e] | Increasing | 1,000,000[c] |
| Western Central Flyway | 107,000 | Increasing | 110,000 |
| Wrangel Island (U.S.S.R.) | no estimate | Stable | 120,000[c] |
| Western Canadian Arctic lesser | 185,000[b] | Stable | 200,000[c] |
| Ross' Goose | 106,000 | Increasing | 100,000 |
| White-fronted goose | | | |
| Eastern midcontinent | 71,000 | Increasing | 65,000 |
| Western midcontinent | 201,000 | Increasing | 250,000 |
| Tule | 5,000 | Stable | 5,000 |
| Pacific Flyway | 100,000 | Stable | 300,000 |
| Brant | | | |
| Atlantic | 146,000 | Increasing | 124,000 |
| Pacific | 145,000 | Increasing | 185,000 |

Source: North American Waterfowl Plan (Department of the Interior 1986c)

[a] The emperor goose is found only in Alaska and will not be considered in this plan. The Vancouver Canada goose population is also not considered.

[b] Breeding population information only available.

[c] Breeding population goals.

[d] Currently listed as an endangered species. Recovery plan specifies maintaining a wild population at a level of 1,200 or greater and to reestablish self-sustaining populations of geese (50 breeding pairs per area) on three former breeding areas in addition to Buldir Island.

[e] Spring inventory.

- Protect and improve 1,084,000 additional acres of mallard and pintail breeding habitat in the north central United States. A major goal of land management there would be to reduce predation on nesting birds and achieve a nest hatching success of 50 percent. Cost: $237 million.

- Protect 686,000 acres of mallard and pintail migration and wintering habitat in the lower Mississippi River-Gulf Coast region and 80,000 acres of wintering habitat for pintails in the Central Valley of California. Cost: $217 million.
- Protect 50,000 acres of black duck migration and wintering habitat along the U.S. East Coast and 10,000 acres in the Great Lakes-St. Lawrence lowlands. Estimated cost: $23 million.
- Protect 60,000 acres for black ducks and mallards in the Great Lakes-St. Lawrence lowlands of Canada. Cost: $20 million (Canadian dollars).
- Protect 10,000 acres of black duck migration and wintering habitat in the Atlantic region of Canada. Cost: $5 million (Canadian dollars).
- Prepare by 1987 specific plans, including habitat-protection recommendations, for the management of cackling, dusky, and Aleutian Canada geese, Pacific white-front geese, Pacific brant, and the trumpeter swan.

**Ongoing Implementation.** A joint U.S.-Canada committee, the North American Waterfowl Management Plan Committee, has been established to promote concrete actions to implement the plan. Work already is under way on three joint ventures: Canadian prairie-habitat protection, black duck conservation, and Arctic-goose conservation.

**Funding.** Although it calls for the expenditure of approximately $1.5 billion over the next 15 years, the plan offers no specific funding strategy to assure success. Instead, it calls for a shared government-private sector funding effort and says that the primary source of funding "must be private organizations and individuals who enjoy and benefit from achieving and maintaining the waterfowl population levels" identified in the plan. In short, the U.S. and Canadian governments are challenging the private sector to raise most of the money necessary to protect public resources.

Ducks Unlimited has challenged other conservation organizations to help fund the plan by contributing $2 for every $1 spent by Ducks Unlimited over the next 15 years. Ducks Unlimited will spend approximately $550 to $585 million during that period. However, the challenge so far has fallen on deaf ears, according to a Ducks Unlimited official.

Informal discussions now are taking place regarding the funding issue among interested corporations, hunting and conservation groups, and federal officials, but where these discussions will lead is anyone's guess. The first practical test of paying for habitat protection will come once the Canadian prairie protection joint-venture team submits detailed plans for conserving Canadian wetlands and grasslands. Some of these plans should be ready for implementation by 1987.

One thorny problem is spending of U.S. government funds in Canada. The plan recommends that 75 percent of the $1 billion spent to protect waterfowl habitat in prairie Canada come from U.S. sources, because U.S. hunters take about 80 percent of the annual North American duck kill and 70 to 75 percent of the goose kill. Expenditure of federal funds in Canada would require congressional approval, but expenditure of privately raised funds would not.

## LEGISLATION

### Emergency Wetlands Resources Act (S. 740)

After four years of deliberation, Congress in 1986 approved the first significant waterfowl-conservation measure since the Wetlands Loan Act of 1961. The new measure, the Emergency Wetlands Resources Act (P.L. 99-645), is designed to increase the acquisition and protection of wetlands not only for the benefit of migratory waterfowl, but also for wildlife in general, commercial and sport fisheries, water quality and supply, flood control, and outdoor recreation.

According to the committee report accompanying the bill, S.740, the continued loss of wetlands is "one of the most serious environmental problems facing the Nation today" (U.S. Congress, Senate 1986). The legislation attacks this problem on a broad number of fronts. It

- increases the amount of federal funds available annually for the acquisition of migratory bird habitat to about $40 million;

- amends the Land and Water Conservation Fund Act to authorize the appropriation of fund monies to states and federal agencies for wetlands acquisition; acquisition efforts are guided by a national wetlands priority conservation plan to be developed by the secretary of the Interior;

- mandates an accelerated schedule for completing the National Wetlands Inventory and for producing wetlands maps for the entire United States;

- requires a report on the status, condition, and trends of wetlands in the lower Mississippi alluvial plain and the prairie-pothole region, and a second report on all other U.S. wetlands; it also requires a detailed study of the environmental and economic benefits and costs of federal programs that impact wetlands.

***Wetlands Acquisition.***   Under current law, FWS acquisitions of migratory bird habitat are financed by the sale of duck stamps, which generates about $14 million annually, and by special appropriations under the Wetlands Loan Act, which vary from year to year. Revenues from both sources are put in the Migratory Bird Conservation Fund and withdrawn as needed by FWS.

The Emergency Wetlands Act augments the amount of money going into the fund by (1) gradually raising the price of a duck stamp from $7.50 to $15 by 1991; (2) authorizing the secretary of the Interior to charge entrance fees at refuges with high visitation and to place 70 percent of collected revenues into the fund; and (3) transferring from the general Treasury to the fund an amount equal to the custom duties collected annually on imported arms and ammunition, about $10 million. Altogether, about $40 million annually will accrue to the Migratory Bird Conservation Fund from all sources.

In addition, the act reauthorizes the Wetlands Loan Act through fiscal year 1988 and repeals the requirement that funds appropriated under that law be repaid from duck-stamp receipts after the loan program expires. Some $196 million of the $200 million authorized for appropriation by the loan act has been spent. The repayment requirement was repealed primarily because it was recognized that all future duck-stamp receipts are needed to buy even more wetlands before they are lost.

**Land and Water Conservation Fund Amendments.** The primary national land-acquisition tool of both federal and state conservation agencies is the Land and Water Conservation Fund. The Emergency Wetlands Act makes several changes in the fund's authorizing statute in order to place a higher emphasis on wetlands acquisition.

First, the act requires the secretary of the Interior to prepare a new "national wetlands priority conservation plan" that identifies the types of wetlands that should be given priority in federal and state acquisition programs. The secretary must consider the broadest range of wetland values in setting priorities. Thus, priority wetlands would be those that provide contributions with respect to wildlife, commercial and sport fisheries, water quality and supply, flood control, and outdoor recreation.

Second, the act requires the states in their comprehensive outdoor-recreation plans[9] to address wetlands as an important outdoor-recreation resource. This requirement takes effect in fiscal year 1988. Alternatively, a state may prepare a wetlands priority plan in consultation with the state fish and wildlife agency. According to the committee report, wetlands have been given low priority by the states in their use of federal matching funds for land acquisition. The Emergency Wetlands Act also amends the Land and Water Conserva-

9. Each state must prepare a State Comprehensive Outdoor Recreation Plan as a condition for receiving federal grants from the Land and Water Conservation Fund.

tion Fund Act to allow use of fund revenues specifically for the purchase of wetlands by federal agencies as long as these purchases are consistent with the national wetlands priority plan. In contrast, FWS acquisitions made with Migratory Bird Conservation Fund revenues do not have to be identified in the national priority plan.

*Wetlands Inventory.* FWS currently conducts the National Wetlands Inventory, a project designed to map all wetlands in the United States by type. These maps are useful in estimating the status and trends of wetlands destruction and in planning public and private development projects. So far, FWS has mapped about 46 percent of the high-priority wetlands in the contiguous states but only 12 percent of the wetlands in Alaska.

The Emergency Wetlands Act requires FWS to complete the mapping of all priority areas by the end of fiscal 1988, all remaining areas by the end of fiscal 1998, and of Alaska and other noncontiguous portions of the U.S. "as soon as possible." The act also mandates a new report on wetlands status and trends every 10 years beginning in 1990.

*Additional Reports.* The act mandates two detailed status reports to Congress: one on wetlands in the Mississippi alluvial plain and the prairie-pothole region, the other on all other wetlands in the United States. Both reports are to be submitted in 1987 and are to contain detailed analyses of the factors responsible for wetlands destruction, degradation, protection, and enhancement.

In addition, the reports are to contain analyses of the environmental and economic impacts of eliminating federal expenditures and financial-assistance programs that directly or indirectly encourage wetlands destruction. Conservation organizations urged Congress to add to the Emergency Wetlands Act provisions that eliminate certain federal activities that adversely affect wetlands. However, the House and Senate authorizing committees wanted to obtain more data before acting. The reports are likely to provide the basis for new wetlands-protection measures in the 100th Congress.

## Fish and Wildlife Coordination Act Amendments (H.R. 2704)

Amendments to the Fish and Wildlife Coordination Act that had passed the House in 1985 died in the Senate Environment and Public Works Committee with the end of the 99th Congress. The Senate did not even hold hearings on the act.

The coordination act requires water-resource agencies such as the Corps of Engineers to consult with the secretary of the Interior regarding the impact of proposed development projects on fish and wildlife, to include wildlife protection or enhancement measures in these projects if feasible, and to mitigate any losses that do occur. Among other things, the bill:

- made clear that water-resource agencies must consult with both FWS and the National Marine Fisheries Service (NMFS) over the impacts of water projects on fish and wildlife resources, although only FWS is mentioned specifically in the law at present;
- mandated the transfer of funds from water-development agencies to FWS and NMFS, as appropriate, to pay for biological studies; although the transfer of such funds is authorized by current law, the mandate is necessary because the "transfer of funds has not always proceeded in a consistent and reliable fashion" (U.S. Congress, House 1985).
- authorized fish and wildlife mitigation measures on lands outside a project area and defined mitigation to be consistent with regulations implementing the National Environmental Policy Act;[10]
- required follow-up studies by FWS, NMFS, and water-resource agencies to determine the extent to which recommended fish and wildlife measures are incorporated in project plans and actually carried out; a 1982 study by NMFS showed that noncompliance with its recommendations for southeastern-region projects ran as high as 25 percent (Lindall and Thayer 1982);
- authorized the secretaries of Commerce and the Interior to negotiate long-term plans that reconcile fish- and wildlife-conservation objectives with water-resource-development objectives; the goal is to provide assurance to biological resource agencies, private developers, and government development agencies that, once designed and under way, a project will proceed without further delays, and each party will know precisely what its obligations and responsibilities are (a similar planning provision was added to the Endangered Species Act in 1982).

According to one FWS official, the effect of the proposed amendments would be minor because they do not address the central need of the coordination act: providing FWS with status equal to that of the water-development agencies, thus giving it the clout to better promote wildlife conservation throughout the project-planning process.

---

10. This provision, according to the House Merchant Marine and Fisheries Committee, would facilitate the use of innovative conflict-resolution techniques such as mitigation banking, a procedure whereby a private developer is allowed to establish "habitat credits" by protecting or managing certain areas for the benefit of wildlife. These credits may then be used to offset habitat losses caused by the developer in another location. The report accompanying H.R. 2704 states that mitigation banking cannot "be used to circumvent existing regulations or policies relative to development in wetlands areas" (U.S. Congress, House 1985).

It is not clear whether the House Merchant Marine and Fisheries Committee will take up coordination-act amendments again in the 100th Congress. The House twice passed the bill only to see it die in the Senate. The measure's sponsor, Representative John Breaux (D-LA), has been elected to the U.S. Senate. According to a Senate source, no compelling need for the legislation exists, a major reason for lack of Senate interest.

**Tax Code Changes That Promote Conservation**

A measure introduced by Senator John Chafee (R-RI) that would deny tax deductions or tax credits to individuals or corporations that develop designated areas of ecological significance – called "environmental zones" – died in the Senate Finance Committee (S. 1839).

According to Chafee, the bill would end federal financial support for development activities that take place within certain environmental zones, including wetlands, that the government is trying to protect under conservation programs. The measure defines "environmental zone" to include any area:

- within a critical habitat designated under the Endangered Species Act;
- authorized by Congress or designated by the secretaries of the Interior or Agriculture for inclusion, but not yet included in, the national park, national wildlife refuge, or national forest systems;
- within a unit of the Coastal Barrier Resources System; designated as a national natural landmark under the Historic Sites, Buildings, and Antiquities Act; or
- authorized by Congress for study as a potential unit of the Wild and Scenic River System.

Although the bill would deny certain tax subsidies for development activities on private lands within environmental zones, it does not prohibit a private party from undertaking the development activity.

The Finance Committee held one hearing on the measure, but the bill was never reported. Opposition to the proposal came from the timber, oil, gas, and real-estate industries.

The last time a conservation tax measure was approved was in 1980, when Congress reauthorized on a permanent basis the conservation easement law. Since that time, several other tax bills have been introduced to benefit conservation but none of them has ever been reported out of committee. However, the Tax Reform Act of 1986 made a number of changes to the federal tax code which eliminate certain tax incentives for wetlands conversion, particularly for agricultural use (see the Wetlands chapter for further details).

# LEGAL DEVELOPMENTS

## Subsistence Hunting of Alaskan Geese

Over the past 20 years, a steady decline in the Pacific Flyway populations of four goose species that breed in Alaska—greater white front, brant, emperor, and cackling Canada—has led to controversy over the proper management of these species. After FWS signed a goose-management agreement[11] with Native American organizations and state wildlife agencies in 1983, two Alaskan sport-hunting organizations filed suit because the plan did not completely ban the taking of goose eggs and birds by Alaskan Native Americans in the Yukon-Kuskokwim Delta during the nesting season. These species traditionally have been hunted by Native Alaskans in spring and summer. The nesting birds offer the first available source of fresh meat after the winter and hence are an important part of the Native diet. The sportsmen's groups alleged that the taking of the birds at that time is a major factor contributing to the goose decline and that FWS is required by the Migratory Bird Treaty Act (16 U.S.C.A. 703 *et. seq.*) to prohibit the hunting of all migratory birds during the nesting season, including hunting for subsistence purposes.

Early in 1986, the U.S. District Court for the District of Alaska found that "Congress has authorized Alaska Natives to harvest migratory waterfowl under the Alaska Game Act of 1925 (43 Stat. 739) . . . during any season of the year, including but not limited to the spring and summer months, when they or members of their family are in need of food and other sufficient food is not available" (*Alaska Fish and Wildlife Federation and Outdoor Council, Inc.* et al. v. *Robert Jantzen, Director, U.S. Fish and Wildlife Service,* et al., No. J 84-013 (D-Alaska). This ruling surprised FWS officials who had assumed all along that the Migratory Bird Treaty Act did apply in Alaska, but did not enforce its provisions for political and other reasons. Among other things, the court held that:

- the Migratory Bird Treaty Act does not apply to the subsistence hunting of migratory birds in Alaska because the act was superseded by the Alaska Game Law of 1925; the treaty act, however, does apply in Alaska in all other respects;
- the Alaska Game Law authorized the secretary of Agriculture (later the secretary of the Interior) to regulate the taking of game and nongame birds, but provided that no regulation "shall prohibit any Indian or Eskimo, prospector, or traveler to take

11. This plan, referred to as the "Hooper Bay Agreement," was signed in January 1984. Subsequently, the plan was revised and renamed "The Yukon-Kuskokwim Delta Goose Management Plan" in March 1985 (Department of the Interior 1985).

animals or birds during the close [sic] season when he is in absolute need of food and other food is not available . . ."
- in 1940, the emergency provision in the Game Law was expanded to create a broader subsistence exception when Congress amended the 1925 act to allow Natives to take birds and animals out of season "when . . . in need of food and other sufficient food is not available;"
- the subsistence hunting of migratory birds for nutritional reasons, as opposed to cultural or other reasons, is legal.

The court declined to address whether or not the secretary has authority to regulate subsistence hunting of migratory birds under the Fish and Wildlife Improvement Act of 1978 (16 U.S.C.A. 712[1]). The Alaska Natives intervening in the case alleged that he does, but the court said that since no regulations had been issued, any opinion would be only advisory. Subsequent to the court ruling, in 1986 FWS issued a notice of its intent to propose regulations governing subsistence hunting of migratory birds in Alaska (51 *Federal Register* 18349) pursuant to the Fish and Wildlife Improvement Act, which states:

> In accordance with the various migratory bird treaties and conventions with Canada, Japan, Mexico and the Union of Soviet Socialist Republics, the Secretary of the Interior is authorized to issue such regulations as may be necessary to assure that taking of migratory birds and the collection of their eggs, by the indigenous inhabitants of the State of Alaska, shall be permitted for their own nutritional and other essential needs, as determined by the Secretary of the Interior, during seasons established so as to provide for the preservation and maintenance of stocks of migratory birds.

According to FWS, the subsistence-hunting regulations will apply to both Native and non-Native residents of rural Alaska because Alaska law does not permit legal distinctions based on race. FWS intends the regulations to take effect prior to the spring 1988 nesting season. The regulations will provide general management guidelines for subsistence taking throughout the state as well as more specific regulations for particular populations of birds that are in jeopardy, such as those in the Yukon-Kuskokwim Delta.

## REFERENCES

Lindall, W.N., Jr. and G.W. Thayer. 1982. "Quantification of National Marine Fisheries Service Habitat Conservation Efforts in the Southeast Region of the United States," *Marine Fisheries Review* 44(12):18-22.

U.S. Congress, House. 1985. Report of the Committee on Merchant Marine and Fisheries to accompany H.R. 2704, 99th Congress, 1st Session, House Report 99-392.

U.S. Congress, Senate. 1986. Report of the Committee on Environment and Public Works to accompany S. 740, 99th Congress, 2nd Session, Senate Report 99-445.

U.S. Department of the Interior, Fish and Wildlife Service. 1976. *Final Environmental Impact Statement: Proposed Use of Steel Shot for Hunting Waterfowl in the United States*. Washington, D.C.

U.S. Fish and Wildlife Service, Department of the Interior 1985a. *Draft Supplemental Environmental Impact Statement on the Use of Lead Shot for Hunting Migratory Birds in the United States*. Washington, D.C.

U.S. Fish and Wildlife Service, Department of the Interior. 1985b. The Yukon-Kuskokwim Delta Goose Management Plan. Unpublished.

U.S. Fish and Wildlife Service Department of the Interior. 1986a. *Final Supplemental Environmental Impact Statement: Use of Lead Shot for Hunting Migratory Birds in the United States*. Washington, D.C.

U.S. Fish and Wildlife Service, Department of the Interior. 1986b. *Status of Waterfowl and Fall Flight Forecast 1986*. Washington, D.C.

U.S. Fish and Wildlife Service and Environment Canada. 1986c. *North American Waterfowl Management Plan*. Washington, D.C.

*William J. Chandler is president of W.J. Chandler Associates, a Washington D.C. environmental policy and government relations consulting firm.*

A fisheries biologist at Mingo National Wildlife Refuge in Missouri measures water clarity and quality. Federal inland fisheries management focuses on 109 species. *U.S. Fish and Wildlife Service*

# Federal Inland Fisheries Management

William J. Chandler

and

Richard Magder

## OVERVIEW

While the states   and Indian tribes have primary management authority[1] over fish within their territorial waters, the federal government has a long history of involvement in fisheries management. Beginning in 1871 with the appointment of a U.S. Commissioner of Fish and Fisheries, federal fishery policy has evolved into two distinct bodies of authority: one for inland-fishery resources,[2] implemented

---

1. This authority includes the key power to regulate the commercial and sport taking of fish. Congress can preempt state authority through its treaty-making power and under the commerce and property clauses of the Constitution. However, the federal government has chosen to preempt state authority over fish in state territorial waters only under the Endangered Species Act (16 U.S.C.A. 1531, *et seq.*) and in a few instances under provisions of the Fishery Conservation and Management Act of 1976 (16 U.S.C.A. 1801, *et seq.*) which regulates ocean fisheries. In addition, the Atlantic Striped Bass Conservation Act (16 U.S.C.A. 1851) authorizes the secretaries of Commerce and Interior jointly to declare a moratorium on catching Atlantic striped bass in the coastal waters of states failing to comply with the salmon management plan adopted by the Atlantic States Marine Fisheries Commission.

2. "Inland fish" generally is used to mean all fish species found in the internal freshwaters of the United States, including those in lakes, rivers, streams, ponds, and

Audubon Wildlife Report 1987

principally by the U.S. Fish and Wildlife Service (FWS), Department of the Interior; and one for ocean fisheries, implemented by the National Marine Fisheries Service (NMFS), an agency of the National Oceanic and Atmospheric Administration, Department of Commerce (for a discussion of NMFS activities, see the chapter on marine fisheries).

The principal exception to this division of responsibility is jurisdiction over anadromous fish—migratory species, such as salmon and shad, that spend part of their lives in freshwater and part in estuarine and ocean waters. Over the years, both FWS and NMFS have been given various responsibilities—some exclusive, some overlapping, and some joint—for anadromous species.

In addition, federal land-managing agencies such as the Forest Service and National Park Service cooperate with state fish and wildlife departments to manage fish in waters that lie within federally owned lands. In this situation, the taking of fish usually is regulated by the state.[3] The federal land agencies concentrate their efforts on habitat management: protecting streams from bank erosion and siltation, removing barriers to stream flow, monitoring fish stocks, stocking waters to improve sport fisheries, and providing vegetative cover, gravel, or artificial structures to improve spawning.

About 750 species of fish, including anadromous species, are found in U.S. inland waters. FWS management programs concentrate on about 40 species and groups of species, principally those with commercial, sport, or Indian cultural value, and on another 69 species that have been listed under the Endangered Species Act as threatened or endangered with extinction.[4]

FWS propagates fish for stocking, conducts research, provides technical assistance to federal and state agencies and Indian tribes, administers a program of federal grants to the states for anadromous-species conservation, mitigates fishery losses caused by federal water-resource projects, and enforces federal fish-conservation laws. Approximately 50 percent of the fishery-resources budget for fiscal year 1987 was allocated to fish propagation at federal hatcheries and another 23 percent to research.

---

estuaries. "Ocean fish" includes marine species caught in coastal, ocean, and high-seas fisheries.

3. The secretary of the Interior determines fishing regulations for national wildlife refuges. These regulations must be compatible with the purposes of the refuge and, to the maximum extent practicable, consistent with state laws and regulations. Furthermore, fishing is prohibited in most national parks. When it is allowed, it is done so in conformance with federal and state laws. Also, Indians are responsible for fishing regulations on tribal lands (48 *Federal Register* 11642-11645 [1983]).

4. The number of listed fish species is current to November 21, 1986. All endangered species, including fish, are the responsibility of the FWS Endangered Species Office.

# CURRENT DEVELOPMENTS

## The Federal Role in Fishery Management

Two reviews of federal fishery policy were issued in 1986, one by the National Oceanic and Atmospheric Administration and one by the American Fisheries Society, a nonprofit organization. The agency's study assesses the effectiveness of the Magnuson Fishery Conservation and Management Act, which governs ocean fisheries overseen by NMFS. However, some of its findings have relevance for FWS fishery-management programs. The American Fisheries Society study addresses the larger subject of fisheries management by all federal agencies.

***National Oceanic and Atmospheric Administration Study.***  One major conclusion of the agency report is that federal and state management responsibilities for shared fishery resources, including anadromous species, have never been defined clearly. This in turn has "materially weakened Federal and State commitments to fund and carry forward the planning, data collection, relevant research and enforcement that are essential . . ." (Department of Commerce 1985). The study calls for a precise delineation of agency responsibilities and for federal standards for coordinated management of certain interjurisdictional fisheries so that fish stocks may be maintained adequately (for a further discussion of this study, see the marine fisheries chapter).

***American Fisheries Society Study.***  The society study reviews all existing federal-agency authorities and programs for fishery management, defines the ideal federal fisheries mission, identifies problems that need correcting, and makes a variety of recommendations to correct them. According to the American Fisheries Society, "The Federal mission for fishery-related functions and services is to achieve wise management and optimum use of fishery resources on a long-term continuing basis for the benefit of the Nation."

Accomplishment of the mission, says the Society, is hindered by eight major problems:

- "Collection, analysis, and dissemination of information on fish stocks, populations, and habitats are inadequate in quantity, quality, and timeliness for effective management of the Nation's fishery resources."
- "Basic researches in fishery biology, community ecology, and fishery applications from other disciplines do not receive the sustained support essential to expand our knowledge base as an investment in future resource productivity . . ."
- "Protection and enhancement of fish habitats and adjacent wetlands, including riparian habitats, and control of airborne

and waterborne contaminants, have not been sufficiently effective to assure the productive future of those critical habitats in the face of increasing encroachments by incompatible uses and impacts."

- "Free and unlimited access to economically valuable publicly owned and managed fishery resources ultimately results in the 'tragedy of the commons,' with economically disastrous over-extension of user operations and production, adverse impacts on fish stocks and habitats, and excessive public costs."
- "The relative roles and responsibilities of Federal, State, Tribal, and local governments lack the definition and the sustained support necessary for effectively coordinated conservation and management throughout their range of fisheries subject to multiple jurisdictions."
- "Federal authority to conserve and manage the Nation's fisheries and their habitats is so fragmented that strong leadership to formulate and implement coherent national policies and programs is lacking. As a result, Federal actions in fishery affairs may be compromised due to lack of effective interagency coordination; moreover, clear accountability for actions taken is diffused and uncertain."
- "In Federal agencies where fishery-related functions are only one of the agency's management responsibilities (e.g. Bureau of Land Management, National Park Service, Forest Service, Corps of Engineers, Environmental Protection Agency, and some twenty others), priorities for support of fishery research and management are diluted by overriding concerns for the remainder of the agency's mission."
- "The role of aquaculture in Federal fishery policy is not clearly defined or directed, and suffers from lack of a centralized governmental effort both to provide national leadership for aquaculture research and development, and to reduce scientific, technological, and institutional impediments to developing the United States potential for commercial aquaculture, and for managing its productivity" (American Fisheries Society 1986).

To help solve these problems, the American Fisheries Society calls for a consolidation of the fishery-related programs of NMFS and FWS into a single federal fishery agency, and the development of effective mechanisms for coordinating the work of the new agency with other federal agencies, the states, Indian tribes, and the private sector.

## Pacific Salmon Treaty

After 15 years of negotiations, the United States and Canada in 1985 signed the Pacific Salmon Treaty. The agreement is expected to end years of sometimes bitter competition between the two countries over the fishing of Pacific salmon stocks along the northwest coast and to provide a basis for cooperative management. The treaty establishes principles for managing the fishery and creates a bilateral commission to make annual catch and conservation recommendations.

At the center of the dispute between the two countries is the issue of "interceptions." Pacific salmon hatch in freshwater streams, but spend their adult lives in the ocean, often migrating thousands of miles before returning to their natal streams to spawn. During these migrations, stocks originating in the waters of one country are intercepted by fishermen from the other. For example, in recent years it is estimated that 20 to 35 percent of the catch of pink and sockeye salmon stocks originating in the Fraser River, Canada's most productive salmon-spawning river, were caught by U.S. fishermen. Similarly, it is estimated that in 1984, 50 percent or more of upper Columbia River and Puget Sound fall chinook salmon stocks were caught by Canadian trollers (U.S.-Canada Treaty Coalition 1985). Over the years, Canadian interceptions, as well as those by Alaskan fishermen, have had a significant adverse impact on salmon stocks in the Columbia River basin (see Table 1).

In an attempt to rebuild stocks in the region through hatchery production and conservation measures, the federal government, the states, and Native American tribes spend about $87 million yearly. Another $800 million has been invested for mitigating the damage caused by hydroelectric facilities and $750 million has been committed by the Northwest Power Planning Council for salmon restoration (U.S.-Canada Treaty Coalition 1985). Northwestern state fishery managers and fishermen consider these investments wasted when only Canadian and Alaskan fishermen catch most of the fish.

**TABLE 1**
**Status of Columbia River Basin Anadromous Fish Stocks**

| | State Population Goals (Pre-McNary Dam)[a] (Base run size) | *Current Run Levels* (5-yr. average) 1975–79 | Fishery Reduction since McNary Dam Construction |
|---|---|---|---|
| Spring chinook | 300,000 | 101,000 | −199,000 (66%) |
| Summer chinook | 200,000 | 41,000 | −159,000 (79%) |
| Fall chinook | 400,000 | 294,000 | −106,000 (26%) |
| Sockeye | 200,000 | 55,000 | −145,000 (72%) |
| Coho | 164,000 | 45,600 | −118,400 (72%) |
| Summer steelhead | 400,000 | 124,000 | −276,000 (69%) |

Source: "Columbia River Basin Fish and Wildlife Program" (Pacific NW Electric Power and Conservation Planning Council 1984)

[a] These goals are represented by state wildlife agencies as the run sizes of the various stocks *which could have been maintained prior to the construction of McNary Dam in 1953.* In the case of coho, the goal was based on the size of the run in 1967.

Under the Pacific Salmon Treaty, each country is directed to conduct its fisheries and salmon enhancement programs to prevent overfishing and to provide for optimum salmon production. Each nation expects to receive benefits equivalent to the amount of salmon originating in its waters. Interceptions will be permitted only if the country producing the intercepted fish is compensated with a like number of fish. In addition, a coast-wide stock assessment and management data system will be developed to investigate the status of stocks of common concern and the effects of interceptions.

The Pacific Salmon Treaty does not set specific catch levels for most Pacific salmon stocks after the 1986 season. To negotiate future limits, the treaty establishes the Pacific Salmon Commission, composed of four commissioners from each country. Each nation is allotted one vote, and all commission recommendations and decisions must be approved by both parties. The commission is assisted by three regional panels with equal U.S. and Canadian representation: a northern panel, a southern panel, and a Fraser River panel. The panels review information and recommend to the commission fishery-management regimes for stocks originating in their jurisdiction.

Creation of the commission is considered a major step in the efforts to restore Pacific salmon stocks to the Columbia River basin and coastal areas of Oregon and Washington. But some observers contend that the real test for the commission and the treaty will come after the 1986 fishing season, when the commission has to set catch levels for most stocks. Most agree that continued support and cooperation from all parties will be necessary for the treaty to meet its lofty goals.

**Atlantic-Salmon Restoration**

A long-standing state and federal cooperative effort to restore naturally spawning populations of Atlantic salmon to the rivers of New England is threatened by the construction of new hydroelectric dams, increasing water acidity, and excessive fishing of Atlantic salmon stocks in ocean fisheries. The goal of the program is to restore self-sustaining populations of salmon in 18 rivers, especially the Merrimack, Connecticut, and Penobscot. The restoration objective of 54,000 returning adults by the year 2000 would yield an annual sport take of some 12,000 salmon and provide an estimated 140,000 angler-days of recreation.

One of the principal threats to the restoration effort is the continued federal licensing of hydroelectric dams on rivers targeted for restoration. Dams block salmon migration to and from spawning grounds. The Federal Energy Regulatory Commission, which grants hydroelectric facilities operating licenses under the Federal Power Act, already has issued licenses or license exemptions for 53 dams in the Merrimack River basin. Another 13 major and minor dam license requests are now under consideration.[5]

One particularly controversial dam — a 4.95 megawatt structure 19 feet high — is proposed for construction at Sewalls Falls on the Merrimack River near Concord, New Hampshire. Conservation organizations, the state of Massachusetts, NMFS, and FWS oppose construction of the dam. Power from the dam is not needed, say dam opponents, but since public utilities are required by federal law to buy small-hydro-produced electricity at favorable prices, an artificial incentive spurs building of the dam. Conservationists view the Sewalls Falls dam as a test case that will determine how serious the federal government is about the salmon-restoration effort. Federal Energy Regulatory Commission approval of the dam would have a significant negative impact on the ability of the Merrimack mainstem to support a self-sustaining salmon population, according to the FWS regional office.

The Federal Energy Regulatory Commission accepted the license application for the Sewalls Falls dam October 31, 1983, and now is studying how to address the issue of the cumulative environmental impacts of all dams in the Merrimack Basin, including the Sewalls Falls facility. Eventually, the commission may decide to conduct a formal cluster impact assessment in the basin to determine the basin-wide impacts of all hydroelectric facilities, existing and proposed. Alternatively, the commission may decide that only a site-specific environmental assessment or impact statement need be prepared for the Sewalls Falls dam. Exactly when the commission will make its decision is unpredictable.

Another problem hampering Atlantic-salmon restoration is the high catch of U.S.-spawned salmon by Canadian and Greenland fishermen in the Atlantic Ocean. In 1982, the United States signed a treaty that established the North Atlantic Salmon Conservation Organization, whose purpose is to regulate the salmon take better and implement needed conservation measures.[6] A major U.S. goal in joining the organization was to reduce ocean interceptions of U.S.-spawned salmon that otherwise would return to New England rivers. U.S.-spawned salmon are taken principally on their feeding grounds off west Greenland and Newfoundland-Labrador. In recent years, some 90 percent of Canada's entire salmon catch has come from the Newfoundland-Labrador area, compared with about 50 percent 10 years ago.

5. As of September 15, 1986.

6. Other treaty signators are Canada, Denmark, the European Economic Community, Iceland, Norway, and Sweden.

In response to this situation, U.S. representatives to the North Atlantic Salmon Conservation Organization in 1986 sought and obtained a shortening of the Canadian fall fishing season in the Newfoundland-Labrador fishery. Canada agreed to close the season October 15 instead of the usual December 31. This change is expected to reduce the Canadian take of U.S.-spawned salmon by at least 15 percent.

Yet to be resolved is the problem of illegal fishing for salmon in the rivers and coastal waters of European nations, where Atlantic salmon also spawn. As fewer European-spawned salmon migrate to the west Greenland fishery and mix with North American-spawned stocks, Greenland fishermen take proportionally more U.S. and Canadian-spawned fish to meet their annual catch quota. It is estimated that the illegal world take of Atlantic salmon totaled 3,070 tons in 1985 — about half the legal catch.

## Toxic Pollutants and Fish

Toxic contamination continues to threaten the health of fish stocks nationwide, despite federal laws enacted in the 1970s to curb the use of pesticides and restrict the use of industrial chemicals such as PCBs (polychlorinated biphenyls). According to a 1986 FWS report, toxic contaminants are found in fish in every region of the country (Department of the Interior 1986). While levels of some substances such as DDT are declining, concentrations of other contaminants are increasing. The implications for fish and wildlife health are serious. Recent research provides strong evidence indicating that toxic contaminants impede reproduction in many fish species and in some cases cause death.

The FWS report, covering samples taken through 1981, reveals both encouraging and alarming trends.[7] A dramatic improvement is shown in levels of the pesticide DDT, banned for general use in the 1970s. The national average DDT concentration in fish tissue declined from one part per million in 1970 to 0.3 parts per million in 1981. FWS also found that levels of a major byproduct of the pesticide chlordane decreased by 50 percent between 1976 and 1981. However, the contam-

7. The federal government has been monitoring contaminants since 1964 when FWS, in cooperation with several other agencies, initiated the National Pesticide Monitoring Program. Each agency went its own way, however, and the original promise of a cooperative effort was never realized. FWS expanded its portion of the program to monitor other contaminants in addition to pesticides and several years ago renamed its program the National Contaminant Biomonitoring Program. FWS collects data on fish contamination every two to three years at more than 100 sampling sites around the country.

inant still was detected at nearly all monitoring sites. Chlordane, like DDT, was used widely in the 1960s and early 1970s before its use was restricted.

The occurrence in fish tissue of toxaphene, a pesticide used extensively on cotton in the Southwest and Southeast, is increasing steadily. Between 1976 and 1979, toxaphene was found in fish at only 60 percent of the monitoring stations. In 1981, it was discovered at 88 percent of the stations. Also alarming is the continued widespread presence of PCBs, used as coolants in hydraulic systems, capacitors, and transformers and as ingredients in certain paints, inks, and plastics. Although PCB use was highly restricted in 1976 by the Toxic Substances Act, the report indicates that PCB levels are unchanged at 102 of 117 monitoring sites. PCB concentrations have decreased, however, where they were previously highest. In the Hudson River, for example, levels declined from 70.6 parts per million to 11.3 parts per million between 1976 and 1981.

Biologists also are concerned about the presence in aquatic systems of naturally occurring inorganic metals, although inorganic metals were not discussed in the report. Of special interest is the metal selenium, which has been leached from western soils by intensive irrigation. High concentrations of selenium also are being discovered in numerous reservoirs associated with coal power plants in the East and Southeast where fly ash or coal residue is believed to be the primary source. Selenium in high concentrations has proved to be lethal to fish and wildlife at Kesterson National Wildlife Refuge in California (for more details, see the wildlife refuge and water projects chapters of this volume).

Biologists likewise are concerned about the presence of aluminum in Northeast aquatic systems. Though research has been limited, aluminum apparently is being dissolved out of the soil by acid rain and may be killing or otherwise harming fish.

Toxic contamination of fish from inorganic metals and organic compounds can have serious consequences not only for fish and wildlife, but also for human health. The Environmental Protection Agency reports that in 1984, 88 fish-consumption advisories were posted by 13 states, and 42 fish-consumption bans were imposed by 10 states (U.S. Environmental Protection Agency 1985). These figures, the agency contends, probably underestimate the total number of closures and warnings, since not all the states provided a complete list. Moreover, closures, warnings, and periodic spot checks of fish by state public-health agencies do not prevent contaminated fish from ending up on restaurant tables, according to some fishery managers. They point out that the Food and Drug Administration generally examines commercial fish catches only when interstate commerce is involved and that the states are reluctant to close any fishery because of the possible impact closure may have on their sport or commercial fishing industries.

In response to the ecological and public health consequences of toxic contamination, Congress passed numerous laws in the 1970s to keep toxic substances out of the environment. But despite passage of the Toxic Substances Control Act, the Clean Water Act, and Superfund, among others, contamination problems persist. Conservationists argue that generally the laws are adequate, but have not been implemented to the fullest extent. On the other hand, conservationists agree that tremendous gains in public awareness have been made in recent years. This makes the problem appear to be getting worse, they say, because biologists and the public are looking more closely for and discovering more sources of contamination.

What is clear is that the FWS contaminant-monitoring program is absolutely vital. Once detected, a contaminant problem can sometimes be solved, as exemplified by the DDT case.

## LEGISLATION

### Atlantic Striped Bass Conservation

In 1985-86, Congress continued its oversight of striped bass management by Atlantic coastal states and passed amendments to the Atlantic Striped Bass Conservation Act of 1984 (16 U.S.C.A 1851). Federal intervention in the management of this interjurisdictional fishery has occurred because of the inability of the states, acting through the Atlantic States Marine Fisheries Commission, to conserve striped bass populations effectively.

The annual commercial catch of striped bass has declined 90 percent in 10 years, from 14.7 million pounds in 1973 to 1.6 million in 1983. Overfishing, chemical contamination of spawning and nursery grounds (especially in the Hudson River and Chesapeake Bay), and episodic reductions in pH levels appear to be the dominant factors causing the decline.

In 1983, the Atlantic States Marine Fisheries Commission finally recognized that the catch of juvenile-sized fish needed to be curtailed so that more adults could survive to spawn. The commission amended its striped bass management plan to require a 55 percent reduction in the total annual take, but lacked authority to assure compliance by member states.

Consequently, Congress in 1984 passed the Atlantic Striped Bass Conservation Act to ensure that all states complied with the commission plan. The act required by July 1, 1985 a 55-percent reduction in striped bass take from Maine to North Carolina and directed the commission to monitor state compliance. It also authorized the secretary of Commerce to declare a moratorium on catching striped bass in a state's coastal waters if the commission determines that the state failed to meet the 55-percent catch reduction or failed to adopt other regulatory measures necessary to fully implement the plan. In addition, the act directed the secretaries of Interior and Commerce to review state-by-state implementation of the commission's striped bass plan and to report to Congress on the potential for achieving the purposes of the act.

The joint Commerce-Interior report reviewing the Atlantic States Marine Fisheries Commission's plan was transmitted to Congress on May 7, 1985 (Department of Commerce and Department of the Interior 1985). The report concluded that the plan then in effect was deficient in several respects, but that compliance with it would be adequate to conserve bass stocks if the commission were to further restrict the catch of female fish.

Subsequently, in October 1985, the commission amended its plan to require the states to prohibit the taking of females of the relatively abundant Chesapeake Bay 1982 year class and of females of all subsequent year classes of Chesapeake Bay stocks in order to allow 95 percent of these fish to reproduce at least once.[8] Effectively, this will require the states to gradually increase the minimum-length catch requirements from 24 inches to 33 inches by April 1988.

Meanwhile, no states were preempted by the secretary of Commerce for noncompliance with the act in 1985. However, at a July 19, 1985, hearing before the Senate Subcommittee on Environmental Pollution of the Committee on Environment and Public Works, several witnesses contended that certain states were not meeting the requirements of the act. Dick Russell, president of the Striped Bass Emergency Council, a private nonprofit organization, told the subcommittee, "New York's harvest of striped bass in 1984 represented 40 percent of the total for the entire East Coast, higher than any other state's catch . . . but there is no closure at all during the month of November . . . when over 75-percent of the recorded landings customarily take place" (Russell 1985). FWS representatives agreed that New York had yet to institute regulations to fully comply with the act and added that New Jersey, Maine, and Connecticut had failed to impose sufficiently tough restrictions on their recreational catches (Kutkuhn 1985).

---

8. The amendment would stay in effect until the three-year running average of the Maryland young-of-the-year index attains 8.0. In 1985, the three-year running index was 2.9. The index is an indicator of the rate of spawning success in a geographically distinct area as measured by the average number of immature fish found in various seine-net samples.

In part because of concern that some states were doing more than others to protect striped bass, and in part because of uncertainty about whether the commission plan does enough to conserve the fish, Senator John Chafee (R-RI) and Representatives Gerry Studds (D-MA) and John Breaux (D-LA) introduced legislation (S.1813, H.R. 3358) designed to keep pressure on the states to conserve and manage bass stocks adequately. As finally passed, the Atlantic Striped Bass Conservation Act Amendments of 1986 (P.L. 99-432):

- continue the Atlantic States Marine Fisheries Commission's authority to determine whether its member states are in compliance with the striped bass plan and are enforcing it adequately in state waters;
- endorse the commission's catch restrictions on females and the implementation timetable as part of the plan;
- require that the secretaries of Commerce and Interior jointly verify state noncompliance with the act after receiving notification from the Atlantic States Marine Fisheries Commission that a state may be in noncompliance;
- require the secretaries jointly to declare a moratorium on striped bass take in the waters of a noncomplying state; once the state has taken remedial action to comply, the moratorium may be lifted; and
- extend the Atlantic Striped Bass Conservation Act through fiscal year 1988 and authorize additional funding of the Emergency Striped Bass Study; continuation of the study, first authorized in 1979, will allow for additional research to monitor reproduction, stock size, and factors affecting the biological health of the fish.

Recovery of the striped bass population ultimately depends on the production of more dominant-year classes on a regular basis. The new amendments are directed toward that goal, but their success remains to be seen.

### Hydroelectric Dams and Fish

In 1986, Congress adopted amendments to the Federal Power Act and the Public Utilities Regulatory Policies Act that substantially increase the protection afforded fishery and other environmental resources during the dam-licensing process. Conservationists have long complained about the inadequate treatment of environmental concerns in the Federal Energy Regulatory Commission's licensing process and about the commission's failure to include in issued licenses and exemptions adequate protection and mitigation requirements for fish. The new amendments, contained in the Electric Consumers Protection Act of 1986 (P.L. 99-495), provide extensive new guidance to the

Federal Energy Regulatory Commission regarding its environmental responsibilities.

***Power Project Purposes.*** The new law amends the Federal Power Act to make environmental values more equal to those of power and development in the hydroelectric-facility licensing process. In deciding whether to issue any license, the Federal Energy Regulatory Commission is required to give "equal consideration to the purposes of energy conservation, the protection, investigation, and enhancement of fish and wildilfe (including related spawning grounds and habitat), the protection of recreational opportunities, and the preservation of other aspects of environmental quality."

***Comprehensive Planning.*** Under the Federal Power Act, the Federal Energy Regulatory Commission is supposed to ensure that all licensed projects "will be best adapted to a comprehensive plan for improving or developing a waterway or waterways for the use or benefit of interstate or foreign commerce, for the improvement and utilization of water-power development, and for other beneficial uses, including recreational purposes . . ." Critics allege that the commission has not paid sufficient attention to this multiple-use mandate and generally has leaned toward power uses in its licensing decisions. To redress this imbalance, and to ensure that any approved project is compatible with the comprehensive plan, the new law requires the commission to ensure that adequate protection, mitigation, and enhancement of fish and wildlife is included in the comprehensive planning process for waterways, and to consider among other things:

- the extent to which the project is consistent with any comprehensive waterway plan prepared by either a federal agency or the state where the facility is located; and
- the recommendations of federal and state agencies and Indian tribes regarding flood control, navigation, irrigation, recreation, culture, and other relevant resources affected by the project.

***Fish and Wildlife Mitigation.*** According to the conference report on the bill (U.S. Congress, House 1986), the amendments "expressly identify fish and wildlife protection, mitigation and enhancement, recreational opportunities, and energy conservation as nondevelopmental values that must be adequately considered by FERC when it decides whether and under what conditions to issue a hydroelectric license for a project." These nondevelopment values, says the law, must receive "equal consideration" in the licensing process. With regard to fish and wildlife values the act:

- requires the Federal Energy Regulatory Commission specifically to consider the recommendations of federal and state fish and wildlife agencies regarding each license application;

- provides that each license issued include conditions for the protection, mitigation, and enhancement of fish and wildlife affected by the hydroelectric facility; the conditions included are to be based on agency recommendations made under the Fish and Wildlife Coordination Act by FWS, NMFS, and state fish and wildlife agencies;
- creates a dispute-resolution procedure in cases where the Federal Energy Regulatory Commission disagrees with any of the fish and wildlife agencies' recommendations. If the commission does not adopt in whole or in part any recommendation of those agencies, it must publish a formal finding, with explanation, that the recommendation is "inconsistent" with existing law and that the conditions actually selected by the commission for inclusion in the license comply with the act's requirements for protecting, mitigating, and enhancing fish and wildlife;
- requires prospective license applicants to consult with fish and wildlife agencies and conduct appropriate studies with those agencies; and
- requires license applicants to pay fees to reimburse fish and wildlife agencies for the costs associated with environmental reviews and studies.

Taken together, these provisions clearly strengthen the position of fish and wildlife agencies in the hydroelectric planning and licensing process. While such agencies are not given a veto over the Federal Energy Regulatory Commission licensing decisions, their enhanced position should enable them to convince the commission that some original project licenses should not be issued because of negative effects the projects will have on fish and wildlife resources and that issued licenses should carry tough restrictions to protect environmental values (U.S. Congress, House 1986).

***Public Utilities Regulatory Policies Act Benefits.*** The Electric Consumers Protection Act also contains environmental provisions relating to hydroelectric facilities 80 megawatts in size or smaller that may be eligible for financial benefits under Section 210 of the Public Utilities Regulatory Policies Act. The Federal Energy Regulatory Commission has interpreted the policies act so as to provide its financial benefits to qualifying hydroelectric projects at all sites, both at existing dams and totally new sites, whereas conservationists contend that Congress intended benefits to be available only for hydroelectric facilities constructed at existing dams. The commission's broader interpretation of the law, say conservationists, combined with the incentives of the act, unleashed a flood of proposals for new dams and diversions. Between 1978, when the Public Utilities Regulatory Policies Act was passed, and 1987, about 10,000 applications for hydroelectric projects were submitted to the Federal Energy Regulatory Commission. Most of these applications, says David Conrad of Friends of the Earth, were driven by the act.

Congress addressed this situation by amending the act to limit the number of hydroelectric facilities eligible for benefits under the act. Among other things, Section 8 of the act:

- defines "new dam or diversion" to mean "a dam or diversion which requires, for purposes of installing any hydroelectric power project, any construction, or any enlargement of any impoundment or diversion structure (other than repairs or reconstruction . . .);"
- prohibits the granting of Public Utilities Regulatory Policies Act benefits to new dams or diversions unless the project meets all of the following conditions:

  1. The Federal Energy Regulatory Act finds that the project "will not have substantial adverse effects on the environment, including recreation and water quality."
  2. The project, at the time the license application is accepted by the commission, is not located on any segment of a natural watercourse included in or designated for potential inclusion in a state or national wild and scenic river system, or on any segment which the state has determined "to possess unique natural, recreational, cultural or scenic attributes which would be adversely affected by hydroelectric development."
  3. The project meets the terms and conditions set by federal and state fish and wildlife agencies in recommendations to the Federal Energy Regulatory Act in accordance with the Fish and Wildlife Coordination Act.

- exempts new dams and diversions already in some stage of the application process from having to meet some or all of the environmental conditions listed above; and
- declares a moratorium on the granting of Public Utilities Regulatory Act benefits to any new dam or diversion project for which a license or exemption is issued after enactment of the act.

The moratorium is to remain in effect while the Federal Energy Regulatory Commission prepares an environmental impact statement on whether the benefits of Section 210 of the Public Utilities Regulatory Policies Act should be applied to future projects utilizing new dams or diversions and reports its findings to Congress.

After Congress receives the report, it will once again re-examine the issue of whether the Public Utilities Regulatory Policies Act has spawned too many environmentally unsound hydroelectric dams.

Meanwhile, say conservationists, the new law should severely restrict the number of new small hydroelectric facilities eligible to receive the act's benefits and put a chill on the small hydro boom.

***Comprehensive Planning.*** The new law updates the comprehensive planning provision of the Federal Power Act, adding the requirement that fish and wildlife protection, mitigation, and enhancement be included as considerations in the planning process. However, the law does not require that they be treated with consideration equal to that given other factors in the planning process (U.S. Congress, House 1986).

### Klamath River Fishery Restoration

Congress passed legislation in 1986 that establishes a 20-year restoration program for anadromous fish that spawn in the Klamath River Basin of California. The new law (P.L. 99-552), sponsored by Representative Douglas Bosco (D-CA), addresses the full range of problems affecting the basin's anadromous fishery, including habitat conservation, fish production, catch management, and user allocations.

Chinook fall-salmon populations in the basin have declined by 80 percent from historic levels and steelhead trout also have been reduced significantly. Diminishing stocks have predictably increased conflicts between Indian and non-Indian sport and commercial fishermen.

The legislation establishes a Klamath River Basin Conservation Area and requires the secretary of the Interior to restore anadromous populations to optimum levels. The secretary is to consult with all concerned parties to develop a fish-conservation program that includes monitoring and coordinating research, improving and restoring habitat, improving hatchery production, rehabilitating problem watersheds, implementing an intensive short-term stocking program, and removing obstacles to fish passage. To the extent practicable, restoration work is to be performed by unemployed commercial and Indian fishermen. A total of $42 million is needed to pay for the program, of which the federal government will provide half and California or its political subdivisions, half.

A unique feature of the bill is its establishment of a fishery advisory council to the secretary which is intended to resolve disputes between federal and state management agencies and sport and commercial fishermen. The council's major duty is to develop in-river-take and ocean-take recommendations for ratification by the management agencies responsible for setting catch levels. Both the management agencies and the user groups have representatives on the council.

The Interior Department expressed concern about the inclusion of commercial- and sport-fishing representatives on the council because they might push for maximum catch limits. Only the several fishery-management agencies should be on the council, said Interior, because they are obligated to pursue the general public goal of conservation.[9]

The House Merchant Marine and Fisheries Committee rejected this argument in favor of a combined management-agency, user-group council. While the committee views user groups as important players in Klamath fishery management, it emphasized the advisory nature of the council and reaffirmed the ultimate authority of management agencies to set actual catch levels.

## Aquaculture Act Reauthorization

Congress reauthorized the National Aquaculture Act through fiscal year 1988 as part of the 1985 Farm Bill (P.L. 99-198). Originally passed in 1980, the Aquaculture Act establishes a national aquaculture policy and coordinates the research and development activities of several federal agencies. Its purpose is to encourage the development of private aquaculture and reduce the U.S. trade deficit in fish and fish products, which was $4.9 billion in 1984 (U.S. Congress, House 1985).

Congress has never appropriated funds to implement the act, even though a joint Interior, Agriculture, and Commerce Department National Aquaculture Development plan was completed in 1983. The Reagan administration consistently has opposed implementation of the act on the grounds that it duplicates existing authorities. Congress, on the other hand, has continued to reauthorize the program.

In addition to reauthorizing the program through fiscal 1988, Congress amended the 1980 act to give the secretary of Agriculture the lead role in aquaculture development while maintaining cooperative roles for the departments of Commerce and Interior. The bill also establishes the secretary of Agriculture as permanent chairman of the interagency Joint Subcommittee on Aquaculture, establishes a National Aquaculture Information Center within the Department of Agriculture, and requires the secretary of the Interior to submit a report to Congress by December 31, 1987, on the benefits and impacts of exotic species introduced for aquaculture purposes.

## Anadromous Fish Grants

The federal grant-in-aid program authorized by Section 4 of the Anadromous Fish Conservation Act was reauthorized in 1986 for three

---

9. Interior's concern about users helping to set harvest levels is shared by the authors of the National Oceanic and Atmospheric Administration study, who found that ocean fishery management by NMFS would be markedly improved by a clear separation between conservation and allocation decisions. "If the resource is to be maintained," said the report, "conservation decisions must precede and be unchanged by allocation decisions. When the two processes are combined in one decision, the pressures are always to . . . serve the interests of more users" (Department of Commerce 1986).

fiscal years as part of a larger measure reauthorizing a variety of National Oceanic and Atmospheric Administration programs (P.L. 99-659). Section 4 technically expired at the end of fiscal 1985, but Congress continued to appropriate grant funds despite the opposition of the Reagan administration, which argued that the original purpose of the program had been fulfilled and that any further state anadromous-fish work could be paid for by states with federal grants provided under the Dingell-Johnson Act. The reauthorization measure provides up to $7.7 million for fiscal year 1987, $7.9 million for fiscal year 1988, and $8.1 million for fiscal year 1989. The funds are distributed by NMFS and FWS to states on a matching basis to restore depleted anadromous-fish stocks that have been affected adversely by federal, state, and private water resource projects or other causes.[10] Over $95 million has been made available to the states during the period from fiscal year 1966 to fiscal year 1985, about half by FWS and half by NMFS. FWS estimates that the annual economic return on its share of these grants is $81 million yearly.

## National Hatchery System

In response to the Reagan administration initiative to close or transfer numerous federal fish hatcheries, Representative Breaux introduced a bill (H.R. 3167) in 1985 to establish a National Fish Hatchery System.[11] A principal reason for hatchery closures, Breaux said, is the perception that federal fish hatcheries have not addressed federal priorities (U.S. Congress, House 1985b). H.R. 3167 would provide explicit policy directives for federal hatchery management.

The measure as it was reported would establish a national fish hatchery system to be administered by FWS to include all FWS hatcheries and other federally supported hatcheries. State-managed hatcheries that fulfill federal objectives specified in the bill also would be incorporated in the system. The measure requires that federal hatchery terminations be authorized specifically by law, rather than through executive branch budget cuts.

The hatchery system would produce fish to meet five primary goals: to mitigate the impacts of federal water projects; to restore species of historical, recreational, commercial, and ecological significance; to stock waters to fulfill international treaty or Indian treaty obligations; to carry out research and development; and to implement endangered species recovery plans. However, the bill prohibits the production of fish within the hatchery system for restoration and

---

10. The act does not apply to anadromous-fish-conservation projects in the Columbia River Basin because other laws cover that area.

11. A similar measure was introduced by Breaux in 1984.

mitigation purposes unless the secretary of the Interior approves a mitigation or restoration plan for the affected stocks within four years after the act passes.

In addition, the bill requires that beneficiaries of federal water projects reimburse the federal government for the costs of producing fish for mitigation purposes. The amount of these reimbursements would increase gradually so that by September 30, 1989, beneficiaries would pay 100 percent of the costs. States and private individuals that receive fish from federal hatcheries for nonfederal objectives would be required to reimburse the federal government for 100 percent of fish production costs by September 30, 1987.

The House Merchant Marine Subcommittee on Fisheries, Wildlife Conservation and the Environment, which Breaux chaired, held a hearing on the hatchery bill on October 2, 1985. FWS, NMFS, conservation groups, and some states declared support for the bill but suggested technical changes. Several witnesses from Pacific Northwest states opposed some provisions of the measure out of concern that the bill would conflict with conservation plans and fish-production funding agreements already in place for the management of the salmon fishery in the Northwest. The bill was reported by the House subcommittee but no further action was taken. No companion bill was introduced in the Senate.

## Coordination Act Amendments

The House passed H.R. 2704 on December 2, 1985, to amend the Fish and Wildlife Coordination Act, but the measure died in the Senate. The House bill made several minor amendments to the Coordination Act, but the Senate Environment Committee never took up the measure because it saw little need for it (for further details, see the legislation section of the migratory bird chapter).

# LEGAL DEVELOPMENTS

## Indian Fishery Rights

In a series of recent decisions, the Ninth Circuit Court of Appeals continued to elucidate the extent of Indian fishing rights. In *U.S. v. Sohappy* (770 F.2nd 816 [9th Cir. 1985]), the United States prosecuted 13 Indians for selling fish taken in violation of various state and tribal laws. The Indians were convicted and appealed. The court held that Indians are subject to Lacey Act prohibitions against transporting, selling, or acquiring fish taken or possessed in violation of state or tribal law. The court said that Congress intended the Lacey Act to apply to Indians and that the tribes do not have exclusive jurisdiction over fishing offenses committed by Indians. When the federal government's prosecution rests on state regulations, however, the government has the burden of proving that the state regulations are reasonable and necessary conservation measures and that their application to Indians is necessary to the interests of conservation.

Since 1968, several states and Indian tribes have been in litigation over the allocation of fishing rights in the Columbia River. In *U.S. v. Oregon* (769 F.2nd 1410 [9th Cir. 1985]), the tribes challenged fishing regulations promulgated under the Columbia River Compact, arguing that they violated Indian treaty rights. The district court agreed, enjoining implementation of the regulations. The court of appeals affirmed the lower court and held that when treaty rights are violated, the district court has the power not only to enjoin enforcement of the offending regulation, but also to adopt guidelines proposed by the tribes.

*U.S. v. Washington* (759 F.2nd 1353 [9th Cir. 1985]), is the latest iteration in the protracted litigation between the United States, suing as trustee for the Indians, and Washington state over Indian fishing rights. In 1980, the district court resolved two of the issues in the litigation by declaratory judgment, holding that (1) hatchery fish, produced by the state, are included in the fish to be apportioned by treaty between Indian tribes and the states; and (2) the Indian treaty right to take fish necessarily includes the right to have those fish protected from human-caused destruction and that the states therefore have a duty to refrain from degrading or authorizing the degradation of fish habitat to an extent that would deprive the Indians of their moderate living needs.

The Ninth Circuit affirmed the judgment that hatchery fish were subject to Indian treaty rights. As to the state's duty to protect fish habitat, however, the court held that the lower court's granting of declaratory relief was improper because it was too "imprecise in definition and uncertain in dimension."

The case was remanded to the district court on this issue for the development of a more precise situation in which fish habitat was being degraded to the detriment of the Indians.

In *U.S. v. Washington* (761 F.2nd 1404 [9th Cir. 1985]), Washington State objected to an interim plan, recommended by the district court's Fishery Technical Advisory, that allowed the tribes to take more than their treaty allocation of 50 percent by catching fish allocated to, but not taken by, the state's hook-and-line sportsmen. The sport fishery is located upstream from the tribes. The state wished to dedicate its share of the catch to the sport fishery. While many fish escape the sport fishery, the state claimed that this did not justify giving the Indians more than 50 percent of the total catch. The tribes argued that the district court's policy against waste of fish suitable for take overrode the state's interest. The circuit court held for the state, saying that the opportunity to catch fish, not the actual catch, should determine the extent of the right for the sport fishery.

## Hudson River Striped Bass

A serious threat to striped bass stocks was averted in 1985 when proponents of New York City's Westway highway project finally gave up their plans after a long court battle. The proposed highway and real-estate development off lower Manhattan would have created 169 acres of land in the Hudson River, adversely affecting a major nursery area for striped bass. This could have proved a serious loss because, as the Chesapeake Bay striped bass population has declined, the Hudson's importance as a breeding ground has increased. Estimates are that between 20 and 50 percent of the striped bass found from North Carolina to Maine may now come from the Hudson. The Army Corps of Engineers estimated that 20 to 33 percent of the Hudson's bass population would have been displaced by Westway. FWS suggested that losses would have been higher (U.S. Army and U.S. Department of Transportation 1984).

Nevertheless, the Corps in 1981 issued a landfill permit for the project under Section 404 of the Clean Water Act. Environmental organizations immediately filed suit challenging the Corps' decision. The district court in 1982 ruled that the Corps did not consider adequately the project's effects on striped bass and blocked the permit (536 F. Supp. 1225 [S.D. N.Y. 1982]). After completing an environmental impact statement, the Corps issued a new permit in March 1985. But in August 1985, the court permanently voided the landfill permit, citing discrepancies between the Corp's draft environmental impact statement, which stated that the project would have a "significant and adverse" impact on striped bass, and the final environmental impact statement, which deleted that finding. A federal appeals court upheld the district court decision in September 1985. New York state leaders, faced with a September 30 congressional deadline after which funds appropriated for Westway would be lost, decided to trade in the federal Westway funds in exchange for $1.7 billion in federal funds to finance substitute highway and mass-transit projects, essentially killing the Westway proposal (*N.Y. Times*, October 1, 1985).

## NMFS Fishery Recommendations for Hydropower Facilities

In *The Steamboaters v. The Federal Energy Regulatory Commission* (759 F.2nd [9th Cir. 1985]), conservation groups and NMFS challenged the Federal Energy Regulatory Commission's decision to permit the building of a hydropower plant in Oregon's Umpqua Basin, a major spawning ground for anadromous fish. NMFS argued that, under section 30 of the Federal Power Act, the Federal Energy Regulatory Commission is required to impose the conditions recommended by NMFS to protect anadromous fish from hydropower projects exempted from licensing. The court of appeals, however, found that section 30 required the Federal Energy Regulatory Commission to impose only the conditions proposed by FWS or the corresponding state agency.

## REFERENCES

American Fisheries Society. 1986. Final Report of the *ad hoc* Federal Fisheries Responsibilities Committee of the American Fisheries Society.

Kutkuhn, Dr. Joseph. 1985. Associate Director Fishery Resources, U.S. Fish and Wildlife Service, Testimony before the Senate Subcommittee on Environmental Pollution. July 19.

Pacific Northwest Electric Power and Conservation Planning Council. 1984. Columbia River Basin Fish and Wildlife Program. Portland, Oregon.

Russell, Dick. President, Striped Bass Emergency Council. Testimony before the Senate Subcommittee on Environmental Pollution, July 19.

U.S. Army Corps of Engineers and U.S. Department of Transportation. 1984. *Final Supplemental Environmental Impact Statement - Westway Highway Project*. Vols. II and III. Washington, D.C.

U.S.-Canada Treaty Coalition, Northwest Indian Fisheries Commission, Columbia River Inter-Tribal Fish Commission, Washington State Department of Fisheries, and Oregon Department of Fish and Wildlife. 1985. *Brief on the U.S.-Canada Salmon Interception Treaty*.

U.S. Congress, House, Committee on Merchant Marine and Fisheries. 1985 National Aquaculture Improvement Act, Report to Accompany House Report 1544, the 99th Congress, 1st Session. House Report 99-105, Part 1.

U.S. Congress, House. 1986. Conference report to accompany S.426, Electric Consumers Protection Act of 1986. House Report 99-934.

U.S. Department of Commerce and U.S. Department of the Interior. 1985. Evaluation of the Interstate Fishery Management Plan for Striped Bass. Unpublished report to Congress. Washington, D.C.

U.S. Department of Commerce, National Oceanic and Atmospheric Administration. 1986. NOAA Fishery Management Study. Washington, D.C.

U.S. Department of the Interior, Fish and Wildlife Service. 1986. *Monitoring Fish and Wildlife for Environmental Contaminants: the National Contaminant Biomonitoring Program*. Washington, D.C.

U.S. Environmental Protection Agency, Office of Water Regulations and Standards. 1985. *National Water Quality Inventory: 1984 Report to Congress*. Washington, D.C.

*William J. Chandler is president of W.J. Chandler Associates, a Washington D.C. environmental policy and government relations consulting firm.*

*Richard Magder is a staff writer for W.J. Chandler Associates.*

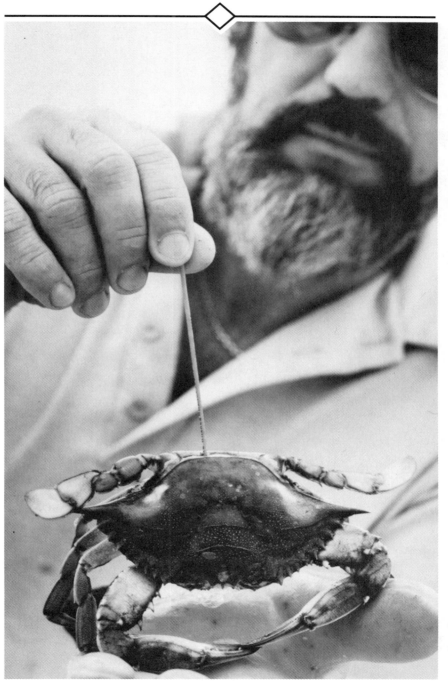

A marine biologist tags a Chesapeake Bay blue crab in a study of migration patterns. Federal marine fisheries management encompasses both national and international interests. *Lowell Georgia/Photo Researchers*

# Federal Marine Fisheries Management

Michael Weber

## OVERVIEW

The first decade of federal marine-fisheries management under the Magnuson Fishery Conservation and Management Act (16 U.S.C.A. 1801-1822) ended in 1986 with mixed results. On the one hand, commercial and sport fishing have continued to be important activities, particularly to local and regional economies. In 1985, nearly a quarter-million people made a living from fishing for more than 300 species of marine fish and shellfish and received more than $2.5 billion at the dock for their catches. Seventeen million people spent more than $7.5 billion to take more than 70 million saltwater fishing trips to catch 425 million fish (U.S. Department of Commerce 1986b).

On the other hand, one recent assessment of federal fisheries management identified 19 groups of finfish and shellfish that were being overfished, although they were covered by management plans developed under the Magnuson Fishery Act. The same assessment identified 22 fisheries in which more vessels participated than were necessary to make the allowable catch (U.S. Department of Commerce 1986a).

Audubon Wildlife Report 1987

131

Congress passed the Magnuson Fishery Conservation Management Act in 1976 in response to several crises in U.S. fisheries. The most politically potent of these was the depletion of fish populations off the East Coast by foreign factory trawlers. Since 1976, efforts to reduce foreign fishing in U.S. waters and to build up the domestic fishing industry have yielded some results. In 1985, foreign fishermen caught 2.6 billion pounds of fish in U.S. waters, compared to 7.1 billion pounds in 1971. However, the foreign take still accounted for 25 percent of the catch in U.S. waters (U.S. Department of Commerce 1986b).

The Magnuson Fishery Act also established a new mechanism for making fisheries-management decisions within U.S. waters. Until the act was passed, the role of the National Marine Fisheries Service (NMFS)—the nation's principal marine fisheries agency—had been limited largely to research and to representation of U.S. interests in international treaty negotiations. Domestic fisheries were managed only to the extent that individual states might choose to manage fishing activities within their own waters.[1] Three regional fisheries commissions, previously established by Congress and still operating, sought to coordinate state management activities, but exercised no authority over them.

For the most part, the act did not alter the management authority of the states or the operations of the regional fisheries commissions. It did require that the secretary of Commerce, acting through NMFS, and eight regional fishery management councils share management responsibility for fishing activities in the fishery conservation zone, which extends from state territorial waters to a boundary 200 miles from the shoreline. The regional councils are composed of federal and state representatives and private citizens. These councils determine which fisheries require conservation and management and submit to the secretary of Commerce a fishery management plan and proposed regulations for implementing the plan. The secretary of Commerce approves, partially approves, or disapproves a proposed fishery management plan and implements the plan by promulgating regulations. By January 1986, 25 fishery management plans had been fully approved and implemented.

A key requirement of the act is that fisheries be managed for optimum yield. This is a difficult concept, both theoretically and practically, which combines a determination of the biological optimum with social, economic, and ecological factors. Indeed, the determination of optimum yield is often the locus for the greatest controversy within fishery management councils and between the councils and NMFS.

---

1. Territorial waters extend three miles from shore, with the exception of the territorial waters of Texas and western Florida, which extend nine miles offshore.

# CURRENT DEVELOPMENTS

## Review of Federal Marine Fisheries Management

In 1986, as the Magnuson Fish Conservation and Management Act reached its 10-year anniversary, several comprehensive reviews of its operation were issued. The administration conducted two reviews of federal marine-fisheries management in order to suggest amendments to the act in 1987 (U.S. Department of Commerce 1986a and 1985a).[2] The first study was conducted in 1985 by two members of regional councils and by the NMFS staff person responsible for development of the regulations initially implementing the act. This study more or less accepted the current structure established by the fishery act and called for administrative changes in the implementation of the act rather than for legislative amendments.

The second study — called the Calio study after Anthony Calio, the administrator of the National Oceanic and Atmospheric Administration, NMFS parent agency — challenges several of the basic features of current federal fisheries management under the act. The study concludes that "because of the significant defects in the way the act has operated, the Study finds that some major conceptual and operational changes are necessary" (U.S. Department of Commerce 1986a).

While the Calio study noted certain accomplishments, it concentrated upon deficiencies in fisheries management under the act. In the panel's opinion, these deficiencies include continued overfishing of some stocks (see Table 1), a lack of coordination between the regional councils and NMFS in setting research agendas, conflicts among users, the vulnerability of the fishery-management plan process to delays and political influence, lack of accountability, inconsistency in management measures in federal and state waters, and adoption of unenforceable management measures. A key conclusion of the panel, one hotly disputed by the fishing industry, is that the regional councils have allowed the short-term economic needs of fishermen to influence the determination of optimum biological catch levels (U.S. Department of Commerce 1986a).

To address these problems, the Calio study made several recommendations.

***Conservation and Allocation Decisions:*** The fishery conservation act requires that fishery management plans include a determination of the optimum yield of a fishery. In the past, the regional councils have been responsible not only for determining the biological optimum, but also for allocating this yield among users, including recreational and commercial fishermen.

2. Some private interests also issued reviews of federal marine fisheries management (Harville 1986, Gutting 1986).

**TABLE 1**

**Representative List of Stocks Under Management Currently Estimated to be Overfished and/or Overcapitalized[a], June 1986**

| Geographic Area | Overfished | Overcapitalized |
|---|---|---|
| New England | haddock, yellowtail flounder, sea scallops, striped bass | haddock, yellowtail flounder, American lobster |
| Mid-Atlantic | swordfish, scallops | swordfish, scallops, surf clams, ocean quahogs |
| South Atlantic | Spanish mackerel | Atlantic shrimp |
| Gulf of Mexico | Spanish mackerel, king mackerel, Gulf of Mexico reef fish (notably red snapper) | spiny lobster, shrimp, stone crab |
| Caribbean | shallow water reef fish (Nassau grouper and possibly certain trunkfishes) | spiny lobster |
| Pacific | chinook and coho salmon (selected stocks), Pacific ocean perch | chinook and coho salmon, groundfish (except Pacific whiting) |
| North Pacific | red king and gulf croaker, Tanner crab, Pacific ocean perch | sablefish, halibut, high seas salmon, king and Tanner crab |
| Western Pacific | seamount groundfish | bottomfish, lobster |

Source: U.S. Department of Commerce, 1986a, Appendix 1

[a] The Calio study defines these terms as follows: "*Overfishing*, as defined by NOAA under the Magnuson Act, is a level of fishing mortality that jeopardizes the capacity of a stock(s) to recover to a level at which it can produce maximum biological yield or economic value on a long-term basis under prevailing biological and environmental conditions . . . *Overcapitalization* is an overcapacity concept, i.e., more vessel and processing capability is brought to bear in a fishery than is required to take the allowable harvest . . ." The study notes that the decision to list a fishery under either category is "valid only for the time when the decision to categorize was made."

The Calio study proposes separating conservation or biological decisions from allocation decisions. According to the panel, "when the two processes are combined in one decision, the pressures are always to add more effort to serve the interests of more users." The study proposes that the National Oceanic and Atmospheric Administration rather than the regional councils make the conservation decision in the form of a determination of the allowable biological catch as currently required by the fishery conservation act. The regional councils then would allocate this catch among the users with little involvement from NMFS. Under this scheme, the allocation decisions and not optimum-yield determinations will be the basis for fishery management plans (U.S. Department of Commerce 1986a).

This proposal has provoked sharp criticism from commercial fishermen, some of whom regard it as a thinly veiled attempt by NMFS to take over fisheries management entirely (*National Fisherman*, October 1986). The proposal would certainly insulate NMFS from the more political aspects of fisheries management and would allow the agency to assume more of a scientific role, one more in keeping with the agency's profile before the enactment of the fishery conservation act.

**Limited Entry.** The Calio study identifies 22 fisheries in which the allowable catch could be caught by fewer vessels than now participate in the fisheries. Excessive catch capacity, as it is called, not only reduces profits for individual fishermen but also increases pressure on fishery stocks, some of which already are overfished. For many years, fishery managers have discussed using restrictions on the number of fishing licenses or imposing poundage fees on commercial fishermen as ways to reduce the amount of fishing effort expended within an individual fishery. Just as frequently, however, commercial fishermen and their advocates in Congress have objected to such limited entry schemes, sometimes viewing them as attempts by the federal government to exercise even greater control over fishing activities. The imposition of entry restrictions is further complicated by the fishery conservation act, which requires that a number of separate findings be made before a limited-entry scheme can be approved. The Calio study suggests removing the act's impediments to limited entry.

**Interjurisdictional Management.** Marine-fish populations quite often move between state and federal waters. In such situations, state and federal agencies sometimes have imposed different and conflicting restrictions on fishing. Although Congress was aware of recurring inconsistencies in the management of interjurisdictional fisheries, it restricted federal authority to federal waters for the most part, dividing management between state and federal waters.

The Calio study found long-term inconsistencies in management measures for fisheries that straddle or move between state and federal waters and called for clearly defining the roles of the various levels of government. More dramatically, the study urges setting federal standards for management of interjurisdictional fisheries. If the states fail to adhere to these standards, the federal government could extend its management authority into state waters.

**Highly Migratory Species.** Since the tuna wars of the 1960s — when U.S. tuna boats were regularly seized in waters claimed by nations bordering the eastern tropical Pacific—the U.S. government has held that highly migratory species, which pass through the jurisdictions of many countries, should be managed not by individual nations but by international agreement. This policy was incorporated into the fishery conservation act (16 U.S.C.A. 1813). The only group of fish formally considered highly migratory are some tunas, although other species are, biologically speaking, highly migratory as well.[3]

The Calio study calls for the repeal of the fishery conservation act's provisions that exclude highly migratory species from U.S. management control. The study argues that this policy "has had unintended and severe resource management and political repercussions" and notes that the State Department has used the policy several times to block a fishery management plan for billfish in the Atlantic because it would restrict the incidental catch of tuna in U.S. waters by Japanese billfish fishermen.[4]

***Outlook.*** The Calio study also offered recommendations on a wide range of other matters, including research, habitat conservation, the regional council system, and license and other fees. In a rather ominous concluding statement, the Calio study warns:

> The American public . . . has not recognized the perilous and inefficient situation in their nearby seas. Throughout history the seas have been regarded as indestructable [sic] and its creatures as inexhaustible. It just happens that our generation is the first to be able to destroy a sea and to wipe out species of its creatures (U.S. Department of Commerce 1986a).

If the uproar from the commercial-fishing community is any indication, the recommendations of the Calio study and other recent reviews may spark a considerable amount of discussion but little real change. Nearly every one of the study's recommendations has an influential constituency against it. The lack of broad public interest in the issues raised by the studies virtually assures that the interests of commercial and recreational fishermen will continue to dominate discussions about federal fisheries management.

## The Redfish Craze

Since 1984, the commercial catch of adult redfish (or red drum) has increased dramatically to supply restaurants serving Cajun cuisine. These increased catches, principally from the adult spawning stock, have combined with a poor understanding of redfish biology to create

---

3. For example, various species of billfish, including marlin and sailfish.

4. The Calio study points out that only the United States and Japan maintain that highly migratory species cannot be managed by individual countries.

**TABLE 2**
**Red Drum Landings from the Gulf of Mexico 1979-1985 (thousands of pounds)**

| YEAR | RECREATIONAL LANDINGS | | COMMERCIAL LANDINGS | |
|---|---|---|---|---|
| | Pounds | Percentage from Federal Waters | Pounds | Percentage from Federal Waters |
| 1979 | 8,567 | 0.7 | 2,773 | NA[a] |
| 1980 | 8,330 | 3.2 | 1,615 | 3.3 |
| 1981 | 4,875 | 3.8 | 2,136 | 1.9 |
| 1982 | 12,066 | 1.2 | 2,425 | 3.5 |
| 1983 | 7,602 | 9.3 | 3,087 | 7.0 |
| 1984 | 6,560 | 5.3 | 4,335 | 22.8 |
| 1985 | 5,430 | NA | 6,334 | 54.5 |
| 1986 (Jan.-June) | NA | NA | 6,000[b] | 87.0 |

Source: 51 *Federal Register* 23552 (June 30, 1986)
[a]Not Available
[b]Preliminary data

an unprecedented fisheries management crisis in the Gulf of Mexico.[5] Members of Congress, NMFS, and state fishing agencies are concerned that redfish in the Gulf of Mexico may be fished out before enough data is available for proper management. Recreational fishermen are accusing commercial purse-seine fishermen of depleting what has been predominantly a recreational fishery. And for the first time in the history of the fishery conservation act, the Department of Commerce has preempted the role of a regional council and prepared a fishery management plan of its own (see Table 2).

Although commercial fishermen have for many years caught redfish either directly or incidentally while fishing for other species such as shrimp, the catch level remained quite low until 1984. As recently as 1983, recreational fishermen caught twice as much redfish, principally juveniles, as did commercial fishermen. But by 1985, after "blackened" redfish had become fashionable, commercial purse-seine fishermen had learned how to locate large schools of the bigger, adult redfish in deeper water and were catching more redfish than were recreational fishermen. In federal waters alone, the commercial catch of bull reds, as the adults are called, increased from 210,000 pounds in 1983 to 5.2 million pounds in the first half of 1986. In less than three years, then, the spawning stock of a species whose biology and population dynamics are not well understood came under unprecedented fishing pressure.

The dramatic increase in fishing effort did not long go unnoticed. The Gulf of Mexico Fishery Management Council reviewed the

5. When asked by Representative Billy Tauzin (D-LA) whether there was a substitute for "blackened" redfish, the popularizer of the Cajun dish, Mr. Paul Prudhomme, replied: "Pompano is wonderful for that cooking method. So is salmon, but what has gotten the reputation is redfish. That's what people understand."

situation in 1984, but declined to prepare a fishery management plan. As the crisis deepened and as rivalry between commercial and recreational fishermen came to the fore, Representative John Breaux (D-LA), chairman of the House Subcommittee on Fisheries and Wildlife Conservation and the Environment, introduced a bill, H.R. 4960, that would have banned catching redfish in the federal waters of the Gulf of Mexico until the secretary of Commerce had developed a fishery management plan.

With the congressional prodding, NMFS, acting on behalf of the secretary of Commerce, set about preparing the first fishery management plan ever prepared by the secretary rather than by a fishery management council. The fishery conservation act allows the secretary to prepare a plan for a fishery that requires conservation and management if a regional council fails to do so (16 U.S.C.A. 1854 [c]). Although the Gulf Council eventually reversed its earlier decision not to prepare a plan, NMFS decided not to wait for the council plan, since its preparation would normally take about two years.

On June 25, 1986, NMFS issued an emergency interim rule (51 *Federal Register* 23551-23556) to reduce the risk of depleting the Gulf's spawning stock of redfish and to allow time for development of a secretarial plan. The emergency rule set a quota of one million pounds for purse-seine fishermen for the remainder of the season. This quota was reached soon afterward, and the fishery was closed July 20 (51 *Federal Register* 26554). On September 10, 1986, NMFS issued its plan for the management of redfish in the Gulf of Mexico (U.S. Department of Commerce 1986c), and on October 9, NMFS proposed regulations for implementing the plan (51 *Federal Register* 36035).

The secretarial plan proposes prohibiting commercial take in federal waters except for fishermen who have permits issued by NMFS as part of a resource-assessment program aimed at increasing biological understanding of redfish.[6] The plan limits landings from the resource-assessment program to one million pounds in 1987 and places no restrictions on recreational catch in the fishery conservation zone. The plan also includes a procedure for setting quotas after 1987 and suggests steps that the states should take to make their management measures consistent.[7]

The dramatic increase in the commercial catch of redfish demonstrates how quickly modern fishing technology, in this case purse

6. The secretarial plan allows for an incidental catch of 300,000 pounds of redfish in other commercial fisheries, such as shrimp trawling. Until the purse seiners entered the red-drum fishery in 1983, five times more redfish were caught in Alabama in shrimp trawls than in all other gear combined (U.S Department of Commerce 1986c).

7. On November 7, 1986, Florida imposed a ban on the recreational and commercial catching and sale of redfish in the state from November 13, 1986, through February 4, 1987.

seining, can create a crisis in a fishery, and how slowly the fishery conservation act's management process may react. This lack of responsiveness is of particular concern with long-lived species such as redfish, since the effects of management decisions upon them may not be seen for many years.

## Gulf and South Atlantic Shrimp

The issue of requiring special gear to exclude sea turtles and finfish from shrimp nets in the Gulf and south Atlantic appeared to be heading toward some resolution as 1986 ended. For many years, commercial shrimp trawlers have incidentally captured thousands of endangered and threatened sea turtles and billions of pounds of unutilized finfish each year. By 1984, after several years of research, NMFS had perfected the Trawling Efficiency Device (TED), which reduces sea turtle captures by 97 percent and finfish by-catch by 50 to 70 percent. Recently, some commercial shrimpers have promoted other devices that seem to reduce sea turtle captures substantially but are less effective in reducing finfish by-catch.

In 1985, conservationists — who believed NMFS efforts to promote voluntary use of TEDs were ineffective — began pushing for regulations that would require use of gear that would reduce both turtle and finfish by-catch substantially. The shrimp industry, the Gulf of Mexico and South Atlantic regional councils, state fisheries agencies, and NMFS have been seeking a more gradual approach. They have argued that the conservation of endangered species must be balanced with the economic health of the shrimp industry. Conservationists and the U.S. Fish and Wildlife Service have insisted that neither the fishery conservation act nor the Endangered Species Act authorize such a balancing.[8]

NMFS estimates that nearly 48,000 endangered and threatened sea turtles are captured in the south Atlantic and Gulf shrimp fishery yearly and that of these, nearly 12,000 die. Conservationists are most concerned by the capture and death of Kemp's ridley sea turtles, whose population of nesting females — already less than one percent of its size as recently as 1947 — has been declining by three percent yearly since 1978 despite very successful international efforts to protect the species' nesting beaches. Conservationists also are concerned by the capture and death of thousands of loggerhead sea turtles, principally in the south Atlantic. Although this species is in less danger than is the Kemp's ridley, those nesting populations of loggerheads most studied along the Atlantic coast seem to be declining at a steady rate.

8. Under the Endangered Species Act and a memorandum of understanding, NMFS and the U.S. Fish and Wildlife Service share responsibility for some marine species, including sea turtles. Generally, NMFS is responsible for the animals while they are in the water and FWS is responsible for them while they are on land.

Conservationists, including sport-fishing organizations, also have been pressing for use of the NMFS TED because it reduces the incidental catch of finfish in shrimp trawls. Each year in the Gulf alone, an estimated 1.5 billion pounds of finfish are captured in the shrimp fishery, about 10 pounds of finfish for every pound of shrimp (Tarnas 1986). Most of the finfish are spot, croaker, sea trout, and other species of recreational or commercial importance.

The incidental capture of sea turtles and finfish has received some attention from the Gulf and South Atlantic fishery management councils. The Gulf shrimp-fishery management plan called for the development and use of gear to reduce finfish bycatch as appropriate (Gulf of Mexico Fishery Management Council 1981). However, the Gulf Council has resisted taking any steps to require the NMFS TED under the shrimp plan, although it seems to be the type of gear called for by the shrimp plan. The South Atlantic Council voted at its August 1986 meeting to require use of turtle-excluder gear in particular areas at particular times as part of a shrimp-fishery management plan that it is now preparing. However, since this plan must yet be written and reviewed by the public and the secretary of Commerce before implementation, the council's vote has little effect.

Citing the lack of voluntary use of excluder gear and the reluctance of the regional councils to require TED use, the conservation community stepped up its demands for action by the federal government. On August 22, 1986, the Center for Environmental Education notified the secretary of Commerce of its intention to file suit in federal court if the TED is not required in all shrimp trawls by 1987.

In an effort to avert a lawsuit, NMFS initiated a series of mediated meetings among representatives of the conservation community and the shrimp industry, with a view to developing a consensus on phasing in use of TEDs in the shrimp fishery. Whether or not the disputing parties reach an agreement, NMFS has committed itself to proposing regulations to require use of TEDs in particular areas beginning in 1987. It is likely that these regulations will require use of gear to reduce sea turtle bycatch but not finfish bycatch. Public hearings are to be held in late 1986 and early 1987.

## Trends in Catch and Effort in U.S. Waters

***Domestic Commercial Fishery Trends.*** During 1985, U.S. commercial fishermen caught 8.7 billion pounds of fish and shellfish, an increase of more than three billion pounds over the commercial catch in 1976 when Congress passed the Magnuson Fishery Conservation and Management Act. Much of this growth resulted from the sale and transfer of two billion pounds of fish to foreign processing vessels in joint ventures (see Table 3 and Table 4). By comparison, such joint-venture transfers amounted to only 23.3 million pounds in 1979.

**TABLE ᵓ**
**U.S. Commercial Landings of Fish and Shell-**
**fish 1976—1985**

| Year | Million Pounds | Million Dollars |
|---|---|---|
| 1976 | 5,388 | $1,349 |
| 1977 | 5,271 | 1,554 |
| 1978 | 6,028 | 1,854 |
| 1979ᵃ | 6,267 | 2,234 |
| 1980ᵃ | 6,482 | 2,237 |
| 1981ᵃ | 5,977 | 2,388 |
| 1982ᵃ | 6,367 | 2,390 |
| 1983ᵃ | 6,439 | 2,355 |
| 1984ᵃ | 6,438 | 2,350 |
| 1985ᵃ | 6,258 | 2,326 |

Source: U.S. Department of Commerce, 1986c, p. 6
ᵃPreliminary data

The United States continued to rank fourth among major fishing nations behind Japan, the Soviet Union, and China. Once again, Louisiana led all states in volume with 1.7 billion pounds, while Alaska led all states in value of its landings at $590.8 million.

As in the past, menhaden led all other species in quantity, with landings of 2.7 billion pounds. Salmon was the second most important in quantity and value. Shrimp were fourth in quantity, but first in value at $473 million. The leading species in joint ventures were flounder, atka mackerel, and Alaska pollock.

Since 1976, the number of commercial fishermen has increased from nearly 175,000 to more than 230,000, while the number of fishing boats has increased from some 100,000 to more than 127,000 (U.S. Department of Commerce 1986b).

***Recreational Fishery Trends.*** Marine-recreational-fishing indicators remained stable in 1985. Excluding Alaska, Hawaii, and Pacific-salmon fisheries, for which data is not available, recreational fishermen caught

**TABLE 4**
**Joint Venture Catches by U.S. Flag Vessels**
**1982-1985**

| Year | Thousand Pounds | Thousand Dollars |
|---|---|---|
| 1982 | 561,389 | $ 36,401 |
| 1983 | 958,887 | 51,250 |
| 1984 | 1,465,084 | 79,042 |
| 1985 | 2,008,889 | 104,320 |

Source: U.S. Department of Commerce, 1986b, p. 12

an estimated 425 million fish weighing 717.3 million pounds in 1985. The recreational catch made up nearly a third of total finfish landings used for food. As in the past, more than 80 percent of the recreational catch off the Gulf and Atlantic coasts and more than 60 percent of the catch off the Pacific coast was taken within state waters.

The dominant species in the Gulf and Atlantic fisheries in 1985 was winter flounder, whereas in earlier years, bluefish or summer flounder dominated. The recreational catch of some species, such as bluefish, spotted seatrout, and king mackerel, exceeded commercial catches. In the Pacific fishery, Pacific mackerel dominated.

***Foreign Fishing Trends.*** In 1985, foreign fishermen caught 2.6 billion pounds of fish and shellfish in U.S. waters, 14 percent less than the level in 1984 and 33 percent less than the level in 1978. As in the past, more than 90 percent of the foreign catch was in waters off Alaska. Alaska pollock continued to dominate the foreign catch, contributing 73 percent. Also, Japan continued to lead all other nations, taking 1.8 billion pounds in U.S. waters.

The United States continues to depend heavily upon the importation of fishery products for edible and industrial purposes. The value of imported fishery products reached a record level of $6.7 billion in 1985. The U.S. fishing industry apparently cannot meet the continued growth in *per capita* consumption of fish in the United States since imports, principally from Canada, still provide nearly two-thirds of all edible fishery products consumed in the United States, or a record $4.1 billion in 1985. Nearly 18 percent of these imports, $1.2 billion, was shrimp, chiefly from Mexico. In 1985, the U.S. government collected record import duties of $191 million on these imported fish products.

In 1985, U.S. fishery exports were valued at $1.1 billion. More than half of this, $700 million worth, was imported by Japan.

# LEGISLATION

## Reauthorization of the Magnuson Fishery Conservation and Management Act

On November 14, 1986, President Reagan signed P.L. 99-659, a package of marine-fisheries legislation. Among other things, P.L. 99-659 reauthorized the Magnuson Fishery Conservation and Management Act through 1989 and amended a number of its provisions. One important amendment strengthens the role of the regional councils in ensuring protection of fishery habitats, although the law does not go as far as conservationists had hoped. Specifically, Congress amended Section 302 of the fishery conservation act (16 U.S.C.A. 1952) so that a regional council may comment upon state and federal actions that may affect the habitat of a fishery resource under its jurisdiction. These actions could include federal approval of permits for dredge or fill disposal in wetlands and other waters under Section 404 of the Clean Water Act, ocean incineration of hazardous wastes, and offshore oil and gas leasing. Federal agencies must respond in detail to such comments within 45 days. Congress also added a requirement to Section 303 that fishery management plans include information regarding the significance of habitat to a fishery and an assessment of the effects that changes to that habitat might have on the fishery resource.

Other amendments to the fishery conservation act cover a wide range of topics, including foreign fishing permits, coordination of NMFS and regional-council research activities, health and safety standards on foreign vessels accompanied by U.S. observers, qualifications of regional-fishery-management-council members, review of fishery management plans by the secretary of Commerce, confidential statistics, and civil penalties for violations of the fishery conservation act. P.L. 99-659 establishes funding authorization limits of $69 million in fiscal 1986, $70.8 million in 1987, $72.9 million in 1988, and $75 million in 1989.

P.L. 99-659 does not include several amendments found in earlier bills. These include a provision in H.R. 1533 that would have required that any management-plan provisions limiting access to a fishery, through licenses or poundage fees for instance, would have to receive the approval of three-fourths of the members of a regional council and two-thirds of the fishermen in the affected fishery. Also, P.L. 99-659 does not include provisions phasing out foreign fishing in U.S. waters, as Senators Ted Stevens (R-AK) and Slade Gorton (R-WA) had sought.

P.L. 99-659 includes provisions affecting other fisheries legislation and programs. Title II establishes a National Fish and Seafood Promotion Council to assist the domestic fishing industry in marketing its products and authorizes the establishment of species-specific promotional councils at industry expense. Title III is the Interjurisdictional Fisheries Act, which replaces the Commercial Fisheries Research and Development Act (16 U.S.C.A. 779). For each of the fiscal years 1987, 1988, and 1989, the Interjurisdictional Fisheries Act authorizes up to $7.5 million for matching grants to the states to support management research on certain types of species as follows:

- species that migrate between state and federal waters and are subject to a fishery management plan under the fishery conservation act;

- species that migrate across state waters and are subject to a fishery management plan developed by one of the interstate marine-fisheries commissions; or
- species that migrate across the waters of the Great Lakes states.

Title III also authorizes up to $350,000 yearly for development of interjurisdictional management plans by the three regional marine-fisheries commissions.

Title IV includes miscellaneous provisions, such as reauthorization of the Atlantic Tunas Convention Act through 1989 (16 U.S.C.A. 971-971 [i]); reauthorization of the Anadromous Fish Conservation Act (16 U.S.C.A. 757g [d]), described briefly in the inland fisheries chapter, and amendments to the Marine Mammal Protection Act and the Endangered Species Act, which are discussed in the marine mammal protection chapter.

In separate legislation, Congress also reauthorized the Atlantic Striped Bass Conservation Act through 1988 (16 U.S.C.A 757g [d]) (see the inland fisheries chapter for details).

**North Pacific Drift-net Fisheries**

Foreign drift-net fisheries in the North Pacific have attracted increasing attention. About 1,700 vessels from Japan, South Korea, and Taiwan deploy nets nine to 20 miles long to catch billfish, salmon, and squid in the North Pacific. Initially, marine-mammal and sea-bird conservationists sounded an alarm over the incidental capture and drowning in these nets of thousands of Dall's porpoises and North Pacific fur seals and hundreds of thousands of sea birds. More recently, western Alaska salmon fishermen have protested the interception by these foreign vessels of up to eight million salmon yearly from North American streams.

In June 1986, Senator Ted Stevens (R-AK) introduced a bill, S. 2611, to address some of these concerns. The bill and its House counterpart, H.R. 5208, would have required nations wishing to use drift nets in U.S. waters to enter into an agreement with the U.S. government to provide for monitoring and assessment of the impacts of their drift nets. The bill also would require the secretary of Commerce to prepare a report on the impact of drift-net fisheries and to submit recommendations on methods for marking and identifying the sources of abandoned nets. S.2611 also would have provided for a bounty system for retrieval of abandoned nets and would have established a sea-bird protection zone surrounding the Aleutian Islands where no drift-net fishing would be permitted.

Because of objections raised by the administration and by New England fishermen, the Senate dropped this bill from the fisheries package discussed above, P.L. 99-659. New England fishermen feared that Canada would use the legislation as a precedent to restrict U.S. fishermen operating near Canadian waters on Georges Bank. Senator Stevens is expected to introduce the bill again in the 100th Congress.

## REFERENCES

Gutting, Richard E. 1986. A Review of U.S. Fishery Policy. Unpublished manuscript.

Harville, John P. 1986. "Summary report and recommendations: AFS Committee on federal fisheries responsibilities," *Fisheries* 11, no. 4:2-6.

Tarnas, David. 1986. Memorandum to Bo Bricklemyer, "By-catch and discard in the Gulf of Mexico by trawl gear, predominantly as utilized in the Gulf commercial shrimp fleet." May 23, 1986.

U.S. Department of Commerce, National Oceanic and Atmospheric Administration, National Marine Fisheries Service. 1986a. *NOAA Fishery Management Study*. Washington, D.C. 63 pp.

U.S. Department of Commerce, National Oceanic and Atmospheric Administration, National Marine Fisheries Service. 1986b. *Fisheries of the United States, 1985*. Washington, D.C. 121 pp.

U.S Department of Commerce, National Oceanic and Atmospheric Administration, National Marine Fisheries Service. 1986c. *Proposed Secretarial Fishery Management Plan, Regulatory Impact Review, Initial Regulatory Flexibility Analysis, and Draft Environmental Impact Statement for the Red Drum Fishery of the Gulf of Mexico*. Washington, D.C. 198 pp.

U.S Department of Commerce, National Oceanic and Atmospheric Administration, National Marine Fisheries Service. 1985a. *An Evaluation of the Implementation of the Magnuson Fishery Conservation and Management Act*. Washington, D.C. 51 pp.

*Michael Weber, vice president for programs of the Center for Environmental Education, is a coauthor of* A Nation of Oceans.

Topa-Topa, captured as an abandoned young bird in 1967, was the first condor brought into the current captive breeding program. Such efforts are a major part of federal endangered species work. *U. S. Fish and Wildlife Service/Jeff Foott*

# The Federal Endangered Species Program

Michael J. Bean

## OVERVIEW

About 930 species of plants and animals, including about 400 that occur within the United States and its territories, receive protection under the Endangered Species Act of 1973. The protected species list has grown steadily since the act's passage, with a recent average of about 50 new listings each year. The overwhelming majority of listed species, and particularly of recently listed species, are the management responsibility of the U.S. Fish and Wildlife Service (FWS). The remainder, for which the National Marine Fisheries Service (NMFS) is responsible, are marine animals.

The listing of any species as "threatened" or "endangered" sets in play a variety of actions intended to serve the act's ultimate objective of restoring the species to a point at which it no longer needs the act's protection. These actions include the enforcement of prohibitions against hunting, collecting, and commercial trading of listed species. For U.S. species, the appropriate agency also frequently designates "critical habitat" in which federal activities are carefully controlled and prepares a written "recovery plan" that identifies the research, management, law enforcement, land acquisition and other measures

Audubon Wildlife Report 1987

that are needed for the species' recovery. These plans serve as guides for future agency actions and related budgetary planning.


## CURRENT DEVELOPMENTS

### New Regulations to Implement Section 7

On June 3, 1986, FWS and NMFS jointly published a set of long awaited and long overdue regulations governing compliance with Section 7 of the Endangered Species Act (51 *Federal Register* 19926). Section 7, in the view of most informed observers, is the act's key provision. It imposes a very stringent set of duties on all federal agencies. Specifically, it prohibits them from authorizing, funding, or carrying out any action likely to jeopardize the continued existence of any threatened or endangered species or causing the adverse modification of any area that has been designated as the critical habitat of any such species.

Backed up by the act's provision allowing private citizens to sue to enforce its requirements, Section 7 has had a major influence on the activities of many federal agencies. Section 7 halted, at least temporarily, the construction of Tellico Dam by the Tennessee Valley Authority in the mid-1970s. It also forced the redesign of Interstate 10 in Mississippi so as to avoid adverse impacts on the endangered Mississippi sandhill crane. The Environmental Protection Agency's inability to satisfy the requirements of Section 7 with regard to bald eagles and endangered right whales prevented it from issuing permits necessary for the construction of the Pittston oil refinery near Eastport, Maine. In addition to these rather dramatic examples, Section 7 routinely influences, in less visible ways, the planning for, and execution of, a myriad of federal government activities.

Because of its great importance, Section 7 is often at the center of controversies involving the Endangered Species Act. As a result, Congress frequently has refined and embellished it. While its central mandate has remained intact, the procedures through which that mandate is implemented were revised by Congress in 1978, 1979, and 1982. Basically, those procedures require FWS and NMFS to consult with other federal agencies about the effects of planned agency activities in order to determine whether the activities are compatible with Section 7.

Because of the frequent congressional tinkering with Section 7, FWS and NMFS have been hard pressed to keep up with the changes. The regulations published in June 1986 revise regulations adopted prior to the 1978 amendments. Thus, for the past eight years the two services' implementing regulations have not reflected the important changes made by Congress on three subsequent occasions. The 1986 regulations were themselves the product of a rulemaking that began in 1983. The unusual delay that attended the promulgation of the Section 7 regulations was a reflection of their importance and of the many controversies within the federal government about them.

Penetrating the new regulations is a daunting task for anyone not already steeped in the complexities of Section 7. They comprise nearly 40 pages of triple-columned, fine-print text and explanatory material in the *Federal Register*. The summary that follows therefore necessarily touches only on some of the major and more controversial points that the regulations resolve.

***Geographical Scope.*** On one key substantive point, the new regulations reverse an interpretation of Section 7 reflected in the prior regulations. The old regulations purported to apply Section 7 to all federal activities, including U.S. government activities that took place in foreign counties. For example, the granting of foreign assistance for development projects by the Agency for International Development, activities at U.S. military bases abroad, and foreign technical cooperation projects such as those of the Army Corps of Engineers and Bureau of Reclamation were all subject to Section 7 under the former regulations. The 1986 regulations, however, limit Section 7 to federal actions occurring within the United States and its territorial waters or on the high seas. In so doing, the new regulations embrace an Interior Department legal opinion that effectively narrowed Section 7 shortly after the Reagan administration took office (Memorandum of Associate Solicitor J. Roy Spradley, Jr. to the assistant secretary for Fish and Wildlife and Parks, Aug. 31, 1981). Thus, the new regulations only conform to what has been FWS practice for several years. Not long after the new regulations were published, Defenders of Wildlife and other organizations filed suit to challenge the new interpretation. A decision on the suit is likely in 1987.

***Actions Hurting Recovery.*** A second controversial issue concerns whether federal actions that impair a species' prospects for recovery, but do not necessarily diminish its likelihood of survival, violate Section 7. The 1986 regulations emphasize that, except in exceptional circumstances, an action that hinders recovery would not violate Section 7. Many conservationists had urged FWS and NMFS to treat actions that diminished species survival or recovery as prohibited. The difference between the two views, in practical terms, is most likely to arise in connection with federal actions that affect areas not currently occupied by an endangered species but potentially important to its future recovery. Under the FWS and NMFS view, such actions, even if they destroy the suitability of the area for future expansion and recovery of the species, will rarely, if ever, run afoul of Section 7. This view seriously restricts the value of Section 7 in recovering to their full biological potential any species that currently occupy only a very tiny portion of their historic or potential range. For species that exist entirely as self-sustaining captive populations, such as the Guam rail and the red wolf (and, in the future, possibly the California condor and the black-footed ferret) the view reflected in the regulations may negate Section 7 usefulness altogether.

***Consideration of Cumulative Effects.*** A final area of much contention concerns the issue of cumulative effects. The National Environmental Policy Act requires federal agencies to discuss in environmental impact statements the environmental effects of their major actions. The question that FWS and NMFS faced in drafting the new Section 7 regulations was whether consultations over particular planned federal actions should encompass a broader examination of the cumulative effects of other reasonably foreseeable actions within the same area. Illustrative is the example of water diversions from western rivers. Except in unusual circumstances, the depletion of water associated with any one diversion is unlikely to jeopardize the continued existence of a fish or other endangered species dependent upon flows in that river. However, the cumulative effect of a series of diversions could be to diminish flows to such an extent that jeopardy, or even extinction, would be almost unavoidable.

Whereas the National Environmental Policy Act requires federal agencies to consider the cumulative effects of the planned action and other "reasonably foreseeable" activities, FWS and NMFS opted for a substantially narrower consideration of cumulative effects in the course of Section 7 consultations. Specifically, their regulations require that they consider only the cumulative effects of other actions that "are reasonably certain to occur," a deliberately more restrictive standard. Moreover, this standard applies only to other actions undertaken by state or private parties rather than by the federal government. The exclusion of other *federal* activities was based on the belief that they would themselves be subject to Section 7 consultations at a later date. The regulations thus foster a piecemeal approach under Section 7 consultation procedures and set the stage for incremental erosion of the status of listed species until they finally reach the point that any further erosion would constitute jeopardy to the species. By that time, however, opportunities to avoid further adverse effects to the species may be sorely limited. However, despite the constraints imposed by the new Section 7 regulations, some novel approaches attempt a more comprehensive, systematic look at the conservation needs of listed species. Those new approaches are examined in the following section.

**New Approaches for Comprehensive Conservation Planning**

One of the vexing problems that has long confronted conservationists is that of securing permanent protection for wildlife habitat. Public acquisition of habitat is the method that seems to offer the greatest security, but it is also typically quite expensive. Moreover, it is increasingly evident that public ownership and careful management of valuable wildlife habitat does not guarantee its protection. Threats can arise from incompatible land uses adjacent to the nominally protected area. A good example is the Devil's Hole portion of Death Valley National Monument.

Devil's Hole is a rocky chasm in the desert of western Nevada. At its bottom is a small pool fed by groundwater. That pool is the only place in the world in which an endangered fish, the Devil's Hole pupfish, lives. The site was added to Death Valley National Monument to give it and the rare fish permanent protection. However, groundwater pumping by an adjoining rancher so lowered the water table that the pupfish was nearly extirpated. A last minute lawsuit by the government in the 1970s limited the amount of pumping the rancher could do. That victory may have been only temporary, however, for the ranch was subsequently sold and subdivided. Thus, whereas once the government had to deal with but a single landowner to protect the pupfish, it must now deal with a multitude of different owners.

The pupfish example illustrates another problem. While conservation interests have scored a good number of successes against particular land-use proposals, seldom do those victories guarantee long-term habitat protection. The landowner or his successor is free to come back again with a new proposal or series of proposals that chip away in less dramatic, but no less certain, fashion the wildlife-habitat value of his land.

Successes in the recovery of endangered species are likely to be limited until effective means are found to implement comprehensive plans for the conservation of endangered species throughout their ranges. FWS and NMFS have prepared formal recovery plans for most of the U.S. species protected by the Endangered Species Act. These plans typically identify, at least in a general way, the research, management, and law-enforcement measures needed to secure the recovery of the species. What the plans characteristically lack, however, is a clearcut mechanism for translating recommendations into action. Because of that key omission, new methods of comprehensive conservation planning are emerging within the federal endangered-species program either parallel to, or in some cases entirely independent of, the traditional recovery-planning process.

One of the most important of these is the ongoing effort to negotiate among relevant state and federal agencies and private developmental and environmental interests a comprehensive plan for the conservation and recovery of three endangered fish species that occur in the upper Colorado River basin—the Colorado River squawfish, the humpback chub, and the bony tail chub. This process got under way in 1985 and continued throughout 1986. The broad approach of the agreement that has emerged from these negotiations is to identify key stretches of the Colorado and its tributaries where water must be maintained at specified flows for the fish, and to establish a mechanism for ensuring that those flows will be maintained.

The mechanism for protecting critical water flows entails the acquisition by state and federal agencies of sufficient water rights for fish-conservation purposes. Funds for water-rights acquisition are to come in part from a start-up appropriation provided by Congress and in part from charges assessed against water developers in the basin on the basis of the amount of water depletion their projects entail.

Once water rights are acquired, projects located outside the key stretches where flows are maintained for fish conservation can be assured of favorable opinions from FWS under Section 7. Thus, the advantage to the water developers is the elimination of uncertainty about the acceptability of their projects. The corresponding advantage to conservation interests is that the process enables them to plan and act comprehensively for the needs of the endangered fish rather than opportunistically attempt to protect them through a series of piece-meal Section 7 consultations.

A somewhat similar effort at broad-scale endangered species conservation planning was encouraged by a provision added to the Endangered Species Act in 1982. That provision allows the appropriate service to issue a permit authorizing the incidental taking of threatened or endangered species in the course of otherwise lawful development activities, provided that the development is accompanied by a conservation plan to mitigate and minimize the impacts of such takings. The provision was designed specially to accommodate a major residential development plan for San Bruno Mountain south of San Francisco. Because the earth moving and other activities associated with the development would have caused the destruction of at least some mission blue butterflies, an endangered species, the act's prohibition against taking could have blocked the project altogether (see the mission blue butterfly chapter in this volume). However, the developers and affected city and county agencies put together a conservation plan that satisfied FWS that the butterfly's future might actually be more secure as a result of the development and the implementation of the plan than it would have been without the development. The plan was largely complete before the 1982 amendments were enacted, and those amendments were tailored specifically to ratify it. The important question, however, is whether the San Bruno experience was unique or whether it provides a model that might help reconcile endangered species and development conflicts elsewhere.

In 1986, one other similar plan was completed and two others were well under way. The completed plan seeks to reconcile future growth in the area of Palm Springs, California, with the conservation needs of the Coachella Valley fringe-toed lizard, an endangered species. Past growth in the area had by 1984 already consumed about two-thirds of the roughly 200 square miles of lizard habitat in the arid region. Projected growth for the rest of the century threatened more than half of what remained. Again because of the uncertainty that development interests faced in planning future projects, the local governments of Riverside County and nine of its cities launched a joint planning effort for future development that would qualify for an Endangered Species Act incidental-taking permit.

The resulting conservation plan calls for the establishment of three preserves to be managed for the lizard's benefit by FWS, the California Department of Fish and Game, and The Nature Conservancy. The cost of managing these areas and part of the cost of acquiring them is to be met by development fees of up to $600 per acre for developing lands outside the preserves but within the overall plan area. The total of such fees is expected to be about $10 million over the 30-year life of the plan. Certain of the lands outside the preserves also will be subject to zoning restrictions designed to ensure that growth there does not adversely affect the areas set aside for the lizard.

Elsewhere in California, work on a third conservation plan has begun under the authority of the 1982 amendments. This plan seeks to reconcile future development in southern California with the conservation needs of the least Bell's vireo, a bird that nests in riparian willow trees. Because of the loss of such habitats, the vireo has suffered one of the most serious recent declines of any songbird in North America. Across the continent, former Florida Governor Bob Graham—now a U.S. senator—has stimulated a similar effort in North Key Largo to accommodate both development interests and the survival needs of several endangered species, including the American crocodile, the Key Largo woodrat, and the Key Largo cotton mouse.

Each of the efforts described has had its share of critics. None of the plans strictly prohibits any taking or injury to threatened or endangered species, as the Endangered Species Act once literally required. Yet, the gulf between the literal words of that statute and the realities imposed by severely limited governmental resources for detection and enforcement has always been wide. The measure of the success or failure of these novel efforts therefore should be whether they in fact give a species greater assurance of long-term survival and recovery than it would otherwise have enjoyed. On that ultimate question, the jury is still out. Nevertheless, the fact that these novel approaches are being tried in order to solve some of the problems that have long vexed endangered-species-conservation efforts is itself an auspicious development.

### Reintroducing Endangered Species into Former Habitats: An Issue of Growing Controversy

For many endangered species, recovery will require their reestablishment in areas from which they have been extirpated. Recovery plans for certain species, such as the California sea otter, specifically call for reintroduction as a measure to ensure against the loss of the only remaining natural populations. For others that exist only in captivity, such as the Guam rail, red wolf, California condor, and black-footed ferret, reintroduction is the only possible means for reestablishing populations in the wild.

Despite the need for species reintroductions, proposals to carry them out often have met with stiff opposition. For example, reintroduction of the northern Rocky Mountain wolf is perceived by some as a potential danger to human life or property. In other cases, the species may compete with human interests. For example, commercial and recreational shellfishermen have long been leery of proposals to establish new sea otter colonies because of the otter's reputation as a voracious eater of abalone and other shellfish. For nearly all listed species, the act's often exaggerated potential to restrict private development, either indirectly through Section 7 or as a result of the taking prohibition, also fuels local opposition to reintroduction proposals. Much of the opposition to the possible reintroduction of Florida panthers into the northern part of the state stems from such fears.

In 1982, the Endangered Species Act was amended to make experimental reintroduction efforts more palatable by relaxing some of the restrictions that would otherwise have applied to the reintroduced animals. While not stemming opposition altogether, the amendments have helped make it possible to advance a number of controversial reintroduction proposals.

*California Sea Otter.* One of the more enduring reintroduction controversies concerns the California sea otter. The only naturally occurring population occupies the near-shore waters along a 200-mile stretch of the central California coast. This lone population is vulnerable to a single catastrophic oil spill or other calamity. As a result, establishing one or more new otter populations has long been a central feature of plans for the otter's recovery. Such plans have not been popular with either shellfishermen or oil interests, who fear new restrictions on exploration and development.

Because of the intensity of the opposition, FWS long delayed implementing this key provision of the sea otter recovery plan. Late in

1986, however, Congress amended the Endangered Species Act specifically for sea otter reintroduction. The amendment was the product of negotiations among oil, shellfishing, and otter-conservation interests. The key feature of the agreement is the commitment to contain the relocated animals within the relocation area. Any animals that disperse from the area will be returned either to it or to the area already occupied by the coastal population. While taking this approach obviously limits the future growth and expansion of the relocated population, it was essential to win the support of the often hostile oil and shellfishing interests. Actual implementation of the relocation effort will begin in 1987. See the sea otter chapter for more details.

**Red Wolf.** Somewhat similar controversies accompanied a proposal to reintroduce red wolves, which exist only in captivity, into the Alligator River National Wildlife Refuge in North Carolina. The principal concern was the possibility that once red wolves were reintroduced, their presence would necessitate restrictions on the type and amount of hunting that would be permitted in the area. Most attention focused on the practice of deer hunting with the use of dogs. Despite these concerns, FWS found that the flexibility afforded by the 1982 amendments was sufficient to win local acceptance of the reintroduction plan. By late 1986, FWS was preparing to introduce the first red wolves into the wild since their disappearance many years earlier.

**Rocky Mountain Wolf.** Yellowstone National Park, site of much controversy already because of differences of opinion over the proper management of grizzly bears, is likely to become the site of the next major reintroduction controversy. The northern Rocky Mountain wolf, once persecuted in the park by the National Park Service itself, may be reintroduced there sometime in the next several years. Although any reintroduction attempt is likely to be years away, debate over the wisdom of reintroducing wolves to the park began in earnest in 1986. Ranchers on nearby lands are concerned about predation on their livestock, and big-game hunters worry that the wolves will thin the ranks of game animals. Add to that the seemingly pervasive fear of wolves, and all the ingredients for a major controversy are present. In 1986, most attention focused on the wolf recovery plan, which, with its recommendation for reestablishing wolves in the park, was still awaiting approval on the desk of the FWS director as the year drew near to a close. Assuming he approves the plan, the next year or two are likely to be spent drafting and debating an environmental impact statement that assesses the planned reintroduction effort.

If reintroductions such as these succeed, both in terms of aiding the recovery of the species and of reassuring local populations that they can live compatibly with endangered species, they are likely to open the way for still other reintroduction efforts. In 1986, all or nearly all the remaining black-footed ferrets and California condors were taken into captivity. The rationale for these and similar captive-breeding efforts has been, at least in part, to establish a self-sustaining captive population from which to repopulate suitable habitats in the wild. The challenges of successfully breeding such animals in captivity are great, but they ultimately may be dwarfed by the challenge of securing local support for the animals' reestablishment.

## LEGISLATION

### Reauthorization of the Endangered Species Act

Legislation to reauthorize the Endangered Species Act was passed by the House in 1985 (H.R. 1027) and reported out of the Senate Committee on Environment and Public Works in 1986 (S. 725). However, the Senate bill never came to the floor for a vote prior to adjournment. Thus, for the second consecutive year Congress failed to extend the basic authorization for the act. However, the program is very much alive since Congress has continued to appropriate money for it.

The reasons for the Senate's failure were several. Senators Steven Symms (R-ID) and Alan Simpson (R-WY) had a variety of concerns about the management of threatened grizzly bears. While their staffs attempted to negotiate resolutions for these concerns, the two senators placed "holds" on the Senate bill, a procedural device peculiar to the Senate that allows an individual member to block consideration of a measure on the Senate floor. Senator Howell Heflin (D-AL) also placed a hold on the Senate bill, apparently in response to the proposed listing of the Alabama flattened musk turtle as a threatened species. The turtle occurs in the Black Warrior River basin of Alabama, the heart of the state's coal industry. The turtle has declined significantly in recent years as a result of deteriorating water quality, and the state's coal interests feared that its listing would impose new requirements on them to reduce their contribution to the pollution of the turtle's waters. Heflin's efforts succeeded in persuading FWS Director Frank Dunkle to postpone a final decision on the turtle's listing until 1987 and to appoint a panel of experts to advise him on whether to list the turtle.

A fourth Senator who held up action on the reauthorizing bill was Senator Lloyd Bentsen (D-TX). Bentsen was concerned that the proposed listing of the Concho water snake might result in a finding that the construction of the Stacy Dam and Reservoir on Texas' Colorado River would violate Section 7 of the act. At one point Bentsen introduced a bill (S. 2347) that would have effectively exempted that project from the act. Subsequently, he was given assurances that FWS was not likely to conclude that construction of the dam was incompatible with the conservation of the snake. He therefore never pushed for action on his bill.

Despite congressional failure to reauthorize the Endangered Species Act in 1986, two substantive provisions of the House-passed bill were stripped from it and added to other measures that passed in the waning days of the 99th Congress. The most important of these provided a detailed framework for the translocation of an experimental population of threatened California sea otters to San Nicholas Island. This provision was added to an unrelated bill for wetlands protection and approved by Congress in late October (P. L. 99-625). Similarly treated was a provision that eliminated certain technical disparities in the treatment of incidental taking of threatened or endangered marine mammals under the Endangered Species Act and Marine Mammal Protection Act. This measure was added to an unrelated fisheries bill just before Congress adjourned (P. L. 99-659).

Legislation to extend the authorization of the act seems likely in 1987. The shift of control in the Senate to the Democratic party will likely lessen the influence of the western Republicans whose concerns about grizzly bear management were a major impediment to Senate action in 1986. Although other issues will generate debate, the chances for action on the long overdue reauthorization appear very good.

***California-Nevada Interstate Water Compact.***  One measure that could have significantly affected endangered species was a bill (S. 2457) introduced by Senator Paul Laxalt to ratify a 1971 interstate compact between the states of California and Nevada. The compact apportions the waters of the Truckee River, which originates in California and discharges into Nevada's Pyramid Lake, home of the endangered cui-ui and threatened Lahontan cutthroat trout. The lake is located on the reservation of the Pyramid Lake Tribe of Paiute Indians. For years the Indians have been seeking to establish their right to waters of the Truckee for fish-conservation purposes in the lake. The compact would have severely undercut the legal bases for their claims. Allied with Audubon, the Environmental Defense Fund, and other conservation groups, the Indians strongly fought the Laxalt measure. The substance of the bill was at one point in September incorporated into a continuing resolution of appropriations that was ready for Senate floor action. Apparently sensing that the provision might be defeated, however, Senator Laxalt withdrew it from the resolution, and the compact was not ratified.

## LEGAL DEVELOPMENTS

In *United States v. Dion* (106 S. Ct. 2216), the Supreme Court decided that Indian treaty hunting rights do not protect Indians from prosecution for killing bald eagles, which are protected by the Endangered Species Act and the Bald Eagle Protection Act. The case arose in South Dakota as a result of an FWS undercover operation to infiltrate the illegal market for feathers and other parts of eagles and other protected birds. One of the individuals arrested in that operation was Dwight Dion, Sr., a Yankton-Sioux Indian who sold several bald and golden eagles to the undercover agents. When charged with killing eagles in violation of the two federal laws, Dion contended that an 1858 treaty gave him the right to hunt on his reservation, where he claimed to have killed the eagles in question, and that neither of the eagle-protection laws had terminated or restricted that right. A divided, *en banc* panel of the United States Court of Appeals agreed with Dion. The United States asked the Supreme Court to review that ruling.

The Supreme Court's unanimous decision, delivered June 11, 1986, reversed the Eighth Circuit's ruling. The court held that the legislative history of the 1940 Bald Eagle Protection Act and its 1962 amendments evidenced a clear congressional intent to abrogate any preexisting Indian treaty rights to kill bald or golden eagles. With respect to the Endangered Species Act, the court's holding was based on the narrowest possible grounds. It declined to address the question of whether the legislative history of the act also indicated a congressional intent to abrogate Indian treaty rights to hunt endangered species. Rather, the court instead reasoned that the earlier congressional abrogation of treaty rights with respect to bald eagles prevented Dion from asserting that treaty rights blocked his prosecution under the Endangered Species Act. Thus, the court left open the question of whether Indians with treaty hunting rights may lawfully hunt other endangered species notwithstanding the prohibitions of the Endangered Species Act. The court also left open the question of whether an Indian who hunted eagles for religious uses, as Dion had not, could be prosecuted under either statute. Despite the carefully limited nature of the court's unanimous decision, it represented a very significant departure from a long line of recent Supreme Court decisions upholding the treaty rights of American Indians to hunt and fish largely free of government regulation.

In *National Wildlife Federation v. Hodel* (unreported) (E.D.Cal. 1986), the National Wildlife Federation sought, by the fall 1987 hunting season, to ban the use of lead shot in migratory waterfowl hunting throughout the lower 48 states. The suit was intended to broaden the successful 1985 federation suit that had compelled the use of steel shot as a substitute for lead in portions of five states. In those areas, evidence suggested that bald eagles had died of lead poisoning as a result of eating ducks that had been struck with lead pellets.

The court dismissed the federation's 1986 suit after the Interior Department's last-minute announcement that it would phase out the use of lead shot in waterfowl hunting by the autumn of 1991. The court regarded Interior's proposed action as allowing for an orderly transition from lead to steel shot. Thus, although the federation did not prevail in its suit, its action did prompt Interior finally to act on a serious source of indirect mortality not only to endangered and threatened bald eagles but to waterfowl as well (see the migratory bird chapter for further details on the lead-shot issue).

In *Palila v. Hawaii Department of Land and Natural Resources,* 649 F. Supp. 1070 (D. Ha. 1986), the Sierra Club Legal Defense Fund sought to enlarge upon its pathbreaking 1979 suit that had directed the Hawaii Department of Land and Natural Resources to remove feral goats and sheep from a state game-management area on the slopes of Mauna Kea. In the original suit, the fund had contended successfully that the maintenance of feral sheep and goat populations was resulting in the taking of palilas, an endangered bird found only on Mauna Kea, because the sheep and goats destroyed the vegetation of the native mamane-naio forests on which the palila depended. The state had been managing the feral animals for sport hunting, but the suit forced the state to remove them from the area.

The relief granted in the original suit did not extend to mouflon sheep, an introduced wild sheep also present on Mauna Kea. However, in the intervening years, evidence mounted that implicated mouflon sheep in the destruction of the palila's habitat. Consequently, in 1985 the Sierra Club Legal Defense Fund amended its original complaint to include mouflon sheep and asked the court to order their removal as well. In November 1986, the court ruled, following a full trial, that the mouflon sheep also were harming the palila and therefore had to be removed.

In the course of its ruling, the court resolved an important issue. The original decision had concluded that destruction of the palila's habitat constituted a prohibited taking under the Endangered Species Act because it harmed the palila. "Harm" was a term that had been defined in an FWS administrative regulation to include adverse environmental modification. Subsequent to that original ruling, FWS amended its administrative definition and contended that under the new definition the alleged damage to the birds' habitat could no longer be considered to "harm" the bird. However, the court rejected that contention, concluding that no substantial change had been effected by the redefinition of the term.

In *National Audubon Society v. Hester,* 801 F.2d 405 (D.C. Cir. 1986), the National Audubon Society's challenge to FWS plans to bring all remaining wild California condors into captivity was rejected. Early in the year, Audubon had obtained a preliminary injunction against the capture effort from the United States District Court for the District of Columbia. Audubon persuaded that court that the FWS about-face from earlier plans to keep a small population of birds in the wild to facilitate the reintroduction of birds from the captive population had been unaccompanied by any reasoned explanation. However, the Court of Appeals on June 10 reversed that decision, paving the way for the capture of the handful of condors then still in the wild.

In *Bob Marshall Alliance v. Watt* (16 ELR 20759), the Bob Marshall Alliance and the Wilderness Society persuaded the United States District Court for Montana to set aside certain oil and gas leases in the Lewis and Clark National Forest. The Bureau of Land Management (BLM) had issued a number of leases on the basis of a very preliminary assessment of their impact on the grizzly bear, gray wolf, peregrine falcon, and bald eagle. The government contended that it could, prior to approving any development plans in the event that oil or gas were discovered, impose appropriate mitigating conditions that would pro-tect adequately any threatened or endangered species. A similar, phased approach to Section 7 compliance has been accepted by several courts presented with challenges to oil and gas leasing on the outer continental shelf. The government's arguments would have extended those earlier rulings to onshore leasing as well. The court held instead that BLM had a duty to gather additional data about the likelihood of affecting these species before it could issue the leases. The decision is thus an important one because it reflects an unwillingness to extend the step-by-step method of compliance with the Endangered Species Act beyond the outer continental shelf leasing context.

*Michael J. Bean is chairman of the Environmental Defense Fund's Wildlife Program and author of* The Evolution of National Wildlife Law

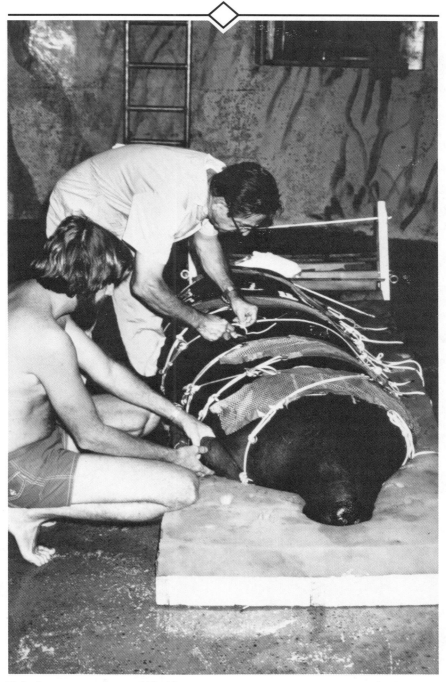

Biologists tag an endangered Florida manatee to monitor its movements. Federal marine mammal protection covers whales, polar bears, seals, and sea lions as well as manatees.
*Charles R. Smith/Photo Researchers*

# Marine Mammal Protection

## Michael Weber

## OVERVIEW

Reckless commercial exploitation of whale populations and incidental capture of porpoises in the U.S. tuna fishery so outraged the American public that in 1972 Congress passed the Marine Mammal Protection Act (16 U.S.C.A. 1361-1407) to ensure the conservation of these species. Among other things, the act imposes a moratorium on the taking and importing of virtually all marine mammals.[1] Only after determining the status of a species and how any proposed taking will affect it can the responsible federal agencies waive the moratorium.

Preempting state authority for marine-mammal conservation, the Marine Mammal Protection Act divided federal responsibility for marine mammals between the Department of Commerce and the Department of the Interior. The Commerce Department's National

---

1. The Marine Mammal Protection Act defines take as "to harass, hunt, capture, or kill." The U.S. Fish and Wildlife Service has defined harassment as negligent or intentional acts resulting in the disturbing or molesting of a marine mammal (50 C.F.R. 216.1 and 50 C.F.R. 18.1). The National Marine Fisheries Service has not issued regulations defining harassment.

Audubon Wildlife Report 1987

Marine Fisheries Service (NMFS) has responsibility for the protection of whales, dolphins, seals and sea lions. Responsibility for the protection of dugongs, manatees, polar bears, sea otters, marine otters, and walruses rests with the Department of the Interior's Fish and Wildlife Service (FWS). The act also established the Marine Mammal Commission, supported by a Committee of Scientific Advisors. The commission functions as an independent agency responsible for overseeing implementation of the act.

At least eleven species of seals and sea lions and 45 species of whales and dolphins commonly occur in U.S. waters (Breiwick and Braham 1984). Polar bears, walruses, sea otters, and West Indian manatees also are found in U.S. coastal waters.

Nineteen species of marine mammals are listed under the Endangered Species Act (16 U.S.C.A. 1531-1543). This act reinforces several of the protective provisions of the Marine Mammal Protection Act and amplifies its general authority to protect marine-mammal habitat. Several other federal laws and programs, such as the Marine Protection, Research, and Sanctuaries Act of 1972 (33 U.S.C.A. 1401-1444 and 16 U.S.C.A. 1431-1434), provide additional means for protecting habitat important to the conservation of marine-mammal populations.

Many marine mammals, such as the highly migratory great whales, have been reduced greatly in numbers by commercial hunting. In response, the United States and other nations have entered into international agreements for the conservation of many marine-mammal populations. Indeed, before passage of the Marine Mammal Protection Act, the federal role in marine-mammal matters was restricted largely to research and participation in international commissions, such as the International Whaling Commission and the North Pacific Fur Seal Commission. For the most part, this participation continues today to play an important role in marine-mammal protection and requires considerable attention and effort from NMFS, Congress, and concerned conservation, industry, and Alaskan Native groups.

For more details on the history and administration of federal marine mammal protection, see the *Audubon Wildlife Report 1985.*

## CURRENT DEVELOPMENTS

### Commercial Whaling

In 1982, the International Whaling Commission amended its regulations to end all commercial whaling, commencing with the 1985-86 season for pelagic whaling and the 1986 season for coastal whaling.

The new provision also provided that, by 1990 at the latest, the commission would undertake a comprehensive assessment of the effect of this decision on whale stocks and consider establishing new catch limits.

Although several nations filed objections to the moratorium, thereby releasing themselves from its obligations, all but Japan, the Soviet Union, and Norway eventually agreed, at the urging of the United States and many other commission members, to cease commercial whaling and comply with the moratorium. Japan and Norway continued whaling in 1986, but agreed to halt commercial operations in the near future. The outlook on Soviet whaling remains uncertain.

***Japan and the Moratorium on Whaling.*** Japanese nationals who continue whaling in opposition to the moratorium remain subject to sanctions under provisions of two U.S. laws: the Packwood-Magnuson Amendment to the Magnuson Fishery Conservation and Management Act and the Pelly Amendment to the Fisherman's Protective Act.

Under the Pelly Amendment, the president may place an embargo on the importation of fish products from any nation if the secretary of Commerce certifies that the nation's actions "diminish the effectiveness" of an international conservation program, such as that of the International Whaling Commission. In addition, the Packwood-Magnuson Amendment directs that the secretary of State at least halve the fishing allocations in U.S. waters of any nation certified as diminishing the effectiveness of the International Whaling Commission conservation program. If the certified country does not correct its offending activities, the secretary of State, after consultations with the secretary of Commerce, may reduce the allocations further.

In an effort to force Japanese compliance, conservationists in the United States claimed that Japan's hunt of sperm, Bryde's, and minke whales and its refusal to abide by the moratorium diminished the effectiveness of the International Whaling Commission. The conservationists argued that the United States was required to impose economic sanctions. Nevertheless, the United States chose not to certify Japan. Instead, the government entered into an agreement with the Japanese in late 1984 that allowed Japan to continue whaling at a reduced level until 1988, when Japanese whalers would commence observing the moratorium. In a challenge to this agreement, conservationists filed suit in federal court and won at the district and appellate court levels but lost before the Supreme Court (see the discussion of *American Cetacean Society v. Baldridge* below). Immediately after the Supreme Court decision, Japan notified the United States that it would cease its southern-ocean minke whaling in March 1987, its coastal whaling on Bryde's and minke whales in October 1987, and its coastal sperm whaling in March 1988.

**Soviet Whaling.**   The Soviet Union in 1982 filed a formal objection to the moratorium provision. In addition, in 1984 the Soviet fleet exceeded its share of the quota for minke whales in the southern ocean. In response to the exceeded quota, the secretary of Commerce in April 1985 certified the Soviet Union under the Pelly Amendment as diminishing the effectiveness of the International Whaling Commission. The United States then reduced the Soviet fishing allocation in U.S. waters by 50 percent, although it did not embargo Soviet fishery products. However, because its fishery allocation in 1985 was so small, the Soviets chose not to fish in U.S. waters. In 1986, the Soviets did not apply for an allocation.

At the 1985 meeting of the International Whaling Commission, the Soviets said that their whaling fleet would cease operations temporarily in 1987. For many years, the principal economic benefit from the Soviet whaling operation has been derived from the sale of meat to Japan. Observers believe that the Soviets decided to cease whaling because the United States probably would certify Japan if it purchased meat from a country violating the moratorium provision.

**Norwegian Whaling.**   Norway, which conducts commercial whaling on minke whales in the North Atlantic, filed objections to the moratorium and also to the whaling commission's classification of the northeast Atlantic minke stock as a "protection stock" on which whaling is prohibited. Under these objections, Norwegian whalers continued their whaling practices during 1986.

In response, in June 1986 the secretary of Commerce certified that Norway's continued whaling was diminishing the whaling commission's effectiveness. In July, with the imposition of economic sanctions imminent, Norway announced that it would cease whaling after the 1987 whaling season. The announced phase-out paralleled the terms of the U.S.-Japan agreement. Therefore, the Reagan administration chose not to embargo Norway's fishery products. Norwegian fish exports to the United States in 1985 amounted to 75 million pounds, worth $144 million. Since Norway does not fish in U.S. waters, the mandatory provisions of the Packwood-Magnuson Amendment are not relevant.

Unlike Japan, Norway has not formally notified the International Whaling Commission that it will withdraw its objections. Therefore, the secretary of Commerce has not withdrawn his certification of Norway.

**Whaling with Scientific Research Permits.**   The International Convention for the Regulation of Whaling provides that member countries may take whales for scientific research provided that the International Whaling Commission's Scientific Committee is given an opportunity to review the proposed research. Recent interest by whaling nations in taking whales under the research provisions and then selling the whale meat on the international market has sparked controversy. Accordingly, the U.S. delegation to the 1986 whaling-commission meeting led efforts to ensure that the meat of whales taken for research purposes does not enter international commercial trade. This action resulted in a resolution calling upon member nations to use whale meat and other products from research whaling primarily for domestic purposes. However, this resolution only limits, but does not prevent, international trade in by-products from research whaling.

In 1985, Iceland informed the International Whaling Commission that it intended to take 80 fin whales, 80 minke whales, and 40 sei whales for scientific purposes. Similarly, South Korea proposed to kill 200 minke whales from the northwest Pacific stock, which the commission had classified as a protection stock. Both Iceland and South Korea intended to sell the meat and other products from the whales to Japan. The United States urged both countries to wait until the 1986 meeting for commission action on the topic of whaling under special scientific permits.

Iceland conducted its research whaling anyway, taking close to 120 whales in 1986. There is no indication that Iceland intends to cease these operations. Iceland apparently hopes to avoid economic sanctions under the Pelly Amendment by adhering to the technical conditions of the commission's scientific-whaling resolution. To meet the resolution's requirement that whale meat and other products from research whaling be used primarily for local consumption, Iceland substantially increased domestic whale-meat consumption and announced that it would export the remaining 49 percent of the meat to Japan. In August, the secretary of Commerce expressed disappointment in Iceland's behavior but did not certify Iceland or Japan under the Pelly Amendment since they were in technical compliance with whaling-commission requirements. In 1985, Iceland exported $208 million and Japan nearly $590 million of fishery products to the United States.

South Korea announced that it would halt its research whaling in 1986, although only after South Korean whalers had taken 69 whales that year. South Korea has not issued a final decision as to whether it will conduct research whaling in the future.

**Prognosis.** It is likely that the final years of this decade will see a cessation in commercial whaling. However, some whaling countries may continue to take a reduced number of whales for research purposes. Thus, the goal of a complete halt of commercial whaling — long sought by conservationists and by the United States — may not be fully achieved.

The question remains, however, whether large-scale commercial whaling will resume in 1990 or afterward. The International Whaling Commission is committed to conducting a comprehensive assessment of whale stocks and to considering establishment of new quotas. This commitment was necessary in order to achieve sufficient support within the commission for the moratorium. However, the likelihood of resumed commercial whaling under the whaling commission seems remote, since many difficult scientific and policy matters, such as which population models or risk factors should be used, have yet to be settled.

Several whaling nations have indicated interest in pursuing whaling under authorities other than commercial whaling. Even before the moratorium was approved, the Japanese suggested that their coastal hunting of sperm whales really should be considered similar to the Alaskan Eskimos' subsistence hunting for bowhead.

Conservationists also must be concerned about the possibility that some of the newer commission members who supported the moratorium, believing that their job is done and that continued commission membership is too expensive, might resign. This would leave commission politics to the whaling countries. Regardless of the outcome of the scientific assessment of stocks, the continuance of the moratorium will depend upon the votes of member countries. The conservation countries will need one vote more than a quarter of the votes cast to prevent a return to commercial whaling. The recent trend of voting by consensus promotes trade-offs and compromises and adds further complications to the renewal of the moratorium on commercial whaling.

Finally, it is unlikely that the cessation of commercial whaling will lead to a swift recovery of depleted whale populations. A recent review of the status of great whales protected under the Endangered Species Act since 1970 indicates that only two populations may have recovered to levels similar to those that existed before commercial whaling began (see Table 1).

## The Northern Fur Seal Hunt

In 1985, nearly two centuries of commercial exploitation of northern fur seals came to an end. This domestic hunt of seals was so accepted that the Marine Mammal Protection Act specifically exempted it from the moratorium on the taking of marine mammals.

The termination of the commercial hunt was precipitated by Senate failure to renew through 1988 the Interim Convention for the Conservation of North Pacific Fur Seals (8 U.S.T. 2283, T.I.A.S. 3948), which authorized the hunt. Declining markets for fur seal skins and corresponding losses in revenue over the previous four or five years

**TABLE 1**
**Whale Status Chart**
A generalized evaluation of the possible recovery of endangered whales by stock(s) or regional groupings.

| Status |
| --- |
| Perhaps recovered[a] |
|     Eastern North Pacific gray whale |
|     Western North Atlantic humpback whale |
| Status uncertain[b] |
|     North Pacific sei whale |
|     North Atlantic sperm whale |
|     North Pacific sperm whale |
|     Southern Hemisphere sperm whale |
| Depleted[c] |
|     All stocks of blue whales |
|     Davis Strait bowhead whale |
|     Sea of Okhotsk bowhead whale |
|     Western Arctic bowhead whale |
|     North Pacific humpback whale |
|     Southern Hemisphere humpback whale |
|     Antarctic fin whale |
|     North Pacific fin whale |
|     Western North Atlantic fin whale |
|     Western Norway/Faeroe Islands fin whale |
|     Southern Hemisphere right whale |
|     Southern Hemisphere sei whale |
| Nearing extinction |
|     East Greenland-Spitsbergen bowhead whale |
|     Western North Pacific gray whale |
|     North Pacific right whale |
| Insufficient data for judgment |
|     Hudson Bay bowhead whale |
|     Denmark Strait fin whale |
|     North Norway fin whale |
|     Spain-Portugal-British Isles fin whale |
|     Eastern North Atlantic humpback whale |
|     Northern Indian Ocean humpback whale |
|     North Atlantic sei whale |
|     North Atlantic right whale |

Source: Braham, 1984

[a] To estimated population size prior to commercial whaling.

[b] Possibly above or near 60 percent of estimated initial population size.

[c] Well below initial population size estimates, but may include low populations that have shown some increase (e.g., Southern Hemisphere right whales and western Arctic bowhead whale).

made continuation of the hunt commercially unattractive. Had the commercial take been conducted, federal subsidies would have been required to make up for financial losses.

A coalition of animal protection groups used these facts to their advantage in lobbying for cessation of the hunt. These groups obtained the signatures of 60 senators on a letter opposing the treaty's renewal.

That clearly doomed any chance that the treaty would be approved by the required two-thirds vote.

Without the treaty renewal, the Department of Commerce was compelled to end the commercial hunt. However, a subsistence hunt of seals continues under authority of the Fur Seal Act of 1966 (16 U.S.C.A. 1151, *et. seq.*). The Department of Commerce issued an emergency interim rule under the act to govern the hunt in 1985 (50 *Federal Register* 27914-27922 [July 8, 1985]). This rule allowed a hunt of subadult male fur seals during a limited time in the summer, during which the Pribilovians killed 3,713 animals.

In 1986, the Commerce Department issued permanent regulations to govern the subsistence hunt (51 *Federal Register* 24828-24821 [July 9, 1986]). These regulations require NMFS to set an allowable range on the number of fur seals that can be taken on St. Paul and St. George islands to meet subsistence needs. The hunt ends automatically when the lower limit of the range is reached. If a review of hunt data indicates that the subsistence needs of Alaskan Natives have not been met, NMFS may extend the harvest. If hunting is extended beyond August 8, the regulations impose certain requirements to minimize the taking of female fur seals coming ashore at that time.

For the 1986 hunt, NMFS established a range of 2,400 to 8,000 fur seals for St. Paul Island and 800 to 1,800 fur seals for St. George Island. By the end of the hunt, 1,299 fur seals had been taken on St. Paul and 124 on St. George.

Fur seal populations are declining at an estimated rate of four to eight percent yearly. If this decline continues, the population will have fallen from a peak of at least two million animals in 1942 to about 400,000 animals by the turn of the century, nearly the level reached when the Fur Seal Treaty was first concluded in 1911. However, most scientists believe that the commercial hunting of juvenile males has not been a contributing factor to this decline. Rather, entanglement of fur seals in discarded fishing gear and plastic is thought to be the major cause. Thus, the recent changes in the hunt are not likely to reverse the decline in the Pribilof Island fur seal population.

### Marine Mammal/Fishery Conflicts

*Capture of Porpoises in Tuna Nets.* Since the early 1960s, tuna fishermen have set purse-seine nets around schools of porpoises in order to catch large yellowfin tuna swimming beneath the porpoises. When the nets are retrieved, porpoises may be captured incidentally and killed.

The incidental capture and drowning of hundreds of thousands of porpoises in purse-seine nets was a focus of concern in drafting the Marine Mammal Protection Act in 1972. In that year, an estimated

368,600 porpoises, principally spotted, spinner, and common dolphins, were incidentally captured by U.S. tuna fishermen operating in the eastern tropical Pacific (Marine Mammal Commission 1986). The Marine Mammal Protection Act called for the reduction of injury and mortality rates to insignificant levels approaching zero.

As a result of gear improvements and of aggressive implementation of the act that resulted from a lawsuit filed by animal welfare groups in 1975, tuna fishermen reduced their capture to 15,305 porpoises in 1980.[2] That year, NMFS set a quota of 20,500 annual incidental takes from 1981 to 1985. This quota was extended indefinitely in the 1984 amendments to the Marine Mammal Protection Act.

Porpoise captures reached an all-time low in 1983, when 9,589 animals were killed or injured. As the fishing effort of the U.S. tuna fleet in the eastern tropical Pacific increased again and experienced skippers left to operate under foreign flags, the estimated kill and injury of porpoises increased to 17,732 in 1984 and 19,173 in 1985.

Preliminary figures indicate that the kill rate increased once again during 1986, as the U.S. fleet caught much more yellowfin tuna by setting on porpoises than in previous years. By early September, with two months left in the season, the fleet had killed as estimated 19,806 porpoises. Conservationists threatened to sue if NMFS did not enforce its limit of 20,500 by prohibiting fishermen from setting on porpoise during the rest of 1986. Subsequently, NMFS issued regulations, applicable in 1986 only, that placed restrictions on the tuna fleet once the limit was reached (51 *Federal Register* 32786 [September 16, 1986]). Among other things, the regulations prohibited the capture, possession, or landing of yellowfin or bigeye tuna unless the capturing vessel carried a NMFS observer to verify that the vessel did not set on porpoises.

***Capture of Porpoises in Foreign Fisheries.***   While the size of the U.S. tuna fleet has declined in recent years, the size of the foreign fleet setting on porpoises has increased. Today, the U.S. fleet comprises 34 vessels, compared to the foreign fleet's 73. Mexico's fleet alone includes 49 vessels (51 *Federal Register* 28963 [August 13, 1986]). Because little effort is made to collect the information, the level of porpoise mortality caused by foreign fleets is largely unknown. Based upon limited research, however, the Inter-American Tropical Tuna Commission estimated that foreign and U.S. fleets together killed 43,984 porpoises in 1984 (Marine Mammal Commission 1986), with foreign fleets responsible for the majority of the losses.

Congress addressed this problem in the 1984 reauthorization of the Marine Mammal Protection Act by requiring that any nation

---

2. Porpoise mortality rates are based upon reports of observers who accompany a percentage of the fishing trips made by the U.S. fleet.

exporting tuna from the eastern tropical Pacific into the United States have a marine-mammal program comparable to that of the United States and that the average rate of incidental take of porpoises be comparable to that of U.S. fishing operations. In August 1986, NMFS proposed regulations to implement these amendments (51 *Federal Register* 28963-28968 [August 13, 1986]), which should become final in fiscal 1987.

In May, the Reagan administration lifted an embargo on Mexican tuna that had resulted from the failure of Mexico to comply with the old Marine Mammal Protection Act regulations (51 *Federal Register* 18644-18645 [May 21, 1986]). The administration did so without making assessments of the Mexican tuna-porpoise program or the rate of incidental capture in the Mexican fishery. The administration later lifted a second embargo that had been imposed under the Magnuson Fishery Conservation and Management Act as the result of Mexico's seizure of U.S. tuna boats several years ago (51 *Federal Register* 29183 [August 14, 1986]). Conservationists are concerned that Mexico's fleet will continue to kill a disproportionately large number of porpoises. Government officials argue that by lifting the embargo, the U.S. will be able to influence Mexico to improve its marine-mammal program (Holing 1986).

**Incidental Drowning of Dall's Porpoises in Driftnets.**  The 1982 amendments to the North Pacific Fisheries Act (16 U.S.C.A. 1021) extended a permit issued to the Japan Salmon Fisheries Cooperative Association in 1981 to take 5,500 Dall's porpoises, 25 northern sea lions, and 450 northern fur seals in the course of fishing with drift nets for salmon in the north Pacific. Since this permit expires in June 1987, the association applied for a permit under the Marine Mammal Protection Act to take these marine mammals incidentally. In response, NMFS proposed extending the existing permit, issued a draft environmental impact statement, and scheduled a December hearing on the proposal before an administrative law judge (51 *Federal Register* 29674-29677 [August 20, 1986]).

This fishery is one of several large drift-net fisheries in the north Pacific that incidentally capture marine mammals, sea birds, and nontarget fish. The issuance of the permit and its terms and conditions will be contested by marine-mammal and seabird conservationists as well as by western Alaska salmon fishermen who fear loss of fish to Japanese competition.

**Drowning of Marine Mammals in Gill Nets in California.**  The use of gill and trammel nets in California coastal waters has increased considerably in the past 10 years. On the average, an estimated 105 threatened southern sea otters were killed yearly in such nets from

1973 to 1984 (Marine Mammal Commission 1986). These nets also catch and drown harbor porpoises, birds, and nontarget fish. In response to widespread concern, the California Department of Fish and Game and the state legislature began limiting the use of such nets during 1985 (for more details see the sea otter chapter).

***Translocation of Southern Sea Otters.*** The southern sea otter population, which is distributed along the central California coast, is listed as threatened under the Endangered Species Act. Because of the vulnerability of the remaining southern sea otter population, the species' recovery plan calls for the establishment of at least one additional breeding population within the species' historical range, but far enough outside the current range so that it would not be affected by an oil spill or other catastrophic incident. In August 1986, FWS proposed to relocate as many as 250 southern sea otters to an area near San Nicholas Island, California (51 *Federal Register* 29362-29383) (for more details see the sea otter chapter).

# LEGISLATION

## Endangered Species Act Amendments

Although efforts to reauthorize the Endangered Species Act in 1986 stalled in the Senate, Congress did approve two sets of amendments that concern marine-mammal conservation. Both amendments were included initially in the House version of the Endangered Species Act in July 1985. These amendments were attached to other bills when it became clear that the Senate would not act on endangered-species legislation.

One amendment, passed on October 14 as part of a package of legislation (H.R.4531), encourages FWS to develop and implement the plan discussed above to translocate some southern sea otters in order to establish an experimental population separate from the current population.

On October 18, Congress approved other amendments to the Endangered Species Act and to the Marine Mammal Protection Act as part of a package of marine-fisheries provisions in S.991. Section 411 of S.991 amends both laws to allow the incidental taking of marine mammals listed as endangered or threatened under the Endangered Species Act—and therefore depleted under the Marine Mammal Protection Act—if it is judged that the taking would not jeopardize the species' continued existence and if the parties concerned take steps to minimize and mitigate the impact.

## LEGAL DEVELOPMENTS

### Discretionary Nature of U.S. Whaling Sanctions

The International Whaling Commission in 1982 set zero quotas for North Pacific sperm whales beginning in October 1984 and for all whales by 1986. Japan subsequently filed a formal objection, thereby releasing itself from any obligation to abide by the commission's decision. Japan then continued its whaling operations after the zero quotas had become effective.

In November 1984, Japan entered into an executive agreement with the United States under which the secretary of Commerce agreed not to impose economic sanctions if the Japanese limited their whaling to certain levels and filed a notice of intent to observe the moratorium on commercial whaling by 1988. Conservationists disputed the federal government's authority to make such an agreement and filed suit (*American Cetacean Society v. Baldridge* [768 D.C. Cir. 426, 604 F.Supp. 1398]). The conservation groups argued that the Pelly and Packwood-Magnuson amendments required the secretaries of Commerce and of State to impose sanctions upon Japan since it was whaling contrary to a decision of the International Whaling Commission.

The district and appellate courts agreed with the conservation groups. But in a 5-4 ruling issued June 30, 1986, the Supreme Court reversed the lower courts' decisions. In an opinion written for the majority, Justice White concluded,

> Congress granted the Secretary the authority to determine whether a foreign nation's whaling in excess of quotas diminishes the effectiveness of the IWC, and we find no reason to impose a mandatory obligation upon the Secretary to certify that every quota violation necessarily fails that standard (S.Ct. Nos. 85-954/85-955, *Opinion*, p.19).

Some conservationists believe that the Supreme Court has weakened the Pelly and Packwood-Magnuson amendments by acknowledging broad administrative discretion in their application. However, the court left untouched the requirement that the fishery allocations of an offending nation be reduced once it is certified under the Packwood-Magnuson Amendment. Thus, the amendments still offer the United States a unique and powerful tool for supporting actions taken by the International Whaling Commission. The behavior of Japan, Iceland, Norway, and South Korea since the Supreme Court decision indicate that they still take the threat of reduced fish allocations quite seriously.

### Sea World Permit Overturned

In 1984, NMFS issued a permit to Sea World, Inc. to conduct scientific research on as many as 100 killer whales and to permanently retain up to 10 of them for public display and captive breeding. The permit request generated unusually broad public attention, including the involvement of the Alaska legislature. In *Jones v. Gordon* (Civ. No. J84-011 [D. Alaska]; No.85-3729 and 85-3767 [9th Cir.]) environmental groups and the state of Alaska challenged the issuance of the permit. The district court agreed with the plaintiffs that NMFS had violated the National Environmental Policy Act in not preparing an environmental impact statement on the effects of its action.

In August 1986, the appellate court agreed in the main with the district court. The government has decided not to appeal the case. Sea World has not announced whether it will continue to pursue the permit. Clearly, the appellate court decision will compel a fuller public review of the permit request if Sea World does renew it.

## Critical Habitat for the Hawaiian Monk Seal

The Hawaiian monk seal has been listed since 1976 as endangered under the Endangered Species Act and as depleted under the Marine Mammal Protection Act. NMFS itself had considered proposing critical habitat as early as 1977, but opposition from the state of Hawaii and commercial fishing interests persuaded NMFS not to issue a final designation.

In January 1985, NMFS finally proposed critical habitat (50 *Federal Register* 1088 [January 9, 1985]), but delayed taking final action. On February 20, 1986, Greenpeace challenged NMFS' failure to designate critical habitat for Hawaiian monk seals in a timely manner (*Greenpeace International, Inc. v. Baldrige*, Civ. No.86-0129 [D. Hawaii]). The plaintiffs alleged that NMFS violated the requirement of the Endangered Species Act that a final determination on critical habitat be issued within a year after critical habitat is proposed.

The plaintiffs also took issue with the substance of the NMFS proposal, which designates critical habitat to a depth of 10 fathoms. They charge that NMFS violated the Endangered Species Act by failing to follow the recovery plan recommendation that critical habitat be designated to a depth of 20 fathoms around the northwestern Hawaiian Islands. They also maintain that NMFS violated a requirement of the Marine Mammal Protection Act that the agency provide a detailed explanation for deviating from a recommendation of the Marine Mammal Commission (16 U.S.C.A. 1402[d]). The commission also had recommended designation of critical habitat to 20 fathoms.

The question of whether NMFS acted in a timely manner became moot when the agency issued a final designation of critical habitat in April 1986. This was the first such designation by NMFS for a marine-mammal population (51 *Federal Register* 16047-16057 [April 30, 1986]). However, the substance of the designation itself is still under challenge. The case is scheduled for a hearing in 1987.

## REFERENCES

Braham, Howard W. 1984. "The status of endangered whales: an overview," *Marine Fisheries Review* 46(4):2-6.

Holing, Dwight. 1986. "The tuna-porpoise issue resurfaces," *Pacific Discovery*. July-September. pp. 4-12.

Marine Mammal Commission. 1986. *Annual Report of the Marine Mammal Commission, Calendar Year 1985*. Washington, D.C. 180pp.

North Pacific Fur Seal Commission. 1985. *Proceedings of the Tokyo Meeting, April 15-18, 1985*. Washington, D.C. 180pp.

U.S. Department of Commerce, National Oceanic and Atmospheric Administration, National Marine Fisheries Service. 1985a. *Strategic Plan for the National Marine Fisheries Service*. Washington, D.C.

U.S. Department of Commerce, National Oceanic and Atmospheric Administration, National Marine Fisheries Service. 1985b. *Final Environmental Impact Statement: Proposed Amendments to Regulations Governing the Taking of Marine Mammals Associated with Tuna Purse Seining Operations*. Washington, D.C. 115pp.

*Michael Weber, vice president for programs of the Center for Environmental Education, is a coauthor of* **A Nation of Oceans.**

The little green heron is among many wading birds whose survival is linked to wetlands. The federal government is adopting new measures to save the nation's vanishing wetlands areas. *Leonard Lee Rue III*

# Federal Wetlands Protection Programs

◇

Katherine Barton

## OVERVIEW

The 95 million acres of wetlands remaining in the conterminous United States[1] represent only five percent of the nation's land surface, but provide some of its most important wildlife habitat. Approximately 5,000 species of plants, 190 species of amphibians, and a third of all bird species in the nation occur in wetlands. Two-thirds of the 10 to 12 million waterfowl in the lower 48 states reproduce in the prairie potholes of the Midwest, and millions of ducks winter in the bottomland hardwoods of the south-central states. More than half of the marine sport fish caught in the United States are dependent on wetland estuaries, and roughly two-thirds of the major U.S. commercial fish are dependent on estuaries and salt marshes for nursery or spawning grounds. Wetlands also serve a variety of other ecological functions, depending on their type and location, such as maintaining water quality, stabilizing shorelines, reducing floodwaters, and trapping sediments and other pollutants.

---

1. The U.S. Fish and Wildlife Service estimate as of 1985.

Audubon Wildlife Report 1987

Despite their value, a majority of the original wetlands in the lower 48 states have been destroyed. According to the U.S. Fish and Wildlife Service (FWS), less than 46 percent of the nation's original wetland acreage remains, and the loss continues at a rate of 300,000 to 450,000 acres per year (Tiner 1984, Office of Technology Assessment 1984). The losses have been particularly severe in certain critical areas. For example, the bottomland-hardwood wetlands of the lower Mississippi Valley have been reduced 80 percent, California's wetlands 90 percent, and Iowa's 95 percent.

The federal government holds an estimated 12.5 million acres of wetlands outside Alaska (Heimlich and Langner 1986), about 13 percent of the nation's total. However, a significant portion of these are on lands under multiple-use management, so their protection is not guaranteed. The vast majority of the nation's wetlands, some 65 million acres, are in private hands (Heimlich and Langner 1986).

The federal government does regulate certain activities on privately owned wetlands, primarily under Section 404 of the Clean Water Act (33 U.S.C.A. 1344). Section 404 requires the issuance of a federal permit for the disposal of dredged or fill material in most of the nation's wetlands and waterways.[2] This program, jointly administered by the Army Corps of Engineers and the Environmental Protection Agency, has helped slow wetlands losses, although exactly to what extent is unknown. Nevertheless, extensive wetland losses have continued despite the 404 program, which has been especially ineffective in controlling losses from agricultural conversion. This conversion was the cause of 87 percent of wetlands losses from the mid-1950s to the mid-1970s (Tiner 1984). A variety of other environmental laws, such as the National Environmental Policy Act, the Wilderness Act, and the Endangered Species Act, indirectly provide some additional protection for wetlands (see Figure 1).

## CURRENT DEVELOPMENTS

### Removing Federal Incentives for Wetlands Destruction: The Swampbuster Provision and Tax Reform

The 99th Congress (1985-86) enacted two new laws intended to eliminate a number of federal policies that aid and encourage the destruction of wetlands, particularly from agricultural conversion. The

2. Under the Clean Water Act, the 404 program applies in the "waters of the United States." The extent of this jurisdiction has been debated repeatedly and litigated since the program's inception. It is currently under litigation again in *National Wildlife Federation v. Laubscher* and is discussed in the litigation section of this chapter.

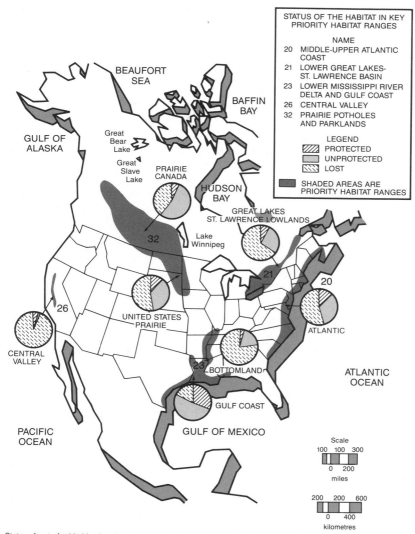

Status of waterfowl habitat in priority breeding and wintering areas of Canada and the United States.
Source: North American Waterfowl Management Plan, (Department of the Interior, 1986C).

Figure 1

1985 farm bill (the Food Security Act of 1985, P.L. 99-198) included a
"swampbuster" provision (Title XII, Subtitle C) that denies federal
price supports, payments, certain loans, and other benefits to farmers
who grow crops on newly converted wetlands. In 1986, the Tax Reform
Act (P.L. 99-514) repealed or altered several provisions of the tax code
that provided incentives for converting wetlands into cropland. These
new laws go a long way toward resolving inconsistencies in federal

policy, which has sought to conserve wetlands at the same time that is has encouraged their conversion.

***Swampbuster.*** The enactment of the swampbuster provision was greeted enthusiastically by fish and wildlife interests, who were optimistic that it would significantly slow the conversion of some five million acres of wetlands that have high to medium potential for conversion to agriculture (U.S. Department of Agriculture 1986). As the Department of Agriculture began implementing the law in 1986, however, conservationist optimism turned to outrage. Agriculture's interpretation of the law, conservationists said, has provided a major loophole for wetlands conversion (see Table 1).

The key controversy is over the department's interpretation of a provision of the law that exempts a person from the swampbuster penalty for growing crops on converted wetlands if the conversion was commenced before enactment of the act on December 23, 1985. In its interim final regulations issued in June 1986 (51 *Federal Register* 23496, June 27, 1986), the Department of Agriculture said that wetlands conversion would be considered to have commenced before the law's enactment if earth moving had been started or if substantial funds had been contractually committed for the conversion. Fish and wildlife interests charged that this definition was too broad.

In the meantime, Senator Mark Andrews of North Dakota — a Republican facing a tight reelection race — pressed to further broaden

**TABLE 1**
**Conversion Potential of Wetlands in Critical Problem Areas, 1982**

| Area | High | Medium | Unlikely | Other[a] | Total |
|---|---|---|---|---|---|
| | | | 1,000 acres | | |
| South Florida palustrine wetlands | 62 | 321 | 1,566 | 1,455 | 4,470 |
| Prairie pothole emergent wetlands | 98 | 472 | 1,540 | 2,103 | 4,888 |
| Nebraska sandhills and rainwater basin | 26 | 105 | 479 | 173 | 859 |
| Lower Mississippi alluvial plain | 96 | 302 | 1,724 | 1,415 | 4,264 |
| Coastal pocosins | 18 | 271 | 2,578 | 3,183 | 7,754 |
| Western riparian | 2 | 33 | 166 | 1,125 | 1,441 |
| Total | 302 | 1,504 | 8,053 | 9,454 | 23,676 |
| Total non-federal | 813 | 4,371 | 28,467 | 25,986 | 78,384 |
| | | | Percentage | | |
| Percentage of non-federal | 37 | 34 | 28 | 36 | 30 |

Source: R.E. Heimlich, and L.L. Langner. 1986. *Swampbusting: Wetland Conversion and Farm Programs.* U.S. Department of Agriculture. Washington, D.C.

[a]Includes wetlands with no conversion potential and where conversion potential was not estimated.

the Department of Agriculture's "commenced" definition, since the proposed definition threatened to cut off federal farm benefits for a number of North Dakota farmers who were planning drainage projects. Two days after Andrews threatened to introduce an amendment to withhold funding for implementation of the swampbuster program in 1987, the Department of Agriculture agreed that wetlands conversion also would be considered to have commenced if a drainage plan had been approved before the law's enactment through a vote of landowners in the drainage area. Fish and wildlife interests say this could exempt multiple projects planned over the past three or four decades, including as much as 10,000 to 20,000 acres of wetlands in the prairie-pothole region.

A second key area of controversy in the regulations was the definition of converted wetlands. This definition determines the circumstances under which a farmer who drains land becomes ineligible for farm-support programs. The interim regulations issued in June stated that a wetland would be considered converted only if the conversion was caused or permitted by "the producer or any of the producer's predecessors in interest." Conservationists charged that this definition provided a loophole for farmers to find third parties to convert their wetlands. In particular, they charged the regulation would exempt wetlands drained by local drainage districts.

The Department of Agriculture said the provision was intended only to avoid penalizing farmers for farming wetlands where the conversion was out of their control—for example, if a neighboring farmer's drainage of wetlands on his property caused drainage on an adjacent farm as well. To clarify this provision, the Department of Agriculture issued guidance to its field staff specifying that a drainage-district conversion would be attributed to the farmers in the drainage district who paid for the cost of the conversion. However, conservationists maintained that so much wetland conversion by drainage districts could proceed without sanctions under the Agriculture Department's new "commenced" definition that this latter change was rendered largely meaningless.

The Department of Agriculture says the changes are not final. The Department will review public comments on the interim regulations and could revise them when final regulations are issued sometime in the future.

*Tax Reform.*    Prior to the passage of tax-reform legislation in 1986, the tax code contained a number of income-tax deductions and credits that provided incentives for farmers to clear and drain wetlands. At the same time, the increased value of drained land was taxed at the lower rate for capital gains. These provisions, and the ability to write off a variety of losses, made agriculture an attractive tax shelter as well.

The Tax Reform Act of 1986 has eliminated a number of these incentives for wetland drainage. One important change is the elimination of the preferential reduced tax rate for capital gains. Under tax reform, after a one-year transition, capital gains will be taxed at the same rates as other income, receiving no preferential treatment. In addition, the law explicitly denies capital gains treatment on income derived from the sale of highly erodible cropland and converted wetlands, which provides some assurance that gains from these activities will continue to be taxed at regular income rates even if preferential treatment for capital gains is restored in the future.

Under the old tax code the costs of land clearing—including the moving of earth and the diversion of streams and waterways—were deductible up to $5,000 or 25 percent of taxable income. This provision was repealed by the new law. Formerly, deductions also were allowed for certain soil-conservation and water-conservation costs, including the filling of wetlands. The new law allows deductions of expenses only for activities included in conservation plans approved by the Soil Conservation Service or a comparable agency and specifically excludes deductions for agricultural conversion of wetlands. The new law also eliminates the 10-percent investment tax credit, which helped offset the costs of certain drainage activities such as the installation of drainage tile, and includes provisions intended to make agricultural investment less attractive as a tax shelter.

The extent to which the new changes will discourage wetlands conversion is unknown.[3] Prior to tax reform, FWS had contracted for studies on the impact of tax policies on agricultural conversion in the prairie potholes and in lower Mississippi Valley bottomland hardwoods. Results are expected to be released in early 1987.

### The 404 Permit Program: Environmental Guidelines Disputed

Under Section 404 of the Clean Water Act, the Army Corps of Engineers is responsible for issuing permits for the disposal of dredged or fill material into U.S. waters. The Corps administers the program jointly with the Environmental Protection Agency (EPA), which sets the environmental standards that projects must meet to receive a permit, as authorized in Section 404(b)(1). EPA also which has a virtual veto over Corps permit decisions under Section 404(c), which authorizes EPA to prohibit or restrict the use of an area as a disposal site for dredged or fill material if the discharge will have unacceptable adverse effects on municipal water supplies, shellfish beds and fishery areas, wildlife, or recreational areas. In addition, the Corps must consult with

3. However, see Heimlich and Langner 1986, Office of Technology Assessment 1984 and "Economics of Wetland Conversion: Farm Programs and Income Tax," by R.E. Heimlich, *National Wetlands Newsletter*, Vol. 8, No. 4, July-August, 1986, p.7.

EPA, FWS, the National Marine Fisheries Service, and state fish and wildlife agencies before issuing a permit.

The Corps and conservation groups have battled over the 404 program since its inception. The Corps generally has interpreted the program narrowly in terms of both the types of water bodies and the types of activities to which the program applies, while conservationists have pressed for and frequently won expansion of the program. Controversy has intensified since 1981, when the Presidential Task Force on Regulatory Relief identified the 404 program as a top priority for reform. Over the past five years, the Army has made numerous proposals for changes in the program, most of which have been opposed by fish and wildlife interests. Some of the proposals have been blocked, blunted, or overturned by lawsuits or as a result of congressional pressure. However, many others have taken effect or are still in the works. Administration of the 404 program, regulatory relief efforts, and previous 404(b)(1) controversies are discussed further in the 1985 and 1986 *Audubon Wildlife Reports*.

In 1986, most of the debate over the 404 program focused on the 404(b)(1) environmental guidelines, targeted for reform by the Task Force on Regulatory Relief in 1981, when the Army attempted to modify the guidelines by having them revised or demoted to advisory status only. These efforts were stalled when EPA, after soliciting public comment, determined that the need for changes in the guidelines was not substantiated, and when, as a result of a legal settlement of a conservationist lawsuit (*National Wildlife Federation v. Marsh*), the Corps issued regulations prohibiting the issuance of a 404 permit unless the project compiled with the 404(b)(1) guidelines.

With the guidelines unchanged and clearly mandatory, the debate has shifted to disputes over their interpretation. The primary focus of this dispute is a decision in 1985 by the Corps of Engineers to issue a permit for the construction of a shopping mall in South Attleboro, Massachusetts. In 1986, EPA used its 404(c) authority to overrule the Corps' decision and rebutted some of the Corps' reasoning in regard to the guidelines. However, EPA's action has been appealed in court by the developer (see litigation section). Disagreements over applications of the guidelines are likely to continue for some time.

Among other things, the guidelines generally provide that a discharge of dredged or fill material will not be permitted if there is a practicable alternative that would have less adverse impacts on the aquatic ecosystem, providing the alternative does not have other significant adverse environmental consequences. For discharges in wetlands and other specific "special aquatic sites," the guidelines impose a stricter standard, generally called the "water dependency test." This test, considered by many to be the cornerstone of wetlands protection under the 404 program, states that: (1) an activity that is not dependent on being located near water may be presumed to have practicable alternatives that do not involve wetlands or other special aquatic sites; and (2) that in all cases, alternatives that do not discharge into special aquatic sites may be presumed to have less adverse impacts on the aquatic ecosystem. Only if a developer can show that these presumptions are incorrect in his particular case can a permit be issued for his project.

The Attleboro Mall case deals with two important areas of controversy over the 404(b)(1) guidelines: how mitigation should be considered in permit review and what constitutes a practicable alternative.

***Mitigation.*** In constructing its shopping mall in South Attleboro, Pyramid Companies proposed to fill or alter 45 acres of forested wetlands. To compensate for this loss, Pyramid proposed to construct 35 to 50 acres of wetlands at another, upland site—although the resulting wetlands would be of a type different from those being destroyed—and to enhance some existing wetlands on the project site. The Corps maintained that this mitigation would fully compensate for the lost wetlands, that the project therefore would have no net adverse environmental effects, and that in any case, no practicable alternatives to the site existed. For these reasons, the Corps said, Pyramid has successfully rebutted both presumptions of the water-dependency test.

In a statement explaining its 404(c) determination, EPA disagreed with the Corps. EPA maintained that the difficulty of artificial wetlands creation made the success of the proposed mitigation so uncertain that the Corps must seriously investigate whether a practicable alternative to the project exists. In fact, as discussed below, EPA identified what might be a practicable alternative site that contained only one acre of wetlands. Moreover, EPA said that the guidelines do not allow mitigation to be used as a remedy for destroying wetlands when a practicable alternative exists.

Disagreement between the Corps and EPA over the mitigation may heat up in 1987. EPA began developing mitigation guidance in 1985, but halted the effort in response to an Army request that the two agencies work together to develop joint guidance. In the meantime, the Corps decided to include its own existing mitigation policy in a set of regulations due to come out in fiscal year 1987. EPA objected on the grounds that the Corps mitigation policy might not be consistent with the 404(b)(1) guidelines. At the beginning of fiscal year 1987, EPA and the Army were negotiating clarifications aimed at addressing these concerns. If the development of joint mitigation guidance is not successful, EPA has indicated it may finalize and issue its own mitigation guidance to EPA field personnel.[4]

***Practicable Alternatives.***   A secondary issue in the Attleboro Mall case was whether a practicable alternative to the project existed. The debate focused on whether a site at North Attleboro—located three miles from the South Attleboro site and containing less than one acre of wetlands—was a practicable alternative. The issue of what constitutes a practicable alternative has been addressed in several lawsuits and has been controversial in a number of cases aside from Attleboro.

Under the 404(b)(1) guidelines, an alternative is considered practicable when it is both feasible and available. The Corps said the North Attleboro site was not feasible because it did not fulfill the project's basic purposes from the applicant's point of view. Also, the Corps said that the site was not available because the site was owned by another developer at the time of the permit application.

EPA disagreed. In determining feasibility, EPA said the applicant's proposal should be the starting point for identifying the basic project purpose. However, the agency added that the 404(b)(1) guidelines do not demand an acceptance of everything a developer wants. EPA said that "project purpose" refers to the general function of an activity. However, EPA said that in this particular case it did not need to address how broadly the project purpose could be construed (for example, whether the purpose was increased shopping versus a new, quality shopping mall), since the alternative site at North Attleboro was capable of serving a "strikingly similar project." This was suggested by the plans of the competing developer to construct at the alternative site a mall quite similar to Pyramid's. EPA also said that Pyramid had not met the burden of proving that the North Attleboro site was unavailable. In fact, the land was for sale when Pyramid was selecting a site.

Pyramid has sued the federal government to overturn EPA's determination and to require issuance of a 404 permit. Meanwhile, the Corps and EPA also have been debating the interpretation of a 1985 court ruling that dealt with the practicable alternatives test. The court had ruled that the Corps has a duty to consider the applicant's objectives in its alternatives analysis (*Louisiana Wildlife Federation v. York*, 761 F.2d 1044, 5th Cir. [1986]), but EPA and the Corps have disagreed to what extent the Corps is to rely on the applicant's point of view in determining if a practicable alternative exists. After an exchange of letters and Senate hearings on the matter, the Corps

4. For further details on mitigation, see the September/October 1986 *National Wetlands Newsletter* and the proceedings of the October 1986 Mitigation Conference by the National Association of State Wetland Managers.

agreed to revise its guidance on the issue, making it clear that in determining whether a practicable alternative exists, the Corps is not restricted only to what the applicant prefers or to the alternative that maximizes profits. The guidance will be submitted to EPA for review and is expected to be issued in fiscal year 1987.

## NMFS Studies on Permit Recommendations

The Southeast Region of the National Marine Fisheries Service (NMFS) has completed a series of studies on wetlands losses resulting from Corps' permit decisions and on Corps treatment of NMFS recommendations in making those decisions.[5] The studies are important because almost no information of this type has been collected to date.

Although the studies show that the Corps' accepts NMFS recommendations in most cases, they also show that (1) substantial wetland alteration—about 50,000 acres in five years—has occurred without any objection from NMFS; (2) Corps districts are highly variable in their treatment of NMFS recommendations; and (3) projects that individually seem to involve insignificant habitat loss are causing significant cumulative losses (see Table 2).

From 1981 through 1985, the Southeast Region commented on 23,292 wetlands-alteration proposals. Of these, NMFS studied 5,385 for which it collected detailed habitat information. Of the 184,187 acres of wetlands proposed for alteration, NMFS recommendations would have conserved 135,687, 74 percent of the total. NMFS did not object to the alteration of 48,500 acres—26 percent of the total—although it did recommend that these habitat losses be offset by the restoration or creation of 110,406 acres, more than twice the total lost (Mager and Thayer, in press).

NMFS then further analyzed 857 of the permit applications to determine the degree to which the Corps accepted NMFS recommendations. Of 22,054 acres of wetland habitat proposed for alteration, NMFS recommendations would have allowed the alteration of 9,060 acres or 41 percent. The Corps permitted the alteration of 11,614 acres—28 percent more acreage than the NMFS recommendations and 53 percent of the total. The Corps was closer to NMFS recommendations on mitigation, approving 56,758 acres of mitigation, just 432 acres short of the 57,190 NMFS recommended. The analysis showed the Corps fully accepted NMFS recommendations half of the time, partially accepted recommendations 24 percent of the time, and rejected them 26 percent of the time (Mager and Thayer, in press).

5. These include primarily 404 permit decisions.

**TABLE 2**
**Treatment of NMFS Recommendations on Permit Applications by the Corps of Engineers from 1981 through 1985, by District**

| COE District | N | NMFS comments accepted | NMFS comments partially accepted | NMFS comments rejected | Acreage proposed by applicant | Acreage accepted by NMFS | Acreage permitted by COE | Acreage R/G recom. | Acreage R/G permitted |
|---|---|---|---|---|---|---|---|---|---|
| New Orleans | 120 | 47 (39%) | 70 (58%) | 3 (3%) | 9,552 | 7,540 (79%) | 7,914 (83%) | 53,688 | 53,456 (99%) |
| Galveston | 144 | 80 (56%) | 45 (31%) | 19 (13%) | 7,273 | 625 (9%) | 1,895 (26%) | 3,031 | 3,054 (101%) |
| Mobile | 59 | 28 (48%) | 17 (29%) | 14 (24%) | 164 | 33 (20%) | 68 (41%) | 15 | 47 (313%) |
| Jacksonville | 268 | 54 (20%) | 56 (21%) | 158 (59%) | 2,050 | 703 (34%) | 1,492 (73%) | 334 | 104 (31%) |
| Savannah | 26 | 23 (89%) | 0 (0%) | 3 (12%) | 423 | 13 (3%) | 58 (14%) | 44 | 16 (36%) |
| Charleston | 121 | 97 (80%) | 8 (7%) | 16 (13%) | 2,379 | 88 (4%) | 111 (5%) | 21 | 24 (114%) |
| Wilmington | 119 | 103 (87%) | 9 (8%) | 7 (6%) | 213 | 60 (28%) | 79 (37%) | 59 | 59 (100%) |
| Total | 857 | 432 (50%) | 205 (24%) | 220 (26%) | 22,054 | 9,061 (41%) | 11,617 (53%) | 57,192 | 56,760 (99%) |

Source: A. Mager, 1986. *Treatment of National Marine Fisheries Service Recommendations by the Corps of Engineers in the Southeast Region of the United States from 1981-1985.* National Marine Fisheries Service. St. Petersburg, Florida.
N refers to the number of permits sampled.
Percentages for columns 1-3 are % of N.
Percentages for columns 5-6 are % of column 4.
Percentages for column 8 are % of column 7.
R/G refers to wetlands recommended for restoration and generation.

NMFS also found extreme variability in how the various Corps districts responded to NMFS recommendations[6] on these 857 permit applications (Mager 1986). The percent of NMFS recommendations fully accepted ranged from 89 percent in the Savannah District to 20 percent in the Jacksonville district. The Charleston District permitted the alteration of only one percent more acreage than recommended by NMFS, while the Jacksonville District permitted 39 percent more. Except for Jacksonville and Savannah, however, all districts permitted more mitigation acreage than NMFS recommended.

Over the five-year period, NMFS also tracked applicant compliance with mitigation requirements in 584 issued permits. Overall, applicants complied with permit stipulations 80 percent of the time. Compliance was highest in the Wilmington District at 90.8 percent and lowest in the Mobile District at 56.5 percent. However, NMFS did not study whether these mitigation efforts were successful in achieving their goals (Mager and Thayer, in press).

Finally, the Southeast Region analyzed permit applications reviewed in 1985 to determine the extent of habitat losses from projects for which NMFS registered no objection. The purpose was to determine if these very small projects, which individually seemed insignificant, might cumulatively cause significant losses (Mager and Hardy, in press).

Of 4,435 permit applications reviewed in 1985, NMFS had no objection to 3,133 or 71 percent. Of these, 61 percent involved habitat losses. NMFS further reviewed 1,802 projects for which acreage information was available. Of the 65,671 acres proposed for alterations by these projects, NMFS did not object to the alteration of 11,162 acres or 17 percent. However, the review showed that 7,864 of these acres—70 percent of the acreage loss not objected to—involved significant habitat losses.[7] NMFS recommended 19,200 acres of mitigation to offset these losses, most apparently accepted by the Corps, but, NMFS stresses, habitat restoration and creation efforts are still experimental and may not be successful (Mager and Thayer, in press).

Considering that NMFS did not object to the alteration of almost 50,000 acres over five years, these cumulative impacts may be substantial.

One major concern of NMFS personnel is that while the studies show that large amounts of mitigation are recommended by NMFS and frequently required by the Corps, success of mitigation is not exam-

6. The study found that NMFS treatment of permits was remarkably consistent, and therefore attributed the variability to how the different Corps districts responded to NMFS recommendations.

7. The other 30 percent of the acreage includes, among other things, projects located in wetlands not under NMFS jurisdiction, but that may involve some significant habitat losses under the purview of other agencies.

ined. NMFS staff recommend studying the results of past mitigation efforts and exploring those that have high potential for success.


## Other Developments

*National Wetlands Inventory.*    The National Wetlands Inventory continues its production of topical maps of the nation's key wetlands. The 1988 inventory goal for mapping is still on schedule for all identified priority areas in the lower 48 states and Alaska. The inventory's wetland plant lists are now complete and, with the previously completed soil lists, are available for each state. The inventory also has begun to issue detailed state reports summarizing the findings of the inventory and other existing wetland information. Reports for New Jersey and Delaware have been issued and others are expected (U.S. Department of the Interior 1985a, 1985b).

*Wetlands Assessments.*    Scientists and federal agencies have been working for years to develop methodologies for assessing wetlands functions and values in order to help in making management decisions and setting wetlands-protection priorities. A methodology originally developed by Paul Adamus for the Federal Highway Administration is being revised and is scheduled to be released in April 1987 as an operational draft. The use of wetland assessments has been somewhat controversial. Fish and wildlife interests are concerned that the varied and complex functions of wetlands are difficult to compare and that wetlands with lower values will be considered expendable even though all remaining wetlands in an area may be of intrinsically high importance. The revised methodology will be field tested by various state and federal users and may eventually undergo additional revisions.

*Up-front Planning for Wetlands Protection.*    Efforts to use the 404 program as a planning and education tool for wetlands protection advanced in 1986 and are likely to accelerate in coming years. EPA, under a provision in the 404(b)(1) guidelines (40 CFR 230.80), is conducting "advanced identification" efforts in a number of areas, including Nebraska's Rainwater Basin, Chincoteague Island in Virginia, and Havensack Meadows in New Jersey. Under the advanced identification program, EPA works with the Corps of Engineers to designate wetlands as potentially suitable or unsuitable for disposal of dredged or fill material in advance of permit applications. This does not guarantee the issuance or denial of permits, but is intended to guide projects away from sensitive wetlands and the jurisdiction of the 404 program, as well as to speed permit review. In addition, the Corps of Engineers is conducting a number of Special Area Management

Planning efforts in which local, state, and federal agencies develop a comprehensive management plan to improve predictability in wetlands regulation. These planning efforts are intended to identify areas that EPA can designate as unsuitable under the advanced identification program or as off-limits to disposal under its 404(c) authority and to identify allowable activities or disposal areas that could be covered by a general permit. Both EPA and the Corps expect to issue guidance in fiscal year 1987 to their field staff on their respective programs.

***Regulation of Solid Waste Under 404.*** In January 1986, EPA and the Corps of Engineers reached an interim agreement on the regulation of solid-waste disposal in wetlands. Under a legal settlement agreement (*National Wildlife Federation v. Marsh*), the Environmental Protection Agency and the Corps were to resolve this question by issuing a joint definition of fill by May 1984. Unable to reach a permanent agreement, the agencies developed an interim arrangement that will remain in effect until EPA determines if solid-waste disposal in wetlands ultimately should be regulated under the Resource Conservation and Recovery Act. The interim agreement is oriented primarily toward stopping unauthorized discharges, which will be administrated primarily by EPA. Where permits are required, EPA — under its permitting authority for point-source discharges in Section 402 of the Clean Water Act — will regulate disposal of homogeneous industrial wastes such as mining wastes. The Army, under Section 404, will regulate heterogeneous materials, such as garbage and construction waste. The regulation of discharges previously covered by Sections 404 and 402 is not intended to change.

***Pending 404 Issues.*** A number of long-standing issues surrounding the 404 permit program remained unresolved at the end of fiscal year 1986. EPA and the Corps continued to negotiate over revisions of regulations implementing Corps responsibilities under the National Environmental Policy Act. These regulations play an important role in the effectiveness of the 404 program. Issuance of the regulations was blocked in 1985, when EPA argued before the Council on Environmental Quality that the proposed regulations would have an adverse effect on EPA's ability to prevent unacceptable discharges under the 404 program. The regulations should be issued in fiscal year 1987.

Two additional sets of regulations are expected in fiscal year 1987: EPA regulations simplifying procedures and requirements for state assumption of permit permitting responsibilities, and the Corps' consolidated 404 regulations, a compilation of regulatory changes made over the past few years. The consolidated regulations also will finalize some new and possibly controversial regulatory changes. Various internal policy matters also await resolution: an agreement between the Corps and EPA on how to delineate wetlands boundaries in the field; a memorandum of understanding between EPA and the Corps clarifying each agency's role in establishing geographic jurisdiction over the 404 program; and EPA's policy on bottomland hardwoods.

## LEGISLATION

Congress enacted several important pieces of legislation that should improve wetlands protection. The Emergency Wetlands Resources Act, covered in the migratory birds chapter, provides an additional $40 million yearly for federal wetland acquisition through various mechanisms. The act extends the Wetlands Loan Act through fiscal year 1988, allowing Congress to appropriate the approximately $3.5 million remaining in the loan advance, and forgives repayment of the loan, allowing all duck-stamp receipts to continue to be used for acquisition of migratory-bird habitat. The Tax Reform Act of 1986, discussed earlier in this chapter, removes various incentives for agricultural wetland conversion. The Water Resources Policy Act of 1985 (P.L. 99-662), covered in the federal water projects chapter, authorizes $175 million worth of fish and wildlife mitigation at existing Corps water projects, strengthens mitigation requirements for future projects, and generally should result in fewer and less environmentally destructive water projects because of the increased cost-sharing burden it places on local project sponsors. Congress also authorized administrative penalties for the 404 program in the Clean Water Act, but this bill was vetoed by President Reagan.

Finally, the House passed a package of amendments to the Fish and Wildlife Coordination Act (H.R. 2704), but the legislation died in the Senate for the second consecutive time. Future action is uncertain. The Fish and Wildlife Coordination Act requires federal agencies such as the Corps of Engineers and Bureau of Reclamation, to give full consideration to the views of fish and wildlife agencies when planning water projects or reviewing 404 permits and to include all justifiable mitigation. The amendments would make only relatively minor changes in existing law, somewhat strengthening the role of the fish and wildlife agencies. This legislation is discussed in detail in the migratory birds chapter.

## LEGAL DEVELOPMENTS

### Section 404 Taking Decision Overturned

On May 14, 1986, the U.S. Court of Appeals for the Federal Circuit ruled that Corps denial of a 404 permit for a limestone mining project in south Florida did not make the Corps liable for compensation of the owner simply because the Corps deprived the owner of his immediate use of the property (*Florida Rock Industries, Inc. v. United States*, Nos. 85-2588, 84-2609 [Fed. Cir. May 14, 1986]). The ruling was significant for overturning a claims court decision awarding the property owners $1.029 million from the federal government.

The case involved a 1,560-acre tract of land in Dade County, Florida, purchased in 1972 by a limestone mining company, Florida Rock Industries, for nearly $3 million. The tract is part of the Everglades system and contains wetlands that are used by wildlife and that recharge the Biscayne aquifer, used by Miami for drinking water. In October 1980, the Corps denied a 404 permit for discharges associated with the mining of 98 acres. The permit was opposed by EPA, the National Park Service, FWS, the state, and Dade County on the grounds that the project would cause irremediable loss of wetlands and temporary water pollution associated with limestone mining. Florida Rock maintained that the tract had no viable economic use other than mining and that the government should compensate it for the entire tract.

In the key portion of the ruling, the appeals court said that a previous case, *U.S. v. Riverside Bayview Homes* (106 S.Ct. 455 [1985]), made it clear that compensation could be required if a 404 permit denial severely limited a landowner's ability to use his property. However, the appeals court ruled that the trial court erred in the method it used to determine the severity of the economic impact caused by the denial. The trial court had taken the position that, if there was no allowable and practicable immediate use of the property, this established a taking, regardless of the impact of the permit denial on the property's fair market value. The appeals court said the owner's opportunity to recoup his investment by selling the property could not be ignored and that the trial court should consider the relationship between the owner's investment and the property's fair market value before and after the permit denial. The appeals court also said the lower court had erred in accepting the testimony of Florida Rock's economic expert, who maintained that the property had no fair market value because anyone who bought the supposedly worthless tract would be a victim of fraud. A real estate appraiser testifying for the government in the appeals court assigned a value of $5.466 million to the tract and said that speculators would purchase it in hopes that the regulation would change. In fact, Florida Rock had turned down a $6-million offer for the property.

Nevertheless, the appeals court said there was a substantial possibility that, under the legal standards set forth in its decision, compensation should be made to Florida Rock. Consequently, it remanded the case to the lower court for reconsideration. In September, however, Florida Rock requested that the Supreme Court review the appeals court ruling. The company argued that the proper standard for determining whether compensation is deserved is whether the Corps denies the owner economically viable use of his land.

## Isolated Wetlands and the Extent of 404 Jurisdiction

The National Wildlife Federation, along with the Sierra Club and the Frontera Audubon Society, has filed suit in the U.S. District Court for the Southern District of Texas against the Department of the Army and EPA. The plaintiffs charged that the Corps and EPA have failed to apply the 404 program to isolated wetlands and waters that Congress intended for regulation under the law (*National Wildlife Federation v. Laubscher*, No. 6-86-37). Isolated wetlands include millions of acres of high-value waters, such as prairie potholes, playa lakes, wet meadows, and deep bogs in ancient glacial lakes. All of these wetlands provide important migratory-waterfowl habitat.

The overriding authority for federal regulation of activities in waterways and wetlands, such as the 404 permit program, comes from the Commerce Clause of the Constitution, which grants Congress the power to regulate interstate commerce. The plaintiffs ask the court to rule that Congress, under the Commerce Clause, has the power to regulate all wetlands. By contrast, the Corps and EPA presently determine on a case-by-case basis whether a particular isolated wetlands has sufficient connection to interstate commerce, such as use by migratory birds, to fall under 404 jurisdiction. Furthermore, the plaintiffs ask the court to find that Congress fully exercised the power to regulate wetlands as a class in enacting Section 404 and that the Corps and EPA are prohibited from applying their case-by-case approach.

The National Wildlife Federation maintains that the case-by-case approach to determining 404 jurisdiction—plus Corps failure to provide clear guidance on how to make this determination—has resulted in confusion, delays, and inconsistent 404 application from district to district and in the failure to regulate wetlands that Congress intended to be covered by 404. The federation cites as an example a 30-acre wetland in South Texas, called Pond 12, which the Corps refused to regulate under 404 jurisdiction even though FWS reported that the lake was used by 84 species covered by the Migratory Bird Treaty Act, including 17 species of game birds. The wetland subsequently was destroyed drainage activities that would have been prohibited by 404 regulations. Thus, the plaintiffs also seek a ruling that Pond 12 was covered by 404 and that its destruction violated the Clean Water Act. If the court rules favorably on this count, the plaintiffs will seek restoration of Pond 12 to its natural state.

The federal government has sought to have the case dismissed on the grounds that the court lacks jurisdiction over the questions raised by the plaintiffs and that the National Wildlife Federation lacks standing to bring the suit. Furthermore, the government maintains that it has applied the Commerce Clause principles correctly and that the Clean Water Act does not mandate that the Corps and EPA extend 404 jurisdiction over all wetlands.

Finally, the agencies say their actions over the past year to ensure that all Corps districts and divisions exercise fully their regulatory jurisdiction make moot the federation's charges that they have implemented the 404 program inadequately. In this series of actions, the Corps distributed an EPA legal opinion finding that 404 jurisdiction extends to wetlands that are or could be used by migratory birds; surveyed its districts and divisions and concluded that they were following EPA guidance; and, overturning the earlier Corps ruling on Pond 12, determined that it was a water regulated under 404 prior to being drained. The Corps does not, however, propose to seek restoration of Pond 12. Further EPA-Corps guidance on isolated waters is expected in 1987.

### Attleboro Mall and the 404(b)(1) Guidelines

On July 1, 1986, Pyramid Companies filed suit in the U.S. District Court for the Northern District of New York against EPA, seeking to overturn an EPA 404(c) denial of a permit for construction of a shopping mall in South Attleboro, Massachusetts (*Bersani v. U.S. EPA*, No. 86-CV-772). The background of the case, and the reasoning in EPA's 404(c) determination, were discussed earlier in this chapter.

The case deals primarily with the interpretation of the 404(b)(1) guidelines. Pyramid alleges that EPA determination of a practicable alternative site to South Attleboro was arbitrary and capricious. The company maintains that the alternative site was neither practicable for its project nor available for purchase by the company. Pyramid also charges that EPA determination that the project will have avoidable, adverse effects on the aquatic ecosystem was arbitrary and capricious. The company maintains that its project will have a net positive environmental effect on the aquatic ecosystem and that the alternative site is more environmentally sensitive than the Pyramid site. Pyramid asks the court to require EPA to rescind the 404(c) determination and to require the Corps to issue the company a 404 permit for its project.

Since Pyramid filed its suit, a Massachusetts state court has applied a state regulation to the mall project that could make it very difficult for Pyramid to get a state construction permit. It is unclear what effect this will have on the federal lawsuit.

**Other Wetlands Litigation**

In *U.S. v. Akers* (785 F.2d 814 [9th Cir. 1986]), the federal appeals court upheld a district court's ruling that the appellant's conversion of a wetland to agricultural use was not exempt from the 404 permit requirement. Although Section 404(f)(1) exempts a number of farming activities, the court ruled that the appellant's activities were not exempt because they were incidental to an effort to convert wetlands to upland for agriculture.

In *Track 12, Inc. v. District Engineer* (618 F. Supp. 448 [D.Minn. 1985]), the district court ruled that the Corps of Engineers had 404 jurisdiction over artificially created wetlands as long as the wetlands were not created by the Corps. An earlier ruling had said that granting the Corps jurisdiction over wetlands it created would allow the Corps to extend its jurisdiction beyond the scope intended by Congress (*U.S. v. City of Fort Pierre* 747 F.2d 464 [8th Cir. 1984]).

In *National Wildlife Federation v. Hanson* (623 F. Supp. 1539 [E.D.N.C. 1985]), a federal district court ruled that a Corps determination that a 14,000-acre tract in North Carolina was not a wetland was arbitrary and capricious. The court said that when it is not obvious whether an area is a wetland or not—as was the case with this partially drained tract—the Corps must make its determination based on sound scientific analysis. The court said the record showed no scientific basis for the Corps determination. The court did not, however, agree with the plaintiff's request to instruct the Corps on how to make the redetermination. On remand, the Corps is now undertaking a new jurisdictional determination.

In *Friends of the Earth v. Hintz* (No. 84-4176, D.C. No. C83-260T [9th Cir., 1986]), the Ninth Circuit Court of Appeals upheld a Corps of Engineers decision to issue a Section 404 permit for an already completed fill in Grays Harbor on the Washington coast, a valuable wetlands habitat. The court used a highly deferential standard of review of the Corps' decision, citing a previous Ninth Circuit Court ruling that the court may not set aside agency action as arbitrary and capricious under the Administrative Procedures Act "unless there is no rational basis for the action." Using this strict standard of review, the court did not find a basis for overruling any of the Corps' determinations challenged in the case. These included a determination that the project—a log storage facility—was a water-dependent activity because the company, ITT Rayonier, wanted to locate it near its shipping facility and a determination, in which the Corps placed heavy reliance on information submitted by the permit applicant, that there were no practicable alternatives to the proposed project. The court also held that the Corps did not err when it considered the cost to the applicant in determining whether alternatives were practicable. It also said that off-site mitigation—compensating for wetlands loss by the creation of new wetlands elsewhere—may constitute mitigation that relieves the Corps of the obligation to prepare an environmental impact statement on a proposed permit. The decision appeared to add little new interpretation to the 404 program, but indicated it may be difficult to overturn Corps' 404 permit decisions in the Ninth Circuit.

## REFERENCES

Heimlich, R.E. 1986. "Economics of Wetland Conversion: Farm Programs and Income Tax," *National Wetlands Newsletter* 8 (4):7. July-August.

Heimlich, R.E. and L.L. Langner. 1986. *Swampbusting: Wetland Conversion and Farm Programs.* U.S. Department of Agriculture, Agricultural Economic Report Number 551. Washington, D.C.

Mager, A. 1986. *Treatment of National Marine Fisheries Service Recommendations by the Corps of Engineers in the Southeast Region of the United States from 1981 through 1985.* National Marine Fisheries Service. St. Petersburg, Florida.

Mager, A. and G.W. Thayer. "National Marine Fisheries Service habitat conservation efforts in the southeast region of the United States from 1981 through 1985," *Marine Fisheries Review.* In press.

Mager, A. and L.H. Hardy. "National Marine Fisheries Service Habitat Conservation Efforts in the Southeast Region of the United States for 1985 and an Analysis of Recommendations." Manuscript prepared for the National Symposium: Mitigation of Impacts and Losses. October 8-10, 1986. New Orleans, Louisiana. In press.

Tiner, R.W. 1984. *Wetlands of the United States: Current Status and Recent Trends.* U.S. Department of the Interior. Washington, D.C.

U.S. Congress, Office of Technology Assessment. 1984. *Wetlands: Their Use and Regulation.* Government Printing Office. Washington, D.C.

U.S. Department of Agriculture. 1986. *Environmental Assessment for the Regulations Implementing the Wetland Conservation Provisions of the Food Security Act of 1985.* U.S. Department of Agriculture. Washington, D.C.

Wilson, J.J. 1986. *Final Determination of the Assistant Administrator for External Affairs Concerning the Sweedens Swamp Site in Attleboro, Massachusetts Pursuant to Section 404(c) of the Clean Water Act.* U.S. Environmental Protection Agency. Washington, D.C.

*Katherine Barton, a freelance writer who specializes in conservation issues, is based in Washington, D.C.*

Columbus Lock and Dam on the Tennessee-Tombigbee Waterway, which is the nation's largest water project. Federal budget tightening is slowing development of these wildlife-destructive projects. *U.S. Army Corps of Engineers*

# Water Projects
# and
# Wildlife

Ruth Norris

## OVERVIEW

Water projects often have significant adverse environmental effects. The anadromous fisheries of the Pacific Northwest are nearly gone, with the catch only eight percent of its size a century ago, because more than three dozen dams have blocked fish migrations and inundated spawning areas of the Columbia River and its tributaries (Getches 1984). More than half the woody riparian plant communities of the lower 48 states have been destroyed. Nearly a fifth of the nation's million miles of streams have been altered by reservoirs, channelization, dredging, and water diversions. Meanders, oxbow lakes, islands, and other valuable resting and nesting areas for migratory birds have been destroyed. Rock riprap has replaced riparian vegetation, making streams inaccessible to deer and other wildlife.

The landscape of the West has been altered radically. Water projects have changed 10 million acres of deserts to farm fields, cities, and industrial areas. California's Central Valley, once home to thousands of grizzly bears and elk, has become one vast irrigated farm (Reisner 1986). Ninety percent of the valley's seasonal wetlands and

Audubon Wildlife Report 1987

201

ninety percent of its salmon streams are gone. Its wintering waterfowl populations have been reduced from 10 million to four million.

Although much wildlife habitat has been destroyed by water projects, new and different kinds of habitat also have been created. For example, disposal of dredge spoils can create islands used as rookeries by wading birds. Reservoirs have become prime spots for trout, bass, and other species. Water used to irrigate crops has provided feeding and resting habitat in previously dry areas for species that can adapt to living in an agricultural environment.

Four federal agencies carry primary responsibility for the construction and maintenance of water projects:

- The U.S. Army Corps of Engineers, which constructs and manages projects for navigation improvement, hydroelectric power generation, flood control, beach-erosion control, urban water supply, hurricane protection, and other purposes.
- The Bureau of Reclamation, an agency of the Department of the Interior created by the Reclamation Act of 1902 to develop water resources, primarily irrigation projects, for the western states. Today, the Bureau of Reclamation not only builds dams and irrigation systems but assists a variety of nonfederal entities, such as states, counties, and irrigation districts, to develop and manage water for municipalities, industry, hydroelectric projects, and recreation.
- The Tennessee Valley Authority, created by Congress in 1933 to improve navigation, prevent floods, and assist in development along the Tennessee River and its tributaries. The Tennessee basin covers some 40,910 square miles and parts of seven southeastern states.
- The Soil Conservation Service, an agency of the Department of Agriculture, which administers the small-watershed program established by the Watershed Protection and Flood Prevention Act of 1954. The program has authorized about 1,300 projects in watersheds no greater than 250,000 acres; 597 of these projects have been completed. The small-watershed program's emphasis has shifted somewhat from the large flood-control dams of the 1960s and 1970s to land-treatment projects for managing erosion, sedimentation, and runoff (Bouchard 1986).

By 1985, annual water-project spending by the Corps of Engineers, Bureau of Reclamation, and Soil Conservation Service had reached $4.3 billion. Collectively, these agencies operate 850 major dams, 25,000 miles of inland waterways, and 240 navigation locks. They dredge 200 commercial harbors, generate about six percent of the nation's electricity, and supply 11 million acres of cropland and pasture with 40 million acre-feet of irrigation water.[1] These agencies also supply 10 million acre-feet of water to cities and industries and monitor 3,400 miles of flood-control levees (Office of Management and Budget 1985). In addition, the Tennessee Valley Authority operates nine dams on the Tennessee and 22 on its tributaries, as well as hydroelectric, coal, and nuclear generating facilities.

Many federal water projects now in operation or under construction have their roots in problems and needs identified decades ago— opening the West for development, creating jobs, preventing flood damage, and alleviating the drought conditions of the 1930s. These missions largely have been filled. In the meantime, the cost of water projects has escalated, water-use patterns have shifted, and concern for protecting water resources in their natural conditions has grown. Moreover, the flow of federal construction dollars is slowing, the best damsites already are dammed, and some irrigation projects have been stalled because of costs, massive agricultural surpluses, and emerging evidence about project-related environmental damage, including water pollution and toxic contamination (Adams *et al.* 1985, Driver 1986). Thus water agencies will be looking for new roles in coming decades, perhaps shifting focus to emphasize water management more strongly than water development. Such changes in U.S. water policy bring with them major implications for wildlife.

## CURRENT DEVELOPMENTS

### Mitigation

Congress since the 1920s has attempted to prevent and mitigate the adverse impacts of water projects on wildlife. Some of these laws are comprehensive and apply to all federal actions. Others are specific to individual water projects or to the fish and wildlife resources affected. Examples are the Fish and Wildlife Coordination Act, which requires federal agencies to consult with the U.S. Fish and Wildlife Service on the potential impacts of proposed projects on wildlife and habitat and encourages mitigation measures that will minimize adverse impacts; and the Endangered Species Act, which generally prohibits federal actions that result in the taking of endangered species or destruction of their habitat (see Table 1).

Policy statements from water-project agencies generally affirm the value of wildlife habitat and resources and closely follow the stated

1. An acre-foot is the amount of water needed to cover an acre to the depth of one foot. This is roughly 325,000 gallons, or about what an average family uses in two years.

**TABLE 1**
*Federal Laws Imposing Environmental Restraints on Water Projects*

The Clean Water Act (33 U.S.C.A. §1251-1376)

sets standards and requires permits for the discharge of pollutants into the nation's waters and (in Section 404) requires permits from the Army Corps of Engineers for dredging and filling in waterways and adjacent wetlands (e.g., for construction and dam projects).

Section 7 of the Endangered Species Act (16 U.S.C.A. §1534)

mandates preservation of endangered-species habitat.

The National Environmental Policy Act of 1969 (42 U.S.C.A §4331-44)

requires environmental impact statements assessing the impact of federal projects before construction.

The Fish and Wildlife Coordination Act (16 U.S.C.A §661-66c)

requires federal agencies sponsoring or issuing permits for water projects to consult with the U.S. Fish and Wildlife Service "with a view to the conservation of wildlife resources" and encourages project developers to include measures to maximize overall project benefits, including mitigation measures to minimize adverse impacts.

The Wild and Scenic Rivers Act (16 USCA §1271-87)

mandates preservation in a free-flowing condition of certain rivers possessing outstanding "scenic, recreational, geologic, fish and wildlife, historic, cultural, and other similar values." Dams and water projects may not be licensed on rivers so designated (Getches 1984).

Pacific Northwest Electric Power Planning and Conservation Act (16 U.S.C.A §839)

contains significant requirements for preserving and restoring anadromous fish resources in the Pacific Northwest.

objectives of Congress and the federal Council on Environmental Quality for the recognition and protection of these resources. Thus, the U.S. Army Corps of Engineers planning regulation on environmental resources states, "It is national policy that fish and wildlife resources conservation be given equal consideration with other study purposes in the formulation and evaluation of alternative plans." Also, project planners are directed to give "full consideration" to the recommendations of federal and state wildlife agencies and to "demonstrate that damages to significant fish and wildlife resources have been avoided or minimized to the maximum extent practicable, and that unavoidable damages have been compensated to the extent justified . . ." (U.S. Department of the Army 1984).

In implementing this policy, the Corps sets out this sequence of protective steps:

- avoiding impacts altogether by not taking a specified action,
- minimizing impacts by limiting the degree or magnitude of the action,
- rectifying the impact by restoring the affected environment,
- reducing the impact over time by preservation and maintenance operations during the life of the action, and
- compensating for the impact by replacing or providing substitute resources (U.S. Department of the Army 1984).

The Bureau of Reclamation has set a goal similar to that of the Corps:

> The objectives of Reclamation with regard to fish and wildlife resources are to afford Federal and State fish and wildlife agencies the opportunity to participate actively in the planning for projects that could affect fish and wildlife resources, to ensure that the public is fully informed regarding fish and wildlife resource matters and that their views are considered, and to ensure that fish and wildlife resources are fully considered in Reclamation's decisionmaking process . . . (Bureau of Reclamation 1986)

In practice, however mitigation is an inexact science, its limits exacerbated by the difficulty and expense of generating data on existing wildlife resources, probable impacts of proposed projects, and probable outcomes of mitigation programs. Also, construction agencies legally are required only to consider, not to implement, U.S. Fish and Wildlife Service recommendations on mitigation or modifications of projects. "Often, in the view of many, the Corps failed to recommend adequate fish and wildlife mitigation programs," said Senator Robert Stafford during debate on the Water Resources Development Act of 1986. "The Corps simply refused to own up to the environmental dislocation produced by its projects. On other occasions, the mitigation work was often proposed after the project was completed. In such instances, the mitigation — which often involved land purchases for providing wildlife cover — ran into opposition from local developers. The retort: We have our project, why give those bird-and-bunny people anything?"

The Upper Mississippi River System is an example of a case where steps only recently have been taken to mitigate the cumulative impacts of a series of navigation projects. The system includes some 1,300 commercially navigable miles of the upper Mississippi and its tributaries. Its heavily forested floodplains and islands, together with varied river and backwater habitats, support more than 150 species of fish, 50 species of freshwater mussels, 300 species of migratory birds, and uncounted mammals, reptiles, and amphibians, including 10 federally listed endangered or threatened species (Carmody *et al.* 1986).

The upper Mississippi and its tributaries also serve as a major transportation system. The Corps of Engineers operates 26 locks and dams that keep barge traffic moving up and down the Mississippi. Some environmentalists believe that dramatic fish, wildlife, and habitat losses would result from any further increases in barge traffic. Towboat propellers, with total water intakes that match those of the region's hydroelectric plants, kill fish and larvae and increase both water turbidity and stream-bank erosion. Noise and disturbance also alters wildlife behavior, and port development destroys habitat.

For 15 years, Corps plans to expand navigation on the Upper Mississippi have been controversial (Hansen 1986). Replacement and enlargement of Lock and Dam 26 at Alton, Illinois, which effectively controls the rate of barge traffic upriver on the Illinois and Mississippi, was halted by environmental litigation in 1974 but allowed to proceed in 1978 concurrent with development of a master plan for the management of the Upper Mississippi River System. When Congress approved the construction of a second new lock in 1985, it ordered the Corps to develop and implement an environmental management plan for the system, concurrently and on equal fiscal footing with lock construction. Although the Corps has spent close to three-quarters of a billion dollars on the first lock and soon will start constructing the $285 million second lock, the environmental plan, strongly opposed by the Army's Assistant Secretary for Civil Works Robert Dawson, has languished. Late in 1986, an environmental impact statement on the second lock was issued. Conservationists believe the report ignores important adverse impacts that could result from increased barge traffic following lock construction. Congress, in an indication of its lack of faith in previous Corps evaluations of wildlife impacts, authorized as part of the Water Resources Development Act of 1986 the spending of $47 million over the next three years for fish and wildlife habitat studies and improvements on the Upper Mississippi.

Similar unmet fish and wildlife mitigation needs are associated with the biggest of all navigation projects, the Tennessee-Tombigbee Waterway. This 234-mile-long barge canal, built at a cost of $8 million per mile, allows barges traveling the Tennessee River to shortcut toward the Gulf by going down the Tombigbee across west-central Alabama and northeastern Mississippi. Although the project was completed in 1985, wildlife mitigation measures still are pending. The Water Resources Development Act of 1986 authorizes $60 million for restoring wildlife habitat and specifically directs that 88,000 acres be acquired for mitigation. In addition, the act requires in-kind replacement of the 34,000 acres of bottomland hardwoods destroyed by the project. This means the Corps must restore and protect *equivalent* habitats, as opposed to substituting habitat of a different type or undertaking other mitigation measures.

Perhaps the most dramatic incident in which unforeseen project impacts have required extensive correction is found in south Florida. Alterations of the state's natural waterways, including channelization of the Kissimmee River, so disrupted the seasonal flows of water into the Everglades that extensive ecological damage has resulted. To correct this, Congress has authorized a Corps study, now under way, on the feasibility of restoring the river to its pre-water-project, free-flowing state. Although no recommendation has been made by the Corps, the state has installed a temporary dam to conduct experiments on the effect of restoring "natural" water flows.

Some water projects, however, especially newer projects, are notable for creative approaches to mitigation. The recently completed Charles River Project in Massachusetts is an example of the Corps working with nature instead of trying to change it. To prevent flooding on the Charles that would threaten downtown Boston and Cambridge, the Corps bought and preserved some 9,000 acres of upstream meadows and wetlands that help to soak up and hold runoff. The land is managed by the Massachusetts Fisheries and Wildlife Division. Preserving the wetlands has prevented flooding so far, while benefiting wildlife as well (Purcell 1982).

## Economics

Economic issues affecting water projects are numerous and complicated. Because the federal government has paid the entire cost of water projects for flood protection, navigation, and erosion control, project beneficiaries for the most part have been insulated from the costs incurred to meet their water needs. Costs for water-supply projects for agriculture originally were envisioned as being repaid by user fees, but in fact many of these costs have been covered by sales of electricity generated at dams, by including flood control and recreational benefits as project purposes to be paid for by the federal government, and by the very generous terms of water-supply contracts. Typically, these contracts feature low interest rates and long, often repeatedly extended, repayment periods, together with water prices limited by a farmer's ability to pay, so that irrigators typically pay back less than 10 percent of project costs. The central point of water-project economics is that these subsidies encourage construction of many unneeded and environmentally destructive projects that would not be constructed if users had to pay a more realistic share of project costs.

Conservation groups are becoming increasingly sophisticated in water-project economics, because it is in economic considerations that water projects are most vulnerable. More and more frequently, conservationists are joining forces with fiscal conservatives and taxpayer groups to oppose particularly damaging projects. North Dakota's

Garrison Diversion Unit, which would have damaged a dozen national wildlife refuges and tens of thousands of acres of important waterfowl breeding areas, was redesigned and much of the project deauthorized after a protracted battle hinging as much on the project's economic viability as on concerns for wildlife and the environment. Similarly, citizen groups have challenged in court some federal subsidies for Cliff Dam, which would cost $380 million; inundate a stretch of the Verde River, Arizona's only designated wild and scenic river; and destroy nesting habitat of North America's only desert-nesting bald eagles. Citizen groups have documented that the dam's alleged flood-control measures are meant to benefit structures that have not yet been built and that the measures are, in fact, a subsidy to real-estate developers.

In water resources, as in other federal programs, pressure is growing to stop uneconomic practices and reduce or terminate subsidies to special-interest groups. President Jimmy Carter fired the opening salvo in this battle a decade ago when he identified 19 western water projects as too expensive and tried to have them deauthorized. He failed, but until 1986 a *de facto* moratorium halted most new water-project authorizations. Although appropriations for fiscal 1986 were up slightly over 1985, water projects have continued to slip in the competition for scarce federal dollars. Federal funds spent on Corps of Engineers construction work have dropped 78 percent, not counting inflation, since the mid-1960s (Council on Environmental Quality 1985). By the end of fiscal 1986, the Corps had a backlog of 911 authorized projects requiring $28.3 billion to complete. The Corps' entire civil-works budget is about $3 billion yearly (Council on Environmental Quality 1985).

Although Congress authorized nearly 300 new projects in 1986, questions remain about how these projects will be funded.[2] The Water Resources Development Act of 1986 requires project beneficiaries to pay 25 to 50 percent of the costs of new Corps of Engineers projects, and both conservationists and fiscal conservatives continue to advocate improvements in the Bureau of Reclamation's cost-sharing procedures to bring about a similar policy. This should make it more difficult for the boondoggles to survive.

A case in point is the proposed Yazoo pumping station in Mississippi, which would drain 100 square miles of seasonal wetlands — important winter waterfowl habitat — for agriculture. Since the crops to be produced, including cotton, soybeans, and wheat, are only marginally profitable and in surplus already, the additional income gained by benefiting farmers would not be sufficient to cover the station's $187

2. The authorization of water projects and the appropriation of funds for their construction and maintenance are separate legislative processes. Thus it is possible to kill funding for a project in any given year, but leave the project intact.

million cost. The project was supported strongly by potential beneficiaries when it was authorized with the federal government paying 100 percent of its cost. Whether the project will proceed under new rules that will require beneficiaries to pay 25 percent of its cost remains to be seen.

Increased cost sharing on federal water projects has been one of the major policy goals of the Reagan administration. Robert Dawson, assistant secretary of the Army for Civil Works, told the *Journal of Soil and Water Conservation* that cost sharing was critical to the future of federal water-resources programs, adding that new cost-sharing requirements would reduce Corps expenditures in two ways: by reducing the number and size of projects constructed and by reducing the federal cost of each project (Mosher 1986). In addition, cost-sharing requirements will boost nonstructural alternatives for flood control — measures such as moving buildings out of a floodplain or protecting upstream wetlands to hold floodwaters, as opposed to building dams. Under the new law, nonfederal beneficiaries of flood-control dams are required to pay at least five percent of the total project cost in cash during construction. Those who opt for nonstructural alternatives still must share costs, but are not required to pay cash up front.

Two potential outcomes of the trend toward economic efficiency bear careful watching by wildlife interests. One is a possible trend toward state and private construction of high-return projects, such as those that provide municipal/industrial supplies and hydropower generation. These projects pose special problems because they are less subject than federal projects to federal laws spelling out environmental protections. Another potential problem is that as beneficiaries are asked to pay a greater share of project costs, it becomes increasingly difficult to find support for the mitigation and wildlife expenditures which new Corps rules require to be cost-shared on the same basis as project construction. Beneficiaries want the most project for their money and can be expected to balk at "subsidizing" wildlife benefits for the general good.

The trend toward cost sharing coincides with the expiration of the 30-year and 40-year water-supply contracts originally negotiated for many Bureau of Reclamation projects. Many of the agency's earlier projects did not explicitly include wildlife benefits among their purposes, and thus no provision is made for water recipients to pay back wildlife mitigation and management expenditures. The negotiation of new contracts provides an opportunity for the federal government to insert provisions that will mitigate some of the wildlife losses and prevent future losses. Conservationists, however, expect that such provisions will be far from routine and that continuing involvement by wildlife interests, together with cooperation from irrigation districts, will be necessary if they are to be included.

With the federal government less able to provide water for free or at vastly reduced costs, the nature of water development increasingly will be determined by market forces. Urban and industrial users can afford to pay a great deal more for water than can agricultural users. The direct impacts on wildlife of increases in urban water development and decreases in new agricultural development are difficult to assess. A shift to more efficient, urban uses of water will not necessarily mean more water available for instream flows. Urban growth and development may quickly swallow whatever water is saved. Urban development affects a smaller area than agricultural development, but its effects are more intense. The full impact of these economic forces on wildlife habitat can only be guessed.

## Western Water Rights Issues

Over the past 20 years, the West has experienced dramatic growth and change. Increased urbanization, expanding economic development, more need for recreational facilities, and the insistence that environmental values be protected have placed unprecedented demands on the West's water system. Development of new water sources generally has taken precedence over the conservation and efficient use of existing supplies, but the best water-development sites already are developed, and those remaining pose economic and environmental problems. Two things are certain: Growth will continue, and pressures to use water wisely and efficiently will mount (Driver 1986).

Although most water developments in the West have focused on supplying agriculture — in Nevada, California, Texas, Montana, and Arizona, farmers use up to 98 percent of the water supply — farmers and ranchers are finding that their water rights are more valuable than their crops or livestock. As cost of delivering new water supplies escalates, cities and industries have turned to buying farmland in order to secure its water rights. Urban users, who can afford higher rates than farmers, are becoming the prime customers of projects proposed by private developers. In addition, opposition has grown to delivery of federally subsidized water for production of surplus crops (a fifth of U.S. cropland is now withdrawn from production with federal compensation to its owners in efforts to reduce crop surpluses) (Welsh 1985). The first surplus-crop penalty to be attached to a water-project reauthorization was enacted in 1986, and legislation applying this sort of penalty to other projects is expected in the 100th Congress (see Legislative Developments, the Garrison Diversion Reformulation).

The increasing costs of water and the scarcity of new sources to develop also have fueled a movement toward an obvious alternative source: conservation. Present irrigation practices are not geared to conserving water. One reason is that water is provided cheaply so the economic returns for conservation are not sufficient to pay back investments. Also, under the "prior appropriation" doctrine of water law in the western states, incentives for conservation are few. Water rights under this doctrine are granted to those who first use them. These rights can be retained only as long as the water continues to be used. A farmer who withdraws less water than he is entitled to loses his rights to the unused water. Thus, any water saved by one party and allowed to return to a stream will simply become the property of downstream users.

Water from federal projects is priced well below what it would bring on an open market, but a farmer is not allowed to resell any water that might be conserved, so again there is no conservation incentive. Thus, conservationists contend, enormous amounts of water are wasted on every farm, enough to supply several times over all the needs of nearby cities and industries. It has been estimated that a seven to 10 percent reduction in agricultural water use in the West could eliminate the need to supply any "new" water even if all other uses increase by 100 percent (Welsh 1985). The Bureau of Reclamation, however, estimates that only about six percent of total diversions actually are consumed or lost to further use and that massive changes in irrigation systems to promote efficient use would make available less than four percent more water (Engelbert and Scheuring 1985, Willardson 1985).

In 1986, the Western Governors Association adopted a report calling for establishment of economic efficiency as a primary objective in water development. Among the potential benefits cited was "avoidance of building what could be vastly expensive, environmentally damaging water projects" (Driver 1986).

Among the new options recommended by the report are policies facilitating the sale or sharing of water rights, encouraging salvage and conservation of water, coordinating the use of water supplies that can be substituted for each other, and providing adequate alternative supplies of water to holders of senior water rights. The governors recommended broadening the focus of the U.S. Bureau of Reclamation from that of a builder of big water projects to that of an agency that assists the West in improving the efficiency with which Bureau-provided water is used. One area where this concept may be applicable is southern California, which has been taking water from the Colorado River that legally has been allocated to Arizona. Until this year, Arizona did not have the ability to withdraw its share, but with the completion of the Central Arizona Project's Granite Reef Aqueduct, designed to divert Colorado River water into Arizona, the state begun to increase its withdrawals. San Diego, which has drawn some of its municipal water from the Arizona share, will have to find alternate supplies.

The governors' report has prompted creation of a working group of Interior Department officials allied with the governors' association to map out strategies for implementing the recommendations of the report. Another Bureau of Reclamation working group is studying the general issue of conservation, efficiency, and water marketing. Among wildlife interests, these developments have been received with enthusiasm, but also with a certain wariness. Better use of existing water supplies, if it serves to avoid the need for massive new projects, will benefit wildlife. But it remains to be seen whether these water-conservation techniques will themselves be good or bad for wildlife. For example, a farmer who lines irrigation canals to conserve water may eliminate marshes along the canals that have been fed by leakage. And if western water becomes almost literally "liquid gold," it may be harder to ensure that enough is left for streams, wetlands, and other valuable habitat areas.

## Kesterson and Long-term Offsite Impacts

The issue of farm-drainage pollution reached a boil in 1985 when drainage canals from 42,000 acres of California's San Joaquin Valley farmland were closed because of the high selenium content of the water. Selenium is toxic in high concentrations and was linked to significant birth defects and deaths among waterfowl at Kesterson National Wildlife Refuge, where the farm drainage collected. Drainage into the refuge was stopped in June 1986. For background on problems at Kesterson and on toxic contamination of wildlife refuges generally, see the wildlife refuges chapter in this volume and in the *Audubon Wildlife Reports* 1985 and 1986.

Various agencies scurried throughout 1985 and 1986 to study ways to clean up the Kesterson disaster, to find ways to keep farmers from having to shut down, and to avoid similar problems in other areas. Almost all Bureau of Reclamation projects[3] generate drainage and return flows. Eight currently are being studied for potential problems similar to Kesterson's, and 10 more studies are slated to begin in 1987. Still, the San Luis Drain, which carries water to Kesterson, remains a prime example of the wildlife costs incurred when development plans ignore environmental concerns. The Bureau of Reclamation has been sharply criticized for putting the short-term economic benefit of a few irrigators ahead of long-term costs to taxpayers and natural resources. Planners of the irrigation project—the nation's largest—knew that it would create problems because the valley soil is underlain by an impermeable clay layer—like a flowerpot without a hole. Unless

---

3. The number of projects ranges from 220 to 470, depending on how single and multi-featured dams are classified. For example, a multi-feature dam that includes 10 subunits could be tabulated as one or 10 projects.

disposed of, irrigation runoff laden with leached salts and minerals would saturate the plant root zone, poisoning the plants. But, since adding the cost of a drain to the irrigation project would have made the projects cost exceed its benefits, the question of wastewater disposal was deferred and the project built. After irrigation began, pollution problems quickly escalated to emergency proportions. The drainage system, once considered too costly for the original project, became the solution. The Bureau of Reclamation began construction of a drain that would have dumped all runoff into San Francisco Bay's delta region. However, this plan was halted midway to completion because of fears over how the drainwater would affect the delta's water quality. The Bureau of Reclamation subsequently decided to dump the runoff into Kesterson (Mosher 1986).

Aside from potential damage to the delta, the drain had another problem: massive cost overruns that could have amounted to $5,000 per acre of irrigated land, or more than the land was worth. So the builders charged some $30 million to the federal government—by calculating that amount as the value of the wildlife benefits to be realized by creating drainwater wetlands for waterfowl at Kesterson and other areas.

In 1986, attempts were made to reduce the contamination. Congress authorized a plan that requires California's Central Valley Project and State Water Project to be operated in accordance with clean-water standards, thus blocking the discharge of excess toxic contaminants into San Francisco Bay. The plan requires new projects to be preceded by research on soil conditions that could lead to toxic contamination.

### Campaign to Protect the Platte River

Each spring, about 80 percent of the lesser sandhill cranes in North America stop for several weeks along the Platte River in central Nebraska, en route to their breeding grounds in Canada, Alaska, and the Soviet Union. The Platte stopover is vital to crane survival. There the birds rest and feed, obtaining nutrients essential to the completion of migration and breeding. The Platte also is important habitat for large numbers of migrating waterfowl and other birds, including such endangered species as the interior least tern, piping plover, whooping crane, and bald eagle. The river has been designated as critical habitat for whoopers.

The Platte, however, is one of the most intensively used of western rivers. Its waters are withdrawn for irrigation and other uses, returned to the river as runoff, and withdrawn again as many as 18 times over. The river is in a state of decline. Its flows have been depleted by 70 percent from historic levels, and the river has been reduced to 20 percent of its former width in some stretches. Waterfowl have crowded into the remnant habitat in such concentrations that diseases such as avian cholera have become epidemic. Although no new major water projects have been built on the Platte in 16 years, more than a dozen proposed projects are pending. Several have reached the final permitting or funding stage preceding construction.

The National Audubon Society and other wildlife groups have launched a major effort to protect and restore the Platte's habitat. As of late 1986, goals include keeping withdrawals at their current level or lower until a comprehensive plan is developed and implemented to ensure adequate supplies both of water and of the sediments that scour the river's banks. This scouring keeps sandbars clear of the vegetation that otherwise would choke the open wetlands required by cranes.

Projects approaching the final development stage include:

1. Wyoming's proposed dam and reservoir on Deer Creek, a North Platte River tributary near Casper. This is a project for municipal water supplies.
2. The relicensing of the hydropower plant at Kingsley Dam on the Platte.
3. Potential enlargement of the Seminole Reservoir on the North Platte in Wyoming.
4. The Denver Water Board's proposed Two Forks Dam and Reservoir, an urban-supply project on the South Platte just upstream from Denver.
5. The Bureau of Reclamation's congressionally authorized Narrows Dam, an irrigation, flood control, and municipal supply project on the South Platte halfway between Denver and the Nebraska state line. This dam was on President Carter's "hit list" and has been criticized for its similarity, both in design and in the geology of its proposed site, to Teton Dam, the Bureau of Reclamation dam in Idaho that collapsed as its reservoir was being filled in 1976.
6. The Bureau of Reclamation's Prairie Bend project, which would divert Platte River water to recharge the depleted Ogallalla Aquifer. For fiscal year 1987, Congress provided $300,000 for studies of irrigation, instream flow, and sediment on the central Platte.

## LEGISLATIVE DEVELOPMENTS

### The Water Resources Development Act of 1986

On October 17, Congress passed the Water Resources Development Act of 1986, authorizing 262 new dams, ports, and waterway projects with an estimated federal cost of $16.3 billion. The bill establishes new cost-sharing formulas that will increase the amount to be contributed by nonfederal beneficiaries of Corps of Engineers projects, including both newly authorized projects and unconstructed segments of previously authorized projects. This reform is expected to curb both environmental damage and federal spending. Under this bill:

- Nonfederal beneficiaries of harbor-deepening projects will pay a share that increases with the depth of the harbor. The result is likely to be fewer and less extensive harbor projects.
- Inland waterways, which have been constructed at 100 percent federal cost, will be subject to a 50-percent cost share by beneficiaries.
- Wildlife mitigation will have to be carried out *concurrent with* project construction. Mitigation costs are to be shared on the same basis as other project costs, although certain wildlife-enhancement programs carried out for the benefit of the nation as a whole will be paid in full by the federal government.
- Some 300 unbuilt projects, including unconstructed portions of previously authorized projects, with a total authorized cost of $11.1 billion, are deauthorized — including such once hotly debated projects as the Cross Florida Barge Canal and Dickey Dam and Lincoln School Dam in Maine. Lands once acquired for the Cross Florida Barge Canal are to become a conservation area. Provisions have been made for automatic deauthorization of projects authorized by this act if no funds are appropriated within five years. Previously authorized projects also are automatically deauthorized if they go unfunded for 10 years.

The act permits construction to proceed on a number of previously authorized projects whose continued funding had been made conditional upon enactment of cost-sharing reforms. In addition, several special provisions affect wildlife:

- The Interior Department is directed to establish a research and development program to address the overdrafting of the Ogallalla Aquifer, the underground water supply of the central plains.
- The secretary of the Army is directed to study the Corps' capability to conserve fish and wildlife and their habitats, consulting with the heads of resource agencies and reporting to Congress by April 1989. The Corps also is directed to establish an Office of Environmental Policy.
- The act incorporates the Upper Mississippi Management Act of 1986, endorsing the 1982 Master Plan prepared by the Upper Mississippi River Basin Commission as a guideline and authorizing three years of environmental studies.

- In addition, the act provides numerous other fish and wildlife studies and benefits.

## Appropriations

Water-project appropriations for fiscal 1987 passed as part of the continuing resolution enacted October 17. In general, funding for water projects, although up slightly from fiscal 1986, followed a pattern consistent with previous years. The Corps of Engineers' budget for civil works shows a slight shift in balance, with operation and maintenance funds increasing while construction funds decrease. Although specific records are not kept, the Corps estimates that about three and a half percent of its civil works budget is for wildlife-related expenditures, a figure that is relatively constant from year to year. The Bureau of Reclamation analyzes fish and wildlife conservation as a part of the total budget on a year-to-year basis, but the latest year for which figures are available is 1983 (see Table 2 and Table 3).

## The Garrison Reformulation

On May 12, the president signed the Garrison Diversion Unit Reformulation Act of 1986, bringing nearer to a close one of the most acrimonious water-project conflicts in history. Although the full impact of this legislation will depend on the success of its implementation, the reformulation is important for a number of reasons. Not least of these is its symbolic value: One of the biggest, most expensive, most environmentally damaging irrigation projects ever conceived by the Bureau of Reclamation was redesigned to accommodate environmental concerns and the changing needs of the benefiting community. The new project still contains an irrigation element, but will supply water primarily for municipal and industrial uses. The bill contains

**TABLE 2**
**Civil Works Construction and Operations Budgets, U.S. Army Corps of Engineers (in millions of dollars)**

| Year | Construction | Operation and Maintenance | Total[a] |
|------|--------------|---------------------------|----------|
| 1982 | $1,429 | $1,025 | $3,001 |
| 1983 | 1,508 | 1,201 | 3,421 |
| 1984 | 926 | 1,184 | 2,691 |
| 1985 | 955 | 1,307 | 2,901 |
| 1986 | 919 | 1,319 | 2,831 |
| 1987 | 1,152 | 1,389 | 3,135 |

Source: U.S Army Corps of Engineers.
[a]Also includes separate funds for general expenditures, emergencies, revolving fund, and permanent appropriations.

**TABLE 3**
**Annual Funds Available, Bureau of Reclamation (In millions of dollars)**

| Year | Construction | Operation and Maintenance | Total[b] |
|------|-------------|---------------------------|----------|
| 1978 | $545 | $180 | $756 |
| | 41[a] | 4[a] | |
| 1979 | 422 | 158 | 681 |
| | 24.5[a] | 3.7[a] | |
| 1980 | 462 | 167 | 703 |
| | 21.9[a] | 3.7[a] | |
| 1981 | 587 | 180 | 871 |
| | 32.6[a] | 4.8[a] | |
| 1982 | 544 | 208 | 853 |
| | 29.3[a] | 4.4[a] | |
| 1983 | 579 | 150 | 858 |
| (partial) | 39.6[a] | 3.2[a] | |

Source: Budget Office, U.S. Bureau of Reclamation.
[a]Amount represents funds for fish and wildlife.
[b]Includes additional funds not identified on chart, e.g. discretionary funds, etc.

significant reforms of the type that conservationists have long been trying to make standard procedure. And the project's potential adverse impact on the prairie wetlands of North Dakota—essential habitat for millions of migratory birds—has been vastly reduced (National Audubon Society 1986).

The change came about as a result of negotiations with state officials and congressional representatives initiated in 1984 by the National Audubon Society, which for more than a decade had led the fight to stop the project. Construction was about to begin on one of Garrison's most controversial features—a dam at one end of the Lonetree Valley, a key wildlife area. As a result of the negotiations, Congress passed legislation that year that continued funding for the project but required the secretary of the Interior to convene a special commission to determine whether the Garrison project adequately served North Dakota's contemporary water supply needs and, if not, to develop an alternative project. The commission made its recommendations in December 1984. The legislation enacted 17 months later was based on those recommendations and subsequent negotiations.

The reformulation bill:

- shifts project emphasis away from irrigation and toward municipal and industrial supplies, deauthorizing some 850,000 acres of planned irrigation and reducing the number of acres included in project construction components from 250,000 to roughly 100,000, and provides that municipal and industrial supply features will be built first;
- establishes a federal- and state-funded Wetlands Trust to protect, enhance, restore, and manage prairie-pothole wetlands;

- creates a "surplus-crops-production charge" to be levied on farmers who use project water to grow crops that the secretary of Agriculture has determined to be in surplus, the charge is 10 percent of the *full* cost of delivering water; if a similar charge were applied to all proposed Bureau of Reclamation projects, a number of them would most likely lose local support;
- establishes explicit limits on appropriations for individual project components (the usual practice is establishing overall spending limits for projects but not specific limits for individual components);
- does not allow automatic increases in authorization ceilings in order to meet higher costs caused by inflation; the new procedure requires project sponsors to come back to Congress to have spending ceilings raised as the project proceeds, thus building in opportunities for periodic review by authorizing committees;[4]
- authorizes creation of a new national wildlife refuge to protect outstanding wildlife resources in the Kraft Slough area, avoids many of the massive effects of reservoirs and irrigation, and requires acre-for-acre mitigation of wildlife-habitat losses, concurrent with or in advance of project construction.

Garrison has been called a unique case. But a similar negotiation process taking place at the same time as the latest phase of the Garrison reformulation has resulted in a proposal to reformulate the O'Neill irrigation project. This project, located on the Niobrara River in Nebraska, was designed to supply irrigation water to 77,000 acres in an area where groundwater levels are declining. Criticisms of that project are similar to criticisms of Garrison: it is outmoded, too costly, too environmentally destructive. Project backers now have agreed to scrap the project's $407 million Norden Dam and substitute a $200 million groundwater recharge system.

### California-Nevada Interstate Compact, S.2457

The Senate Judiciary Committee's Constitution Subcommittee considered but did not report S.2457, which would grant consent of Congress to a compact to allocate for agricultural and other uses water from the Lake Tahoe basin, the Truckee River basin, and two adjacent watersheds. The dispute that this legislation proposed to settle is one of the longest in reclamation history, arising from the Bureau of Reclamation's first water-diversion project, begun in 1905. This project

---

4. When Garrison was reauthorized in 1965, its approved cost was $204 million. By 1986, however, the estimated cost to complete the project was $1.6 billion. This was considered within the authorized limit because the limit was "indexed," i.e. allowed to increase automatically with inflation.

diverted the waters of the Truckee River, which flows out of Lake Tahoe and into the arid Great Basin of western Nevada, to the Carson River to supply irrigation. Lakes that had received the Truckee's waters were altered drastically. Winnemucca Lake, a rich wildlife habitat and national wildlife refuge, was dry by 1938 and was removed from the National Wildlife Refuge System in 1966. Pyramid Lake's level declined some 80 feet. Its native cutthroat trout became extinct in the 1940s.

At the center of the present controversy is the cui-ui, a sucker-like fish found only in Pyramid Lake (see the cui-ui chapter in this volume). Conservationists want provisions added to any water-allocation compact to ensure adequate allocations for the survival of Pyramid Lake and its fish and other wildlife and of the surrounding wetlands of Carson Lake and Stillwater National Wildlife Refuge. The compact, ratified by California and Nevada in 1970, was opposed by environmental groups when it was presented for Congressional ratification. Conservationists say the compact has not been reviewed and made consistent with federal environmental-protection laws. Also they say it subordinates federal water rights and wildlife interests to state and local decisions and does not provide for protection of endangered and threatened species (Defenders *et al.* 1986). With the failure of this bill in the 99th Congress and the retirement of its chief sponsor, Senator Paul Laxalt (R-NV), prospects for ratification of this compact appeared dim.

## H.R. 3113, Coordinated Operating Agreement on State Water Project and Central Valley Project

This law, in addition to requiring that Central Valley irrigation projects be operated in accordance with California water-quality standards for discharge into San Francisco Bay and the San Joaquin/Sacramento delta, reauthorizes the Small Reclamation Projects Act of 1956, which provides loans to nonfederal entities for the construction and operation of small reclamation projects. H.R. 3113 raises ceiling on federal funds authorized for loans from $600 million to $1.2 billion. The law also diverts the program policy from one of dam construction to one of rehabilitation and betterment of existing projects. The bill also requires that soil surveys be conducted to determine the potential for toxic runoff before a project is undertaken and limits the amount of water that can be used to produce surplus crops (irrigation of more than 320 acres of such crops will require repayment on water contracts at market interest rates, while the first 320 acres is interest free). Another title of the act establishes an agreement for the preservation of Suisun Marsh, an important wildlife area.

## LEGAL DEVELOPMENTS

### The Public Trust Doctrine

The courts have been the primary arena for the emergence of a powerful tool for the protection of environmental and wildlife values threatened by water-project development: the public trust doctrine, which provides that the the states hold title to all tidelands and navigable waters in trust for the benefit of the people (Connors 1986). A number of recent court decisions (*Marks v. Whitney*, [491 P. 2d 374 Cal. 1971], *National Audubon Society v. Superior Court of Alpine County*, [104 S. Ct. 413 Cal. 1983], and others) have broadened the applicability of the doctrine. Traditionally, it has limited the states' ability to permit their lands and waters to be used in such a way as to impair commerce, navigation, or fishing. More recently, the public trust doctrine has been interpreted by the courts as conferring upon the states duties to protect aesthetic, recreational, and ecological values. In the Mono Lake case, *National Audubon Society v. Superior Court of Alpine County*, the California Supreme Court held that the California Division of Natural Resources and the Los Angeles Department of Water and Power should not have licensed water diversions from streams feeding Mono Lake — a scenic water body and important bird nesting area — because the diversion reduced the lake's area by a third, thus endangering scenic and zoological values. The case is even more significant because it extended the public trust doctrine to nonnavigable waters when actions affecting them also affect navigable waters downstream. Mono Lake itself is navigable, but the tributary streams affected by the diversions are not.

### Current Litigation

No precedent-setting water-project cases with direct impacts on wildlife were decided in 1986. A number of cases on water rights (for example, *Wyoming v. Nebraska*, over rights to Platte River water, and *Sierra Club v. Block*, a case that involves securing water rights for wilderness areas) are pending, and a number of water-project proposals (Cliff Dam in Arizona, the Dolores River Project in Colorado) are in litigation on procedural and other grounds.

## REFERENCES

Adams, John H., L.C. Dunlap, J.D. Hair, F.D. Krupp, J. Lorenz, J.M. McCloskey, R.W. Peterson, P.C. Pritchard, W. A. Turnage, and K. Wendelowski. 1985. *An Environmental Agenda for the Future*. Agenda Press. Washington, D.C. 155 pp.

Bouchard, Carl E. 1986. Program Status of PL 83-566 Land Treatment Projects. Paper presented at 1986 summer meeting, American Society of Agricultural Engineers. California Polytechnic Institute. San Luis Obispo, California.

Carmody, Gail A., G. Bade, and J.L. Rasmussen. 1986. Fish and Wildlife Coordination Act Report for Lock and Dam 26 (Replacement), Second Lock, Draft EIS. Prepared for U.S. Army Corps of Engineers, St. Louis District. U.S. Fish and Wildlife Service. Rock Island, Illinois.

Connors, Donald L. 1986. The Public Trust Doctrine: A Primer for the 1980s. Unpublished manuscript. 32 pp.

Council on Environmental Quality. 1985. *Environmental Quality 1984: The Fifteenth Annual Report of the Council on Environmental Quality*. U.S. Government Printing Office. Washington, D.C. 719 pp.

Defenders of Wildlife, Environmental Defense Fund, Environmental Policy Institute, Natural Resources Defense Council, National Audubon Society, Northern California Council of the Federation of Fly Fishers, and Sierra Club. 1986. Statement before the Constitution Subcommittee of the Senate Committee on the Judiciary. July 15, 1986.

Driver, Bruce. 1986. *The Report to the Western Governors' Association from the Water Efficiency Task Force*. 81 pp.

Getches, David H. 1984. *Water Law in a Nutshell*. West Publishing Company. St. Paul, Minnesota. 439 pp.

Englebert, Ernest A. and A.F. Scheuring. 1985. *Water Scarcity Impacts on Western Agriculture*. University of California Press. Berkeley, California.

Hansen, Paul. 1986. White Papers on Upper Mississippi River System. Izaak Walton League of America, Inc. Arlington, Virginia.

Mosher, Lawrence. 1986. "Federal Water Development: Going, Going . . .," *Journal of Soil and Water Conservation*: 164-166. Ankeny, Iowa. May/June.

National Audubon Society. 1986. Correspondence with Members of House Interior Committee on Garrison Diversion Unit. Letters dated March 18, 1986.

National Water Commission. 1973. *Water Policies for the Future*. U.S. Government Printing Office. Washington, D.C. 579pp.

Purcell, David. 1982. "Towns find new ways to foil floods," *Christian Science Monitor*:1. November 30.

Reisner, Marc. 1986. *Cadillac Desert: The American West and its Disappearing Water*. Viking Penguin Books. New York. 582 pp.

U.S. Department of the Army, Corps of Engineers. 1977. The U.S. Army Corps of Engineers and the Environment. Document EP-360-1-10. 16pp.

U.S. Department of the Army, Corps of Engineers. 1984. Document ER-1105-2-50. Planning: Environmental Resources. Washington, D.C.

U.S. Department of the Interior, Bureau of Reclamation. 1986. Release No. 376-26, Transmittal of Reclamation Instructions, Chapter 13, Fish and Wildlife Coordination Act.

U.S. Office of Management and Budget. 1985. "Supplement to Special Analysis D, A Report required by the Federal Capital Investment Program Information Act of 1984 (Title II of Public Law 98-501)," in *Environmental Quality 1984: The Fifteenth Annual Report of the Council on Environmental Quality*. U.S. Government Printing Office. Washington, D.C. 719 pp.

Welsh, Frank. 1985. *How to Create a Water Crisis*. Johnson Books. Boulder, Colorado. 238 pp.

Willardson, L.S. 1985. "Basin-wide impacts of irrigation efficiency," *Journal of Irrigation and Drainage Engineering* 3:241-246. Vol. III.

*Ruth Norris, a former editor of* Audubon *magazine, is now publications editor for* The Nature Conservancy International.

Herders fasten rubber collars filled with deadly Compound 1080 to sheep. Coyotes are supposed to be killed if they attack the livestock. *U.S. Fish and Wildlife Service*

# The Federal Animal Damage Control Program

Ruth Norris

## OVERVIEW

When people establish homes, farms, and livestock in territory occupied by wildlife, conflicts often arise. Deer, rabbits, and squirrels consume garden produce, ornamental plants, and agricultural crops. Blackbirds eat cultivated corn, sunflowers, and rice. Geese eat winter wheat. Beaver dams can cause flooding. Birds may be an aviation hazard at airports. Diseases such as rabies can be transmitted by skunks and raccoons. Livestock may be taken by predators, and domestic pets may be injured or killed as well.

Prevention and control of wildlife damage generally is considered an essential part of wildlife management, but as practiced by federal and state governments, it often is a source of considerable controversy. The federal animal damage control (ADC) program's cost-effectiveness is not supported by data. Conservationists have criticized the federal ADC program for its emphasis on lethal animal controls rather than on nonlethal and preventive means of avoiding wildlife damage. Its heavy emphasis on coyote control brings charges that the program functions as a subsidy to the wool industry. Inhumane means of controlling and killing problem wildlife have come under fire from animal rights

Audubon Wildlife Report 1987

groups. Opposition to the highly toxic and slow-acting poisons used to kill predators and rodents is particularly intense, primarily because these poisons kill other wildlife in addition to the intended targets.

In the past two years, controversy has flared up over which agency should be responsible for carrying out federal ADC activities. By appropriating ADC funds to the Agriculture Department rather than the Interior Department in the continuing resolution of December 19, 1985, Congress moved the federal program from the U.S. Fish and Wildlife Service (FWS) to the U.S. Department of Agriculture's Animal and Plant Health Inspection Service (APHIS). Observers on both sides of the issue predicted major changes in federal activities when the program was moved from an agency whose primary mission is wildlife management to one whose primary mission is the protection of agricultural interests. To date, however, no major changes have materialized.

In determining what the future directions of the animal damage control program will be, APHIS faces a variety of challenges. Crop and livestock producers seek increased federal assistance in controlling damage by such animals as blackbirds, wolves, bears, coyotes, and beavers. Increasing numbers of urban, suburban, and rural residents also expect help and advice (Bromley 1985). The groups who argued most forcefully for the transfer of ADC to the Agriculture Department — primarily western livestock producers — anticipate greater responsiveness to their needs. However, because some of the programs most important to them, such as predator control, are opposed strongly by conservationists, increases in ADC funding may be difficult to obtain. Furthermore, some problems have no readily acceptable solutions regardless of the agency dealing with them. Blackbirds, for example, cause significant crop depredations. Destroying roosts merely moves the birds to another location, and also drives away other, desirable bird species. Killing blackbirds in large numbers has provoked intense public outcry.

The Animal Damage Control Act of 1931 authorizes and directs the federal government to develop techniques for the control of injurious wildlife on public and private land. In accordance with the provisions of the act, animal control is carried out by the federal government only at the request of states, communities, or private individuals, and then under a cooperative, cost-sharing program. The federal budget for these activities at the time of the transfer to APHIS was about $20 million yearly. This generally is estimated to be about half the annual public expenditure on animal damage control, with additional efforts carried out and funded by private citizens and organizations. ADC programs apply to the control of vertebrate anmals only. Additional millions are spent by other agencies, such as the

Division of Plant Protection and Quarantine, on control of insects and other pests.

Historically, ADC programs in the eastern states have centered on extension education — teaching people about wildlife and helping them cope with whatever problems they may experience. On a local scale, nuisances created by animals such as birds, beavers, bats, and snakes can be controlled by such habitat alterations as fencing, clearing, or thinning vegetation; closing entrance holes; and stopping people who may have been feeding or otherwise attracting the wildlife that has become a nuisance. In cases of crop damage, states or counties may issue permits for the removal or killing of the offending animal, while extension agents teach and recommend effective techniques for accomplishing these tasks. In the western states, crop and livestock producers have turned to government agents not just for advice but for practical solutions. ADC programs in western states conduct trapping, poisoning, and other control operations. Extension assistance is supplied when appropriate, but lethal control of individuals and of local wildlife populations by government ADC agents has been the major element of these programs.

For detailed information about the history and legal background of animal damage control, please see the *Audubon Wildlife Report 1985.*

## CURRENT DEVELOPMENTS

### Transfer from Interior to Agriculture

Although many conservation groups have been critical of how FWS handled the animal damage control program, most strenuously objected to the transfer to the Department of Agriculture. They believe that ADC belongs in an agency administered primarily for wildlife management, rather than in one organized to support agriculture and in which wildlife has seldom received attention except as an afterthought. It is too early to draw conclusions about the long-term impacts of the shift, but no wholesale program changes have been apparent. ADC programs were transferred largely intact in a four-month transition period, with 530 employees transferring directly from FWS to APHIS. Administration was consolidated: Where FWS operated from seven regional offices, APHIS established two, one in Denver and one in Nashville, Tennessee. The federal wildlife research center, which provides research assistance to the ADC program, remains in Denver, although it, too, has been moved from FWS to APHIS.

When the program was moved, APHIS continued FWS policies and regulations, but began a systematic review to study and implement changes as needed. Manuals are being reviewed and revised as necessary. The difference in APHIS versus FWS administration, says the APHIS assistant deputy administrator for ADC, "is likely to be in the level of congressional support. FWS used the ADC program to further more general wildlife goals. With a return to the basic function of protecting livestock, crops, other resources, and health and safety, we'll probably see more direct support, particularly since we now have Agriculture Department people working directly with congressional agriculture and agriculture appropriations committees, rather than interior and interior appropriations committees. Also, we're much more lean in administrative structure than ADC was in the FWS. What we save we put back into the program, so there's an incentive to be efficient."

APHIS will appoint a national ADC advisory committee with representatives from various groups interested in animal damage control, including producers, conservationists, and academics. The committee, chaired by the assistant secretary for Marketing and Inspection Services, with the APHIS administrator as executive secretary, will provide policy advice to the secretary of Agriculture. It is similar in structure and function to a number of advisory committees serving Agriculture Department agencies. APHIS officials see this committee as a major policy initiative to improve participation by interested and affected parties. They expect the committee to serve as the major public forum for raising issues concerning ADC activities.

APHIS national technical support staff, to include 10 or 11 biologists, statisticians, and specialists in pesticides and other technical areas, is headed by Dr. Dale A. Wade, hired in September from Texas A&M University. All ADC programs will be analyzed by this staff for environmental, biological, and economic feasibility considerations.

ADC activities will be coordinated by a policy group composed of agencies within the Agriculture Department: the Forest Service, Extension Service, Agricultural Research Service, Economic Research Service, and Cooperative State Research Service. This group will define the role each organization will play in ADC activities and will advise the ADC administrator on policy matters.

When ADC was conducted by the Interior Department, the Agriculture Department conducted a complementary program through its Cooperative Extension Service[1] and research services. The Extension Service distributed educational materials, provided information

---

1. The Cooperative Extension Service is an "extension" of the land-grant university in each state. Its employees include university faculty (specialists) and professional agents in every county in every state.

about regulations affecting wildlife management and damage control, interpreted research, and demonstrated control techniques to an audience of landowners and managers. The Extension Service, even after the ADC shift to the Department of Agriculture, has no regulatory responsibility and does not actually conduct ADC operations. Clients seeking professional assistance in controlling wildlife are referred to private trappers, exterminators, and other commercial services, or to state and federal ADC programs. Although Extension supports lethal control methods, including the use of traps and registered poisons, Extension agents generally stress preventive control measures. In many cases, this involves nothing more than informing landowners that the species they are concerned about does not cause significant problems (Byford 1985). When serious problems exist, the Extension agent often can show the landowner how to control the problem without killing wildlife — for example, by using large helium-filled balloons and other devices to frighten flocks of depredating birds away from grainfields or by improving livestock husbandry to avoid losses to predators.

Conservationists have argued that Extension's preventative approach to animal damage control ought to replace the ADC program's traditional emphasis on lethal controls. One of the main advantages of an Extension approach from a public-expense point of view is that it requires fewer employees and is less costly than direct control services. Moreover, because under the Extension approach time and equipment costs are borne by the beneficiary, a built-in incentive to reduce cost helps limit control to cases in which it is most needed and cost effective (U.S. Fish and Wildlife Service 1978). However, ADC officials state that although extension assistance is useful under certain conditions, such assistance cannot adequately address damage problems resulting from overpopulations of depredating animals or damage problems in which prevention would be too costly.

As the ADC programs are integrated within the Agriculture Department, questions arise as to the balance that can be struck between lethal and preventative damage controls. Several trends, in addition to increased federal funding, suggest that the direct federal role in wildlife damage control will increase in coming years. Among these trends are the movement of urban people into rural settings, with concurrent increases in human/wildlife conflicts; expansion of wildlife populations into new habitats in urban and suburban environments; emergence of the coyote as a prominent predator in the East; and dramatic changes in agricultural technology, causing shifts in production patterns that will open new areas of potential conflict. For example, advances in technology have made it possible to grow specialty crops, such as grapes and Christmas trees, in previously uncultivated desert areas of Texas and Arizona.

Recent developments in eastern states indicate that federal activities may concentrate even more on cooperative operational programs. Pennsylvania, Wisconsin, Louisiana, and other states where the federal role so far has been primarily advisory have requested cooperative programs. In these states, the primary problems include control of blackbirds, starlings, and birds that cause safety problems at airports; beavers that transmit giardia, damage forests, and dam and flood roadways, levees, and other structures; and coyotes that prey on livestock. As of late 1986, cooperative agreements for federal coyote control had been signed by New York and New Hampshire, and interest in concluding such agreements was expressed by Maine and Virginia. In addition, federal agents had begun trapping coyotes in West Virginia.

ADC staff foresee no major expansion of their programs or budgets to accommodate these additional programs, but envision, rather, a shifting of focus within existing or slightly expanded limits. A major reason for this shift of focus is that the Department of Agriculture's ADC managers see their mission in a somewhat different context than did their FWS predecessors. Also, the rapid and fundamental changes in American agriculture are making it possible to introduce new crops and livestock into areas where they were not previously considered suitable and creating a potential for increased animal-damage problems. Moreover, farmers and ranchers are tending to consider risk management more carefully and to analyze probable costs and benefits of production. In some cases, this may mean a more realistic factoring in of the inevitable cost of doing business in wildlife territories and, perhaps, a scaling back of production schemes that require arduous ADC efforts to survive. In other cases, particularly where established production patterns are suffering from low profitability, the result is likely to be continued and increased reliance on federal ADC programs.

## Predator Control

***The Philosophical Debate.*** The most bitterly fought controversy involving ADC operations centers on the predator-control program, which for 70 years has attempted to protect livestock, primarily sheep, by killing tens of thousands of coyotes and other predators in western states each year (Wilson 1985). Every lethal method has been used against the coyote: trapping, snaring, aerial hunting, denning (killing adults and pups in their dens), and poisoning with such compounds as strychnine, sodium cyanide, and sodium monofluoroacetate (Compound 1080). When FWS in 1978 prepared an in-depth analysis of coyote management in the West, it estimated that in the previous fiscal year, its agents killed 83,790 coyotes at an average cost of $75.82 per coyote (U.S. Fish and Wildlife Service 1978). Today, killing one coyote by shooting it from a helicopter can cost several hundred dollars.

Over the past two decades, none of these efforts has significantly reduced either coyote numbers or coyote depredations, although ADC officials point out that no method exists to demonstrate what coyote populations might have been in the absence of ADC. Coyote populations remain high even in the face of stringent controls because coyotes have the reproductive capacity to recover rapidly after population reductions occur. Consequently, control of coyote depredations is rarely successful for a long period of time when the basic problem is vulnerable livestock. As long as the emphasis of control efforts is on removing and killing individual animals, controls must be repeated each time surviving coyotes fill the niches left by those removed.

"Coyote control is at best an excessively optimistic proposition," rancher/author Glen Martin recently wrote in *Audubon*. "Even at the height of the most aggressive control measures—bait stations heavily dosed with thallium sulfate or 1080, and aerial hunting—coyotes continued to expand in both range and numbers. The base number of coyotes may never be reduced significantly. But it does appear that aggressive control can check troublesome coyote populations on a restricted regional basis so that domestic livestock or affected wildlife are offered some relief" (Martin 1985). Some critics disagree even with that assessment, insisting that proper livestock husbandry, together with acceptance of the notion that loss levels simply may be a part of the cost of doing business in coyote country, is the answer to the predator-control problem.

The predator-control issue can be seen as a tug of war between the western sheep industry and the wildlife, environmental, and humane community. Sheepmen contend that coyotes are putting them out of business, that coyote populations and livestock losses to coyotes are increasing dramatically, and that poisons as well as shooting and trapping should be employed in the battle against coyotes. Environmentalists, on the other hand, contend that declines in the sheep industry have not been caused by predators; that coyote populations and total sheep losses have remained stable since the poison ban; that existing methods of control, coupled with better livestock husbandry, can control losses adequately; and that nontarget species are likely to be killed by poisons.

The public at large is strongly opposed to the use of toxicants and highly critical of the predator-control program in general. A survey conducted in 1979 by Yale University professor Stephen Kellert for FWS revealed that 92 percent of the informed general public disapproved of the use of slow-acting poisons for predator control if other animals in addition to coyotes might be killed, even though poisons were the least expensive method of control (Wilson 1985). Another option, "Shoot or trap as many coyotes as possible," was disapproved by 62 percent of the general public.

The persistence of the federal predator-control program despite heavy opposition among nonfarming members of the public and relatively low interest by members of Congress outside the western states can be explained in part by the political power of the sheep industry in the West. Sheep owners apply pressure to their elected representatives who in turn keep up the pressure for ADC predator-control activities and for the approval of lethal poisons by the Environmental Protection Agency.[2] Another part of the explanation is historical. Until recently, predators were considered worthless varmints that destroyed valuable animals. Hardly anyone opposed killing them. The Animal Damage Control Act of 1931 called for eradication of coyotes, a goal the Agriculture Department, which then had charge of the program, thought it could accomplish in a decade if it were given a million dollars a year. The department got its appropriations, but the coyote proved difficult to eradicate. Still, the statutory goal technically remains. Although the 1931 act has been effectively modified by subsequent laws such as the Endangered Species Act, it remains in force despite dramatic changes in public opinion (Wilson 1985).

## Lethal Versus Nonlethal Controls

Conservation and humane groups continue to advocate increased reliance on nonlethal predator-control methods, which include use of guarding dogs, fencing, improved husbandry practices, and taste aversion.[3] One oft-cited example of success with this approach is the Kansas animal damage control program, which since 1968 has been operated by the state Cooperative Extension Service. Kansas is a major agricultural and livestock producing state, with some 1.7 million calves born yearly and a sheep population of some 250,000 ewes. Unlike most western states, Kansas has an increasing number of sheep producers and one of the lowest rates of livestock losses to coyotes in the nation.

The Kansas ADC program concentrates on training farmers and ranchers to cope with their own problems — by killing depredating animals where appropriate, but primarily by avoiding losses through good husbandry. Farmers are encouraged to keep sheep in lighted pens at night, to dispose of carcasses properly, to avoid lambing in pastures,

2. The Environmental Protection Agency, as the federal agency in charge of pesticide registration, has authority over the pesticide compounds used for animal damage control. Under the Federal Insecticide, Fungicide, and Rodenticide Act, chemicals may be cleared for use throughout the country, subject to label limitations and state restrictions (under Section 3); for time-limited experimental use (under Section 5); and for emergency uses (Section 18) and special local needs (Section 24c).

3. Treating "prey" animals with chemicals such as lithium chloride, which will make coyotes ill and cause them to avoid similar prey.

and to use guard animals. The annual cost of providing these training services is $60,000, about five percent of what neighboring Oklahoma spends annually on its ADC program. The explanation, says the director of the Kansas program, is that *animal* control as practiced in Oklahoma and other states is the wrong approach. *Damage* control is what the Kansas program stresses. "It comes down to husbandry," he says. "You can't control coyote numbers. You can train people who raise sheep how to avoid coyote losses. But if you tell them they can call in a government trapper to kill coyotes whenever they have a problem, they're not going to pay attention to husbandry."

***The 1080 Controversy.*** In the past few years, a major issue in predator control has been the lifting of a long-standing federal ban on the use of sodium monofluoroacetate, better known as Compound 1080, to kill predators. An extremely toxic, colorless, odorless, and tasteless poison, 1080 was used widely for coyote control in the West before being banned by the Nixon administration in 1972 because it killed foxes, hawks, eagles, and many other nontarget animals in addition to coyotes, including many endangered species. While the environmental community has not been in total agreement on the overall issue of predator control, opposition to use of 1080 as a predacide has been nearly unanimous, including sportsmen's groups such as the National Wildlife Federation, the Izaak Walton League, and the humane-oriented Friends of Animals.

In 1985, the Environmental Protection Agency reregistered Compound 1080 for use in livestock protection collars. A fuller account of the controversy leading up to this decision can be found in the *Audubon Wildlife Report 1985*. Major events were as follows.

In 1981, livestockmen succeeded in persuading Interior Secretary James Watt and Environmental Protection Agency Administrator Anne Gorsuch Burford to reopen the case on 1080, claiming there was substantial new evidence about 1080 since the 1972 ban which would justify its resurrection as a predacide. In 1982, a federal judge ruled that there was no justification for reversing the ban on "bait stations" (poisoned carcasses set out to kill whatever came along to feed on them). But, the judge said, use of 1080 in single-lethal-dose (SLD) baits and toxic collars might help farmers in certain areas.[4]

Through 1984 and 1985, environmentalists appealed this decision, which was substantially upheld in September 1985 by the U.S. Court of Appeals in Denver. This opened the way for the states to train and certify ranchers to use the collars with certain restrictions, such as

4. The toxic collar is a rubber pouch containing 1080 in liquid form, which is placed around the neck of target animals. The theory is that since coyotes usually attack the neck of sheep or lambs, they will receive a lethal dose. SLD baits are small cubes of meat or fat containing a lethal dose—three to five milligrams—of 1080.

disposal of damaged or leaking collars and regulated monitoring of collared sheep. A Defenders of Wildlife survey conducted in the summer of 1986 showed that while only Wyoming had approved use of toxic collars, Idaho, Montana, Nebraska, Texas, and both Dakotas were planning to approve use, and Alaska, Nevada, Oklahoma, Tennessee, Virginia, West Virginia, Washington, Arizona, and Utah were considering such a move (Defenders 1986).

Use of 1080 in SLD baits has been more controversial, and additional litigation has occurred over how much 1080 should be contained in one SLD bait. With this and other assorted problems, some observers now believe the SLD may never be used against coyotes. An APHIS official said in November 1986 that not enough research has been completed to meet EPA data requirements for registration of 1080 in single-lethal-dose baits. Emergency use of 1080 in SLD baits has been allowed for control of rabid feral cats on Guam and to control Arctic foxes preying on the endangered Aleutian Canada geese on Kiska Island, Alaska. Some environmentalists expressed fear that bald eagles would be among the victims of SLD baits on Kiska Island, but in the first year of use, no eagles were killed.[5]

Compound 1080 currently is registered for use in rodent control in all states and for use against prairie dogs, ground squirrels, meadow mice, deer mice, wood rats, and chipmunks in California, Colorado, Nevada, and Oregon. Although no legal challenges have been brought against continued rodenticidal use of 1080, controversy has flared because when used against rodents, 1080 has posed a lethal threat to endangered species such as the black-footed ferret. Also, Compound 1080 legally obtained for rodent control was used illegally in Wyoming in the mid-1970s for predator control.

## Leghold Trap Ban

Some humane and animal rights groups still seek to ban the leghold trap, arguing that it causes unnecessary suffering and kills too many nontarget animals. No federal legislative activity occurred on this issue in 1986, but state legislatures, as in New York, have considered trap bans. Research published in 1986 tended to show that one alternative to the standard leghold trap, a padded version, did cause fewer leg and foot injuries to trapped animals but was somewhat less effective than the standard trap (Linhart *et al.* undated, Olson *et al.* 1986).

5. Responsibility for ADC activities aimed at protecting endangered species and other wildlife was a source of some controversy immediately after the ADC transfer to the Agriculture Department. APHIS at first took the position that those duties remained with FWS, but it was determined that legislative language had in fact placed responsibility for all ADC activities in APHIS.

**Research**

ADC research is conducted by the Denver Wildlife Research Center, a former FWS unit moved to the Department of Agriculture with the rest of the ADC program. The research program provides APHIS and the public with the means for reducing wildlife damage to crops and other resources and helps transfer existing technology to broader uses in animal damage control. Research activities include assessing damage caused by wildlife, laboratory and field studies of damaging species, and development and testing of chemical, physical, biological, and cultural methods for minimizing damages and health-related hazards. The program is organized into three branches: the Wildlife Damage Branch, which develops techniques to control problems caused by birds and nonpredatory mammals; the Branch of Predator Studies, which researches the coyote and methods for its control; and the Research Support Branch, which provides computing, library, statistical, and scientific services.

A high priority in the Wildlife Damage Branch is development of an effective toxicant to kill grain-depredating blackbirds at their roost sites. The work of this branch also includes evaluation of wildlife depredations on agricultural crops, rangelands, forests, livestock feeds, and residential and industrial facilities, and development and testing of methods for control of these depredations.

The Branch of Predator Studies has a staff of 22 and a budget of $1.2 million. This includes some funding passed on to outside agencies for designated projects: $90,000 to Hampshire College in Massachusetts for a study of sheep-guarding dogs and $90,000 to Arizona State University for studies of nonlethal coyote controls in three western states. This branch has three sections: Depredations Control, Chemical Methods Research and Evaluation, and Ecology and Behavior. Its employees study control methods including poisons, scare devices, traps, fences, and taste aversion. About 60 percent of the research center's in-house work is devoted to lethal controls and 40 percent to nonlethal controls. However, the center includes trapping in the nonlethal category, even though trapping is ultimately lethal. Adding in work performed by outside consultants and universities, the balance is closer to 50-50, but still favors lethal controls.

APHIS has requested assistance from the American Society of Testing and Materials to review current ADC research and evaluate additional research needs and priorities.[6] To meet this purpose, the Society has convened a Vertebrate Control Agents task force, open to anyone affected by and interested in the ADC program. In addition,

6. ASTM, headquartered in Philadelphia, is a nonprofit corporation for the development of voluntary consensus standards for materials, products, systems, and services.

recommendations on research priorities have been sought from state ADC directors and will be sought from the Agriculture Department's national ADC advisory committee. Critics of the ADC research program conducted by FWS have welcomed this review and reevaluation as long overdue. However, some skepticism exists about the effectiveness of the Agriculture Department's advisory committees in general, and at the end of 1986 the ADC committee had not been appointed and no meeting was scheduled.

Problems not yet adequately addressed by ADC research include:

***Difficulties in Gathering Loss Data.*** Federal ADC officials are unable to provide data showing whether livestock and crop losses to predators and birds are increasing or decreasing. In the western states, where most of the very large sheep flocks are raised, keeping accurate loss statistics is difficult even for trained researchers, who must rely on information supplied by farmers and ranchers themselves. Most ranchers do not keep written records on losses or what causes them. Large numbers of sheep and lambs simply disappear. Often, losses are blamed on predators even when weather, disease, theft, accidents, or other causes may be to blame. A few case studies show that coyote control can reduce livestock losses effectively in specific situations, but these are acknowledged to be atypical cases and are too few in number to permit statistically meaningful generalizations (U.S. Fish and Wildlife Service 1978).

***Killing of Nontarget Species.*** Bobcats, foxes, badgers, skunks, opossums, raccoons, porcupines, dogs, cats, deer, bears, raptors, and other migratory birds — to name a few — have been captured accidentally or killed by control measures taken against other species. While data documenting the number of nontarget animals killed is collected at the state level, it is infrequently compiled into meaningful regional or national reports. The only comprehensive report on the subject is a 1979 FWS environmental impact statement on the ADC program (Elfring 1985).

Proponents of poisons such as Compound 1080 often point out that few cases of nontarget poisonings are documented. But this is to be expected, given that very little time and effort has been devoted to searching for and analyzing carcasses of nontarget species. Moreover, until recently government trappers were not required to report nontarget fatalities, and internal FWS memoranda requiring accidental-kill reports have not been consistently enforced. Nontarget kills have been treated for the most part as a public relations problem (Wilson 1985).

## The Animal Rights Issue

Once widely considered to be an extremist phenomenon, the animal-rights movement has become more mainstream through the past decade, attracting thousands of members and funding hundreds of local and national organizations. In the spring of 1984, 2,500 animal-rights activists gathered at the Lincoln Memorial in Washington, D.C., for a protest against the leghold trap.

Chief among the convictions of animal-rights activists is the belief that animals possess consciousness and the ability to experience pleasure and pain. From this, they argue, animals derive rights of survival and humane treatment. Research on public attitudes about the predator-control program conducted by the Agriculture Department in 1978 (Stuby *et al.* 1978) showed that the general public is more concerned about animal suffering and about the possibility that non-depredating animals may be killed than it is about problem animals being killed or about the program's cost. Asked to rank control methods on a 0 to 10 scale, with 10 rating "extremely acceptable" and 0 "not acceptable at all," survey respondents ranked only guarding dogs, repellent chemicals, and birth control at five or above. Leghold traps and slow-acting poisons such as 1080 were ranked among the least acceptable options.

## LEGISLATIVE DEVELOPMENTS

### The Shift to Agriculture

The transfer of animal damage control programs to the Agriculture Department was made possible by House Joint Resolution 465 (Report 99-439), which authorized appropriations for agriculture, rural development, and related agencies for the fiscal year ending September 30, 1986. It had been debated throughout 1985, primarily in budget and appropriations committees, and passed December 19.

Considerable debate has centered on whether language in an appropriations bill can permanently transfer the agency or whether permanent transfer will require additional Congressional authorization. ADC officials say the transfer is "as good as permanent, or as good as any program that requires annual appropriations." Nevertheless, the controversial nature of the transfer and the attendant publicity may have put pressure on APHIS to exercise caution in making any significant changes before the transfer is authorized as permanent. In any case, continued requests for increases in ADC funding are likely to come under closer scrutiny as competition for federal dollars intensifies in coming years.

### Federal Insecticide, Fungicide, and Rodenticide Act

A proposed reauthorization of the Federal Insecticide, Fungicide, and Rodenticide Act, which provides for the registration, regulation, and use of pesticides, including the poisons used to control predators and rodents, failed in the closing days of the 99th Congress. The act has been extended on a year-to-year basis pending full reauthorization. Some of the issues to be addressed when the act is reauthorized will affect ADC activities. For example, chemicals not previously tested fully will have to be retested and reregistered, and training requirements for those who use poisons may be changed.

## LEGAL DEVELOPMENTS

After a seven-year procedure known as RPAR[7], the Environmental Protection Agency in 1983 announced its intention to cancel most above-ground uses of strychnine, then reversed itself after a hearing requested by western states and the Farm Bureau Federation, in which no additional evidence was taken. A subsequent court case, *Defenders of Wildlife, Sierra Club, and Friends of Animals and their Environment v. Administrator, Environmental Protection Agency, and Secretary, U.S. Department of the Interior*, was filed August 27, 1986. It asks for a ban on the above-ground use of products containing strychnine and strychnine sulfate, which are used to control prairie dogs and other rodents, as well as coyotes. Plaintiffs charge that the administrator and secretary have violated the Endangered Species Act, Bald and Golden Eagle Protection Act, National Environmental Policy Act, Migratory Bird Treaty Act, and Administrative Procedures Act by allowing continued use of strychnine.

Papers filed by the plaintiffs in the Fourth Division District Court in Minnesota cite a strychnine threat to black-footed ferrets, sandhill cranes, Utah prairie dogs, San Joaquin kit foxes, gray wolves, and grizzly bears and allege that documented evidence shows that strychnine has poisoned bald eagles, peregrine falcons, California condors, golden eagles, other migratory birds, black bears, dogs, and humans.

## REFERENCES

Bromley, Peter T., ed. 1985. *Proceedings of the Second Eastern Wildlife Damage Control Conference.* North Carolina State University. Raleigh, North Carolina. 275pp.

Byford, James L. 1985. "Role and responsibilities of state cooperative extension services for wildlife damage control," in, P.T. Bromley ed., *Proceedings of the Second Eastern*

7. Rebuttable Presumption Against Registration, a FIFRA-authorized process whereby a pesticide's registration is canceled unless evidence can be presented proving that it should not be.

*Wildlife Damage Control Conference.* North Carolina State University. Raleigh, North Carolina. 275pp.

Defenders of Wildlife. 1986. "Status of State Replies to Toxic Collar' Intents' request," July 9, 1986.

Elfring, Chris. 1985. "Federal animal damage control programs." Unpublished chapter for *Audubon Wildlife Report 1986.*

Linhart, S.B., J.G. Dasch, C.B. Male, and R.M. Engeman. "Efficacy of unpadded and padded steel foothold traps for capturing coyotes," *Wildlife Society Bulletin* 14:212-218.

Martin, Glen. 1985. "A plethora of coyotes," *Audubon*:144-48. November.

Olsen, G.H., S.B. Linhart, R.A. Holmes, G.J. Dasch, and C.B. Male. 1986. "Injuries to coyotes caught in padded and unpadded steel foothold traps," *Wildlife Society Bulletin* 14: 215-223.

Starr, Douglas. 1984. "Equal rights," *Audubon*:30-35. November.

Stuby, R.G., E.H. Carpenter, and L.M. Arthur. 1978. *Public Attitudes Toward Coyote Control.* U.S. Department of Agriculture Economic Statistic Cooperative Service. Washington, DC.

U.S. Fish and Wildlife Service, Department of the Interior. 1978. *Predator Damage in the West: A Study of Coyote Management Alternatives.* U.S. Government Printing Office. Washington, D.C. 168 pp.

Wilson, Cynthia E. 1985. *The 1080 Controversy: A Dilemma in Public Policy Making.* Report to the Wild Wings Foundation. 31 pp.

*Ruth Norris, a former editor of* Audubon *magazine, is now publications editor for* The Nature Conservancy International.

Greater and lesser yellowlegs find feeding grounds at Chincoteague National Wildlife Refuge, important habitat for waterfowl as well as shorebirds. Controversy has flared at the refuge over heavy recreational use. *Page Chichester*

# The National Wildlife Refuge System

Ruth Norris

and

Cynthia Lenhart

## OVERVIEW

The National Wildlife Refuge System contains more than 90 million acres of lands and waters set aside to protect and perpetuate wildlife. Although the system lacks a congressionally authorized long-term goal or mandate, the U.S. Fish and Wildlife Service (FWS), the agency that oversees the refuge system, has developed this mission statement to guide its operation: "to provide, manage, and safeguard a national network of lands and waters sufficient in size, diversity, and location to make available, now and in the future, public benefits that are associated with wildlife over which the federal government has responsibility, particularly migratory birds and endangered species" (U.S. Fish and Wildlife Service 1976).

Among the wildlife that the system seeks to protect, special attention and priority are given to threatened or endangered species and to migratory birds. Four hundred thirty-seven refuges are run primarily by professional wildlife managers and biologists, who are charged not only with ensuring healthy habitats for wildlife but, at some refuges, with managing myriad unrelated activities—grazing, logging, mining and mineral development, farming, and recreational activities such as

Audubon Wildlife Report 1987

fishing, boating, birdwatching, and hunting. Often these activities were begun on a refuge as a relatively low-cost management tool to assist in population or habitat objectives. However, in many instances the use of the "tool" has grown beyond its originally intended purpose and exists as much for the economic interest involved as for wildlife. Although the National Wildlife Refuge System Administration Act (16 USCA 668 dd and ee) and other federal laws and regulations require that all refuge use be compatible with the wildlife purposes for which the refuge was established, the growing trend toward maximizing use of the refuge system worries a number of observers. Unlike the national forests, national parks, and other federal lands set aside to serve recreational, aesthetic, and commercial needs, the refuges are unique in being established primarily for the restoration and protection of wildlife habitats and of the fish and wildlife populations they support.

Today, the system appears, in frequently cited statistical summaries, to be acheiving its stated mission. Although the National Wildlife Refuge System is clearly the most far-flung and comprehensive program of wildlife-habitat protection existing on Earth, lesser known statistics cast a shadow on this heroic accomplishment. For instance, 77 million acres of the system are located in 16 refuge units in a single state (Alaska). The remaining 13 million acres are scattered across the other four-fifths of America, often consisting of unmanned, underfunded, postage-stamp-size areas where external conditions and activities are threatening their fundamental capability to provide havens for wildlife.

Recent years have brought a number of warning signs that the system is not in itself capable of sustaining wildlife populations: Waterfowl numbers have plummeted, pollution has taken its toll on the refuges themselves and on surrounding lands, and FWS has had difficulty in controlling activities such as grazing and drilling that adversely affect refuge wildlife.

Five new refuges were added to the system in 1986, bringing total refuge acres to 88,337,012. The entire system, including waterfowl production areas managed but not owned by FWS, is 90,493,084 acres. A number of designated refuges contain plots of land that remain in private ownership because of insufficient federal acquisition funds. Also in 1986, FWS organizational changes following the appointment of Frank Dunkle as director confirmed a line of authority in which refuge managers report through regional directors to the FWS director. From 1973 until the early 1980s, refuge managers reported to area directors who in turn reported to regional directors. The authority of the regional directors has been enhanced in the reorganization, and field staff in general are being increased while headquarters staff in Washington is being cut back (see Figure 1).

Major work ongoing in the refuge system during 1986 included continuing surveys and assessment of toxic-contamination problems; updating of the refuge system's programmatic environmental impact statement, which has been in effect for 10 years and is due for a major overhaul; and completion of the Interior Department's draft report on management of the coastal plain of the Arctic National Wildlife Refuge in Alaska. The latter, together with comprehensive planning and consideration of wilderness status for a number of refuge areas in Alaska, is expected to be one of the major conservation issues before the 100th Congress.

# CURRENT DEVELOPMENTS

## Water Quality/Toxic Contamination

One of every five national wildlife refuges is affected by contaminant issues requiring management attention, according to an FWS report released in April 1986. The report, *Contaminant Issues of Concern, National Wildlife Refuges,* is the first systematic attempt FWS has made at a consolidated national listing of refuge pollution problems. The issues identified by this study include toxic contamination of refuge lands and waters by industrial wastes and agricultural drainwater; ordinance and wastes left on refuges after military activities; municipal discharges; and leachate from mines and toxic-waste dumps.

Selenium, the widely publicized trace metal that accumulated in toxic quantities at Kesterson National Wildlife Refuge in California's San Joaquin Valley, killing water birds and forcing a shutoff of the agricultural drainwater that fed the refuge, has been found at elevated levels in 20 other refuges as well.[1] In all, 84 refuges are identified as having or appearing likely to have serious contamination problems. Nine refuges, including Kesterson, have significant, Category A contamination problems.[2] Thirty refuges fall into the lower-priority Category B. Fifty-seven are Category C (some appear in more than one category for different contaminants). Managers of the affected refuges have been asked to submit action plans for further monitoring, evaluation, or cleanup (see Table 1).

1. For detailed information about Kesterson and about problems associated with irrigation projects, please see the *Audubon Wildlife Report 1986* and the water projects chapter of this volume.
2. The categories are as follows: Category A—evidence indicates the need for corrective action; Category B—on-site, direct evidence indicates the need for in-depth monitoring and analysis of impacts; Category C—on or off-site circumstantial evidence indicates a priority need for additional reconnaissance monitoring.

The National Wildlife Refuge System
Figure 1

242

**TABLE 1**
**Contaminant Issues of Concern on National Wildlife Refuges**

| State | Refuge(s) | Contaminant Issue of Concern |
|---|---|---|
| Category A: Evidence indicates the need for corrective action | | |
| AL | Wheeler NWR | Industrial wastes (DDT) |
| AK | Kenai NWR | Industrial wastes (PCBs) |
| CA | Kesterson NWR | Agricultural drainwater (selenium, other trace elements) |
| CA | Seal Beach NWR | Military activities |
| HI | Johnston Island NWR | Military activities (nerve and mustard gas, dioxin, and plutonium) |
| IL | Crab Orchard NWR | Area 9 industrial wastes (PCBs) |
| NJ | Great Swamp NWR | Asbestos dump |
| VA | Eastern Shore of Virginia NWR | Asbestos insulation in refuge buildings |
| VA | Fisherman Island NWR | Military activities (DDT) |
| Category B: On-site, direct evidence indicates the need for in-depth monitoring and analysis of impacts | | |
| AK | Alaska Maritime NWR | Military/industrial wastes and discharges |
| AK | Alaska Maritime NWR | Military activities on Amchitka and Atka Islands |
| AZ | Cibola, Havasu, and Imperial NWR | Agricultural drainwater (ag-chemicals, selenium, other trace elements) |
| CA | Grasslands Wildlife Management Area | Agricultural drainwater (selenium, other trace elements) |
| CA | Salton Sea NWR | Agricultural drainwater and municipal/industrial discharges |
| CA | San Luis NWR | Agricultural drainwater (trace elements, eg-chemicals) |
| CA | Tijuana Slough NWR | Municipal/industrial discharges |
| FL | Loxahatchee NWR | Agricultural/municipal drainwater (ag-chemicals) |
| GA | Savannah and Tybee NWRs | Municipal/industrial discharges |
| HI | Baker Island and Howland Island NWR | Drums of petroleum |
| LA | Tensas River NWR | Agricultural drainwater (ag-chemicals) |
| MA | Great Meadows NWR | Hazardous waste dumps (heavy metals) |

*(continued)*

**TABLE 1** *(Continued)*

| State | Refuge(s) | Contaminant Issue of Concern |
|---|---|---|
| MS | Yazoo NWR | Agricultural drainwater (ag-chemicals) |
| MT | Benton Lake NWR | Agricultural drainwater (selenium) |
| MT | Bowdoin NWR | Agricultural drainwater (selenium) |
| NV | Stillwater Wildlife Management Area | Agricultural drainwater (selenium, arsenic, mercury) |
| NJ | Great Swamp NWR | Rolling Knolls landfill effluents |
| NC | Alligator River NWR | Landfill effluent (mercury, nutrients) |
| OK | Sequoyah NWR | Agricultural drainwater and industrial/municipal discharges |
| OK | Wichita Mountains Wildlife Refuge | Mining activities (mercury, arsenic, other trace elements) |
| OR | Malheur NWR | Agricultural drainwater (mercury, arsenic, boron) |
| PA | Tinicum National Environmental Center | Folcroft landfill (heavy metals, pesticides, cyanide) |
| TX | Aransas NWR | Oil and grease (polyaeromatic hydrocarbons and heavy metals) |
| TX | Buffalo Lake NWR | Cattle feedlots (nutrients) |
| TX | Laguna Atascosa NWR | Agricultural drainwater (ag-chemicals, trace elements) |
| WA | San Juan Islands NWR | Municipal/industrial discharges (PCBs, trace elements, metals) |

Category C: On or off-site, circumstantial evidence indicates a priority need for additional reconnaissance monitoring

| | | |
|---|---|---|
| AK | Alaska Maritime NWR | Industrial air pollution |
| AK | Alaska Maritime, Arctic, Togiak, Yukon Delta NWRs | Military activities (PCBs and fuel drums) |
| AK | Innoko, Kanuti, Koyukuk, Nowitna, Selawik, Yukon Delta and Yukon Flats NWRs | Placer mining |
| AK | Kenai NWR | Oil and gas activities |
| AK | Tetlin NWR | Industrial dump (petroleum by-products) |
| AR | Big Lake NWR | Agricultural drainwater (ag-chemicals) |
| AR | Overflow NWR | Agricultural drainwater (ag-chemicals) |

*(continued)*

**TABLE 1** *(Continued)*

| State | Refuge(s) | Contaminant Issue of Concern |
|---|---|---|
| Category C: On and off-side, circumstantial evidence indicates a priority need for additional reconnaissance monitoring. | | |
| AR | White River NWR | Agricultural drainwater (ag-chemicals |
| AZ | Kofa NWR | Mining activities (cyanide) |
| AZ | San Bernadino NWR | Industrial discharges (copper smelter/acid rain) |
| CA | Butte Sink, Colusa, Delevan, Sacramento and Sutter NWRs | Agricultural drainwater (ag-chemicals, trace elements) |
| CA | Humboldt Bay NWR | Inactive landfill dump |
| CA | Lower Klamath and Tule Lake NWRs | Agricultural drainwater (ag-chemicals) |
| CA | Salinas River WMA | Agricultural drainwater (ag-chemicals) |
| CA | San Francisco Bay NWR | Municipal/industrial/ agricultural activities and landfill effluent (trace elements) |
| CA | San Pablo Bay NWR | Municipal/industrial discharges (trace elements) |
| CO | Browns Park NWR | Agricultural drainwater (selenium) |
| FL | National Key Deer Refuge | Mosquito control spraying (chemicals) |
| ID | Bear Lake NWR | Agricultural/municipal drainwater |
| IL | Crab Orchard NWR | Other industrial wastes (on refuge) |
| IL | Crab Orchard NWR | Municipal wastes (off refuge) |
| LA | Lacassine NWR | Agricultural drainwater (ag-chemicals) |
| LA | Sabine NWR | Industrial discharges (mercury) |
| MI | Shiawassee NWR | Agricultural drainwater and municipal/industrial discharges |
| NJ | Edwin B. Forsythe NWR | Buried drums (unknown contents) |
| NJ | Great Swamp NWR | Harding landfill effluents |
| NM | Bitter Lake NWR | Agricultural drainwater (ag-chemical, trace elements) |
| NM | Bosque del Apache NWR | Agricultural drainwater (ag-chemicals, trace elements) |
| NY | Iroquois NWR | Buried drums (ag-chemicals) |
| NY | Montezuma NWR | Buried drums (ag-chemicals) |
| OK | Salt Plains NWR | Agricultural drainwater (ag-chemicals, other trace elements) |

*(continued)*

**TABLE 1** *(Continued)*

| State | Refuge(s) | Contaminant Issue of Concern |
|---|---|---|
| Category C: On and off-side, circumstantial evidence indicates a priority need for additional reconnaissance monitoring | | |
| OK | Tishomingo NWR | Agricultural drainwater (ag-chemicals) |
| PA | Tinicum National Environmental Center | Clearview landfill (poly-chlorinated compounds) |
| RI | Ninigret NWR | Military dumps |
| RI | Sachuest Point NWR | Municipal landfill |
| TX | Anahuac NWR | Agricultural drainwater (ag-chemicals) |
| TX | Aransas NWR | Agricultural drainwater (ag-chemicals) |
| TX | Santa Ana and Lower Rio Grande Valley NWRs | Agricultural drainwater and municipal/industrial discharges (nutrients, toxic chemicals, and metals) |
| UT | Ouray NWR | Agricultural drainwater (selenium) |
| VA | Great Dismal Swamp NWR | Suffolk landfill |
| WA | Nisqually NWR | Municipal/industrial discharges (heavy metals, chemicals) |
| WI | Horicon NWR | Agricultural drainwater (ag-chemicals) |

Contamination affects refuge wildlife in a variety of ways. Birds in the Lower Rio Grande Valley refuge have died after eating insects poisoned with pesticide. Elevated levels of DDE and toxaphene have been found in the tissues of birds and fish at Texas' Laguna Atascosa refuge. At Crab Orchard refuge, wildlife lives amid PCB-laden soils. Oil and gas spills, together with road building and other activities associated with oil and gas development, have had adverse effects on Kenai National Wildlife Refuge in Alaska. Soil at Kenai has been contaminated with PCBs. Fish in the waters of Stillwater National Wildlife Management Area in Nevada contain mercury levels up to four times the maximum suggested for human consumption. Bird and fish die-offs from various causes are not uncommon there. In 1983, workers counted 50,000 dead ducks on Stillwater's grounds. Selenium and other toxic chemicals associated with drainage of agricultural irrigation water in the West have caused birth deformities and death in water birds, and research has shown a correlation between exposure to these chemicals and susceptibility to diseases such as botulism and avian cholera (Dolan 1986). Acid rain has damaged fish habitat and may be affecting waterfowl reproductive success.

Environmental groups are concerned that contamination problems are more serious than current reports indicate. Because the FWS report was based on questionnaires answered by refuge managers, with follow-up calls and visits to refuges where problems were apparent, built-in inconsistencies occur in the ranking of problems. A problem considered unimportant at one refuge may have been rated very important at another. Also, no means was available for determining the seriousness of problems where obvious evidence has not surfaced and no monitoring has been done. Many of the studies required to determine the nature of contamination are time-consuming and expensive. The National Audubon Society obtained copies of the questionnaires used in compiling the report and noted that problems frequently were assigned a category B or C ranking when substantial evidence suggested that contamination was occurring but no funds were available to monitor for confirmation.

Although the Interior Department did not request additional funds, Congress provided a fiscal 1987 budget increase of $4.5 million above fiscal year 1986 appropriations for dealing with contamination issues. Of this, $2 million went directly to the refuges— $1.5 million "to move aggressively to initiate necessary studies, to accelerate the analysis of refuge samples, and to continue to develop and implement strategies to clean up affected refuges and initiate cleanup actions where appropriate," and $500,000 for repetitive sampling where needed for training and other purposes. The remaining $2.5 million was appropriated for research and development purposes: $500,000 to assess the effects of new contaminants; $550,000 to begin a long-term study on the Upper Mississippi River; $450,000 for a long-term study of contaminants and diving ducks on the Gulf Coast; $400,000 for a long-term study of San Francisco Bay; and $600,000 for development of a strategy to coordinate federal contaminant-monitoring activities and to assure quality control in nonfederal analyses.

**Compatibility Issues**

Under the National Wildlife Refuge System Administration Act of 1966, a refuge manager may permit use of a refuge by the public or by private interests for commercial or noncommercial purposes "whenever he determines that such uses are compatible with the major purposes for which such areas were established." A number of other laws, regulations, and executive orders establish criteria for regulating certain types of uses and protecting key resources on the refuge system, including the Refuge Recreation Act of 1962, Alaska National Interest Lands Conservation Act of 1980, Endangered Species Act, and National Historic Preservation Act.

Determining whether a proposed use of a refuge is compatible with refuge purposes can be and often is a matter of some dispute. Conflicts have been especially sharp when the issue is hunting, mineral development, logging, grazing, or other commercial enterprises. In May 1986, FWS issued a new chapter for its *Refuge Manual*, "Compatibility Determination," to provide guidance for refuge managers on determining the compatibility of proposed refuge uses. In general, this is determined by the refuge manager on a site-specific basis. When written reports are required in addition to other required reports, such as environmental assessments or environmental impact statements on proposed activities, or when a written report is prepared at the manager's discretion, the report is expected to identify refuge purposes, anticipated impact of the proposed use, stipulations required to ensure compatibility, and justification for a finding that the use is or is not compatible (U.S. Fish and Wildlife Service 1986).

Compatibility issues of major concern in 1986 included:

**Hunting, Fishing, and Trapping:** Hunting of some kind is permitted on some portion of 260 of the 437 refuges. More than 400,000 animals are killed yearly on the refuges by hunters and trappers (Miller 1986), and 1.5 to 3 million birds die on and off the refuge system from lead poisoning after ingesting spent shot.

FWS opened an additional seven refuges to hunting and 11 to fishing in 1986, continuing a program designed to expand hunting and fishing opportunities on the refuge system.[3] The ongoing controversies over impacts on wildlife of specific hunting programs and over philosophical issues relating to whether hunting should be permitted at all also continued.

A lawsuit by the Humane Society of the United States (*The Humane Society v. Hodel*, case no. 84-3630, D.C. District Court), seeking to prevent FWS from implementing its 1984 revision of refuge hunting regulations, was dismissed. The court ruled that the Humane Society is not an organization created to protect wildlife on national wildlife refuges and thus lacked standing to sue. The Humane Society has pursued a separate procedural issue and plans to appeal the decision in an attempt to gain a hearing of the substantial issues, which include:

---

3. Refuges that were opened to hunting and fishing in 1986 were: Migratory bird and upland game hunting: San Bernardino, Arizona; San Pablo Bay, California; Ash Meadows, Nevada; Chickasaw, Tennessee; and Bandon Marsh, Oregon. Sport fishing: Prime Hook, Delaware; Hanalei and Kakahaia, Hawaii; Pond Island, Maine; Nantucket, Massachusetts; Cedar Island and Swanquarter, North Carolina; Cedar Point and Ottawa, Ohio; Bandon Marsh, Oregon; and Johnson Atoll, Pacific Islands. Big game hunting: Eufala, Alabama; Bear Valley, Oregon; and Chickasaw, Tennessee.

- whether the new regulations, which replace refuge-by-refuge rulemaking with generalized codification basically adopting state hunting regulations, were studied adequately and open to public comment;
- whether authority, manpower, and funds have been diverted illegally;
- whether FWS conducted adequate studies before determining that hunting was compatible with refuge purposes on refuges opened to hunting; and
- whether historical limitations on refuge hunting have been circumvented.

The Humane Society objected to all the proposed new hunting plans and notified the Interior Department of its intent to sue if they were not canceled. Other conservationists objected to the proposed migratory-bird and upland-game hunting at Ash Meadows National Wildlife Refuge in Nevada, a unique desert refuge established to protect more than a dozen endangered species, including many plants whose critical habitat occurs in the refuge. Under threat of litigation by Defenders of Wildlife and the Sierra Club Legal Defense Fund as well as the Humane Society, FWS agreed to take specific measures to protect Ash Meadows' plants, such as assigning a full-time refuge manager on site, closing certain roads to vehicular traffic, and posting signs to inform hunters of the presence of endangered species and requirements for their protection.

Hunting of snow geese on Bosque del Apache National Wildlife Refuge, New Mexico, continued in 1986. Bosque del Apache is the winter home of an experimental flock of whooping cranes. The whoopers are raised from eggs placed in sandhill crane nests at Grays Lake National Wildlife Refuge in Idaho. They migrate and winter with their foster parents at Bosque del Apache. Because snow geese and whooping cranes are similar in appearance, the refuge requires hunters to complete a certification program to assure that they are able to distinguish geese from cranes and other birds such as herons.

Bosque del Apache's master plan (U.S. Fish and Wildlife Service 1982) states that the foremost goal of the refuge is "to provide habitat and protection for endangered species with special emphasis on the whooping crane . . . Crane maintenance is considered the most important management activity at this refuge." Although the snow goose hunt is carefully regulated—limited in 1986 to 14 weekdays during midday hours when cranes normally are feeding off the refuge—the recovery team believes that the hunt still poses a threat.

If the whoopers habituate to feeding and wintering off the refuge because of the disturbance caused by hunting—which, according to one FWS biologist monitoring the cranes, already is happening— added threats such as shooting and lead poisoning will reduce the flock's chances of survival. The lead-poisoning problem should diminish over time as the result of new regulations established for nearby hunting areas in 1986, however. Nontoxic-shot zones were established for lands along the Rio Grande Valley in two counties, Valencia and Socorro, stretching north from Bosque del Apache to Albuquerque.

**Livestock Grazing.** In 1986, FWS took steps to reduce grazing by a third on the Charles M. Russell National Wildlife Refuge in Montana. Livestock grazing has been blamed for deterioration of the refuge's rangelands and for reducing the amount of forage available to wildlife. Reductions will come in a phased program beginning in 1987 and continuing through 1990. When the program is complete, wildlife will get about 63 percent of the forage available on the million-acre refuge and livestock about 37 percent. These reductions follow nearly a decade of agency review, which has been under way since joint Bureau of Land Management-FWS management of the refuge was terminated in favor of full responsibility for FWS in 1976. During that time, a series of court cases clarified legal requirements for grazing allocations. In addition to reducing the amount of forage consumed by livestock, FWS plans to prepare habitat management plans for each of the 65 grazing allotments on the refuge.

**Oil and Gas Drilling.** Drilling activities on D'Arbonne National Wildlife Refuge, Louisiana, were modified slightly in response to 1986 environmental litigation, although the major portion of the lawsuit was decided in favor of the drilling company. The drilling activity was challenged on the grounds that it was harming endangered red-cockaded woodpeckers in violation of the Endangered Species Act as well as on procedural grounds under the National Environmental Policy Act (*Michael J. Caire, M.D.,* et al. *v. Lee J. Fulton* et al., U.S. District Court, West District, Louisiana, Monroe Division, 1986). Environmentalists and the federal government contended that the drilling company, TerrOnne Corporation, was required by the act to obtain a permit before drilling on the refuge. TerrOnne held mineral rights that had been reserved when the federal government acquired surface rights for the refuge.

The D'Arbonne case[4] originally was seen as precedent setting and likely to determine how much control FWS could exercise over development of mineral rights on refuge lands held by outside parties. FWS was planning a comprehensive review of its regulations governing such activities, pending outcome of the D'Arbonne case. But the outcome left the larger question up in the air. Judge F.A. Little, Jr. ruled

4. Background for the case is covered in detail in the *Audubon Wildlife Report 1986.*

that FWS did not have authority to require TerrOnne to secure a permit before developing its oil and gas rights. The decision was based on terms specific to the acquisition of D'Arbonne. The court did not address the question of whether the Refuge Administration Act and other federal laws give FWS general authority to require permits for the development of privately held mineral rights underlying refuge lands.[5] After the ruling, the plaintiffs—Sierra Club Legal Defense Fund and the Justice Department—initially filed notices of appeal, but later withdrew. The Justice Department also withdrew a similar suit pending against a firm drilling in the Upper Ouachita National Wildlife Refuge. Instead of pursuing further litigation, conservationists will seek federal legislation explicitly giving FWS regulatory authority over development of privately held mineral resources underlying its lands.

Although the National Environmental Policy Act claim was not upheld in the D'Arbonne case, Sierra Club Legal Defense Fund pursued a second claim against TerrOnne, alleging that drilling activities constituted a taking of an endangered species, the red-cockaded woodpecker, in violation of the Endangered Species Act. In December 1986, Sierra Club Legal Defense Fund and TerrOnne signed a settlement agreement. TerrOnne agreed not to drill within 200 feet of any established woodpecker colony; not to conduct any activities within 1,000 feet of an active nest site during breeding season, April to July; to minimize activities in habitat areas suitable for woodpeckers whenever feasible; to limit the size of clearings cut for wells to a third of an acre; to consult with the refuge manager on locating new well sites; and to relocate five of its proposed wells closest to the main woodpecker colony to an area that is not prime habitat.

**Public Use.** A master plan for Chincoteague National Wildlife Refuge, on the eastern shore of Virginia, was due to be issued in draft in the fall of 1986, but was delayed. A draft for public comment was expected to be issued in early 1987. Meanwhile, the controversy over future use of the refuge has continued to heat up.

Chincoteague's beaches attract extensive recreational use, making it the second most visited refuge in the National Wildlife Refuge System. Refuge managers have struggled to limit recreational use to a level compatible with the refuge's wildlife purposes, but are opposed by business and real-estate interests and the mayor of the town of Chincoteague, which lies at the entrance of the refuge and harbors aspirations toward development of a major beach resort. One of the issues to be addressed in the refuge master plan is vehicular use.

5. FWS estimates that outside parties hold rights to oil and gas under 1.6 million refuge acres, coal under 1.2 million acres, and other minerals under 1.7 million acres. These figures include overlapping lands and rights to uneconomic resources not likely to be developed.

Conservationists had hoped to forestall any adjustments before the plan was completed, but under pressure from the local community and Representative Herbert Bateman (R-VA), the refuge allowed construction of an additional parking lot surfaced with oyster shells in the summer of 1986. In September, the Environmental Protection Agency and U.S. Army Corps of Engineers released a study of wetlands on Chincoteague Island, adjacent to the refuge, identifying some as suitable for development but the majority as unsuitable for dredging and filling. A public hearing on the report in October provoked heated exchanges between pro-development interests who claimed that their property rights were in jeopardy and moderates who favor reasonable controls. The wetland issue, although not related directly to the refuge, was widely seen as foreshadowing controversies to come when the refuge master plan is released for public comment.

## Alaska Issues

In the Alaska National Interest Lands Conservation Act (ANILCA) of 1980, Congress designated nine new national wildlife refuges and enlarged and redesignated seven more. Thus, Alaska now has 16 national wildlife refuges. These total 77 million acres, or 85 percent of the refuge system.[6]

Two issues were of particular concern during 1986: refuge planning and wilderness recommendations, and a study on future management of the Arctic National Wildlife Refuge.

*Planning and Wilderness.* ANILCA designated 13 refuge wilderness areas totaling 18.5 million acres and directed FWS to study the wilderness potential of other Alaskan refuge lands and recommend to the president areas suitable for preservation as wilderness. The president is to advise Congress on his recommendations by 1987. In addition, each Alaska refuge is to have a "comprehensive conservation plan." But despite dedicated work by agency professionals, the refuge plans and wilderness-suitability reviews are behind schedule and, conservationists believe, seriously deficient.

The National Audubon Society has identified these specific problems (National Audubon Society 1986):

- refuge plans fail to subject all major activities on refuges to compatibility determinations as required by the National Wildlife Refuge Administration Act of 1966;
- in a futile attempt to meet the demands of increasing numbers of sport and subsistence hunters and trappers, FWS has allowed

6. Alaska refuges and refuge issues also are covered in the *Audubon Wildlife Report 1986*.

moose, various furbearers, and geese to be overhunted severely on certain units; pressures on sport-fishery resources also are increasing dramatically on many refuges;

- use and development is being permitted to expand without knowledge of effects or monitoring to determine effects;
- the question of refuge-regulation applicability to native-owned village inholdings remains unresolved after 15 years;
- wilderness recommendations have been limited and arbitrary because of policies restricting them to areas that may have been overlooked inadvertently by Congress and to established areas requiring boundary adjustments;
- administration policy encourages accommodation of oil and gas exploration on refuges, even in areas suitable for wilderness designation;
- refuge fish- and wildlife-management responsibility has been delegated to the state of Alaska through a joint memorandum of understanding with the Alaska Department of Fish and Game; and
- refuge plans place undue emphasis on management of game species rather than on conserving natural diversity as required in the law.

Congress responded to concerns about the lagging conservation plans by earmarking $960,000 in fiscal year 1987 appropriations for operations and maintenance at Alaska refuges, encouraging the planning process to proceed with all due speed.

***Arctic National Wildlife Refuge.*** Congress designated this refuge and doubled its size in ANILCA, identifying its principal purpose as conservation of wildlife and fish populations and habitat in their natural diversity. Congress also designated eight million of its 18 million acres as wilderness, including 40 miles of arctic coastline. The remaining 10 million acres were to be studied for wilderness designation. The refuge, which is the second largest unit in the refuge system, is habitat for the 180,000 caribou of the Porcupine herd, whose calving ground is on the coastal plain, as well as for many other species, including polar bears, grizzly bears, musk-ox, Dall sheep, wolves, wolverines, snow geese, peregrine falcons, Arctic char, and grayling.

Portions of the coastal plain are reported to possess high potential for discovery of major commercial deposits of oil and gas. Consequently, Congress in section 1002 of ANILCA directed that 1.5 million acres of the two-million-acre coastal plain be subjected to a comprehensive and continuing assessment of fish and wildlife values and to a government-guided oil and gas exploration program, although with no drilling permitted.

While the exploration and studies were in progress, conservationists were concerned by evidence of unnecessary damage to soil and vegetation during seismic exploration activities; evidence that Interior was negotiating possible assignment of mineral rights on the refuge to native corporations in exchange for surface holdings elsewhere; and indications that overall refuge purposes were being neglected because the 1002 study consumed as much as 90 percent of refuge staff time and budget (National Audubon Society 1986).

The Interior Department released a draft of the 1002 report on November 24. It recommends opening the entire 1.5 million acres of coastal plain to oil and gas leasing and development (Department of Interior 1986). The department's geologic analysis predicts that the area may contain 4.8 billion barrels of oil and 11.5 trillion cubic feet of natural gas, or, stated in terms of recoverable reserves, roughly a third to a half of the resources of the Prudhoe Bay area. The refuge's reserves could be even larger, perhaps many times larger, than Prudhoe Bay's. But the figures are hypothetical. Chances for discovery and recovery of these potentially large reserves are somewhat less than one in five.

The Interior Department projects that development of the refuge's resources if they can be discovered and recovered could reduce U.S. reliance on foreign oil by almost nine percent in the year 2005. In addition, the report says, "contributions from the 1002 area would enhance the national security of the country, produce a more favorable balance of trade . . . and provide overall enhanced economic benefits to the Nation" (Department of the Interior 1986). The report recommends that the Interior Department be given authority to place restrictions on oil and gas activities when necessary to avoid adverse effects on wildlife. It also recommends that the caribou herd's core calving area be opened for leasing last, so that development there would have the benefit of knowledge gained in other areas.

Conservationists objected immediately to the recommendations, as did a number of congressional sponsors of the ANILCA legislation. Representative Morris K. Udall (D-AZ) said he would again introduce Alaska wilderness legislation in the 100th Congress calling for designation of the Arctic National Wildlife Refuge's entire coastal plain as wilderness.

The public comment period on the 1002 report extended until January 23, after which Interior Secretary Donald Hodel was to make a final recommendation to Congress. Unless Congress approves opening new areas, the *status quo*—no drilling permitted—remains in effect.

## Flood Control at Malheur National Wildlife Refuge

In September 1986, the Corps of Engineers released a draft environmental impact statement on alternatives for flood control in the

Malheur Basin in Harney County, Oregon. The basin encompasses Malheur National Wildlife Refuge, a 183,000-acre freshwater marsh that is the largest migratory-waterfowl refuge in the lower 48 states (Puchy 1986). Increased precipitation and runoff in recent years have raised the level of the basin's three lakes substantially above their historic high-water mark. Lake surface area has increased from a usual variation between 40,000 and 60,000 acres to more than 100,000 acres. The flooding has damaged farms, roads, utilities, and a branch line of the Union Pacific Railroad in addition to submerging major portions of the refuge. Estimated damage through 1985 is $17.3 million.

Several structural and nonstructural alternatives for reducing flood damage have been studied. The Corps' draft environmental impact statement focuses on two alternatives: (1) construction of a 17-mile canal to drain Malheur Lake into the South Fork of the Malheur River; and (2) relocation of the railroad, which has sustained most of the damages, to higher ground, with federal purchase and addition to the refuge of some low-lying private lands. Conservationists support the second alternative because it would reduce flood damage without altering the basin's basic hydrology. The canal, they argue, would change Malheur's natural water-level fluctuations, which are necessary to maintain a healthy ecosystem. The canal also would open the way for water diversions for agriculture and hydropower—an economic benefit to the area in wet years, but potentially troublesome if those uses were to become established and prevented the refuge from receiving sufficient water in dry years. And a canal would be likely to cause erosion, pollution, and rough-fish problems. The Corps is considering public comments and in 1987 will issue a final environmental impact statement recommending a course of action. Congressional approval of a structural alternative, which would be necessary if the canal were to be built, is considered unlikely.

## Operations and Maintenance

In one of its federal budget cutting moves, the Reagan administration proposed to cut back its Accelerated Refuge Maintenance and Management program by 53 percent for fiscal 1987. However, this move was rejected by Congress, which appropriated more than $12 million above administration requests for refuge maintenance and operations. The Accelerated Refuge Maintenance and Management program was launched by Interior in 1984 as a major effort to reduce the tremendous backlog of refuge maintenance projects nationwide. Its goal was to build up to the $55 million needed yearly for this purpose, but after three years total program funding has been less than $60 million.

Although FWS has budgeted modest increases for operations and maintenance at new and existing refuges, it has not followed congressional directives to increase staff at refuges where additional personnel are needed to manage wildlife resources adequately. Both House and Senate appropriations committees added directives to committee reports on appropriations, instructing FWS to restore 100 full-time equivalents to the refuge system, and threatened to add more specific and binding language to appropriations for fiscal 1988 if the directive were not followed.

## Land Acquisition

For fiscal 1987, as for five of the past six budget years, the Reagan administration proposed zero funds for acquisition of lands for the National Wildlife Refuge System. Congress, however, appropriated $42.425 million from the Land and Water Conservation Fund, which provides the overwhelming majority of funds for refuge acquisitions including $1 million for acquisition of inholdings within the refuge system. Congress also advanced another $21 million from the Migratory Bird Conservation Fund.

In January 1987, the federal Office of Management and Budget proposed a recission of unobligated Land and Water Conservation Fund monies for fiscal 1987. This proposal would effectively reduce the fiscal 1987 Land and Water Conservation Fund acquisition budget to $26.762 million. Such a recission must be approved by Congress within 60 days in order to become effective (see Table 2).

## Environmental Impact Statement on the Operation of the Refuge System

An update and major overhaul of the refuge system programmatic environmental impact statement was announced in 1986. Although originally expected for public review and comment in September, the update was delayed until early 1987. This statement goes beyond the current, 1976 environmental impact statement, which examined the potential impacts on refuge management and habitat of various funding levels. The new environmental impact statement, according to FWS, will evaluate the environmental and wildlife impact of current management programs and also of potential alternative policies.

## Land Exchange for Florida Panther National Wildlife Refuge

Federal acquisition of 15,000 acres of Florida wetlands for a national wildlife refuge to protect the endangered Florida panther and 20,000 acres for a refuge in the Ten Thousand Island area on Florida's Gulf Coast, together with major additions to Big Cypress National Preserve,

**TABLE 2**
**FY 1987 Land and Water Conservation Fund, Fish and Wildlife Service**

| | |
|---|---|
| Inholdings | $ 1,000,000 |
| Acquisition management | 1,750,000 |
| Alligator River NWR, NC | 650,000 |
| Aransas NWR, TX | 3,000,000 |
| Ash Meadows NWR, NV | 500,000 |
| Bayou Sauvage NWR, LA (subject to auth.) | 3,000,000 |
| Bogue Chitto NWR, LA | 1,000,000 |
| Bon Secour NWR, AL | 500,000 |
| Connecticut Coastal NWR, CT | 600,000 |
| Eastern Shore NWR, VA | 375,000 |
| Finnegan Cut, CA | 1,100,000 |
| Florida Panther NWR, FL | 3,000,000 |
| Great Dismal Swamp NWR, NC | 750,000 |
| Hakalau Forest, HI | 3,000,000 |
| Kirtlands Warbler, MI | 300,000 |
| Lower Rio Grande NWR, TX | 6,000,000 |
| Lower Suwanee NWR, FL | 1,500,000 |
| Minnesota Valley NWR, MN | 1,500,000 |
| National Key Deer NWR, FL | 2,000,000 |
| Rachel Carson NWR, ME | 900,000 |
| Red Rocks Lake Refuge, MT | 2,000,000 |
| Sacramento NWR, CA | 2,200,000 |
| San Francisco Bay NWR, CA | 1,500,000 |
| Tensas River NWR, LA | 1,000,000 |
| Willapa NWR, WA | 3,300,000 |
| Total | 42,425,000 |

was set back in the summer of 1986. A land swap proposed to accomplish the acquisition was shelved after arousing intense controversy.

The Interior Department proposed to trade 108 acres currently occupied by an Indian school in Phoenix, Arizona, for the Florida land, which is owned by Collier Enterprises and Barron Collier Companies of Naples, Florida. Both have major real-estate and development interests in addition to vast landholdings, oil fields, vegetable and citrus farms, cattle ranches, and a newspaper. The Collier companies agreed to deed to the federal government approximately 145,000 acres they own in the national preserve area and pay $50 million in cash in return for the Phoenix property, which they would develop for mixed residential and commercial use.

The swap ran into opposition from the Arizona congressional delegation and from Phoenix officials, who had plans to develop the site as a park if the federal government closed the Indian school. Congress would have to approve the swap before it could take place, so the prospects for acquisition of the Florida property remained clouded. The House of Representatives had approved legislation authorizing purchase of the Collier properties before the proposed swap was made public, but a Senate bill authorizing purchase was put on hold pending resolution of the swap issue. No action was taken by the 99th Congress before adjournment.

## Revision of Easement Regulations

In a final rule published in the *Federal Register* of March 5, 1986, FWS clarified the application of refuge-system regulations to lands not owned by FWS but managed under easements as waterfowl production areas and for other purposes. The new rule places these easement areas in a separate category of refuge-system units and ends the regulation there of activities that do not directly affect wildlife purposes, such as prohibitions on drinking, gambling, and other social activities.

# LEGISLATION

### Emergency Wetlands Resources Act of 1986 (P.L. 99-645)[7]

In its final days, the 99th Congress passed legislation to step up the pace of wetland preservation nationwide by providing additional sources of revenue for federal and state acquisition of wetlands for refuges, parks, national forests, and other conservation purposes. The Emergency Wetlands Resources Act amends the federal Land and Water Conservation Fund Act of 1965 specifically to authorize appropriation of money from the fund for wetlands acquisition. The fund, which is generated by federal revenues from property sales, user fees, motorboat fuel taxes, and offshore oil and gas activities, has been used to acquire more than half a million acres of refuge lands over the years.

The Emergency Wetlands Resources Act also increases the amount of money available through the Migratory Bird Conservation Fund, which is made up primarily of duck-stamp fees. The price of a duck stamp will be raised from $7.50 to $15 over the next five years. In addition, the Emergency Wetlands Resources Act authorizes entrance fees at certain wildlife refuges, with 70 percent of revenues to go to the Migratory Bird Conservation Fund, and authorizes the transfer to that fund of an amount equaling federal duties collected on imported arms and ammunition. Finally, the act extends for two years the availability of Wetlands Loan Act monies for wetland acquisition and eliminates the requirement that such loans be repaid from future duck-stamp revenues.

7. For further discussion of this legislation, see the wetlands and migratory bird chapters in this volume and in the *Audubon Wildlife Report 1986*.

## Military Lands Withdrawal Act of 1985 (P.L. 99-606)

A number of refuges are affected by military activities, particularly weapons testing and training, that take place on, near, or in the airspace over refuge lands. The military withdraws these lands from the public domain for its use for a specified period of time. The effects include disturbance of wildlife by aircraft and explosives, safety hazards created by the presence of unexploded bombs within and outside of target areas, and contamination of refuge lands and waters by weapons, explosives, and wastes.

Since 1958, under authority of the Engle Act (72 Stat. 27, U.S.C. 155-58, 2-28-58), the military has been required to have Congressional sanction for withdrawals of public lands of more than 5,000 acres. As withdrawals came up for renewal, they also became subject to the terms of the National Environmental Policy Act and Federal Land Policy and Management Act requiring that a number of environmental assessments be prepared. For the most part, these assessments were completed by 1982. Most analyzed the impacts of withdrawal renewal based on the assumption that no change in level or type of activities from the past would occur (The Wilderness Society 1986).

In 1984, the administration forwarded to Congress a series of bills to withdraw several military areas whose withdrawal had lapsed. Over the next two years, these bills were debated individually and attempts were made to pass an omnibus bill with generalized provisions. The House bill, H.R. 1790, was introduced by Representative Beverly Byron (D-MD) in 1985, and the Senate bill, S. 2412, by Senator James McClure (R-ID) in May 1986. The total number of acres to be withdrawn was about eight million. Conservationists expressed concerns about several of the bills' provisions and about two specific withdrawals: Nellis Air Force Range in Nevada, which encompasses more than half of Desert National Wildlife Refuge, and the Luke Air Force Range in Arizona, whose activities affect Cabeza Prieta National Wildlife Refuge.

Desert National Wildlife Refuge is the largest refuge in the lower 48 states, encompassing more than 1.5 million acres of mountains, desert, pine forest, and stands of joshua trees. It was established in 1936 to protect remnant populations of the desert bighorn sheep and today supports the largest existing population of this species, as well as bobcats, mountain lions, mule deer, desert tortoises, some 227 species of birds, and the endangered Pahrump killifish.

Although the eastern mountain ranges of the refuge are popular areas for hiking and backcountry use, the western two-thirds of the refuge, first withdrawn temporarily for use as a bombing and gunnery range during World War II, remains closed to most public use. Even refuge personnel must receive permission from the Air Force to enter the western portion. Military use of the airspace over the refuge has intensified since an air combat maneuvering instrumentation range was installed at Nellis in 1975. Sonic booms have been reported at the rate of 5,000 per year. About 16 percent of the refuge's low-elevation lands are used as target sites. Aircraft are required to fly above 2,000 feet when practical, but can and do fly as low as 100 feet above ground level. A major bighorn watering hole has been strafed (Eno 1986). Problems at Cabeza Prieta are similar: Wildlife is disturbed by aircraft and other activities, and weapons pose continuing hazards.

Conservationists did not object to the withdrawals *per se*, but asked for provisions to ensure that primary jurisdiction for refuge lands would remain, as in the current memorandum of understanding, with the Department of the Interior rather than be taken over by the military; to assure that contamination resulting from military activities would be cleaned up; to limit withdrawals to 10 years, with public review and comment on management practices at renewal time; and for environmental impact statements. As passed, the bill maintains primary jurisdiction within Interior, requires a continuation of decontamination work ongoing in fiscal year 1986, establishes withdrawals of 15 years, and requires all areas to prepare an environmental impact statement after 12 years. Nevada sites will be required to issue a report including cumulative effects analysis after five years.

### Bayou Sauvage Urban National Wildlife Refuge

Congress authorized the designation of this refuge in 1986 and appropriated $3 million for land acquisition. The refuge, located within minutes of downtown New Orleans, has the potential to become a major environmental education center. It also has a unique history. In 1985, South Point, Inc., a subsidiary of the financial firm Merrill Lynch, applied for a permit to drain and develop some 13,000 acres of a 23,450-acre parcel of land it owned in eastern New Orleans. After threat of an environmentalist lawsuit, discussions were initiated by environmentalists, city officials, and representatives of the business community. South Point, Inc., decided to convey some 19,000 acres of the property to FWS for establishment of the refuge. In return, plans will go ahead for development of the remaining acreage. Negotiators still are working to establish agreement on the precise acreage to be conveyed and on the selling price.

## LEGAL DEVELOPMENTS

*The Humane Society* v. *Hodel*, discussed in the current developments section of this chapter, was dismissed. The ruling that the Humane

Society of the United States had no standing to sue precluded consideration of substantive issues, which focused on FWS authority to allow additional hunting on the national wildlife refuges. An appeal is expected.

*Caire v. Fulton*, involving D'Arbonne National Wildlife Refuge, also discussed under current developments, was decided in March. The court ruled that the Interior Department does not have regulatory authority to require a special-use permit for drilling by TerrOnne Corporation on D'Arbonne National Wildlife Refuge. The U.S. Department of Justice and Sierra Club Legal Defense Fund withdrew plans to appeal, and a similar case against IMC Corporation, drilling on the Upper Ouachita National Wildlife Refuge, was dropped. Conservationists will seek legislation to give FWS authority to require special-use permits for development of mineral rights held by outside parties but underlying refuge lands.

## REFERENCES

Dolan, Maura. 1986. Pollution endangers U.S. refuges. *Los Angeles Times*, July 6.

Eno, Amos S. 1986. Testimony before the Subcommittee on Public Lands and National Parks, Committee on Interior and Insular Affairs. U.S. House of Representatives, August 6.

Miller, J.A. 1986. "Wildlife refuge system: refuge for whom?" *Science News*:183. March 22, 1986.

National Audubon Society. 1986. Briefing Papers on Planning and Wilderness on National Wildlife Refuges in Alaska (July 10, 1986) and Arctic National Wildlife Refuge (July 15, 1986). Anchorage, Alaska. 4 pp. each.

Puchy, Claire A. 1986. "Malheur threatened," *Outdoors West*, newsletter of the Federation of Western Outdoor Clubs. Seattle, Washington. Winter.

U.S. Department of Interior. 1986. *Draft Arctic National Wildlife Refuge, Alaska, Coastal Plain Resource Assessment*. Executive summary. Washington, D.C. 10 pp.

U.S. Fish and Wildlife Service. Department of the Interior. 1976. *Environmental Impact Statement on the Operation of the National Wildlife Refuge System*. U.S.Government Printing Office. Washington, D.C.

U.S. Department of Interior. Fish and Wildlife Service. 1982. *Master Plan for Bosque del Apache National Wildlife Refuge*. Albuquerque, N.M. 282 pp.

U.S. Fish and Wildlife Service. Department of the Interior. 1986. *Contaminant Issues of Concern, National Wildlife Refuges*. Washington, D.C. 170 pp.

U.S. Fish and Wildlife Service. Department of the Interior. 1986. *Refuge Manual*. Release No. 014, May 8. Washington, D.C. 90 pp.

The Wilderness Society. 1986. Background Information, Military Land Withdrawal Legislation. Washington, D.C. 14 pp.

*Ruth Norris, a former editor of* Audubon *magazine, is now publications editor for The Nature Conservancy International.*

*Cynthia Lenhart is with the National Audubon Society's wildlife issues staff in Washington D.C.*

A forester for the U.S. Forest Service uses an increment borer to extract a core sample from which tree age and health will be determined. *U.S. Forest Service*

# Wildlife and the U.S. Forest Service

Katherine Barton

## OVERVIEW

The Forest Service manages a wealth of wildlife and other natural resources on the 191 million acres in the National Forest System. The system provides habitat for about 3,000 species of fish and wildlife, contains half of the big-game and cold-water-fish habitat in the nation, and supports 41 percent of the recreational use on all federal lands. It provides habitat for 129 species listed as endangered or threatened and for an additional 682 species under consideration for listing. The national forests, in some cases together with national parks, provide the last refuges for species requiring large undisturbed areas, such as the grizzly bear, California condor, and gray wolf, and species inhabiting old-growth or mature forests, such as the northern spotted owl, the Sitka black-tailed deer, and the red-cockaded woodpecker.

The National Forest System provides a variety of resources in addition to wildlife habitat, including timber for commercial harvest, mineral and energy resources, and forage for livestock grazing. The Forest Service is required to manage its lands for all these multiple uses, with no particular use specified to receive top priority.

Audubon Wildlife Report 1987

Until the 1950s, demands on the National Forest System were low and the conflicts relatively minor. But beginning in the 1950s, as the nation's population and economy boomed, new demands were placed on forest resources to provide increased timber supplies, recreational opportunities, and energy and mineral resources. As conflicting demands increased, wildlife and other conservation interests began to believe that National Forest System management had skewed heavily in favor of commodity uses, particularly timber harvest. Timber sales accelerated rapidly from 3.4 billion board feet in 1950 to 12 billion board feet yearly in the 1960s. In 1964, the fear that this emphasis would result in the loss of wilderness areas to timber harvest led to the enactment of the Wilderness Act (16 U.S.C. 1131-1136). This act established the National Wilderness Preservation System, in which areas designated by Congress would be off-limits to timber production and most other commodity uses. In 1976, public concern over extensive clearcutting in the national forests during the late 1960s and early 1970s resulted in passage of the National Forest Management Act (16 U.S.C. 1601-1614). This legislation set certain limitations and restrictions on logging and required the Forest Service to prepare comprehensive, detailed forest plans, developed with public participation, to guide forest-system management.

Today, a decade after passage of the National Forest Management Act, the Forest Service is completing the first 10- to 15-year forest plans required by the law. These plans will make critical decisions about fish-and-wildlife management on the National Forest System, such as how much old-growth habitat will be maintained or restored, the extent of road construction in currently unroaded areas, levels of timber sales and intensity of timber management, and what types of fish and wildlife species will be emphasized and at what population levels they will be maintained.

As the plans have been issued, conservation organizations in almost every instance have charged that the plans favor commodity production on the national forests and that they do not meet the National Forest Management Act requirements regarding fish and wildlife, recreation, soil protection, and water management. Conservationists maintain that the intent of the law was to bring other uses of the national forests into balance with timber management, and they expect the plans to show an increased emphasis on fish and wildlife habitat and recreation. Timber interests, on the other hand, have charged that the plans are not providing for necessary increases in timber availability.

The National Forest Management Act also requires a new approach to fish- and wildlife-habitat management on the National Forest System by directing the forest plans to provide for a diversity of animal and plant communities. Under this requirement, along with other environmental laws of the 1970s, the Forest Service has moved away from focusing management primarily on big-game species to a more ecological approach. But conservation organizations still charge that many of the forest plans fail to meet the biological-diversity requirement adequately.

At the root of the controversy are different views about what functions the National Forest System should serve. Some interests believe National Forest System management should emphasize and increase timber production to meet the large increases in timber demand projected by the Department of Agriculture and to support the economies of certain local communities. Most conservation organizations, however, believe the National Forest System should focus on providing resources not available on private and industrial timber lands, such as old-growth habitat, maintenance of biological diversity, protection of healthy watersheds for fisheries, management of relatively undisturbed ecosystems, dispersed recreation, and habitat for species sensitive to human disturbance. Some conservation groups believe that true multiple-use management would be achieved only by reducing current timber-harvest levels and road mileage. To help meet the nation's timber needs, these organizations believe the federal government should concentrate on assisting production on nonindustrial private forest lands, which have the greatest potential for increased harvests of softwood timber.

## CURRENT DEVELOPMENTS

### Spotted Owl/Old-Growth Management in the Pacific Northwest

One of the most contentious forest-management issues — how much old growth to preserve or cut in the national forests of the Pacific Northwest — continued to build in 1986, with more divisive and heated debates looming in the future. The main focus of this debate is the northern spotted owl, a medium-sized owl that lives in old-growth forests or mixed forests of old-growth and mature trees in the Pacific Northwest and part of the Sierra Nevada mountains. According to the Forest Service, habitat for the northern spotted owl has declined from 15 million acres in the early 1800s to 4.79 million acres today.[1] With almost all old-growth eliminated from privately-owned forest lands, 96 percent of the owl's remaining habitat is on federal lands, and 76 percent is on national forests in Oregon and Washington. The owl's population has been declining — at an estimated rate of almost one

1. Many conservationists believe the habitat loss has been even greater than Forest Service data show.

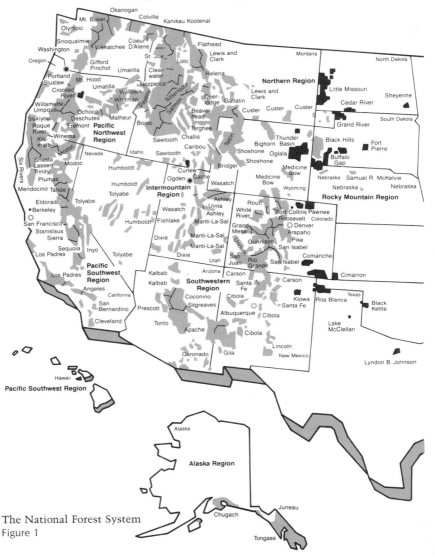

The National Forest System
Figure 1

percent yearly in Oregon (Forsman and Meslow 1986)—primarily because of the cutting of old-growth forests. The species is classified as "sensitive" by the Forest Service and is listed as threatened under state laws in Oregon and Washington.

But more is at stake than just the survival of the spotted owl. Because of the close linkage of the owl with old-growth Douglas-fir forests, the Forest Service has designated it as a "management indicator species," meaning that changes in its populations are expected to indicate changes in the health and extent of this forest type. The owl's

Legend:

- ▨ National Forests
- ▮ National Grasslands
- ▬ Regional Boundaries
- ◎ Regional Headquarters
- • Forest and Range Experiment Station Headquarters
- ▲ Forest Products Laboratory
- ☐ State and Private Forestry Area Headquarters (in other Regions S.&P.F. activities are directed from Regional headquarters)

decline may be a sign that other old-growth components are failing. In addition, recent research by the Bureau of Land Management and Forest Service scientists indicates that old-growth forest may support an array of functions, such as making nutrients in the forest system available to other plants and animals, that are of fundamental and long-term importance to the ecology of the region (Maser and Trappe 1984).

One of the major problems in spotted owl management has been lack of information on questions such as how many owls there are, how many pairs need to be maintained, and the type, amount, and distribution of habitat needed for each pair. A spotted owl management plan developed by state and federal agencies in the early 1970s initially required protection of 300 acres of old-growth per pair of owls, a figure later increased to 1,000 acres. In the 1984 regional guide establishing standards and guidelines for forest plans in the Forest Service Pacific Northwest Region (Oregon and Washington), the Forest Service adopted the 1,000-acre requirement of the interagency plan. At that time, however, new research was showing that larger amounts of old-growth were used by each pair.

In 1984, four conservation groups[2] appealed the regional guide, arguing in part that its management provisions for the spotted owl were inadequate to maintain the long-term viability of the bird. In March 1985, the deputy assistant secretary of Agriculture directed the Forest Service to prepare a supplemental environmental impact statement on its regional guide in order to give more adequate consideration to recent biological information and issues associated with spotted owl management.

***Audubon's Independent Panel of Scientists.*** In the meantime, the National Audubon Society asked the American Ornithological Union and the Cooper Ornithological Society to assemble an independent panel of ecologists and ornithologists not previously involved in the northern spotted owl controversy. The panel's report, released in May 1986, recommended a conservative approach to owl management, noting that "if the number of owls is reduced below some as yet undetermined minimum, extinction might ensue so quickly that no action could stop it" (National Audubon Society 1986). The report recommended that 1,500 pairs of owls be maintained throughout the owl's range, saying this is the "absolute minimum" for providing any prospect of long-term survival. In addition, the panel said recent findings suggest that the area of old-growth required in spotted owl home ranges increases from south to north and recommended protection of different amounts of old-growth depending on the location: 1,400 acres per pair of owls in the Sierra Nevada, 2,500 acres per pair in Oregon and northwest California, and 4,500 acres in Washington. The report noted that the current population of spotted owls is as low or lower than some species on the federal endangered species list. It warned that, depending on the management alternative adopted, the population could be reduced by half.

***Forest Service Spotted Owl Guidelines.*** In August 1986, the Forest Service released for public comment a draft of the supplemental environmental impact statement on spotted owl guidelines for the

2. National Wildlife Federation, Oregon Wildlife Federation, Lane County Audubon Society, and Oregon Natural Resources Council.

regional guide (U.S. Department of Agriculture 1986a). The Forest Service's preferred alternative, Alternative F, would not change the number of habitat areas targeted for protection under the regional guide: 550 areas in Oregon and Washington. However, in response to the findings that spotted owls may use more than 1,000 acres of old growth, this alternative establishes a scheme to protect up to 2,200 acres of old-growth for each pair of owls over the 10- to 15-year life of the plan, while additional research is conducted to determine how much old-growth habitat the owls need. The Forest Service would preserve 1,000 acres of old-growth per pair by excluding this acreage from the "suitable" timber land base, which determines how much timber may be sold in a given area. An additional 1,200 acres of old growth per pair would not be scheduled for any timber sales during the 10- to 15-year cycle of the plan, but this acreage would not be removed from the suitable timber base and would not reduce the allowable timber-sale quantity on a forest. To the greatest extent possible, spotted owl habitat areas would be located on lands already unavailable for timber harvest. This approach allows the Forest Service to protect additional spotted owl habitat without reducing timber-sale levels from its original proposal.

Under this alternative, habitat capability for the owl on the national forests in Oregon and Washington is expected to drop from 1,248 pairs of owls to 929 pairs over the next 15 years and to 501 to 592 pairs over 50 years. Making certain assumptions about habitat management on other federal lands in these states, as well as in northern California and the Sierra Nevada, habitat capability throughout the owl's range is projected to drop from the current Forest Service estimate of 3,085 pairs to two-thirds this level in 15 years and to less than half the current population in 50 years. The Forest Service estimates that the probability that Alternative F will maintain a well-distributed population of owls in Oregon and Washington is high over the next 15 years, high to medium over the next 50 years, medium to low over the next 100 years, and low in 150 years. However, the Forest Service says that owl management will be revised in future forest plans as necessary to ensure that minimum viable owl populations are maintained into perpetuity.

In comments on the supplemental environmental impact statement, conservation groups, including the National Audubon Society, the National Wildlife Federation, and the Wilderness Society, disagreed with the Forest Service's recommendation for a variety of reasons. They maintained that the preferred alternative provides for too few habitat areas of too small a size and will not maintain the minimum population levels or provide the amount of protected habitat recommended by the National Audubon Society's independent advisory panel. In summary, they said that the Forest Service is required by its own regulations, which call for it to *ensure* the maintenance of viable populations of existing species on the national forests, to choose an alternative that has a high probability of maintaining owl populations for at least 100 years. These groups recommended the Forest Service adopt an interim timber-management program in the region that defers logging in old-growth forest areas identified as spotted owl habitat for five years while additional research is conducted and a long-term spotted owl management plan is adopted.

***Bureau of Land Management Spotted Owl Management.*** While the public debate focused primarily on the National Forest System, research showed that timber harvesting on Bureau of Land Management (BLM) lands in western Oregon—the Oregon and California grant lands—may be a more immediate threat to the spotted owl. Both the National Audubon Society report and a report by BLM wildlife scientists found that these BLM lands may provide a critical link between owl populations in the national forests on the Oregon coast and in the Oregon Cascades, a link that may be necessary to maintain a self-sustaining breeding population (U.S. Department of the Interior 1986). The BLM report, shelved by the Department of the Interior but leaked to the National Audubon Society, said research suggested that if current cutting levels continue on BLM lands for the next four years, habitat on BLM lands may not be sufficient to provide this vital link. Under these circumstances, the report warned, there is a high probability that the spotted owl will be federally listed as threatened or endangered in four to six years and that by then little suitable habitat will remain for owl management on BLM lands.

To complicate matters, the Interior Department has interpreted the Oregon and California Grant Lands Act[3] (43 U.S.C. 1181 *et seq.*) as giving high priority to timber harvesting and as sharply constraining BLM's ability to set aside commercial timber lands for uses such as the spotted owl. BLM has said it will continue managing for 90 pairs of owls on its lands until 1988 in accordance with the interagency spotted owl management plan, but has agreed to protect an old-growth core area of only 300 acres for each pair. Furthermore, in a recent BLM survey pairs of owls were found in only half of the protected areas.[4]

***Congressional Action.*** Congress is starting to struggle with the issue of the spotted owl and timber management in the Pacific Northwest, although it has taken little substantive action to date. The conference

3. This act is the primary authority governing timber management on BLM's Oregon and California grant lands.

4. BLM's management of the spotted owl is covered in more detail in the *Audubon Wildlife Report 1985*. See also the Forest Service wildlife issues chapter and the spotted owl chapter in the *Audubon Wildlife Report 1986*.

report accompanying legislation appropriating 1987 funding for the federal government directed the Forest Service to maintain the region's high timber-sales offering, directed the Service to begin advanced work necessary to maintain the option of continuing historic sales levels, and added $15 million to the Forest Service road budget for the advanced engineering and design activities to assist in this effort. However, the report directed the Service not to accelerate unduly road access into roadless areas released from wilderness consideration. The conference report also prohibited BLM from modifying its land-use plans so as to reduce the allowable timber cut more than one million board feet in any master unit (U.S. Congress 1986a).

***Outlook.*** The Forest Service is expected to release its final supplemental environmental impact statement on the spotted owl management guidelines in 1987, and the various forest plans for the Pacific Northwest region should continue to be released in draft and final form throughout the year. Those plans are expected to recommend reductions in timber harvesting, in part but not solely because of spotted owl management requirements. Conservationists, however, are concerned that the timber industry will seek to delay implementation of the plans. BLM, for its part, is revising its spotted owl report for possible release in fiscal 1987 and is gearing up for the preparation of resource management plans for lands in western Oregon, scheduled for completion by 1990. Guidance to BLM state directors, which should set standards for BLM districts to consider in planning for spotted owl management, is scheduled for issuance in June 1987.

In the meantime, it is possible that someone will petition the U.S. Fish and Wildlife Service to list the northern spotted owl as threatened or endangered under the Endangered Species Act. Currently, Forest Service management for the owl is guided by the National Forest Management Act, which requires forest plans to provide for a diversity of plant and animal communities, and by Forest Service regulations, which require the plans to maintain viable and well-distributed populations of existing species. BLM believes it has no legal requirement to protect the owl. The Endangered Species Act could provide a clearer and more enforceable mandate for protecting the owl since it prohibits federal agencies from taking actions that would jeopardize the continued existence of a listed species or its critical habitat. Any attempt to use the Endangered Species Act to protect the owl, however, would likely be perceived as a threat to timber production and in all probability would be stiffly resisted.

## Tongass National Forest

Controversy over timber management on the Tongass National Forest in southeast Alaska heated up in 1986 as the Forest Service issued a congressionally mandated report on the status of the Tongass (U.S. Department of Agriculture 1986b). At the same time, the Wilderness Society, with the publication of a 215-page study that was highly critical of the Tongass timber program, launched a major campaign to reform the forest's management. Calling the Tongass one of the last largely intact rain forests in the world's temperate latitudes, the Wilderness Society and other conservation organizations charge that congressionally mandated timber subsidies and supply goals — combined with improper Forest Service implementation of the Tongass timber program — are causing excessive harvesting of old-growth forest, are threatening wildlife and recreation, and are costing taxpayers tens of millions of dollars yearly.

The Tongass is the nation's largest national forest, larger than all of West Virginia. It also is notable for its abundant fish and wildlife populations. It supports the greatest concentrations of bald eagles and grizzly bears left in America. The forest also supports significant populations of black bear, Sitka black-tailed deer, mountain goats, wolves, and a variety of birds and furbearers. The freshwater fisheries of southeast Alaska, including a salmon fishery vital to the local economy, largely depend on the streams and lakes within the Tongass.

The Tongass is managed in accordance with special provisions included in Section 705 of the Alaska National Interest Lands Conservation Act of 1980 (16 U.S.C.A. 539d, 1604). Section 705 essentially ratified the Forest Service's 1979 land-management plan for the Tongass and was intended to guarantee the continued availability of timber at existing sales levels after 5.4 million acres of the Tongass were designated as wilderness in the Alaska Lands Act. Under Section 705(a), Congress set a goal of supplying 4.5 billion board feet of timber per decade from the Tongass to dependent industry.

To ensure that the Forest Service would have the funds necessary to prepare this level of timber sales, Section 705(a) provided the Service a minimum appropriation of $40 million yearly, called the Tongass Supply Fund. Unlike most other federal expenditures, these funds are available to the Forest Service automatically, without annual appropriation by Congress. Recognizing that the Forest Service, in order to maintain the mandated level of timber availability, might have to sell timber from lands that normally would not be considered suitable for commercial logging, Congress in Section 705(d) of the act exempted the Tongass from Section 6(k) of the National Forest Management Act. Section 6(k) provides that lands identified as physically or economically unsuitable for timber production be placed off limits to commercial sales. Section 706(b) of the Alaska Lands Act requires the Forest Service, in consultation with various Alaska interests, to report on the status of the Tongass in 1985 and every two years thereafter. The first report required under this provision was issued in early 1986 (U.S. Department of Agriculture 1986b).

In general, fish and wildlife interests charge that old-growth harvest levels and associated road construction anticipated in the Tongass land-management plan will harm fish and wildlife resources. But more at issue is the *quality* of the old growth to be harvested. The Forest Service categorizes old-growth stands as low, medium, or high volume. The higher volume stands not only provide the most productive timber, but also provide some of the best wildlife habitat. Of approximately 4.7 million acres of old-growth forest on the Tongass that has sufficient volume for timber production, only about 640,000 acres have stands of medium to high volume, and only about 160,000 acres of these stands are protected as wilderness or backcountry lands (see Figure 2). According to the Wilderness Society report, 75 percent of the medium-volume and high-volume stands will either be logged or disturbed by timber roads under the long-range plan for the Tongass.

Of particular concern are the 100,000 acres of high-volume old-growth. The Sitka black-tailed deer, the most popular game animal in the forest, depends during winter on these limited, high-volume old-growth stands. The uneven canopy in these stands provides shelter from deep winter snows while still allowing sufficient sunlight to reach the forest floor to produce plenty of forage. The Tongass plan would result in the harvest of 66 percent of the remaining high-volume acreage. This would cause an 80-percent loss in this habitat type when compared with 1950 levels. The Alaska Department of Fish and Game says that planned harvests of old-growth forest habitat will cause the Sitka black-tailed deer population to decline by more than 50 percent in three-fourths of the watersheds scheduled for eventual logging. Other wildlife and fish species also are likely to suffer adverse impacts from the old-growth harvest, including moose, black bear, brown bear (grizzlies), mountain goats, martens, wolves, land otters, and cavity-nesting birds (State of Alaska 1985). Logging also could cause reductions in salmon and trout reproduction on the Tongass, which produces 80 to 85 percent of the salmonids commercially harvested in Alaska. The Forest Service, however, says that fishery-enhancement projects, constructed largely by the Forest Service from 1980 to 1984, will add six million pounds of salmon yearly to the region's fisheries. The state of Alaska, commercial fishermen, and the region's Alaska Native Corporation, Sealaska, have urged improved management for fish and wildlife on the forest.

Another key criticism of the Tongass timber program is that it is losing millions of dollars yearly at the taxpayers' expense. According to the Congressional Research Service, between 1970 and 1984 the Forest Service spent $375 million to sell timber from the Tongass and

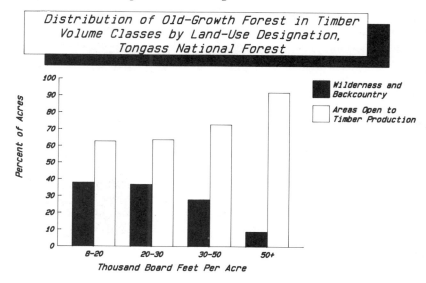

Distribution of Old-Growth Forest in Timber
Volume Classes by Land-Use Designation,
Tongass National Forest

Source: The Wilderness Society. 1986.
America's Vanishing Rain Forests. A Report on Federal
Timber Management in Southeast Alaska.

Figure 2

received $62.6 million in timber-sale revenues, for a loss of $312 million (Southeast Alaska Conservation Council 1986). In 1984 alone, the program lost $54 million, a loss of 93 cents on every dollar spent (The Wilderness Society 1986a).

Conservationists also maintain that the Tongass timber harvest is an effort to prop up an industry whose decline is due to factors beyond the Forest Service's control. Timber sales on the Tongass have plunged in recent years, from 450 million board feet in 1980 to 250 million board feet in 1984. Timber-industry jobs have declined from 3,000 full-time-equivalent jobs in 1980 to fewer than 1,800 in 1986. Several factors are responsible for the decline, including increased timber sales from lands owned by Alaska Natives, competition from British Columbia, and a poor market for Alaska's lumber products and dissolving pulp, 90 percent of which is exported. Furthermore, conservation organizations charge that timber production is a short-term industry in Alaska because second-growth trees will not be commercially valuable. In the meantime, they maintain that timber harvest on the Tongass threatens commercial fisheries and the tourism industry, which are southeast Alaska's economic future, as well as the local subsistence economy.

Conservation groups advocate several changes in the management of the Tongass. They have called for repeal of Section 705(a) to eliminate the timber supply goal and the Tongass Timber Supply Fund, and repeal of Section 705(d) so that the Tongass will be subject to the suitability requirements of the National Forest Management Act. They seek termination of the 50-year contracts between the Forest Service and two large timber companies which, they say, have promoted waste, fraud, and abuse on the forest.[5] And they seek revision of the Tongass forest plan. In the interim, they also have called for various reforms in management of the forest.

Congress took some initial steps toward addressing complaints about the Tongass timber program in 1986. The House Interior Subcommittee on Public Lands, chaired by Representative John Seiberling (D-OH), held oversight hearings on the Tongass in the spring. Interior Committee Chairman Morris Udall (D-AZ) wrote the secretary of Agriculture requesting several reforms to the Forest Service's implementation of the Tongass program (Udall 1986). The House Appropriations Committee directed its surveys and investigations staff to study "contentions raised by various interests" regarding the Tongass Timber Supply Fund and the forest's management and to report back to the committee within six months (U.S. Congress 1986b). The committee also directed the Forest Service to prepare a plan that provides for more efficient expenditure of the Tongass Timber Supply Fund and to include an explanation of actions taken to address these concerns in its fiscal year 1988 budget submission. The committee also urged the authorizing committees to address these issues, including the continued appropriateness of providing funding through the Tongass Timber Supply Fund rather than as part of the annual appropriations process. Finally, Representative Robert Mrazek (D-NY) introduced legislation, H.R.5291, to repeal sections 705(a) and 705(d) of the Alaska Lands Act. No action was taken on the bill, but conservationists think action is likely on similar legislation in both the House and Senate in 1987.

## The 1985 Resources Planning Act Program

In the fall of 1986, the administration released the long-overdue 1985 update of the Resources Planning Act program, a 50-year national plan for Forest Service programs (U.S. Department of Agriculture 1986c). The program was criticized from all sides: by members of the House of Representatives, who objected to its approach of recommending a range of activity and output levels, constrained by high and low bounds, rather than recommending a single, optimum program; by conservationists, who charged the program maintains and even expands the dominance of commodity production on the national forests; and by the timber industry, which argued that timber supply

5. Discussed in more detail in the *Audubon Wildlife Report 1986.*

from the national forests in the first decades of the program is scheduled to increase at a far slower rate than projected timber demand.

The Forest Service is directed by the Forest and Rangeland Renewable Resources Planning Act of 1974 (16 U.S.C. 1600-1614) to prepare and update every 10 years a renewable-resource assessment describing the nation's overall renewable-resource situation, including both government and private lands. Based on the findings of the assessment, the Forest Service is to develop a long-range renewable-resource program every five years covering 40 to 50 years and outlining goals and objectives for the Forest Service's three major programs: the National Forest System, State and Private Forestry, and Research. The president transmits the recommended program to Congress along with a Statement of Policy intended to be used in framing budget requests for the next five to 10 years. The submitted program is considered operative unless either house of Congress modifies or disapproves it within 90 days while Congress is in session.

The release of the 1985 program was delayed for more than a year by the Office of Management and Budget, which was concerned about the spending levels called for in the Forest Service's proposed program. The program finally submitted to Congress included both a low-bound program, essentially the program favored by Office of Management and Budget, and a high-bound program, which for the most part is the program the Forest Service would like to see. At the low bound, Forest Service programs would decline until 1990 both in funding and in outputs—such as timber-sale offerings, recreation and wildlife user days, and animal unit months of livestock grazing—and then would begin to expand. Under the high bound, new investments would begin immediately and would continue to increase throughout the planning period.

***Fish and Wildlife Habitat Management.*** For the wildlife and fish element of the program, the Forest Service sets objectives for wildlife and fish user days and commercial anadromous-fish production. Under the low-bound program, fish and wildlife funding would remain relatively constant until 1990. Wildlife and fish user days would drop from 23 million in 1986 to 20 million in 1990, and commercial anadromous-fish production would drop from 106 million pounds to 103 million pounds. Under the high-bound program, funding would more than double by 1990. User days would increase to 28 million, and commercial anadromous-fish production would increase to 114 million pounds. Habitat carrying capacity for species that are hunted or fished is expected to increase by the year 2000 under the high-bound program and to decrease under the low-bound program (see Figure 3).

Under the high-bound program, two aspects of wildlife- and

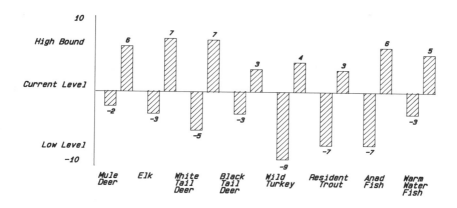

Projected Change in Habitat Capability, 1985–2000: Comparison Between RPA High and Low Bound Programs

*Source:   U.S. Forest Service*
Figure 3

fish-habitat management would receive special emphasis beginning in 1988: endangered species and anadromous fisheries. Under the endangered-species initiative, accelerated funding would be provided to ensure that the Forest Service can complete recovery schedules for listed species by 2000. There are 141 species listed or proposed as threatened or endangered on the National Forest System, and 80 recovery plans have been written to date. The fiscal 1988 cost for this program is $5.3 million, compared with appropriations of $3.5 million in fiscal 1987. Without this accelerated funding, the Forest Service will not be able to manage effectively for endangered species, and the resulting litigation and mitigation requirements are expected to cause sharply increased costs for the Forest Service. Only 65 percent of the Forest Service's share of recovery schedules would be completed by 2000 without this accelerated funding.

Under the anadromous-fish initiative, the Forest Service, in cooperation with various states, would restore key salmon and steelhead habitat that has been damaged by past logging, mining, and road construction. Anadromous fish produced on the National Forest System account for approximately 21 percent of the direct economic value from U.S. commercial anadromous fisheries. The fiscal year 1988 cost of the initiative would be $17.1 million, compared with appropriations of $4.5 million for anadromous fish in 1987. With this initiative, commercial anadromous-fish production would increase from 106 million pounds yearly to 142 million pounds by 2000. Without the initiative, production is projected to decline until 1990 and regain current levels by the year 2000.

**Timber and Roads.** The 1985 Resources Planning Act program recommends dramatic increases in road construction and timber-sale offerings over the long-term. These increases are expected to have adverse impacts on fish and wildlife. The high-bound program calls for annual timber-sale offerings of 20 billion board feet by 2030, a huge increase over current sale-offering levels of 11.2 billion board feet and more than a doubling of the average sales-offering level of 9.6 billion board feet over the past decade. The 20 billion-board-feet level has been attacked as politically and ideologically motivated, since it is the level former Assistant Agriculture Secretary John Crowell advocated and was derived by including an arbitrary add-on of 4.39 billion board feet to be achieved through the development of unspecified "new technology." Without this add-on, the high-bound timber level would be 15.6 billion board feet, which is the timber-sales offering level that the Forest Service expects will be included in the aggregated forest plans. The low-bound level for timber is 15.6 billion board feet, including .8 billion board feet to be derived from "new technology." This level is roughly equal to the high-bound level in the previous 1980 Resources Planning Act program. The program document says timber management under the 1985 Resources Planning Act program will improve wildlife habitat for species that favor younger forest habitat, but that species requiring mature or old-growth forest habitat, particularly in Oregon, Washington, and northern California, may suffer population declines from increased harvest levels. Habitat capability for species requiring mature or old-growth habitat is projected to decline 11 percent by the year 2000 under the low-bound program and by 15 percent under the high-bound.

Road mileage in the National Forest System also is targeted for dramatic increases. Road construction and reconstruction is scheduled to increase from 7,762 miles in 1986 to 12,900 miles in 2030 under the low-bound program and to 15,270 miles under the high-bound program. Under the high-bound program, 580,751 miles of roads would be built between 1986 and 2030. Approximately 260,000 miles would be new roads and would almost double current National Forest System road mileage from 343,000 miles to more than 600,000 miles. Impacts of this road construction are not discussed in the 1985 program document.

**Significance of the Resources Planning Act Program.** What actual effect the Resources Planning Act program will have on forest management or Forest Service funding is unclear. The 1980 program aimed to balance the Forest Service's emphasis on timber by holding timber funding roughly level between 1980 and 1985 while providing increased funding for most other programs. However, the Reagan administration did not follow the 1980 program in formulating its budget requests, nor did Congress appropriate funds according to the program's priorities. In fact, the priorities were almost reversed. Timber funding increased about seven percent in constant dollars over those five years, while most other funding dropped. Timber and road construction consistently achieved nearly 100 percent of the 1980 program goals, while wildlife-habitat improvement achieved an average of 29 percent of its goals (see Table 1).

Furthermore, it is unclear how the Resources Planning Act program is to relate to the individual forest plans now in preparation. One of the major concerns expressed by timber-industry representatives at congressional hearings was that while the Resources Planning Act program called for increases in timber-sale offerings, many of the plans are not fully achieving the Resources Planning Act timber objectives. Congress began to respond to these concerns in late 1986 by including a number of directives in the conference report on the continuing resolution funding the government for fiscal 1987 (U.S. Congress 1986a).

The House Agriculture Subcommittee on Forest, Family Farms, and Energy has asked the Department of Agriculture to revise the 1985 program to eliminate the high- and low-bound approach and to submit a single recommendation in January 1987 (Whitley 1986). The subcommittee also asked the department to explain how its 1988 budget request differs from the Resources Planning Act program's recommendations. Congress could revise the Resources Planning Act Program when it begins work in 1987.

## Florida National Forests and Biological Diversity

In February 1986, eight conservation organizations, including the National Wildlife Federation and the National Audubon Society, filed an administrative appeal[6] on the forest plan for the Florida national forests[7] on two basic grounds: that it fails to provide for and maintain diversity of natural communities on the forest, and that it fails to maintain and recover the endangered red-cockaded woodpecker. The National Forest Management Act and Forest Service regulations require forest plans to maintain biological diversity on the national forests. If the Forest Service does not alter the Florida plan, the

6. Individuals or organizations dissatisfied with a decision in a forest plan may appeal to the chief of the Forest Service to have that decision reviewed.

7. The three national forests in Florida—the Apalachicola, the Osceola, and the Ocala—are covered by this one plan.

**TABLE 1**
**Goals for 1985 RPA Program, Selected Activities**

| | 1986 | 1990 | | 2000 | | 2030 | |
|---|---|---|---|---|---|---|---|
| | | low-bound | high-bound | low-bound | high-bound | low-bound | high-bound |
| Timber (sales offered, bbf) | 11.4 | 9.0 | 11.6 | 11.8 | 14.0 | 15.6 | 20.0 |
| Grazing (in millions of animal unit months) | 11.3 | 9.8 | 9.8 | 9.8 | 10.0 | 10.3 | |
| Wildlife and Fish (millions of user days) | 23 | 20 | 28 | 23 | 35 | 28 | 40 |
| Anadromous Fish (commercial harvest, millions of pounds) | 106 | 103 | 114 | 107 | 142 | 135 | 177 |
| Wilderness Acreage (in millions) | 32 | 35 | 37 | 35 | 38 | 35 | 40 |
| Road Construction/reconstruction (in miles per year) | 7,762 | 6,879 | 11,296 | 9,600 | 12,191 | 12,900 | 15,270 |

Source: U.S. Department of Agriculture, Forest Service. 1986. *A Recommended Renewable Resources Program: 1985-2030 (1985 update)*. U.S. Department of Agriculture. Washington, D.C.

conservation groups may use the plan as a test case to determine in court what these requirements entail.

The conservationists' major concern is the Forest Service's proposal to cut and convert much of the Florida national forests' longleaf-pine forest. Longleaf-pine forest, with its native wiregrass and associated groundcover, is one of the most biologically diverse natural communities in the Southeast. According to the appeal, only 14 percent of the original longleaf-forest acreage on the coastal plan remains. The appeal charges that nearly a fourth of the Florida national forests have been converted to tree farms by intensive forestry practices in recent decades and that the plan, which calls for clearcutting on short rotations and artificial regeneration using mechanical site preparation, will result in conversion of most of the remaining pine forest. The appellants maintain that this will virtually eliminate the remaining longleaf pine/wiregrass natural community in the Florida national forests and thus will violate the National Forest Management Act and Forest Service regulations on biological diversity. Forest Service regulations allow reductions in diversity only where needed to meet overall multiple-use objectives. The appellants say the only reason for reducing longleaf-pine communities is to increase timber outputs, which does not meet the multiple-use criterion.

The appeal also charges that the plan will not provide adequate habitat to maintain viable populations of the endangered red-cockaded woodpecker on any of the Florida national forests. On the Apalachicola National Forest, which appellants say probably supports the only viable population of red-cockaded woodpeckers in the world, conservationists charge that the plan fails to protect sufficient mature pines older than 60 years, which are necessary for foraging habitat. They also say that the amount of pine to be managed on rotations of 70 to 80 years on the Apalachicola is inadequate to protect red-cockaded woodpecker colony sites. On the other two national forests covered by the plan, the Osceola and the Ocala, the appellants charge that red-cockaded woodpecker population goals are insufficient. The appellants charge that the plan violates the Endangered Species Act as well as Forest Service regulations which require that viable populations of existing wildlife species be maintained and that, where possible, the plans provide for recovery of threatened and endangered species. The appeal was still pending at the end of fiscal 1986.

## Caribbean National Forest and the Puerto Rican Parrot

In 1986, the Forest Service proposed to develop a commercial timber program on the Caribbean National Forest in Puerto Rico, the only tropical rain forest in the National Forest System. The proposal, however, was strongly opposed by numerous interests in Puerto Rico and by national conservation organizations. At the end of the year, the Forest Service reversed its decision.

The Caribbean National Forest provides the only habitat for the Puerto Rican parrot, one of the most critically endangered species in the world and the last native species of parrot surviving in U.S territory. The forest also provides habitat for the endangered Puerto Rican boa, six plant species proposed for federally endangered status, three other wildlife species considered by Puerto Rico to be threatened, and 62 plant species identified as critical. Since the 1930s, the Forest Service has managed the forest primarily as a site for research on tropical forest ecology. Under a captive-breeding program, the U.S. Fish and Wildlife Service and the Forest Service have increased Puerto Rican parrot populations on the forest from 16 birds in 1971 to 31 in 1986, and the captive population has increased from three to 38.

The Forest Service's plan for the Caribbean National Forest proposed to begin a commercial timber-production program on the forest in order to demonstrate tropical-forest silviculture. The plan classified 21 percent of the forest as suitable for intensive timber production, including six percent of the area determined by the Forest Service to be critical parrot habitat. Twelve environmental organizations, including eight in Puerto Rico, appealed the plan, saying that commercial timber production and road construction would affect forest wildlife, recreation, and watershed values adversely. A variety of experts also warned that the timber program appeared to be uneconomical and thus would do little to demonstrate to other countries the feasibility of developing self-sufficient, local wood-products industries.

In late 1986, the Forest Service announced that the regional forester for the Southern Region, in response to a request by the governor of the Commonwealth of Puerto Rico, decided to eliminate the proposal for commercial harvest of timber on the forest. Instead, the forest will continue to be managed for protection of its natural and recreational values and for recovery of the Puerto Rican parrot. The Service also will use the forest to demonstrate proper tropical-forest management techniques. The forest plan will be modified accordingly.

## Woodland Caribou

Forest Service plans to reestablish a stable woodland caribou population in the United States by transplanting animals from Canada into northwestern Idaho are scheduled to proceed in the winter of 1986-87. The transplant proposal ran into trouble in late 1985 when timber interests objected to the transplant out of concern that caribou management would interfere with timber production. A compromise developed with the assistance of Senator James McClure (R-ID), however, paved the way for the transplant program.

The woodland caribou exists in healthy populations across central Canada, but has disappeared almost completely from the conterminous United States. The exception is a small remnant population of about 25 animals located in the Selkirk Mountains of southern British Columbia, northeastern Washington, and northwestern Idaho, where it is federally listed as an endangered species. The recovery plan for the woodland caribou anticipates augmenting the population in the United States by transplanting 18 to 36 animals from another population in Canada over a three-year period.

## Other Developments

***Endangered Species Information Tracking System.*** In 1986, the Forest Service installed a computerized system for tracking information and management progress on species listed as threatened or endangered, species proposed for listing as threatened or endangered, and category 1 and 2 species—species that appear to warrant consideration for listing but for which additional data are first required.[8] The system tracks species in the above categories that occur in the national forest system—811 species in all—and includes information such as whether a recovery plan has been prepared for the species, the key goals of Forest Service management included in each recovery plan, and the progress made toward accomplishing the goals. A printout of this information can be obtained from the wildlife and fisheries staff at the Forest Service's Washington office. The Forest Service is the first federal agency to install such a system, which may provide a model for other agencies.

***Below-Cost Timber Sales.*** The below-cost timber sales controversy continued to simmer in 1986, but took a back seat to debate over other aspects of national-forest management. Fish and wildlife interests have opposed many below-cost sales on the grounds that these timber harvests and associated roads frequently have adverse impacts on fish and wildlife habitat and at the same time are not economically justified. In 1986, the Forest Service released a draft of its timber-sales accounting system, prepared at the request of Congress for use in identifying uneconomic sales. The proposed accounting system was criticized by the General Accounting Office, the Natural Resources Defense Council, other conservation groups, and both the House and Senate appropriations committees. The House Appropriations Committee directed the Forest Service to work with the General Accounting Office to refine the system and directed the Service to delay

8. The Forest Service refers to these as "PETC" species, an acronym for "proposed, endangered, threatened, category 1 and 2."

implementing a new system until this effort with the General Accounting Office has been completed. It is expected to be released in 1987.

***Road Construction.*** Continued efforts by fish, wildlife, and other conservation interests to slow national forest road construction failed in 1986, but only after a near win that may indicate that these interests will be more successful in the future. The president's budget requested $178.5 million for forest-road construction, including $143.8 million for construction of roads to access timber sales. The House of Representatives, charging that the Forest Service for the past five years had exceeded its planned and funded goals for road construction and reconstruction despite funding reductions, cut $44 million from the budget for timber-road construction. The Senate Appropriations Committee countered by adding $66.7 million to the president's request for timber roads. The full Senate rejected this increase and approved an amendment by Senator William Proxmire (D-WI) to cut the timber-road budget to a level below the president's request, but this vote was reversed after political maneuvering by Senator James McClure (R-ID), chairman of the Interior Appropriations Subcommittee. In the final appropriations act, Congress provided $180 million for Forest Service timber-road construction in fiscal 1987, $36.2 million above the president's request. However, the conference report on the appropriations bill addressed one conservationist complaint about the road program by directing forest supervisors to make available for public review the location, mileage, and cost of timber roads planned for construction each year.

## LEGISLATION

### Wilderness Legislation

Congress passed wilderness bills for four states in 1986, designating 42,300 acres of national-forest wilderness in Georgia (P.L. 99-555), 33,700 acres in Tennessee (P.L. 99-490), and 8,100 acres in Nebraska (P.L. 99-504). The Nebraska bill also designated a 6,600-acre Pine Ridge National Recreation Area. Congress also adjusted the boundaries of five wilderness areas in Texas (P.L. 99-584), adding about 1,000 acres to existing wilderness. Bills designating national-forest wilderness in several other states were introduced and in some cases received some action, but were not completed by Congress. Bills for Nevada, Michigan, and Alabama passed in the House but were stalled for various reasons. A bill for Montana was introduced by Senator John Melcher

(D-MT), but saw no action. No legislation was introduced for Idaho or Colorado national-forest wilderness.

## LEGAL DEVELOPMENTS

### Pine Beetle Suppression and the Red-Cockaded Woodpecker

Environmental organizations have brought two lawsuits to prevent the Forest Service from cutting trees in designated wilderness as part of its efforts to suppress southern pine beetle infestations. No significant legal action occurred on these pending suits in fiscal year 1986. However, the Forest Service did release a court-ordered draft environmental impact statement on the program, paving the way for further action on the litigation or perhaps a resolution of the issue in 1987.

Although timber cutting is seldom allowed in wilderness, the Wilderness Act authorizes the Forest Service to take such measures as necessary to control fire, insects, and diseases. It has been Forest Service policy to cut trees infested with southern pine beetles, including trees in wilderness areas, to prevent the beetles from spreading to other forested areas. The plaintiffs—the Sierra Club Legal Defense Fund, joined by the Wilderness Society on one of the suits—charge that the Wilderness Act's authorization of such measures "as necessary to control" insects means that the measures must be necessary and efficacious, and charge that the Forest Service has never proved that cutting of infected trees is efficacious. They also maintain that the Forest Service did not comply with the requirement of the National Environmental Policy Act for an assessment of the environmental impacts of the pine beetle suppression program.

The issue is complicated by the fact that in some areas, red-cockaded woodpecker habitat overlaps with wilderness areas that have been infested by southern pine beetles. In these areas, the Forest Service has said that it must cut the trees to prevent southern pine beetles from further infesting red-cockaded woodpecker habitat. The Service maintains that the beetles kill the trees, forcing the woodpeckers, which depend on live trees for food, to relocate. The plaintiffs, however, charge that such tree cutting has actually damaged red-cockaded woodpecker habitat and thus has violated the Endangered Species Act.

In 1985, initial preliminary injunctions against the suppression program in wilderness were issued in Texas (*Sierra Club v. Block*, 614 F.Supp. 488 [D. Tex. 1985]) and in Arkansas, Louisiana, and Mississippi (*Sierra Club and the Wilderness Society v. Block*, 614 F.Supp. 134 [D. D.C. 1985]). In the latter case, the Forest Service was directed to prepare an environmental impact statement on the pine beetle suppression program. In 1986, the Forest Service issued a draft environmental impact statement covering the entire Forest Service Southern Region. The preferred alternative proposed the cutting of trees in wilderness as part of the pine beetle suppression program in only two cases: in order to protect essential colony sites and foraging areas for the red-cockaded woodpecker and to protect adjacent state and private lands. However, Forest Service sources say an alternative that would allow no cutting in wilderness also is receiving serious consideration. The Service is awaiting a formal opinion from the Fish and Wildlife Service as to whether failure to cut trees to protect red-cockaded woodpecker habitat would violate the Endangered Species Act requirement that federal agencies not jeopardize the continued existence of endangered species or their critical habitat. The final environment impact statement on pine beetle suppression was scheduled for release in February 1987. Further action on the lawsuits was likely to be delayed until that time.

## REFERENCES

Forsman, E. and E. C. Meslow. 1986. "The Spotted Owl," *in* Roger Di Silvestro ed., *Audubon Wildlife Report 1986*. National Audubon Society. New York, New York.

Maser, C. and J.M. Trappe. 1984. "The Seen and Unseen World of the Fallen Tree." General Technical Report PNW-164. Pacific Northwest Forest and Range Experiment Station, U.S. Department of Agriculture, in cooperation with the Bureau of Land Management, U.S. Department of the Interior. Portland, Oregon.

National Audubon Society. 1986. *Report of the Advisory Panel on the Spotted Owl*. New York, New York.

Norse, E. A. *et al.* 1986. *Conserving Biological Diversity in Our National Forests*. The Wilderness Society. Washington, D.C.

Southeast Alaska Conservation Council. 1986. *Last Stand for the Tongass National Forest*. Juneau, Alaska.

State of Alaska. 1985. "Views of the State of Alaska: The Effects of the Alaska National Interest Lands Conservation Act and its Implementation on Southeast Alaska" in *Status of the Tongass National Forest 1985 Report*. U.S. Department of Agriculture, Forest Service, Alaska Region. 1986. Admin. Doc. Number 153.

The Wilderness Society. 1986a. *American's Vanishing Rain Forest: A Report on Federal Timber Management in Southeast Alaska*. The Wilderness Society. Washington, D.C.

Udall, M. K. 1986. Letter from Morris K. Udall, Chairman, Committee on Interior and Insular Affairs, U.S. House of Representatives, to Richard E. Lyng, Secretary, U.S. Department of Agriculture, July 31, 1986.

U.S. Congress, U.S. House of Representatives. 1986a. Making Continuing Appropriations for Fiscal Year 1987, Conference Report to accompany House Joint Resolution 738, House Report 99-1005, October 15, 1986. Government Printing Office. Washington, D.C.

U.S. Congress, U.S. House of Representatives, Committee on Appropriations. 1986b. Report on Department of the Interior and Related Agencies Appropriations Bill, 1987,

House Report 99-714, July 24, 1986. Government Printing Office. Washington, D.C.

U.S. Department of Agriculture, Forest Service, Pacific Northwest Region. 1986a. *Draft Supplement to the Environmental Impact Statement for an Amendment to the Pacific Northwest Regional Guide, Vols. 1 and 2, Spotted Owl Guidelines*. Washington, D.C.

U.S. Department of Agriculture, Forest Service, Alaska Region. 1986b. *Status of the Tongass National Forest: 1985 Report*. Admin. Doc. Number 153. Washington, D.C.

U.S. Department of Agriculture, Forest Service. 1986c. *A Recommended Renewable Resources Program: 1985-2030*. Washington, D.C.

U.S. Department of Agriculture, Forest Service. 1986d. *National Forest System Threatened and Endangered Species Program: A Brief*. Washington, D.C.

U.S. Department of the Interior, Bureau of Land Management. 1986. "Northern Spotted Owl Analysis, May 8, 1986." Unpublished report. Washington, D.C.

Whitley, C. O. and Sid Morrison. 1986. Letter from Charles O. Whitley, Chairman, and Sid Morrison, Ranking Minority Member, Subcommittee on Forests, Family Farms, and Energy, Committee on Agriculture, U.S. House of Representatives, to George Dunlop, Assistant Secretary for National Resources and Environment, October 16, 1986.

*Katherine Barton, a freelance writer who specializes in conservation issues, is based in Washington D.C.*

Mount Gould towers above a field of bear grass at Glacier National Park, one of 337 areas managed by the National Park Service. *National Park Service/Photo by Hileman*

# Wildlife and the National Park Service

Richard C. Curry

## OVERVIEW

The National Park Service manages 337 areas totaling 74.8 million acres in 49 states. Natural areas of the National Park System range in size and location from the 880-acre Buck Island Reef National Monument in the U.S. Virgin Islands to the 13.2-million-acre Wrangell-St. Elias National Park and Preserve in Alaska. By design, the National Park System is intended to include representations of every significant element of the rich mosaic of native U.S. flora and fauna. Park Service Director William Mott, Jr., refers to the system as a "Library of the Wild," "a fragile treasure of species that can keep the planet alive and well" (*National Parks*, January-February 1986). Although there is no complete central inventory of all the wildlife species that inhabit the system, nearly a third of the rare and endangered animal species in the United States occur in units of the park system.

The management mandate of the Park Service is eloquently simple:

. . .to conserve the scenery and the natural and historical objects and the wildlife therein and to provide for the enjoyment of the same in such

Audubon Wildlife Report 1987

manner and by such means as will leave them unimpaired for the enjoyment of future generations (16 U.S.C.A. 1, 2-3).

Yet the achievement of that mandate has proved to be extraordinarily difficult. Visitor use and enjoyment must be incorporated into the resource-management scheme. In the abstract, limiting activities within the park to those that will not significantly impair park resources seems easy. In reality, the Service lacks standards by which to judge when uses are causing unacceptable damage and faces great pressure to satisfy demands for public use and access.

Even if the parks were strictly protected, some conservationists still fear that park ecosystems will be unable to sustain themselves in the long run. In 1915, when the Park Service received its management mandate, the parks were so remote and inaccessible that Stephen T. Mather, the first director, promoted the use of trains and automobiles as means for opening up the parks for public use and enjoyment. Now, most parks either are or soon will be encircled by some level of development immediately adjacent to the park boundary.

Each unit of the park system is under the day-to-day direction of a resident superintendent. Each unit has a core of base funding that supports continuing programs. The percentage of the base that is allocated to resource management is one measure of the commitment to wildlife preservation, since wildlife management is a component of the resource-management program. In fiscal 1987, about 6.4 percent of the total Park Service funds will be allocated to resource management and less than one percent of the permanent workforce will be involved full time with natural-resources management (Department of Interior 1985a). No estimate is available for the portion of the resource-management budget dedicated to wildlife.

## CURRENT DEVELOPMENTS

### Director Mott's 12-Point Plan

In summer 1985, the newly appointed director of the National Park Service, William Penn Mott, Jr., presented a 12-point plan and accompanying objectives for improving park management. The plan was designed to promote a rededication by the National Park Service "to the protection, preservation, and perpetuation of all units of the National Park System . . ." (Department of Interior 1985b).

Thirty-two "action elements" were developed as a means of implementing each of the plan's 12 points. In 1986, several initiatives were taken that would improve the management of wildlife resources in the parks. These include actions to:

- improve wilderness management;
- create usable resource inventories for each park;
- establish a blue-ribbon panel to examine National Park Service policies on natural and cultural resources and to recommend how these policies may be improved.

***Improving Wilderness Management.*** The management of wilderness areas is a critical element of wildlife management in the national parks. In many parks where wilderness designation covers up to 80 percent of the acreage, vast areas subject to heavy visitor use must be managed in strict conformance to wilderness standards. Visitors have great potential for altering the behavior and habitat of park wildlife. For example, methods must be devised to keep backpacker food supplies away from bears; maintain the natural distribution, ecology, and behavior of bears; and minimize threats to human safety and property. Yet these bear-management measures must be implemented so as not to degrade the wilderness quality of the area.

Under its action plan, "The Park Service will complete a comprehensive review of its wilderness-management policies and practices by 1987, and needed changes will be made in management, interpretation, and planning. The goal will be to ensure that designated, potential, and proposed wilderness areas in the National Park System are managed according to the principles of the Wilderness Act, and in Alaska according to the Alaska National Interest Lands Conservation Act . . ." (Department of Interior 1986a).

In addition, the plan calls for specific steps to improve coordination and consistency in the management of all wilderness areas; to monitor human use, air quality, and noise trends in wilderness areas; to develop a program of interpretation and public information to explain the role of wilderness in society; and to develop a systematic resource-management strategy for wilderness areas.

A Task Force on Wilderness Management and Policy was appointed by the director to analyse the Service's wilderness policy. The task force includes, in addition to National Park Service personnel, representatives of the other federal agencies managing wilderness areas (U.S. Forest Service, Bureau of Land Management, and U.S. Fish and Wildlife Service) and several national conservation organizations (National Audubon Society, National Parks and Conservation Association, and the Conservation Foundation).

The task force met early in 1986 and established the five-year management action program developed by the Steering Committee of the First National Wilderness Management Workshop, convened by the University of Idaho in 1985, as a sound basis for developing the National Park Service program (Department of Interior 1986b). The task force also found that the Service's wilderness-management policies were adequate and in accord with basic legislative mandates. However, the task force concluded that there is a lack of consistency between the Service's wilderness policy and the actual management of National Park Service wilderness areas. This inconsistency was attributed to such factors as variations in managers' interpretation of policy, the lack of central coordination, the absence of guidance on specific management issues, and insufficient exchange of information about wilderness management issues and problems both within the agency and with other federal land-managing agencies.

The task force recommended that action be taken in six areas: policy coordination through the designation of agency personnel with a specific mandate to facilitate consistency; improvement of management techniques; determination of appropriate uses and the development of a capacity to assess user impacts; education and training of wilderness management personnel; development of public knowledge and understanding of wilderness-resource values, uses and ethics; and facilitation of interagency coordination and consistency through the establishment of a National Wilderness Coordination Committee.

The first priority of the task force is the designation of wilderness coordinators at both the Washington and regional office levels. A second level of priority is assigned to the training of service personnel and the development of a National Wilderness Coordination Group. In addition, the development of public information and materials is viewed by the task force as a prerequisite to the strengthening of use-management and resource-protection efforts.

In a related development, the University of Idaho Wilderness Center began a study to identify and evaluate indicators that can be used to monitor human-caused change in wilderness conditions. The purpose of the study is to identify the characteristics of wilderness that are most sensitive to human impacts and narrow the number of indicators that need to be monitored so that an efficient and effective monitoring program can be developed. More than 200 indicators were identified and organized under three basic wilderness components: biological (vegetation and wildlife/fish), physical (soil, water, and air), and human (visitor population description and experience).

The study so far has winnowed down the range of potential indicators to about 32. However, the indicators that appear to offer the most potential now must be tested in the field.

***Usable Resource Inventories for Each Park.*** In 1972, the Service initiated a program to have all park units develop a natural resource management plan that would provide an inventory of the resources in a park, an understanding of the relationships between those resources, and an action plan to protect them. A park natural-resource-management plan might include components on the management of fisheries, wildlife, vegetation, air-resources and nonnative (exotic) species and protection of endangered and/or threatened species.

Although all national parks have some type of inventory, few, if any, of the inventories are complete and current. Consequently, one of the highest priorities of all park units is inventory completion. The recently established parks in Alaska are ranked as the highest priority for securing complete inventories. The continuing resolution for fiscal 1987 appropriations (P.L. 99-591) specifically addressed this need in two ways. A half-million dollars was added to the Service's budget to obtain baseline data for the Alaska park units, and $1.14 million was appropriated to provide air-quality monitoring equipment at eight Class I national parks lacking such equipment. Class I parks, 48 in number, were identified by Congress in the Clean Air Act as pristine areas which should be protected from significant deterioration of their current air quality. Monitoring is essential to assess the impacts of pollution on park resources, analyze the impact of proposed developments on park areas, and develop long-range protection strategies.

***Expert Policy-Review Panel.*** The action plan recommends that a panel of outside experts be convened to review Park Service management policies for both natural and cultural resources. The plan recommends that the panel begin its task by developing a holistic approach to park management that recognizes and values parks as remnant ecosystems, gene pools, cultural benchmarks, and places for recreational and spiritual renewal.

The overall trend toward the insularization of the parks by development, coupled with the fact that political park boundaries may be meaningless with regard to the management of certain resources, especially wildlife, necessitates review of the 1963 Leopold Report as part of the panel's charge. The Leopold Report, the primary basis for current Park Service wildlife-management policies, is the product of an advisory commission chaired by A. Starker Leopold (Department of Interior 1963). The report requires review because in the 23 years since its issuance, the park system has grown dramatically, and the park units themselves exist in a sharply altered overall environment.

In September 1986, a Park Service Committee met to identify specific issues that presumably would serve as a possible agenda for the panel of experts. However, the panel has yet to be appointed.

***Biological Diversity.*** In a related development, the Service sponsored a Biological Diversity Workshop that met in Washington D.C. under the leadership of Dr. Christine Schonewald Cox. The central focus was the Park Service's role in the conservation of biological diversity and education of the public about the importance of national parks in preserving gene pools. The workshop presented a summary of their findings to the director and recommended that the Park Service:

- identify the current range of biological diversity in parks and what changes are occurring in genetic materials as well as the causes of those changes;
- work with other agencies and organizations to establish a nation-wide cooperative program for the conservation of biological diversity;
- educate park managers about biological diversity and their role in its conservation and protection;
- develop technical expertise within the Park Service to carry out its conservation role.

The proceedings of the conference and the technical papers presented will be published in 1987.

**Service-wide Information System**

The Information and Data Systems Division is completing the initial development phase of a Service-wide automated information base containing key information on each park unit. The Service-wide system, called COMMON, is a corporate data base. Park-by-park summaries of such subjects as land status, budget and visitation information, law-enforcement data, personnel information, and natural- and cultural-resources data is easily accessible by park, regional, and Washington personnel.

In addition to the general information collected for all park-system units, specialized bodies of information or modules are being developed, several of which relate specifically to wildlife management. The BIOSCI module contains general descriptive natural-resource information about the parks, including resource features, resource threats, ecological classifications, status of baseline inventories, ownership/management of adjacent lands, park surface water and wetlands, stream and river length, Clean Air Act status, and an inventory of air quality, acid rain, and weather monitoring stations.

The BIOSCI module also will contain information about the region-wide Natural Science Program. Information from this program includes the status of park and regional natural-resources personnel; status of park and regional natural-resources funding; and park natural-resources five-year project priorities and funding needs. It is anticipated that this information, which is the basis of a region's annual resource-management report, will be online by May 1987.

Other modules of interest include TEX, which contains information on the occurrence of threatened, endangered, and exotic species in parks; NP FLORA, the flora data base of 141 parks that will be transferred to the COMMON data base in February 1987; PESTS, containing information on park pest-management problems and treatments; and the Integrated Pest Management Decision Tree Module, which can be used to help identify the source of an observed pest problem and retrieve current, nonchemical pest-treatment information.

When COMMON is fully operational it will be easier for those dealing with Service wildlife-management programs to acquire information about units with similar problems and the type of research that is available. It also will be easier to monitor the allocation of dollar and staff resources to specific management activities.


## Water Rights

In the 17 semi-arid states of the West, water rights are based on use. Anyone who first uses a water source establishes a right to the water until it is no longer used. When the water available is insufficient to meet the needs of all users, priority is based chronologically on who first put the water to use. The priority date is important because it guarantees the senior appropriator the entire quantity of water to which he is entitled prior to delivery of any water to a more junior appropriator. This is the "prior appropriation" or "first use'" doctrine.

Water rights are appropriated by the states, and the federal government's water rights are subject to this process. In reviewing water-rights cases, the courts have recognized two types of federal lands: those withdrawn or designated by Congress for special purposes such as parks, refuges, or forests, and those in the public domain. Federal water use on public-domain lands must be secured by appropriation. However, water needed to administer special-purpose lands is reserved when Congress first sets them aside.[1] The courts have ruled that the agency managing reserved lands must quantify the amount of water that must be set aside to carry out the purposes for which Congress established the area.

In *Sierra Club v. Block* (622 Fed. Supp. 842) the Federal District Court for Colorado held that Congress in passing the Wilderness Act in 1965 reserved to the U.S. government previously unappropriated water for management of the Colorado wilderness areas of the U.S. Forest Service. It is reasonable to assume that this ruling will lead to the claim of reserved water rights for wilderness areas managed by the Fish and Wildlife Service, the Bureau of Land Management, and the National Park Service as well.

In the *United States v. Denver* (Colo. 658 P.2d 1 1982) the Supreme Court of Colorado affirmed the Colorado Water Court's ruling that no instream-flow water right exists for recreational boating on the Yampa River within Dinosaur National Monument. The court held that the monument was created by Congress for the purpose of preserving

---

1. If the federal government acquires private land for parks, water rights are based on the appropriation rights established by the private owner.

outstanding objects of historic and scientific interest and not for recreational purposes. Consequently, the federal government is not entitled to reserved water for recreational purposes. With respect to reserving some instream flows for the purpose of preserving fish habitat, the court held that the National Park Organic Act mandate (16 U.S.C. 1) to protect park wildlife could not be used to expand monument purposes. Rather, any claim of reserved water rights is dependent upon the purposes described in the text of the 1938 proclamation creating the monument.

At present, the Park Service has not fully assessed the amount of water it needs to guarantee protection of park resources, including wildlife, in perpetuity for any unit in which reserved water rights are at issue. However, many projects are under way. In 1987, the National Park Service will be faced with litigating 25 to 30 water-rights cases in four states. It is anticipated that the Service will be involved in 70 to 80 cases in 17 states requiring administrative or judicial allocation of water rights in the next few years. For example, Arizona hopes to adjudicate water rights for the entire state no later than the mid-1990s.

In fiscal year 1987, Congress appropriated an additional $1 million to the Water Resources Unit to enable the Service to respond to water-rights adjudication proceedings. In making this appropriation, Congress issued the following guidelines to the Service in the preparation of its claims for reserved water:

- water quantity needs are to be determined according to the minimum amounts required to protect the primary purposes of a given unit;
- primary purposes are those established in the legislation or proclamation that established a given unit;
- such legislation or proclamation establishes the priority date for a given unit;
- negotiated settlements will be the first means used to resolve conflicts among multiple claimants;
- the National Park Service will use state courts and state proceedings in accordance with state law to resolve conflicts among claimants.

## Restoration of Species

In 1986, the National Park Service continued several species-restoration programs, such as the Peregrine Falcon Program and the Sierra Nevada Bighorn Sheep Recovery and Conservation Plan. With respect to peregrines, 10 birds were released in May at Acadia National Park in Maine.

Reintroduction of bighorn sheep into Yosemite National Park was undertaken with the assistance of the adjacent Inyo National Forest. In

April 1986, approximately 25 sheep were released in the Inyo Forest adjacent to the park boundary near Lee Vining, California. All but two were radio collared in order to monitor the group. Six collared sheep died and the two noncollared animals have not been sighted and are presumed dead. However, seven lambs were born, thus maintaining the overall population.

In early 1987, the environmental assessment of the management plan for the reintroduction of bighorn sheep in Sequoia National Park will be released for public comment. The Service anticipates being able to reintroduce bighorns to the Sawtooth Peak-Farewell Gap area of the park. This area historically has been the prime bighorn sheep habitat in Sierra Nevada range.

Park Service efforts to reintroduce elk herds at Theodore Roosevelt National Park and Wind Cave National Monument, both in North Dakota, have been successful. Between 1984 and 1986 the herd has almost doubled.

A critical objective at Olympic National Park is the restoration of anadromous fish to the Elwha River system. An Elwha Restoration Steering Committee serves to integrate the efforts of the National Park Service and the U.S. Fish and Wildlife Service with the short and long-term catch-management planning of the state of Washington and the Klallam Indian tribe. Prior to the construction of the Elwha Dams in the early 1900s, five species of salmonids spawned in the Elwha and its tributary streams. Since construction of the dams, no anadromous fish have passed upstream beyond those barriers. The restoration of this fishery can have a significant and positive effect on Olympic National Park's ecosystem by restoring a major protein source for wildlife, contributing to the preservation of wild genetic stocks and natural runs of salmon and steelhead, and providing a significant addition to the anadromous fishery stocks of the state of Washington (Department of Interior 1985c).

Gulf Islands National Seashore is one of five locations where bald eagles are being reestablished in the southeastern United States. A hack tower has been located near Horn Island, Mississippi, in a historic bald eagle nesting area. The location offers the dual protection of being located both within the seashore and within designated wilderness. Four fledglings released last winter remained in the immediate area for longer than 10 weeks before dispersing as a group. If funding is maintained, 100 birds will be released in each of the next five years. Each site will receive 50 to 60 fledglings for one of the five years in an effort to increase the size of the breeding cohort that would return to the release areas.

## Control of Exotics

The National Park Service continues to wage a never-ending battle to control exotic flora and fauna that have invaded the system. Some of the invasions have been self inflicted, some have been inherited, some have arisen because of activities outside the parks. All exotic species invasions have posed a major management challenge.

In Death Valley, a three-year burro removal program completed in 1986 succeeded in removing 5,787 burros, 87 horses, and five mules (Department of Interior 1986c). Captured animals were distributed to private individuals in an adoption program operated in cooperation with the Bureau of Land Management. The removal of the burros appears to be having a positive impact on the monument's desert bighorn sheep restoration program. Bighorns have been sighted for the first time in many years in areas from which burros have been removed.

Research efforts are continuing in Olympic National Park in support of an environmental assessment of mountain goat management. The research program includes studies of the impact of goats on vegetation and soil erosion, methods of sterilization, population numbers and dynamics, and control and removal methods.

Over the years, persistent pressure to expand and/or maintain recreational fishing in park units by stocking threatens park aquatic ecosystems. The National Park Service currently is struggling to affirm its basic policy of maintaining natural conditions and populations in aquatic ecosystems. In the North Cascades Complex, the National Park Service is trying to avoid introducing fish into fish-free waters or stocking areas with nonindigenous sport fish that would have adverse impacts on native fish species. An attempt is being made to establish and enforce three categories of waters in the North Cascades Complex: natural fish-free waters that will remain fish free; self-sustaining fish-population waters, previously stocked where fisheries will be allowed to perpetuate themselves or revert to fish-free status; and continue-to-stock waters, which will be restocked for the purposes of enhancing recreational fishing activities (Mott 1986).

## Conflicts with Park Neighbors

As adjacent lands are developed, parks and their resident wildlife populations are subjected to an ever-increasing number of adverse impacts. In 1986, many existing problems continued and the potential for new conflicts arose:

- Cattlemen in the Yellowstone ecosystem continued to be concerned about the bison that wander out of the park because of the threat of transmission of brucellosis to their cattle.
- Ranchers in the vicinity of Carlsbad Caverns and Guadalupe Mountains National Park whose herds suffer predation from mountain lions wanted to pursue the cats into the park. The

Service refused. A recently concluded three-year study and environmental assessment clearly demonstrated that "hot pursuit" of predators should continue to be banned, and that hunting of mountain lions outside the park is threatening the long-term vitality of the park population (Harvey and Stanley Associates 1986).

- Livestock interests are one of the major obstacles to the reintroduction of the wolf to the Yellowstone ecosystem.
- In Shenandoah National Park concern exists that park black bears may be forced into developed areas of the park and to adjacent land in increasing numbers by the invasion of the gypsy moth, which defoliates vegetation. A study is being developed to compare bear activity in the moth-invaded northern district of the park with bear activity in the unaffected central district.
- Adjacent-land uses continue to reduce the wintering range for elk in Grand Teton and Rocky Mountain national parks.
- At Valley Forge National Historic Park development has claimed the entire perimeter of the park. Lack of routes by which wildlife can move beyond the park boundary has created the need for total control of resident species.
- Grazing in some park units is a significant problem. In Fossil Butte National Monument, Glen Canyon National Recreation Area, Capitol Reef National Park, Dinosaur National Monument, and Grand Teton and Zion national parks grazing leases due to terminate have been extended legislatively while a congressionally mandated study to assess the economic, social, and ecological impacts of grazing is conducted.

## Rare and Endangered Species Programs

The National Park Service is cooperating with the U.S. Fish and Wildlife Service in an overall recovery program for the piping plover. In January 1986, the U.S. Fish and Wildlife Service officially listed the species as endangered in the Great Lakes Watershed, including New York and Pennsylvania, and as threatened from the Canadian Maritime Provinces down the Atlantic Coast. Gateway National Recreation Area and Fire Island National Seashore in New York, Cape Cod National Seashore in Massachusetts, and Assateague National Seashore in Virginia and Maryland are all participating units. At Cape Cod, a census of breeding pairs and an investigation of the possible effects of beach development, human recreation, and predators as factors affecting nesting success and chick survival are being pursued.

In Florida, an interagency panel consisting of the Florida Department of Natural Resources, Florida Game and Fresh Water Fish

Commission, U.S. Fish and Wildlife Service, and National Park Service are coordinating efforts to protect the Florida panther. Two studies have been initiated in 1986 because of concern about the effectiveness of recovery actions taken to date. One study will be of the panther population in Everglades National Park. The study objective is to determine basic population parameters such as population size and distribution, age structure, sex ratio, reproductive success, and recruitment rate. The study will seek to determine behavioral and ecological requirements including food habits, habitat preference and utilization, social organization, and behavior. The general health and genetic condition of the population also will be assessed (Robertson and Bass 1986).

In a companion study, the white-tailed deer will be examined in the Everglades and Big Cypress National Reserve. The study will provide an opportunity to assess predator-prey relationships (Eisenberg and Sunquist 1986). In the Everglades, the deer studied are hunted only by the Florida panther, whereas in the Big Cypress National Preserve sport hunting is permitted and occurred prior to the establishment of the area as a unit of the National Park System.

In Yellowstone National Park a biological study concluded that the Fishing Bridge area, which provides prime grizzly bear habitat, also possesses extraordinary ecological diversity that makes it unique (Department of Interior 1986). Development and intensive use of the area, said the report, would continue to affect Yellowstone's grizzly population adversely. The report recommended removal of the visitor facilities now in the Fishing Bridge area. Nevertheless, political pressure has prompted the preparation of an environmental impact statement that will include an analysis of the effect that relocating visitor facilities will have on surrounding communities and on the tax revenues of Park and Teton counties. Release of the draft environmental statement is scheduled for early 1987.

In a counter move, the National Wildlife Federation filed suit in the U.S. District Court of Wyoming on March 27, 1986. The Federation is suing the National Park Service, U.S. Fish and Wildlife Service, and Department of the Interior to implement removal of the Fishing Bridge facilities.

## LEGISLATIVE DEVELOPMENTS

The most significant action in 1986 involved congressional approval of a boundary adjustment to Olympic National Park that was supported by the National Park Service, Forest Service, U.S. Fish and Wildlife Service, and the state of Washington. The boundary adjustment between the park and the adjacent forest produced several wildlife benefits. The park acquired critical spotted owl and elk habitat, the key trout spawning watershed for Lake Crescent, and two national wildlife refuges, Quillayute Needles and Flattery Rocks, which had no on-site management. The state of Washington relinquished its ownership of lands along the coastline. As a result, 57 miles of coastline including very important tidepools will be managed as part of the park. This action should eliminate the steady increase of vandalism that is occurring to the tidepools.

## LEGAL DEVELOPMENTS

***Trapping in the Parks.*** Between 1982 and 1984, the Park Service undertook a revision of its regulations, including those governing hunting and trapping. This revision was prompted by language inserted by Congress into the Redwood Expansion Act of 1978 to the effect that the management mandate of the National Park Service Organic Act of 1916 (16 U.S.C.A. 1) applied to all areas of the park system unless Congress directly and specifically provided otherwise. The Service interpreted this as a directive to manage park resources such as wildlife in a uniform manner throughout the system without regard to the unit's classification and declared hunting and trapping prohibited in parks and historic areas but permitted in recreation areas.

Generally, in the legislation establishing various national recreation areas, Congress specified whether hunting was to be allowed. This was especially true in cases where hunting had occurred prior to enactment of park legislation. However, with regard to hunting in some recreation areas the enabling legislation was silent. Under the old regulations, when the legislation was silent, as in Cuyahoga National Recreation Area, Santa Monica Mountains National Recreation Area, and Indiana Dunes National Lakeshore, hunting was permissible at the superintendents' discretion. The new regulations prohibited hunting or trapping in these areas unless *specifically* provided for by Congress. As a result, trapping was forbidden in all recreation areas except Buffalo National River, Arkansas; Ozark National Scenic Riverways, Missouri; Saint Croix National Scenic Riverway, Wisconsin and Minnesota; and Delaware Water Gap National Recreation Area, Pennsylvania and New Jersey.

The National Rifle Association filed suit seeking to prevent implementation of the regulations, alleging that the regulations prohibiting trapping were arbitrary and capricious and that trapping was a form of hunting and therefore should be allowed in units where Congress had authorized hunting. The court in *National Rifle Associ-*

*ation* et al. v. *Arnett* (628 F. Supp. 903) held that trapping was a separate and distinct activity from hunting and that if Congress had wanted to permit trapping it would have so specified. The court also affirmed the Service's interpretation of its management mandates as clarified by the Redwood Park Act.

At present, trapping is allowed only in the Ozarks National Riverway. The Missouri Trappers Association secured a preliminary injunction staying the application of the new regulations in that unit. This issue will be litigated in 1987.

**Commercial Fishing in Parks.** On June 6, 1986, the U.S. Supreme Court declined to review a 1985 ruling of the 11th Circuit Court of Appeals in the case of the *Organization of Florida Fisherman v. Hodel* (775 F.2d, 1544). In this case, commercial fisherman challenged the authority of the Service to eliminate commercial fishing in the waters of Everglades National Park. The fisherman based their right to remain in the park on written and verbal assurances made by park personnel at the time the park was established. The fisherman further alleged that there were insufficient scientific data to support the regulations, which were alleged to be arbitrary and capricious. The Service argued that its data showed that commercial fishing was affecting park resources adversely. The Circuit Court ruled that the Service had the authority to regulate fishing and that its regulations were reasonable and based on sound research.

**Insect Control in Parks.** In *U.S. v. Moore* et al. (Civil Action No. 2:86-0724) the National Park Service sought an injunction to prevent West Virginia from conducting its black fly nuisance-control program within the boundaries of New River Gorge National River. The Service argued that the black fly is a species native to the park and an integral part of the park ecosystem. The United States District Court for the Southern District of West Virginia issued a restraining order in 1986 that blocked the spraying program. The National Park Service sought to enjoin state action completely because West Virginia had not applied for a permit to proceed with the spraying within the boundaries of the national river. The U.S. District Court ruled that the state was indeed required to obtain a permit and that the National Park Service was required to process the application with due diligence.

The real issue—the role of the fly in the natural ecosystem—is to be joined at a future date. As long as the black fly remains merely a nuisance and not a public health threat, the National Park Service will seek to protect it as part of the park's ecosystem. However, in the absence of data supporting the role of the black fly in the ecosystem, and unless sport fishermen rally to oppose the state's plan, the National Park Service may be pressured by park neighbors and their representatives to permit the state to proceed with spraying.

# REFERENCES

Eisenberg, John F. and Mervin E. Sunquist. 1986. "Ecology of White Tailed Deer in Everglades National Park." Research proposal to the National Park Service.

Harvey and Stanley Associates, Inc. 1986. "Mountain Lions in the Vicinity of Carlsbad Caverns and Guadalupe Mountains National Parks - An Ecological Study." Unpublished report to the National Park Service.

Mott, William Penn Jr. 1986. Letter to Senator Slade Gorton, Washington. August 15, 1986.

Newmark, William Dubois. 1986. "Mammalian Richness, Colonization and Extinction in Western North American National Parks," Ph.D. dissertation. University of Michigan, Department of Natural Resources.

Robertson Jr., William B. and Oron L. Bass, Jr. 1986. "Ecology and Population Dynamics of the Florida Panther in Everglades National Park." Research Proposal to the National Park Service.

U.S. Department of Interior, National Park Service. 1985a. Budget Justifications for FY1987: The National Park Service. Washington, D.C.

U.S. Department of Interior, National Park Service. 1985b. "The 12-point Plan: The Challenge." Washington, D.C.

U.S. Department of Interior, National Park Service. 1986a. "The 12-point Plan: The Challenge, The Actions." Washington, D.C.

U.S. Department of Interior, National Park Service. 1986b. *1986 Wilderness Task Force Report.* Washington, D.C.

U.S. Department of Interior, Secretary of the Interior. 1963. *1963 Task Force Report, Wildlife Management in the National Parks.* Washington, D.C.

U.S. Department of Interior, National Park Service. 1986c. *1986 Regional Natural Resources Management Report, Western Region.* San Francisco, California.

U.S. Department of Interior, National Park Service. 1986d. *1986 Planning and Development Issues.* Yellowstone National Park. Gardiner, Montana.

Wampler, P.L. *et al.* 1985. "A review of a proposed solution to the problem of migrant salmonid passage by the Elwha River dams." Unpublished report to the National Park Service.

*Richard Curry, a former National Park Service official, is head of Richard Curry Associates, a government relations firm.*

A native of the Mato Grosso jungle offers a jaguar hide for sale. Import of jaguar hides and other rare-animal products into the United States is forbidden by federal law. *George Holton/Photo Researchers*

# International Wildlife Conservation

Michael J. Bean

## OVERVIEW

No single federal agency  or program has exclusive responsibility for
conserving wildlife beyond our nation's borders. Instead, a variety of
agencies, acting under disparate authorities, carry out many different
programs relating to international conservation. The U.S. Fish and
Wildlife Service (FWS) in the Department of the Interior is responsible
for the best known of these. FWS administers a migratory-bird conservation program under authority of four bilateral treaties with Canada,
Mexico, Japan, and the Soviet Union. FWS also has primary responsibility for regulating the import and export of plants and animals
threatened with extinction under the authority of the Convention on
International Trade in Endangered Species of Wild Fauna and Flora, a
responsibility that it shares with the National Marine Fisheries Service
in the Department of Commerce. The Commerce Department also
represents the United States in the International Whaling Commission
and numerous other international bodies that regulate ocean fisheries.
The National Park Service carries out a modest program of technical
assistance and training for foreign park professionals. Numerous other

Audubon Wildlife Report 1987

federal agencies are charged with programs that affect, albeit often indirectly, the wildlife resources of other countries.

Despite the many agencies and programs that exist to promote international wildlife conservation, most recent assessments of the status of wildlife abroad paint an alarming picture. One of the first comprehensive examinations of the future of the world's wildlife, the 1980 *Global 2000* study, predicted direly that a million or more species then in existence might become extinct by the beginning of the next century, primarily as a result of the deforestation of the species-rich tropics (Council on Environmental Quality 1980). Subsequent studies have more or less confirmed that conclusion. Indeed, recent research suggests that far more species live in tropical rainforests than previously imagined, increasing estimates of the numbers of unique life forms that will be lost as rainforests are destroyed (Erwin 1983).

The forces responsible in the destruction of tropical rainforests and other important wildlife habitats in the less developed countries often appear to be beyond the influence of U.S. government agencies and private organizations. Yet, important bonds link institutions in the United States and the fate of wildlife in what has come to be known as the Third World. Among the most important of these are multilateral development institutions such as the World Bank and its three regional counterparts. In 1986, increasing scrutiny was focused on how these institutions and the U.S. agencies responsible for them in part determine the fate of important international wildlife habitats. This chapter examines recent developments in both the traditional international conservation programs of the Interior Department and other agencies and the growing controversy over the role of multilateral development agencies in the destruction of the world's richest remaining wildlife habitats.

## CURRENT DEVELOPMENTS

### Regulating International Trade in Endangered Plants and Animals

The 1973 Convention on International Trade in Endangered Species of Wild Fauna and Flora, more frequently known by the acronym "CITES," is an international treaty to which the United States and 92 other countries subscribe (27 U.S.T. 1086, March 3, 1973). The purpose of CITES is to protect endangered and threatened wild plant and animal species by regulating international trade in them. Its effectiveness is constrained by two things: (1) the degree to which trade itself is a contributing factor to the endangerment of any species (for most species, destruction of habitat is a far more significant factor), and (2) the extent to which the controls imposed by CITES are actually carried out by its member states.

Close scrutiny of member-state implementation arose in 1986 while the United States was considering a CITES amendment that had been negotiated in 1983 at a special meeting of the CITES parties. The amendment's purpose was to allow so-called "regional economic integration organizations," specifically the European Economic Community, to become members of CITES in their own right. Currently, only nations can be members of CITES. The amendment, if it ever becomes effective, would allow the European Economic Community and similar regional organizations to take over from their member states the responsibility of controlling international trade in CITES-protected species.

Despite having voted for the amendment at the special 1983 meeting, the United States did not formally consider its ratification until 1986. Ratification by two-thirds of the 80 countries who were parties to CITES at the time the amendment was adopted is necessary to bring it into force. Currently, only 11 nations have ratified the amendment, including just three of the six European Economic Community member states who were CITES members in 1983.

The Subcommittee on International Economic Policy, Oceans, and Environment of the Senate Foreign Relations Committee held a hearing in March 1986 to consider the Reagan administration's request that the Senate ratify the amendment. At that hearing, environmental organizations[1] raised concerns about the quality of implementation of CITES within the European Economic Community, which is particularly critical to the overall effectiveness of CITES because Europe is perhaps the world's largest market for cat and reptile skins as well as other wildlife products. These groups objected emphatically to the stated plans of the European Economic Community to drop from annual CITES trade reports any information about the trade of CITES-protected species between Community member states.

One of the important sources of information about patterns of trade in CITES-protected species is the annual report that each member country is required to prepare. These reports, and the trade records from which they are compiled, can provide information useful in investigations of treaty violations. The European Economic Community, however, maintains that its 12 European member nations, and many of their overseas territories, that comprise it should be treated as a single unit for purposes of CITES implementation. Only trade between the entire Community and countries outside it should be subjected to CITES controls and included in annual CITES reports.

---

1. Statement by the Environmental Defense Fund on behalf of itself, World Wildlife Fund-U.S., National Audubon Society, Natural Resources Defense Council, Humane Society of the United States, Defenders of Wildlife, and Center for Environmental Education.

The testimony of the environmental groups persuaded the Senate committee to defer action on the amendment pending further evaluation of the quality of CITES implementation within the European Economic Community. In May, the Community submitted to the CITES Secretariat an annual report on CITES trade for all of its member states. World Wildlife Fund-U.S. undertook an analysis of the report that confirmed the criticisms earlier voiced at the Senate hearing and showed continuing European trade in CITES Appendix I species, the category of the most endangered species (World Wildlife Fund 1986). In addition, the report highlighted problems stemming from lax trade enforcement in overseas territories such as French Guiana, said by World Wildlife Fund to be "a funnel for illegal wildlife from the entire South American continent to the EEC." The report also underscored the CITES loopholes provided by freeports such as Hamburg, West Germany, where lax to nonexistent controls enable wildlife products to enter the European Economic Community from all over the world. Under the "single unit" concept proposed by the Community, CITES trade controls throughout Europe would sink to the level of the lowest common denominator. That is, if South American smugglers can slip their contraband across jungle borders into French Guiana, they have effectively entered Europe. The failure of the European Economic Community to monitor and report thereafter the movement of those wildlife products renders nearly useless the enforcement efforts of European nations that diligently police their borders (see Table 1).

At this writing, the ultimate resolution of the controversy spurred by the European Economic Community amendment is uncertain. U.S. ratification of the amendment has been postponed until at least 1987, and ratification by the required 54 parties to bring the amendment into force seems even further away. The controversy clearly has put pressure on the Community to take action to remedy the implementation problems prior to the next meeting of the CITES parties in Canada in July 1987. The controversy also may rekindle efforts to formalize a review of CITES infractions by member states. A proposal put forward by Saint Lucia at the last meeting in 1985 to set up a permanent mechanism for reviewing infractions was rejected. The CITES Secretariat is expected to present a new infractions proposal at the 1987 meeting.

Since the 1986 Senate hearing, the United States has taken the lead in pressing the European Economic Community to correct its implementation problems and to resume the reporting of intra-Community trade. Another sign of stiffened U.S. resolve to improve the effectiveness of CITES was an FWS decision on September 25, 1986, to ban all further wildlife imports from Singapore (51 *Federal Register* 34159). Singapore is neither a member of CITES nor a country in which

**TABLE 1**
**European Economic Community Trade in CITES**
**Appendix I Species**
**(as revealed by 1984 European Economic Community CITES Report)**

| | | |
|---|---|---|
| France | African slender-snouted crocodile | 2,050 skins |
| | Hawksbill sea turtle | 550 lb. of shell |
| | Green sea turtle | 3,873 cans of soup |
| | Peregrine falcon | 21 birds |
| | Leopard | 9 skulls |
| Germany | Chimpanzee | 2 animals |
| | Cheetah | 7 skins |
| | Green sea turtle | 920 lb. of meat |
| | Hawksbill sea turtle | 595 lb. of shell |
| Italy | Green sea turtle | 2,375 lb. of oil |
| | Nile crocodile | 345 skins |
| Denmark | Sperm whale | 1,430 lb. of bone |
| United Kingdom | Yellow monitor lizard | 97 skins |
| | Sperm whale | 22 lb. of wax |
| | Green sea turtle | 14,180 lb. meat and calipee |
| | Vicuna | 5,400 yard of cloth |

Source: World Wildlife Fund 1986.

much native wildlife exists. It is, however, a major conduit for trade in CITES-protected species from all over the world. It is believed to be a major supplier of rhino horn, elephant ivory, and other rare wildlife products throughout the world.

By agreement among them, CITES parties are to accept imports from nonparty countries only if they are accompanied by documentation substantially identical to that required of CITES member countries, showing that the wildlife was legally obtained and exported from its country of origin. Singapore, however, has failed consistently to provide such documentation and in particular has failed to identify the countries of origin for the nonnative wildlife that it reexports. Thus, the unusual action by the United States signals a crackdown on a major source of wildlife trade of dubious legality.

## Wildlife and the Multilateral Development Banks

The frequently ruthless exploitation of endangered wildlife in international commercial trade often is depicted vividly in both the popular and environmental press. In part because of the shocking cruelty often associated with wildlife trade, CITES itself has benefited from a committed and active constituency of both governmental and nongovernmental organizations interested in its effective implementation. At the same time, however, other, less visible, more destructive forces are affecting wildlife. The transformation of the natural habitats upon which the world's wildlife depends, particularly the destruction of the tropical rainforests, threatens a true cataclysm of species extinctions unlike any the world has experienced since man first set foot upon it (Caufield 1984).

Though they cover only seven percent of the Earth's land surface, tropical forests probably harbor well over half the species of plants and animals in the world. These forests are being chopped, burned, or inundated at a dizzying speed. A 1981 study estimated that by the year 2000, all the primary rainforest in Nigeria and the Ivory Coast would be gone; 80 percent of the remaining rainforest in Costa Rica and 60 percent of the rainforest in Thailand also would be gone (Food and Agriculture Organization 1981). Even where significant acreages of rainforest remain, as in Brazil and Indonesia, the loss of rainforest-associated species is likely to be high. The fragmentation of once vast, continuous forests into multiple, discontinuous components creates habitat "islands" unable to support species that require larger territories or more abundant populations for survival. Roads that penetrate deep into the interior of the largest forest tracts open up inaccessible areas to the poachers and traders who are the initial links in the chain of illicit international wildlife trade. In this way, the forces of habitat destruction and unrelenting commercial trade work hand in hand.

An appreciation of the gravity of the problem of tropical deforestation and the rapidity with which it is progressing has come about only recently. Even more recent, however, is recognition of the role played by multilateral development institutions, of which the United States is a key member. In fact, some of the most dramatic, large-scale projects entailing the destruction of huge areas of tropical rainforests and other wildlife habitats are supported by these institutions. Thus, American tax dollars are being spent to subsidize the destruction of some of the last, best places on Earth for the conservation of the world's wildlife.

Four so-called multilateral development banks support a variety of development projects throughout the Third World. The biggest and best known of these is the World Bank, headquartered in Washington, D.C. Created by the Treaty of Bretton Woods in the aftermath of World War II, the World Bank is an autonomous international organization beyond the exclusive control of any one nation. Individual governments contribute financial resources to the bank, and their voting power within the institution is proportional to their financial commitments to it.

The United States is the largest contributor to the World Bank, accounting for nearly a fifth of the voting power on the individual loans and policy decisions that come before the bank's board of governors or its board of executive directors, the smaller operating board to which many of the formal powers of the board of governors are delegated. The next largest shareholder, Japan, exercises voting rights equal to about seven percent of the total. Together, the western nations of Japan, Great Britain, West Germany, France, and the United States account for more than 40 percent of the voting power. The Soviet Union does not participate in the World Bank, though there are recent indications that it may seek to do so in the future. The president of the World Bank, by tradition an American citizen, is Barber Conable, a respected former Congressman who assumed the presidency in 1986.

Paralleling the World Bank are three similar regional institutions, the Inter-American Development Bank, the Asian Development Bank, and the African Development Bank. Each of these is much smaller than the World Bank. Indeed, the World Bank's annual lending of around $15 billion is more than twice the amounts lent by the other three banks combined. The United States has very prominent influence within the regional banks as well. It controls 35 percent of the voting power within the Inter-American Development Bank, sufficient to veto low-interest loans made through the bank's "soft loan" window; shares with Japan the role of primary shareholder in the Asian Development Bank; and is second only to Nigeria in voting power within the African Development Bank.

The U.S. representatives at these various institutions receive their instructions from the Treasury Department. Within Treasury, the assistant secretary for International Affairs and, under him, the deputy assistant secretary for Developing Nations and an Office of Multilateral Development Banks are the key policy posts. Because of the obvious connection between bank activities and the foreign-policy interests of the United States, the Department of State cooperates closely with Treasury. With respect to environmental matters, State's role is handled by the assistant secretary for the Bureau of Oceans and International Environmental and Scientific Affairs and, under him, the Office of Food and Natural Resources and the Office of Environment and Health. In addition, U.S. policy on multilateral development banks is coordinated by the special interagency Working Group on Multilateral Assistance, which consists of representatives of Treasury and State, the Agency for International Development, the United States Trade Representative, the Federal Reserve Board, and the departments of Agriculture, Interior, Labor, and Commerce.

The various multilateral development banks provide loans, often at below market rates, for projects intended to promote economic development within the recipient country by improving its production of exportable agricultural commodities; building dams, highways, and other infrastructure; or solving other significant development problems. Some of these projects have had devastating consequences for the environment and wildlife of the recipient countries. In Botswana, for example, once magnificent herds of wildebeest and other big game have been put at grave risk by the World Bank's efforts to boost that arid country's production and export of beef. In Brazil, a series of major dams in the Amazon basin has destroyed vast areas of pristine rainforest.

Critics, including some within the recipient countries, maintain that the banks have failed to take environmental considerations adequately into account when reviewing potential projects and in any event lack the resources necessary to ensure fair attention to environmental factors (Rich 1985, Sierra Club 1986). They point to the fact that of the World Bank's roughly 7,000 employees, only seven are assigned to the Bank's Office of Environmental and Scientific Affairs. Of these, just three have the task of reviewing the environmental aspects of the more than 300 new projects that the bank funds each year. The critics also maintain that the multilateral development banks fail to involve the requisite environmental officials of the recipient countries in project planning and seldom monitor effectively the actual implementation of approved projects to ensure that whatever environmental safeguards are supposed to accompany each project are in fact carried out (see Table 2).

These criticisms increasingly have drawn the attention of key Congressional committees. In the past few years, more than a dozen congressional hearings have considered the environmental effects of bank policies and projects. The principal congressional bodies currently in the forefront of this effort are the subcommittees of the House and Senate Appropriations Committees responsible for initially determining the level of U.S. contributions to the banks. Somewhat surprisingly, the leaders in this effort span the spectrum of political philosophy. The chairman of the Subcommittee on Foreign Assistance and Related Programs of the Senate Appropriations Committee is Robert Kasten, a generally conservative Republican. His counterpart in the House, the chairman of the Subcommittee on Foreign Operations and Related Agencies of the House Appropriations Committee, is David Obey, a liberal Democrat. Both have aggressively encouraged environmental reform in the Treasury Department and, through it, in the multilateral development banks themselves.

**TABLE 2**
**World Bank Lending in 1985**

|  | Percentage |
| --- | --- |
| Agriculture and rural development | 26.1 |
| Energy (other than oil, gas, and coal) | 15.6 |
| Transportation | 14.9 |
| Education | 6.4 |
| Population, health and nutrition | 1.3 |
| Other | 35.7 |

Source: Sierra Club 1986.

Since the multilateral development banks are not agencies of the United States government, Congress has no direct legislative authority over them. However, it does have legislative authority over the Treasury Department, the U.S. representative to the banks. Thus, through legislation directed at the Treasury Department, Congress can influence or even control the way in which the United States exercises its voting power within the banks. In both 1985 and 1986, the annual foreign-assistance appropriations bill has been the vehicle for increasing the congressional control of how the United States deals with important environmental issues within the banks.

In December 1985, Congress directed the secretary of the Treasury to instruct the United States executive directors of each of the multilateral development banks to pursue a variety of bank reforms (P. L. 99-190). This legislation distilled the most important elements of some 19 nonbinding recommendations that the Subcommittee on International Development Institutions and Finance of the House Committee on Banking, Finance, and Urban affairs had promulgated in 1984 (House of Representatives 1984). The new legislative directives included seeking a commitment for a stronger professionally trained staff that will review the environmental effects of proposed projects; encouraging the participation of recipient-country health and environmental ministries, as well as nongovernmental conservation and indigenous peoples' organizations, in the planning and preparation of projects; and promoting a commitment to increase the funding of so-called "environmentally beneficial projects," such as agroforestry, watershed management and rehabilitation, integrated pest-management systems, and programs to improve energy and irrigation efficiency.

To ensure attention to these matters, the legislation also directed the Treasury secretary to instruct the U.S. executive directors to seek special meetings of the bank boards of executive directors for discussion of their environmental performance and ways to improve it. The U.S. executive director of the World Bank presented these reform proposals to the bank's board at a spring meeting in 1986. The U.S. proposals were supported by most of the directors representing major industrialized countries, as well as some representing less developed nations, including the People's Republic of China. As a result, the bank is preparing an internal directive requiring that recipient-country ministries of environment and health be consulted on projects that may affect those concerns and is undertaking a study that may result in a reorganized, strengthened environmental review unit within the bank.

Congressional concern about the environmental impacts of multilateral-development-bank projects also has begun to affect the way in which the U.S. is exercising its voting power within the bank. In mid-1986, the World Bank considered a half-billion dollar loan to the Brazilian state electric utility for construction of a series of mammoth hydroelectric dams on tributaries of the Amazon. One of the dams, if completed, would flood an Indian reserve that had been created specifically to mitigate the effects of an earlier bank-supported dam. Describing the new loan as "pure folly," the U.S. executive director cast a rare vote in opposition to the loan on environmental and economic grounds. However, because the U.S. vote had the support only of the Scandanavian representative, the loan request was approved.

Greater success had been achieved in 1985 in the Interamerican Development Bank when, as a result of U.S. action, the bank denied a loan for a three-hundred-mile extension of a road into the Amazonian rainforest. The road extension would have added to the devastation of an earlier World Bank settlement and road-construction project known as the Polonoroeste Project. The Polonoroeste Project has led to the deforestation of an area of pristine tropical rainforest nearly the size of Great Britain. The extension road, because it was to be funded through the Interamerican Bank's soft-loan window, required approval from two-thirds of the Bank's voting representatives. The United States, with nearly 35 percent of the voting power, abstained from the vote and thus effectively vetoed the loan, the first time in the Bank's 26 year history that the United States voted against a loan to Brazil.

Despite this evidence of increased U.S. attentiveness to the environmental consequences of multilateral-development-bank-funded projects, much controversy still attends the role of the banks in supporting development activities that threaten the destruction of rainforests and other ecologically important habitats. The World Bank's annual meeting in Washington in September 1986 was greeted with street demonstrations by environmental activists concerned about ecological destruction. They point to World Bank-supported projects such as the planned transmigration of literally millions of Indonesians from the densely populated islands of Java and Bali to sparsely populated and mostly forested areas such as Irian Jaya, the western half of the island of New Guinea (*The Ecologist* 1986). In India, in which most forests already have been destroyed, the Narmada Valley Dam Project includes plans for 30 major dams and more than 3,000 smaller ones that will flood nearly a million acres of wildlife-rich forests. In Botswana, wildlife experts invariably rate the overabundance of cattle as the principal threat to the environment of that arid nation and its extraordinary wildlife. Yet the World Bank, after two earlier, mostly unsuccessful cattle ventures, is supporting a third aimed at increasing Botswanan beef exports.

The seemingly endless parade of environmentally troublesome projects that the World Bank and its regional counterparts are supporting assures a continuing high priority for those institutions on the agendas of many environmental organizations. The banks also will likely continue to attract close scrutiny by the Congressional committees that have made environmental reform within the banks a key objective. The continuing resolution of appropriations signed into law in October 1986 contains a number of still further reforms that Congress wants to promote within the banks (P. L 99-591). These include measures that seek to loosen the banks' traditionally tight restrictions on the release of information about the projects they fund and their environmental effects. With the freer flow of information the new law seeks to secure, the controversy over the role of the banks in the destruction of some of the world's most important ecological resources is likely to increase rather than abate.

## LEGISLATION

In addition to the legislative developments discussed in the previous section, 1986 witnessed a number of other important legislative developments for international wildlife conservation.

***Tropical Forests and Biological Diversity.*** In October 1986, President Reagan signed into law the Child Survival Act, Title III of which combined two unrelated bills that sought to promote the conservation of tropical forests and biological diversity in U.S. foreign assistance programs (P. L. 99-529). Title III amends the Foreign Assistance Act of 1961, the basic legislative authority under which the United States provides assistance to developing countries through the U.S. Agency for International Development.

The amended law directs the President, when providing assistance to developing countries, to place "a high priority on conservation and sustainable management of tropical forests." In particular, it directs him "to the fullest extent feasible" to support projects and activities that (1) help developing countries identify and implement alternatives to colonizing forested areas, (2) increase the capacity of developing countries to improve the management of their forests, (3) help end destructive slash-and-burn agriculture, (4) increase production on lands already cleared or degraded, (5) rehabilitate degraded forest lands through reforestation, soil conservation, and related activities, and (6) promote research in agroforestry and sustainable management of natural forests.

In addition, the legislation seeks to support the establishment of "a representative network of protected tropical forest ecosystems on a world wide basis" by, among other things, "making the establishment of protected areas a condition of support for activities involving forest clearance or degradation." It also prohibits actions that significantly degrade national parks or similar protected areas that contain tropical forests, result in the conversion of forest lands for the raising of livestock, flood relatively undegraded forest lands, or result in their colonization. All of these prohibitions are subject to the qualification that activities in the prohibited class may be supported if "an environmental assessment indicates that the proposed activity will contribute significantly and directly to improving the livelihood of the rural poor and will be conducted in an environmentally sound manner." The extent to which this effort will change the approach of the U.S. Agency for International Development remains to be seen. If it is successful in improving the environmental soundness of U.S. foreign assistance, the legislation may provide a useful model for adoption by the multilateral development banks as well.

A separate provision of the amended statute addresses the subject of biological diversity. It specifically earmarks $2.5 million of the U.S. Agency for International Development funds for new activities designed to promote the conservation of biological diversity in developing countries. The provision encourages the administrator of the Agency for International Development to carry out these new activities under the management of appropriate nongovernmental organizations and directs him to "look to the World Conservation Strategy[2] as an overall guide for actions to conserve biological diversity." The new legislation thus confers a potentially important formal endorsement of the Strategy as a guide for future U.S. development assistance.

**Unsound Natural-Resources Exploitation as a Form of Unfair Trade Practice.** HR 4681, introduced by Representative John Seiberling (D-OH), sought to remedy what is perceived to be the unfair trade advantage derived by some countries from the exploitation of their environment or the unsound development of their natural resources. The bill directed the president to seek the adoption, within the General Agreement on Trade and Tariffs, of international trade standards tied to basic standards for preventing air and water pollution, soil erosion, hazardous-waste contamination, or endangerment of species and degradation of natural resources. The premise of the legislation was that countries that enforce rigorous environmental standards impose costs on their industries that put them at a disadvantage relative to the same industries in other countries with less stringent or

---

2. The Strategy is a 1980 document prepared by the International Union for the Conservation of Nature and Natural Resources and the World Wildlife Fund that articulates a general prescription for promoting environmentally sustainable economic development.

no standards. Seiberling's rather novel idea died in the House Ways and Means Committee, and thus did not make it to the House floor before the 99th Congress adjourned.

***H.R. 4568 — A Bill to Strengthen the International Authorities of the Interior Department.*** This bill, also introduced by Representative Seiberling, sought to clarify and strengthen the authority of the secretary of the Interior to provide to other countries technical assistance relating to conservation and natural resources and direction for such activities. The bill was reported out of the House Committee on Interior and Insular Affairs, but Congress adjourned without voting on it on the House floor. The retirement of Representative Seiberling casts considerable doubt on the question of whether either of these two bills, so closely identified with him, will be pursued again in the 100th Congress.

## REFERENCES

Caufield, C. 1984. *In the Rainforest.* University of Chicago Press. Chicago, Illinois.

Council on Environmental Quality. 1980. *The Global 2000 Report to the President.* Government Printing Office. Washington, D.C.

*The Ecologist.* 1986. "Indonesia's transmigration programme: a special report in collaboration with Survival International and Tapol." Vol. 16(2/3).

Erwin, T.L. 1983. "Beetles and other insects of tropical forest canopies at Manaus, Brazil, sampled by insecticidal fogging," pp. 59-75, *in* S.L. Sutton, T.C. Whitmore, and A.C. Chadwick eds., *Tropical Rain Forest: Ecology and Management.* Blackwell Scientific Publications. Edinburgh, United Kingdom.

Food and Agriculture Organization. 1981. *Tropical Forest Resources.* Forestry Paper 30. Rome.

House of Representatives. 1984. Recommendations of the Subcommittee on International Development Institutions and Finance of the House Committee on Banking, Finance and Urban Affairs. Washington, D.C.

Rich, B. 1985. "The multilateral development banks, environmental policy and the United States," *Ecology Law Quarterly* 12:681.

Sierra Club. 1986. *Bankrolling Disaster: International Development Banks and the Global Environment.* San Francisco, California.

World Wildlife Fund. 1986. The EEC Annual CITES Report for 1984: A Preliminary Assessment of the Implementation of CITES in the European Economic Community. Washington, D.C.

*Michael J. Bean is chairman of the Environmental Defense Fund's Wildlife Program and author of* The Evolution of National Wildlife Law.

A U.S. Fish and Wildlife Service biologist examines a young sandhill crane. Critical federal wildlife programs have been threatened with severe budget cuts in recent years. *U.S. Fish and Wildlife Service/William Radke*

# Federal Fish and Wildlife Agency Budgets

Katherine Barton

## OVERVIEW

Five federal agencies have responsibility for the management of extensive amounts of fish and wildlife habitat or of certain fish and wildlife species. These are the U.S. Fish and Wildlife Service (FWS), the National Marine Fisheries Service (NMFS), the National Park Service, the Forest Service, and the Bureau of Land Management (BLM). Budgets for these agencies range from about $160 million to more than $2 billion, although most of these agencies also fund activities other than fish and wildlife conservation.

Despite efforts to cut federal spending to reduce the budget deficit, all of these agencies received small increases in 1987 appropriations over 1986 levels,[1] and their budgets were increased or remained about even with 1986 levels in constant dollars. Wildlife-related programs generally remained at about 1986 levels except in the Forest Service, where wildlife- and fish-habitat management and wildlife-related research received significant increases over 1986 levels.

---

1. All 1986 budget figures include the 4.3 percent reduction from the congressionally appropriated level required by the Gramm-Rudman deficit-reduction law.

During the past five or six years,[2] however, the budgets of all these agencies except NMFS and FWS have been reduced in constant-dollar spending power. The NMFS budget has remained about even in spending power since 1982. FWS is the only agency of the five for which the 1987 budget is higher in constant dollars than the 1981 levels. However, although the overall Forest Service budget is down, funding for wildlife- and fish-habitat management on the National Forest System is up slightly in constant dollars from 1981 levels. Similarly, while the Park Service budget is reduced from 1982 levels, funding for natural-resources management has increased 22 percent in constant dollars. On the other hand, while the BLM 1987 budget is five to 10 percent below the 1981 level in constant dollars, wildlife-habitat management is down 21 percent in constant dollars over the same period.

With the exception of BLM, therefore, most wildlife-related federal spending is about even or somewhat above 1981 or 1982 levels. In general, this is in spite of substantial reductions proposed for these programs in the president's annual budget submissions and is the result of Congress' refusal to make cuts as deep as those the administration has requested. Nevertheless, many federal fish and wildlife programs have felt a significant squeeze as new responsibilities have been added and as personnel have been reduced.[3]

## FISH AND WILDLIFE SERVICE

FWS is responsible for the management of 73 national fish hatcheries, all migratory birds, most threatened and endangered species, and the 90-million-acre National Wildlife Refuge System. It enforces various federal wildlife laws, consults with other federal agencies on the impacts of water-resource development on fish and wildlife, and administers federal grants-in-aid to state fish and wildlife agencies for use in fish and wildlife restoration and enhancement. It conducts fish and wildlife research at 11 laboratories and is inventorying and mapping the nation's wetlands. The FWS 1987 budget is $674 million and the agency employs the equivalent of approximately 6,500 full-time personnel.

The major elements of the FWS budget are federal grants-in-aid, which form 37 percent of the total budget, and resource management, which accounts for 47 percent (see Figure 1). Federal grants-in-aid are

2. All budget-trend comparisons are based on 1981 funding levels except for the budgets for National Park Service and NMFS, which had structural budget changes that make comparisons difficult for years prior to 1982.

3. The impacts of budget and personnel changes are discussed in other chapters where they are a significant issue.

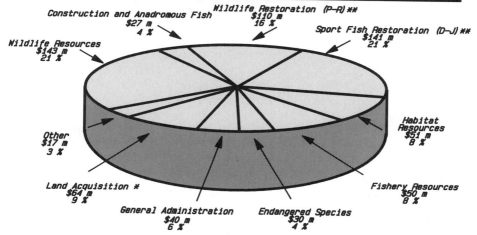

Fish and Wildlife Service Budget, Fiscal Year 1987
Total = $674 Million

Construction and Anadromous Fish
$27 m
4 %

Wildlife Restoration (P-R)**
$110 m
16 %

Sport Fish Restoration (D-J)**
$141 m
21 %

Wildlife Resources
$143 m
21 %

Habitat Resources
$51 m
8 %

Other
$17 m
3 %

Fishery Resources
$50 m
8 %

Land Acquisition *
$64 m
9 %

General Administration
$40 m
6 %

Endangered Species
$30 m
4 %

*Land acquisition includes $42.4 million appropriated from the Land and Water Conservation Fund, $7.0 million appropriated under the Wetlands Loan Act, and an estimated $14.4 million in duck stamp receipts.

**Federal Grants-in-Aid, $251 m, 37 %

Source: FWS

Figure 1

funded primarily by excise taxes on certain types of sporting equipment and motorboat fuel. All receipts are distributed to the states, except for a small amount to cover FWS administration costs. The resource management account funds most FWS management activities and is divided into five subcategories of spending: habitat resources, wildlife resources, fishery resources, endangered species, and general administration. Wildlife resources is the largest subcategory, accounting for 45 percent of the resource management account and 21 percent of the total FWS budget in 1987. Other significant appropriations in the FWS budget are for land acquisition under the Land and Water Conservation Fund and the Wetlands Loan Act and for "Construction and Anadromous Fish," which includes funding for construction of refuge, hatchery, and research facilities and grants to states for anadromous fish efforts.

## Total FWS Budget

Congress appropriated $674 million for FWS in 1987, a small increase in constant dollars above the 1986 budget of $635 million.[4] About 41

4. Throughout this chapter, comparisons in funding levels between different years are made in constant dollars to account for inflation and allow more accurate compari-

percent of the FWS budget is funded by permanent and trust funds. These funds fluctuate depending on receipts from excise taxes and certain other sources. Congress generally does not direct specific spending levels for these programs. Not including permanent and trust funds, Congress appropriated $396 million for FWS in 1987. This provided some small program increases over the 1986 level of $365 million, primarily in construction and in programs to address contaminants and declining waterfowl breeding populations. Congress appropriated about a third more funding than the president's request of $295 million, rejecting the administration's proposals to cut back refuge maintenance funding, halt appropriations for land acquisition, and eliminate all construction except that needed to ensure dam safety.

Since 1981, the total FWS budget has increased from $437 million to $674 million, about a 22 percent increase in constant dollars. Much of this increase, about $110 million, has been in federal grants-in-aid to the states for fish restoration under the Dingell-Johnson program and is due to the enactment of legislation in 1984 expanding the program's funding sources. Not including federal grants-in-aid and other permanent and trust funds, the FWS budget increased from $288 million in 1981 to $396 million in 1986, about an eight percent increase in constant dollars. This includes significant increases in refuge operations and maintenance, which has nearly doubled in funding, and in land acquisition under the Land and Water Conservation Fund. Most other programs currently are funded at about 1981 levels in constant dollars or have experienced small funding declines.

**Habitat Resources**

Habitat resources includes FWS consultation with other agencies regarding the impacts of federally licensed, permitted, or constructed projects; monitoring of contaminants; the national wetlands inventory; and research on the impacts of human activities on fish and wildlife habitat. Congress appropriated $51.4 million for habitat resources in 1987, a nine percent increase in constant dollars above the 1986 level of $45.7 million (see Figure 2). Habitat-resources funding has increased $7.6 million since 1981, but has declined eight percent in constant dollars (see Figure 3).

---

sons of purchasing power. Constant-dollar conversions were made using the Gross National Product implicit price deflators reported by the Bureau of Economic Analysis for the years 1981 through 1986 and the Congressional Budget Office's projected Gross National Project price deflator of 2.9 for 1987. Percentage changes are calculated by converting fiscal year appropriations into dollars of the fiscal year with which they are being compared. For example, in comparisons with 1986 appropriations, 1987 appropriations are converted into fiscal year 1986 dollars. For comparisons with 1981 appropriations, 1987 appropriations are converted into fiscal year 1981 dollars.

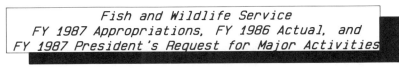

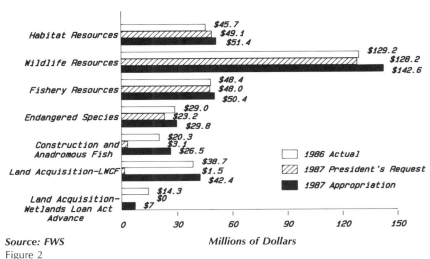

Source: FWS

Figure 2

*Millions of Dollars*

Most of the increase in 1987 was to address the problem of contaminants in critical hot spots — such as California's Central Valley, the Texas Gulf Coast, the Upper Mississippi River, and the Great Lakes — and for contaminant research. Congress also approved an increase of $280,000, requested by the administration, to allow FWS to study the effectiveness of the recommendations it makes for mitigating the adverse impacts of water-resource projects on fish and wildlife. Funding for the national wetlands inventory, $5.3 million, remained about even with 1986 levels, but is the one area in habitat resources that has increased in constant dollars since 1981, when it was funded at $2.4 million.

## Wildlife Resources

This account provides most of the funding for management of the National Wildlife Refuge System, migratory birds, and marine mammals under FWS jurisdiction, as well as for wildlife research in these areas. Congress appropriated $142.6 million for wildlife resources in 1987, a seven percent increase in constant dollars from the 1986 level of $129.2 million.

Congress approved the president's request to increase refuge-operation funding by $2.4 million, primarily to cover management

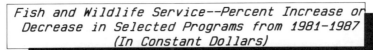

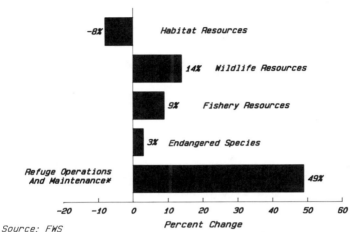

Source: FWS
*Includes some funding under Wildlife and Fishery Resources
Figure 3

costs at recently established refuges, and added $1 million for Alaska refuges and $2 million to address contaminant problems on refuges. Congress approved $4 million of the administration's request for a $5-million increase to respond to the decline in waterfowl breeding populations, which in 1985 hit their lowest level in 31 years.

Congress rejected the president's proposal to cut the administration's refuge-maintenance initiative and the Accelerated Refuge Maintenance Management Program by more than 50 percent and provided $8.8 million to return the effort approximately to the 1986 level of $18 million. Congress noted that the accelerated maintenance program originally was to be funded at $55 million yearly for five years, but so far has received only a total of $50 million over three years (see Table 1).

Wildlife resources funding has increased $44 million from its 1981 level of $98.6 million, a 14-percent increase in constant dollars. In fact, because FWS animal damage control responsibilities were transferred to the Department of Agriculture in 1985, causing a reduction of about $15 million in program responsibilities, the effective increase has been about 26 percent in constant dollars. The increase has been entirely in refuge operations and maintenance, which has increased from $57 million in 1981 to $109 million in 1987, a 50-percent increase in

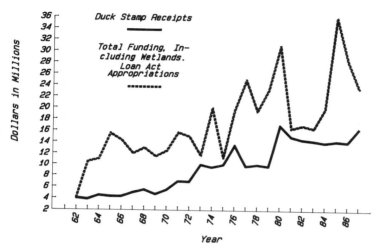

Total Migratory Bird Conservation Fund Funding, 1962 - 1987

Source: FWS

Figure 4

constant dollars. Other activities under wildlife resources have declined somewhat in constant dollars during the same period: law enforcement by 10 percent and research and development by 16 percent.

## Fishery Resources

Fishery resources funds a variety of FWS management responsibilities for inland and anadromous fish, including the operation and mainte- nance of federal fish hatcheries, promotion of fishing on the refuge system, enforcement of federal fish-protection laws, fishery research and development, and implementation of the Lower Snake River Compensation Plan, a program to mitigate damage to fishery resources caused by four federal dams in Washington. Congress provided $50.4 million for fishery resources in 1987, a slight increase over the 1986 level of $48.4 million, but about the same as the 1986 funding level in constant dollars. Congress rejected the administration's recommenda- tion to cut $2.1 million by transferring or closing six national fish hatcheries, reducing maintenance and interpretive activities, and decreasing various other activities. Congress restored funding for all

**TABLE 1**

Migratory Bird Conservation Fund — Appropriations and Acquisition History, FY 1962[a] to FY 1987

| Year | Duck Stamp Receipts | Loan Act Advance | Obligated Funds | Acres Acquired Easement | Acres Acquired Fee | Acres Acquired Total |
|---|---|---|---|---|---|---|
| 1962 | $ 4,094,874 | — | $ 2,678,858 | 4,968 | 30,579 | 35,565 |
| 1963 | 3,418,638 | $ 7,000,000 | 9,008,961 | 12,774 | 75,807 | 88,581 |
| 1964 | 4,559,564 | 10,000,000 | 8,748,887 | 71,575 | 65,819 | 137,394 |
| 1965 | 4,622,688 | 8,000,000 | 12,018,535 | 177,796 | 76,356 | 254,152 |
| 1966 | 4,684,908 | 7,500,000 | 11,669,999 | 146,031 | 79,556 | 225,587 |
| 1967 | 5,385,069 | 6,000,000 | 9,060,515 | 106,954 | 54,967 | 161,921 |
| 1968 | 5,825,238 | 7,500,000 | 10,466,989 | 87,770 | 65,645 | 153,415 |
| 1969 | 5,562,303 | 7,500,000 | 8,720,734 | 61,354 | 51,577 | 112,931 |
| 1970 | 6,107,280 | 5,800,000 | 9,319,380 | 100,411 | 59,186 | 159,597 |
| 1971 | 7,181,256 | 7,500,000 | 11,749,588 | 60,258 | 72,023 | 132,281 |
| 1972 | 7,351,425 | 7,500,000 | 10,227,624 | 51,349 | 50,927 | 102,279 |
| 1973 | 10,734,313 | 7,100,000 | 7,843,144 | 58,289 | 35,157 | 93,446 |
| 1974 | 10,219,685 | 3,500,000 | 15,561,186 | 57,149 | 35,118 | 92,267 |
| 1975 | 11,019,133 | 1,000,000 | 7,283,502 | 34,072 | 19,886 | 53,958 |
| 1976 | 13,700,270 | 7,500,000 | 14,002,727 | 28,472 | 46,911 | 75,383 |
| 1977 | 10,667,020 | 14,000,000 | 18,577,782 | 36,796 | 38,156 | 74,952 |
| 1978 | 11,144,449 | 10,000,000 | 13,909,035 | 23,216 | 32,580 | 55,796 |
| 1979 | 11,079,528 | 10,000,000 | 16,106,843 | 17,015 | 38,525 | 55,540 |
| 1980 | 16,638,831 | 15,000,000 | 22,725,644 | 16,168 | 66,263 | 82,431 |
| 1981 | 14,916,720 | 1,250,000 | 9,387,646 | 14,320 | 10,029 | 24,349 |
| 1982 | 14,598,651 | 1,200,000 | 11,418,673 | 16,535 | 16,003 | 32,538 |
| 1983 | 14,663,828 | 2,000,000 | 11,550,802 | 9,413 | 16,852 | 26,265 |
| 1984 | 13,789,613 | 7,000,000 | 14,439,201 | 8,312 | 21,477 | 29,789 |
| 1985 | 14,411,748 | 21,266,000 | 29,621,265 | 14,692 | 38,755 | 53,447 |
| 1986 | 14,129,308 | 14,323,000 | 21,370,151 | 12,027 | 22,239 | 34,266 |
| 1987 | 14,400,000[b] | 7,000,000[c] | N/A | N/A | N/A | N/A |
| TOTAL | 254,906,340 | 196,493,000 | 317,469,671 | 1,227,716 | 1,120,411 | 2,348,127 |

Source: U.S. Department of the Interior, Fish and Wildlife Service, Division of Realty.

[a] Since passage of the Wetlands Loan Act

[b] Projected receipts

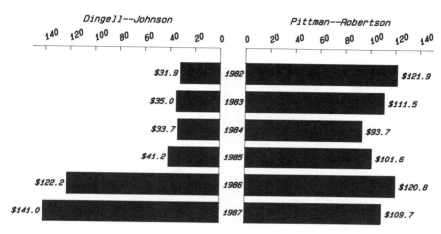

Appropriations, Federal Aid in Wildlife and
Fish Restoration, Fiscal Year 1982-87
(Dollars in Millions)

| | Dingell--Johnson | | Pittman--Robertson |
|---|---|---|---|
| 1982 | $31.9 | | $121.9 |
| 1983 | $35.0 | | $111.5 |
| 1984 | $33.7 | | $93.7 |
| 1985 | $41.2 | | $101.6 |
| 1986 | $122.2 | | $120.8 |
| 1987 | $141.0 | | $109.7 |

*Source: FWS*
Figure 5

facilities except hatcheries in Kentucky and Ohio, which will be transferred to these states. Inreases wereprovided for the Lower Snake River Compensation Plan and for fishery research and development.

The 1987 funding level of $50.4 million for fishery resources was about a nine-percent increase in constant dollars over the 1981 level of $36.4 million. This increase, however, is due to the initiation of the Lower Snake River Compensation Plan in 1984. Excluding funds for this new program, fishery resources funding actually has declined about three percen in constant dollars sine 1981. Endangered Species

## Endangered Species

The endangered species program is the smallest portion of the resource management account and comprises about four percent of the FWS budget. It includes funding for listing and recovery of threatened and endangered species, consultation with other agencies on the impacts of their activities on listed species, law enforcement, research, and grants to assist states in initiating endangered-species conservation programs in cooperation with FWS.[5]

5. Other funding for endangered species is included in budgets for NMFS, BLM, and the Forest Service, and in land-acquisition funds for FWS, BLM, and the Forest Service.

Congress appropriated $29.8 million for endangered species in 1987, a small cut in constant dollars from the 1986 level but a substantial increase over the administration's request for $23 million. Compared with 1986 levels, Congress provided small increases for pre-listing in order to arrest the decline of species not yet qualified for listing; for consultation with other agencies regarding the impacts of their actions on listed species; for research and development; and for the recovery of certain listed species. Congress rejected the administration's proposal to eliminate state assistance and instead provided $4.3 million for this program, about the 1986 level.

The 1987 funding level for the endangered species program is about the same as the 1981 level in constant dollars, while the number of listed species has grown from 748 to 927. Funds have shifted over time, with some reduction in funds for listing species and increases for recovery efforts and research and development.

## Construction and Anadromous Fish

Congress appropriated $26.5 million for this account, compared with $20.3 million in 1986 and $3.1 million in the president's request. Congress provided $24.5 million for construction of hatchery, research, and refuge facilities, a 29-percent increase in constant dollars over 1986 construction funding and a rejection of the president's proposal to fund only construction related to dam safety. Congress also rejected the administration's proposal to halt anadromous fish grants to the states and provided $2 million for the program, maintaining it at about 1986 levels. Construction is 40 percent below the 1981 funding level in constant dollars — although it is higher than funding levels in most years since 1981 — and anadromous fish grants are 55 percent below 1981 levels.

## Land Acquisition

FWS acquires land using three funding sources: funds appropriated under the Land and Water Conservation Fund; revenues collected from the sale of migratory bird conservation stamps, called duck stamps; and funds appropriated under the Wetlands Loan Act, which authorizes a $200-million loan advance against future duck-stamp receipts. In 1987, the president's budget proposed no funding for new land acquisition except for lands acquired with duck-stamp receipts. Congress rejected this proposal. Instead, it appropriated $7 million under the Wetlands Loan Act, about half the 1986 level. This leaves about $3.6 million of the $200-million loan advance available for appropriation in 1988. Congress also appropriated $42.4 million from the Land and

Water Conservation Fund, a small increase over the 1986 level of $38.7 million. Duck stamps are expected to yield about $14.4 million in 1986.

Altogether, the $64 million for land acquisition in 1987 is slightly below the 1986 level of $67.4 million, but well above the $26.8 million available in 1981, a particularly low year for acquisition funding. Over the past decade, appropriations from the Land and Water Conservation Fund have ranged from $9.5 million to $70.3 million, appropriations from the Wetlands Loan Act from $1.2 million to $21.3 million, and duck stamp receipts from $11 million to $16.4 million (see Table 1 and Figure 4). Total land-acquisition funds have averaged $56 million yearly. The $64 million available in 1987 is somewhat above this in current dollars, but is reduced substantially from levels in the late 1970s in purchasing power.

### Federal Aid in Fish and Wildlife Restoration

Receipts to these state-assistance programs totaled $251 million in 1987, up from $223 million in 1986 and more than double the 1981 level of $124 million (see Figure 5). The increase is primarily in sport-fish restoration, which has grown from $33.6 million in 1981 to $141 million in 1987, a 230-percent increase in constant dollars. Wildlife-restoration funds have increased from $90.7 million in 1981 to $109.7 million in 1987, but have decreased about five percent in constant dollars. Together, these programs have grown as a proportion of the total FWS budget as well, from 28 percent in 1981 to 37 percent in 1987.

## FOREST SERVICE

The Forest Service is responsible for management of the 191-million-acre National Forest System; conducts research to assist in the management of the nation's 1.6 billion acres of forest and range land, including federal and private lands; and cooperates with the states to provide assistance to improve management and production on nonindustrial private forest lands. The Forest Service 1987 budget is $2.324 billion, and the service employs the equivalent of approximately 38,000 full-time personnel.

About 28 percent of the Forest Service budget is permanent and trust funds. More than half of these funds are used to support activities on the National Forest System, including a small portion used for fish- and wildlife-habitat improvement. The remainder are used to pay states and counties their share of receipts from commercial production

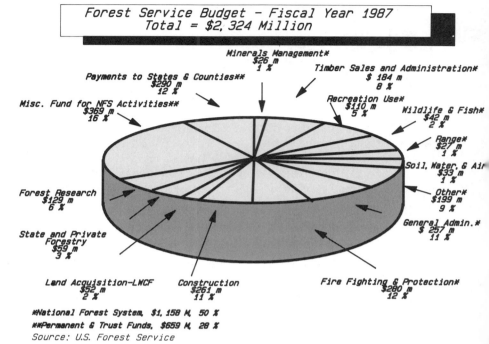

**Forest Service Budget – Fiscal Year 1987**
**Total = $2,324 Million**

Minerals Management*
$26 m
1 %

Timber Sales and Administration*
$ 184 m
8 %

Payments to States & Counties**
$290 m
12 %

Recreation Use*
$110 m
5 %

Misc. Fund for NFS Activities**
$369 m
16 %

Wildlife & Fish*
$42 m
2 %

Range*
$27 m
1 %

Soil, Water, & Air
$33 m
1 %

Forest Research
$129 m
6 %

Other*
$199 m
9 %

State and Private
Forestry
$59 m
3 %

General Admin.*
$ 257 m
11 %

Land Acquisition–LWCF
$52 m
2 %

Construction
$261 m
11 %

Fire Fighting & Protection*
$290 m
12 %

*National Forest System, $1,158 M, 50 %
**Permanent & Trust Funds, $659 M, 28 %
Source: U.S. Forest Service

Figure 6

on forest-system lands. The remainder of the Forest Service budget, about $1.666 billion in 1987, is divided among five major accounts, forest research, state and private forestry, the National Forest System, construction, and land acquisition (Land and Water Conservation Fund) – plus several smaller miscellaneous accounts (see Figure 6). The National Forest System account forms 50 percent of the total Forest Service budget and funds most forest-system management activities, including fish- and wildlife-habitat management, which comprises about two percent of the total Forest Service budget. The largest program on the National Forest System is the timber program. Including funds for road construction and for the planning and mitigation needed to protect other resources or activities from the impacts of timber production, the Forest Service estimates that the timber program accounts for about 28 percent of the total budge.[6]

## Total Forest Service Budget

The total Forest Service budget of $2.32 billion in 1987 is substantially above the president's request of $1.74 billion and is about a four percent increase in constant dollars from the 1986 level of $2.16

6. Based on 1985 appropriations.

billion. Excluding permanent and trust funds, Congress appropriated $1.666 billion for the Forest Service in 1987, compared with $1.287 billion in the president's request. This about even with the 1986 level of $1.625 billion in constant dollars.

These total figures are misleading, however, because the 1987 budget includes a $40 million decrease for firefighting—an activity that fluctuates substantially from year to year—and a $30 million decrease in appropriations from general revenues for reforestation—a reduction that is compensated for by $30 million from the Reforestation Trust Fund. In fact, a number of Forest Service programs received meaningful increases in 1987. Congress provided funding levels above the president's request, and above 1986 levels in constant-dollar purchasing power, for wildlife- and fish-habitat management; wildlife, range, and fish-habitat research; soil, water, and air management; recreation use; land acquisition; timber sales and administration; and road construction. Range management and minerals-area management were funded at close to 1986 levels and thus decreased somewhat in constant dollars (see Figure 7).

Since 1981, the total Forest Service budget has increased from $2.113 billion to $2.324 billion, but has declined about 14 percent in constant dollars. Not including permanent and trust funds, Forest Service appropriations have increased from $1.592 billion in 1981 to $1.666 billion in 1986, but have declined 18 percent in constant dollars. Funding for most National Forest System programs also has declined in constant dollars since 1981, including funding for land acquisition; recreation use; the range-betterment fund; range management; soil, water, and air management; and timber-sales administration and management. With the 1987 increase, however, wildlife-habitat management and wildlife, range, and fish-habitat research are up somewhat from 1981 levels in constant dollars. Only funding for minerals-area management has increased significantly since 1981, up about 36 percent in constant dollars. But at $26.3 million in 1987, this program remains a small portion of the total Forest Service budget.

Funding trends over the past six years diverge substantially from the goals set by the 1980 Resources Planning Act program, which established funding and output goals for the Forest Service through 1985 and beyond.[7] Under the 1980 program, appropriations for timber were projected to remain relatively steady in constant dollars, while almost all other programs were projected to increase. For example, between 1981 and 1985, range funding was scheduled to increase 28

7. The 1980 Resources Planning Act program was updated by the administration in 1986, although Congress could alter the recommended program in 1987. See the Forest Service chapter for details.

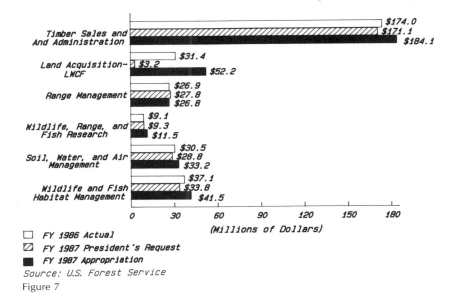

Forest Service—FY 1987 Appropriations Compared
With FY 1986 Actual and FY 1987 President's
Request--Selected Programs

*(Millions of Dollars)*

☐ FY 1986 Actual
▨ FY 1987 President's Request
■ FY 1987 Appropriation

*Source: U.S. Forest Service*

Figure 7

percent, recreation 42 percent, water 67 percent, and fish and wildlife 112 percent.

A change in administrations and policies, however, and pressures to increase returns to the federal treasury and reduce federal outlays in order to address the budget deficit, has meant that few programs except timber have come close to meeting the 1980 Resources Planning Act program goals. Timber spending has remained relatively steady since 1981, and the timber program accomplished an average of 97 percent of its annual Resources Planning Act program goals from 1981 to 1984. In contrast, other programs received only small funding increases or were cut in funding and thus have fallen far below their 1980 program goals. The fish and wildlife habitat program, for example, accomplished an average of only 28 percent of its 1980 program goals for habitat improvement from 1981 to 1984.

### Wildlife and Fish Habitat Management

Congress appropriated $41.5 million for wildlife and fish habitat management on the National Forest System in 1987, a substantial increase from the president's request for $33.8 million and a nine

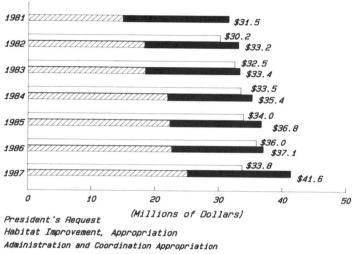

Forest Service Wildlife and Fish Habitat Management Appropriations FY 1981--1987

President's Request
Habitat Improvement. Appropriation
Administration and Coordination Appropriation

Source: U.S. Forest Service
Figure 8

percent increase in constant dollars over the 1986 level of $37.1 million. With this funding boost, funding for wildlife- and fish-habitat management in 1987 for the first time exceeded 1981 levels in constant dollars. The 1987 level is about three percent above the 1981 level of $31.5 million in constant dollars (see Figure 8).

The increases for 1987 included $1 million to conduct inventories of the northern spotted owl, the species that is at the center of controversy over old-growth timber management in the Pacific Northwest.[8] Congress also provided $1.5 million to continue the challenge grant program started last year. Under this program, federally appropriated dollars are matched with state, private, or other federal funds to carry out habitat-management activities on the National Forest System. The Forest Service estimates it received $1.6 million in contributions in 1986, exceeding the $903,695 in Forest Service challenge grant funds available that year. All activities funded as part of the Forest Service's wildlife- and fish-habitat management program received increases in 1986 except resident fish-habitat improvement. Funding for endangered species was increased from $2.4 million in 1986 to $3.5 million in 1987.

8. Discussed in the Forest Service chapter.

Another source of fish- and wildlife-habitat funds is deposits made by timber purchasers under the Knutson-Vandenberg Act. These funds are used for habitat-improvement measures on the timber-sale area for which the deposits are made. Approximately $9.1 million is available from Knutson-Vandenburg funds for fish- and wildlife-habitat improvements in 1987, bringing total fish and wildlife funding to $50.6 million.

### Wildlife and Fish Research

Research for wildlife, range, and fish habitat was funded at $11.5 million in 1987, up 23 percent in constant dollars from the 1986 level of $9.1 million. Congress included $1.5 million for research on the northern spotted owl, to be matched by $500,000 in private funds. Other increases were provided for research on endangered species, trout productivity, semi-arid habitat, moose habitat, and tropical wildlife in Puerto Rico.

### Range Management and Improvements

Forest-range-management funds consist of dollars appropriated under the range management activity in the Forest Service budget and the Range Betterment Fund, which consists of 50 percent of fee receipts from grazing on the National Forest System. Congress appropriated $26.8 million for range management in 1987, about even with the 1986 level of $26.9 million, but the distribution of the funds was changed. At the administration's request, Congress specified that almost two-thirds of the $2 million previously used for range improvements be used for grazing management. This reflects the Forest Service's judgment that increased management of livestock grazing is a more cost-effective approach to improving range condition than are capital investments in improvement projects. Appropriations for range management in 1987 were only slightly above the 1981 level of $25.6 million and were 18 percent below the 1981 level in constant dollars.

The Range Betterment Fund, totaling $3.8 million in 1987, remained at about the 1986 funding level. However, Range Betterment funds have declined from a high of $6.9 million in 1981 as National Forest System grazing fees have dropped. The 1987 level is 57 percent below 1981 levels in constant-dollar purchasing power (see Figure 9).

### Soil, Water, and Air Management

Congress appropriated $33.2 million for soil, water, and air management, a six-percent increase in constant dollars over the 1986 level of

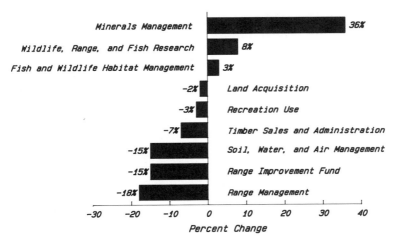

**Forest Service–Percent Increase or Decrease in Appropriations from FY 1981–FY 1987 for Selected Programs (In Constant Dollars)**

*Source: U.S. Forest Services*
Figure 9

$30.5 million. This is an all-time high for the program in current dollars, but represents a 15-percent decline in constant dollars from the 1981 level of $30.6 million.

### Recreation Use

Congress rejected an administration proposal to increase national-forest recreation fees and to fund $52 million of the recreation program from these fees. Congress appropriated $110.2 million for recreation-use programs, an eight percent increase in constant dollars over the 1986 funding level of $99 million. The 1987 funding level is a significant increase above the 1981 level of $89.4 million in current dollars, but constitutes a three-percent decline in constant dollars.

### Land Acquisition

Congress appropriated $52.2 million from the Land and Water Conservation Fund for National Forest System land acquisition, a substantial increase above the 1986 level of $31.4 million and a rejection of the administration's proposal to halt new land acquisition. Over the past decade, Forest Service land-acquisition funds under the Land and Water

Conservation Fund have fluctuated from a low of $26.3 million in 1982 to a high of $90 million in 1978, averaging about $48 million yearly. The 1987 funding level is slightly above this average, but as land prices have increased, the purchasing power of land-acquisition funds has declined.

## Timber Sales and Road Construction

Congress appropriated $184.1 million for timber sales and administration and directed the Forest Service to offer 11.2 billion board feet of timber for sale. This is a three-percent increase in constant dollars over the 1986 funding level of $174 million, but it funds a slightly lower sales offering level than the 11.4 billion board feet offered in 1986. Funding for timber sales and administration was about $30 million above the 1981 level of $155.3 million, but was about seven percent below the 1981 level in constant dollars. This decline is in part because the 1987 timber-sale offering level of 11.2 billion board feet is below the 1981 level of 12.2 billion board feet. It also is the result of reduced costs in recent years for preparing timber sales in areas that were purchased by timber producers at high prices in the late 1970s and early 1980s but were retracted by the Forest Service in an economic-aid effort after the 1982-84 recession caused timber prices to slump.[9] Some of these sale areas are largely ready for resale without additional preparation.

The largest increase in the 1987 Forest Service budget was in funding under the Forest Road Program for road construction on the National Forest System. In most years, almost the entire road-construction budget is used to construct timber roads. In 1987, Congress appropriated $228.8 million for road construction, compared with $178.5 million requested in the president's budget and $181 million in 1986. This included a $36.2 million increase over the president's budget for timber roads and an increase of $14.1 million for recreation roads and other nontimber items. An effort by the House of Representatives to cut the funding for construction of timber roads was defeated in the Senate (see the Forest Service chapter for further discussion).

Funding for road construction under the Forest Road Program in 1987 was about even with the 1981 funding level of $224.8 million, but was significantly below 1981 levels in constant dollars. However, miles of roads constructed or reconstructed under the Forest Roads Program has increased during this period as the Forest Service has lowered road and construction standards and thus has reduced construction costs.

9. This timber buy-back was authorized by Congress in the Timber Contract Modification Act of 1984 (16 U.S.C. 619) and is discussed further in *Audubon Wildlife Report 1986*, pp. 57–58.

The Forest Service also says that a larger portion of current road construction is reconstruction of old roads rather than construction of new roads. Although road-construction dollars from 1981 to 1985 declined 15 percent in constant dollars, miles of roads constructed or reconstructed increased 53 percent, from 1,217 miles to 1,858 miles.[10]

## BUREAU OF LAND MANAGEMENT

BLM is a multiple-use agency responsible for managing fish and wildlife habitat and a variety of other resources and activities on 270 million acres of public land located primarily in the 11 westernmost states and Alaska. BLM also administers energy and mineral-leasing and development laws on an additional 300 million acres managed by federal agencies and on other lands where the federal government owns subsurface mineral rights. The 1987 BLM budget is $717 million, and BLM employs the equivalent of approximately 10,000 full-time personnel.

About half of the BLM budget is allocated to land-management activities. Renewable-resources management accounts for 17 percent of the total BLM budget and includes fish- and wildlife-habitat management, which accounts for two percent of the total BLM budget. Eleven percent of the budget is allocated to energy and minerals management and eight percent to the management of timber harvesting on BLM lands in western Oregon. The other half of the BLM budget is spent on firefighting and general administration and to make legally required payments to states and counties (see Figure 10).

### Total BLM Budget

The total 1987 BLM budget of $717 million was significantly above the president's request of $600 million and the 1986 level of $564 million. Not including permanent and trust funds, which have fluctuated widely in recent years and thus complicate budget comparisons, BLM was appropriated $664 million in 1987, compared with the 1986 level of $550 million and the president's 1987 budget request of $547 million. Most of this apparent increase, however, is due to an irregu-

10. Roads also are constructed under the purchaser credit program, in which timber purchasers construct roads in exchange for national forest timber (a cost that is not included in the Forest Service budget), and under the purchaser election program, in which the Forest Service uses timber-sale receipts to build roads to access national forest timber sales purchased by certain small timber producers. Purchaser election funds are provided under the permanent funds section of the budget. Including these funding sources, road-construction funding decreased from $488.7 million in 1981 to $339.8 million in 1985 and total construction miles declined from 10,053 miles to 8,043 miles.

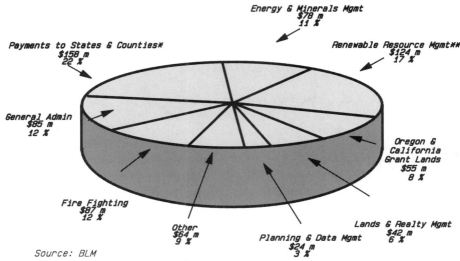

Bureau of Land Management Budget, Fiscal Year 1987
Total = $717 Million

Energy & Minerals Mgmt
$78 m
11 %

Payments to States & Counties*
$158 m
22 %

Renewable Resource Mgmt**
$124 m
17 %

General Admin
$85 m
12 %

Oregon &
California
Grant Lands
$55 m
8 %

Fire Fighting
$87 m
12 %

Other
$64 m
9 %

Planning & Data Mgmt
$24 m
3 %

Lands & Realty Mgmt
$42 m
6 %

Source: BLM

*Includes payments to states for their 25 percent share of receipts from economic activities on BLM lands and payments to counties that contain BLM lands. These payments are made to compensate for taxes the counties would have collected had the lands been in private ownership.

**Includes forest management, wildlife habitat management, range management, recreation management. fire management, and soil, water, and air management.

Figure 10

larity in firefighting appropriations that caused 1986 firefighting costs to be reflected in 1987 appropriations. Discounting this difference, 1987 appropriations for BLM are about $31 million higher than the 1986 level, a slight increase in constant-dollar spending power. As in the past, Congress rejected the president's request for significant cuts in most renewable-resource programs and in fact provided small increases over the 1986 budget for wildlife-habitat management, grazing management, recreation management, and land acquisition. Funding for energy and minerals management, the range-improvement fund, and soil, water, and air management was slightly reduced from 1986 levels (see Figure 11).

The 1987 funding level of $664 million was nearly $120 million above the 1981 level of $547 million.[11] In constant dollars, however, BLM appropriations have decreased about five percent and, when funding for new minerals responsibilities assumed by the Bureau in

11. For more accurate comparison, permanent and trust funds and funds for offshore oil and gas leasing, which are no longer included in BLM's budget, are not included here.

1983 and 1984 are subtracted, the Bureau's effective budget has decreased nearly 10 percent. Most of the renewable-resource programs have been particularly hard hit: wildlife-habitat management has been cut 21 percent in constant dollars, grazing management by 32 percent, soil, water, and air management 42 percent, and the range-improvement fund 45 percent. Of all the federal agencies with wildlife-management responsibilities—and BLM manages more habitat than any other agency—BLM's renewable-resource programs have suffered the greatest budget reductions during this period (see Figure 13).

## Wildlife Habitat Management

Congress provided $16.1 million for fish- and wildlife-habitat management in 1987, a 17-percent increase above the president's request and about even in constant dollars with the 1986 level of $15.4 million. Congress added $1 million to the president's request for endangered and threatened species to restore this activity to $3.9 million, the 1986

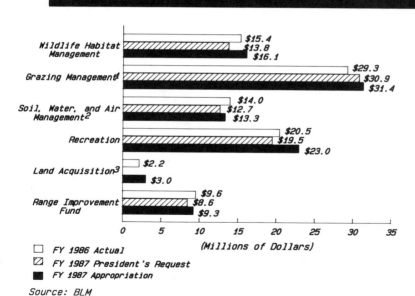

Bureau of Land Management–FY 1987 Appropriations Compared with FY 1986 Actual and FY 1987 President's Request--Selected Programs

□ FY 1986 Actual
▨ FY 1987 President's Request
■ FY 1987 Appropriation

*Source: BLM*

[1]*1987 appropriation does not include $5 million add-on for grasshopper control.*
[2]*Does not include funds for hazardous waste management.*
[3]*1987 appropriation of $6.22 million offset in part by $3.2 million recision of funds appropriated in 1984, for a total of $3.02 million.*

Figure 11

funding level prior to Gramm-Rudman reductions. Congress also included $450,000 in challenge grant funds to be used to obtain state and private matching contributions for wildlife- and fish-habitat management activities. Challenge grants in the past three years have allowed BLM to conduct substantial improvement and reintroduction activities for the desert bighorn sheep, and Congress specified that up to $300,000 of the 1987 challenge grant funds may be used to continue this effort.

In addition, the House Appropriations Committee expressed concern that BLM is paying insufficient attention to the identification and protection of critical plant species and habitats and urged BLM to maintain or bolster its staff of botanists. In 1986, BLM had eight botanists.

After years of depressed finding levels, in 1987 the wildlife-habitat-management budget was boosted to an all-time high of $16.1 million. Nevertheless, the wildlife program is 21 percent below 1981 levels in constant dollars (see Figures 12 and 13).

### Range Management and Improvements

Congress appropriated $54.1 million for range management in 1987, a substantial increase over the 1986 level of $45.6 million and the

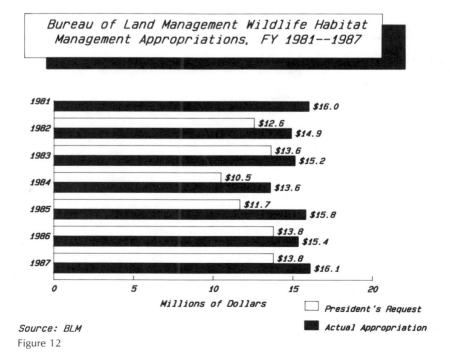

Bureau of Land Management Wildlife Habitat Management Appropriations, FY 1981--1987

Source: BLM

Figure 12

president's request of $46.1 million. Very little of this increase, however, was for the management of livestock grazing. Congress added $5 million for grasshopper control—not previously funded in this account—and $2.5 million for wild horse and burro management which, at $17.8 million, was funded at an all-time high.

Grazing management was funded at $31.4 million, including a $385,000 increase over the 1986 level for planning of range-improvement projects. This was about a four-percent increase in constant dollars over the 1986 level of $29.3 million. Nevertheless, grazing-management funding remains substantially below the 1981 level of $36.1 million and has decreased 32 percent in constant-dollar spending power during this period.

Congress appropriated $9.3 million for the range-improvement fund, which is paid for primarily with 50 percent of receipts from grazing fees on public lands. This is the first year that Congress has not appropriated the $10-million minimum level provided for the fund in the Public Rangelands Improvement Act. That provision was intended to keep range-improvement funds from falling below $10 million even if grazing fees dropped so low that the receipts no longer yielded this amount to the fund. Grazing-fee deposits to the range-improvement fund have not totaled $10 million since 1983. Range-improvement funds have declined from $13.1 million in 1981, a 45-percent decrease in constant dollars.

**Soil, Water, and Air Management**

This account funds traditional soil, water, and air inventory, monitoring, and improvement activities, as well as the hazardous-waste-management program. Congress provided the administration's request of $1.8 million for hazardous-waste management, but increased soil, water, and air funding $650,000 over the president's budget for a total of $13.3 million. This was still a decrease of $567,000 from the 1986 level and a seven-percent decrease from 1986 in constant dollars. The 1987 funding level is substantially below the 1981 level of $18 million and constitutes a 42-percent decrease in spending power in the past six years.

**Recreation Management**

Congress appropriated $23 million for recreation management in 1987, compared with the president's request of $19.5 million and the 1986 level of $20.5 million. This was about a nine-percent increase above the 1986 level in constant dollars. Of note for wildlife is $400,000 appropriated for inventories and management planning in the San Pedro Riparian Area in Arizona, established by Congress in 1986 as the

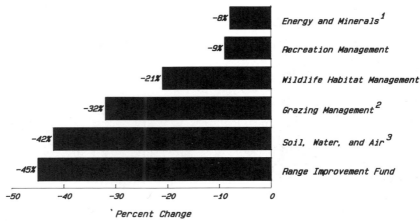

Bureau of Land Management Percent Decrease In Appropriations Between FY 1981 and FY 1987 for Selected Activities (In Constant Dollars)

Source: BLM

[1]Shows percentage change from 1984–1987. Merger of new mineral responsibilities into BLM in 1983 and 1984 makes comparison with earlier years inappropriate.

[2]$5.0 million for grasshopper control in 1987 not included.

[3]Hazardous waste management funds not included.

Figure 13

country's first Riparian Area. The 1987 funding increase brought recreation-management funding above the 1981 level of $19.7 million, but the program is eight percent below the 1981 level in constant dollars.

**Land Acquisition**

BLM land acquisition under the Land and Water Conservation Fund received a significant boost in 1987. Congress appropriated $6.2 million for acquisition in various recreation and wildlife areas, compared with $2.2 million in 1986 and the president's request for no funding. This increase was offset in part by a recision of $3.2 million appropriated in 1984 for cash equalization payments for the Navajo-Hopi land exchange. With this offset, total BLM land-acquisition appropriations were $3 million for 1987. This was substantially above the 1981 level of $1 million, but acquisition funds have fluctuated significantly over the years, and this does not represent a general upward trend.

## Energy and Minerals Management

Energy- and minerals-management funding was reduced slightly from $80.3 million in 1986 to $77.9 million in 1987, primarily because of a decline in coal leasing and the elimination of oil-shale and tar-sands leasing due to lack of demand. Oil and gas leasing and mining law administration received small increases over the president's budget request for inspection, enforcement, and environmental-assessment activities.

Energy and minerals funding has increased since 1981 from $53 million to $77.9 million.[12] However, a 1983 merger with the Minerals Management Service gave BLM additional energy and minerals responsibilities that may account for all of this increase or more. Since 1984, the earliest year with which accurate comparisons in the energy and minerals budget can be made, funding for energy and minerals management has decreased eight percent in constant dollars, a smaller decrease than that of most of the renewable-resource programs and one largely due to lack of demand for energy development in recent years.

# NATIONAL PARK SERVICE

The National Park Service is responsible for the preservation and management of 337 parks, monuments, historic sites, and other areas, some 75 million acres. The Park Service's 1987 budget is $909 million, and the Service employs the equivalent of roughly 16,000 full-time personnel. Three quarters of the current Park Service budget is allocated to operation of the National Park System. Other significant expenditures are for park land acquisition, construction and repair of park facilities, and matching grants to states for historic preservation and outdoor-recreation efforts.

The National Park Service budget does not track funds spent specifically on the management of fish and wildlife populations or habitat. Few activities conducted by park personnel are focused exclusively on wildlife, although the Park Service maintains that its ecosystem approach to management integrates wildlife concerns into all management activities. In addition, park personnel typically have many varied duties, and it is difficult to account for all staff time spent on wildlife-related activities. Most funding for direct fish- and wildlife-habitat efforts is appropriated under natural resources management, a subdivision of the resources management line item under park management in the Operation of the National Park System account.

---

12. Not including offshore oil and gas leasing funds in 1981, since these funds are no longer included in BLM's budget.

Natural resources management funding accounts for about six percent of the total Park Service budget and eight percent of the operating funds (see Figure 14).

### Total National Park Service Budget

The 1987 Park Service budget of $909 million was substantially higher than the president's request of $734 million and about even in constant dollars with the 1986 level of $880 million. Congress rejected administration proposals to halt new land acquisition, terminate state-assistance grants under the Land and Water Conservation Fund, eliminate funding for the Historic Preservation Fund, and defer most construction. Congress did approve reductions from the 1986 levels for construction and Land and Water Conservation Fund state assistance, while increasing funds for park management.

Excluding permanent and trust funds in order to allow more accurate comparisons, the 1987 Park Service budget was $889 million, significantly above the 1982 level of $801 million but a six-percent decrease from the 1982 level in constant dollars. The major decreases have been in land acquisition, construction, and the urban park and recreation fund, which was terminated in 1985. The 1987 level is

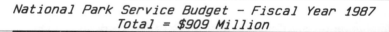

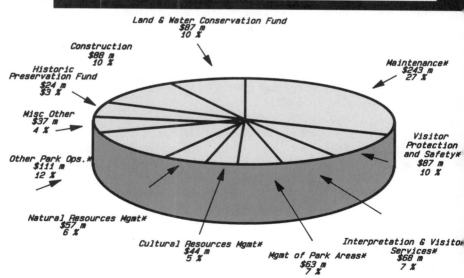

National Park Service Budget - Fiscal Year 1987
Total = $909 Million

Land & Water Conservation Fund
$87 m
10 %

Construction
$88 m
10 %

Historic
Preservation Fund
$24 m
$3 %

Misc Other
$37 m
4 %

Other Park Ops.*
$111 m
12 %

Natural Resources Mgmt*
$57 m
6 %

Cultural Resources Mgmt*
$44 m
5 %

Mgmt of Park Areas*
$63 m
7 %

Interpretation & Visitor
Services*
$68 m
7 %

Maintenance*
$243 m
27 %

Visitor
Protection
and Safety*
$87 m
10 %

*Operation of the National Park System, $673 M, 74 %
*Source: National Park Service*

Figure 14

substantially below Park Service budgets from 1983 to 1985, when an administration initiative to improve park facilities temporarily swelled construction and maintenance funding and when Land and Water Conservation Fund appropriations were substantially higher than at present. However, funding for park management actually has increased since 1982, as has funding for natural-resources management.

**Park Management and Natural Resources**

Congress funded the park-management account at $585 million in 1987, up about seven percent in constant dollars from the 1986 level of $531 million. The most significant change in park-management funding resulted from the enactment of legislation to increase existing park entrance fees and to charge fees at certain parks that have no fees. Under this legislation, park fee receipts would no longer be deposited in the Land and Water Conservation Fund for use in acquiring land, but instead would be used to support park operations.

The entrance-fee legislation, long sought by the administration, was advanced in the president's budget. The president requested appropriations of $521 million for park management, significantly below the 1986 program levels, but proposed to supplement this

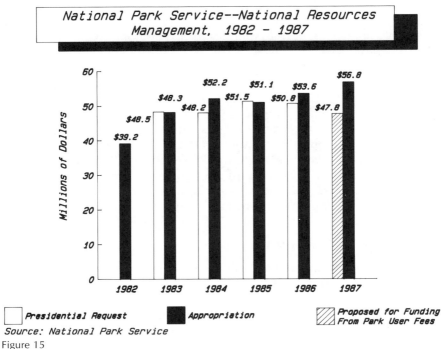

Source: National Park Service

Figure 15

appropriation by returning 80 percent of anticipated entrance-fee revenues—$59 million—to the Park Service. Part of the $59 million was to be used to restore park-management activities to their 1986 levels and to fund the collection of fees. In addition, the president proposed that $14.7 million of entrance-fee receipts be allocated generally to "enhance park operations."

Congress enacted legislation authorizing additional and increased park entrance fees for one year, although it approved smaller increases than the administration proposed and treated the revenues differently. Instead of earmarking 80 percent of fee receipts for park operations, Congress directed that all fee receipts be returned to the general treasury and then appropriated the additional funds anticipated to be derived from these receipts. Congress retained the administration's proposal for a general appropriation to enhance park operations, funded at $15 million and to be used for resource protection, research, interpretation, and maintenance activities related to resource protection. Of this $15 million, half will be allocated among park system units in proportion to each unit's operating expenses, and half will be provided to units with entrance fees based on each unit's proportion of the total entrance fees collected.

Within the park-management funding, Congress appropriated $56.8 million for natural-resources management, providing small increases over 1986 for air-quality monitoring and several other specific activities. However, additional funds could be allocated to natural-resources management from the $15 million appropriated for enhanced park operations.

In constant dollars, the 1987 appropriation of $585 million for park management is five-percent above the 1982 level of $470 million. Natural-resources-management appropriations have increased significantly from the 1982 level of $29 million, a 22-percent increase in constant dollars. Natural-resources-management funding has increased as a proportion of total National Park Service appropriations—from 4.8 percent in 1982 to 6.4 percent in 1987. Nevertheless, natural-resources-management funding remains a small portion of the budget of the agency whose mission is to preserve some of the rarest and most spectacular natural resources in the nation (see Figure 15).

## Land and Water Conservation Fund

Appropriations from the Land and Water Conservation Fund are used for land acquisition and matching grants to states for outdoor-recreation programs. The president's budget repeatedly has proposed to terminate appropriations for both these efforts as a deficit-reduction measure. Congress has consistently rejected the administration's proposal, although it has reduced funding levels for these programs.

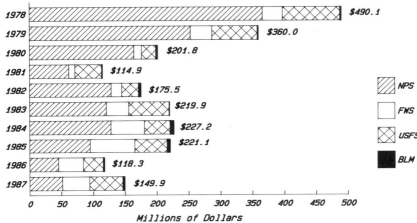

Source: NPS, FWS, USFS, BLM

Figure 16

In 1987, Congress provided $52.3 million for land acquisition, substantially above the president's request of $13 million and slightly above the 1986 level of $46 million. However, the 1987 level is substantially below historic levels for Park Service land acquisition, which was funded at $129 million in 1982 and at two to three times this level in the late 1970s. The $35 million appropriated in 1987 for state-assistance grants was significantly above the president's request of $2.3 million but was below the 1986 level of $47.7 million. It also was substantially below funding levels in most prior years (see Figure 16).

## NATIONAL MARINE FISHERIES SERVICE

The National Marine Fisheries Service (NMFS) is responsible for the management of marine fisheries within the U.S. fishery conservation zone, which extends from the states' territorial waters — usually three miles offshore — to 200 miles from the U.S. coastline. NMFS also is responsible for protection and management of certain threatened and endangered species, marine mammals, and anadromous fish stocks. NMFS consults with other federal agencies regarding the impacts of their activities on marine-fisheries habitat and conducts surveys and research on resources under its jurisdiction.

NMFS is funded in the budget for the National Oceanic and Atmospheric Administration. All NMFS resource-management funds are appropriated under the Marine Fishery Resource Programs activity in the Operations, Research, and Facilities account. Certain other special funds to assist the commercial fishing industry, itemized elsewhere in the National Oceanic and Atmospheric Administration budget, are administered by NMFS but are not covered here because they do not affect the agency's ability to meet its resource-management responsibilities. NMFS has a small budget, $162 million in 1987, and employs the equivalent of about 2,000 full-time personnel.

The NMFS budget is divided into three subactivities: information collection and analysis; conservation and management operations; and state and industry programs. Federal involvement in marine fisheries traditionally has focused on research—NMFS did not gain general commercial-fisheries management authority until 1976—and research activities, funded under information collection and analysis, still account for 61 percent of the NMFS budget in 1987. Conservation and management operations account for just over a quarter of the budget, and state and industry programs for 13 percent (see Figure 17).

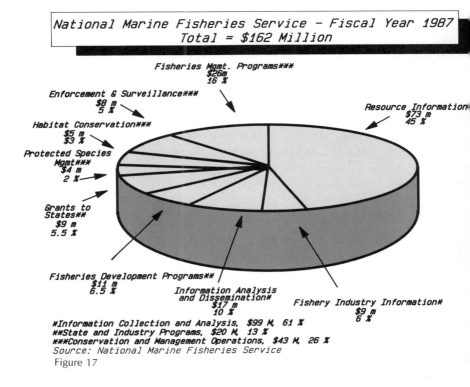

**National Marine Fisheries Service – Fiscal Year 1987**
**Total = $162 Million**

Fisheries Mgmt. Programs***
$26m
16 %

Enforcement & Surveillance***
$8 m
5 %

Habitat Conservation***
$5 m
3 %

Protected Species
Mgmt***
$4 m
2 %

Grants to
States**
$9 m
5.5 %

Resource Information
$73 m
45 %

Fisheries Development Programs**
$11 m
6.5 %

Information Analysis
and Dissemination*
$17 m
10 %

Fishery Industry Information*
$9 m
6 %

*Information Collection and Analysis, $99 M, 61 %
**State and Industry Programs, $20 M, 13 %
***Conservation and Management Operations, $43 M, 26 %
Source: National Marine Fisheries Service
Figure 17

**Total NMFS Budget**

Among the federal agencies with fish- and wildlife-management responsibilities, NMFS repeatedly has been targeted by the Reagan administration for the sharpest cuts. The president's 1987 budget requested a 37-percent cut from 1986 levels, from $155.4 million to $96.7 million. Congress repeatedly has rejected these cuts and in general has provided small increases for the NMFS budget. Congress appropriated $162.1 million for NMFS in 1987, about even with the 1986 level in constant dollars. Almost all of the increase was for research and survey activities.

The NMFS budget changed in structure in 1983, and the agency also has altered how funds are allocated among various line items in recent years, making it difficult to compare funding levels from year to year. The 1987 level of $162 million is substantially above the 1982[13] level of $129 million, but much of this apparent increase is because fisheries-development programs, an $11-million line item under state and industry programs, was funded in a different part of the National Oceanic and Atmospheric Administration budget in 1982. Correcting for this difference, the 1987 NMFS budget is about even with 1981 funding levels in constant dollars. The allocation of funds, however, has shifted somewhat away from conservation and management operations to research and survey work.

**Information Collection and Analysis**

Funding under this subactivity is divided among three line items: resource information, which funds the collection of biological and environmental data on living marine resources and their environment; fisheries-industry information, which includes the collection of economic and commercial-fisheries statistics; and information dissemination and analysis, which includes analytical research.

Congress appropriated $98.9 million for information collection and analysis in 1987, restoring most of the cuts proposed in the president's request of $65.4 million and providing some increases to boost funding about six percent in constant dollars above the 1986 level of $90.5 million. All the increases were in resource information and included $2 million for the Antarctic Marine Living Resources Program and more than $1 million for anadromous-fisheries research. The 1987 budget includes approximately $6.5 million for protected species research, a $150,000 reduction from 1986; $13.5 million for habitat research, about $1.5 million below the 1986 level; and $16.8 million for anadromous-fish research, up about $1 million from 1986.

13. NMFS budget documents restructured the 1982 budget to fit the 1983 format for comparison purposes.

Funding for fisheries-industry information and for information dissemination and analysis was maintained at 1986 levels (see Figure 18).

Information collection and analysis has increased from $70.5 million in 1981 to $98.9 million in 1987. It also has increased as a proportion of the NMFS budget, from 50 percent in 1982 to 61 percent in 1987. NMFS budget officials say this is in part due to a change in accounting procedures that caused funds previously reflected under conservation and management operations to be currently reflected under information collection and analysis. However, they also say that some real shift in emphasis toward research and data collection has occurred.

### Conservation and Management Operations

Under this subactivity, NMFS funds management activities related to marine and anadromous fisheries, endangered species, and marine mammals and conducts limited habitat-conservation efforts. Funding is divided among four line items: fisheries-management programs, which accounts for almost two-thirds of the funding under conservation and management operations; protected species (endangered species and marine mammals); habitat conservation; and enforcement and surveillance.

Congress provided $43.2 million for conservation and management operations in 1987, substantially above the president's request of $28.3 million and about a one-percent decrease in constant dollars from the 1986 level of $24.3 million. This included a $750,000 reduction in fishery-management programs due to the termination of the salmon vessel buy-back program in which NMFS purchased salmon vessels or licenses to reduce overcapacity of fishing effort. Habitat conservation was reduced by $269,000 for environmental-impact analysis and mitigation work. Enforcement and surveillance and protected-species management were maintained at 1986 levels.

Funding for conservation management and operations has declined 28 percent in constant dollars since 1982, although much of this is because of the shift in accounting procedures. NMFS budget officials say habitat conservation and protected species funding probably has remained about level since 1982, perhaps eroding a little in purchasing power as a result of inflation.

### State and Industry Programs

Prior to 1987, this subactivity included three line items: grants to states, which fund research and development efforts on commercial-fishery resources, disaster aid, anadromous-fish conservation projects and striped bass research; fisheries-development programs, which fund various activities to promote the development of U.S. fisheries and to ensure the quality of U.S. fishery products; and financial-services-programs administration, which funds NMFS costs in administering special industry-assistance funds included elsewhere in the budget.

The Reagan administration, maintaining that these activities would be more appropriately or efficiently carried out by the states, industry, and the private sector, proposed to terminate all funding except $3 million to maintain a core program in product quality and safety research. Congress rejected most the administration's proposals and appropriated $20 million for state and industry programs, a 14-percent reduction in constant dollars from the 1986 level of $22.6 million. Congress did approve the administration's request to terminate funding for administration of the financial-services programs ($628,000 in 1986), but did not agree to terminate the programs themselves, which means that NMFS will have to use funds appropriated to other programs to cover these administrative costs.

Repeated Reagan administration requests to terminate funding for state and industry programs has had little impact on the NMFS budget. Since 1982, grants to states have increased from $7.4 million to $9

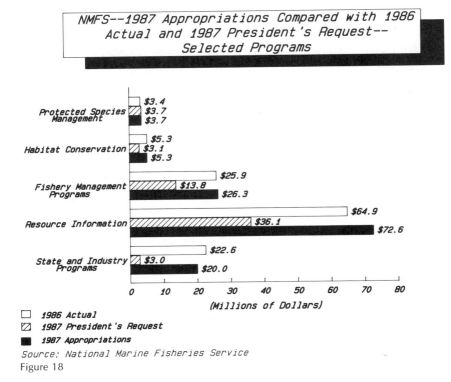

NMFS--1987 Appropriations Compared with 1986 Actual and 1987 President's Request-- Selected Programs

Source: National Marine Fisheries Service

Figure 18

million in 1987, about even in constant dollars. Funding for fisheries-development programs has increased from $10.3 million in 1983[14] to $11 million in 1987, a slight decrease in constant dollars.

14. Fisheries development programs were not funded in this portion of the NOAA budget in 1982.

*Katherine Barton, a freelance writer who specializes in conservation issues, is based in Washington D.C.*

# Part Three

## Species Accounts

The walrus is one of the largest pinnipeds; adult males weigh up to two tons. Increased hunting pressure is contributing to the decline of Pacific walrus populations. *Stephen J. Kraseman/Photo Researchers*

# The Walrus

John L. Sease

and

Francis H. Fay
*University of Alaska*

## SPECIES DESCRIPTION AND NATURAL HISTORY

The walrus, like the polar bear a symbol of the arctic, occurs in several discrete populations around the Northern Hemisphere. Two subspecies are recognized: the Atlantic walrus (*Odobenus rosmarus rosmarus*), which occurs from Hudson Bay and the eastern Canadian arctic to Greenland, Spitzbergen, and Barents and Kara seas, and the Pacific walrus (*O. rosmarus divergens*), which occurs primarily in the Bering and Chukchi seas (Allen 1880, Smirnov 1929). Some Soviet authorities recognize the small, isolated population in the Laptev Sea as a third subspecies (*O. rosmarus laptevi*) (Chapskii 1940, Arsen'ev 1976).

The Pacific walrus population was estimated in 1980 at about 250,000 individuals, 80 percent or more of the total world population (Fay 1981). The largest portion of the Atlantic population, residing in the Canadian arctic and western Greenland, probably numbers about 25,000 (Mansfield 1966, Reeves 1978). The Laptev population includes about 4,000 to 5,000 individuals (Arsen'ev 1976). The Pacific walrus population is the only one that occurs in U.S. waters. For that reason, the following description is mainly about that population.

Audubon Wildlife Report 1987

**Physical Characteristics**

The walrus is one of the largest of the pinnipeds, exceeded in size only by male elephant seals (*Mirounga* spp.) (Ridgeway and Harrison 1981, King 1983). Pacific walruses tend to be slightly larger than those of the Atlantic and Laptev populations. Newborn calves average four feet in length and about 130 pounds. Adults are sexually dimorphic: males average slightly more than ten feet long and nearly two tons, females average about eight feet and nearly a ton (Fay 1982).

Walruses are most similar in general appearance to Steller sea lions. The body is basically the same fusiform shape, although the neck and shoulders are somewhat heavier. The tusks and truncated snout, however, are distinctive. The snout, broad and blunt, is covered with several hundred short, stout vibrissae. Both sexes have tusks, but the tusks are somewhat longer and heavier in males than in females of equal age. Their exposed length in mature animals ranges from about one to two feet. The roots are about six to eight inches long. The tusks grow rapidly at first. In older age the growth slows gradually but never stops. The rate of wear and breakage equals or exceeds annual growth in old animals, especially females, so their tusks tend to be shorter (Fay 1982). Tusks are used in a variety of ways, but their major function is for agonistic displays and in fighting for positions of dominance (Miller 1975, 1976).

The skin on the neck and shoulders of mature males typically is nodular, with numerous rounded lumps, each about one to one and an half inches in diameter and about a half inch thicker than surrounding skin (Fay 1982). These bosses begin to develop as males reach sexual maturity, leading some workers to assume that they are a secondary sexual character (Chapskii 1936, Nikulin 1941, Brooks 1954, Sokolov 1960). Other researchers suggest that they are simply scars, probably caused by tusk strikes from other males (Brown 1868, Loughrey 1959).

Skin and pelage color generally is cinnamon-brown overall, although this varies with age and sex. Young animals tend to be darker than old animals and adult females generally are darker than adult males. Calves may appear almost black, while some old males are pale enough to seem albinistic (Fay 1982). This light color is accentuated during immersion in cold water because blood flow to the skin is restricted. Basking in the sun, especially in warm weather, causes increased blood flow to the skin. The resulting rosy color, especially of molting animals, frequently has been attributed incorrectly to sunburn (Fay and Ray 1968).Walruses appear awkward and ponderous on land or ice, where they use a quadrupedal locomotion similar to that of sea lions and fur seals. The weight of the posterior parts is borne by the hind limbs. The rest of the animal's weight is carried by the forelimbs and chest. Forward progression is accomplished by coordinating movements of the head and torso with the limbs to haul the body along. In water, walruses move easily, and locomotion is like that of the seals: The hind limbs are used for propulsion and the forelimbs for steering (Ray 1963). Maximum "sprint" speed in water may be greater than 20 miles per hour (Fay 1981).

## Distribution and Migration

The Pacific walrus population inhabits primarily the shelf waters of the Bering and Chukchi seas, where its distribution is closely tied to the pack ice. In winter, the walruses concentrate in the Bering Sea in two major areas: southwest of St. Lawrence Island and in Bristol and Kuskokwim bays. As the pack ice breaks up and melts during spring, all of the females and most of the young males migrate northward through Bering Strait into the Chukchi Sea. Most of the subadult and adult males do not participate in that migration, but remain in the Bering Sea throughout the summer, especially in Bristol Bay, Anadyr Gulf, and Bering Strait. During the return migration in autumn, the walruses that summered in the Chukchi Sea swim southward ahead of the reforming ice. They arrive back in their wintering areas in the Bering Sea by December (Fay 1982).

Walruses spend about two-thirds of their time in the water (Fay and Ray 1968). They haul out on ice and land to rest, molt, and bear young. Ice is the preferred substrate, but haulouts on shore are used during migration and in summering areas where ice is not accessible. The males that remain in the Bering Sea during summer haul out by the thousands on certain islands and sand spits in Bristol Bay, Anadyr Gulf, and Bering Strait.

## Reproduction

Female walruses reach breeding age principally at six or seven years. Males typically become fertile at nine or 10, but they usually are excluded from breeding until about 15 years old and large enough to compete successfully with other adult males (Fay 1982).

Mating takes place during January and February, when the walruses are concentrated in their wintering area in the Bering Sea. The polygynous adults congregate in traditional areas where males continually vocalize and display before the females. The displays take place in the water, alongside the floes where the females haul out to rest (Fay *et al.* 1984b). Presumably, mating takes place in the water.

Implantation of the embryo is delayed three to four months, until June. Birth occurs the following spring, mainly in May (Belopol'ski 1939, Krylov 1969). Since pregnancy lasts 15 to 16 months, annual breeding is not possible. Biennial breeding is typical for females in their reproductive prime (nine to 10 years old), but older females may breed at intervals of three, four, or more years (Krylov 1962). For this reason, the reproductive potential of walruses is much lower than that of other pinnipeds.

Walruses often give birth in isolation. A day or two after birth they congregate in large, compact "nursery herds" (Burns 1965, 1970). The cow-calf bond is stronger in walruses than in other pinnipeds and cows are extremely protective of their young. Calves are dependent primarily on their mother's milk during the first year of life and are weaned gradually during the second year. Orphaned calves may be fostered by adult females but most of them probably perish. Young males usually remain with the female herds for two to five years after weaning, then join the all-male herds. Young females remain with the herds of adult females (Fay 1981).

**Diet**

Walruses feed almost exclusively on invertebrates that live on the sea bottom. More than 60 genera of marine organisms have been identified from stomach contents. Several kinds of bivalve mollusks appear to be the preferred or most important prey. Daily food intake is at least five to seven percent of total body weight (Fay 1982, Gehnrich 1984). Some walruses, primarily males, feed on seals occasionally. Most seal eating may be predation, rather than scavenging on carrion (Lowry and Fay 1984).

Contrary to the popular myth, walruses do not use their tusks to dig clams from the sea bottom. Abrasion patterns on the tusks and vibrissae indicate that walruses "root-out" buried prey with their snouts, while the tusks drag along the bottom, like sled runners. Food items are located with the sensitive facial vibrissae. Soft parts of mollusks are removed from the shells by suction and ingested whole, without chewing. Shells rarely are ingested. Walruses are known to feed in water as deep as 250 feet (Vibe 1950).

## SIGNIFICANCE OF THE SPECIES

Walruses appear to have a structuring effect on sea-bottom fauna by selective predation on the mature age classes of a few species, especially of bivalve mollusks (Vibe 1950, Fay *et al.* 1977). Foraging by walruses also causes massive mixing of the bottom sediments (Ray 1973, Fay *et al.* 1977, Oliver *et al.* 1983). This releases nutrients that may be beneficial to other organisms, but it may also have a disruptive effect by interfering with colonization by invertebrate larvae.

Walrus calves may be an important source of food for polar bears in summer. The significance of this relationship is unknown, but the bears do catch and eat calves and tend to gather where female walruses and young congregate during summer months (Fay 1982). The effect of this predation on the walrus population may be negligible.

Walruses are extremely important economically for Alaskan Eskimos and for the Eskimos and coastal Chukchi of eastern Siberia. For thousands of years before the arrival of Europeans in the Bering-Chukchi region, the origins and entire cultures of some communities were centered around the hunting of walruses (Collins 1937, Rudenko 1947, Arutiunov and Sergeev 1968). Dependence on the walrus is still very high in the coastal areas.

## HISTORICAL PERSPECTIVE

Prior to contact with Europeans in the 18th century, the Pacific walrus population probably numbered at least 200,000 (Fay 1957). Taking of walruses by aborigines is believed to have had less impact on the walrus population at that time than did other natural mortality factors (Allen 1895, Fay 1982). The impact of hunting increased somewhat when Russia expanded its influence into the Bering Sea and was greatly increased when the Yankee whaling fleet began to operate in Bering Strait in the mid-19th century. From 1869 to 1880 the average walrus take by whalers was about 11,000 yearly. The kill may have been as large as 35,000 in 1876 (Bockstoce and Botkin 1982). By 1880, the Pacific walrus population was estimated to have been reduced to about half its former size, and about a third of the dependent natives in the Bering Strait region had died from starvation (Nelson and True 1887, Allen 1895). By that time, commercial hunting was no longer profitable for the whalers, either (Bockstoce and Botkin 1982).

The walrus population probably recovered somewhat in the late 19th century and early 20th century after several decades of reduced take. In the 1930s, however, the Soviet Union commenced ship-based hunting of walruses, and their numbers decreased again. By the mid-1950s, depletion of the Pacific walrus population was recognized in both the United States and the Soviet Union (Fay 1957, Geller 1957, Kleinenberg 1957). Over the next six years the Soviets phased out ship-based hunting in the Bering and Chukchi seas (Krylov 1968). At about the same time, the newly established state of Alaska restricted the taking of walruses by Alaskan Eskimos. Given that protection, the Pacific walrus population increased from about 100,000 animals in the mid-1950s to its pre-contact level of about 250,000 by 1980 (DeMaster 1984, Fay *et al.* 1984a).

## CURRENT TRENDS

Overhunting had kept the Pacific walrus population well below 200,000 animals for nearly 100 years as of the mid-20th century. With the protection initiated in the 1960s, the population increased rapidly and surpassed the 200,000 level sometime during the mid- to late 1970s. In a period of about 30 years, from the mid-1950s to the mid-1980s, the walrus has reoccupied virtually all its former range.

Major density dependent changes were evident after the early to mid-1970s. These included changes in kinds and sizes of prey consumed, greater incidence in the diet of alternate prey such as non-molluscan, sea-bottom dwellers, fishes, and seals; decreased thickness of blubber; lowered fecundity; and increased natural mortality (Fay and Kelly 1980, Fay and Stoker 1982a, Fay and Stoker 1982b, Fay *et al.* 1984a, Sease 1986). An increase in the mean age of walruses taken by Alaskan Eskimos also took place during the 1960s and 1970s. This trend may be explained in part by a change in the age-composition of the population at large. The greater availability of old walruses as the population increased also may have played a part in the trend, for in most cases hunters preferentially select walruses with large tusks, which equates to selection for old animals (Fay *et al.* 1984a, Sease 1986).

At St. Lawrence Island, where hunters preferentially select female walruses with calves, tusk size is of secondary importance. The hides of calves are preferred for making very strong rawhide ropes, and the meat traditionally is dried for human consumption (Fay 1958). Because of this unique selection, the mean ages of female walruses taken by the St. Lawrence Islanders each year tended to cluster around the age of maximal fecundity (nine to 10 years) during the 1950s and 1960s. This changed very little until about 1972, when the mean age of taken females increased steadily. These findings imply that age-specific fecundity has been changing since that time and that the age at which females attain maximal fecundity has shifted upward (Fay *et al.* 1984a, Sease 1986). This usually occurs in populations that have reached the upper limit of growth and may indicate crowding.

The productivity of the Pacific walrus population has decreased and become more erratic at least since the late 1970s. Calf production has been extremely low during some years but remarkably high during others. Part of this is attributable to the older age of the animals, but several other factors, such as lowered nutrition and infectious disease, may be involved (Fay *et al.* 1984a). Calf production was especially poor during 1980 (Fay and Stoker 1982b), and calf survival also was exceptionally low that year (Fay *et al.* 1984a, Sease 1986). Even in years when production was high, survival apparently was very low. From 1981 to 1984, the observed proportion of adult females accompanied by two-month-old calves ranged from three to 15 percent, rather than the expected 30 percent or more. This indicates very low recruitment of cohorts into the adult population for at least a decade, a condition expected to persist for several more years.

Coupled with the increase in size and range of the Pacific walrus population has been an increase in size of the annual take in both Soviet and American waters. Walrus harvests were restricted on both sides in the 1960s but have been liberalized during recent years and allowed to increase. The average number of walruses taken annually by Alaskan Eskimos rose from about 1,500 during the early 1970s to about 3,500 by the early 1980s. The Soviet take rose from about 1,000 to 4,000 during the same period. The total kill of walruses, including Soviet and Alaskan catches together with estimated losses of sunken and mortally wounded animals, has been at least 10,000 each year since 1981 (Fay *et al.* 1984a, Sease 1986). Since this is believed to have exceeded recruitment in several recent years, the population presently may be in decline.

## MANAGEMENT

Enactment by Congress of the Marine Mammal Protection Act in 1972 included taking jurisdiction over Pacific walruses away from the Alaska Department of Fish and Game and placing it in the hands of the U.S. Fish and Wildlife Service (FWS). Alaska regained management authority for a short time in the 1970s but relinquished it in 1979 when, beset by federal restrictions, the state managers were unable to take appropriate management actions. The state has investigated the possibilities for regaining management of walruses in recent years, but for political reasons apparently has decided against it at this time.

Under the provisions of the Marine Mammal Protection Act, walruses may be taken in Alaskan water by Eskimos, Indians, and Aleuts. Walruses are to be taken only for subsistence purposes or for the production of authentic articles of native handicraft and must be taken in a nonwasteful manner. The act does not include any provisions for regulating the size or composition of the walrus take or for specifying the manner of taking, unless the walrus population becomes depleted.

On the Soviet side, about two-thirds of the annual quota set by the Ministry of Fisheries is allotted to the shore-based natives and a third to ship-based government hunters. The entire catch must be taken only from herds on the ice. Hunting of walruses in the water and on shore is not permitted. Harvests are monitored by the Okhotsk branch of the Fishery Inspection Agency. FWS currently monitors the spring walrus hunt in Alaska and, based on the spring kills, estimates the total number and sex ratio of animals taken each year. Tooth samples are collected yearly to estimate the age distribution of killed walruses. Samples of stomach contents and of reproductive organs from adult females are collected at five-year intervals. FWS, in cooperation with the Magadan Section of the Soviet Union's Pacific Institute of Fisheries and Oceanography, also conducts aerial surveys every five years. The most recent survey was in autumn 1985.

## PROGNOSIS

The observed changes in feeding habits, blubber thickness, age structure, reproduction, and recruitment of the Pacific walrus are consistent with changes that would be expected when a population nears or exceeds the carrying capacity of its environment (Fowler *et al.* 1980). Lowered productivity and increased juvenile mortality eventually would bring recruitment into equilibrium with total mortality, yielding a population fluctuating naturally at the carrying capacity of the environment. In the absence of human intervention, the population would remain in a stable relationship with its resource base but would be very susceptible to perturbation.

Ironically, hunting pressure on both sides of the Bering Sea began to increase at the same time that the signs of depressed recruitment began to be recognized. That is, the catches increased just as the population was becoming less resistant to increased mortality. The annual kill plus other losses probably has exceeded recruitment for at least the past five years. The Pacific walrus population probably is in a decline that will continue until annual takes are reduced and recruitment is increased.

## RECOMMENDATIONS

A sound management program for any species is dependent on a constant flow of information from field studies that monitor population status. Present methods for monitoring the Pacific walrus population on both sides of the Bering Sea consist of sampling from the yearly kills and conducting periodic aerial surveys. While both of those methods are important and useful for detecting major trends, their biases and potential errors are many and largely uncontrollable. Hence they can show the trends only in a very general way and only in retrospect, several years or even decades after data are collected. This long lag between the research and the interpretation of results often has led to management responses being too much, too late. The consequences have been that the walrus population has fluctuated greatly in numbers due to its being alternately overhunted and over-protected. One obvious need is for newer, more sensitive methods for population monitoring. These should provide some advanced warning of potential problems and allow appropriate actions to be taken quickly enough to maintain the population at a more stable, optimal level.

Computer modeling of the Pacific walrus population is in the forefront of needed efforts to develop that predictive ability. But before that can be accomplished, some additional, basic information about the population is needed. For example, some recent models have assumed that the sex ratio of the entire population is one male to one female, based on extrapolation from the sex ratio at birth. That assumption is not valid for polygynous species, in which the females usually outnumber the males (Carrick *et al.* 1962, Chapman 1964, Ralls *et al.* 1980). A measurement of the real sex ratio of adults will be needed for the predictive model, as will several other parameters of the population that still are unknown.

All of the proposed offshore oil lease areas on the Bering-Chukchi shelf lie within the range of the Pacific walrus, but the effects that their development may have on walruses are largely unknown. Contamination from oil spills could have long-term, adverse effects on food resources by lowering productivity or altering the species composition of the sea-bottom fauna. Organisms in the immediate vicinity of a spill could be killed directly, and, because of the slow maturation rates of many of the species, especially bivalves, recovery could take many years (Hansen 1985).

Drilling platform activity and support vessels could impinge on major mating areas in winter, calving areas and migration corridors in spring, nursery areas in summer, and feeding areas and migration corridors in autumn. Ship and aircraft traffic in the immediate vicinity of walruses may cause them to flee into the water, potentially resulting in injury or abandonment of calves (Fay *et al.* 1984a). Future management plans should include means to assess the magnitude of disturbance from oil development as well as the means to mitigate adverse effects.

The Pacific walrus population is a resource of equal value to both the United States and the Soviet Union. For this reason alone it should be managed jointly and by mutual consent, rather than separately and unilaterally as it is now. For the sake of the resource and of the people who are dependent on it, an international agreement for management of the Pacific walrus is needed. The Soviets agree in principle with this need, but reject the idea of negotiating a formal agreement with the

United States. They recognize that, on the one hand, the Marine Mammal Protection Act does not include any realistic options for federal management on the American side, and, on the other hand, that it overly protects economically important and abundant marine mammal resources. At present, the act allows neither regulation of native walrus hunts nor complete protection of the animals on any but a few state and federal refuges. Furthermore, the kills have been increasing steadily, and the waste is unconscionable. To the Soviets, the walrus situation in the United States appears chaotic and uncontrolled. Understandably, they want no part of it and insist that the United States bring the chaos under control before even suggesting any further negotiations toward a management agreement.

## REFERENCES

Allen, J.A. 1880. *History of North American Pinnipeds, a Monograph of the Walruses, Sea Lions, Sea Bears and Seals of North America.* U.S. Geological Survey of the Territories, Miscellaneous Publication 12. 785 pp.

―――. 1895. "A Synopsis of the pinnipeds, or seals and walruses, in relation to their commercial history and products," in *Fur Seal Arbitration,* vol. 1, U.S. Government Printing Office. 53rd Congress, 2nd Session, Senate Exec. Doc. 177. pp. 367-391.

Arsen'ev, V.A. 1976. "Walruses, genus *Odobenus* Brisson, 1762," in V.G. Heptner, K.K. Chapskii, V.A. Arsen'ev, and V.E. Sokolov, eds., *Mlekopitaiushcie Sovietskogo Soiuza.* Tom. 2, vyp. 3 Vysshaia Shkola, Moscow. pp. 27-51.

Arutiunov, S.A. and D.A. Sergeev. 1968. "Two millennia of cultural evolution of the Bering Sea hunter," *Arctic Anthropology* 5:72-75.

Belopol'ski, L.O. 1939. "On the migrations and ecology of reproduction of the Pacific walrus (*Odobenus rosmarus divergens* Illiger)," *Zool. Zh.* (Moscow) 18: 762-774.

Bockstoce, J.R. and D.B. Botkin. 1982. "The harvest of Pacific walruses by the pelagic whaling industry, 1848 to 1914," *Arctic and Alpine Research* 14:183-188.

Brooks, J.W. 1954. *A Contribution to the Life History and Ecology of the Pacific Walrus.* Alaska Cooperative Wildlife Research Unit, University of Alaska, Fairbanks, Special Report 1. 103 pp.

Brown, R. 1868. "Notes on the history and geographical relations of the Pinnipedia frequenting the spitzbergen and Greenland seas," *Proceedings of the Zoological Society* (London) 1868:405-440.

Burns, J.J. 1965. *The Walrus in Alaska, Its Ecology and Management.* Alaska Department of Fish and Game. Juneau, Alaska. 48 pp.

Burns, J.J. 1970. "Remarks on the distribution and natural history of pagophilic pinnipeds in the Bering and Chukchi seas," *Journal of Mammalogy* 51:445-454.

Carrick, R., S.E. Scordas, and S.E. Ingham. 1962. "Studies of the southern elephant seal, *Mirounga leonina* (L.). IV. Breeding and Development," *C.S.I.R.O. Wildlife Research* 7:161-197.

Chapman, D.G. 1964. "A critical study of Pribilof fur seal population estimates," *Fisheries Bulletin* 63:657-669.

Chapskii, K.K. 1936. "The walrus of the Kara Sea," *Trudy Vsesoiuz. Arkt. Inst.* (Leningrad) 67:1-124.

Chapskii, K.K. 1940. "Distribution of the walrus in the Laptev and East Siberian seas," *Problemy Severa* (Leningrad) 9:231-268.

Collins, H.B. 1937. "Archaeology of St. Lawrence Island, Alaska," *Smithsonian Miscellaneous Collections* 96:1-431.

DeMaster, D.P. 1984. "An analysis of a hypothetical population of walruses," in F.H. Fay and G.A. Fedoseev, eds., *Soviet-American Cooperative Research on Marine Mammals.* vol. 1. *Pinnipeds.* National Marine Fisheries Service Technical Report. 104 pp.

Fay, F.H. 1957. "History and present status of the Pacific walrus population," *Transactions of the North American Wildlife Conference* 22:431-443.

———. 1958. Pacific walrus investigations on St. Lawrence Island, Alaska. Unpublished Report. Arctic Health Research Center. Anchorage, Alaska. 54 pp.

———. and G.C. Ray. 1968. "Influence of climate on the distribution of walruses, *Odobenus rosmarus* (Linnaeus). I. Evidence from thermoregulatory behavior," *Zoologica* 53:1-18.

———., H.M. Feder, and S.W. Stoker. 1977. *An Estimate of the Impact of the Pacific Walrus Population on its Food Resources in the Bering Sea.* U.S. Department of Commerce, National Technical Information Service, (Springfield, Va.) PB-273-505. 38 pp.

———. and B.P.Kelly. 1980. "Mass natural mortality of walruses (*Odobenus rosmarus*) at St. Lawrence Island, Bering Sea, Autumn, 1978," *Arctic* 33:226-245.

———. 1981. "Walrus *Odobenus rosmarus* (Linnaeus, 1758)," in S.H. Ridgway and R.J. Harrison, eds., *Handbook of Marine Mammals,* vol. 1. *The Walrus, Sea Lions, Fur Seals and Sea Otter.* Academic Press. New York. pp. 1-23.

———. 1982. "Ecology and biology of the Pacific walrus," *Odobenus rosmarus divergens Illiger.* North American Fauna 74. 279 pp.

———. and S.W. Stoker. 1982a. *Analysis of Reproductive Organs and Stomach Contents from Walruses Taken in the Alaskan Native Harvest, Spring 1980.* Final Report Contract 14-16-0007-81-5216. U.S. Fish and Wildlife Service, Anchorage, Alaska. 86 pp.

———. and S.W. Stoker. 1982b. *Reproductive Success and Feeding Habits of Walruses Taken in the 1982 Spring Harvest, with Comparisons from Previous Years.* Eskimo Walrus Commission. Nome, Alaska. 91 pp.

———., B.P. Kelly, P.H. Gehnrich, J.L. Sease, and A.A. Hoover. 1984a. *Modern Populations, Migrations, Demography, Trophics, and Historical Status of the Pacific Walrus.* Final Report R.U. #611. National Oceanic and Atmospheric Administration Outer Continental Shelf Environmental Assessment Program. Anchorage, Alaska. 142 pp.

———., G.C. Ray, and A.A. Kibal'chich. 1984b. "Time and location of mating and associated behavior of the Pacific walrus, *Odobenus rosmarus divergens* Illiger," in F.H. Fay and G.A. Fedoseev, eds., *Soviet-American Cooperative Research on Marine Mammals.* vol. 1, *Pinnipeds.* National Marine Fisheries Service Technical Report. pp. 89-99.

Fowler, C.W., W.T. Bunderson, M.B. Cherry, R.J. Ryel, and B.B. Steele. 1980. *Comparative Population Dynamics of Large Mammals: A Search for Management Criteria.* U.S. Department of Commerce, National Technical Information Service. Springfield, Virginia. PB80-178627. 330 pp.

Gehnrich, P.H. 1984. Nutritional and behavioral aspects of reproduction in walruses. Unpublished M.S. Thesis. University of Alaska, Fairbanks. 147 pp.

Geller, M. Kh. 1957. "On the protection of harvested marine mammals of Chukotka," *Okhrana Prirody Zapoved.* Moscow 1957: 108-117.

Hansen, D.J. 1985. *The Potential Effects of Oil Spills and Other Chemical Pollutants on Marine Mammals Occurring in Alaskan Waters.* U.S. Department of Interior MMS OCS Report. Anchorage, Alaska. 22 pp.

King, J.E. 1983. *Seals of the World.* Cornell University Press. Ithaca, New York. 240 pp.

Kleinenberg, S.E. 1957. "On protection of the walrus," *Priroda* (Moscow) 1957:101-103.

Krylov, V.I. 1962. "Rates of reproduction of the Pacific walrus," *Zool. Zh.* (Moscow) 41:116-120.

Krylov, V.I. 1968. "Present condition of the Pacific walrus stocks and prospects of their rational exploitation," in V.A. Arsen'ev and K.I. Panin, eds. *Lastonogie Severnoi Chasti Tikhogo Okeana.* Pihschevaya Promyshlennost', Moscow. pp. 189-204.

———. 1969. "The period of mating and pupping of the Pacific walrus," in V.A. Arsen'ev, B.A. Zenkovich, and K.K. Chapskii, eds. *Morskie Mlekopitaiuschie.* Nauka, Moscow. pp. 275-285.

Loughrey, A.G. 1959. "Preliminary investigation of the Atlantic walrus, *Odobenus rosmarus rosmarus* (Linnaeus)," *Wildlife Management Bulletin* 14, Ser. 1. Canadian Wildlife Service. 123 pp.

Lowry L.F. and F.H. Fay. 1984. "Seal eating by walruses in the Bering and Chukchi seas," *Polar Biology* 3:11-18.

Mansfield, A.W. 1966. "The walrus in Canada's Arctic," *Canadian Geographic Journal* 72: 88-95.

Miller, E.H. 1975. "Walrus ethology. I. The social role of tusks and applications of multidimensional scaling," *Canadian Journal of Zoology* 53:590-613.

———. 1976. "Walrus ethology. II. Herd structure and activity budgets of summering males," *Canadian Journal of Zoology* 54:704-715.

Nelson, E.W. and F.W. True. 1887. "Mammals of northern Alaska," in E.W. Nelson, ed., *Report Upon Natural History Collections Made in Alaska Between the Years 1877 and 1881.* No. III Arctic Series Publications Signal Service, U.S. Army. U.S. Government Printing Office. pp. 227-293.

Nikulin, P.G. 1941. "The Chukchi Walrus," *Izv. TINRO* (Vladivostok) 20:21-59.

Oliver, J.S., P.N. Slattery, E.F. O'Connor, and L.F. Lowry. 1983. "Walrus, *Odobenus rosmarus*, feeding in the Bering Sea: a benthic perspective," *Fisheries Bulletin* 81:501-512.

Reeves, R.R. 1978. *Atlantic Walrus (*Odobenus rosmarus rosmarus*): A Literature Survey and Status Report.* U.S. Fish and Wildlife Service Wildlife Research Report 10. 41 pp.

Ralls, K., R.L. Brownell, Jr., and J. Ballou. 1980. *Differential Mortality by Sex and Age in Mammals with, 22 Specific References to the Sperm Whale.* Report of the International Whaling Commission. (Special issue 2) 1980:233-243.

Ray, G.C. 1963. "Locomotion in Pinnipeds," *Natural History* 72:10-21.

Ray, G.C. 1973. "Underwater observation increases understanding of marine mammals," *Marine Technical Society Journal* 7:16-20.

Ridgway, S.H. and R.J. Harrison, eds. 1981. *Handbook of Marine Mammals*, vol. 1, *The Walrus, Sea Lions, Fur Seals and Sea Otter.* Academic Press. New York. 235 pp.

Rudenko, S.I. 1947. "The ancient culture of the Bering Sea and the Eskimo problem," *Anthropology North: Translation from Russian Sources 1.* Arctic Institute North America, Montreal, 1961. 186 pp.

Sease, J.L. 1986. Historical status and population dynamics of the Pacific walrus. Unpublished M.S. Thesis. University of Alaska, Fairbanks.

Smirnov, N.A. 1929. "A Review of the Pinnipedia of Europe and northern Asia," *Isv. Otd. Priklad. Ikhtiol.* 9:231-268.

Sokolov, V.E. 1960. "Structure of the cutaneous integument of the Pinnipedia, pt. 2," *Biul. Mosk. Obsch. Isp. Prirody, Otd. Biol.* 65:5-17.

Vibe, C. 1950. "The marine mammals and the marine fauna in the Thule District (Northwest Greenland) with observations on ice conditions in 1939-41," *Medd. om. Gronl.* 150:1-115.

*John L. Sease, a graduate student at the University of Alaska in Fairbanks, has studied walruses since 1981.*

*Francis H. Fay is a professor of marine science at the University of Alaska who began studying walruses on St. Lawrence Island in 1952.*

The mission blue butterfly, perched here on a lupine plant, has been at the center of some creative solutions to resolving conflicts between endangered-species management and development. *Richard Arnold*

# The Mission Blue Butterfly

Richard A. Arnold

*Entomological Consulting Services*

## SPECIES DESCRIPTION AND NATURAL HISTORY

The mission blue butterfly (*Plebejus [ = Icaricia] icarioides missionensis*) is one of 12 subspecies of Boisduval's blue found in the western cordilleran region of North America. Adult butterflies are small, with a wingspan varying from one to 1.5 inches. Uppersides of the male's wings are colored a brillant silvery-blue, with slightly darker wing veins and darker borders. In the female, the upperside is often completely brown, but many individuals have some blue nearer the wing bases. Undersides of both sexes have a background color of pale or silvery-gray with numerous black spots that vary in intensity. On the hindwings, the black spots frequently have white halos.

### Breeding

The mission blue has one generation each year. Its adult flight season, protracted because of the moderate coastal climate, occurs from early March until early July, depending on the location. Individual adults apparently live about six to 10 days during a flight season that may last eight weeks or more at a particular locality (Arnold 1983).

Many aspects of the mission blue's life cycle occur in association with larval, i.e. caterpillar, food plants. These are three perennial species of lupine, the varied lupine (*Lupinus variicolor*), silver bush lupine (*L. albifrons*), and summer lupine (*L. formosus*). Adults eat the nectar primarily of naked stemmed buckwheat (*Eriogonum latifolium*), golden aster (*Chrysopsis villosa*), blue dicks (*Brodiaea pulchella*), and ithuriel's spear (*B. laxa*), plus occasionally other plants. Nectar fulfills their nutrient, water, and energy needs.

Males and females spend much of their adult lives flying from one patch of lupine to another looking for mates, a behavior referred to as patrolling. Upon locating a receptive mate, a brief courtship flight ensues and mating often occurs on the lupine or nearby vegetation. Females usually lay single eggs on the lupine's foliage, stems, flowers, and seed pods, although small clusters of eggs are observed periodically. Eggs hatch within several days and young larvae feed briefly on the lupine's leaves before entering an obligate diapause, a quiescent stage in which they remain inactive for the rest of the summer, fall, and winter. Partially grown larvae resume feeding the following spring and complete their development in about four to six weeks. Mature larvae are tended by several species of ants which apparently discover the larvae as the caterpillars are feeding on the lupines. Larvae possess an abdominal gland that secretes honeydew, a sugary solution that ants readily drink. In return for receiving this food source, tending ants protect mission blue larvae from other insect predators and parasites. Fully developed larvae form a chrysalis among leaf litter near the base of the lupine food plant. During this stage of the life cycle, larvae metamorphose and give rise to the adult butterfly within a few weeks.

## Range

At the time it was recognized as an endangered species in 1976, the mission blue was known from only three localities. Two of the sites, San Bruno Mountain in San Mateo County immediately south of San Francisco, California, and Twin Peaks in San Francisco, are situated in the northern portion of the San Francisco peninsula. The third locality is just north of the Golden Gate Bridge at Fort Baker in southern Marin County. Subsequent field surveys have discovered four additional localities on the peninsula in San Mateo County. Three are located east and southeast of Pacifica, including Sweeney Ridge, Milagra Ridge-Sharp Park area, and Skyline College. The fourth is in the vicinity of San Andreas Dam near Hillsborough (Murphy 1985). The primary vegetation type at all seven sites is coastal grassland with an influx of numerous weeds and annual grasses. Prior to the spread of extensive urbanization, this habitat type, and presumably the butterfly, were much more widespread on the San Francisco peninsula. Today, the mission blue is restricted to approximately 2,500 acres of grassland habitat at its seven remaining localities.

## SIGNIFICANCE OF THE SPECIES

The mission blue was among the first insects recognized as endangered by the U.S. Fish and Wildlife Service (FWS) under the Endangered Species Act of 1973 (U.S. Fish and Wildlife 1976). However, it is probably better known for the confrontation it caused among politicians, environmentalists, several government agencies, and the landowners and developers of the butterfly's habitat on San Bruno Mountain. This conflict resulted in the Section 10a incidental take amendment to the Endangered Species Act during the act's 1982 reauthorization (Arnold 1985, Drabelle 1985). The amendment authorizes FWS to issue permits for the taking of listed species by private parties otherwise prohibited from take by other sections of the Endangered Species Act. Applicants for such permits must submit a habitat conservation plan that specifies the impacts that likely will result from the incidental take and that describes the steps the applicant will employ to minimize and mitigate those impacts. FWS will then issue a permit for incidental take if the applicant can demonstrate that the taking will not appreciably reduce chances for the survival and recovery of the species.

Butterflies are excellent indicators of the health of ecological systems because of their obligate dependence on specific larval and adult food plants and their ease of monitoring. The mission blue is no exception. Its status, determined through careful monitoring, can serve as an indicator of problems that might affect other vulnerable species in the area. This could prove critical since San Bruno Mountain harbors major populations of several other endangered or candidate animals and plants, plus numerous endemics. The mountain also has been recognized as a "threatened community" by the International Union for the Conservation of Nature (Wells *et al.* 1983). Federally listed endangered species include the San Bruno elfin butterfly (*Callophrys mossii bayensis*) and possibly the San Francisco garter snake (*Thamnophis sirtalis tetrataenia*). Two other butterflies and a moth are candidates for federal listing as endangered or threatened species. Twelve plant species are recognized by the California Native Plant Society (Smith and York 1984) as rare or endangered. Noteworthy among the plants are three manzanita (*Arctostaphylos*) species, including the Pacific manzanita (*A. pacifica*), restricted only to San Bruno Mountain, where it is represented by just two individuals on one rocky outcrop; the San Bruno Mountain manzanita (*A. imbricata*), known from just seven sites on the mountain; and the Montara Mountain manzanita (*A. montarensis*), known only from a limited number of rocky hilltops in San Mateo County.

Wing color and spot patterns in the mission blue and related populations of *Plebejus icarioides* are quite variable. Hovanitz (1937) suggested that environmental factors were probably at least partially responsible for the observed variability. For example, butterflies tend to be darker in foggy areas, presumably an adaptation to allow for more heat absorption from the sun. Such findings can help scientists to better understand the evolution of all species.

## HISTORICAL PERSPECTIVE

William Hovanitz first collected the mission blue and described it as a new subspecies in 1937, using specimens from Twin Peaks, located in the Mission District of San Francisco. Although Twin Peaks still supports a small population of the endangered butterfly, all other historical localities in San Francisco have been extirpated by urbanization. Some years later, the butterfly was discovered on San Bruno Mountain, where it ranges throughout nearly 2,000 acres of coastal grassland on the eastern portion of the mountain and to a lesser extent in the coastal sage-scrub habitat prevalent on the western portion. At the other six mission blue localities, a collective total of only 500 acres of the coastal grassland habitat remains.

Urbanization of the San Francisco peninsula since the butterfly's description has been so rapid and extensive that the butterfly's complete former range and population numbers are unknown. However, prior to the peninsula's urbanization, the coastal grassland habitat favored by mission blues was much more widely distributed. Thus, it is likely that the butterfly also was more widespread and abundant on the peninsula. Residential development, industrialization, agriculture, quarrying, and highway construction have reduced the coastal grassland habitat.

Even before rampant urbanization of the San Francisco peninsula occurred, the composition and diversity of plant species in the coastal grasslands had been altered by the grazing and other ranching practices of Spanish settlers. As a result of these practices, native perennial grasses have been replaced largely by annual grasses, which, along with other weedy forbs, limit seedling establishment, grow faster, and out compete perennial lupines used by the mission blue. Today, remnant habitat sites are still threatened by numerous exotics, notably European gorse (*Ulex europa*) and several species of annual grasses. For example, approximately 158 exotic plant species now reside on San Bruno Mountain, comprising nearly 30 percent of the flora (McClintock *et al.* 1968).

## CURRENT TRENDS

FWS in 1976 listed the mission blue butterfly as endangered. Critical habitat at San Bruno Mountain and Twin Peaks was proposed in 1977

(U.S. Fish and Wildlife Service 1977), but withdrawn two years later because of procedural changes in the listing process (U.S. Fish and Wildlife Service 1979). These changes, imposed by the 1978 amendments to the Endangered Species Act, required among other things that an economic analysis of listing impacts be prepared for each possible listing and that proposed rulemakings be finalized within two years or the proposal killed. Failure to meet the two-year deadline caused failure to designate critical habitat for the mission blue. New information or a new petition would be necessary to repropose critical habitat. A recovery plan for the mission blue (Arnold 1984) recently was approved by FWS.

Despite the recent discovery of four new colonies, the major stronghold for the mission blue continues to be San Bruno Mountain, which supports roughly 70 to 75 percent of the entire known population. A capture-recapture census of the mission blue at San Bruno Mountain in 1981 indicates a population of about 18,000 individuals (Thomas Reid Associates 1981). However, this estimate may not be reliable because of the low recapture rate. Population estimates for other colonies range from a few hundred to a few thousand individuals (Murphy 1985, Arnold unpubl. data).

Transect counts on San Bruno Mountain for the period 1982 to 1985 suggest that butterfly numbers fluctuate dramatically from year to year in response to varying climatic conditions (Thomas Reid Associates 1985). Arnold (unpubl. data) has monitored for 10 years the relationship between lupines and mission blues at one site on San Bruno Mountain and noted a 28 percent decline in lupine and a 52-percent decline in butterfly numbers in areas where habitat quality has deteriorated.

## MANAGEMENT

Adoption of the San Bruno Mountain Habitat Conservation Plan and issuance of the 30-year incidental take permit by FWS in March 1983 were widely acclaimed as landmark compromises among FWS, environmentalists, and developers. Under the plan, approximately 80 percent of the remaining open space on the mountain will become parkland, while about 20 percent, including some prime mission blue habitat, will be used for residential and commercial developments. Landowners, developers, and owners of the new homes and businesses provide operating funds for the habitat conservation plan.

The San Bruno Mountain plan, a joint agreement among federal, state, county, and local government agencies, allows some development of remaining open space on San Bruno Mountain and the use of funds generated by these projects to protect and manage remaining habitat areas to benefit the mission blue and other organisms indigenous to the mountain. Undeveloped areas will be protected by transferring ownership to public agencies. Vegetation in protected areas will be managed to minimize the spread of exotic plants and weeds that threaten lupines and other native flora. Status of the mission blue and progress of rehabilitation efforts will be monitored annually.

Six of the seven known mission blue localities are owned by government agencies, but public ownership does not guarantee that the natural processes necessary for maintenance of the grassland habitat will continue to operate. Grassland is a disclimax community, i.e., maintenance and regeneration of the plants characteristic of this ecosystem are dependent upon perturbations that preclude normal succession. The lupine larval food plants of the mission blue are pioneer species. Under natural conditions, they are distributed widely throughout the grassland at low density, but tend to grow in higher-density patches at sites of recent localized disturbance (mud or rock slides, fires, rodent burrows, etc.) or at early stages of grassland succession. But these higher-density patches may deteriorate as they are invaded by weeds, annual grasses, or later successional-stage plants unless an irregular disturbance regime occurs to permit the lupines to regenerate. Thus, the disturbances that allow for colonization by lupine and, subsequently, the butterfly, are dynamic, and the location of many lupine patches varies from year to year because the patches generally are short lived. Mission blues opportunistically use localized dense patches of lupine as long as they exist, but as these patches age and decline in quality the butterflies must find and colonize newly created patches. Clearly, maintenance of the lupine's patch dynamics is an important aspect in conservation of the mission blue.

Since 1983, the San Bruno Mountain Habitat Conservation Plan has called for the control of several alien plants that are displacing native flora, but it is still too early to draw conclusions about the success of control efforts. A variety of management techniques has been tested to control European gorse, eucalyptus trees (*Eucalyptus globulus*), broom (*Cytisus*), and ice plants (*Carpobrotus*). Revegetation of graded areas with native plants at three development sites was initiated in 1985 (Thomas Reid Associates 1985).

In addition to the controversial and precedent-setting habitat conservation plan, the firm Quarry Products, Inc., has initiated a long-term reclamation plan for its rock quarry on San Bruno Mountain. This plan includes considerable restoration of coastal sage-scrub and grassland habitats to benefit the mission blue. The butterfly's larval and adult food plants, along with several other floral species characteristic of these habitats, have been propagated and planted in areas where quarry operations have ceased. These reclaimed areas are being monitored to determine if the butterflies will recolonize and breed there.

## PROGNOSIS

The long-term outlook for the mission blue is guardedly optimistic. At San Bruno Mountain, this prognosis could change depending upon the success of the habitat conservation plan. Construction of most of the primary development projects approved by the plan has been delayed, thus also delaying loss of significant mission blue breeding habitat. The mission blue's prognosis should be reevaluated after these developments are completed and their impact on the butterfly can be better assessed.

Although major habitat areas on San Bruno Mountain have been protected from development, many exotic plants must be controlled or eradicated to ensure the butterfly's survival. Populations at the other six localities may be more vulnerable because their smaller numbers and more limited habitat areas leave them extremely vulnerable to catastrophic events. If vegetation management programs are not implemented successfully at all remaining habitat sites, the mission blue could become extinct, as did its close relative, the pheres blue (*Plebejus icarioides pheres*), which formerly inhabited sand dunes on the San Francisco peninsula.

## RECOMMENDATIONS

As most of the mission blue localities are in public ownership, control of several encroaching exotic plants is the primary problem requiring immediate and long-term attention to ensure the mission blue's continued survival. Although the habitat conservation plan at San Bruno Mountain has been under way since 1983, similar programs emphasizing vegetation management are sorely needed at the butterfly's other locations. As the plan includes a significant experimental component to determine cost-effective methods to control exotic plants, the results of vegetation management trials should be closely monitored.

Most of the sites that support the endangered butterfly are county or state parklands that until recently received little use by the general public. An exception is Twin Peaks in San Francisco, which is a popular tourist attraction. However, portions of San Bruno Mountain,

Milagra Ridge, and Sweeney Ridge recently have been improved to better serve an anticipated increase in visitors and their recreational needs. The last two areas eventually will be incorporated into Golden Gate National Recreation Area. The impacts of increased visits and recreational activities on these sensitive habitat areas need to be monitored carefully.

## REFERENCES

Arnold, R.A. 1983. "Ecological studies of six endangered butterflies (Lepidoptera:Lycaenidae); island biogeography, patch dynamics, and the design of habitat preserves," *University of California Publication in Entomology* 99:1-161.

———. 1984. *Recovery Plan for the San Bruno Elfin and Mission Blue Butterflies.* U.S. Fish and Wildlife Service. Portland, Oregon. 81 pp.

———. 1985. "Private and government-funded conservation programs for endangered insects in California," *Natural Areas Journal* 5(2):28-39.

Drabelle, D. 1985. "The endangered species program," in Roger Di Silvestro, ed., *Audubon Wildlife Report 1985.* National Audubon Society. New York, New York. pp. 72-91.

Hovanitz, W. 1937. "Concerning the *Plebejus icarioides* rassenkreis," *Pan-Pac. Entomologist* 13:184-189.

McClintock, E., W. Knight and N. Fahy. 1968. "A flora of the San Bruno Mountains, San Mateo County, California," *Proceedings of the California Academy of Sciences* 32(20):587-677.

Murphy, D.D. 1985. *Report on the Status of* Plebejus icarioides missionensis *in the Skyline College Vicinity of San Mateo County, California.* Final Report for U.S. Fish and Wildlife Service contract #SE-0013-5. 22 pp.

Smith, J.P., Jr. and R. York. 1984. *Inventory of Rare and Endangered Vascular Plants of California.* California Native Plant Society Special Publication 1, third edition. 174 pp.

Thomas Reid Associates. 1981. *Endangered Species Survey: San Bruno Mountain Biological Study—1981.* Unpublished draft report prepared for San Mateo County. 260 pp.

———. 1985. *San Bruno Mountain Area Habitat Conservation Plan Activities Report—1985.* Unpublished report prepared for San Mateo County. 24 pp.

U.S. Fish and Wildlife Service. 1976. "Final rulemaking - determination that six species of butterflies are endangered species," *Federal Register* 41:22041-22044.

U.S. Fish and Wildlife Service. 1977. "Proposed determination of critical habitat for six butterflies and two plants," *Federal Register* 42:7972-7975.

U.S. Fish and Wildlife Service. 1979. "Withdrawal of critical habitat proposals," *Federal Register* 44:12382.

Wells, S.M., R.M. Pyle and N.M. Collins. 1983. *The IUCN Invertebrate Red Data Book.* International Union for the Conservation of Nature and Natural Resources. Gland, Switzerland. 632 pp.

*Richard A. Arnold, a research associate of the Entomology Department at the University of California, Berkeley and the Los Angeles County Museum of Natural History, has conducted research on 11 of the 13 federally listed U.S. endangered insects.*

A wood duck drake perches at the entrance to a nest cavity. Once very low in numbers, the wood duck has rebounded; continued success depends on protection of southern bottomlands and of streams throughout its range. *Leonard Lee Rue III*

# The Wood Duck

### Frank C. Bellrose

*Illinois Natural History Survey*

and

### Robert A. Heister

*University of Illinois*

## SPECIES DESCRIPTION AND NATURAL HISTORY

The wood duck drake (*Aix sponsa*) is the most brilliantly colored of all native North American waterfowl. The hen, although more drab than the male, is still more attractively colored than the mottled-brown hens of other dabbling duck species. Both the male and female wood duck have noticeably crested heads when in nuptial plumage, but the crest of the male is purplish green and laced with two white stripes, in contrast to the sooty-gray crest of the female. The drake has two prongs of white extending upward from its white throat onto the side and back of the purplish head. The colorful head is further accentuated by the red eye and the red base of the bill. The hen bears a white, tear-shaped mark extending from the back of the eye to the back of its gray head. The burgundy breast of the male is streaked with rows of white spots, and the grayish-brown breast of the female is streaked with white dashes that increase in size along the gray sides. The male's bronze sides are vermiculated with fine black lines and his upper side feathers are margined in black and white. Both male and female have white bellies.

Audubon Wildlife Report 1987

381

Adult wood ducks wear an eclipse, or basic, plumage from early summer into fall, a period when the brownish male looks much like the female except for his white facial marks, red eye, and red bill base. In eclipse plumage, the bellies of both sexes are streaked with brown, and neither sex bears a crest.

Males in juvenile plumage resemble adults in eclipse plumage, but lack the red eye and red on the bill. Juvenile females have a narrow white ring around the eye, but lack the tear-shaped white dash of the adults for several months.

Wood ducks ride more buoyantly on the water than do other species, their large, square tails often raised at an angle. When swimming, they frequently nod their heads, reminiscent of the coot. On the wing, the large crested head, short neck, large tail, and broad wings give the wood duck a compressed rather than elongated appearance.

More than most ducks, it bobs its head in flight, appearing to look downward as if endeavoring to view the landscape more clearly. Its rapid and agile flight can be most appreciated when the wood duck is observed zigzagging through a labyrinth of trees in order to avoid branches and limbs. The wood duck is both alert and jumpy. Often, the casual observer's first sight of a wood duck is its hasty departure, with the female's loud, squealing "wee-e-e-eek, wee-e-e-eek" marking its passage. On such occasions, the white trailing edge of the secondaries on the almost black wings provides a hasty visual cue.

## Range

The wood duck is confined almost entirely to the contiguous United States. Relatively small numbers cross the border into Canada to breed in the Maritime Provinces and in Quebec, Ontario, Manitoba, and British Columbia. Although a scattering of wood ducks breeds across Montana, the state serves largely as a dividing line between two distinct wood duck populations: one east of the Great Plains and one that includes the Pacific Northwest and California. The population east of the Great Plains is 10 to 20 times larger than the western population.

The eastern population breeds as far south as the Gulf of Mexico, excluding only the tip of Florida. In California, breeding grounds extend over most of the state north of the Tehachapi Mountains, which lie between Los Angeles and Bakersfield.

During winter, eastern wood ducks in the northern part of their range join their cousins below 35 degrees latitude in the region east of the Great Plains. In the West, most retreat to the Central Valley of California, particularly the Butte Sink area north of Sacramento.

For both breeding and wintering, wood ducks prefer wooded creeks, rivers, lakes, ponds, and swamps and marshes adjacent to woodlands. Their principal requirements are an adequate food supply and sufficient nest sites. Wood ducks prefer placid waters, rather than those subject to turbulence from wind and current. Unless there are lengthy pools of calm water, only limited numbers of wood ducks frequent streams that have extensive rapids and riffles. Beaver ponds, especially near extensive deciduous growth, often provide ideal habitat. On a larger scale, bottomland swamps dotted with lakes, ponds, and sloughs provide optimum breeding and wintering habitat.

Basic to quality habitat is the wooded cover that occurs dispersed through or overhanging the margin of water areas. Buttonbush and swamp privet are two important shrubs that, along with young willows, maples, gums, and other trees, provide sought-after cover. Indeed, wood ducks appear uncomfortable and insecure where cover is lacking. In summer, marsh vegetation may provide an alternate source of cover. American lotus, spatterdock, arrow arum, duck potato, and marsh smartweed are particularly suited to their needs during this season.

## Breeding

Wood ducks nest in tree cavities usually located within a mile, rarely more, of the wetlands that will provide their food and cover for their broods. Although thousands of nest houses erected by federal and state agencies and by private citizens are a valuable adjunct to them, tree cavities still provide the bulk of nest production. Wood ducks also use the abandoned nest sites of the pileated woodpecker, but to what degree is uncertain. In many towns and cities, wood ducks nest either in natural cavities or in nest houses, much to the delight of interested citizens.

Most wood ducks nest for the first time as yearlings, but not all yearlings nest. Data from web-tagged broods indicate that ducklings that hatch late in the season often do not show up as breeding birds until their second year. In Massachusetts, Grice and Rogers (1965) found that 40 percent of the breeding females were adults that had nested previously, 48 percent were yearlings, and 12 percent were two-year-olds nesting for the first time. In Illinois, yearlings nest approximately two weeks later than older birds (Bellrose 1976), but in southeastern Missouri, Hansen (1971) reported a difference of almost one month (see Figure 1).

In the deep South, nesting activities commence early in February and may not reach a peak until two months later, although late nests may be started from the middle to the end of June (Cunningham 1969). Some 500 miles to the north, wood ducks in Missouri begin nesting in late February or early March, reach a peak in mid-March, but do not complete nest initiation until late June (Hansen 1971). In central

**Wood Duck Range**

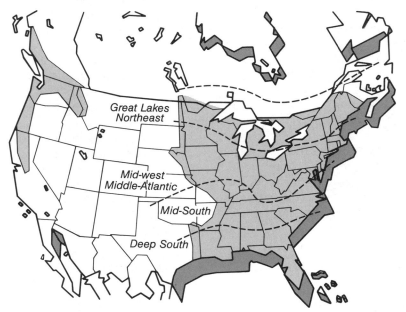

*Source: Frank Bellrose*
Figure 1

Illinois, nesting usually begins in early April, peaks in late April, and terminates in late June. Another 500 miles to the north, in central Minnesota and at similar latitudes in the Northeast, wood ducks begin nesting in mid-April, but still cease nest initiation in late June (Fiedler 1966). Although the period of nest initiation varies a great deal with latitude, the cessation of activities occurs at about the same date throughout wood duck breeding range: Nesting spans about 140 days in the South, but only about 60 days in the North.

Analysis of banding data from incubating wood duck hens reveals that almost 50 percent survive and return to initiate nesting activities at the same nesting area the following year (Bellrose 1976). This survival rate is further supported by analysis of bands recovered by hunters. In many cases the females return to the same nesting site at which they nested successfully the year before. The hen will move to a new site if the former one is destroyed or occupied by another bird, such as a starling or another wood duck. Some yearlings tend to return to their natal areas, but not as precisely as their mothers. Many yearlings will pioneer into new areas.

Once a nesting site is selected, the female returns to it several times before commencing to lay. Normally, she lays one egg per day, but her laying may be interrupted by cold weather or any other factor that temporarily reduces her energy level. At first, the eggs are covered by the material at the base of the nest—dead wood, leaves, or even sawdust if the nest is in a nest house—but about the time that she deposits the sixth egg, the hen begins to pluck down from her breast and add it to the covering. Immediately before the clutch is completed, she spends as much as two hours plucking down. By the time the clutch is completed, the eggs are covered with a thick layer of down during periods when the hen is absent.

Average clutch size is about 12 eggs, but an individual nest may have from a few eggs—as in a nest that has been preyed upon or resulted from a late renesting hen—to as many as 50 or more eggs—as in a nest where several hens have contributed eggs. The latter instance is known as a compound nest because of the dumping of eggs by several females at a single nest site. Usually, any clutch with more than 15 eggs is considered likely to contain eggs from more than one female. Dump nesting is particularly prevalent in areas with a high density of breeding wood ducks, but rather infrequent where the population is sparse. Yearlings seem to be the most actively involved in dump nesting. Most of the females involved in this activity go on to have nests of their own, but with smaller clutches because of the amount of energy they already expended dumping eggs. Dump nesting frequently results in a reduced hatchability of the eggs. In a normal clutch of 12 eggs, only two, on the average, fail to hatch. Most unhatched eggs result from embryos dying within the shell, and infertility accounts for about a third. In dump nests, tremendous wasting of eggs can occur— anywhere from 50 percent to 90 percent may fail to hatch. This can result from eggs being laid during incubation by one or more intruding hens or from insufficient warmth being applied to so many eggs.

Incubation varies from 28 days to 38 days after the laying of the last egg, with the average incubation period lasting about 30 days. The length of time involved in incubation is dependent upon the consistency of the heat provided by the hen and by the outside temperature. If the hen is extremely attentive, incubation will be minimal. However, if the female is absent from the nest a great deal of the time and outside temperatures are relatively low, the period of incubation will extend toward the maximum.

Incubating wood duck hens usually leave the nest twice a day: once in the morning shortly after daybreak and again in the afternoon or evening. They are gone from the nest anywhere from half an hour to two hours. The length of absences may be dependent upon air temperature, the availability of food, or the stage of incubation. The hens leave to replenish their energy, which they generally lose at the rate of a half percent of body weight per day during incubation. The male accompanies the female back to the nest site and, as she ducks into the nest cavity, returns to his general waiting area. As incubation progresses, an increasing number of males desert their spouses. By the time the eggs hatch, only a relatively small portion of males are still accompanying their mates. However, wood ducks are much more attentive to their spouses than the ducks of other species. Most other ducks desert their hens in the first days of incubation.

The wide variation in the success of wood duck nests is due to many factors: the density of the nests, the abundance and kind of predators, and whether or not the nests are in natural cavities or in nest houses. Biologists are most concerned with nesting success in tree cavities because most wood ducks nest in that type of site. Although scores of studies have been performed on nests in nest houses, only limited numbers have been conducted on those in natural cavities. Even so, research on natural-cavity nests has shown that nest success reaches 40 percent to 50 percent (Bellrose 1976). Most nest destruction is due to natural predators, such as raccoons, fox squirrels, gray squirrels, bull snakes, flickers, starlings, and, in the South, rat snakes.

Nests in houses have proved more successful than nests in natural cavities when the houses were constructed in a fashion that deterred predators. Nest houses have varied in their value as contributors to nest success from 30 percent to 95 percent (Bellrose 1976). But even with the best constructed and erected nest houses, it is seldom possible to prevent all predation. For example, starlings and flickers have been able to victimize wood duck nests in almost every type of house that has been constructed. In the long run, whether or not nest houses will be successful tools for management depends upon the degree to which they ensure nest success.

The young are out of the shell within 24 hours after the eggs show an indication of pipping. The female continues to brood the young for another 24 hours, during which they dry their downy plumage and gather strength. Then the young are ready for departure. While the ducklings were breaking through the shell, the female called repeatedly to them. Now, when they are ready to leave the nest and no danger threatens, the mother repeats these calls from outside the nest, either from a nearby branch or from the ground or water surface below. Upon hearing this call, the young climb up the inside of the nest, jumping six to 12 inches at a time and clinging to the side of the cavity, until they give yet another spring, eventually reaching the entrance. They pause there momentarily before launching themselves into space with tiny wings outspread. They might fall only a few feet or as much as 60 feet. The female waits until most or all of the young have left the nest, their "peeping" calls making her aware of any ducklings still in the nest. Once she has gathered her brood, the female starts for the nearest water, which may be up to a mile away. At this time, the young still have sufficient yolk to maintain themselves for another 48 hours, after which they will have exhausted their energy reserves. By then, they must have found an adequate food supply.

Ducklings weigh about one ounce at hatching and grow rapidly over the first eight weeks. Their growth rate slows after that. During the early part of their development they feed almost entirely on invertebrates, especially the larvae of aquatic and terrestrial insects. After they are a month old, they turn increasingly to plant food, particularly where duckweed and other aquatic plants are available.

In 60 or 70 days, the ducklings have molted from down into juvenile plumage and are able to fly. In another three months they will molt from juvenile plumage into nuptial plumage. Females take somewhat longer than males, as shown by the latent development of the white dash mark behind the eye.

A beginning brood numbers about 10 to 12 ducklings, but attrition takes a heavy toll, especially in the first week or two of life. Some fall prey to predators while others become lost or separated from the female and the brood. By the time they have reached the flying stage, only about half the young remain. The female accompanies the ducklings for about eight or nine weeks, brooding them when it is cold or rainy, warning them of danger, and leading them to food sources. She deserts maturing young as they approach the flying stage. However, a late-nesting female occasionally deserts her brood while they are even younger as she enters the molt leading to the eclipse plumage.

## Molt Leading Into Eclipse Plumage

Males begin showing signs of entering eclipse plumage late in May, when they begin losing their brilliant side colors, followed shortly by loss of their head crests. It appears that the first birds to molt are the males that mated early to successful nesting hens. Males that did not succeed in finding a mate or that mated later in the nesting season appear to be the last to enter the molt. Indeed, some males have been found that still have brilliant plumage in late July.

The females not only enter eclipse plumage later than the males but also exhibit a much more subdued change. The principal reason for the later molt in females is that they spend about three months incubating and attending to the brood before they can expend a lot of energy changing plumage.

After the body plumage is molted, which takes about one month, the wood duck loses its flight feathers. At this "flapper" stage, the bird is flightless for three to four weeks and can only skitter across water. After the wood duck regains its flight feathers, almost another two months elapse before the male completely regains his nuptial plumage. The females lag behind the males because of later entry into the molt. Evidence suggests that a fair portion of the males move north of their breeding grounds into the northern marshes in order to undergo this molt. The females are more prone to enter the molt on or near the areas where they nested.

### Roosting Behavior

Wood ducks are unique among ducks in forming nocturnal roosts during the summer, fall, and winter. Ordinarily, roosts are located in an area that provides suitable overhead cover. In this respect, buttonbush is an ideal plant. Some roosts are reinhabited for many years, whereas others are only temporary expediencies. Whether or not a roost is occupied year after year may depend upon water levels, cover, food, and other conditions that affect local population numbers. An increase in water levels, as in floods, usually disrupts a roost—even one with a long tradition—as the birds scatter over a much more extensive area and adapt to new feeding grounds and routines.

Wood ducks can be observed flying to roosts about mid-July in Illinois, traveling as many as 10 miles to the roost site. Roosts may include from 20 or 30 birds up to several thousand. Where roosts are small, a number of them often occur in a limited area. When there is a large roost, it encompasses the movements of birds over an extensive wetland habitat. Birds commence coming into roosts about 30 or 40 minutes before sunset and continue for about the same length of time after sunset, when it is quite dark. They begin to leave the roost at daybreak. By the time the sun has risen, the roosts, for the most part, are empty. The morning departure extends over a much shorter period than the evening arrival.

Birds fly to roosts as singles, pairs, small groups, and, occasionally, as flocks of some 20 birds. At the peak of activity, flocks arrive almost in a continuous stream. During the late summer months, roosts are made up of local birds, but with the onset of fall, migrants begin to appear and swell the ranks of the inhabitants.

### Flocking

To some degree, flocking occurs throughout the year. Where there is a relatively dense population, wood ducks arrive on the breeding grounds in pairs and small flocks. As females begin incubation, several males can be found banding together. And as brood activities cease, females begin to gather in small clusters. The broods, each having grown up as an entity, tend to remain a unit, each member attached to one or more brood mates. Thus, a nucleus of flocks exists in these early gatherings on the breeding grounds. However, there seem to be many individuals that do not attach themselves permanently to any group, and some small groups fail to attract larger numbers on a permanent basis. Most flocks appear to have a cohesive unit, or hard core, that sticks together, augmented through some attraction of transitory nature by other individuals.

Flocks vary in size between morning and evening as they fly in and out of a roost. But many assemblages do not remain the same from one day to the next during flights to a roost. This seems to indicate that the associations between some individuals and flocks are ephemeral. Except for large aggregations that occur at a particular time or place because of some unusual event, such as a large roost site, wood ducks tend to form rather small flocks, rarely with more than 20 individuals.

**Migration**

In late summer a small number of wood ducks, particularly adult males and immatures of both sexes, fly north from their breeding and natal areas, some as far as Ontario and Quebec. Wood ducks from the southern states may move north into Indiana, Ohio, Illinois, and Missouri (Bellrose 1976). Probably because of this premigration before their departure southward in the fall, wood ducks have dispersed into new habitats and regions, such as the states of the Great Plains, where previously they either were absent or less common.

At the greatest distance, wood ducks are only a thousand miles from their wintering grounds. Most are within 500 miles. Therefore, they have a relatively short migration flight compared with ducks nesting in, for example, the Northwest Territories or Alaska. Because wood ducks migrate a comparatively short distance, their migratory behavior is different from that of most other waterfowl.

In contrast to most other species that make extensive flights along fairly well-defined migration corridors, wood ducks fan out from individual breeding sites so that, at the southern extremity, birds from a single breeding location may disperse laterally several hundred miles. They disperse over much of the region that embraces the southern part of their winter range, except in the Pacific Coast area where they are restricted largely to the Central Valley of California. Wood ducks from northern areas tend to move almost directly to wintering grounds, seldom stopping along the way.

**Diet**

Almost throughout their range, wood ducks feed extensively on acorns. This food is especially important on the southern wintering grounds. Although they prefer acorns that have been inundated by shallow water, wood ducks often fly to oak groves, in both bottomlands and uplands, that are devoid of undergrowth in order to pick up acorns from the ground. They fill their proventriculi and esophagi. Often, biologists have found seven or eight acorns stacked up in a wood duck's esophagus. The seeds of other plants that grow in swamps also are used, including pecans, swamp privet, dogwood, and ash, as well as buttonbush, bald cypress, and arrow arum (Martin *et al.* 1951). When the mast found in swamps is in short supply, wood ducks may fly out to corn and rice fields to feed upon waste grain left by combines.

In spring and early summer, wood ducks feed on mulberries. In late summer they feed on grapes and even rip open the pods of the American lotus to obtain its immature seeds, apparently before the seeds become too hard to digest. Wood ducks also make extensive use of millets, smartweeds, nutgrasses, rice cut-grass, and other moist-soil plants that develop on mud flats during the summer and are flooded during the fall.

## SIGNIFICANCE OF THE SPECIES

The wood duck is unique in North America. Its only close cousin is the Mandarin duck, an Asian species, but since both ducks are so geographically independent, it is difficult to draw conclusions about their similarities. Because of its unique place among North American waterfowl, the wood duck has not served as an indicator of the relative abundance of other species.

The wood duck also is unique for the long-standing interest it has generated as a symbol for our native waterfowl. As far back as colonial times, the wood duck was noted for its beauty, nesting behavior, and abundance along the eastern seaboard during periods when other waterfowl were absent. It has been the subject of a national postage stamp, commemorated in October 1968, as well as several national and state duck stamps. The wood duck continues to intrigue artists and wood carvers who, with meticulous care, render it on canvas and in wood. Today, it evokes much admiration as well as concern on the part of countless observers in populated areas where the wood duck nests. Sights such as the ducklings jumping from the nest and following the mother through a residential area to a water source have endeared it to thousands.

Sportsmen and breeders, too, maintain a high regard for the wood duck. Trout fishermen appreciate the wood duck's barred side feathers, indispensable for tying the Cahill fly, a dry fly noted for its attractiveness to trout. The wood duck is a favorite among aviculturalists because it is easy to raise and, because of its spectacular plumage, attracts much attention. Hunters regard the wood duck highly, never more so than in the 1980s as duck populations from Canadian breeding grounds and the northern U.S. prairies have declined. Indeed, the wood duck was the second most numerous duck in the bag, overall, during the 1983-84 and 1984-85 hunting seasons within the United States, and it was the first duck in the bag along the Atlantic Flyway during the 1980s, although the mallard runs a close second. In the early 1980s, hunters in the United States took about 1,300,000 wood ducks. Of this number, about 400,000 were taken in the Atlantic Flyway and about 800,000 in the Mississippi Flyway, with comparatively small numbers from the Central and Pacific flyways. Overall during this period, the wood duck has composed from 10 percent to 11 percent of the kill of all ducks in the United States. In the Mississippi Flyway it has composed about 15 percent of the kill and in the Atlantic Flyway from 23 percent to 25 percent. Thus, it is quite evident that the homegrown wood duck has contributed significantly to the pleasure of hunters. Without these birds, many a duck hunter would have returned home empty-handed.

## HISTORICAL PERSPECTIVE

Except for a few isolated references to its existence, no one really knows with certainty how abundant the wood duck was in the 19th century and the very beginnings of the 20th century. No censuses were taken. In fact, even today, because of the species' reclusive nature, no field technique can provide any viable index of wood duck populations over an extensive area. For an index of its status, specialists must rely on the trend in kill numbers and on banding information collected from birds taken by hunters.

Sketchy historical evidence, however, does provide some indication of the wood duck's abundance in the eastern United States during the 19th century. For example, in a book on Michigan bird life, Barrows (1912) commented that in 1890 the wood duck was one of the most abundant ducks in Michigan. In Ohio, Trautman (1940) quoted a former market hunter to the effect that it was such an abundant duck during the summers between 1850 and 1890 that a profitable business was made of hunting fledglings and flightless adults in the "flapper" stage. And in south-central Wisconsin, a market hunter reported that the wood duck was the most abundant duck, with the mallard a close second. Also, in a comment describing a spring trip through the lowlands of Arkansas in the 1890s, Askins (1931) observed during a 20-mile horseback ride that the wood duck was never out of sight and that thousands of them were nesting in the trees of the swamplands. He stated that no one envisioned a time when this would not be true.

Looking back at the pristine habitat of the 19th century and earlier, it is easy to conclude that the wood duck probably was the most abundant duck species east of the Appalachian Mountains and, next to the mallard, the most abundant duck north of the coastal marshes of Louisiana in the Mississippi Flyway. But man, shooting for the market and during very long hunting seasons that often ran from September to April, began to deplete this population. By the early 20th century many ornithologists began to be concerned that the wood duck would be exterminated. For example, Cooke (1906) noted, "So persistent has this duck been pursued that in some sections it had been practically exterminated . . . As a result the wood duck has constantly diminishing numbers and soon is likely to be known only from books or by tradition." The famous hunter and naturalist George Grinnell (1901) remarked, "being shot in all seasons of the year they are becoming very scarce and are likely to be exterminated before long." Forbush (1913), an eminent Massachusetts ornithologist, said that "the wood duck . . . is now rapidly growing rare in most of the state," adding that "only the most rigid enforcement of the law can save this most beautiful of all American wild ducks from extermination."

Fortunately, the dire forecast for the wood duck was turned around by the passage of the Migratory Bird Treaty Act in 1918. This act gave the wood duck complete protection from all types of hunting. The closed season continued until 1941, when one wood duck was allowed in the bag in 15 states. The following year the bag limit was extended to all states. Although there had always been an intentional and unintentional kill of wood ducks during the period of complete protection, the wood duck prospered, so that by 1938, it was evident that large numbers of wood ducks were breeding through the central Illinois River valley, as indicated by the numbers of nests found in natural cavities and unusual sites. Later that fall, as many as 10,000 wood ducks were observed feeding in wheat stubble fields near Havana, Illinois. This observation indicated that, for at least part of its range, the wood duck had indeed made a remarkable recovery from the very low populations prevailing in the early 1900s.

Wood ducks were abundant in the East, too, as chronicled by Griscom (1949), who reported that by 1938 the wood duck in Massachusetts had recovered from the very verge of extinction and fully occupied all nesting habitats. In 1942, the Illinois Natural History Survey circulated among several hundred wildlife biologists and ornithologists a questionnaire concerning wood duck status. Two hundred and twenty replied. In the Atlantic Flyway, 64 percent of the respondents reported an increase, 27 percent no apparent change, and only nine percent a decrease in wood duck breeding populations. In the Mississippi Flyway, 62 percent of the observers reported an increase, 31 percent little or no change, and seven percent a decrease. Obviously, the wood duck had come back a long way in the 20 years from the time it was given complete protection in 1918.

In the mid-1950s, for reasons unknown, the wood duck experienced a temporary setback that caused the seasons to be closed in 1954 and 1956 in the Mississippi Flyway and again in certain states in 1957 and 1958. From 1959 up to the mid-1980s, the wood duck has shown a continued increase in abundance, as indicated by its kill in the Atlantic and Mississippi flyways. For example, back in 1959, 249,000 wood ducks were killed in the United States. In 1984, the number was 1,485,000. Again, in the Atlantic Flyway in 1959, the kill was 76,000. By 1984 it had risen to 446,000. In the Mississippi Flyway in 1959, the kill was 144,000. In 1984 it was 855,000.

## CURRENT TRENDS

Direct band recovery data indicate that throughout the period from the mid-1950s to the mid-1980s hunters took about the same proportion of the fall wood duck population. Therefore, the increased number of wood ducks in hunter bags is due solely to an increase in their numbers and not to the possibility that hunters are killing a greater proportion of the population. However, the kill in recent years indicates that the populations may be reaching a plateau. The rate of increase appears to be leveling off.

In the Central Flyway, the wood duck remained at a comparatively low level until the fall of 1969, when 78,000 were taken. Numbers since that time have remained much higher than in prior years, reaching a peak of 90,000 in 1983, but dropping off to 62,000 in 1984. Thus, it appears that a substantial increase in the wood duck as a breeding bird has occurred in the states of the Great Plains.

However, the situation is markedly different in the Pacific Flyway area and gives cause for concern. Pacific Flyway numbers have risen and fallen regularly without showing any real indications of a trend. Since 1980, the kill has declined from 52,000 in 1980 to 23,000 in 1984. The kill in the Pacific Flyway indicates that the wood duck has shown no consistent change in numbers and that its autumn population may be governed more by a favorable yearly increment in the young than by any other factor. Biologists need to determine whether the downward trends are real or just a reflection of hunter success.

In order to better understand recent trends in wood duck populations, waterfowl specialists have concentrated much of their research on wood duck nest houses and on the dynamics of wood duck populations at specific sites. Leigh Frederickson of the University of Missouri and his associates are studying second nesting, behavior, and courtship by wood ducks at Duck Creek, Mingo National Wildlife Refuge and Swamp, Puxico, Missouri. The same research interests are pursued by Frank Bellrose and Robert Crompton, both of the Illinois Natural History Survey, at Quiver Creek and Nauvoo Slough in Illinois. Other nesting studies are being conducted at Muscatatuck National Wildlife Refuge, Indiana; Noxubee National Wildlife Refuge, Mississippi; and Mead Wildlife Area, Wisconsin; McGraw Wildlife Area, Illinois; and near Auburn, Alabama.

A survival study is being conducted by Dick Kasul, formerly of Louisiana State University, Vern Wright of Lousiana State University, and Frank Bellrose from banding data supplied by the U.S. Fish and Wildlife Service (FWS) Bird Banding Laboratory and from state and flyway kill data provided by the administrative reports of the Office of Migratory Bird Management. Much of this research concentrates upon the survival of wood ducks by age and sex classes in the different regions of the United States, how long the birds survive, and the degree to which yearly changes in the survival rate are a reflection of hunter removal.

## MANAGEMENT

Management of the wood duck embraces two different aspects: habitat and population. Habitat is crucial to its status. Basic to this are the overflow swamps, primarily in the southern states, that provide optimum wintering habitat. The overflow bottomlands are particularly important in the so-called Mississippi Delta region extending south from the boot heel of Missouri to New Orleans. On both sides of the Mississippi River are numerous streams that drain the delta country. These usually slow streams tend to parallel the river and at one time had extensive bottomland forests adjacent to them. Unfortunately, much of these bottomland forests have been cleared, and some of the forest loss has been increased by channelization of the streams.

Bayou DeView and the Cache River in Arkansas and the Atchafalaya Swamp west of Baton Rouge, Louisiana, probably are the most important single areas remaining for wood ducks in the Mississippi Flyway. Next in importance are the Yazoo Basin in Mississippi and the Hatchie, Forked Deer, and Obion rivers in Tennessee. All these areas have been threatened by some degree of channelization, from complete channelization to a sectional one. If the current wood duck population in the Mississippi Flyway is to be maintained, these habitats must be preserved.

Greenbelts along stream banks are important both for checking stream-bank erosion and for the welfare of wood ducks. They also are important for providing nest sites as well as the overhanging cover that wood ducks need in order to make the greatest use of the aquatic habitat. The encouragement of beaver populations and the building of farm ponds or small lakes in wooded areas also increase wood duck habitat. Nesting sites can be enhanced by providing nest houses, but nest houses will not be of much value unless they are made or erected to exclude mammalian and snake predators.

Management embraces limiting the kill of wood ducks to the surplus provided by the yearly increment of young. In the past, officials have been admirably conservative in their approach to regulations affecting the kill of wood ducks. The wood duck has had some type of special protection since the season was first opened in 1941: first a limit of one, then two, and then the point system in which the states that adopted this control of the duck bag made wood ducks worth 70 or more points each, limiting the daily kill to no more than two birds.

Wood duck hunting seems to be well controlled. Band recoveries do not indicate any overall excess kill by hunters. Perhaps some local populations are subject to too great a kill, however, because about half of the wood duck take in any one location is made up of local birds. Consequently, if hunting is intense in a particular locality, it is possible to hurt the local population while not affecting the entire state or flyway population. Nevertheless, in the early 1980s several states, mostly in the South, petitioned FWS for an experimental season to coincide with the early season on blue-winged teal. They contended that wood ducks in the South were not being hunted to the extent that the population allowed. FWS, in an effort to study the possibility of changing wood duck hunting regulations, has recognized that several states should experiment with early wood duck seasons to determine if they have any effect on local populations or if wood ducks from farther north might be involved in the kill. All the studies from these special experimental seasons have not been evaluated completely, so it would be premature to draw any conclusions.

Many states are placing nest houses on their waterfowl refuges and public hunting grounds. Numerous federal refuges also are participating. Although the establishment of these nest houses has varied according to the interest of refuge managers, it is hoped that in the future more refuges will erect and monitor the use of wood duck houses.

Louisiana and Mississippi have been making a concerted effort to acquire overflow bottomland swamps for wood ducks, wintering mallards, and other wildlife. FWS likewise has given these habitats high priority in their current and future acquisition programs.

## PROGNOSIS

For a number of reasons, the wood duck has shown a tremendous ability to rebound from a very low population level. First, it lays an extremely large number of eggs and readily renests if its original nest is destroyed. The wood duck has been known to raise two broods to flight stage in the same season, particularly in areas below 39 degrees latitude. The wood duck also has shown a significant ability to adapt to many different types of aquatic and wetland habitats. It has further enhanced its survival through increased nesting at beaver ponds, in sites previously occupied by pileated woodpeckers, and in nest houses provided by concerned individuals.

In recent years, the wood duck has extended its range to areas where it formerly was sparse or unknown. Moreover, the wood duck has shown an increasing tolerance to human use of its waterways. The success of the wood duck is due, in large part, to its adaptability under adverse circumstances. This adaptability, along with an egg-laying productivity unequaled among other game ducks, seems to offer a prognosis of continued prosperity at present levels.

## RECOMMENDATIONS

The greatest need for the future welfare of the wood duck is the acquisition and maintenance of the vast overflow bottomland swamps of the South, particularly those in the Mississippi Basin south of the Ohio River. The necessity for preserving this habitat cannot be overemphasized. Present habitat loss for wood ducks and other waterfowl has reached critical proportions, as evidenced by the almost 6.6 million acres of bottomland hardwood forests lost in the Mississippi Delta region between 1937 and 1978. Probably only 4.6 million of the original 11.8 million acres remain at present (MacDonald et al. 1979).

A second recommendation is to reduce or eliminate the channelization of streams everywhere within the wood duck's range. Channelization destroys the food base, quiet waters, and overhanging cover that the birds need. Channelization is a most destructive practice insofar as wood duck breeding numbers and production of young are concerned. Encouraging and planting trees as greenbelts along the banks of streams would greatly improve the quality of habitat for wood ducks by stabilizing banks that are subject to erosion, thereby creating a better food base, more needed bank cover, and, ultimately, more nest sites as the trees mature.

A third recommendation is to erect nest houses on federal and state refuges and on private wetlands where studies indicate that such a program would be economically feasible.

A fourth recommendation is to maintain the hunter kill of wood ducks at current levels, except where careful studies demonstrate that larger numbers could be taken without harming local populations.

# REFERENCES

Askins, Capt. C. 1931. *Game Bird Shooting*. MacMillan Co. New York, New York. 321 pp.

Barrows, W.B. 1912. "Michigan bird life." *Michigan Agricultural College Special Bulletin*. 822 pp.

Bellrose, F.C. 1976. *Ducks, Geese and Swans of North America*. Stackpole Books. Harrisburg, Pennsylvania. 540 pp.

Cooke, W.W. 1906. "Distribution and migration of North American ducks, geese, and swans." *U.S. Department of Agriculture Bureau of Biological Survey Bulletin* 26. 90 pp.

Cunningham, E.R. 1969. "A three year study of the wood duck on the Yazoo National Wildlife Refuge." *Proceedings of the Annual Conference of the Southeastern Association for Game and Fish Commissioners* 22:145-155.

Fiedler, D. 1966. *Results of Wood Duck Usage of Artificial Nesting Boxes During the 1966 Nesting Season in the Study Area in Morrison County in Central Minnesota — A Progress Report*. Mimeographed report. 12 pp.

Forbush, E.H. 1913. *Useful Birds and Their Protection*. 4th ed. Massachusetts State Board of Agriculture. 451 pp.

Grice, D., and J.P. Rogers. 1965. *The Wood Duck in Massachusetts*. Final Report Project No. W-19-R. Massachusetts Division of Fish and Game. 96 pp.

Grinnell, G.B. 1901. *American Duck Shooting*. Forest and Stream Publishing Company. New York, New York. 627 pp.

Griscom, L. 1949. *The Birds of Concord*. Harvard University Press, Cambridge. 340 pp.

Hansen, J.L. 1971. The role of nest boxes in management of the wood duck on Mingo National Wildlife Refuge. Master's Thesis. University of Missouri, Columbia. 159 pp.

MacDonald, P.O., W.E. Frayer, and J.K. Clauser. 1979. *Documentation, Chronology, and Future Projections of Bottomland Hardwood Habitat Loss in the Lower Mississippi Alluvial Plain. vol. I: Basic Report, November 1979*. United States Department of the Interior, Fish and Wildlife Service, Division of Ecological Services. 133 pp.

Martin, A.C., H.S. Zim, and A.L. Nelson. 1951. *American Wildlife and Plants*. McGraw-Hill, Inc. New York, New York. 500 pp.

Trautman, M.B. 1940. "The Birds of Buckeye Lake, Ohio." *University of Michigan Museum Zoology Miscellaneous Publication* 44. 466 pp.

*Frank C. Bellrose, who has been a waterfowl biologist for 49 years, is principal scientist with the Illinois Natural History Survey.*

*Robert A. Heister is an editor with Agricultural Publications, College of Agriculture, University of Illinois at Urbana–Champaign.*

The future for the bobcat looks bright as researchers illuminate its management needs. However, the species is susceptible to overhunting, overtrapping, and habitat loss to urban sprawl and agriculture. *Leonard Lee Rue III*

# The Bobcat

## Gary Koehler

*University of Idaho*

## SPECIES DESCRIPTION AND NATURAL HISTORY

The bobcat (*Felis rufus*) occurs over much of the United States, throughout southern Canada, and into central Mexico. The bobcat's coat varies in color with geographic regions. In the dense forests of the Pacific Northwest and western Canada, where little sun penetrates, bobcats are a dark reddish-brown. In the more arid regions of the southwestern United States they are light gray-brown. Taxonomists have identified as many as 14 subspecies of bobcats based on these color variations. Today, however, some taxonomists recognize only three: *Felis rufus fasciatus* of the Pacific Coast west of the Cascade Mountains, *F.r. pallescens*, which occupies the rest of the range in central Mexico, and *F.r. escuinapae*, which occurs to central Mexico (McCord and Cardoza 1982).

The bobcat bears distinct dark brown or black spots over the back and legs. The belly is white and distinctly spotted with black. The back of the ears are black with a large white spot in the center. The spotted pelage is very effective camouflage in places the sun casts dappled shadows among the undergrowth allowing this elusive predator to meld into its environment.

The bobcat received its name from its "bobbed" tail, which may measure only one to two inches. Its similarity to its close relative, the lynx (*F. lynx*) earned it the nickname "lynx cat" or "bay lynx" in parts of its range.

Bobcats and lynx are indeed similar. Both weigh about the same, with males running 20 to 35 pounds and females 15 to 25. They have the same stubbed tail, facial tufts or "sideburns," and tiny tufts of fur at the tips of the ears. However, the bobcat's ear tufts are smaller, making its ears appear less pointed. Its facial tufts are not as pronounced, either. The bobcat's tail has one or more bars, including one at the end, with the underside of the tail completely white. The lynx's tail is not barred and ends in a dark tip that includes the underside.

Bobcats lack the longer legs and larger feet of the lynx, adaptations to the deep snows of the northern latitudes where the lynx is found. The bobcat is better adapted to more southern latitudes where the snow is less challenging.

## Breeding

Bobcats generally breed from February to April, although they are capable of breeding throughout most of the year (Crowe 1975). The gestation period is about 60 days. Litter size ranges from one to five kittens, with three the average.

Females are able to breed at one and a half years. Males are capable of breeding after two years (Crowe 1975). Bailey found, however, that only resident bobcats with established territories raise litters (Bailey 1972).

Bobcats may live 14 years in the wild. However, mortality can be high among kittens and juveniles. Crowe found that kitten survival ranges from 0 to 71 percent (Crowe 1975). Survival of young is dependent on the abundance and availability of food. Bailey observed that when cottontail rabbit populations are low, kitten survival is low too (Bailey 1972).

Although coyotes (*Canis latrans*) have been implicated as an important bobcat mortality factor (Nunley 1978), it has been demonstrated in Maine and Idaho that little competition or interaction exists between coyotes and bobcats (Bailey 1972, Major 1983). Both can coexist because of differences in habitat, prey selection, and hunting behavior. However, cougars (*F. concolor*) do occasionally kill bobcats for food or in defense of food caches (Ackerman *et al.* 1984, Koehler unpubl. data). Trapping and hunting are major causes of mortality in some areas (Bailey 1972, Major 1983, Rolley 1985).

## Social Organization and Territoriality

Like other solitary felids, bobcats establish well-defined home ranges or territories within which they confine most foraging and breeding activity. In most areas, territories of resident bobcats exclude others of the same sex but overlap with bobcats of the opposite sex. However, territories may be less exclusive during stressful times when food is scarce or weather conditions severe. The size of territories varies from 0.2 of a square mile to greater than 80 square miles (McCord and Cardoza 1982) depending on prey densities, habitat, and weather conditions. Females generally have smaller home ranges than do males.

Only sexually mature individuals occupy territories. Juveniles lack territories, wandering instead through resident territories. When a resident adult moves from its territory or dies, a juvenile may establish itself in the vacated territory (Bailey 1974, Major 1983, Zezulak and Schwab 1979).

The exclusive nature of bobcat territories is maintained by olfactory and visual signs. Bobcats advertise their presence by depositing scats, urine, or exudate from anal scent glands or by making "scrapes," piles of duff or dirt, with their front feet. Sometimes "scrapes" also may be marked with scent or scats (Bailey 1972).

Territoriality maintains the solitary nature of bobcats and provides for an equitable distribution of resources. Territories allow cats to be more effective predators by restricting their hunting to areas with which they are familiar.

Territorial systems act together with prey and habitat conditions to regulate bobcat densities. Densities may range from one bobcat per five square miles to more than seven bobcats per square mile (McCord and Cardoza 1982).

## Habitat

Bobcats occupy a variety of habitats, including subtropical swamplands in the southeastern United States, deserts in Mexico, high mountain ranges in the western United States and Canada, and dense coniferous rain forests on the Pacific Coast. Bobcats are not found in the northern latitudes where deep snow restricts their movements.

Rugged areas with caves, rock outcrops, and ledges provide good habitat for bobcats (Bailey 1974, McCord 1974). These sites are used for resting, natal den sites, and cover for stalking and hunting as well as for protection from man. Where rocky terrain is not available, swamps and thickets can provide adequate escape cover.

Bobcats can live in close proximity to humans. They use agricultural areas if cover and prey are available. Secondary successional forests following fires and logging can provide habitat for prey and can benefit bobcats if adequate escape cover exists. However, they avoid agricultural areas where habitat has been destroyed and prey has been eliminated, as in the Corn Belt of the midwestern United States.

Bobcats frequently use roads and trails for traveling, especially when deep snow begins to restrict their movements.

### Diet

The bobcat's wide range reflects the broad distribution and diversity of its prey. Large rodents, rabbits, and hares are dominant food items, as shown by studies in Alabama (Miller and Speake 1979), Arizona (Jones and Smith 1979), Arkansas (Fritts and Sealander 1978), California (Leach and Frazier 1953), Idaho (Bailey 1972), Maine (Major 1983), Minnesota (Rollings 1945), New England (Pollack 1951), Oregon (Nassbaum and Maser 1975), Texas (Beasom and Moore 1977), Utah and Nevada (Gashwiler *et al.* 1960), Vermont (Hamilton and Hunter 1939), and Virginia and North Carolina (Progulske 1955). Bobcats often select for these items even though other prey may be more abundant (Bailey 1972, Jones and Smith 1979). However, when preferred prey becomes scarce, bobcats may rely more heavily on alternative prey. In the North, deer may become a major portion of the diet. Although bobcats are capable of killing deer (McCord 1974), they more often feed on carrion or deer killed or wounded by hunters during the fall (Hamilton and Hunter 1939). In the South, cotton rats are an important source of food (Beasom and Moore 1977, Miller and Speake 1979). Kangaroo rats are important in California (Leach and Frazier 1953) and gray squirrels in the southern Appalachians (Progulske 1955). Bobcats also prey on a variety of other items, including birds, mice, pack rats, eggs, and reptiles.

## SIGNIFICANCE OF THE SPECIES

Cats are the most highly evolved of all mammalian predators. They have evolved specialized physical adaptations for being effective predators: retractable claws kept sharp for capturing; front paws that can rotate freely for grasping prey; binocular vision for accurately judging distance; pupils that dilate greatly for night vision; and short powerful jaws, sharp canines, and specialized molars for piercing and cutting flesh. The behavior of cats, too, is highly attuned to the detection and pursuit of prey.

Because they are so specialized, felids occupy a niche at the peak of the ecological pyramid, with more generalized predators and prey occupying the lower ecological trophic levels. Wherever felids occur they are present in very low densities. Because of this, and the fact that they are such specialized predators, felids may be vulnerable to exces sive exploitation, habitat alteration, and disruption of prey abundance. This sensitivity to environmental degradation suggests that the presence of felids may be an indication of the quality and quantity of prey and habitat.

The value of felids as indicators of ecological conditions is illustrated by comparing the present range of bobcats and coyotes. Bobcats and coyotes are ecological equivalents preying on similar species and occupying similiar habitats. However, coyotes are generalized predators able to subsist on vegetable material and carrion as well as prey. Bobcats are exclusive flesheaters depending for survival on rodents and rabbits or other prey. Because of their more restrictive requirements, bobcats have been eliminated from portions of their range by excessive exploitation and habitat alterations. By contrast, the more generalized coyote, despite heavy persecution, has expanded its range throughout North America.

Bobcat abundance is dependent on rodent and rabbit abundance (Bailey 1981). Although prey abundance may control bobcat abundance, predation by bobcats generally has little effect on numbers of rodents or other prey. However, when combined with the effects of other predators such as coyotes, hawks, and mustelids, the total effect of predation may help regulate numbers of prey. Exceptions also may occur where bobcat populations fluctuate in response to fluctuations in prey densities. In these situations, bobcats at peak densities may affect the rate and extent of decline in the prey base in a manner similar to the demonstrated lynx-snowshoe hare cycles (Keith and Windberg 1978). Predation by bobcats may at times be an important mortality factor of pronghorn and white-tailed deer fawns (Beale and Smith 1973, Beasom 1974). But often in these situations other environmental factors, such as reduced protective cover for fawns or adverse weather conditions, increase the vulnerability of fawns and may explain the increased predation on them.

Ecologically the bobcat is an important predator. However, they seldom prey on domestic animals or game so they present little if any threat to the livestock business or to management of game animals (Miller and Speake 1979, McCord and Cardoza 1982). Economically the bobcat is presently considered a valuable furbearer, a single pelt may be worth as much as $300.

## HISTORICAL PERSPECTIVE AND CURRENT TRENDS

The distribution of bobcats probably has not changed significantly since Europeans first settled in North America. The range described by Seton (1929) for early 1900 is similar to the current range.

Bobcats have been eliminated from much of the midwestern United States by intensive agricultural activity. In central Mexico the subspecies *F.r. escuinapae* is considered endangered, but in some areas of Canada bobcats have expanded their range (McCord and Cardoza 1982) probably as a result of small scale agricultural and timber harvest practices.

Bobcat numbers increased in the western United States during the 1950s, but have since declined. The increase coincided with efforts to control coyotes by using the poison Compound 1080. It has been suggested that controlling coyotes reduced competition with bobcats, allowing bobcat numbers to increase (Nunley 1978). However, other factors may explain this coincidental observation, since little competition or interaction between the species have been found in Maine or Idaho (Bailey 1972, Major 1983).

Bobcats are vulnerable to trapping and hunting. Where these activities have not been regulated, bobcats have suffered. Now, however, stringent regulations and research into bobcat requirements have been more favorable to bobcats. Presently, bobcats are protected where rare or uncommon, as in Connecticut, Delaware, Illinois, Indiana, Iowa, Kentucky, Maryland, New Jersey, Ohio, Pennsylvania, South Dakota and Rhode Island.

## MANAGEMENT

Prior to 1970, little effort was directed toward the management of bobcats. Although some states regulated bobcat take by trappers and hunters, other states considered the bobcat a predator and paid bounties on it. Little attention was given to bobcat management until the price for pelts skyrocketed from $5 or $10 to $300 a pelt in the mid-1970s.

This sudden increase in price was partly due to the protection given the cheetah, leopard, jaguar and ocelot. During the 1960s, a worldwide demand for garments made from big spotted cats caused these species to be relentlessly hunted for their pelts. When they became threatened with extinction, 54 countries in 1973 signed an international treaty, the Convention on International Trade in Endangered Species of Wild Fauna and Flora (CITES), to protect the cats. Eighty-seven countries now have signed the treaty, giving protection to all spotted cats by prohibiting their trade.

But the treaty did not quell the demand for garments made from spotted furs. The fashion industry began looking for an alternative to the exotic cats of Asia, Africa, and Central and South America. The bobcat provided that source. By 1976, the demand for its fur, with its distinct black spots, increased dramatically.

The sudden change in bobcat status from an undesirable predator to a valuable furbearer caused an unexpected and dramatic increase in the numbers killed. This alarmed conservation groups and wildlife managers. Would the bobcat become threatened, as had the leopard, cheetah, jaguar, and ocelot?

Because all cats are vulnerable to excessive exploitation, the CITES treaty was amended, imposing regulations on all cats. This amendment required signatory countries to produce estimates of felid abundance and to take necessary precautions and impose regulations so that trade would not threaten the survival of the cats. Suddenly the bobcat became an important management and political issue. In order to export bobcat furs, states were required to provide estimates of bobcat numbers and show that commercial trade would not threaten their population.

Conservation groups challenged the management position that adequate data existed on bobcat biology and ecology to safely take this species. Management maintained that they had taken adequate steps to protect bobcats. Wildlife managers and groups representing the fur industry petitioned the CITES treaty to remove the bobcat from consideration, arguing that bobcat populations were healthy and not endangered. They failed. Eventually, Congress settled the matter in 1982 in an amendment to the Endangered Species Act that said the states could not be required to make population estimates.

The debate centered around the fact that bobcats, because they are secretive, are difficult to count. Conservationists still disagree with some of the findings and techniques used by managers to estimate populations. In fact, managers often disagree with each other as to appropriate methods for estimating bobcat numbers.

An adequate estimate of animal numbers is basic for any management program, whether for deer, waterfowl, or bobcats. But bobcats are much more difficult to count than deer or waterfowl. Probably the most accurate method for estimating numbers of these secretive predators involves capture-mark-recapture or radio-telemetry techniques. But these techniques are expensive. Radio-telemetry studies can be done in representative habitats to provide a basis for density estimates as well as to provide information on mortality and productivity. This information, in conjunction with information from harvest records, habitat inventory, and prey density estimates, can provide adequate estimates of numbers for management over the species entire range. But the information must be gathered yearly to reflect changes of bobcat numbers in response to fluctuating prey populations.

Once population estimates are made, regulations are set to limit the take to acceptable levels, generally not to exceed the estimated annual recruitment of 20 percent. Different strategies are used: limiting the number of trapping or hunting licenses sold, setting a ceiling on the number of cats to be taken and closing the season once the quota is met, limiting the number each person can kill, controlling the length of the season and the months the season will occur, and limiting the methods by which cats can be taken.

Private organizations, too, have been instrumental in bobcat management. These groups review management plans and provide input into harvest regulations. They also provide funding for the research needed to assess bobcat densities and prey and habitat requirements. Research not only provides information beneficial to managers, but also provides for a better understanding and appreciation of the bobcat as part of the predator-prey system.

## PROGNOSIS

Prospects for the bobcat's future appear encouraging in part because of the present interest in its management. Bobcats are adaptable, inhabit a wide variety of habitats, and have a relatively high reproductive potential. Because of this they have weathered periods of intensive persecution, such as when they were controlled as predators or heavily trapped for furs.

Research has changed our perspective on the bobcat. Their habitat and prey requirements are more fully understood, and much of the mystery and stigma associated with these predators have been removed. It now is known that bobcats seldom prey on livestock and game animals. Except for localized problems, little need exists to control bobcats.

Bobcats can tolerate human activity. They have expanded their range into areas where limited agriculture and timber harvesting have provided favorable habitat. Where they have been eliminated, reintroducing bobcats may be a promising management option. However, intensive agriculture practices and urban sprawl destroy habitat. Here the survival of the bobcat may continue to be jeopardized. Too, local populations may suffer from overtrapping and overhunting, but these areas can be repopulated with individuals immigrating from adjacent protected areas.

Now that bobcats are in the management spotlight, greater care will be taken to prevent populations from being overhunted. Relief for bobcats may occur when demand for their fur falls from favor. As quickly as prices rose they may plummet, and hunting pressure on bobcats will diminish in response. In the meantime, managers and conservation groups are taking steps to insure the survival of the bobcat.

Bobcats are susceptible to excessive hunting and trapping pressure. Felids have few natural enemies, except for man, and so they had no need to evolve defenses to flee or defend themselves. The lack of defensive adaptations may explain why bobcats and other felids are so vulnerable to trapping and hunting.

## RECOMMENDATIONS

If the objective of management is to maintain reproducing populations in all habitats, regulations must remain flexible to accommodate yearly fluctuations in bobcat numbers. When populations are depressed, limits should be decreased or curtailed to protect resident breeding animals. Regulations also must accommodate for differences in density and productivity in the various habitats. Trapping quotas can be more liberal where bobcat densities are greater (Bailey 1981, Fuller *et al.* 1985, Knick *et al.* 1985, Rolley 1985).

Flexible regulations will pose difficulties for law enforcement personnel. Illegally transferring pelts, falsifying trapping records, or poaching may be expected. But these problems will have a minimal influence on bobcat populations. Flexible regulations will be safest for ensuring the continual survival of bobcats over the long term.

In places where refuges do not already exist, it may be advisable to set aside protected areas. These areas can provide a reproductive nucleus from which dispersing cats can repopulate outlying areas.

Where bobcats have been extirpated and where there is little opportunity for natural repopulation to occur, transplanting bobcats may be necessary. This has been successfully demonstrated in New Jersey.

Bobcats are adaptable predators. They are able to inhabit most areas where prey and cover are available. They have even expanded their range in some regions. Because of their wide distribution and high reproductive potential, they can sustain regulated hunting and trapping. But bobcats are easy to trap, so their populations must be closely monitored and take closely regulated. Ensuring the continued existence of bobcats as an integral part of the predator community of North America requires habitat to be protected, take to be regulated, and the public to be informed about the habits of these secretive predators.

## REFERENCES

Ackerman, B.B., F.G. Lindzey and T.P. Hemker. 1984. "Cougar food habits in southern Utah," *Journal of Wildlife Management* 48(1):147-155.

Bailey, T.N. 1972. Ecology of bobcats with special reference to social organization. Ph.D Dissertation. University of Idaho. Moscow, Idaho. 32 pp.

## 408 ◇ Species Accounts

———. 1974. "Social organization in a bobcat population," *Journal of Wildlife Management* 38:435-460.

Bailey, T.N. 1981. "Factors of bobcat social organization and some management implications," in J. Chapman and D. Pursley, eds., *Proceedings of the Worldwide Furbearer Conference* vol. II. Frostburg, Maryland. pp. 984-1000.

Beale, D.M. and A.D. Smith. 1973. "Mortality of pronghorn antelope fawns in western Utah," *Journal of Wildlife Management* 37 (3):343-352.

Beasom, S.L. 1974. "Relationships between predation removal and white-tailed deer net productivity," *Journal of Wildlife Management* 38(4):854-859.

———. and R.A. Moore. 1977. "Bobcat food habit response to a change in prey abundance," *Southwest Naturalist* 21(4):451-457.

Crowe, D.M. 1975. "A model for exploited bobcat populations in Wyoming," *Journal of Wildlife Management* 39(2):408-415.

Fuller, T.K., W.E. Berg, and D.W. Kuehn. 1985. "Survival rates and mortality factors of adult bobcats in North-Central Minnesota," *Journal of Wildlife Management* 49:292-296.

Fritts, S.H. and J.A. Sealander. 1978. "Diets of bobcats in Arkansas with special reference to age and sex differences," *Journal of Wildlife Management* 42(3):533-539.

Gashwiler, J.S., W.L. Robinette, and O.W. Morris. 1960. "Foods of bobcats in Utah and eastern Nevada," *Journal of Wildlife Management* 24(2):226-229.

Hamilton, W.J. Jr., and R.P. Hunter. 1939. "Fall and winter food habits of Vermont bobcats," *Journal of Wildlife Management* 3(2):99-103.

Jones, J.H. and N.S. Smith. 1979. "Bobcat density and prey selection in Central Arizona," *Journal of Wildlife Management* 43(3):666-672.

Keith, L.B. and L.A. Windberg. 1978. "A demographic analysis of the snowshoe hare cycle," *Wildlife Monograph* No. 58. p. 70.

Knick, S.T., J.D. Brittell, and S.J. Sweeney. 1985. "Population characteristics of bobcats in Washington state," *Journal of Wildlife Management* 49:721-728.

Koehler, G.M. Unpublished data.

Leach, H.R. and W.H. Frazier. 1953. "A study on the possible extent of predation on heavy concentrations of valley quail with special reference to the bobcat," *California Fish and Game* 39(4):527-538.

Major, J.T. 1983. Ecology and interspecific relationships of coyotes, bobcats, and red foxes in western Maine. Ph.D Dissertation. University of Maine. Orono, Maine. 64 pp.

Miller, S.D. and D.W. Speake. 1979. "Prey utilization by bobcats on quail plantations in southern Alabama," *Proceedings on the Annual Conference of the Southeast Associations of Fish and Wildlife Agencies* 32:100-111.

McCord, C.M. 1974. "Selection of winter habitat by bobcats (*Lynx rufus*) on the Quabbin Reservation, Massachusetts," *Journal of Mammalogy* 55(2):428-437.

———. and J.E. Cardoza. 1982. "Bobcat and lynx," in J. A. Chapman and G. A. Feldhamer, eds., *Wild Mammals of North America*. John Hopkins University Press. Baltimore, Maryland. pp. 728-766.

Nassbaum, R.A. and C. Maser. 1975. "Food habits of the bobcat, *Lynx rufus*, in the Coast and Cascade ranges of western Oregon in relation to present management policies," *Northwest Scientist* 49(4):261-266.

Nunley, G.L. 1978. "Present and historical bobcat population trends in New Mexico and the West," *Proceedings of the Vertebrate Pest Conference* 8:177-184.

Pollack, E.M. 1951. "Food habits of the bobcat in the New England states," *Journal of Wildlife Management* 15(2):209-213.

Progulske, D.R. 1955. "Game animals utilized as food by the bobcat in the Southern Appalachians," *Journal of Wildlife Management* 19(2):249-253.

Rolley, R.E. 1985. "Dynamics of a harvested bobcat populations in Oklahoma," *Journal of Wildlife Management* 49(2):283-292.

Rollings, C.T. 1945. "Habits, foods and parasites of the bobcat in Minnesota," *Journal of Wildlife Management* 9(2):131-145.

Seton, E.T. 1929. *Lives of Game Animals, Vol. 1, part 1: Cats, Wolves, and Foxes.* Charles Scribner's Sons. New York. 337 pp.

Zezulak, D.S. and R.G. Schwab. 1979. "A comparison of density, home range and habitat utilization of bobcat populations at Lava Beds and Joshua Tree National Monuments, California," in *Bobcat Resource Conference Proceedings of the National Wildlife Federation Science Technical Serial* 6. pp. 74-79.

*Gary Koehler is a wildlife biologist with the Wildlife Research Institute at the University of Idaho in Moscow.*

A lynx kitten bats its mother's ears. Lynx populations require close monitoring because the cat's fur is popular in the fashion industry. *Photo Researchers*

# The Lynx

## Stephen DeStefano
*University of Idaho*

## SPECIES DESCRIPTION AND NATURAL HISTORY

The lynx (*Felis lynx*) is a predator of the Northern Hemisphere's high-latitude and deep-snow boreal forest ecosystem. Traditionally, North American and Eurasian lynx were considered different species, *Lynx canadensis* and *L. lynx*, respectively. However, many authorities now believe the two are subspecies. A third population, the Spanish lynx of the Iberian Peninsula, is considered a separate species, *Felis pardina*, by some and a subspecies, *F. lynx pardina*, by others. Taxonomic and evolutionary relationships still are not clear (Corbet 1978, Nowak and Paradiso 1983).

### Physical Characteristics

In North America, lynx measure from two to three and a half feet long and weigh 10 to 40 pounds (Banfield 1974, Saunders 1964). Eurasian lynx are somewhat larger, measuring up to four feet long and weighing up to 70 pounds (Novikov 1962). Males generally are larger than females, and weights and physical dimensions also vary geographically (McCord and Cardoza 1982).

Coloration varies from yellowish brown to gray, often with a pattern of dark spots. The short tail may have several dark rings and is tipped with black. Long, ruff-like fur on the lower cheeks and tufts of black hairs on the tips of the ears give the lynx a distinctive face. The legs are relatively long and the paws large and densely furred, an adaptation for moving over snow.

Although similar to the bobcat (*F. rufus*), the lynx can be distinguished by its longer legs, larger feet, and longer ear tufts. It lacks the bobcat's more definite markings over the body, and its tail is black-tipped above and below, while the stubby tail of the bobcat is black only on the upperside of the tip (Murie 1963).

Lynx generally are noctural or crepuscular. Highly resistant to cold, they appear to be affected adversely by hot weather. They have poor endurance and usually ambush rather than chase prey (Banfield 1974).

## Range

Lynx are found throughout Canada except for the northern regions of Labrador, Quebec, and the Northwest Territories; the arctic archipelago; and the coastal mountains of British Columbia (McCord and Cardoza 1982). They inhabit most of Alaska, except for the coastal regions, but in the contiguous United States the only substantial populations are in northern Washington and Idaho and northwestern Montana, with lower densities extending down the Rocky Mountains into Utah and Colorado (McCord and Cardoza 1982). A few live in northern New England. On occasion, especially during periods of high population levels in Canada, lynx are found in the states of the northern plains and upper Great Lakes (Adams 1963). Lynx densities throughout the range vary widely, with highs and lows occurring in the 10-year population cycle. Density estimates are not available for most areas, but in Alberta lynx numbers changed from 10 to two individuals per 40 square miles during a decline in the snowshoe hare (*Lepus americanus*) population (Brand and Keith 1979).

Lynx also are widely distributed in the forest zone of the Soviet Union, the mountains of central Asia, and throughout western mainland Europe (Novikov 1962). The endangered Spanish lynx formerly occurred throughout the Iberian Peninsula, but now is restricted to scattered mountainous areas and the Guadalquivir Delta (Nowak and Paradiso 1983).

Lynx habitat has been described generally as climax boreal forest with a dense undercover of thickets and windfalls. Advanced successional stages of forests and dense conifer stands often are selected as habitat (Banfield 1974). Habitat quality and food abundance can influence home range size, which normally averages from four to 20 square miles per individual and at times up to 80 square miles (Brand *et al.* 1976, Carbyn and Patriquin 1983, Saunders 1963). Lynx reportedly move three to 18 miles a day. A movement of almost 300 miles was recorded for a young female (Mech 1977).

## Reproduction

Mating occurs mainly in February and March, beginning about mid-February in more northerly regions. Females bear a single litter of one to six, usually two or three, young yearly (Saunders 1963). Gestation lasts nine or 10 weeks, and kittens are born mid-May to mid-June.

Lactation can last for five to six months, but some meat is eaten by two- to six-week-old kittens. The young usually remain with their mother until the winter mating season, and siblings may stay together for a while afterward (Nowak and Paradiso 1983).

## Diet

Lynx throughout North America and Europe show remarkable consistency in diet. Little doubt exists that this cat is especially adapted to prey on rabbits. The snowshoe hare is the major prey species in North America, the mountain hare (*L. timidus*) is a primary food source in Europe, and the Old World rabbit (*Oryctolagus cuniculus*) is the basic prey of the Spanish lynx. Hares can comprise some 80 percent of the lynx diet. It has been estimated that lynx make a kill every other day and that an individual lynx may eat 170 to 200 hares yearly, plus a few birds and mice. Lynx sometimes cache prey and return later to feed upon them (Saunders 1963).

Grouse, squirrels, and small rodents can be important alternate prey items for all lynx populations. Ungulates in northern Europe and the Soviet Union and ducks on the Iberian Peninsula often make up a large portion of the diet (Borg 1962, Delibes 1980).

In North America, lynx rely on snowshoe hares more during winter than during summer. Their diet varies more when there is no snow cover, probably because of the greater availability of small mammals. However, snowshoe hares still comprise the majority of prey consumed during summer months. In some parts of Europe, lynx change their diet in early winter from one of hares, small mammals, and birds toward a higher proportion of ungulates (Birkeland and Myrberget 1980). Snow conditions can greatly influence hunting success. When the weight-bearing strength of snow is low, lynx will break through, while hare and grouse prey do not (Nellis and Keith 1968). Soft, deep snow also hinders the hunting ability of lynx. Thus in certain years with poor snow conditions, success can be low even if prey densities are high.

**Population Cycles**

North American lynx population trends probably have been recorded longer than those of any other wildlife species. Fur returns, useful as an index to population growth and decline, were recorded by the Hudson Bay Company for more than two centuries. Several authors have pointed out that fur returns, indicative of the size of the lynx population, fluctuated regularly from extremely high levels to very low levels, about every 10 years. The periods between peaks in population levels vary somewhat, but less than would be expected by chance (Bulmer 1974).

One researcher described the 10-year cycle as follows, "the basic cause of the cycles is the [snowshoe hare] interacting with its vegetable food to produce a predator-prey oscillation. When the rodents decline in numbers, the [lynx] become short of food, prey upon and cause the decrease of the gallinaceous birds of the same region and themselves die of starvation and/or emigrate . . . in large numbers [which] helps to synchronize various regions" (Lack 1954).

The following points about the 10-year cycle also have been made: (1) lynx have followed a 10-year cycle at the continental level for the past 200 years, (2) lynx can remain common in some areas two to three years after the hares decline, though in Alaska, lynx declined immediately after hares declined, (3) lynx fluctuations have been more extreme than those of other furbearers, (4) mass movements of hares, lynx, foxes (*Vulpes vulpes*), martens (*Martes americana*), and other species probably have taken place, and (5) the amplitude of recent lynx cycles has declined markedly as the peaks in the cycle have become lower (Bailey *et al.* 1986, Keith 1963, O'Conner 1984).

# SIGNIFICANCE OF THE SPECIES

The lynx has important economic, recreational, scientific, and aesthetic value. Throughout its range it is classified as a furbearer and provides recreational opportunities and economic returns for trappers. More recently, formal seasons have been established in the northwestern United States for hunters who use hounds to pursue and tree lynx. Pelt values can vary considerably with individual quality and demand, but generally provide some of the highest monetary returns of any fur.

In certain instances, lynx may regulate or influence some prey population levels. Declines of arctic hare (*L. arcticus*) and caribou (*Rangifer tarandus*) on Newfoundland have been attributed to lynx predation pressure (Bergerud 1967, 1971). However, it is generally believed that lynx do not cause the density of their rabbit prey to decline, but rather the level of available prey influences the survival, abundance, and reproductive success of the lynx. Nevertheless, when hare numbers are low, lynx may keep the hare population depressed for two or three years before the increase phase begins.

In some high-elevation forests in the Pacific Northwest the presence of the lynx is considered an indicator of ecosystem integrity. In these areas, lynx generally inhabit the timbered ridgetops and slopes where harvests of such species as lodgepole pine (*Pinus contorta*) are being planned.

The scientific value of the lynx is tremendous. The 10-year cycle is among the most intriguing phenomena in nature. Much can be learned about predator-prey relationships, wildlife population dynamics, and the ecology of predators in general and felids in particular from the study of the lynx. Aesthetic values are nebulous and impossible to quantify realistically, but to many people the lynx's secretive nature, periodic abundance and scarcity, and ability to survive in severe winter cold and deep snow make it a symbol of the boreal forest.

## HISTORICAL PERSPECTIVE

The range of the lynx in North America before European settlement probably was very similar to what it is today, with the exception of its southern edge. It is possible that lynx range once extended south to cover the northern third of the United States. However, lynx were not often distinguished from bobcats in historical or bounty records, so some confusion exists in regard to the southern extent of the former range. Historical records indicate that lynx were found in low to moderate densities throughout forested sections of Wisconsin, New York, Vermont, New Hampshire, Maine, Nova Scotia, and Newfoundland (Orff 1985). Similar densities were present in the western mountains as far south as Oregon and Colorado. Local lynx populations in other parts of Canada and Alaska probably have experienced declines due to agricultural, industrial, and suburban development, but these declines could be considered relatively minor compared to those caused by habitat loss in the northern United States and southeastern Canada.

However, from 1880 to 1920, a time included in the height of wild-fur trade, successive peaks in the lynx cycle showed continued declines (Todd unpubl. report). Throughout this period each new peak in the lynx harvest was lower than those preceding it. In the late 1880s, about 80,000 lynx were pelted, but by the early 1900s the number had dropped to 20,000 (Todd unpubl. report). This trend continued through 1940.

The available evidence suggests that a major decline in lynx abundance occurred during a period of less than 30 years around the turn of the century, when fur-trade trapping was basically unregulated on the western frontier. Intense exploitation is seen as the primary reason for the lynx decline (Elton and Nicholson 1942, Devos and Matel 1952). Pelt prices remained stable throughout this period, so a lack of economic incentive was not responsible for the smaller fur harvests.

Lynx were considered pests in the early 1900s and attempts were made to control their numbers. Bounties were still offered in some states in the 1960s, but lynx are no longer considered undesirable (Siegler 1971).

## CURRENT TRENDS

The lynx had re-occupied much of its former range by the early 1960s. These gains continued into the early 1970s, but data now indicate that the occupied range has shrunk again (Todd unpubl. report).

In the early 1980s, lynx were present in 14 states and all Canadian provinces and territories except Prince Edward Island (Deems and Pursley 1983). Accurate, or even rough estimates, of lynx numbers do not exist because of this cat's secretive nature, generally low densities, and confounding population dynamics. However, the best compendium on the status of the lynx in North America can be found in Jorgensen and Mech (1971). Status reports are included for Alaska, British Columbia, Saskatchewan, Wisconsin, New Hampshire, and the northwestern states. These reports suggest that trapping was not the only factor involved in local declines of lynx populations. They also indicate that, in general, lynx populations are secure in Canada and Alaska, but withdrawing from the heavily human-populated southern fringe of the species' range. State reports from New England, New York, Wisconsin, and Wyoming indicate that lynx are present but in very low densities.

Research in Canada and Alaska indicates that increased trapping pressure and habitat alteration and destruction are still having negative impacts on lynx populations in some areas. This is particularly true for lynx along the southern edge of the range, where densities are low and access to trap lines is high. The implications seem to be that heavy trapping, spurred by large jumps in pelt prices, is largely responsible for the decline in lynx abundance throughout much of the range. Only remote regions in the Yukon and Northwest Territories have shown actual increases in the latest cyclic peaks compared to previous peaks

(Todd unpubl. report). Habitat loss is considered of secondary importance and is probably more critical along the southern edge of the range.

Some researchers believe that intense trapping when lynx are at low levels could be a form of additive mortality, removing adult lynx that normally would survive during the cyclic lows and reproduce when snowshoe hares increase (Brand and Keith 1979). A similar increase in mortality also could occur when adult lynx are isolated in "pockets" of suitable habitat and adequate food supply during low-density years, especially if large numbers of trappers have access to these pockets (Berrie 1974, Todd unpubl. report). Maintaining an adequate breeding stock during low population years is critical to ensure a swift and substantial increase in lynx numbers during the increase phase of the 10-year cycle. If this management objective is not attained, the major long-term impact seems to point toward lynx populations that cycle about a lower mean level and that show markedly reduced population peaks.

Although trapping and poisoning of lynx were once widely practiced in Europe and Russia, regulated hunting and trapping seasons now exist. Scandinavian and Finnish-Russian lynx populations are once again becoming contiguous, possibly because of reduced hunting, better food conditions, and reduced competition from wolves. Reintroduction of lynx has been carried out in parts of Germany, Austria, Switzerland, Italy, and Yugoslavia (Heggberget and Myrberget 1980, Smit and Van Wijngaarden 1976).

The Spanish lynx is classified as endangered and is confined to isolated, mainly mountainous areas in central and southern Spain and Portugal. The total population is estimated at 1,000 to 1,500, but is rapidly declining because of habitat loss, disease, and accidental kills (Delibes 1979).

## MANAGEMENT

Lynx management generally focuses on regulating the yearly kill, with trapping and hunting confined to specified seasons during the winter months. In Canada, trappers are required to operate on registered trap lines or areas. In Washington, lynx can be pursued with hounds on a limited basis and both trappers and hunters are required to register lynx pelts with the Department of Game. Currently lynx are subjected to limited harvest in six states and 10 provinces and territories and are receiving total protection in nine states and one province. The lynx is on the endangered species lists of Colorado, New Hampshire, and Wisconsin and is listed in Appendix II of the Convention on International Trade and Endangered Species of Wild Flora and Fauna treaty (Defenders of Wildlife 1984), giving it some protection from the international fur trade.

Many states and provinces currently are monitoring or planning to monitor lynx populations. Private organizations, such as Defenders of Wildlife, urge that the status of the lynx throughout its range be carefully monitored and that management be reevaluated, taking into account the rise in pelt prices (Defenders of Wildlife 1984).

Published accounts on habitat management for lynx are scarce. Research is being conducted in the northwestern states to determine habitat use and to evaluate the impact of timber harvest on lynx distribution on national forest lands.

## PROGNOSIS

Research suggests that lynx populations are relatively stable throughout much of the North American range. However, in some regions local populations have declined to levels lower than the apparent normal cyclic lows of the recent past. Many researchers believe that more effective management will have to be developed and applied if exploitation of this species increases. The extreme fluctuations in numbers, coupled with the ease with which the species can be trapped, could contribute to severe local reductions of breeding stock. Although the lynx may be considered safe throughout much of its range, populations levels should be watched closely. Increasing economic value of lynx pelts could influence pressure on local populations (Jorgensen and Mech 1971).

The influence of pelt value on lynx harvests is of critical importance. As recently as the 1984-85 season the price on a prime lynx pelt soared to over $1,000. Average pelt price was $650 (Haefer, Moscow Hide and Fur, pers. comm.). With price tags such as these the incentive is created to sacrifice conservation and long-term economic productivity for short-term economic gain (Todd unpubl. report).

It is possible that local populations, and possibly populations over broad parts of the range, will decline if pelt prices continue to rise and trapping pressure intensifies along with increased habitat loss. Some biologists believe that these trends will continue and, therefore, that the concept of a lynx surplus suitable for trapping will have to be reevaluated (Bailey unpubl. summ.). They also suggest that new management strategies for lynx need to be developed because lynx occur in fluctuating and highly unpredictable environments, cycle over eight to 11 year periods, usually are dependent on hares as their sole source of food, and are highly vulnerable to trapping, especially in accessible areas.

One management strategy that has been suggested is to curtail or cease the taking of lynx for three years during the declining phase of the 10-year cycle (Brand and Keith 1979). During this time, recruitment of kittens into the population is very low or nonexistent. The surviving adults therefore play the extremely important role of restocking the population. Reducing trapping mortality for three or more years during the population phase decline would lessen the population crash. In highly accessible areas with few natural refugia, curtailment of trapping up to five years, followed by quotas or shortened seasons, may be necessary to prevent overexploitation (Bailey *et al.* 1986).

Other factors have been named as possible agents involved in reducing lynx abundance. Habitat loss, severe winters, industrial development, and snowshoe hare population levels have had some localized influence, but only contributed a fraction of the total impact.

It is unlikely that the lynx will be classified as endangered throughout its range in the foreseeable future, but it may become increasingly rare in areas accessible to large numbers of trappers and susceptible to habitat alteration or destruction. What is likely is that increasingly stringent trapping regulations will be needed in some areas to ensure that viable local populations continue to exist at or near carrying capacity. A drastic drop in fur prices could improve the outlook in heavily trapped areas.

## RECOMMENDATIONS

Theodore N. Bailey recommended that ideal lynx management should be (1) highly flexible, (2) rapidly responsive to sudden changes in lynx habitat or prey abundance, (3) able to predict the impact of trapping on the entire lynx cycle rather than only on the following year's population, (4) closely tied to snowshoe hare abundance and distribution, (5) able to consider offspring dependence on females by adjusting trapping periods, and (6) able to provide for adequate stocks and distributions of breeding adults during years of low prey abundance (Bailey unpubl. summ.).

Several trapping regulations have been suggested. These include closing the season for three to five years once lynx and hare populations have peaked, shorter and later seasons, quotas and permits based on management areas, untrapped sanctuaries, and perhaps restricting the use of exposed bait, flag, and cubby sets during other furbearer seasons to reduce incidental lynx capture (Bailey *et al.* 1986, Brand and Keith 1979). Continued and improved monitoring of lynx populations throughout the range is essential to developing proper base-line data from which management decisions can be made.

In 1978, several biologists reviewed whether international trade in species listed under Appendix II of CITES was detrimental to the survival of those species (Mech 1978). They recommended that each state review its lynx research and management programs and seek to improve them in order to help ensure continued lynx survival. This directive still can be considered a timely one today.

Virtually every aspect of lynx biology, ecology, and management is in need of further research. The impact of trapping, habitat alteration, and human interference on local population levels and social organization is vital to the management of this species, especially on the southern edge of lynx range where numbers may be declining. Studies designed to remove certain individuals and to manipulate habitat could provide answers about man's influence on lynx populations. Individuals which are taken from a population during removal studies could be introduced into low-density areas, thereby providing information on possible stocking programs. Concurrent studies on lynx and bobcats could help determine whether the species compete for the same resources or if they are ecologically separated by differences in adaptation or habitat preference. Additional basic knowledge of social organization, predator-prey relationships, and habitat preference also is needed.

The challenge of lynx conservation and management is a multifaceted one. Pelt values and the fur harvest, the 10-year cycle, survival, mortality, changing reproductive parameters, and habitat loss all play a part in the population dynamics of this native cat.

## REFERENCES

Adams, A.W. 1963. "The lynx explosion," *North Dakota Outdoors* 26(5):20-24.

Bailey, T.N. Lynx management: some considerations and suggestions. Unpublished Summ., U.S. Fish and Wildlife Service. Soldotna, Alaska.

———. E.E. Bangs, M.F. Portner, J.C. Malloy, and R.J. McAvinchey. 1986. "An apparent overexploited lynx population on the Kenai Peninsula, Alaska," *Journal of Wildlife Management* 50:279-90.

Banfield, A.W.F. 1974. *The Mammals of Canada*. Nature Museum of Canada. University of Toronto Press. Toronto, Canada. 438 pp.

Bergerud, A.T. 1967. "The distribution and abundance of arctic hares in Newfoundland," *Canadian Field Naturalist* 81:242-248.

Bergerud, A.T. 1971. "The population dynamics of Newfoundland caribou," *Wildlife Monograph* 25. 55 pp.

Berrie, P.M. 1974. "Ecology and status of the lynx in interior Alaska," *in* R.L. Eaton ed., *The World's Cats, Vol. 1*. World Wildlife Safari. Winston, Oregon. 349 pp.

Birkeland, K.H., and S. Myrberget. 1980. "The diet of the lynx *Lynx lynx* in Norway," *Fauna Norv. Ser. A* 1:24-28.

Borg, K. 1962. "Predation on roe deer in Sweden," *Journal of Wildlife Management* 27:384-390.

Brand, C.J., and L.B. Keith. 1979. "Lynx demography during a snowshoe hare decline in Alberta," *Journal of Wildlife Management* 48:827-849.

Brand, C.J., L.B. Keith, and C.A. Fischer. 1976. "Lynx responses to changing snowshoe hare densities in central Alberta," *Journal of Wildlife Management* 40:416-428.

Bulmer, M.G. 1974. "A statistical analysis of the 10-year cycle in Canada," *Journal of Animal Ecology* 43:701-718.

Carbyn, L.N., and D. Patriquin. 1983. "Observations on home range sizes, movements and social organization of lynx, *Lynx canadensis*, in Riding Mountain National Park, Manitoba," *Canadian Field Naturalist* 97:262-267.

Corbet, G.B. 1978. *The Mammals of the Palearctic Region: A Taxonomic Review*. British Museum of Natural History. Cornell University Press. London and Ithaca, New York. 314 pp.

Deems, E.F., Jr. and D. Pursley, eds. 1983. *North American Furbearers*. International Association for Fish and Wildlife Agencies and Maryland Department of Natural Resources - Wildlife Administration. 223 pp.

Defenders of Wildlife. 1984. "Lynx," *Saving Endangered Species: A Report and Plan for Action*. Defenders of Wildlife. Washington, D.C. May 1984.

Delibes, M. 1979. [The lynx in the Iberian Peninsula.] Bulletin Mens. Off. Nation. Chasse No. Sp. Scien. Tech. le Lynx. pp. 41-46. (In French, Eng. Summary)

Delibes, M. 1980. "Feeding ecology of the Spanish lynx in the Coto Donana," *Acta Theriologica* 25(4):309-324.

DeVos, A., and S.E. Matel. 1952. "The status of the lynx in Canada, 1920-1952," *Journal of Forestry* 50:742-745.

Elton, C., and M. Nicholson. 1942. "The ten-year cycle in numbers of the lynx in Canada," *Journal of Animal Ecology* 11:215-244.

Heggberget, T.M., and S. Myrberget. 1980. "The Norwegian lynx *Lynx lynx* population in the 1970's," *Fauna Norvegica Series A*, 1:29-33.

Jorgensen, S.E., and L.D. Mech. 1971. *Proceedings of Symposium on the Native Cats of North America; Their Status and Management*. U.S. Bureau of Sport Fisheries and Wildlife, Portland. 139 pp.

Keith, L.B. 1963. *Wildlife's Ten-Year Cycle*. University of Wisconsin Press. Madison, Wisconsin. 201 pp.

Lack, D. 1954. "Cyclic mortality," *Journal of Wildlife Management* 18:25-37.

McCord, C.M., and J.E. Cardoza. 1982. "Bobcat and lynx," *in* J.A. Chapman and G.A. Feldhamer eds., *Wild Mammals of North America*. John Hopkins University Press. Baltimore, Maryland. pp. 728-766.

Mech, L.D. 1977. "Record movement of a Canadian lynx," *Journal of Mammalogy* 58:676-677.

Mech, L.D. 1978. *Report of the Working Group on Bobcat, Lynx, and River Otter*. National Science Foundation. Washington, D.C. 15 pp.

Murie, A. 1963. *A Naturalist in Alaska*. Devin-Adair Co., New York. 302 pp.

Nellis, C.H., and L.B. Keith. 1968. "Hunting activities and success of lynxes in Alberta," *Journal of Wildlife Management* 32:718-722.

Novikov, G.A. 1962. *Carnivorous Mammals of the Fauna of the USSR*. Israel Program of Scientific Translation, Jerusalem. 284 pp.

Nowak, R.M., and J.L. Paradiso. 1983. *Walker's Mammal's of the World, 4th ed.* John Hopkins University Press. Baltimore, Maryland. 1,362 pp.

O'Conner, R.M. 1984. Population trends, age structures, and reproductive characteristics of female lynx in Alaska, 1961 through 1973. Unpublished master's thesis. University of Alaska, Fairbanks. 111 pp.

Orff, E.P. 1985. Northeast lynx (*Felis lynx*) status report. Unpublished report. New Hampshire Fish and Game Department. Concord, New Hampshire. 2 pp.

Saunders, J.K., Jr. 1963. "Movements and activities of the lynx in Newfoundland," *Journal of Wildlife Management* 27:390-400.

Saunders, J.K., Jr. 1964. "Physical characteristics of the Newfoundland lynx," *Journal of Mammalogy* 45:36-47.

Siegler, H.R. 1971. "The status of wildcats in New Hampshire," *in* S.E. Jorgensen and L.D. Mech eds., *Proceedings of the Symposium on the Native Cats of North America.* U.S. Bureau of Sport, Fish and Wildlife. Portland. 139 pp.

Smit, C.J., and A. Van Wijngaarden. 1976. *Threatened Mammals of Europe.* European Committee for the Conservation of Nature and Natural Resources. 189 pp.

Todd, A.W. no date. The Canada lynx, interesting and valuable wildcat of the North. Unpublished Report. Alberta Fish and Wildlife Division. 16 pp.

*Stephen DeStefano, a research assistant with the University of Idaho's Wildlife Research Institute, participated in a northern Washington lynx study.*

A U.S. Fish and Wildlife Service biologist prepares to release a cui-ui after studying it. The species is at the center of an intense water-rights controversy in Nevada and California. *U.S. Fish and Wildlife Service*

# The Cui-ui

Chester C. Buchanan

and

Mark E. Coleman
*U.S. Fish and Wildlife Service*

## SPECIES DESCRIPTION AND NATURAL HISTORY

The cui-ui (*Chasmistes cujus*), pronounced "kwee-wee," is a large, omnivorous sucker found only in Pyramid Lake, Nevada. The dorsal side of its plump, coarsely-scaled body is blackish-brown, while the ventral side is creamy-white. Female cui-ui can live up to 42 years. Males do not live as long, with few reaching their late twenties. Both sexes grow at about the same rate until they reach maturity between six and 12 years of age. They are approximately four inches long at age one and 12 inches long at age five (Scoppettone *et al.* 1986). At maturity, male growth slows to about a quarter inch per year and female growth to about a half inch per year. Ultimately, some may reach a length of 27 inches.

Though it is a lake-dwelling species, the cui-ui can spawn only in streams. Each spring, adults congregate near the mouth of the Truckee River prior to migration upstream. The spawning run begins in April or May, depending on river inflow and water temperatures, and continues for four to eight weeks. Approximately 80 percent of the fish enter the river over a seven to 14-day period (Coleman 1986).

Audubon Wildlife Report 1987

425

The size of the spawning run depends on the size and year-class structure of the adult population, river accessibility, and river inflow. When lake elevation and spring inflows are high, spawning runs are large.

Cui-ui spawners do not migrate far upstream. Most fish remain in the lower three to six miles of the river, while a few may travel nearly 12 miles. They spend up to 16 days in the river: one to 11 days acclimating before spawning and one to five days after spawning is initiated. Like other suckers, cui-ui spawn in small groups, depositing eggs over a broad area of predominately gravel substrate in water 10 inches to four feet deep, where water velocities are one to two feet per second (Scoppettone *et al.* 1983). Once an adult has finished spawning, it moves within hours back to the lake. Although some cui-ui spawn every year, it is suspected that most spawn only once every three or four years.

Female cui-ui produce large numbers of small eggs. Average fecundity increases from approximately 20,000 eggs for a 16-inch female to 105,000 for a 26-inch fish, but when individuals reach about 30 years of age, egg viability decreases dramatically. Fertilized eggs hatch in one to two weeks, depending on water temperature (Koch 1982). High embryo mortality occurs when daily maximum temperatures exceed 63 degrees. After the eggs hatch, the yolk-sac larvae spend five to 10 days in the gravel before they emerge. Upon emergence most larvae are swept passively downstream to the lake, although a few may find refuge in the river's backwaters for a month or two.

Most larvae, after reaching the lake, remain in the shallow littoral zone feeding on zooplankton. In the late summer they disperse into deeper water, where both larvae and adults feed on zooplankton and benthic invertebrates. Although the movements of larvae and adults in Pyramid Lake are not well known, they commonly are found near the bottom in 50 to 100 feet of water throughout the year.

## SIGNIFICANCE OF THE SPECIES

The cui-ui is the last pure species of the genus *Chasmistes*, giving it a special importance to biologists. Other members of this genus, the June sucker (*C. liorus*) of Utah Lake and the shortnose sucker (*C. brevirostus*) of Upper Klamath Lake have hybridized with other suckers (Sigler *et al.* 1985).

Archaeological evidence indicates that the fishes of Pyramid Lake have been important to man for at least the past 4,000 years (Knach and Stewart 1984). The Kuyuidokado band of the Northern Paiute culture is the latest to center its activities around the lake. Kuyuidokado literally means "cui-ui eaters." The band is known today as the Pyramid Lake Paiute Tribe. Before the cui-ui declined following European contact, these Indians fished from the mouth of the Truckee River to several miles upstream. Cui-ui and the Pyramid Lake strain of Lahontan cutthroat trout (*Salmo clarki henshawi*) were eaten fresh or air-dried for later use.

During the cui-ui spawning run, other Northern Paiute bands would gather with the Kuyuidokado to share in the catch. This was a time of abundant food and celebration (Hummel 1881). Fishing was so much a part of the tribe's cultural heritage that even after the federal government restricted it to a reservation surrounding Pyramid Lake in the 1850s, the Paiutes refused to give up subsistence fishing for farming and ranching. Their resistance was in vain, because the decline of the cui-ui population and extinction of the trout left them no choice. However, the cui-ui is still important to the Kuyuidokado culture, and these people are playing an instrumental role in seeking the restoration of the cui-ui population.

White settlers considered the cui-ui to be quite unpalatable. That attitude may have stemmed from the Indian's fish-drying activities, which created a distinct aroma in the area, or from the fish's ungainly appearance (Knach and Stewart 1984, Hummel 1881). Many people today in the Reno, Sparks, and Fallon areas of Nevada still have a distinct dislike for this plump sucker because they fear that federal protection of the fish will stifle local water-development projects. In fact, cui-ui protection may help the region's water-management agencies to development better water-conservation programs.

## HISTORICAL PERSPECTIVE

At the beginning of the 20th century, cui-ui inhabited Pyramid and Winnemucca lakes. The beds of these lakes lie in adjacent topographically closed basins connected by a shallow channel. Pyramid Lake, covering only 180 square miles, is a remnant of ancient Lake Lahontan, which covered about 8,700 square miles of the Great Basin region of Nevada from about 9,000 to 40,000 years ago (Benson 1978, Galat *et al.* 1981). The Truckee River, fed primarily by melting snows in the Sierra Nevada range nearly 130 river-miles to the west, is the lake's only permanent water source. Before 1930, the river would occasionally split its channel just south of Pyramid and Winnemucca lakes, sending inflow to either or both lakes. Before man began regulating the river, average annual inflow to the lakes was about 600,000 acre-feet, with precipitation adding another 50,000 acre-feet. Current flow has been about halved, with devastating effects on the cui-ui.

It is generally agreed that in the past some cui-ui swam farther up the Truckee River to spawn than they do today. In the 1800s, it was reported that some cui-ui spawned nearly 25 miles upstream, while today they commonly go no further than six to 12 miles (Coleman 1986, Hummel 1881, Snyder 1917). This change in spawning location may be due to the creation of new river habitat in areas previously flooded by Pyramid Lake, a reduced spawning-run size, or both.

Historical sizes of the cui-ui population and spawning runs are not known. Only general observations have been reported, such as that by Snyder in 1917 when he noted that ". . . at times 'cui-ui' appeared in such large and densely packed schools that considerable numbers were crowded out of the water in shallow places . . ." From such descriptions, and the fact that runs fed many people, it seems reasonable to assume that spawning runs may have numbered in the hundreds of thousands and that the lake population was much larger.

Natural flow of the Truckee River has been altered so much in the past 100 years that the continued existence of the cui-ui is in jeopardy. Because of large diversions for agriculture and urban use, in combination with prolonged droughts, the cui-ui population today is only a fraction of what it was historically.

Rights and priorities to these waters were not adjudicated until the Orr Ditch Decree in 1944. This action, which the federal government initiated in 1913, established rights for hydroelectric generation, irrigation, storage, and municipal and other uses, with priority dates ranging from 1859 to 1902. The Pyramid Lake Paiute Tribe was allocated an irrigation right for about five percent of the historic normal flow. The need for water to maintain the lake's fish resources was ignored. The decree affirmed the federal government's actions of storing and diverting the remaining water as needed. With an increasing demand for agricultural and urban water, the future of the cui-ui was threatened.

The single-most detrimental impact on the cui-ui has been the huge water withdrawals for the Bureau of Reclamation's Newlands Project. Under the Newlands Project, Truckee River water since 1907 has been diverted for agricultural and domestic use from Derby Dam, about 20 miles east of Reno, through the Truckee Canal to the Lahontan Valley in the Carson River drainage. Year-round diversions for hydroelectric generation were allowed until 1967. From 1901 through 1970, nearly half or more of the river was diverted for irrigable lands that covered an area about half the size of Pyramid Lake (Sigler *et al.* 1985, Summer 1940).

As a consequence of the Newlands Project diversions and upstream diversions and storage, river flows below Derby Dam during normal-water years were reduced to levels that under natural conditions commonly occurred only during droughts. These diversions, in combination with droughts, caused Pyramid Lake to recede 85 feet in 60 years to its lowest elevation in nearly 4,000 years (Benson 1978). By 1938, Winnemucca Lake, then a national wildlife refuge, had gone dry. If the 1970s average annual inflow of 324,000 acre-feet had continued, Pyramid Lake would have receded another 100 feet more before reaching equilibrium (Brown *et al.* 1986).

Problems associated with declining lake depth already were apparent in the early decades of this century. As the lake receded, a delta formed across the mouth of the Truckee River. By 1926, the delta was so massive that fish became hopelessly stranded in the shallow river channels (Sumner 1940). From then on, cui-ui probably could reproduce only during high-water years, when sufficient flows created a passable channel through the delta (Scoppettone *et al.* 1983).

Until 1964, the maintenance of Pyramid Lake and restoration of the cui-ui were given little consideration in the management of the Truckee River. In that year, the secretary of the Interior formed a task force to recommend ways to resolve water-use conflicts on the Truckee and Carson rivers. Three years later, one of the recommendations led to the first attempt to increase inflow to Pyramid Lake by establishing a set of operating criteria and procedures for controlling the diversion of water from the Truckee River to the farmlands of the Newlands Project. Because of lengthy lawsuits and appeals, the new criteria were not enforced until 1984.

The Newlands Project is not the only irrigation district that has a history of using excessive quantities of Truckee River water. During normal-water years it was common for water districts in the Truckee Meadows area near Reno to allow more water to be diverted than they had a right to divert. These practices not only decreased river flow, they also degraded the water quality and disrupted the timing of flows. The Pyramid Lake Paiute Tribe and the U.S. Justice Department were successful recently in petitioning the U.S. District Court to order the water districts to develop a reasonable program to make diversions consistent with water entitlements. These water-saving measures should help the cui-ui by improving water quality, quantity, and timing.

Another factor in the near collapse of the cui-ui population was the control of Truckee River flows. Court decrees established criteria for maintaining river flows to meet decreed water rights. These regulatory actions were established with no regard for Pyramid Lake, thereby causing the cui-ui to suffer from reduced river flows during their spawning period.

The completion of Stampede Dam and Reservoir on the Little Truckee River, nearly 90 miles upstream of Pyramid Lake, turned out to be of significant importance in reestablishing suitable river flow for cui-ui. Built under the authority of the Washoe Project Act, the dam became operational in 1970. It was designed to store unappropriated seasonal floodwaters for irrigation, power generation, municipal water supply, recreation, and fish and wildlife resources, with particular reference given to fishes of Pyramid Lake. Faulty planning initially over-appropriated the limited water supply of the Little Truckee River so that all planned allocations could not be satisfied. Therefore, the secretary of the Interior, in order to satisy his obligation under the Endangered Species Act and his trust responsibility to the Pyramid Lake Paiute Tribe, ordered that the reservoir be operated only for the benefit of the threatened and endangered fishes of Pyramid Lake and for limited flood control.

Since 1976, the U.S. Fish and Wildlife Service (FWS) has used Stampede storage to supplement river-flow timing and volume to influence cui-ui and Lahontan cutthroat trout spawning runs and to maintain water temperatures suitable for egg incubation.[1] The U.S. District Court for the District of Nevada in 1982 affirmed the secretary's authority by ruling that the secretary was to use ". . . the waters stored in Stampede Reservoir for the benefit of the Pyramid Lake fishery until such time as the cui-ui and Lahontan cutthroat trout are no longer classified as threatened or endangered, or until sufficient water becomes available from other sources to conserve the cui-ui and Lahontan cutthroat trout." The U.S. Ninth Circuit Court of Appeals affirmed this decision, and the U.S. Supreme Court declined to review the case. This gave the cui-ui its only assured water supply.

Also built as part of the Washoe Project Act by the Bureau of Reclamation in 1976 were Marble Bluff Dam and Marble Bluff Fish Facility, which included the Pyramid Lake Fishway. These facilities on the Truckee River three miles upstream of Pyramid Lake were significant restoration actions for the cui-ui because they provide passage around the river delta when lake level is limiting and help control erosion of cui-ui spawning habitat upstream of the dam. When fish can make it over the delta, the facilities provide a means of capture and passage upstream of the dam.

## CURRENT TRENDS

Since cui-ui are long-lived, they have been able to resist man's onslaught long enough to take advantage of the occasional high-water

---

1. Lahontan cutthroat trout, a threatened species, was reintroduced in the 1950s and is maintained by hatchery reproduction.

years that allowed for reproduction. From 1950 to 1980, only two major year-classes of cui-ui were produced, one from 1950 and another from 1969. Today, the few individuals remaining from the 1950 year-class are reproductively impotent, while those of the 1969 year-class are near their reproductive zenith. The 1969 class, roughly 100,000 individuals, dominates the adult population.

Since 1980 six successful cui-ui spawning runs have occurred. These were facilitated by three abnormally wet years that raised the Pyramid Lake level some 30 feet, increased the passage capabilities of the Marble Bluff Fish Facility, and filled Stampede Reservoir to near capacity, making water available for use during the spawning run. The runs averaged 13,600 fish and ranged from 5,000 to 36,300. However, these runs are small compared to historic runs and, although hundreds of millions of larvae were produced by these runs, a lack of statistics precludes prediction of the adequacy of these new year-classes to sustain the population.

As in the past, the threat to cui-ui continues to be water diversions and river-management practices. Even though the full 226,000 acre-foot storage capacity of Stampede Reservoir is potentially available for the fish, it is not adequate to sustain the species. The average usable storage available each year in Stampede is approximately 50,000 acre-feet, as compared to the 400,000 acre-feet required to maintain Pyramid Lake, of which a minimum of 200,000 acre-feet is required during the spring for spawning. These volumes are available during wet years without Stampede supplementation, but usually are not available during normal-water years.

Improvements have been made in the Truckee Meadows diversion operations and in managing Stampede storage, but the efficiency of the Newlands Project delivery system is still extremely low, and controlled flow rates for the Truckee River and upstream reservoir management remain unchanged. In 1985, for example, delivery efficiency for the Newlands Project averaged only 55 percent. The other 45 percent remainder was lost through seepage, spills, and evaporation. Because of this the Bureau of Reclamation implemented a water-conservation and management program that is expected to cut project-wide water losses to 37 percent by 1991. The bureau also is developing new long-term operating criteria and procedures for the Newlands Project that, starting in 1987, will replace the interim criteria used since 1984. The bureau's objective is to limit diversions from the Truckee River within the decreed water rights for the Newlands Project, thereby making additional water available to Pyramid Lake. Physical improvements to the project which could increase delivery efficiences are not proposed at this time because funding is not available.

# MANAGEMENT

Nevada and the federal government have instituted protective measures to ensure the continued existence of the cui-ui. The cui-ui was listed as an endangered species in 1967 and a recovery plan was approved in 1978. It also was listed as endangered by the Nevada Department of Wildlife. The goal of the federal *Cui-ui Recovery Plan* is to restore and maintain an optimum self-sustaining population in the Truckee River/Pyramid Lake system. This will be achieved through proper management of the species and rehabilitation of the species' historical habitat. The FWS management objective is to create opportunities for cui-ui to produce as many year-classes as possible. This is done by managing Stampede Reservoir releases to maximize the occurrence of suitable river and lake conditions during spawning runs and by operating the Marble Bluff Fish Facility. Research goals are to define an optimum self-sustaining population, to determine the number of recruits required to achieve and maintain such a population, and to refine knowledge of environmental stimulants and other requirements. FWS and the Pyramid Lake Paiute Tribe also are trying actively to persuade irrigation districts and/or authorities to improve their water-delivery efficiencies and river-management practices on the Truckee River.

Each year, FWS personnel develop a water release program for using available storage in Stampede Reservoir to create the best possible river flow for cui-ui reproductive success. The flow regimes also help in the collection of cui-ui and cutthroat trout eggs for hatchery incubation. When sufficient water is in storage, it is used to create suitable attraction flows and to supplement background flows below Derby Dam in order to maintain cui-ui spawning habitat. Without such releases, many of the spawning runs since 1976 would not have occurred, and the reproductive success of those that did occur would have been much less.

Until there is some assurance of the cui-ui population becoming self-sustaining, it must be augmented with hatchery rearing. In the early 1970s, FWS, with the assistance of the Pyramid Lake Paiute Tribe, created a small hatchery near Pyramid Lake for developing techniques for spawning and rearing cui-ui. With the completion of the tribe's David Koch Cui-ui Hatchery and training of tribal personnel in cui-ui culture techniques in 1978, FWS turned over to the tribe responsibility for cui-ui hatchery reproduction. Most of the artificially propagated cui-ui have been released in the lower Truckee River or near the delta as larvae one to four weeks old. A small percentage of the larvae are held in the hatchery for up to a year before release. Annual releases from 1982 to 1986 ranged from 7.7 million to 11.7 million larvae.

From 1981 through 1983, FWS had a rather large cui-ui research program. Much was learned of cui-ui life history and habitat requirements. Budget cuts have steadily reduced the program, however. Recent work has centered around refining the temperature requirements of eggs and larvae and estimating larvae emigration. Results obtained from these two activities have been useful in improving the efficient use of Stampede storage and in evaluating the impacts of different operating criteria and procedures on cui-ui reproductive potential. An extensive tagging program has monitored adult population size and the success of fish passage at Marble Bluff Fish Facility. Yearly operational and structural modifications also have been incorporated to improve passage efficiency.

The Pyramid Lake Paiute Tribe has been the cui-ui's champion in its battle for survival. Through intervention and initiation of numerous court cases during the past two decades the tribe has pursued aggressively the water needed to maintain the lake and its fish resources. It was primarily through their actions that Stampede Reservoir storage was secured for cui-ui and cutthroat trout, that the Truckee Meadow irrigation districts are making efforts to control diversions, and that equitable long-term operating criteria and procedures are being sought for the Newlands Project.

## PROGNOSIS

The perpetuation of the cui-ui would be assured if it were possible to return the Truckee River/Pyramid Lake ecosystem to the balanced condition of the early 19th century. Since that cannot be done, the fate of the cui-ui hinges on its reproductive success in recent years and the future availability of water. The immediate health of the population is keyed to the six year-classes produced since 1980. If these year-classes prove to be relatively small, then the population may decrease drastically in the next few years as age gradually takes its toll of the dominant 1969 year-class. Conversely, if the year-classes are relatively large, then they will form a sound foundation for new generations. We do not have the necessary population statistics to assess the reproductive adequacy of these classes. Based on the size of the spawning runs and the low survival of cui-ui larvae, the first five year-classes may be relatively small. The most recent hope of producing a large year-class lies with the large 1986 year-class. Expectations may be overly optimistic, however, because the 1969 year-class probably was produced by two to three times as many spawners as in 1986.

Even if recent spawning runs have produced healthy year-classes, restoration of the species cannot be assured until an adequate water supply is guaranteed. The most significant action to secure this water supply was the acquisition of Stampede Reservoir storage. However, setbacks also have occurred, such as a recent U.S. Supreme Court ruling that the tribe could not re-open the Orr Ditch case to seek any more water for Pyramid Lake. The only remedy available to the tribe for the government's deficient representation of its interest was to sue for damages.

The adequacy of flows below Derby Dam depend upon future urban and agricultural demands for river water. The most consequential factor affecting these flows is the long-term operating criteria and procedures that the Bureau of Reclamation is formulating for the Newlands Project. Depending upon the final diversion criteria and the total allowable diversion selected, the impacts on cui-ui could be detrimental or beneficial. FWS will continue to assist the bureau in designing criteria that will provide decreed water rights to the Newlands Project while fulfilling the government's responsibilities to threatened and endangered species. One program that could benefit farmers and fish is to reduce losses in the Newlands Project's delivery system. Although the bureau has a program for improving delivery efficiencies, its target of 63 percent project-wide will not provide enough additional water to the lower Truckee River to restore the fishery. Efficiencies in the 80 to 85 percent range would benefit the fishery greatly, allow thousands of acre-feet of water each year to remain in the Truckee River, and reduce water-shortage potentials for the farmers. Achieving this goal would require lining the project's dirt canals and ditches with concrete and installing modern regulatory devices. Whether such a project will materialize depends on the availability of sufficient funds, as well the willingness of the farmers to change their historic practices.

Other users have plans for the waters of the Truckee River. Although Nevada is the nation's driest state, it is also one of the fastest growing. As communities along the Truckee River grow, their demand for water will increase. Recent studies suggest that by 1992 the Reno/ Sparks area will experience water shortages during drought years if additional water sources and storage facilities are not found (Firth *et al.* 1985). Sierra Pacific Power Company, the local water and power company, has recommended that storage rights in Stampede Reservoir be obtained. This would require about 50 percent of the reservoir's storage capacity at the expense of the cui-ui. Sierra Pacific Power Company also has applied to the Nevada State Water Engineer for a 175 cubic-feet per second increase in its water allocation from the Truckee River for municipal and domestic use. Washoe County recently applied for 9,000 cubic-feet per second, which far exceeds normal-water-year flows.

On the brighter side, the Pyramid Lake Paiute Tribe is seeking a water right under the Winters Doctrine for all remaining unappropriated water in the Truckee River. Under this doctrine, established in the 1908 court decision *Winters v. the United States*, sufficient water ordinarily is reserved to fulfill the purpose of an Indian reservation. In this case, the Pyramid Lake Paiute Indian Reservation was established to protect and provide access for tribal members to their historic fishing grounds in Pyramid Lake and along the lower Truckee River. Since river flows under normal water conditions are nearly fully appropriated, this would in effect be a right to flood flows. These waters, along with those of Stampede Reservoir and current river flows below Derby Dam, are essential for the cui-ui's restoration.

Just as important as the quantity of water reaching Pyramid Lake is the quality. Clean, cool water is a necessity for successful cui-ui reproduction. Continued urban growth throughout the watershed may degrade water quality. Nutrients and other materials introduced into the river are carried into Pyramid Lake, where they accumulate. The long-term effects of such accumulations may result in water-quality changes that are detrimental to cui-ui survival.

## RECOMMENDATIONS

Recovery and eventual removal of the cui-ui from the endangered species list ultimately will depend upon securing a consistent supply of clean water in the lower Truckee River that will maintain suitable spawning habitat in the river and a certain minimal elevation of Pyramid Lake. A number of actions could be taken, and in some cases are being taken, to accomplish this goal. Among them are: (1) improved delivery efficiences in the Newlands Project; (2) implementation of operating criteria and procedures that will benefit cui-ui; (3) securing of rights to unappropriated water of the Truckee River; (4) removal from production of marginal farmlands in the Newlands Project; (5) secure Stampede Reservoir storage for threatened and endangered fishes; and (6) modification of Floriston rates to better reflect the needs of the species.

Probably the only hope for accomplishing all of these actions and settling the many water-related disputes that have plagued northern Nevada for some 80 years is a sound basin-wide water-management plan that distributes the benefits equitably among all parties. Such a comprehensive solution will be difficult to achieve because of outdated water-management regulations and long-standing animosities. This is not to say that it would be impossible, only that there are entrenched barriers that must be overcome before all parties will sit down and work sincerely for the common good.

# REFERENCES

Benson, L.V. 1978. "Fluctuations in the level of Pluvial Lake Lahontan for the past 40,000 years," *Quarternary Research* 9:300-318.

Brown III, William M., Jon O. Nowlin, Lawrence H. Smith, and Mary R. Flint. 1986. *River-quality Assessment of the Truckee and Carson River System, California and Nevada — Hydrologic Characteristics*. U.S. Geological Survey Open-File Report 84-576. Sacramento, California. 201 pp.

Coleman, Mark E. 1986 *Evaluation of Spawning Runs at the Marble Bluff Fish Facility, Nixon, Nevada: 1978 to 1985*. U.S. Fish and Wildlife Service Report No. FRI/FAO-86-11. Portland, Oregon. 93 pp.

Firth, Robert E., Richard D. Moser, and Janice H. Anderson. 1985. *Sierra Pacific Power Company 1985 - 2005 Water Resource Plan*. Sierra Pacific Power Company, Gas/Water Engineering and Planning Department.

Galat, D.L., E.L. Lider, S. Vigg, and S.R. Robertson. 1981. "Limnology of a large, deep, North American terminal lake, Pyramid Lake, Nevada," *Hydrobiologia* 82:281-317.

Hummel, N.A. 1881. "The Que-oi-wee - The habits of a peculiar fish - The Pelican as a fisherman - graphic description of a Piute pow-wou - etc.," *Reno Evening Gazette*. May 9, 1881.

Knach, Martha C., and Omer C. Stewart. 1984. *As Long As The River Shall Run*. University of California Press. Berkeley, California. 433 pp.

Koch, D.L. 1982. *Temperature Tolerance Evaluation of Various Life Phases of the Cui-ui*. Report to Pyramid Lake Indian Tribal Council, January 8, 1982. Koch and Associates. Reno, Nevada. 20 pp.

Sigler, William F., Steven Vigg, and Mimi Bres. 1985. "Life history of the cui-ui, *Chasmistes cujus* Cope, in Pyramid Lake, Nevada: a review," *The Great Basin Naturalist* 45(4):571-603. October.

Snyder, John O. 1917. "The fishes of the Lahontan system of Nevada and northeastern California," *Bulletin of the U.S. Bureau of Fisheries* 35:31-38.

Sumner, Francis H. 1940. "The decline of the Pyramid Lake fishery," *Transactions of the American Fisheries Society* 69:216-224.

Scoppettone, G. Gary, Gary A. Wedemeyer, Mark E. Coleman, and Howard Burge. 1983. "Reproduction by the endangered cui-ui in the lower Truckee River," *Transactions of the American Fisheries Society* 112(6):788-793. November.

————. Gary A. Wedemeyer, Mark E. Coleman, and Howard Burge. 1983. *Life History Information on the Endangered Cui-ui* (Chasmistes cujus). U.S. Fish and Wildlife Service Annual Report - FY 1983. National Fishery Research Center. Seattle, Washington. 45 pp.

————. Mark E. Coleman, and Gary A. Wedemeyer. 1986. *Life History and Status of the Endangered Cui-ui of Pyramid Lake, Nevada*. U.S. Fish and Wildlife Service Research Report Series. In press.

*Chester C. Buchanan has been the Cui-ui Recovery Coordinator for the U.S. Fish and Wildlife Service since 1981.*

*Mark E. Coleman has been involved actively in fishery restoration projects at Pyramid Lake since 1978, including six years with the U.S. Fish and Wildlife Service.*

Once abundant from Kansas to West Virginia, the running buffalo clover has dwindled to a single wild population of no more than eight plants. Its survival may have been linked to the now-vanished bison herds. *Rodney Bartgis*

# The Running Buffalo Clover

## Judy F. Jacobs
*U.S. Fish and Wildlife Service*

## and

## Rodney L. Bartgis
*West Virginia Department of Natural Resources*

## SPECIES DESCRIPTION AND TAXONOMY

One of five native eastern clovers, the running buffalo clover (*Trifolium stoloniferum*) is a perennial species that forms long stolons that root at their nodes. The plants produce erect flowering stems, typically three to six inches tall with two leaves near the summit, topped by a roundish flowerhead one to 1.5 inches in diameter. The shapes of the white flowers and leaves are typical of the clover genus. *T. stoloniferum* closely resembles two other clover species within its range: another native species, buffalo clover (*T. reflexum*), and the introduced white clover (*T. repens*). Running buffalo clover differs from these species by several distinct morphological characters. Among these are the considerably larger seeds of running buffalo clover, the lack of stolons in buffalo clover, and the lack of leaves on the flowering stems of white clover. Recent examination of living material from West Virginia shows that chromosome morphology and/or number distinguishes running buffalo clover from the other native clovers and from the introduced white clover (Taylor pers. comm.). Other distinguishing features have been summarized recently by Brooks (1983a).

The clover genus *Trifolium* contains about 240 species worldwide (Taylor *et al.* 1979). Within the range of running buffalo clover are two other native clovers, buffalo clover (*T. reflexum*) and Carolina clover (*T. carolinianum*). Kates Mountain clover (*T. virginicum*), a shale barren endemic, and a recently discovered undescribed clover apparently restricted to cedar glades (Collins pers. comm.), are native to the areas immediately east and south.

## SIGNIFICANCE OF THE SPECIES

Clovers belong to the legume family, second only to the grass family in its global economic importance (Vietmeyer 1986). In the United States, about 20 species of clover are important to agriculture as forage, stock feed, and cover crops (Hermann 1953). Nitrogen-fixing bacteria associated with nodules on clover roots are well known for their ability to enrich cropland soils. The potential economic value of running buffalo clover is unknown, but is being studied at the University of Kentucky.

## HISTORICAL PERSPECTIVE

Henry Muhlenberg first identified running buffalo clover as a new species in 1813. In 1818, Amos Eaton validated Muhlenberg's name by publishing a description. The type specimen on which the original description was based is unknown. Brooks (1983b) recently designated a substitute or "neotype."

Running buffalo clover originally ranged across the central eastern United States from Kansas into West Virginia. According to historical accounts, the species was abundant in several areas of the Ohio Valley and adjacent regions prior to European settlement. It may have been a local dominant within the Kentucky bluegrass region (Campbell 1985).

Most collections of running buffalo clover were made from the 1870s to the 1890s, when botanical activity was increasing in the Midwest. At that time, populations apparently were limited and widely scattered. The only two collections made after 1910, one in 1937 and one in 1940, were both from West Virginia. A recent review of the species' status concluded that running buffalo clover was possibly extinct (Brooks 1983a). Subsequently, the U.S. Fish and Wildlife Service (FWS) included the clover as a candidate for endangered or threatened status, noting the possibility that it was already extinct (U.S. Fish and Wildlife Service 1983). In 1983 and 1984, the clover was found at two sites in West Virginia (Bartgis 1985).

The cause of the nearly range-wide disappearance of running buffalo clover is unknown. Historical and circumstantial evidence possibly links its decline to the extermination of bison from the clover's range. Running buffalo clover apparently was adapted to rich soils associated with continual, moderately intense disturbance in areas where open forest met bison-maintained openings, such as trails, licks, or prairies (Campbell 1985). These large herbivores may have provided the right balance of periodic disturbance, soil enrichment, seed dispersal, and, possibly, seed scarification necessary to maintain the clover. Historical and recent sites for the clover in West Virginia are also in the vicinity of known bison traces (Bartgis 1985), although this may mean only that both the clover and migrating bison occupied floodplains. Interestingly, both populations recently discovered in West Virginia are immediately adjacent to human-caused disturbances. It appears that in the absence of disturbance, the clover is unable to compete successfully with adjacent vegetation (Bartgis pers. obser.).

Another factor contributing to the species' demise could have been the clearing of its habitat for pasture and agriculture. For example, by 1850 much of the native vegetation of the Kentucky bluegrass region had been replaced by pasture plants, including bluegrass (Poa pratensis) and introduced white clover. This more aggressive clover may have invaded the habitat of running buffalo clover and out-competed the native species for access to light, space, and nutrients.

Recent observations suggest that certain more subtle interactions with white clover also could have contributed to the running buffalo clover's demise. For example, it appears that the native clover may be susceptible to a virus-like disease transmitted from the non-native white clover (Taylor pers. comm.). Another concern is that clover species often differ in the nitrogen-fixing bacterial species (rhizobia) they require to form the essential root nodules. The introduction into American soils of the rhizobium associated with white clover could have reduced the likelihood of, or even prevented, nodule formation in running buffalo clover by its own rhizobial associate. Such rhizobial competition has been observed among native and introduced clover species in California (Taylor pers. comm.). The role of rhizobial competition in the case of the running buffalo is speculative. However, it is supported by the observation that neither the clover plants used to establish the greenhouse population nor any of the plants presently in cultivation have produced nodules. Possibly, the bison also played a role in the rhizobial inoculation process. Whatever the reason for their loss, the nodules must be restored, since they are essential for the species' long-term survival and recovery.

## CURRENT TRENDS

As stated above, two populations of running buffalo clover were found recently in West Virginia (Bartgis 1985). At the time of their discovery, each population contained two plants with numerous stoloniferous offshoots. One population, which bordered plowed ground, is believed to be a relocation of the 1940 collection site. During the 1984 growing season, this population increased to four plants. The Nature Conservancy negotiated a conservation agreement with the landowner to protect this site. However, for unknown reasons, the four clover plants disappeared during the summer of 1985 and have not reappeared.

The single known remaining population, located adjacent to an off-road vehicle trail in alluvial woods, has been disturbed repeatedly by recreational vehicles. By 1985, this disturbance had separated the stolons from the parent plants, converting the population to 21 smaller plants. Two of these were removed to establish a greenhouse population at the University of Kentucky.

Endangered status was proposed for *T. stoloniferum* on March 10, 1986 (U.S. Fish and Wildlife Service 1986). However, by the summer of 1986, continued disturbance had reduced the wild population to fewer than eight plants. Following this event, The Nature Conservancy, the landowner, and FWS agreed to close the trail. In September 1986, the landowner and the West Virginia Department of Natural Resources announced that the site would be protected formally.

## MANAGEMENT

The most pressing management needs for this rare clover are protection of the existing population, establishment and protection of additional populations, and further survey work to locate any surviving populations.

Often, a substantial interval occurs between the time a species is recognized as a candidate for the endangered species list and the time that it is listed officially and the federal recovery process is initiated. However, candidate species need not be neglected while they await listing. Thus, although running buffalo clover, as of late 1986, remains only a proposed species, many of its recovery needs are clear and certain recovery actions already have been taken. For example, thorough searches have been made for the clover in appropriate habitat in West Virginia, eastern Kentucky, and Ohio. Botanists are searching for other wild populations farther west in the clover's original range. Such populations, if found, would be important in expanding the genetic base of the population, which may now consist of only a single genotype.

The plants in cultivation at the University of Kentucky have done very well, producing many offspring vegetatively and, more recently, from seed. Running buffalo clover is not known to have been cultivated or studied previously. Therefore, much has been learned and more questions have surfaced about its habits and requirements. For example, the remaining wild plants have set seed successfully but have produced only two seedlings, neither of which survived (Bartgis pers. obser.). In cultivation, a period of winter cold has been found necessary to stimulate flower production. Plants are self-fertile, and seed germination is improved greatly by scarification (Campbell and Taylor pers. comm.). Cultivation of this clover also has shed light on possible causes of the species' decline and of poor seedling survival—the putative pathogen introduced from white clover and the lack of nodules on running buffalo clover, as mentioned previously. Current research at the University of Kentucky focuses on the life history, ecology, and genetics of this clover. The plants also are being grown and studied at West Virginia University, where tissue culture methods have been used to increase the population (Baker pers. comm.).

In late 1986, some offspring from the University of Kentucky plants were planted on National Park Service land, not far from the one known remaining wild population in West Virginia. Another population was established at the Core Arboretum in Morgantown, West Virginia, near a historical collection. Since only an eastern genotype is known, reintroductions will be discouraged in the western half of the clover's range until a western population is found or it appears that one will not be found. Following final listing, all reestablished populations will receive full federal protection. This includes prohibiting collection from federal land and ensures that the actions of federal agencies will not jeopardize the clover. However, the clover presently is not protected under West Virginia law. Protection of the existing natural population must continue, including the exclusion of motor vehicles, control of aggressive weedy vegetation, and continuation of other necessary management measures.

## PROGNOSIS

Under the present conditions of cultivation, running buffalo clover appears to be a vigorous and prolific plant. However, the causes for the species' disastrous decline must be pinpointed before recovery can be expected. In addition, the very limited genetic diversity of the cultivated plants may present problems in reestablishing wild populations. New information will be gained from ongoing research, as well as from every attempted management action. At present, running buffalo clover is virtually extinct in the wild. If the causes of its near extirpation can be determined, or if its requirements can be met in modern-day environments, the clover's chances for survival and recovery are good.

## RECOMMENDATIONS

1. Continue protection and monitoring of the single known remaining natural population.
2. Continue to search for natural populations in likely habitat, particularly in the western part of the clover's original range. Also, obtain protection for newly discovered populations in cooperation with landowners and federal, state, and private conservation agencies.
3. Continue research on the species' cultivation requirements, microbial associates, genetics, and limiting factors.
4. Continue reestablishment efforts, focusing particularly on federal lands in the eastern part of the species' range.

## REFERENCES

Bartgis, R. 1985. "Rediscovery of *Trifolium stoloniferum* Muhl. A. Eaton," *Rhodora* 87:425-429.

Brooks, R. 1983a. "*Trifolium stoloniferum*, running buffalo clover. Description, distribution and current status," *Rhodora* 85:343-54.

———. 1983b. "Neotypification of *Trifolium stoloniferum*. Muhl. ex. A. Eaton (Fabaceae)," *Taxon* 32:454-455.

Campbell, J. 1985. The land of cane and clover: Pre-settlement vegetation in the so-called Bluegrass Region of Kentucky. Unpublished manuscript. University of Kentucky. Lexington, Kentucky.

Eaton, A. 1818. *Manual of Botany for the Northern and Middle States*, second edition. Webster and Skinners. Albany, New York.

Hermann, F. 1953. "A botanical synopsis of the cultivated clovers (*Trifolium*)," *Agricultural Monographs* 22. U.S. Department of Agriculture.

Muhlenberg, G.H.E. 1813. *Catalogus Plantarum Americae Septentrionalis Hucusque Cognitarium Indiginarum et Circurum*. W. Hamilton, Lancaster, Pennsylvania.

Taylor, N., K. Quesenberry and M. Anderson. 1979. "Genetic systems in *Trifolium*," *Economic Botany* 33:431-441.

U.S. Fish and Wildlife Service. 1983. "Endangered and threatened wildlife and plants; supplement to review of plant taxa for listing," *Federal Register* 48(229):53640-53670.

———. 1986. "Proposal to determine *Trifolium stoloniferum* (running buffalo clover) to be an endangered species," *Federal Register* 51(46):8217-8220.

Vietmeyer, N.D. 1986. "Lesser-known plants of potential use in agriculture and forestry," *Science* 232:1379-1394.

*Judy Jacobs, a biologist with the U.S. Fish and Wildlife Service Endangered Species Program in Maryland, wrote the* Federal Register *documents listing the running buffalo clover as an endangered species.*

*Rodney L. Bartgis, former director of science for the West Virginia field office of The Nature Conservancy, rediscovered the running buffalo clover in West Virginia in 1983. He is currently a zoologist with the West Virginia Department of Natural Resources Heritage Program.*

The black-footed ferret may be the rarest mammal on Earth. The only known population, in Wyoming, has been decimated by disease and the 17 known survivors taken into captivity. *Dean Biggins/U.S. Fish and Wildlife Service*

# The Black-Footed Ferret

Max Schroeder
*U.S. Fish and Wildlife Service*

## SPECIES DESCRIPTION AND NATURAL HISTORY

Black-footed ferrets (*Mustela nigripes*) are long, slender-bodied animals similar in size to mink. They are noctural carnivores and members of the weasel family, Mustelidae (Anderson *et al.* 1986). The species is characterized by a brown, almost black, mask across the face, black feet and legs, and a black tip on the tail. Henderson *et al.* (1969) described their pelage as pale yellow buff becoming lighter on the underparts of the body. The forehead, muzzle, and throat are light, occasionally whitish. The head is brownish and the middle of the back has brown-tipped guard hairs that create the appearance of a dark saddle. The fur is short, with guard hairs averaging less than an inch long. Adult ferrets weigh 1.4 to three pounds. Adult males average slightly more than 1.5 feet long and have a tail length of four to five inches. Females average about 10 percent smaller than males (Hall and Kelson 1959).

### Distribution

Original black-footed ferret range was extensive and included the Great Plains of Canada, the intermontane regions of the interior Rocky

Mountains, and the southwestern United States (Anderson *et al.* 1986). The range was coextensive with that of three species of prairie dog, including the black-tailed prairie dog (*Cynomysludovicianus*), white-tailed prairie dog (*C. leucurus*), and Gunnison's prairie dog (*C. gunnisoni*) with which it coexisted (Hubbard and Schmitt 1984). It is believed that ferret distribution has been reduced greatly since 1900 as a direct result of the reduction of prairie dog populations throughout much of the original range. Currently, the only known ferret population is one near Meeteetse, Wyoming, in a white-tailed prairie dog complex restricted to about 60 square miles (Anderson *et al.* 1986).

**Diet**

Although their typical prey consists of prairie dogs, black-footed ferrets appear to be opportunistic feeders. In feeding trials, ferrets consumed thirteen-lined ground squirrels (*Spermophilus tridecemlineatus*), cottontail rabbits (*Sylvilagus floridanus*), white-footed mice (*Peromyscus* spp.), and small birds offered to them both alive and dead (Hillman 1968). Studies of foods taken by wild black-footed ferrets in South Dakota indicate that prairie dog remains were found in 91 percent of 82 ferret scats and mouse remains in 26 percent (Sheets *et al.* 1972). This agreed closely with the results of an examination of 86 Wyoming ferret scats by Campbell *et al.* (1987), who found that 86 percent of the scats contained prairie dog remains and less than ten percent contained small rodent remains. Campbell *et al.* also found small amounts of cottontail and jackrabbit (*Lepus* spp.) remains in the scats.

**Activity**

Black-footed ferrets are active throughout the year. Observations of individual ferrets and their tracks on snow indicate that individuals are solitary in late fall, winter, and spring (Henderson *et al.* 1969, Forrest *et al.* 1985a). Biggins *et al.* (1985, 1986) investigated the activity of two radio-tagged ferrets in Wyoming during the fall of 1981 and 1982 and found the male was active nearly three hours nightly, compared to two hours for the female. They discussed movements of a young female that moved a maximum of 3,600 yards in one night and averaged 1,200 yards of linear movement each night. This animal's activity area covered 130 acres, about half of that occupied by the adult male. The portions of the area used most intensively by the female were characterized by high densities of prairie dog burrows and short-grass vegetation.

Forrest *et al.* (1985a) studied winter movements of ferrets by following and recording their tracks in snow. They discovered that in winter, ferrets cover distances up to 4.3 miles in a single night and that movement of 1.25 miles or more per night were common. As in summer, ferret winter activities were mostly nocturnal, but Clark *et al.* (1986) found evidence that in winter ferrets are often active after sunrise.

Black-footed ferrets are active in cold temperatures and inclement conditions. Henderson *et al.* (1969) reported that a captive ferret did not hibernate and ventured outside in temperatures as low as -18 degrees Fahrenheit. Clark *et al.* (1986) reported that ferrets moved during rain and snow storms, in temperatures as low as -36 degrees Fahrenheit, and in winds up to 30 miles per hour.

## Breeding

The breeding behavior of wild black-footed ferrets has not been observed, but ferrets in captivity have bred during February and March (Carpenter and Hillman 1979, E.T. Thorne, pers. comm.). The young are born after a 42-day gestation period but are not seen above ground until they are about six weeks old. Observations of 11 litters in South Dakota from 1964 through 1972 and 55 litters in Wyoming from 1982 through 1984 revealed that the litter size of wild ferrets found above ground varies from one to five and averages 3.4 (Linder *et al.* 1972, Forrest *et al.* 1985b). When first observed above ground, young ferrets appear from a third to three-quarters of adult size, and their sex ratio is believed to be equal (Clark *et al.* 1986, Hillman 1968, Henderson *et al.* 1969, Forrest *et al.* 1985b).

The adult male does not contribute to the care of the young, and the female and young remain together until about mid-August. At that time, the female begins to separate siblings into different burrows. From August through early September the young become increasingly solitary. By early October they are independent.

## Longevity

Forrest *et al.* (1985b) suggested that the average life span of black-footed ferrets is less than a year. This is supported by evidence of high juvenile mortality in the population near Meeteetse, Wyoming. The cause of losses in the wild are not well documented. Predation by golden eagles (*Aquila chrysaetos*), great horned owls (*Bubo virginianus*), hawks, badgers (*Taxidea taxus*), coyotes (*Canis latrans*), and bobcats (*Lynx rufus*) is believed to be a principal factor. Disease contributes to both indirect and direct loss of ferrets. Carpenter *et al.* (1981) discussed the occurrence of diabetes mellitus, monorchidism, breeding disorders, and malignant tumors in ferrets captured in South Dakota. He suggested that these disorders could be attributed to a loss of genetic viability in the population or could be in part the result of advanced age in the captive animals.

Sylvatic plague is not believed to affect ferrets directly, but epidemics in prairie dog populations can destroy the ferret's prey base over large areas. Canine distemper is fatal to ferrets. As this disease spread with the arrival of European man and his domestic animals, it may have been partly responsible for the historic reduction in wild ferret numbers throughout the range.

The relationship of parasites to ferret populations is not known. Both fleas and ticks are found commonly on ferrets, but their relation to disease transmission has not been studied.

## SIGNIFICANCE OF THE SPECIES

The black-footed ferret was first introduced to science in 1851, when John Audubon and John Bachman described the species from an imperfect skin sent to them from near Fort Laramie, Wyoming. Although a secretive, seldom observed animal, the black-footed ferret was believed to have been widely distributed throughout the Great Plains and was held in special regard by the American Indian. Ferret hides were used in headdresses worn by tribal chiefs and as tobacco pouches, sacred objects, and symbols of influence by several tribes of plains Indians (Henderson *et al.* 1969).

The black-footed ferret is unique in that it is the only native ferret presently found in North America and is believed to be the rarest mammal in the world. It is a federally listed endangered species.

## HISTORICAL PERSPECTIVE

Anderson (1973) studied the Pleistocene fossil record of ferrets. She found that black-footed ferrets are most closely related to the Siberian polecat (*Mustela eversmanii michonoi*), a species found in the Trans-baikal region of Siberia.

Originating in the Old World, ferrets entered North America across the Bering land bridge and spread southward throughout the Great Plains. Evidence exists showing that both this species and the Siberian polecat existed in North America during the Pleistocene.

Prior to 1900, the mid-grass and short-grass prairies of the Great Plains supported several hundred million acres of prairie dog towns, providing prey and habitat for the black-footed ferret. The number of ferrets that existed at the peak of their population remains unknown. Because of their nocturnal habits and use of burrows for shelter and raising young, black-footed ferret activities are seldom observed by man. Flath and Clark (1984) noted that only about 1,000 reports of live black-footed ferrets have been recorded. No doubt many others have been seen but not recorded.

Until recently, it was believed that the ferret had always been relatively rare, but Choate *et al.* (1982) reported that the species may have been more common than once suspected. In Kansas, 26 specimens were collected from Trego and Gove counties from 1891 through 1894. Linder *et al.* (1972) referred to an employee of the Bureau of Biological Survey who concluded in 1923 that the species was not uncommon in parts of South Dakota. During a five year period following his statement, 42 ferrets were taken by the Bureau in South Dakota (Hubbard and Schmitt 1984).

When European settlers first arrived, they changed vast acreages of the Great Plains grasslands to farmland, a process that destroyed many acres of prairie dog colonies. In the early 1900s, private land managers were assisted in their efforts to reduce prairie dog numbers when federal and state agencies joined in an intensive effort to eliminate prairie dogs on public rangelands. As a result of these efforts, millions of prairie dogs were killed, resulting in extensive loss of the ferret's prey base and habitat. Black-footed ferrets became unintended victims and dwindled to the point that the species qualified as a charter member of the first federal endangered species list, developed in 1964.

## CURRENT TRENDS

From 1972 to 1981, no black-footed ferrets were found in the wild, and some biologists were beginning to speculate that the species was extinct. Then, in September 1981, an adult male black-footed ferret was killed by a farm dog on the John Hogg ranch west of Meeteetse. This was the first wild black-footed ferret found since 1972 and soon led to discovery of a wild population (Schroeder and Martin 1982). Since then, thousands of hours have been spent searching for ferrets. Many sightings have been reported and dirt diggings characteristic of the species have been found, but no ferret has been verified outside of the area near Meeteetse.

From 1981 through 1984, the Meeteetse ferret population appeared to be increasing. At its peak in 1984, nearly 130 ferrets were counted on the study site (Clark 1986). Then, in 1985, canine distemper diminished the isolated population to only a few ferrets. In October 1985, canine distemper was found in two of six ferrets captured to start a captive breeding population at the Wyoming Game and Fish Department's Sybille Wildlife Research Unit. Shortly after their capture, all of these ferrets died of canine distemper. Six additional ferrets were then captured for the facility, and these have remained healthy.

During the summer of 1985, sylvatic plaque seriously diminished parts of the prairie dog colonies on the study site. Surveys of prairie dog habitat in this area showed that though many prairie dogs were lost, adequate habitat remains to support ferrets. However, population biologists were concerned that not enough ferrets had survived the distemper outbreak to repopulate the site. To determine how many wild ferrets remained on the study area, surveys were started. In July 1986, searchers found two adult females, each with a litter of five young, and three isolated animals believed to be males. In August 1986, personnel of the Wyoming Game and Fish Department met to review the available data. At this meeting they determined that too few ferrets remained in the wild to prevent their extinction. To prevent further losses from this fragile population, it was agreed to capture as many of the ferrets from the Meeteetse study area as possible. Currently, 18 ferrets are in captivity at the department's Sybille Wildlife Research Unit near Wheatland. In addition, a few wild ferrets are still believed to remain in the Meeteetse area.

## MANAGEMENT

Present recovery efforts include preservation of remaining ferrets, attempts to breed the species in captivity, attempts to locate new populations, and conservation of prairie dog habitat for the future establishment of new populations.

In March 1982, the U.S. Fish and Wildlife Service (FWS) transferred responsibility for the administration of black-footed ferret research and management activities in Wyoming to the Wyoming Game and Fish Department. For assistance with this, the department appointed a black-footed ferret advisory team representing landowners, state and federal resource agencies, a national wildlife organization, and the University of Wyoming. This team was charged with the responsibility to review research and management activities, define black-footed ferret research needs, review ferret research proposals, establish a cooperative research fund for the black-footed ferret, and recommend management strategies based on the results of ferret research. Since its establishment, the team has encouraged research directed toward determining the number of ferrets in the Meeteetse population, the area of occupied prairie dog habitat, ferret reproductive success, time of ferret dispersal, and fate of dispersing animals.

Future management of wild black-footed ferrets will depend on the success of captive propagation and the reintroduction of captive ferrets into the wild or on locating other populations of wild ferrets. State and federal land-management agencies have been encouraged to identify and maintain adequate prairie dog habitat to sustain future populations of captive-reared black-footed ferrets. To protect against losses of small populations to epizootic disease and other natural or manmade problems, several isolated populations would be desirable.

Successful reproduction of black-footed ferrets in captivity may be achieved in the near future. To assist with this, FWS and the Wyoming Game and Fish Department requested that the Captive Breeding Specialist Group of the International Union for the Conservation of Nature and Natural Resources serve as a technical advisory group. This group has been very active in developing recommendations and providing assistance to the recovery effort. Management strategies to breed ferrets and raise their young successfully, minimize the problems of genetic inbreeding, increase the population size, and distribute ferrets into other facilities are being developed with the assistance of the technical advisory group.

## PROGNOSIS

Since discovery of canine distemper in the ferret population near Meeteetse, the direction of research has changed. The current focus of black-footed ferret management is on locating additional populations and on captive propagation. State and federal natural-resource agencies continue to survey for ferrets and to identify prairie dog colonies suitable for possible reintroduction of the species. Wildlife Conservation International, a division of the New York Zoological Society, is sponsoring a reward for the discovery of a new black-footed ferret population. Conservation agencies are working with Congress and private groups to locate other sources of funding for ferret research and management. Unless another population is discovered, many believe that too few ferrets exist to sustain genetic fitness in the species. Until other populations of ferrets can be found or captive breeding and reestablishment of the black-footed ferret succeeds, this species must be considered critically endangered.

## RECOMMENDATIONS

Recovery of black-footed ferrets will require a continued commitment by both the public and scientific community to locate additional populations of wild black-footed ferrets, to conduct research to better understand the behavior and reproductive process of the black-footed ferret, and to preserve adequate prairie dog habitat to support wild ferret populations. In 1985, Congress provided additional funds for black-footed ferret research. In addition, FWS and the Wyoming Game and Fish Commission have provided the Wyoming Game and Fish Department sufficient funds to build a black-footed ferret breeding facility at the Sybille Research Unit near Wheatland, Wyoming. A sustained commitment by these agencies will be needed to provide adequate money to support the captive breeding facility, to fund future research, and to continue surveys for other populations of black-footed ferrets. Private landowners and citizens can help. State and federal land-management agencies and private landowners must cooperate to locate and protect large, undisturbed prairie dog colonies suitable for future reintroduction of black-footed ferrets. People aware of unreported ferret populations and those who observe the species in the field should report the animals to state game and fish departments or to FWS. Such reports could lead to the discovery of yet another wild population from which individuals could be recruited to help strengthen the genetic fitness of this rare species.

A vaccine to protect black-footed ferrets against canine distemper is needed before ferrets can be released into the wild. Lack of this protection will subject any small relocated population to risk of exposure by farm animals or other wide-ranging predator species.

At present, adequate habitat remains for the black-footed ferret throughout much of its original range. The prospects for the recovery of this species now depends on our ability to raise this species successfully in captivity and to reintroduce it into its natural habitat.

## REFERENCES

Anderson, E.S. 1973. "Ferret from the Pleistocene of central Alaska," *Journal of Mammalogy* 54:778-779.

———, S.C. Forrest, T.W. Clark, and L. Richardson. 1986. "Paleobiology, biogeography and systematics of the black-footed ferret, (*Mustela nigripes*), Audubon and Bachman 1851," *Great Basin Naturalist Memoirs* 8:11-62.

Biggins, D.E., M.H. Schroeder, S.C. Forrest, and L. Richardson. 1985. "Movements and habitat relations of radio-tagged black-footed ferrets," pp. 1-11, 17, *in* S. Anderson and D. Inkley eds., *Proceedings of the Black-footed Ferret Workshop*. Laramie, Wyoming. September 18-19, 1984. Wyoming Game and Fish Publication.

———. 1986. "Activity of radio-tagged black-footed ferrets," *Great Basin Naturalist Memoirs* 8:135-140.

Campbell, T.M. III, T.W. Clark, L.R. Forrest, and S.C. Forrest. 1987. "Food habits of Wyoming black-footed ferrets," *American Midland Naturalist*. In Press.

Carpenter, J.W., N.N. Meliton and H.E. Kaiser. 1981. "Neoplasia and other disease problems in black-footed ferrets: implications for an endangered species," pp. 739-746, *in* H.E. Kaiser ed., *Neoplasms: Comparative Pathology of Growth in Animals, Plants, and Man*. Raven Press. New York.

————., and C.N. Hillman. 1979. "Husbandry, reproduction, and veterinary care of captive ferrets," pp. 36-47, in *Proceedings of the American Association Zoo Veterinarians*. Knoxville, Tennessee.

Choate, J.R., E.K. Boggess, and F.R. Henderson. 1982. "History and status of the black-footed ferret in Kansas," *Transactions of the Kansas Academy of Science* 85:121-132.

Clark, T.W. 1986. "Guidelines for management of the black-footed ferret," *Great Basin Naturalists Memoirs* 8:160-168.

Clark, T.W., L. Richardson, S.C. Forrest, T.M. Campbell III, D.E. Casey, and K.A. Fagerstone. 1986. "Descriptive ethology and activity patterns of black-footed ferrets," *Great Basin Naturalist Memoirs* 8:115-134.

Flath, D.L. and T.M. Clark. 1984. "Montana: crucial key to ferret recovery," *Montana Outdoors* 15(3):34-37.

Forrest, S.C., T.W. Clark, L. Richardson, T.M. Campbell III. 1985a. "Black-footed ferret habitat: some management and reintroduction considerations," *Wildlife Technical Bulletin Number* 2. Wyoming Bureau of Land Management. Cheyenne, Wyoming. 49 pp.

————., S.C., T.W. Clark, L. Richardson, D. Biggins, K.A. Fagerstone and T.M. Campbell. 1985b. "Life history characteristics of the genus *Mustela*, with special reference to the black-footed ferret, *Mustela nigripes*," pp. 1-23, *in* S. Anderson and D. Inkley eds., *Proceedings of the Black-footed Ferret Workshop*. Laramie, Wyoming, September 18-19, 1984. Wyoming Game and Fish Publication.

Hall, E.R. and K.R. Kelson. 1959. *The Mammals of North America*. Ronald Press. New York. 1162 pp.

Henderson, F.R., R.F. Springer, and R. Adrian. 1969. "The black-footed ferret in South Dakota," *South Dakota Department of Game, Fish and Parks Technical Bulletin No.* 4. 36 pp.

Hillman, C.N. 1968. "Field observations of black-footed ferrets in South Dakota," *Transactions of the North American Wildlife and Natural Resources Conference* 33:433-443.

Hubbard, J.P. and C.G. Schmitt. 1984. *The Black-Footed Ferret in New Mexico*. Final Report to BLM, Santa Fe, New Mexico, under Contract No. NM-910-CTI-7 to Department of Game Fish, Santa Fe and under New Mexico Department of Game and Fish Projects. FW-17-R. 118 pp.

Linder, R., R.B. Dahlgren, and C.N. Hillman. 1972. "Black footed ferret prairie dog interrelationships," pp. 26-36, in *Proceedings of the Symposium on Rare and Endangered Wildlife of the Southwestern U.S.* September 22-23, 1972. New Mexico Department of Game and Fish, Santa Fe. Albuquerque, New Mexico.

Schroeder, M.H. and S.J. Martin. 1982. "Search for the black-footed ferret succeeds," *Wyoming Wildlife* 46(7):8-9.

Sheets, R.G., R.L. Linder, and R.B. Dahlgren. 1972. "Food habits of two litters of black-footed ferrets in South Dakota," *American Midland Naturalist* 87:249-251.

*Max Schroeder is the black-footed ferret coordinator for the Fish and Wildlife Service Region 6 Office.*

The southern sea otter population has not increased and may have declined since the mid-1970s. The otters are found in only a single vulnerable population along 220 miles of California coast. *Richard Bucich*

# The Southern Sea Otter

## Wilbur N. Ladd, Jr.
*U.S. Fish and Wildlife Service*

## and

## Marianne L. Riedman
*Monterey Bay Aquarium*

## SPECIES DESCRIPTION AND NATURAL HISTORY

A long-standing controversy over the taxonomic status of the southern or California sea otter (*Enhydra lutris nereis*) continues unabated and unresolved. The Alaskan and California populations now are believed to be geographically and genetically isolated from one another and probably have been for at least a century. However, biologists have yet to determine whether the morphological and behavioral differences that exist between the southern sea otter and the Alaskan sea otter (*E.l. lutris*) are clinal variations of a single subspecies or the genetic variations of two subspecies that historically mixed in a region of overlap at Prince William Sound. In this chapter, the terms "southern sea otter" and "California sea otter" will be used interchangeably for sea otters currently found along the central California coast.

### Historic and Current Range

The southern sea otter historically ranged from approximately Punta Abreojos in Baja California, Mexico, northward along the California, Oregon, and Washington coast. The northern limit of its historic range

Audubon Wildlife Report 1987

is still debated. Some authors have concluded that the northern limit was the Strait of Juan de Fuca (e.g., Barabash-Nikiforov 1947, Taylor and Shaw 1929, Kenyon 1981), although others recently have suggested that the northern limit, presuming the southern sea otter is a valid subspecies, was Prince William Sound (e.g., Roest 1971, Davis and Lidicker 1975, Rice 1977).

The current range of the California population extends for about 220 miles of coastline, from Ano Nuevo Point to the Santa Maria River. Most of the established population is centered between Sandhill Bluff and the Santa Maria River, with widely scattered individuals or pairs of otters sighted north and south of these limits.

The center of the range, between Monterey Bay and Cayucos, is occupied primarily by females of all ages and pups. In addition, territorial adult males move into female areas in summer and fall, and recently weaned juvenile males may remain in female areas throughout the year until two or three years old. The southern and northern ends of the range are inhabited throughout the year mainly by nonreproductive, immature males and during the winter-spring nonbreeding season by adult males (Benech 1981, Estes and Jameson 1983, Jameson in prep.).

Along the central California coast, sea otters inhabit a narrow zone of shallow, subtidal waters. The majority of the population remains within about a half mile to a mile of the coastline, inshore of the 10-fathom depth curve. Some, however, forage offshore to 20 fathoms or more (Odemar and Wilson 1969, Wild and Ames 1974, Loughlin 1977, Ribic 1982).

Although California sea otters may rest in open water, most of the time they rest in the kelp-bed canopies. These consist of the bull kelp (*Nereocystis leutkeana*) and especially the giant kelp (*Macrocystis pyrifiera*). Kelp appears to be a significant variable influencing sea otter distribution as well as territorial and home-range boundaries (Jameson in prep.).

## Morphology and Physiology

Sea otters are one of the largest members of the weasel family. Measurements of dead adult male and adult female California sea otters average 50.3 inches and 46.7 inches respectively (Ames unpubl. data). Average weights for healthy sea otters are 63.8 pounds for adult males and 43.6 pounds for adult females (Ames *et al.* 1983). Pups weigh between 3.1 and 5.1 pounds at birth (Miller 1974). Little is known of life span. Males probably live up to 15 years, while females appear to live about five years longer.

Unlike most other marine mammals, sea otters have very little subcutaneous fat. Instead, their dense fur insulates against the cold and traps a layer of air that provides buoyancy and allows the skin to remain dry even when immersed in seawater (Kenyon 1969, Morrison *et al.* 1974, Tarasoff 1974, Costa and Kooyman 1982). If 25 to 30 percent of the fur surface, possibly even less, becomes contaminated with oil, the fur loses its insulative qualities and the otter most certainly will die (e.g. Kenyon 1969, Kooyman *et al.* 1977, Williams 1978, Costa and Kooyman 1982, Siniff *et al.* 1982).

## Reproduction

Although mating and pupping may take place throughout the year in California, pupping peaks from January to March (e.g. Fisher 1939, Vandevere 1970, Sandegren *et al.* 1973, Estes and Jameson 1983). Indirect evidence suggests that the breeding season peaks from July to October (Jameson in prep.).

Preliminary observations indicate that California females may reach sexual maturity at four or five years of age (Wendell *et al.* 1984, Jameson unpubl. data). Green (1978) suggested that California males reach sexual maturity at about five years, as do Alaskan males. However, males probably do not establish territories or actively participate in breeding for two or more years after reaching puberty.

Gestation periods have been estimated at four to six months (Loughlin *et al.* 1981, Estes and Jameson 1983), with the reproductive cycle ranging from 11 to 14 months (Loughlin *et al.* 1981, Wendell *et al.* 1984). Females undergo a period of delayed implantation which probably is variable (Sinha *et al.* 1966) and give birth to one pup at a time. Observations made in California indicate that birth may take place in water (Sandegren *et al.* 1973) or on land (Woodward 1981, Jameson 1983).

Pups less than three months old are relatively helpless and dependent on their mothers for nourishment and protection. By age 14 weeks, most pups are able to swim independently, dive proficiently, and groom themselves. They are able to capture and break open hard-shelled prey, using a rock as a hammer, by five to six months (Payne and Jameson 1984).

## Foraging Behavior and Diet

California sea otters forage along the bottoms of rocky and soft-sediment nearshore communities as well as within kelp canopies and understories. In California, otters generally forage at depths less than 90 feet. They capture prey with their forepaws, often storing food items within loose pockets of skin beneath the axilla of each foreleg. Otters use rocks as hammers to dislodge prey underwater and break open hard-shelled mollusks at the surface before consuming them. Siniff and

Ralls (1986) provide detailed information on activity patterns and time budgets in California sea otters. They found that otters spend 37 percent to 48 percent of their time foraging and that variation in time spent feeding was related to age and sex.

The diet of California sea otters consists almost exclusively of a variety of large nearshore invertebrates. In recently reoccupied habitats of central California, the diet consists principally of high-calorie species such as abalones (*Haliotis* spp.), rock crabs (*Cancer* spp.), and sea urchins (*Strongylocentrotus* spp.) (Ebert 1968a Wild and Ames 1974, Benech 1981, Estes *et al.* 1981). As populations of preferred prey are reduced, otters increase consumption of items such as kelp crabs (*Pugettia* spp.), clams (various genera), turban snails (*Tegula* spp.), mussels (*Mytilus* spp.), octopus (*Octopus* spp.), barnacles (*Balanus* spp.), scallops (*Hinnites* spp.), sea stars (*Pisaster* spp.), and chitons (*Cryptochiton* spp.) (e.g. Wild and Ames 1974, Estes 1980, Estes *et al.* 1981, Benech 1981, Ostfeld 1982). However, recent studies show that individual variations in diet and foraging strategies occur among adult California sea otters (Lyons and Estes 1985, Riedman and Estes unpubl. data.).

## SIGNIFICANCE OF THE SPECIES

### Interactions Between Sea Otters and Marine Communities

Sea otters appear to be one of the most important sea urchin predators and have caused significant reductions in sea urchin densities in some areas of the California range (e.g. McLean 1962, Ebert 1968, Lowry and Pearse 1973, Gotshall *et al.* 1976, Benech 1977). This can affect kelp growth because in California sea urchins graze extensively on kelp. Large urchin populations may even cause substantial kelp-bed reductions, limiting the seaward expansion of kelp forests in some areas (McLean 1962, North 1965, North and Pearse 1970, Leighton 1971, Lawrence 1975, Pearse and Hines 1979, Tegner 1980, Tegner and Dayton 1981, Dean *et al.* 1984, Harrold and Reed 1985).

While kelp damage by sea urchins varies considerably in the absence of sea otters, damage apparently rarely occurs where sea otters are well established. Under certain conditions in some areas, the reestablishment and enlargement of kelp canopies may be associated with the presence of sea otters (e.g. McLean 1962, North 1965, VanBlaricom and Jameson 1979, VanBlaricom 1984a, b). In some cases, the reestablishment and expansion of *Macrocystis* kelp beds may help increase some of the finfish associated with kelp forests in California (e.g. Quast 1968, Davies 1968, VanBlaricom 1984a,b, Bodkin 1984), as has occurred in the Aleutian Islands, Alaska (Estes *et al.* 1978,

Simenstad *et al.* 1978). Further research is contributing to better understand the interrelationships of kelp, sea urchins, and sea otters.

Kelp itself, harvested commercially in central and southern California nearshore waters, is economically important. Kelp-industry spokesmen say they have been unable to meet the demand for kelp in about half of the past 10 years. A reduction in urchin densities as a result of sea otter reoccupation of former range may have a beneficial effect on the commercial kelp industry.

## Economic Importance

The presence of sea otters along California's coastline continues to have rather profound economic effects. One of the most publicized is the impact that sea otters have had on California's shellfishing industry. Although many factors can influence shellfish densities, including sport and commercial take, sea otters can cause major reductions in densities and individual sizes of many shellfish species, such as clams and abalone. Otters are so efficient at foraging on these prey species that it is unlikely that sea otters can coexist with most commercial, and probably recreational, shellfisheries (Estes and Van-Blaricom 1985).

This apparent incompatability is exemplified by the decline in California's commercial abalone fishery coincidentally with the natural repopulation of the sea otter into its former range along the central coast (Estes and VanBlaricom 1985, Ault 1985). While the commercial catch has been redirected from primarily red abalone to other abalone species, the total commercial abalone catch in California has declined steadily from about 4.5 million pounds in the mid-1960s to about 1.2 million pounds in 1982 (Ault 1985). However, the sea otter's role in abalone reduction is still poorly understood. For example, the overall density and average size of abalones at Hopkins Marine Life Refuge in Monterey were reduced substantially from that found in areas not occupied by otters. However, the abundance, size, and species composition of the abalones at the refuge had remained stable from 1972 to 1981 after nearly 20 years of sea otter occupation (Hines and Pearse 1982). Similarly, otter predation at Elkhorn Slough in Monterey Bay had no noticeable effect on abundance and size distribution of deep-burrowing clams of the species *Tresus nuttalli* and *Saxidomus nuttalli* (Kvitek *et al.* 1985).

The presence of sea otters recently has had a socio-economic impact on the nearshore commercial set-net halibut fishery (California Department of Fish and Game n.d.). In order to minimize the chance of otters being drowned in the set nets, the California Department of Fish and Game and the state legislature have invoked emergency and permanent closures that prohibit commercial set-net fishing within essentially the entire sea otter range out to a depth of at least 15 fathoms (see below). The closures have significantly reduced the halibut fishery along the central California coast, where the fishery involves primarily small boats and independent operators. According to an analysis by the California Department of Fish and Game, the 15-fathom closure may have resulted in a 28-percent average income reduction among some central coast fishermen. However, this does not take into account the impact on the individual fisherman nor the possibility of shifting effort to other species (California Department of Fish and Game, n.d.). For some fishermen, redirecting their efforts to other fish species is difficult because of the cost of switching gear and vessels.

Because the sea otter is listed as threatened under the Endangered Species Act, all federal agencies must ensure that any activities they permit, fund, or carry out will not jeopardize the animal's continued existence. Thus, potential risks to sea otters from oil spills could affect individual federally permitted offshore oil-and-gas-development projects. Depending on the severity of the risk and the types of reasonable and prudent alternatives determined to be necessary to avoid jeopardizing the species, substantial economic impact could occur. However, the impact may be little more than a delay in the development of offshore resources, since the requirements and restrictions imposed by the Endangered Species Act would be lifted if the sea otter is recovered and delisted. Restrictions placed on outer-continental-shelf development to protect the sea otter could also result in greater protection for other coastal wildlife as well as scenic and human resources.

One economic benefit, currently unquantified, that results from the presence of sea otters is the enhancement of the local tourist industry. Sea otters have become a major tourist attraction along the central California coast, where they are readily observable by the public at many access points.

## HISTORICAL PERSPECTIVE

### Distribution and Abundance

Historically, the sea otter's range extended from the northern Japanese archipelago (*E.l. gracilis*) northeast to the Commander and Pribilof Islands, across the Aleutian Island chain to the Alaskan Peninsula (*E.l. lutris*), and along the Pacific coast of North America south to central Baja California, Mexico (*E.l. nereis*). The worldwide population was estimated at about 150,000 (Kenyon 1969) to 300,000 (Johnson 1982) animals prior to commercial exploitation. The preexploitation population in California was estimated to number between 16,000 and 20,000 (California Department of Fish and Game 1976, Johnson pers. comm. cited in Ralls *et al.* 1983) (see Figure 1).

Intensive commercial exploitation did not begin until 1741, when the Vitus Bering expedition discovered the Commander Islands. Subsequent commercial exploitation in the 18th and 19th centuries severely reduced the entire worldwide population to an estimated 1,000 to 2,000 animals (Ogden 1941, Kenyon 1969). The total California population in 1914 was estimated to be about 50 animals (California Department of Fish and Game 1976). In 1911, the sea otter became fully protected outside the three-mile territorial limit by the International Fur Seal Treaty, and, in 1913, within three miles by California state law. Such protections spurred a slow otter recovery. By 1960, the population was estimated at approximately 1,000 (California Department of Fish and Game 1976) (see Figure 2).

From the late-1930s to the mid-1970s, the California sea otter population appears to have increased at an average rate of four to five percent yearly (California Department of Fish and Game 1976, Estes 1981, Estes and Jameson 1983, Bonnell *et al.* 1983, Ralls *et al.* 1983).

Censuses made over the past decade indicate that at least since the mid-1970s, the population has ceased to increase and may have declined. From 1982 through 1985, population counts ranged between 1,200 and 1,400 otters, including both independent animals and dependent pups. The spring 1986 survey resulted in a total count of 1,570 dependent and independent otters while the fall count was 1,201 (see Table 1).

## Legal Status of the Southern Sea Otter

The California sea otter is classified as depleted under the Marine Mammal Protection Act and, since 1977, as threatened under the Endangered Species Act. These laws protect it from nearly all forms of taking, killing, and harassment unless for scientific research. The California sea otter also is classified as a "fully protected mammal" under state law.

## Contemporary Problems

When the southern sea otter was listed as threatened in 1977, the primary management problems were the drastically reduced population size and range and the high degree of vulnerability to oil spills from tankers. In 1982, the U.S. Fish and Wildlife Service (FWS)

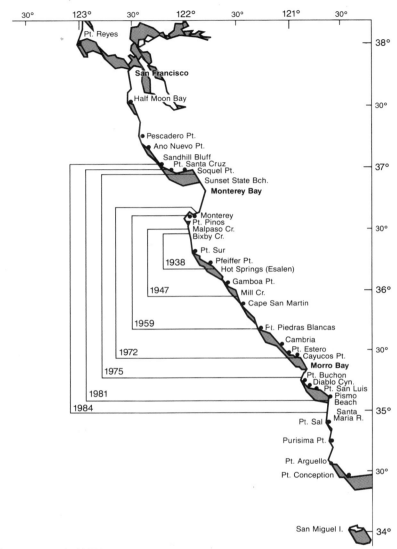

30° 123° 30° 122° 30° 121° 30°

38°

Pt. Reyes

San Francisco

30°

Half Moon Bay

Pescadero Pt.

Ano Nuevo Pt.

Sandhill Bluff
Pt. Santa Cruz
Soquel Pt.

37°

Sunset State Bch.
**Monterey Bay**

Monterey
Pt. Pinos
Malpaso Cr.
Bixby Cr.

30°

Pt. Sur

Pfeiffer Pt.
1938
Hot Springs (Esalen)

Gamboa Pt.
1947
Mill Cr.

36°

Cape San Martin

1959

Pt. Piedras Blancas

Cambria
Pt. Estero
1972
Cayucos Pt.

30°

1975
**Morro Bay**
Pt. Buchon
Diablo Cyn.
Pt. San Luis

1981
Pismo
Beach

1984
Santa
Maria R.

35°

Pt. Sal

Purisima Pt.

Pt. Arguello

30°

Pt. Conception

San Miguel I.

34°

Rate of range expansion (1938-1984) of the California sea otter population
(adapted from California Department of Fish and Game 1976, U.S. Fish and
Wildlife Service 1981).

completed a recovery plan for the sea otter and, two years later,
finished the first comprehensive status review since the species was
listed as threatened. Such reviews are required at least every five years.
The 1984 status review revealed a number of new problems in addition
to the original problems, which were still relevant. The major concerns
identified in 1984 were:

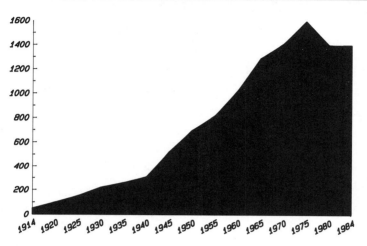

**Growth Rate of the California Sea Otter Population, 1914 - 1984**

*Numerical values are based on CDFG and USFWS population estimates (adapted from Ralls et al. 1981).*

Figure 2

## TABLE 1
### Results of 1982 to 1986 Shore-Ranged California Sea Otter Counts of the Entire Range.

|      |        | Number of Independent Otters | Number of Pups | Total |
|------|--------|------------------------------|----------------|-------|
| 1982 | Spring | 1,124 | 222 | 1,346 |
|      | Fall   | 1,194 | 144 | 1,338 |
| 1983 | Spring | 1,131 | 120 | 1,251 |
|      | Fall   | 1,062 | 164 | 1,226 |
| 1984 | Spring | 1,181 | 123 | 1,304 |
|      | Spring[a] | 1,151 | 52 | 1,203 |
| 1985 | Spring | 1,124 | 236 | 1,360 |
|      | Fall   | 1,066 | 155 | 1,221 |
| 1986 | Spring | 1,345 | 225 | 1,570 |
|      | Fall   | 1,088 | 113 | 1,201 |

Source: Data were cooperatively collected by FWS and the California Department of Fish and Game.

[a] California Department of Fish and Game aerial survey with ground truth stations.

1. population growth had not occurred since at least 1969;
2. the chance of oil tanker spills occurring, though still a major threat, may have decreased somewhat since 1977;
3. the threat of oil spills associated with offshore oil and gas development near the southern end of the otter's range was increasing;
4. incidental entanglement and drowning of significant numbers of otters in commercial gill and trammel set-nets appeared to be a major new problem.

The review concluded that "although the threatened status is still warranted, the overall status of the southern sea otter is probably somewhat worse than at the time of its original listing in 1977" (U.S. Fish and Wildlife Service Five-Year Status Review 1984).

Since 1984, each of the major problems has been analyzed and documented more thoroughly by FWS, the California Department of Fish and Game, and others acting cooperatively. Special observation programs, started in 1980 and intensified from 1982 to 1985, indicate that from 1973 to 1983 otter deaths resulting from commercial fishing operations ranged from 49 to 168 yearly (Wendell *et al.* 1985). Wendell *et al.* (1985) estimate that from June 1982 to June 1984 an average of 80 sea otters drowned in gill and trammel nets each year, an average annual loss of approximately six percent of the population. This was very likely high enough to prevent population growth (see Table 2).

Offshore oil and gas development plans in the federally controlled waters of California's outer continental shelf now include areas within

**TABLE 2**
**Estimates of Incidental Drowning of California Sea Otters in Gill-and-Trammel Nets Calculated from Estimates of Set-Net Effort 1973-1983[a,b]**

| Year | Number of Landings | Estimated Number of Dead Sea Otters |
|------|--------------------|--------------------------------------|
| 1973 | 457 | 49 |
| 1974 | 645 | 69 |
| 1975 | no data | 69 |
| 1976 | 980 | 105 |
| 1977 | 663 | 71 |
| 1978 | 874 | 93 |
| 1979 | 1449 | 154 |
| 1980 | 1407 | 150 |
| 1981 | 1578 | 168 |
| 1982 | 1057 | 113 |
| 1983 | 696 | 73 |

[a] From Wendell *et al.* 1985.
[b] Estimate of effort is based on the number of landings of set-net boats within the sea otter range. Estimated take is based on the rate of take observed in 1983.

the sea otter's range, augmenting the threat from oil spills. However, the potential for a catastrophic spill from a tanker or other large vessel continues to be the greater concern.

Some 100 million barrels of oil and other petroleum products are shipped yearly past otter range. According to U.S. Coast Guard records, more than 3,800 large vessels transit the central California coast adjacent to the otter's range each year. About 19 percent of these are oil tankers. The remainder carry other types of cargo but hold large quantities of their own fuel (U.S. Coast Guard files, 11th and 12th Districts). Sixty percent of the tankers pass within 10 miles of shore.

Oil-spill containment and clean-up technology is not advanced to the point where sizeable spills in moderately rough seas could be contained or cleaned up. Techniques for moving sea otters away from an oil spill have been developed, but not tested in an actual spill. Methods for cleaning and rehabilitating oiled otters are even less developed.

Other problems affecting sea otters, such as illegal shooting and environmental contaminants, have been identified through mortality monitoring studies and other sources, but to date have not been investigated fully or do not appear to have significant impact on the population. Attacks on sea otters by great white sharks (*Carcharodon carcharias*) represent a source of natural mortality to which Ames *et al.* (1983) conservatively attributed roughly 10 percent of the recorded mortality from 1968 to 1984. The significance of this mortality is not known.

## MANAGEMENT

Management responsibility for the southern sea otter within its present range is shared between FWS and the California Department of Fish and Game through a cooperative agreement under the Endangered Species Act. The act requires development and implementation of a recovery program to restore listed species so that they no longer require the special protections of the act.

The sea otter recovery plan identifies five major goals and a variety of tasks that must be accomplished in order to restore the population (U.S. Fish and Wildlife Service 1982):

1. minimize the risk of oil spills from tanker accidents and other sources;
2. minimize the possible effects of oil spills;
3. minimize vandalism, harassment, and incidental take of sea otters;
4. monitor the recovery of the existing population and any new colonies;

5. integrate the recovery plan into the development and management plans of local coastal governments.

In order to minimize the risk of oil spills, comprehensive knowledge is needed on the potential sources of spills and their most likely behavior if they do occur. Better information is also needed on state-of-the-art techniques for preventing and controlling spills to minimize impacts. Once this information is available, steps can be taken to minimize the possibility that serious spills will occur.

The Minerals Management Service in the Department of the Interior, charged with regulating outer-continental-shelf oil and gas development in federal waters (outside of three miles), also is responsible for using its authorities to help recover and enhance species listed as threatened or endangered. The Minerals Management Service establishes safety requirements for all outer-continental-shelf exploration and development activities to minimize the chances and magnitude of a spill.

Through the Section 7 consultation process, the Minerals Management Service consults with FWS on the effects that outer-continental-shelf projects could have on sea otters. A comprehensive analysis of oil-spill risks and of the cumulative impacts on the sea otter is done as part of the consultation process. To date, consultations have been completed for development of the Southern and Central Basin fields and for one platform in the Northern Santa Maria Basin field, none of which indicated that the development would jeopardize the sea otter. A consultation for additional development of the Northern Santa Maria Basin field, which actually overlaps the southern portion of the sea otter's range, was completed in September 1986. That consultation concluded that full development of the Northern Santa Maria Basin would be likely to jeopardize the continued existence of the southern sea otters. Because the analysis was based on hypothetical platforms and models to predict sea otter losses from oil spills, it was deemed prudent to conduct individual consultations as each platform comes forward for approval.

An outgrowth of the outer-continental-shelf oil-development program is an extensive research program on sea otters funded by the Minerals Management Service. The principal projects now under way include a comprehensive tagging and radio telemetry study to further understand population dynamics, movements, and behavior; an evaluation of techniques for cleaning and rehabilitating oiled otters; and an assessment of potential methods for moving or herding sea otters away from an oil spill.

The U.S. Coast Guard is considering establishment of a "fairway" system of travel lanes between San Francisco Bay and the Santa Barbara Channel in which no structures such as oil platforms could be placed.

The Coast Guard believes the lanes would reduce the chance of collisions with obstacles. However, since the lanes would be within about nine miles of Point Sur in the middle of the otter's range, some concern exists that oil-spill risks to sea otters may actually increase if larger vessels that now travel farther offshore move into the fairway. The future of this proposal is uncertain, but the Coast Guard probably will be required to consult with FWS under Section 7 to determine if the sea otter would be jeopardized.

In order to mitigate the possible effects of oil spills, the recovery plan calls for establishment of at least one additional breeding colony outside the present range but within the otter's historic range. It would be located where there would be virtually no chance of a major oil spill affecting both the existing population and the new colony. Based on a three-year study by James Dobbins Associates (1984) FWS is considering three potential sites: San Nicolas Island, California; the northern coast of California to about Cape Mendocino; the southern coast of Oregon from the California border to Cape Blanco. High-quality habitat, a low potential for conflicts with fisheries and oil-related activities, and the potential for containment of the new colony by natural barriers make San Nicolas, about 60 miles off the southern California coast, the preferred site.

In June 1984, FWS formally announced its intent to prepare an environmental impact statement and proposed rulemaking on the establishment and containment of the new breeding colony. The scoping process included extensive interaction with interest groups as well as state and other federal agencies. Several preliminary drafts of the environmental impact statement had been produced by early 1986, but release of a draft to the public was held up pending an amendment to the Endangered Species Act that would specifically authorize the translocation. The amendment (H.R. 1027), passed by the House in 1985, also would require containment of the new colony in order to minimize the impacts of the translocation on other resources and establish ground rules for implementing the translocation. The bill represented general consensus among the various interest groups and state and federal agencies involved. In October 1986 Congress authorized sea otter translocation, and the president signed it into law in November. The plan now awaits approval by the California coastal and fish and game commissions, slated to act in June 1987.

Because the serious threat of an oil spill along California's central coast is increasing, decisions on the proposed translocation should be made as quickly as possible. However, because of potential effects on fisheries and oil development, the translocation proposal is highly controversial and in any event will begin no earlier than fall 1987. The actual translocation, if it occurs at all, may take several years, moving as many as 70 animals to the new site during the first year with small supplements after that if needed to bolster the initial group. At the end of the translocation period, the status of both the new colony and the existing population would be fully evaluated. Conceivably, if all went well, recovery could be accomplished soon after the new colony is established and self-perpetuating. Without translocation, recovery would not be accomplished until the current population inhabits enough coastline to prevent a large oil spill from decimating more than a small proportion of the otters. Even this is contingent upon the population beginning to grow again and may take at least 15 years.

The California Department of Fish and Game, in cooperation with FWS and the Marine Mammal Commission, has taken the lead in minimizing vandalism, harassment, and incidental take of sea otters. The incidental take of sea otters in fishing nets was described previously. California has acted expeditiously over the past four years to curb these losses. Most dramatically, in May 1985 the legislature permanently closed the otter range out to 15 fathoms for set nets with mesh larger than 3.5 inches, except that the area beyond the extreme southern end of the otter range could be opened to fishing by emergency order if it were determined that no otters were likely to be caught. The legislation also encouraged the development of new gear and fishing techniques that would not result in the incidental take of otters, other marine mammals, or seabirds.

Unfortunately, after this new law was in place a series of additional drownings occurred just outside the 15-fathom line, most of them between Cape San Martin and Piedras Blancas. As a result, the California Department of Fish and Game in August 1985 invoked a 120-day emergency closure covering this specific area out to 20 fathoms. No additional drownings were observed during the emergency closure. However, since its expiration the following December at least three entangled otters have been observed. Data since the permanent closure indicate that the 15-fathom closure may have reduced the rate of incidental take by only 40 percent.

At this writing, the state legislature had passed legislation that would extend the ban on large-mesh gill and trammel nets out to 20 fathoms within parts of the state Sea Otter Refuge between Carmel and Piedras Blancas. The legislation, which awaited the governor's signature, also would provide funds for low-interest loans to fishermen so they can purchase experimental or alternative fishing gear. The effects of these closures on the otter population, if implemented will not be known immediately, but biannual counts of the California population and observation of gill-net fishing activity will be continued.

# PROGNOSIS

Recovery and restoration of the California sea otter population is still uncertain, although implementation of several important recovery tasks gives reason for some optimism. The managing agencies not only have discovered the probable cause of the otter population's failure to grow—entanglement and drowning in nearshore gill and trammel-set nets—but also have taken relatively strong measures to eliminate this hazard. Unless some other as yet unidentified factor is constraining population growth, researchers expect to see the population begin growing, possibly at the rate of four to five percent yearly as it did prior to about 1970.

Yet to be definitively reckoned with, however, is the threat of serious oil spills, especially from tanker accidents. Tanker and other large vessel traffic along the coast adjacent to the sea otter range is increasing. Plans for oil development and additional lease sales within and immediately adjacent to the otter range are either on the drawing boards or actually being implemented. Establishment of a separate, additional breeding colony as called for in the recovery plan could lessen the impact of future oil spills on the population.

Regardless of the success of various recovery programs, it is very possible that as long as important shellfisheries remain along the West Coast the southern sea otter will never reoccupy a high percentage of its former habitat, Some form of zonal management program will likely be invoked to designate certain key fishery zones from which sea otters will be excluded. At the same time, the zones designated for otters probably will be unable to support viable commercial or sport shellfisheries because of heavy otter predation on shellfish and may not be available for commercial gill-net and trammel-net fishing.

# RECOMMENDATIONS

1. Minimize potential impacts of a large oil spill by establishing an independent but contained breeding colony within the sea otter's historic range, and evaluate the colony's growth and effects on the ecosystem. Maintain the surrounding area free of otters to minimize the impact of the translocation on fisheries and other important marine-resource uses.
2. Develop practical techniques for herding southern sea otters away from oil spills.
3. Improve nonlethal techniques for controlling the movement of southern sea otters into designated no-otter zones.

4. Further reduce the chances of oil spills from vessel accidents by stationing at least one ocean-going tug within the sea otter range to assist disabled vessels.
5. Improve techniques for controlling open-ocean oil spills that occur during unusually rough sea conditions.
6. Study southern sea otter population dynamics to determine the optimum-sustainable-population level.
7. Continue to monitor and evaluate the extent and the impact of otter entanglement in commercial nets.
8. Assist the gill-net fishing industry to develop techniques that will not entangle southern sea otters and other nontarget species.
9. FWS, in cooperation with Pacific-Coast states, should develop a comprehensive, long-range zonal management plan designed to ensure conservation of the southern sea otter and restoration of the optimum sustainable population and to minimize conflicts with sport and commercial fisheries and other valid uses of the coastal zone. The long-range plan should be implemented at such time as the recovery of the southern sea otter is assured.
10. Develop practical and effective methods to clean and rehabilitate oiled sea otters.
11. Develop and implement a comprehensive public information and education program on the status of the southern sea otter, progress toward otter recovery, and plans for otter management.
12. Initiate research to determine how environmental contaminants — such as petroleum products, discharges from offshore oil development and production activities, and municipal and agricultural wastes — affect sea otters and their prey species. This should be done in conjunction with evaluation and monitoring programs conducted by the Minerals Management Service, Environmental Protection Agency, and state and local government water-quality programs.
13. Investigate taxonomic differences between California sea otters and Alaskan sea otters and determine whether mixing would destroy genetic diversity or improve the long-term viability of both.
14. Continue state and federal efforts to halt illegal shooting of sea otters.

## REFERENCES

Ames, J.A., R.A. Hardy, F.E. Wendell and J.J. Geibel. 1983. Sea otter mortality in California. Draft unpublished report. Marine Resource Branch, California Department of Fish and Game, Monterey. 49 pp.

Ault, J.S. 1985. *Species Profiles: Life Histories and Environmental Requirements of Coastal Fishes and Invertebrates (Pacific Southwest) — Black, Green, and Red Abalones.* U.S. Fish and Wildlife Service Biological Report 82 (11.32). U.S. Army Corps of Engineers, TR EL-82-4. 19 pp.

Barabash-Nikiforov, I.I. 1947. *Kalan (The sea otter).* Soviet Ministry RSFSR. Translated from Russian by Israel Program for Scientific Translation. Jerusalem, Israel. 1982. 227 pp.

Benech, S.V. 1977. Preliminary investigations of the giant red sea urchin resources of San Luis Obispo County, California, *Strongylocentrotus franciscanus* (Agassiz). M.S. Thesis. California Polytechnic State University, San Luis Obispo.

————. 1981. Observations of the sea otter *Enhydra lutris* population between Point Buchon and Rattlesnake Creek, San Luis Obispo, California. January through December 1980. ECOMAR, Inc. VII-6-81. 41 pp.

Bodkin, J.L. 1984. A comparison of fish assemblages in *Macrocystis and Nereocystis* kelp forests off central California. Unpublished M.S. Thesis. California Polytechnic State University, San Luis Obispo. 98 pp.

Bolin, R.L. 1938. "Reappearance of the southern sea otter along the California coast," *Journal of Mammalogy* 19(3):301-303.

Bonnell, M.L., M.O. Pierson, and G.D. Farrens. 1983. *Pinnipeds and Sea Otters of Central and Northern California, 1980-1983: Status, Abundance, and Distribution.* Part I of Investigator's Final Report, Marine Mammal and Seabird Study. Prepared for Pacific OCS Region. Minerals Management Service. Center for Marine Studies, University of California, Santa Cruz.

California Department of Fish and Game. 1976. A proposal for sea otter protection and research, and request for return of management to the State of California. Unpublished report, January 1976. 2 volumes.

————. n.d. Assessment of economic impact on gill and trammel net fisheries associated with a proposed 15-fathom closure within the sea otter's range. Unpublished report prepared for consideration of Senate Bill 89 enacted on May 24, 1985, to restrict gill and trammel net fisheries. 5 pp.

Costa and G.L. Kooyman. 1982. "Oxygen consumption, thermoregulation, and the effect of fur oiling and washing on the sea otter, *Enhydra lutris*," *Canadian Journal of Zoology* 60:2761-2767.

Davies, D.H. 1968. "Statistical analysis of the relation between kelp harvesting and sportfishing in the California kelp beds," pp. 151-222, *in* W.J. North and C.L. Hubbs eds., *Utilization of kelp-bed resources in southern California.* California Department of Fish and Game. Fisheries Bulletin 139.

Davis, J.D. and W.Z. Lidicker, Jr. 1975. "The taxonomic status of the southern sea otter," *Proceedings of the California Academy of Sciences, 4th Series* 40:429-437.

Dean, T.A., S.C. Schneter, and J. Dixon. 1984. "Grazing by red and white sea urchins and its effect on the recruitment and survival of kelp," *Marine Biology* 78:301-313.

Ebert, E.E. 1968. "A food-habits study of the southern sea otter, *Enhydra lutris nereis*," *California Fish and Game* 54(1):33-42.

Estes, J.A. 1980. *Enhydra lutris.* American Society of Mammalogists, Mammalian Species No. 133. 8 pp.

————. 1981. "The case of the sea otter," *in* P. Jewell and S. Holt eds, *Problems in Management of Locally Abundant Wild Mammals.* Academic Press. New York.

————. and J.F. Palmisano. 1974. "Sea otters: Their role in structuring nearshore communities," *Science* 185:1058-1060.

————. and E.E. Ebert. 1981. Sea otters and invertebrate fishery resources: existing and potential conflicts from Canada to Mexico. IUCN workshop on Marine Mammal/Fisheries Interactions, 31 March-2 April, 1981. La Jolla, California.

————. and R.J. Jameson. 1983. *Summary of Available Population Information on California Sea Otters.* POCS Technical Paper No. 83-11. Prepared by the U.S. Fish and

Wildlife Service for the Minerals Management Service. Interagency Agreement N. 14-12-001. 29 pp.

———. and G.R. VanBlaricom. 1985. "Sea otters and shellfishes," pp. 187-235, *in* J.R. Reddington, R.J.H. Beaverton and D.M. Lavigne eds., *Marine Mammals and Fisheries.* George Allen and Unwin. London.

———. N.S. Smith and J.F. Palmisano. 1978. "Sea otter predation and community organization in the Western Aleutian Islands, Alaska," *Ecology* 59(4):822-833.

Fisher, E.M. 1939. "Habits of the southern sea otter," *Journal of Mammalogy* 20(1): 21-36.

Gotshall, D.W., L.L. Laurent, and F.E. Wendell. 1976. Diablo Canyon power plant site ecological study annual report, July 1, 1974-June 30, 1975 and quarterly report No. 8, April 1, 1975 - June 30, 1975, California Department of Fish and Game. Marine Resources Administrative Report 76-8.

Green, B. 1978. Sexual maturity and senescence of the male California sea otter (*Enhydra lutris*). Master's thesis. San Jose State University, California.

Harrold, C., and D.C. Reed. In press. "Food availability, sea urchin grazing, and kelp forest community structure," *Ecology.*

Hines, A.H., and J.S. Pearse. 1982. "Abalones, shells, and sea otters: dynamics of prey populations in central California," *Ecology* 63(5):1547-1560.

James Dobbin Associates. 1984. *Southern Sea Otter: Compilation and Mapping of Available Biological, Ecological and Socio-economic Information Bearing on the Protection, Management and Restoration of the Southern Sea Otter.* Report prepared for the U.S. Fish and Wildlife Service in cooperation with U.S. Marine Mammal Commission, under contract no. 14-16-0009-81-050. 117 pp. [+] 5 appendices.

Jameson, R.J. 1983. "Evidence of birth of a sea otter on land in central California," *California Fish and Game* 69(2):122-123.

———. In prep. Movements, home range, and territories of male sea otters in central California.

Johnson, A.M. 1982. "The sea otter, *Enhydra lutris*," pp. 521-525, in *Mammals of the Sea.* FAO Fisheries Series No. 5, Vol. IV.

Kenyon, K.W. 1969. "The sea otter in the eastern Pacific Ocean," *North American Fauna* 68. Bureau of Sport Fisheries and Wildlife. U.S. Government Printing Office. Washington, D.C. 352 pp.

———. 1981. "Sea otter - *Enhydra lutris*," pp. 209-223, *in* Ridgway and R.J. Harrison eds., *Handbook of Marine Mammals.* Academic Press. New York. 235 pp.

Kooyman, G.L., R.W. Davis and M.A. Castellini. 1977. "Thermal conductance of immersed pinniped and sea otter pelts before and after oiling with Prudhoe Bay crude," pp. 151-157, *in* D.A. Wolfe ed., *Fate and Effects of Petroleum Hydrocarbons in Marine Ecosystems and Organisms.* Proceedings of a Symposium, November 10-12, 1976. Seattle, Washington.

Kvitek, R., A. Fukuyama, B. Anderson and B. Grimm. 1985. *Sea Otter Foraging on Deep-burrowing Bivalves in the Elkhorn Slough, a California Coastal Lagoon.* Paper presented at Western Society of Naturalists. Sixty-sixth Annual Meeting, December 27-30, 1985. Monterey, California. (Abstract).

Lawrence, J.M. 1975. "On the relationship between marine plants and sea urchins," *Ocean Marine Biological Annual Review* 13:213-268.

LeBoeuf, B.J., M.C. Riedman and R.S. Keyes. 1982. "White shark predation on pinnipeds in California coastal waters," *Fishery Bulletin* 80(4):891-895.

Leighton, D.L. 1971. "Grazing activities of benthic invertebrates in southern California kelp beds," pp. 421-453, *in* W.J. North ed., *The Biology of Giant Kelp Beds* (Macrocystis) *in California.* Beiheft Zur Nova Hedwigia Heft 32.

Loughlin, T.R. 1977. Activity patterns, habitat partitioning and grooming behavior of the sea otter, *Enhydra lutris*, in California. Ph.D. thesis. University of California, Los Angeles. 110 pp.

————. 1979. "Radio telemetric determination of the 24-hour feeding activities of sea otters, *Enhydra lutris*," pp. 717-724, *in* C.J. Amlaner and D.W. MacDonald eds., *A Handbook on Biotelemetry and Radiotracking*. Pergamon Press. Oxford and New York.

————. J.A. Ames and J.E. Vandevere. 1981. "Annual reproduction, dependency period, and apparent gestation period in two California sea otters, *Enhydra lutris*," *Fishery Bulletin* 79(2):347-349.

Lowry, L.F. and J.S. Pearse. 1973. "Abalone and sea urchins in an area inhabited by sea otters," *Marine Biology* 23:213-219.

Lyons, K.J. and J.A. Estes. 1985. "Individual variation in diet and foraging strategy in the female California sea otter." Sixth Biennial Conference on the Biology of Marine Mammals, November 22-26, 1985. Vancouver, British Columbia. (Abstract)

McLean, J.H. 1962. "Sublittoral ecology of kelp beds of the open coast near Carmel, California," *Biology Bulletin* 122:213-219.

Miller, D.J. 1974. The sea otter, *Enhydra lutris*: Its life history, taxonomic status, and some ecological relationships. *Marine Resources Leaflet* No. 7. The Resources Agency, State of California, Department of Fish and Game. 13 pp.

Morrison, P., M. Rosenmann and J.A. Estes. 1974. "Metabolism and thermoregulation in the sea otter," *Physiological Zoology* 47(4):218-229.

North, W.J. 1965. "Urchin predation," pp. 57-61, *in* W.J. North ed., *California Institute of Technological Kelp Habitat Improvement Project Annual Report, 1 February 1964-31, March 1965. 70 pp.*

————. and J.S. Pearse. 1970. "Sea Urchin Population explosion in southern California coastal waters," *Science* 167:209.

Odemar, M.W. and K.C. Wilson. 1969. "Results of sea otter capture, tagging and transporting operations by the California Department of Fish and Game," pp. 73-79, *in Proceedings of the Sixth Annual Conference on Biological Sonar and Diving Mammals*. Stanford Research Institute. Menlo Park, California.

Ogden, A. 1941. *The California Sea Otter Trade, 1784-1848*. University of California Press. Berkeley, California 251 pp.

Ostfeld, R.S. 1982. "Foraging strategies and prey switching in the California sea otter," *Oceologia* 53:170-178.

Payne, S.F. and R.J. Jameson. 1984. "Early behavioral development of the sea otter, *Enhydra lutris*," *Journal of Mammalogy* 65(3): 527-531.

Pearse, J.S. and A.H. Hines. 1979. "Expansion of a central California kelp forest following the mass mortality of sea urchins," *Marine Biology* 51:83-91.

Quast, J.C. 1968b. "The effects of kelp harvesting on the fishes of the kelp beds," pp. 143-150, *in* W.J. North and C.L. Hubbs eds., *Utilization of kelp-bed resources in southern California*. California Department of Fish and Game. *Fishery Bulletin* 139.

Ralls, K., J. Ballou and R.L. Brownell, Jr. 1983. "Genetic diversity in California sea otters: theoretical considerations and management implications," *Biology Conservation* 25: 209-232.

Ribic, C. A. 1982. "Autumn activity of sea otters in California," *Journal of Mammalogy* 63(4):702-706.

Rice, D.W. 1977. A list of the Marine Mammals of the World. (Third Edition). National Oceanic and Atmospheric Administration Technical Report. National Marine Fisheries Service SSRF-711.

Roest, A.I. 1971. "A systematic study of the sea otter (*Enhydra lutris*)," pp. 133-135, *in Proceedings of the Eighth Annual Conference on Biological Sonar and Diving Mammals*. Biological Sonar Laboratory, Marine Mammal Study Center. Stanford Research Institute. Menlo Park, California.

Sandegren, F.E., E.W. Chu and J.E. Vandevere. 1973. "Maternal behavior in the California sea otter," *Journal of Mammalogy* 54(3):688-679.

Simenstad, C.A., J.A. Estes and K.W. Kenyon. 1978. "Aleuts, sea otters, and alternates stable-state communities," *Science* 200:403-411.

Siniff, D.B., T.D. Williams, A.M. Johnson and D.L. Garshelis. 1982. "Experiments on the response of sea otters, *Enhydra lutris*, to oil contamination," *Biological Conservation* 2:261-272.

———. and K. Ralls. 1986. *Summary of Infomation Obtained on Sea Otters for Minerals Management Service Study on Population Status of California Sea Otters.* Report to California Department of Fish and Game and U.S. Fish and Wildlife Service Office of Sea Otter Coordination. August 31, 1986. 86 pp.

Sinha, A.A., C.H. Conaway and K.W. Kenyon. 1966. "Reproduction in the female sea otter," *Journal of Wildlife Management* 30(1):121-130.

Tarasoff, F.J. 1974. "Anatomical adaptations in the river otter, sea otter, and harp seal," pp. 111-141, *in* R.J. Harrison ed., *Functional Anatomy of Marine Mammals* 2:1-366. Academic Press. New York.

Taylor, W.P. and W.T. Shaw. 1929. Provisional list of land mammals of the State of Washington. *In* Occasional Papers of the Charles R. Conner Museum, State College of Washington. Pullman, Washington. No. 2.

Tegner, M.J. 1980. "Multispecies considerations of resource management in southern California kelp beds," *Canadian Technical Report of Fisheries and Aquatic Sciences* 954:125-143.

———. and P.K. Dayton. 1981. "Population structure, recruitment, and mortality of two sea urchins (*Strongylocentrotus franciscanus* and *S. purpuratus*) in a kelp forest," *Marine Ecology Progress Series* 5:255-268.

U.S. Fish and Wildlife Service. 1982. Southern Sea Otter Recovery Plan. 66 p.

VanBlaricom, G.R. 1984a. "Relationship of sea otters to living marine resources in California: A new perspective," pp. 361-381, *in* V. Lyle ed., *Collection of Papers Presented at the Ocean Studies Symposium, November 7-10, Asilomar, California.* California Coastal Commission and California Department of Fish and Game. Sacramento, California.

———. 1984b. *Sea Otters Enhance Commercially Valuable Resources in Kelp Forests of Central California.* U.S. Fish and Wildlife Service Research Information Bulletin No. 84-12.

———. and R.J. Jameson. 1979. *Sea Otter Kelp Canopy Relationship in Central California: A Historical Review and A Model.* Paper presented at the Sea Otter Workshop. Santa Barbara Museum of Natural History. Santa Barbara, California. 23-25 August.

Vandevere, J.E. 1970. "Reproduction in the southern sea otter," pp. 221-227, *Proceedings of the Seventh Annual Conference on Biological Sonar and Diving Mammals.* Stanford Research Institute.

Wendell, F.E., J.A. Ames and R.A. Hardy. 1984. "Pup dependency period and length of reproductive cycle: estimates from observations of tagged sea otters, *Enhydra lutris*, in California," *California Fish and Game* 70(2):89-100.

———. R.A. Hardy and J.A. Ames. 1985. Assessment of the accidental take of sea otters, *Enhydra lutris*, in gill and trammel nets. Unpublished Report. Marine Resources Branch. California Department of Fish and Game. 30 pp.

Wild, P.W. and J.A. Ames. 1974. "A report on the sea otter *Enhydra lutris* L., in California," *Marine Resources Technical Report* No. 20. California Department of Fish and Game. 93 pp.

Williams, T.D. 1978. *Chemical Immobilization, Baseline Hematological Parameters, and Oil Contamination in the Sea Otter.* Final Report to the U.S. Marine Mammal Commission in fulfillment of Contract No. MM7AD094. Report No. MMC-77/06. U.S. Department of Commerce. National Technical Information Service PB-283-969. 27 pp.

Woodward, R. 1981. "On-the-rocks birth of a sea otter pup," *The Otter Raft* No. 25.

*Wilbur N. Ladd, Jr. is project leader for the U.S. Fish and Wildlife Service Office of Sea Otter Coordination, which directs the recovery program for southern sea otters.*

*Marianne L. Riedman is a research biologist with the Monterey Bay Aquarium who is now in her fifth year of sea otter research.*

The red-cockaded woodpecker is intricately linked with old-growth pine forests in the South, which are rapidly being logged. *William A. Greer*

# The Red-Cockaded Woodpecker

Jerome A. Jackson

*Mississippi State University*

## SPECIES DESCRIPTION AND NATURAL HISTORY

Perhaps no bird better characterizes the mature, open pine forest ecosystem of the southeastern United States than does the red-cockaded woodpecker (*Picoides borealis*), a diminutive species about 8.5 inches long that is readily identified by its large white cheek patches, ladder back, and querulous social nature. The male bears a red spot—the cockade—on the sides of its head, but this is exhibited only during courtship and agonistic displays. The red-cockaded woodpecker is adapted intimately to the fire-climax, southern pine forests and is endangered today because of man's influence on the forests.

### Distribution and Habitat

The range of the red-cockaded woodpecker today includes portions of 12 southeastern states extending from east Texas and southeastern Oklahoma eastward through the Gulf states, south to the Big Cypress Preserve of south Florida, and north as far as Tennessee, south-central Kentucky, and eastern Virginia. Weather patterns associated with the Gulf of Mexico and the northeastern and eastern Gulf Coast give the

Audubon Wildlife Report 1987

479

woodpecker's range a frequency of electrical storms matched nowhere else in North America and by few places anywhere (Jackson *et al.* 1986). Average thunderstorm frequency ranges from 90 days of storms yearly in central Florida to 60 days yearly in inland portions of the Southeast. In contrast, New York City is exposed to thunderstorms on fewer than 30 days per year and the entire Pacific Coast on fewer than five.

Lightning from these storms starts fires. The soils of the southeastern coastal plain are sandy and drain rapidly, increasing the potential for lightning-started fires to sweep across the landscape. Before the arrival of European man, such fires were an annual event on peninsular Florida and apparently ravaged much of the remaining coastal plain at intervals of three to five years (Komarek 1974). Even the marshes burned as flames raced across the water's surface on the tongues of dried grasses. Only the deep-water swamps and the moist hardwood bottomlands were spared.

This fire-dominated environment played a harsh selective role in forming the southern pine ecosystem that is home to the red-cockaded woodpecker. The southern pines themselves evolved adaptations for fire resistance. Their bark and needles form insulating layers that protect growing tissues. This also benefits the red-cockaded woodpecker. For unlike other woodpeckers, it excavates its nest and roost cavities exclusively in living pines—trees that protect its nests from fire. In fact, the behavioral ecology of the red-cockaded woodpecker is intricately related to the fire that dominates the species' ecosystem. In order to survive, the red-cockaded woodpecker needs:

1. pines 75 to 95 years old for cavity excavation;
2. active resin wells for protection from rat snakes;
3. a relatively dense population, to meet the needs of the species' complex social system; and
4. extensive stands of old, open pine forest for foraging and nesting.

### Cavity Excavation and the Need for Resin Wells

Excavating a hole in a living tree is difficult, and red-cockadeds may take years to complete a cavity (Jackson *et al.* 1979b). Once completed, however, a cavity may be used for decades by the birds and their descendants. Some cavities are known to have been used in excess of 50 years. In contrast, other woodpecker species tend to excavate new nesting cavities each year in a process that takes about two weeks.

Because gum flow could fill the cavity and entrap the bird (Locke *et al.* 1979), the cavity entrance must be excavated slightly upward and through the living tissue into the heartwood. Once into the heartwood, the excavation downward generally is made simpler by the presence of red heart fungus (*Phellinus pini*), which weakens the heartwood of pines age 60 years or older (Jackson 1977a). The average age of red-cockaded woodpecker cavity trees in which a new cavity has been excavated is about 95 years for longleaf pine (*Pinus palustris*) and 75 years for loblolly (*P. taeda*) and other southern pines. These generally have the heart-rot fungus, a reduced gum flow that is less likely to fill cavities, and an adequate diameter to allow excavation of a cavity within the heartwood (Jackson and Jackson 1986).

Typically, red-cockaded woodpeckers excavate their cavities below the lowest branch. Probably this is because the spores of red heart fungus enter the tree through the stubs of branches that are pruned naturally as a result of shading. Above the lowest branches, the presence of the fungus is unlikely and cavity excavation more difficult. The lowest branches average higher in older trees, making the red-cockaded woodpecker cavities safer from fire and climbing predators and keeping them above a potentially encroaching understory.

If the understory reaches cavity heights, the birds tend to abandon the cavity (Beckett 1971, pers. obser.). The reason for abandonment is unclear, but may be related to increased vulnerability to predation or to increased competition from other cavity-nesting birds (Jackson 1978c). Here fire plays an important role, controlling understory vegetation, keeping it from growing to cavity height, and allowing the persistence of colonies over several generations.

Perhaps the most characteristic feature of a red-cockaded woodpecker cavity is the presence of smaller holes, called "resin wells," that the birds excavate above and below their cavities. The flow of wet gum resulting from these wells is a deterrant to climbing gray rat snakes (*Elaphe obsoleta spiloides*), serious predators that have adapted to the fire regime by climbing live pines (Jackson 1974). Cavities placed below the lowest branches would be particularly vulnerable to snake predation without the protective barriers resin wells provide (Jackson 1978d).

## Clan Social System and the Need for Nearby Colonies

Because nesting cavities require investments of time and energy and are critical to survival in an environment that is frequently burnt, it is not surprising that red-cockaded woodpeckers should have a social system that transfers the cavities from father to son through several generations.

The birds that occupy a colony site are called a clan (Jackson and Thompson 1971). Typically, each clan includes a breeding pair, their young of the year, plus additional male young from previous breeding seasons. The additional males assist with incubation, brooding, and feeding of the young; maintenance of resin wells; and excavation of new cavities. Colonies with helpers fledge more young than those without (Lennartz and Harlow 1979, Jackson unpubl. data). Thus, it is important that the colony site and foraging habitat be adequate to support these helpers as well as the breeding pair.

Female young usually leave the colony in late winter and apparently wander in the population until they are accepted into a clan that has lost its breeding female. This departure from the home colony reduces the potential for inbreeding and enhances gene flow among colonies.

The cavities composing a colony provide nest sites, shelter from predators and weather, and a focal point for social behavior. Initiation of a new colony is very rare. Successful new colonies also must be rare, since during excavation of the first cavity at a new colony the colonizing birds have no place to roost except in the open. This makes them vulnerable to predators and bad weather, unless they are commuting from a nearby colony. Once the first cavity is excavated, the male uses it as a roost. However, his mate must roost in the open or commute until a second cavity is completed. To date, initiation of a new colony has been documented only once. This was observed at Noxubee National Wildlife Refuge, Mississippi, where a new colony was initiated by a marked pair from two other colonies (Jackson pers. obser.). It lasted only two years. The red-cockadeds disappeared after one of their cavities was taken over by a red-bellied woodpecker (*Melanerpes carolinus*).

Colony stability is enhanced by increased numbers of useable cavities. These provide alternatives when competing species are present and provide roost sites for helpers, increasing the chances that helpers will survive to assist with the rearing of the young and excavation of additional cavities or to inherit the role of breeding male.

Because of this social system and the dispersal of young females, colonies must occur in groups so floating females will always be available in the population to replace breeding females that die. At site after site across the Southeast, isolated colonies are the colonies most frequently abandoned or most likely to be occupied by lone males. Colony losses at the Savannah River Plant in South Carolina and at Noxubee National Wildlife Refuge proceeded in orderly manner from the most isolated to the least isolated (Jackson pers. obser.). Those remaining on or near Noxubee National Wildlife Refuge were primarily those associated with clusters of six or more colonies.

## Foraging Ecology and the Need for Large Home Ranges

The foraging behavior of red-cockaded woodpeckers is also intimately adapted to the pines. Instead of peering-and-poking into bark crevices or excavating to extract wood-boring insects, the red-cockaded wood-pecker specializes in scaling loose bark from pines to capture insects, centipedes, and spiders hidden beneath. Berries are eaten occasionally, but are a minor portion of the diet. Foraging habitat, as well as nesting habitat, is maintained by fire.

The loose bark of older pines provides optimum foraging conditions using the scaling technique. The bark of younger pines and of hardwood trees adheres more tightly and is not fertile ground for a scaling bird (Jackson 1979a). Thus, studies of the foraging ecology of red-cockaded woodpeckers have found repeatedly that the birds selected the largest pines for foraging and foraged on hardwoods less than 10 percent of the time (Ramey 1980, DeLotelle *et al.* 1983, pers. obser.).

The birds' social system demands a large foraging area. Males dominate females and apparently take the best foraging sites for themselves. At any rate, males forage on the upper trunk, limbs, and smaller branches and females on the lower trunk and occasionally on larger limbs (Ligon 1968, Ramey 1980). Typically, neither sex will forage below the level of a dense forest midstory. Thus, male dominance further enhances the need for older, larger pines. In younger trees, an encroaching midstory may result in inadequate foraging for the female.

The quality of foraging habitat influences the home range a clan will use. With open stands of older pines, the birds may be able to survive with a foraging range of as little as 125 acres (Lennartz and Henry 1985). However, a much larger home range may be needed if the forest is young. For example, the average home range was approximately 1,000 acres for three clans in habitat dominated by a 16-year-old pine plantation at the Savannah River Plant (Jackson pers. observ.). Porter and Labisky (1986) also document the birds' preference for foraging on longleaf as opposed to slash pine. Thus, the tree species composing the habitat, as well as age and openness, must be considered in managing for the birds' needs.

## SIGNIFICANCE OF THE SPECIES

The red-cockaded woodpecker is most unusual because of its social system and other adaptations to the climax pine-forest ecosystems of the Southeast. As a subject for studies of adaptation and sociobiology in vertebrates, the red-cockaded woodpecker offers unparalleled opportunities. But more importantly, the red-cockaded woodpecker is an indicator of a whole ecosystem that is being lost—the mature, open southern pine forest. This conspicious, most interesting bird has drawn our attention to a serious ecological problem that is facing at least hundreds of species that share the ecosystem.

Man, too, is being influenced by the losses. We have come to depend on the southern pines for wood and pulp, but in using these resources we have upset the balance of the ecosystem — often in favor of disease and insect pests. For our own future as well as the future of the red-cockaded woodpecker, we must gain a better understanding of how the ecosystem functions and apply that knowledge to restore it to health. Meeting the needs of the red-cockaded woodpecker may well be the key to maintaining a healthy resource for our own future.

## HISTORICAL PERSPECTIVE

The red-cockaded woodpecker's range once extended to southern Pennsylvania, where Krider (1879) found that it was "more plenty [sic] before the large timber was cut." A specimen was even collected in Hoboken, New Jersey (Lawrence 1867). A small population survived in southcentral Missouri until the 1940s (Cunningham 1946), but it vanished along with the mature, open pine forest. The red-cockaded woodpecker has disappeared recently from Maryland (Devlin *et al.* 1980).

The causes for the decline of the red-cockaded woodpecker are habitat loss and fragmentation. The key to the species' survival is providing the habitat the bird needs — extensive mature open pine forest.

Columnist Jack Anderson wrote that only two kinds of endangered species exist: those that are controversial, and those that are not. The red-cockaded woodpecker is one of the controversial species because its habitat-needs conflict with forest-industry objectives. The majority of remaining populations are on national forest lands, and the dominant force on most federal forest lands in the Southeast is the production of raw materials for the forest industry. Even on some southern national wildlife refuges the production of sawtimber and pulpwood is big business, bringing in revenues that equal a large portion of refuge annual operating budgets.

The most serious problems of the red-cockaded woodpecker are political, economic, and educational. The species' biological problems can be solved, providing that basic long-term research on the species is funded adequately and research results are used in an active management program.

The political problems begin with the forest industry's continued attempts to remove the red-cockaded woodpecker from the endangered species list, to which it was added in 1970. At least once they were nearly successful. But the political problems go far deeper. They surface continually from within the federal agencies responsible for the bird's protection and management. For example, the Red-Cockaded Woodpecker Recovery Team, appointed in 1975, was not permitted to meet after its recovery plan was approved by the secretary of the Interior in 1979 even though federal guidelines specify that teams should meet yearly after acceptance of a plan. Moreover, the team was disbanded in 1982 when the first recovery plan (Jackson *et al.* 1979a) proved unsatisfactory to the forest industry and the Forest Service. Under the original plan, the Forest Service was found in violation of Section 7 of the Endangered Species Act because of its management of red-cockaded woodpecker habitat. A Forest Service biologist, Michael Lennartz, was then given a contract to rewrite the recovery plan, which was accepted in 1985 (Lennartz and Henry 1985).

Problems with the new plan are numerous and detailed in a special report prepared by a committee appointed by the American Ornithologists' Union (Ligon *et al.* 1986). A basic problem with the new plan is that management for the red-cockaded woodpecker is recommended on the basis of how little protection need be given to meet the species' minimum requirements, rather than what can be done to provide optimum conditions for the bird.

The economic problems are tied closely to both the political and educational problems. Basically, the forest industry wants to maximize profits. In order to sell their trees to the forest industry, federal foresters allow a clearcutting practice, similar to that used on private lands, called even-age management.

An incident at the Savannah River Plant, managed by the Forest Service, typifies the problems created by even-age management. On the Savannah River Plant the forests generally are young. Red-cockaded woodpeckers have survived there by using scattered old trees within otherwise young stands. The Forest Service has refused to acknowledge the importance of these older trees to the survival of the birds there and continues to clearcut.

Another issue was rotation age. Throughout the Savannah River Plant, the rotation age had been set at 60 years. After a biologist studying red-cockaded woodpeckers argued for a lengthier rotation, hoping that it would stall cutting as well as allow the birds to survive until the surrounding forest matured, the Forest Service agreed to an 80-year rotation in stands near the existing colonies. Unfortunately, the tree species most used there by the birds is longleaf pine, which is not suitable for the birds until about age 95. Subsequently, the Service created a large clearcut within the home range of a clan of red-cockaded woodpeckers. This area had included several large trees and was used extensively for foraging by the birds. The forest supervisor explained that although the Service had approved an 80-year rotation, the area had to be clearcut so the rotation could start at year zero. The colony is now abandoned.

On southeastern national wildlife refuges, the stated forest management plan involves "all-age" management in even-aged units. Unfortunately, "all age" on the refuges means management to an age that is less than a third of the natural potential longevity of southern pines.

Another problem is the current management of southern pine beetle (*Dendroctonus frontalis*) infestations. When pines are stressed —as is often the case in forests that are overcrowded monocultures— this beetle can kill vast acreages. To stop such infestations, the Forest Service solution is to clearcut. Recently the Service clearcut some 40 percent of the 8,700-acre Kisatchie Wilderness Area, an area occupied by red-cockaded woodpeckers and set aside by Congress to be undisturbed by man (Anon. 1986). This clearcutting of a national wilderness area was *justified* as a measure needed to protect the woodpeckers. The cavity trees remain, but the birds' former range is a clearcut of massive proportions, and the future of the birds is not promising.

The third problem, and perhaps the root of the other two, is education. Forestry departments at our universities are dominated by the need to train foresters to maximize profits. Endangered species and other forest values are glossed over and at times ridiculed. These are the departments that train not only industry foresters, but also those employed by the federal government to manage forests for endangered species. Moreover, university wildlife departments, those that train managers for our national wildlife refuges and wildlife biologists for our national forests, are typically within a school of forest resources. For example, at some universities wildlife students get a degree in forestry with a wildlife option. Within the forestry departments the interests of these wildlife students are of secondary importance, a situation that does not change when the students leave school for employment with the U.S. Forest Service. The foresters set policy and the wildlife biologists do what they can within that framework. Finally, wildlife departments do not offer much training for endangered species biologists. The emphases have always been on game-species management and remain there, although a few fresh winds are blowing within wildlife education and there is hope for change.

This discussion has hit at the roots of the red-cockaded woodpecker's problems, but has spelled out few of the specific troubles. These are so numerous that space does not permit detailing them, but they include:

1. isolation of colonies;
2. lack of prescribed burning at a frequency that will control the understory;

3. forest rotations that are inadequate to provide replacement cavity trees for the birds;

4. failure to consider selective cutting as an alternative to clear-cutting;

5. replacement of preferred tree species (longleaf pine) with species less desirable to the birds, such as slash pine;

6. sale or trading of federal lands that include red-cockaded woodpecker habitat; and,

7. continual compromise and making of exceptions by FWS to allow logging and other projects (e.g. highways, military barracks, and gas wells) to destroy colonies.

## CURRENT TRENDS

No known red-cockaded woodpecker population is increasing or even stable. Numerous local populations have disappeared or declined precipitously. For example, between 1970 and 1981, the number of red-cockaded woodpecker colonies at Tall Timbers Research Station near Tallahassee, Florida, went from 11 to zero (Baker 1983). Between 1974 and 1984, the number of active colonies at the Savannah River Plant went from 18 to two nesting pairs and about six lone males. Between 1970 and 1985, the number of active colonies on Noxubee National Wildlife Refuge declined from 32 to 12. Populations in Oklahoma (Wood 1983), Kentucky (Jackson *et al.* 1976), and Tennessee (Nicholson 1977) are nearly extinct, with perhaps fewer than 50 birds in each state. Elsewhere, the red-cockaded is restricted to small islands of suitable, but often marginal, habitat, mostly on public land.

Based on personal observations, literature records, and data solicited from federal and state agencies and the forest industry, Jackson (1971) estimated that the species totaled a minimum of 2,939 individuals, but probably not as many as 10,000 birds. These figures were revised in 1978, following extensive personal surveys and solicitation of revised data from sources contacted earlier (Jackson 1978b). Many unknown colonies had been identified, and, although many previously counted colonies were then known to be abandoned, the population estimate was revised upward to include between 1,500 and 3,500 colonies and 4,500 to 10,500 birds. Because these estimates were made by collecting whatever data could be obtained from any source, their statistical reliability could not be evaluated.

As early as 1971, the largest populations of the species were on southeastern national forests and other federal lands (Jackson 1971). In 1978, Jackson (1978b) estimated that 83 percent of the colonies were on federal lands. Both Jackson (1978b) and Lennartz *et al.* (1983) found that a strong majority of the colonies on federal lands were on national forests.

## MANAGEMENT

In 1979, FWS and the Forest Service convened a panel of biologists and administrators to discuss the feasibility of a rangewide census that could be used as a foundation for future surveys. The survey, carried out only on federal lands, tallied an estimated 2,677 ± 456 colonies (Lennartz *et al.* 1983). The value of the Lennartz *et al.* survey is that the colonies were mapped and the individual cavity trees tagged to allow accurate future assessment (see Table 1).

The survey estimate was close to the 2,904 active colonies Jackson (1978b) estimated on federal land. However, both figures may be overestimates. Jackson had accepted individual reports of active colonies at face value and used data that were up to 10 years old. Visits to 172 of the colonies he reported revealed that only 77 (44. 7 percent) were really active. The data reported by Lennartz *et al.* are subject to a number of errors:

1. They too were collected by numerous individuals.
2. The decision as to what constituted a colony was not based on location of nest trees or birds. Instead, a colony was defined as two or more cavity trees, at least one of which was active, within a circle 503 yards in diameter. Yet in numerous instances, active cavity trees of a single colony are in excess of 503 yards apart and consequently would have been identified as two colonies.

**TABLE 1**
**Numbers of Red-Cockaded Woodpecker Colonies Reported on the Basis of Land Ownership[a]**

| Land Ownership | Jackson (1978b) | Lennartz *et al.* (1983) |
|---|---|---|
| National Forest | 2,121 | 2,157 |
| Military | 340 | 461 |
| National Wildlife Refuge | 216 | 286 |
| State or Municipal | 300 | – |
| Industry | 138 | – |
| Private | 55 | – |
| Unknown and Other | 76 | – |
| Estimated maximum total | 3,473 | 2,677 + 456[b] |

[a] From Jackson (1978b) and Lennartz *et al.* (1983)
[b] Lennartz *et al.* included estimates only for federal lands.

3. Numbers of colonies given are not the result of a survey of all suitable habitat, but are an extrapolation based on numbers found on a sample of the habitat. Suitable habitat was defined using available land-management data, and areas to be sampled were selected on a statistical basis.

4. Some obvious errors were made and neither corrected nor discussed. For example, the colonies on the Savannah River Plant are mapped, and all suitable habitat has been searched for colonies. The adjusted population estimate in Lennartz *et al.* was $17 \pm 44$ colonies. What was actually there when the census was made were two colonies each with a pair of birds, and three colonies with males only— a total of five active colonies, three of them nonreproductive.

Since the birds range over a large area, most researchers use the colony site as a census unit. This leads to several problems, one of the most serious of which is a public relations problem. The mere mention of "colony" conjures up images of large numbers of birds, giving some managers the notion that the birds are abundant and not really endangered. However, numerous studies over the past 20 years indicate that there is never more than one breeding pair of birds per colony. Jackson and Thompson (1971) restricted the use of the term colony to the several cavity trees that the birds use or have used. A second problem that contributes to a false impression of abundance is that the cavity trees of red-cockaded woodpeckers remain long after a colony has been abandoned. Moreover, the activity of other animals at abandoned cavity trees often causes colonies to be misjudged as active (Jackson 1977b, 1978a).

A final problem occurs because all-male colonies cannot be discerned from those that include a breeding pair except by locating active nests or by capturing birds to determine their sex. Because the cockades of the males are usually concealed, adults cannot be reliably sexed except in the hand. This is an especially serious problem in areas with low concentrations of colonies, because such areas have high frequencies of all-male colonies.

# PROGNOSIS

Thanks to a number of well-written popular articles (e.g., Heinrichs and Heinrichs 1984, Freeman 1984, and Wood and Eichholz 1986) and airing of television programs such as *Marty Stouffer's Wild America,* the British Broadcasting Corporation's *Planet Earth* series, and the National Geographic Special *In the Realm of the Alligator,* the public is becoming aware of the red-cockaded woodpecker and its plight. Conservation organizations such as the National Audubon Society, the Sierra Club, and Defenders of Wildlife also have gone to court and worked behind the scenes in legal battles to help the species. The forestry industry also has made efforts on the species' behalf, saving cavity trees in some areas and funding some research.

If we accept the challenge to preserve and manage the mature southern pine forest ecosystem, we can save the red-cockaded woodpecker. If we continue to flounder in the morass of biopolitics, the species may one day exist only as a showcase population, if at all.

## RECOMMENDATIONS

A great need exists for public pressure that can spur federal agencies to do more to manage for the red-cockaded woodpecker on public lands. Continued habitat losses and fragmentation will make the species more vulnerable to extinction as the populations become increasingly smaller and more isolated. The original recovery plan (Jackson et al. 1979a) and some of Jackson's research (Jackson 1976, 1979b) indicated the dangers of fragmentation and isolation and recommended the establishment of corridors of suitable habitat to link populations together through management of interstate highway rights-of-way. Colonies occur in interstate rights-of-way, and the birds will use such corridors. Jeff Walters (pers. comm.) in 1986 documented the incredible movement of a marked bird from a colony next to a North Carolina highway to another colony more than 50 miles away but next to the same highway. However, Lennartz and Henry (1985) chose not to include corridors in the new recovery plan, over the objections of reviewers. If such corridors are established, forest industry and private landowners could be encouraged to manage forest lands adjacent to corridors in a manner favorable to the birds. Then, instead of saving isolated cavity trees that often are soon abandoned, forest industry and private landowners could make a minimum commitment to an organized program that would facilitate gene flow among populations.

One of the approaches that has been tried as mitigation for destroying red-cockaded woodpecker colonies is the capture and movement of clans. In general, this does not work (Jackson et al. 1983). A specific type of relocation does show promise, however. Because many isolated colonies end up with only males and because young females leave their natal colonies in midwinter, males-only colonies might be revitalized by capturing young females at the time they would normally disperse and introducing them to the males-only colonies. A cooperative effort following this approach currently is under way. If successful, this would be a tool for maintaining small populations and introducing genetic diversity to them.

Corridors and occasional movement of birds may help the red-cockaded woodpecker, but more basic needs exist. These include:

1. greater support for enforcement of endangered-species laws;
2. greater emphasis on endangered- and nongame-species management in university wildlife departments;
3. more public education about the species and its needs;
4. incentives to encourage industry and individual property owners to manage their forests in a manner conducive to survival of the species;
5. concerted efforts to stop massive clearcutting on federal lands in the name of southern pine beetle control and initiation of efforts to practice crisis prevention rather than crisis management;
6. a return to selective cutting as a means of managing pine forests on portions of all public lands; and
7. lengthening forest harvest ages to be more compatible with the needs of the red-cockaded woodpecker.

Finally, a whole new approach to endangered species protection is needed. It is not just the red-cockaded woodpecker that is disappearing. It is an entire ecosystem. The best approach to saving the red-cockaded woodpecker is to practice ecosystem management, not endangered-species management.

# REFERENCES

Anon. 1986. *Control of Southern Pine Beetle in Wilderness Areas*. Oversight hearing before the Subcommittee on Public Lands of the Committee on Interior and Insular Affairs. House of Representatives, 98th Congress. Hearing held in Washington, D.C., March 18. Serial No. 99-22. U.S. Government Printing Office.

Baker, W.W. 1983. "Decline and extirpation of a population of red-cockaded woodpeckers in northwest Florida," pp. 44-45, *in* D.A. Wood ed., *Red-cockaded Woodpecker Symposium II Proceedings*. Florida Game and Fresh Water Fish Commission. Tallahassee, Florida.

Beckett, T. 1971. "A summary of red-cockaded woodpecker observations in South Carolina," pp. 44-59, *in* R.L. Thompson ed., *Ecology and Management of the Red-cockaded Woodpecker*. Bureau of Sport Fisheries and Wildlife, United States Department of the Interior, and Tall Timbers Research Station. Tallahassee, Florida.

Cunningham, J.W. 1946. "Missouri region," *Audubon* 48:124-125.

DeLotelle, R.S., J.R. Newman and A.E. Jerauld. 1983. "Habitat use by red-cockaded woodpeckers in central Florida," pp. 59-67, *in* D.A. Wood ed., *Red-cockaded Woodpecker Symposium II Proceedings*. Florida Game and Fresh Water Fish Commission. Tallahassee, Florida.

Devlin, W.J., J.A. Mosher and G.J. Taylor. 1980. "History and present status of the red-cockaded woodpecker in Maryland," *American Birds* 34:314-316.

Freeman, J.T. 1984. "Woodsman, spare that woodpecker!" *Defenders* 59(6):4-13.

Heinrichs, J. and D.B. Heinrichs. 1984. "Rare birds and big trees: East. The woodpecker and the pines," *American Forests* 90(3):24-26, 46, 48-49.

Jackson, J.A. 1971. "The evolution, taxonomy, distribution, past populations and current status of the red-cockaded woodpecker," pp. 4-29, in R.L. Thompson ed., *The Ecology and Management of the Red-cockaded Woodpecker.* Bureau of Sport Fisheries and Wildlife, United States Department of the Interior, and Tall Timbers Research Station. Tallahassee, Florida.

————. 1974. "Gray rat snakes versus red-cockaded woodpeckers: predator-prey adaptations," *Auk* 91:342-347.

————. 1976. "Rights-of-way management for an endangered species - the red-cockaded woodpecker," pp. 247-252, in R.L. Tillman ed., *Proceedings of the First National Symposium on Environmental Concerns in Rights-of-way Management.* Mississippi State University. Mississippi State, Mississippi.

————. 1977a. "Red-cockaded woodpeckers and pine redheart disease," *Auk* 94:160-163.

————. 1977b. "Determination of the status of red-cockaded woodpecker colonies," *Journal of Wildlife Management* 41:448-452.

————. 1978a. "Pine bark redness as an indicator of red-cockaded woodpecker activity," *Wildlife Society Bulletin* 6:171-172.

————. 1978b. "Analysis of the distribution and population status of the red-cockaded woodpecker," pp. 101-111, in R.R. Odom and L. Landers eds., *Proceedings of the Rare and Endangered Wildlife Symposium.* Georgia Department of Natural Resources, Game and Fish Division, Technical Bulletin WL 4.

————. 1978c. "Competition for cavities and red-cockaded woodpecker management," pp. 103-112, in S.A. Temple ed., *Endangered Birds: Management Techniques for Preserving Threatened Species.* University of Wisconsin Press. Madison, Wisconsin.

————. 1978d. "Predation of a gray rat snake on red-cockaded woodpecker nestlings," *Bird-Banding* 49:187-188.

————. 1979a. "Tree surfaces as foraging substrates for insectivorous birds," pp. 69-93, in J.G. Dickson, R.N. Conner, R.R. Fleet, J.C. Kroll, and J.A. Jackson eds., *The Role of Insectivorous Birds in Forest Ecosystems.* Academic Press. New York.

————. 1979b. "Highways and wildlife - some challenges and opportunities for management," pp. 566-571, in *The Mitigation Symposium: A National Workshop on Mitigating Losses of Fish and Wildlife Habitats.* General Technical Report RM-65. Rocky Mountain Forest and Range Experiment Station, Forest Service, United States Department of Agriculture. Fort Collins, Colorado.

————, W.W. Baker, V. Carter, T. Cherry and M.L. Hopkins. 1979a. *Recovery Plan for the Red-cockaded Woodpecker.* United States Fish and Wildlife Service. Atlanta, Georgia.

————, R.N. Conner and B.J.S. Jackson. 1986. "The effects of wilderness on the endangered red-cockaded woodpecker," pp. 71-78, in D.L. Kulhavy and R.N. Conner eds., *Wilderness and Natural Areas in the Eastern United States: A Management Challenge.* Center for Applied Studies, School of Forestry, Stephen F. Austin State University. Nacogdoches, Texas.

————. and B.J.S. Jackson. 1986. "Why do red-cockaded woodpeckers need old trees?" *Wildlife Society Bulletin* 14:318-322.

————, M.R. Lennartz and R.G. Hooper. 1979b. "Tree age and cavity initiation by red-cockaded woodpeckers," *Journal of Forestry* 77:102-103.

————, B.J. Schardien and P.R. Miller. 1983. "Moving red-cockaded woodpecker colonies: relocation or phased destruction?" *Wildlife Society Bulletin* 11:59-62.

————. and R.L. Thompson. 1971. "A glossary of terms used in association with the red-cockaded woodpecker," pp. 187-188, *in* R.L. Thompson ed., *The Ecology and Management of the Red-cockaded Woodpecker*. Bureau of Sport Fisheries and Wildlife, United States Department of the Interior, and Tall Timbers Research Station. Tallahassee, Florida.

————, R. Weeks and P. Shindala. 1976. "The present status and future of red-cockaded woodpeckers in Kentucky," *Kentucky Warbler* 52:75-80.

Komarek, E.V. 1974. "Effects of fire on temperate forests and related ecosystems: southeastern United States," pp. 251-277, *in* T.T. Kozlowski and C.E. Ahlgren eds., *Fire and Ecosystems*. Academic Press. New York.

Krider, J. 1879. *Forty Years Notes of a Field Ornithologist*. Press of Joseph H. Weston. Philadelphia, Pennsylvania.

Lawrence, G.N. 1867. "Catalogue of birds observed in New York, Long and Staten islands and the adjacent parts of New Jersey," *Annual Lyceum of the Natural History of New York* 8:279-300.

Lennartz, M.R., P.H. Geissler, R.F. Harlow, R.C. Long, K.M. Chitwood and J.A. Jackson. 1983. "Status of the red-cockaded woodpecker on federal lands in the south," pp. 7-12, *in* D.A. Wood ed., *Red-cockaded Woodpecker Symposium II Proceedings* of Florida Game and Fresh Water Fish Commission. Tallahassee, Florida.

————. and R.F. Harlow. 1979. "The role of parent and helper red-cockaded woodpeckers at the nest," *Wilson Bulletin* 91:331-335.

————. and V.G. Henry. 1985. *Endangered Species Recovery Plan. Red-cockaded Woodpecker* Picoides borealis. U. S. Fish and Wildlife Service. Atlanta, Georgia.

Ligon, J.D. 1968. "Sexual differences in foraging behavior in two species of *Dendrocopos* woodpeckers," *Auk* 85:203-215.

————, and P.B. Stacey, R.N. Conner, C.E. Bock, and C.S. Adkisson. 1986. "Report of the American Ornithologists' Union Committee for the Conservation of the Red-cockaded Woodpecker," *Auk* 103:848-855.

Locke, B.A., R.N. Conner and J.C. Kroll. 1979. "Red-cockaded woodpecker stuck in cavity entrance resin," *Bird-Banding* 50:368-369.

Nicholson, C.P. 1977. "The red-cockaded woodpecker in Tennessee," *Migrant* 48:53-62.

Porter, M.L. and R.F. Labisky. 1986. "Home range and foraging habitat of red-cockaded woodpeckers in northern Florida," *Journal of Wildlife Management* 50:239-247.

Ramey, P. 1980. Seasonal, Sexual, and Geographical Variation in the Foraging Ecology of Red-cockaded Woodpeckers (*Picoides borealis*). M.S. thesis. Mississippi State University. Mississippi State, Mississippi.

Wood, D.A. 1983. "Foraging and colony habitat characteristics of the red-cockaded woodpecker in Oklahoma," pp. 51-58, *in* D.A. Wood ed., *Red-cockaded Woodpecker Symposium II Proceedings*. Florida Game and Fresh Water Fish Commission. Tallahassee, Florida.

Wood, D.A. and N. Eichholz. 1986. "Florida's endangered woodpeckers," *Florida Wildlife* 40(2):20-23.

*Jerome A. Jackson is professor of biological sciences at Mississippi State University. From 1975 to 1982 he was leader of the U.S. Fish and Wildlife Service Red-Cockaded Woodpecker Endangered Species Recovery Team.*

Highly valued for sport hunting, elk are well managed and their populations stable. About a half million elk remain, enough for an assured future but only a fragment of the 10 million that once roamed the continent. *Leonard Lee Rue III*

# The Elk

Jack Ward Thomas

and

Larry D. Bryant

*U.S. Forest Service*

## SPECIES DESCRIPTION AND NATURAL HISTORY

Twelve subspecies of elk *Cervus elaphus* are native to Eurasia and six to North America. Of the six subspecies originally found in North America, the eastern elk (*C.e. canadensis*) and the Merriam elk (*C.e. merriami*) are thought to be extinct, and the Tule elk (*C.e. nannodes*) and the Manitoban elk (*C.e. manitobensis*) have been much reduced in range and numbers. Only the Roosevelt elk (*C.e. roosevelti*) and the Rocky Mountain elk (*C.e. nelsoni*), both drastically reduced in range and numbers by the turn of the century, have been returned, through good wildlife management, to much of their original range and now exist in good numbers. The Rocky Mountain and Roosevelt elk are the largest subspecies, with bulls weighing up to 1,051 pounds and 728 pounds respectively. The Tule elk is much smaller — bulls weigh about 550 pounds — and once was identified as a separate species (Bryant and Maser 1982).

Rocky Mountain and Roosevelt elk calves are distinguished by reddish coats with creamy spots. This spotted coat is gradually replaced by the adult coat by the first autumn of life. In summer, adults of both sexes have a dark or reddish-brown coat with a distinct

Audubon Wildlife Report 1987

495

yellowish rump patch. The winter coat, acquired by late summer or early fall, differs distinctly between males and females. The adult male has a cream-colored body that contrasts sharply with a much darker brownish mane and head. The female also has a mane but it is less pronounced, and the general coat color is similar to but noticeably darker than that of the males (Peek 1982).

Only males have antlers. Yearling males usually produce "spikes," antlers with only a single point. However, some yearlings (28 percent in a Colorado study) produce one or both antlers with two or more tines (Boyd 1970). These antlers vary in length from half a foot to three feet (Peek 1982). Antler growth generally increases with age until senescence begins at about 10 to 14 years of age (Bubenik 1982). Most single antlers of fully adult North American males bear six tines— in fact, these subspecies are classified as six-point deer (Geist 1971). However, mature males frequently produce antlers with eight or more points (Peek 1982). Antlers from mature males weigh 30 pounds or more per shed pair (Blood and Lovaas 1966).

Antlers are grown and shed yearly. Antler growth begins in May and terminates in August when the skin (called velvet) covering the antlers dies and is shed. The antlers are carried in this hardened condition until they drop off, usually in March or April (Peek 1982).

## Breeding

Breeding usually begins in late September and sometimes continues into late November. Breeding has been reported in yearling cows, but this evidently is rare and varies from herd to herd and year to year. One calf (twins are very rare) is born in May or June (Peek 1982). Rocky Mountain elk calves range from 19 to 45 pounds and average 32 pounds at birth (Johnson 1951). Pregnancy rates of adult cows are commonly above 90 percent (Greer 1966).

Yearling males can be fertile but ordinarily do not breed if fully mature males are present in adequate numbers. In herds with sex and age ratios badly distorted from a continuing heavy kill of males by hunters, yearlings may do much or most of the breeding. The ramifications of yearlings serving as primary breeders have not been fully explored, but it has been hypothesized that lowered pregnancy and recruitment rates may result because of inexperience in courtship and breeding, lower sperm production, and lesser frequency of copulation. Moreover, the lower numbers of bulls available for breeding may lead to an extended breeding season. If these hypotheses are correct, many calves would enter winter one to three months younger than might be expected when adequate numbers of mature bulls are present. Such calves would have less chance of surviving the winter and place a heavier burden on their dam, lessening her chances of survival or, if she survives, of producing a surviving calf the next spring (Bubenik 1982, Peek 1985).

During breeding season, bull elk advertise their presence by "bugling." This high-pitched call can be heard across long distances and is thought to attract cows. This gathering of cows, called a harem, is then herded by the bull to keep them in close proximity until they are receptive to his sexual advances. Such behavior is thought to enhance breeding and produce high rates of conception during the first estrus. Other bulls also may be attracted, and the dominant bull will defend the harem against their incursions (Geist 1982).

### Diet

Elk are found over a wide variety of vegetational types from the southwestern United States to Canada and Alaska. The food habits of elk are equally varied, and the species exhibits a wide latitude in the kind of plant material it eats and uses effectively—a much wider array of plant species than other North American members of the deer family. For example, the Rocky Mountain elk, throughout its entire range, reportedly consumes 142 species of forbs, ferns, and lichens; 77 species of grasses and grass-like species; and 111 species of shrubs and trees—330 plant species in all (Nelson and Leege 1982).

Elk seem to prefer grazing, particularly on native bunchgrasses, but also thrive where browse makes up a substantial portion of the diet. Yet, elk do show different food preferences on each individual herd range. These preferences vary between seasons and years. Such preferences depend largely on the availability and phenological stage of the vegetation which are, in turn, influenced by climatic conditions—particularly the presence and depth of snow (Nelson and Leege 1982).

In winter, elk move to where snow is absent or relatively shallow and feed on whatever plants are available—grasses or browse or both, although grasses seem to be preferred. When snow buries both grasses and deciduous browse beyond easy reach, elk sometimes eat conifers, damaging commercially valuable trees. Arboreal lichens are an important part of the winter diet in some conifer forests. When spring arrives, elk shift their feeding to new grass growth, though some browse is still consumed. As grasses begin to dry in late summer, elk shift their diets to more woody plant material and forbs. By fall, dried grasses make up most of the diet. In years when fall rains occur, elk feed on regrowth of perennial grasses (Nelson and Leege 1982).

### Movements

Some Roosevelt and Rocky Mountain elk migrate between summer and winter ranges and some do not. Migrations usually occur between

**Elk Range**

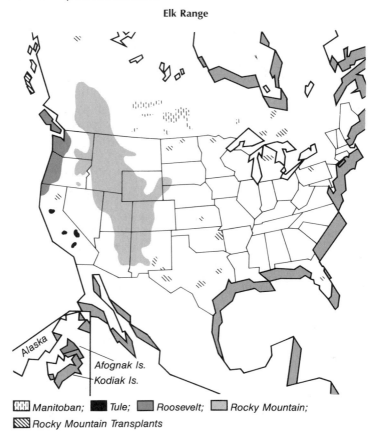

🎦 *Manitoban;* ▇ *Tule;* ▇ *Roosevelt;* ☐ *Rocky Mountain;*
🔲 *Rocky Mountain Transplants*

Figure 1

higher elevation summer ranges through mid-elevation spring-fall ranges to lower elevation winter ranges in the fall or early winter. The reverse occurs in the late winter or early spring. Some of these migrations are quite extensive. For example, the Jackson Hole, Wyoming, herd that winters on the National Elk Refuge covers some 50 miles during migration (Cole 1969). Other migrations may be quite short, but significant in terms of dramatic changes in elevation. However, some groups and some individuals within migratory herds do not migrate and essentially occupy the same general ranges year-round.

Snow depth of 20 to 27 inches seems to trigger migration from higher elevation ranges to winter ranges. Melting snow and decreasing snow depths allow up-slope spring migrations. The cause for both spring and fall migrations is thought to be related to a need for increased food resources (Adams 1982).

The Tule elk is not migratory, and no evidence exists that it ever was (Madson 1966). It is a highly specialized subspecies adapted to open country with semi-desert conditions. However, even the Tule elk exhibits seasonal movements within occupied ranges in response to variations in food availability and palatability. But, these shifts are not considered migrations in the classic sense because summering areas are not made inaccessible by weather, movements are not consistent among herds, and timing of movements varies from herd to herd. These movements are, rather, considered local shifts due to locally occurring conditions (McCullough 1969).

### Habitat Requirements

Roosevelt and Rocky Mountain elk herds, with some rare exceptions, are associated with habitats that contain considerable tree cover. Forests are thought to provide hiding or security cover, protection from the elements, amelioration of ambient temperatures, and food when food sources in openings become unpalatable or are unavailable because of snow depth or other reasons. Commonly, such forests are interspersed with openings created by fire, soil or climatic factors, or such human activities as timber harvest. Where openings exist, elk ordinarily concentrate their use of those openings within 200 yards of forest-opening edges (Lyon and Ward 1982). Where elk are subject to hunting they seem to prefer areas with minimum human disturbances and generally avoid areas adjacent to roads open to vehicular traffic (Perry and Overly 1976).

It is not clear how dependent elk are on free water. Lactating cows, however, seem to need free water. Some evidence suggests that elk distribution, particularly during dry seasons, is highest within a half mile of water (Skovlin 1982).

## SIGNIFICANCE OF THE SPECIES

Elk are large and impressive animals that have become symbols of the North American wilderness. This is somewhat misleading as elk also exist in good numbers in forests managed to produce wood products and sometimes use agricultural lands during severe winters. Some 93 percent of the elk in the United States are found, for at least part of the year, on national forests managed by the U.S. Forest Service. In many of the land-use plans for national forests, elk are identified as either indicator species (a species whose own welfare indicates the general welfare of a group of species and their habitat) or a featured species (one that is selected to receive special management attention) (Thomas and Sirmon 1985).

Elk are highly valued for sport hunting. In 1979, the most recent year for which figures are readily available, 755,179 licenses or hunting permits were issued for hunting elk in North America and 103,781 elk were taken by hunters (Potter 1982). In the late 1970s, the population of elk was estimated at approximately 500,000 (Bryant and Maser 1982). Little reason exists to believe that these numbers have altered much. The species also receives much nonconsumptive recreational use and is sought for viewing by recreationists throughout the western United States and Canada. Elk are a prime attraction in such national parks as Yellowstone, Grand Teton, and Olympic in the United States and Banff and Jasper in Canada.

## HISTORICAL PERSPECTIVE

It has been estimated that some 10 million elk of six subspecies existed in North America at the time of the arrival of Europeans in significant numbers (Seton 1927).

By the late 1880s, the eastern and Merriam elk probably were extinct. The Tule elk had been reduced to fewer than 500 animals and was restricted to a small portion of its former range. Manitoban elk were gone from the Great Plains of the United States and existed only in isolated areas in Canada. Only Rocky Mountain and Roosevelt elk continued to exist in significant numbers, although they, too, were much reduced in both numbers and range. In 1907, it was estimated that the entire elk population in North America was about 100,000 and declining. By 1922, elk numbers were estimated at 90,000, including some 37,000 associated with Yellowstone National Park, Teton National Forest, and portions of Canada (Potter 1982, Bryant and Maser 1982).

These dramatic reductions in elk numbers and range were the result of relentless pursuit by hunters for meat, market, and sport. However, the same result may well have ensued from another source — the incompatibility of large numbers of elk with intensive land conversion for agriculture and human settlement.

The 1920s were the beginning of a modern success story in wildlife management. Elk numbers began to increase following protection from hunting and heavy emphasis on transplanting surplus elk, primarily from Yellowstone National Park, to areas where elk had been extirpated or reduced to very low numbers (Moehler and Toweill 1982). By 1935, elk numbers had recovered to the point where hunting was again permitted and some 3,378 elk were taken legally by hunters. This increased to 19,020 in 1945, 67,454 in 1955, 77,334 in 1965, and 103,830 in 1975 (Potter 1982) (see Table 1).

**Estimated Elk Populations in North America in 1976 by State and Province[a]**

| Nation | State or Province | Subspecies | | | | Total |
|---|---|---|---|---|---|---|
| | | Rocky Mountain | Roosevelt | Manitoban | Tule | |
| Canada | Alberta[b] | 9,500 | — | 9,500 | — | 19,000 |
| | British Columbia[c] | 8,250 | 8,250 | - | — | 16,500 |
| | Manitoba | - | — | 7,500 | — | 7,500 |
| | Ontario | 500 | — | — | — | 500 |
| | Saskatchewan | 2,000 | — | — | — | 2,000 |
| | Yukon Territory | - | — | 50 | — | 50 |
| | | 20,250 | 8,250 | 17,050 | 0 | 45,550 |
| United States | Alaska | — | 450 | — | — | 450 |
| | Arizona | 12,500 | — | — | — | 12,500 |
| | California | 900 | 2,000 | — | 827 | 3,727 |
| | Colorado | 98,000 | — | — | — | 98,000 |
| | Idaho | 51,000 | — | — | — | 51,000 |
| | Michigan | 250 | — | — | — | 250 |
| | Minnesota | 15 | — | — | — | 15 |
| | Montana | 64,000 | — | — | — | 64,000 |
| | Nevada | 650 | — | — | — | 650 |
| | New Mexico | 11,000 | — | — | — | 11,000 |
| | Oklahoma | 350 | — | — | — | 350 |
| | Oregon | 60,000 | 41,000 | — | — | 101,000 |
| | Pennsylvania | 50 | — | — | — | 50 |
| | South Dakota | 2,000 | — | — | — | 2,000 |
| | Texas | 700 | — | — | — | 700 |
| | Utah | 12,000 | — | — | — | 12,000 |
| | Washington | 24,000 | 36,000 | — | — | 60,000 |
| | Wyoming | 65,000 | — | — | — | 65,000 |
| | | 402,415 | 79,450 | 0 | 827 | 482,692 |
| North America Total | | 422,665 | 87,700 | 17,050 | 827 | 528,242 |

[a] From Bryant and Maser (1982).
[b] Reported population of 19,000 containing Rocky Mountain and Manitoban elk arbitrarily divided between the subspecies.
[c] Reported population of 16,500 containing Rocky Mountain and Roosevelt elk arbitrarily divided between the subspecies.

## CURRENT TRENDS

The elk population was estimated at about 500,000 in the late 1970s (Bryant and Maser 1982), the most recent figure available. A 1975 survey of states and provincial fish and wildlife agencies revealed that spokesmen for Alberta, British Columbia, California, Idaho, Montana, South Dakota, Utah, and Washington foresaw further increases in elk numbers. Manitoba, Saskatchewan, Nevada, New Mexico, Oregon, and Wyoming predicted a stable population. Only Arizona and Colorado anticipated decreases in elk numbers (Peek *et al.*1982).

## MANAGEMENT

Under the wildlife laws and customs of the United States, property rights to resident wildlife reside with the states. However, wildlife habitat and access to it for hunting rests with landowners (Lund 1980). Management responsibility for wildlife, therefore, is divided among state conservation departments and private and governmental landowners.

In the late 1970s, 396,000 of the estimated 424,000 elk present in the contiguous 48 states resided at least part of the year on national forests. Moreover, some 89 percent of the national forest land occupied by elk seems likely to be managed under the multiple-use concept to provide grazing for domestic livestock, wood, water, recreation, and wildlife. This makes it very clear that the future of elk in the United States is closely tied to national forest management (Thomas and Sirmon 1985).

The primary habitat components commonly considered by the Forest Service in producing habitat plans for elk management include the size and arrangement of forest stands and openings, the quality and attributes of forest cover, the quality and amount of available forage, and the number of roads open to vehicles per unit of habitat. Such roads serve as a measurement of human disturbance (Thomas *et al.* 1979).

On higher elevation summer and spring-fall ranges, the primary habitat concerns are the amount and pattern of timber harvest, the quality of cover, and the density and management of roads. Forage and browse on such ranges usually are more than adequate.

The primary winter range-management problems appear to be assurance of forage quality and quantity. Many winter ranges are producing forage below the inherent capability of the areas to support ungulates because of a long history of inappropriate grazing. Such situations raise the problem of competition between elk and livestock for available forage. These problems are particularly severe where depleted ranges occur (Peek 1982).

Elk that spend the winter on private lands adjacent to national forests sometimes damage haystacks and fences and consume forage that landowners would prefer to see taken by their livestock. These problems are so pronounced that in some areas the limiting factor on elk numbers is the tolerance that private landowners have for the animals (Peek *et al.*1982). Limitations imposed by landowners may include insistence on control of offending animals in the short-run and reductions in herd numbers over the long-run. Management approaches to reducing elk impacts on private land include feeding elk on selected areas, reducing elk numbers, fencing to control elk access, trapping and transplanting elk, and payment to landowners by state fish and game agencies for damage attributed to elk. None of these approaches has proved to be completely satisfactory, and all are controversial. It seems likely that, as human activities intensify on private lands adjacent to national forests, these problems will increase.

Control of elk numbers and sex and age composition of elk herds usually is accomplished through the manipulation of hunting (time and length of hunting season, hunting methods, and kill limits) and hunter numbers. Management of hunting is the responsibility of the state fish and game agencies and consumes a great deal of their attention. The state agencies establish management objectives for herd numbers after considering the various land management objectives of concerned landowners, both private and governmental; the tolerance of those landowners, particularly private landowners, for the presence and impact of elk; and the demands of the hunting public and other wildlife advocates. This is not an easy task, for these groups are seldom in agreement as to what herd levels should be.

With each passing year, more people want to hunt elk populations that are being held at relatively stable numbers. In many states, the choice has been made to allow hunter numbers to increase and to accept lower hunter success rates. This should slow the increase in hunters, since hunter numbers tend to stabilize when success rates drop below five or six percent (U.S. Forest Service 1975).

This approach has led to a dramatic decline in the number of adult males in some elk herds. For example, post-hunting-season surveys in certain elk management units in Oregon have revealed ratios of two to five antlered males per 100 adult females. This has two ramifications: (1) fewer trophy class bulls are available to hunters and (2) traditional breeding patterns are dramatically altered, with breeding largely accomplished by one-and-a-half and two-and-a-half year-old males instead of older males. The long-term impacts of such a change in breeding behavior is not well understood but has been predicted to cause lowered reproduction and calf survival (Bubenik 1982, Peek 1985).

## PROGNOSIS

The future for elk in North America seems bright. This does not mean that maintaining elk will be easy or that it will occur without human intervention. Elk are big, beautiful, and exciting animals. An animal that stimulates the imagination of so many North Americans will likely continue to receive the management attention it needs to survive in good numbers for the foreseeable future. This does not mean that the *status quo* will be maintained. Some elk herds may decline significantly in numbers because of disturbance from human activities, such as modifications of elk habitat in the course of exploiting natural resources. Some herds may increase, while others may expand their range, thereby producing new herds. It seems inevitable, however, that management of both habitat and hunting will have to be intensified in order to maintain elk numbers.

This means that many of the traditional ways of hunting also will change. There will be ever more people who want to hunt elk, coupled with a stable or decreasing elk population and hunting territory. Rationing of hunting already is under way in many states and is likely to spread and intensify.

The welfare of the elk is inextricably tied to management of the land. If the needs of elk are met in the course of land management, the future for the elk is bright. If they are ignored, if there is failure to recognize the cumulative effects of each land management program on elk, if coordinated management of the various land ownerships within each elk range is not achieved, elk numbers may decline (Peek *et al.* 1982).

> Elk is one wildlife species which significantly interacts with man's other interests and uses of the land. The way we treat these wild creatures which impinge on our other needs can be used as a measure of our humanity, a reflection of the maturity of our society, and an index to our own future. The willingness and ability of people to accept elk as an integral component of the North American landscape will determine whether in the future these wild ungulates will be a curiosity, a memory, or a tribute to compromise and ecological foresight (Peek *et al.* 1982).

## RECOMMENDATIONS

Appropriate management of U.S. national forests and adjoining lands is the key to the welfare of most elk in North America. Just what course of management is to be followed in the national forests is determined through a process of land-use planning and resource allocation that is prescribed by law. The land-use and resource-allocation plans are based upon the issues, concerns, and opportunities identified by the public and the Forest Service itself. Management alternatives are identified and the ecological and economic ramifications of each explored. One alternative is selected and becomes the blueprint for action until the next planning cycle 10 years later. Opportunity for public participation occurs at several stages in the process. Those interested in the welfare of the elk would be well advised to participate effectively in Forest Service land-use planning and resource-allocation activities. After all, habitat is the key to determining the long-term success or failure of an elk herd. All other factors are, in the final analysis, of lesser significance (Thomas and Sirmon 1985).

At the same time, it is critical that adjacent private lands be appropriately managed and that the concern of landowners about the impacts of elk on those lands be addressed. In many cases, the tolerance of such landowners is the factor determining elk herd size. This situation is likely to become more prominent as burgeoning human demands result in intensified land management. Effectively addressing these concerns will require more intensive and more expensive management activities by the state fish and game agencies and by federal land management agencies, particularly the Forest Service.

As the primary purpose for supporting present levels of elk numbers is to furnish game for sport hunting, it seems logical to turn to hunters for the additional resources necessary to carry out the management that will be required. Such revenues can be raised several ways: (1) an increase in hunting license and tag fees; (2) an access fee for hunting on federal lands imposed by the states, under the provision of the Sikes Act; or (3) an access fee for hunting on federal lands imposed by the federal government (Thomas 1984).

An increase in hunter numbers inevitably will make it necessary to tighten the regulation of hunters in order to preserve the quality of hunting and the quality and well-being of elk herds (Peek 1985). This is a serious and growing political issue that must be addressed soon if elk managers are to demonstrate that their primary interest lies with the welfare of elk and not strictly with accommodating increasing hunter numbers and maintaining revenues.

# REFERENCES

Adams, A.W. 1982. "Migration," in J.W. Thomas and D.E Toweill, eds., *Elk of North America — Ecology and Management*. Stackpole Books. Harrisburg, Pennsylvania. pp. 301-322.

Blood, D.A., and A.L. Lovaas. 1966. "Measurements and weight relationships in Manitoba elk," *Journal of Wildlife Management* 30(1):135-140.

Boyd, R.J. 1970. *Elk of the White River Plateau, Colorado.* Colorado Division of Game, Fish and Parks. Denver, Colorado. 121 pp.

Bryant, L.D., and C. Maser. 1982. "Classification and distribution," *in* J.W. Thomas and D.E. Toweill, eds., *Elk of North America—Ecology and Management.* Stackpole Books, Harrisburg, Pennsylvania. pp. 1-60.

Bubenik, A.B. 1982. "Physiology," *in* J.W. Thomas and D.E. Toweill, eds., *Elk of North America—Ecology and Management.* Stackpole Books. Harrisburg, Pennsylvania. pp.125-180.

Cole, G.F. 1969. *The Elk of Grand Teton and Southern Yellowstone National Parks.* U.S. Department of Interior, National Park Service, Research Report GRTE-N-1. 192 pp.

Geist, V. 1971. "The relation of social evolution and dispersal in ungulates during the Pleistocene, with emphasis on the Old World deer and the genus *Bison*," *Quarterly Research* 1 (3):285-315.

Geist, V. 1982. "Adaptive behavioral strategies," *in* J.W. Thomas and D.E. Toweill eds., *Elk of North America—Ecology and Management.* Stackpole Books. Harrisburg, Pennsylvania. pp. 219-277.

Greer, K.R. 1966. "Fertility rates of the northern Yellowstone elk populations," *Proceedings of the Forty-sixth Annual Conference of the Western Association of State Fish and Game Commissioners.* pp. 123-128.

Johnson, D.E. 1951. "Biology of the elk calf, *Cervus canadensis nelsoni,*" *Journal of Wildlife Management* 15 (4):396-410.

Lund, T.A. 1980. *American Wildlife Law.* University of California press. Berkeley and Los Angeles. 179 pp.

Lyon, L.J., and A.L. Ward. 1982. "Elk and land management," *in* J.W. Thomas and D.E: Toweill, eds., *Elk of North America—Ecology and Management.* Stackpole Books. Harrisburg, Pennsylvania. pp. 443-478.

Madson, J. 1966. *The Elk.* Conservation Department, Winchester Western Division, Oling Corporation, East Alton, Illinois. 125 pp.

McCullough, D.R. 1969. "The Tule elk: its history, behavior, and ecology," *University of California Publications in Zoology,* vol. 88. University of California Press. Berkeley and Los Angeles, California. 209 pp.

Moehler, L.L., and D.E. Toweill. 1982. "Regulated elk populations and hunter harvests," *in* J.W. Thomas and D.E. Toweill, eds., *Elk of North America—Ecology and Management.* Stackpole Books. Harrisburg, Pennsylvania. pp. 561-598.

Nelson, J.R., and T.A. Leege. 1982. "Nutritional requirements and food habits," *in* J.W. Thomas and D.E. Toweill, eds., *Elk of North America—Ecology and Management.* Stackpole Books. Harrisburg, Pennsylvania. pp. 323-368.

Peek, J.M. 1982. "Elk," *in* J.A. Chapman and G.A. Feldhamer, eds., *Wild Mammals of North America—Biology, Management, Economics.* The Johns Hopkins University Press. Baltimore, Maryland. pp. 851-861.

Peek, J. 1985. "In defense of the old bull," *Bugle* 2 (3):36-39.

Peek, J.M., R.J. Pedersen, and J.W. Thomas. 1982. "The future of elk and elk hunting," *in* J.W. Thomas and D.E. Toweill, eds., *Elk of North America—Ecology and Management.* Stackpole Books. Harrisburg, Pennsylvania. pp. 599-626.

Perry, C., and R. Overly. 1976. "Impact of roads on big game distribution in portions of the Blue Mountains of Washington," *in* S.R. Hieb ed., *Proceedings of the Elk-logging-roads Symposium.* University of Idaho. Moscow. 142 pp.

Potter, D.R. 1982. "Recreational use of elk," *in* J.W. Thomas and D.E. Toweil, eds., *Elk of North America—Ecology and Management.* Stackpole Books. Harrisburg, Pennsylvania. pp. 509-560.

Seton, E.T. 1927. *Lives of Game Animals.* Volume 3, Part 1. Doubleday, Page and Company. Garden City, New York. 412 pp.

Skovlin, J.M. 1982. "Habitat requirements and evaluation," *in* J.W. Thomas and D.E. Toweill, eds., *Elk of North America—Ecology and Management.* Stackpole Books. Harrisburg, Pennsylvania. pp. 369-414.

Thomas, J.W. 1984. "Fee-hunting on the public's land? — an appraisal," *Transactions of the Forty-ninth North American Wildlife and Natural Resources Conference.* pp. 455-468.

Thomas, J.W. and J.F. Sirmon. 1985. "The national forests and land-use planning — keys to the future of elk and elk hunting," *Bugle* 2(3):22-25.

Thomas, J.W., W.H. Black, Jr., R.J. Scherzinger, and R.J. Pedersen. 1979. "Deer and elk," in J.W. Thomas ed., *Wildlife Habitats in Managed Forests — the Blue Mountains of Oregon and Washington.* Agriculture Handbook Number 553, U.S. Department of Agriculture, Forest Service. Washington, D.C. pp. 104-127.

U.S. Forest Service. 1975. *RPA the Nation's Renewable Resources — An Assessment, 1975.* U.S. Department of Agriculture Forest Service. Washington, D.C. 345 pp.

*Jack Ward Thomas is a U.S. Forest Service wildlife biologist in La Grande, Oregon, and editor of* The Elk in North America. *He has studied elk for 12 years.*

*Larry D. Bryant, also a Forest Service wildlife biologist in La Grande, works on elk with Thomas.*

Only 4,500 piping plovers remain, and they are threatened at many sites by development. If the present population level can be maintained for 10 years, however, biologists will be optimistic about the species' survival. *Harry N. Darrow*

# The Piping Plover

Susan M. Haig

and

Lewis W. Oring
*University of North Dakota*

## SPECIES DESCRIPTION AND NATURAL HISTORY

The piping plover (*Charadrius melodus*) is one of three small North American plover species that nest on wide stretches of open beach. The species' sand-colored upper parts and white undersides are typical of its genus, but its bright orange legs make it easy to distinguish from the snowy plover (*C. alexandrinus*) and the collared plover (*C. collaris*). During the breeding season, the piping plover has a single black band across its breast and forehead. East-coast birds have lighter bands than prairie and Great Lakes birds, and females have lighter bands than males. The black breast band is used in courtship displays and during territorial disputes. In winter, piping plovers lose their breast and forehead bands, orange bill parts, and white eyelines (Haig unpubl. data).

Since piping plovers were described as a species, the American Ornithologists' Union has varied in its designation of inland and Atlantic subspecies (*C. m. circumcinctus* and *C. m. melodus*). Still, insufficient evidence exists to justify separation of piping plovers into distinct populations or subspecies. In this chapter, discussion of

Audubon Wildlife Report 1987

prairie, Great Lakes, and Atlantic Coast birds is done purely in reference to geographic regions and does not imply the existence of biologically distinct populations.

## Range

Currently, piping plovers breed on lakes and alkali wetlands in southeastern Alberta, southern Saskatchewan, southern Manitoba, and North Dakota (see Figure 1). They also breed on gravel spits along major rivers in Montana, North Dakota, South Dakota, and Nebraska. Occasional breeding occurs in Iowa. In the Great Lakes region, birds breed at Lake of the Woods in Minnesota and Ontario and at a few sites on the northern tip of lower Michigan. Breeding occurs on U.S. coastal beaches from Maine to North Carolina and in all the Atlantic provinces of Canada.

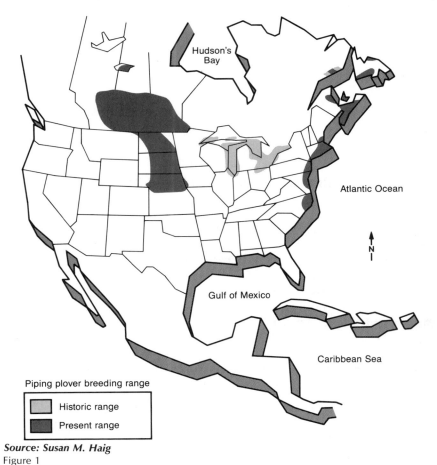

*Source: Susan M. Haig*

Figure 1

Delineation of the winter distribution of the species continues, but recently birds have been sighted on the Atlantic Coast from North Carolina to Florida; on Gulf of Mexico beaches and sandflats from Florida to Brownsville, Texas; and sporadically in Mexico from Matamoros to Veracruz. Few sightings have occurred in the West Indies and little evidence exists to suggest that piping plovers use Central or South American sites. Recent evidence indicates they may winter in Cuba (Haig and Oring 1985).

## Breeding

In spring, piping plovers arrive on breeding grounds in late March on the East Coast (Terwilliger pers. comm. 1986) and during the first two weeks of May in prairie areas (Haig 1985). Most adults return to their previous nest sites, although males exhibit greater site fidelity than do females (Wilcox 1959, Haig 1987, Wiens 1986). Piping plovers are monogamous, but readily change mates and territories following nest failure and between years (Wilcox 1959, Haig 1987, Wiens 1986).

Soon after arrival, males set up and defend territories spaced 25 to 200 yards apart (Wilcox 1959, Cairns 1982). Males also perform aerial courtship displays to lure females onto territories. Both sexes participate in digging a shallow nest scrape in the sand and lining it with tiny shells or pebbles. Eggs are laid every other day until a four-egg clutch is complete. Incubation begins the day the first egg is laid and continues for 25 to 31 days past clutch completion (Cairns 1982, Haig 1987). Both males and females incubate eggs and brood chicks. In Manitoba, females desert broods earlier than do males and often leave broods within the first week after hatching (Haig 1987). Generally, chicks fledge 20 to 32 days after hatch (Cairns 1982, Haig 1987). Chicks are able to breed at one year of age, but less than a fifth of them are seen subsequently at natal sites (Wilcox 1959, Haig 1987, Wiens 1986).

Overall, reproductive success is low and highly variable among sites and years. Many adults do not have a successful nest in a given year, and those that do usually fledge less than two chicks. Piping plovers are sensitive to the presence of people on beaches and have suffered significant losses from vehicles running over nests. In Nova Scotia, fledging success was much greater on isolated beaches than on heavily used beaches (Cairns 1982, Flemming 1984). Studies of nest-site selection at the Chain of Lakes in central North Dakota showed the birds have greater success with nests placed on gravel than on alkali substrate, and on territories with little disturbance and little or highly clumped vegetative cover (Prindiville 1986).

**Post-Breeding**

Adults leave breeding areas as early as the first week of July and continue moving into winter sites through October (Amos pers. comm. 1984). Migratory routes for inland birds are little known. Winter sightings of color-marked birds indicate that post-breeding Atlantic birds move farther south along the Atlantic Coast while prairie and Great Lakes birds frequent the Gulf of Mexico. Banding results also indicate that prairie and Great Lakes birds mix during winter, but Atlantic and inland birds rarely do (Haig and Oring 1985).

Early in the post-breeding period, piping plovers frequent beaches, but later they tend to inhabit ephemeral sandflats found on the back sides of barrier islands. In fact, stabilization of such areas for building projects may be contributing to the decline of the species. In the past, piping plovers may have used beaches more extensively. Now they may be using sandflats in response to increased recreational development of beaches. Current investigations into movements of birds between both habitat types on Dauphin Island, Alabama, may be able to resolve the issue (Johnson 1987).

**Diet**

Little is known about piping plover food habits during any part of the annual cycle. In general, piping plovers eat marine worms, mollusks, crustaceans, and insects (Bent 1929, Quinn and Walden 1966, Palmer 1967). Future investigations of their diet may explain habitat use during all phases of the annual cycle.

## SIGNIFICANCE OF THE SPECIES

The piping plover's value as an indicator species is just beginning to be recognized. Few avian species nest or winter in habitat as ephemeral and vulnerable as that of piping plovers. Throughout their range, they are the first to show the effects of increased recreational activities, fixation of water levels, and stabilization of ephemeral feeding areas. Monitoring the presence of piping plovers on northern Mexican Gulf beaches or the Great Lakes may have yielded a tangible sign that the areas were undergoing detrimental changes that needed more careful assessment.

## HISTORICAL PERSPECTIVE

Piping plovers were first described as a species by Ord in 1824. Little was known about the species until late 19th century and early 20th century expeditions collected specimens (Wilson and Bonaparte undated, Ridgway 1919, Bent 1929). At that time, the breeding range of the inland population extended from central Alberta across Canada to Lake of the Woods, Ontario. The birds were found in northwestern Montana, North Dakota, South Dakota, Nebraska, Iowa, and all states or provinces bordering the Great Lakes. Atlantic Coast birds bred from northern Newfoundland, throughout the Atlantic provinces, and down the Atlantic Coast to South Carolina. Post-breeding birds used beaches along the South Atlantic and Gulf coasts of the United States and Mexico. Occasional sightings of birds in the West Indies indicate that use of the islands may have been more extensive than was documented.

Although attempts to quantify regional or species population numbers did not occur prior to 1980, some evidence suggests that piping plovers never existed in large numbers (Cairns and McLaren 1980). Bent and others reported that intense hunting along the Atlantic Coast caused a serious decline in the number of piping plovers around 1900 (Bent 1929). Passage of the Migratory Bird Treaty Act helped recovery of piping plovers in the 1920s. Following the Depression, extensive construction of homes along Atlantic Coast and Great Lakes beaches once again caused populations to decline. Along with the expansion of human populations came an increase in the number of predators, such as skunks and gulls. Finally, management of water levels on major lakes and rivers throughout the species' breeding and post-breeding ranges became serious threats to previously undisturbed inland sites (Haig 1985).

## CURRENT TRENDS

Since 1900, the species' range has not diminished substantially, but the birds have almost disappeared from the Great Lakes region, where fewer than 20 pairs remain. This loss of birds and breeding sites has formed a major gap in the middle part of the breeding range. On the Atlantic Coast, birds no longer breed on the extreme ends of the range, so those remaining converge on heavily used mid-Atlantic states (Haig and Oring 1985).

Lack of information about the winter distribution of piping plovers makes it difficult to speculate about the current status of post-breeding range. It is known, however, that in the past, piping plovers used northern Gulf of Mexico beaches. Censuses in 1984 could account for only 20 birds in Mexico. Stabilization of sandflats may have curtailed their use (Haig and Oring 1985).

Censuses during the past three years account for 3,500 to 4,200 piping plovers, including 2,137 to 2,684 prairie birds, 28 Great Lakes birds, and 1,370 to 1,435 Atlantic birds. Lack of historic population estimates makes it difficult to put these data into perspective, but comparison with more recent local population figures is useful (Haig and Oring 1985). In a few cases, piping plovers have increased. In Kouchibouguac National Park in New Brunswick, pairs increased from 11 to 21 between 1973 and 1983 (Tull 1984). In 1986, there was a 50 percent increase in nests to 150 at the Chain of Lakes area in North Dakota (Ryan pers. comm. 1986). It is possible this increase was due to a sudden loss of major sites in Saskatchewan, so it may be a temporary phenomenon. Finally, piping plovers were found on Sable Island at Lake of the Woods, Ontario, in 1986 (Hushagen pers. comm. 1986). This discovery removes piping plovers from the list of extirpated birds in Ontario.

While these local increases are encouraging, evidence of a serious population decline continues to grow. Over the past 30 years, piping plovers have been extirpated in Illinois, Indiana, New Hampshire, inland New York, Ohio, Pennsylvania, and possibly Wisconsin. Recent censuses on the Atlantic Coast indicate that the 910 pairs reported in 1980 have decreased 20 to 26 percent to a 1984 estimate of no more than 727 (Haig and Oring 1985).

Traditionally, prairie areas have held the most stable habitat for piping plovers, yet in recent years the prairie region also has experienced a decrease in the number of sites used and birds present. In Manitoba, high water levels and increased recreational use of beaches have resulted in a 35 percent decline in the number of birds to fewer than 80 in 1986, and a loss of three key breeding sites during the past five years (Haig 1986, in press). Likewise, Lake of the Woods, Minnesota, has suffered a 44 percent decline in the number of adult birds over the past three years, reducing them to 21 individuals (Haig and Oring 1986).

Recent censuses in Saskatchewan indicate that major breeding sites may be subject to population declines. The province contains the greatest concentration of piping plovers in North America, some 750 to 2,500 individuals, yet 1986 data indicate the population may have lost up to 1,000 birds since Harris *et al.*'s (1985) censuses in 1984 (Hjertaas pers. comm. 1986). Some 90 percent of the birds known to breed in Saskatchewan are concentrated at five major sites. In the past two years, high water levels have completely inundated nest sites on Lake Diefenbaker, recreational construction threatens birds on Redberry Lake, future industrial development may severely affect birds on Big Quill Lake, and the number of birds at Chaplin Lake has decreased dramatically. Short-term population fluctuations occur for many species, but these significant changes to formerly stable areas demand further attention (Harris *et al.* 1985, Hjertaas pers. comm. 1986, Haig pers. observ.).

## MANAGEMENT

Piping plovers have been experiencing a serious decline since the early part of this century, yet it is only recently that national or international attention has been drawn to the birds. In 1972, the species was listed on the National Audubon Society's Blue List (Tate 1981). Canada was the first country to recognize officially the plight of the piping plover when it assigned the species threatened status in 1978 (Bell 1978). Seven years later, the Committee on the Status of Endangered Wildlife in Canada changed the designation to endangered (Haig 1985). That same year, the U.S. Fish and Wildlife Service listed piping plovers in the Great Lakes area as endangered and in all other areas as threatened (Sidle 1985).

Currently, both the United States and Canada have piping plover recovery teams investigating Atlantic and inland populations. All four teams are working on recovery plans that will be completed by 1987. To further unite the recovery effort, the American Ornithologists' Union ratified a resolution urging the United States, Canada, and other countries where piping plovers are found to cooperate in the development of international conservation strategies (American Ornithologists' Union 1986).

Since the 1985 species' listing in the United States and Canada, census efforts have increased so that most piping plovers have been censused at least once in every state or province where they occur. On the local level, portions of beach have been closed off or protected from the public in Manitoba; Lake of the Woods, Minnesota; Prince Edward Island National Park,; Virginia coastal beaches; and Kouchibouguac National Park, New Brunswick (Haig 1985, Terwilliger pers. comm. 1986, Beach pers. comm. 1985).

In North Dakota, The Nature Conservancy, via its Natural Heritage Program, has initiated purchasing and protection of the Chain of Lakes area. In addition, under the Natural Heritage Programs, The Nature Conservancy has collected data and initiated conservation efforts for piping plovers in every state the bird inhabits. They also have purchased Atlantic Coast barrier islands used by the birds in winter and on migration. Ducks Unlimited (Canada) recently began a pilot project in southern Saskatchewan whereby they hope to draw piping plovers into artificial nesting habitat created by construction of a newly designed, flattened gravel dike. Successful use of this dike may open the door for piping plover habitat enhancement at future Ducks Unlimited projects (Haig 1986).

## PROGNOSIS

Only recently has concern for piping plovers led biologists to take decisive action in protecting the species. While little was known about piping plovers prior to 1980, considerable ground has been covered in the past seven years. It is encouraging that conservation plans have been initiated, recovery teams formed, and international cooperation established before the species reached a point where little could be done to remedy its status. It is essential, however, that progress continue at the current rate. Presently, fewer than 4,500 adult piping plovers remain, and they are distributed in small populations across thousands of miles. It would be easy to ignore a steady loss of seemingly insignificant sites.

At this point, if no protective measures were initiated, piping plovers on prairie rivers would lose nest sites to water-management plans; Great Lakes, Atlantic Coast, and Gulf of Mexico sites would be lost to recreational development; and major Canadian prairie populations would be lost to a variety of development projects.

Objectives for future recovery of piping plover populations will not be finalized by the United States or Canadian recovery teams until late in 1987. However, if current populations can be maintained for the next 10 years, biologists will have achieved an important step in stabilizing the species. Many of the constraints on piping plovers involve extensive alteration of breeding and winter sites. Recovery of piping plovers is possible, but will require the resolution of conflicts on many local sites.

## RECOMMENDATIONS

The following suggestions may enhance recovery efforts already under way:

*1. Life History Parameters:* Breeding studies in recent years, have filled many gaps in our understanding of piping plovers, yet four major issues need to be resolved. First, the diet of the birds must be studied during all parts of the annual cycle. Similarly, delineation of spring and fall migratory pathways of inland birds must be determined. Further research into chick dispersal patterns and into the location and timing of adult pair-bond formation will strengthen reintroduction strategies and evaluation of the genetic status of the species.

*2. Current Distribution and Population Trends:* Censuses of piping plovers during all parts of the year need to be standardized, coordinated, and continued until a more precise picture emerges of the species' status. At that point, less intense monitoring should continue every five years on a continent-wide basis. Currently, documentation of winter distribution needs further attention. More detailed censuses of piping plovers in Alberta, Saskatchewan, and adjacent prairie states also is necessary.

**3. Habitat Needs and Status:** Evaluation of winter and migratory habitat is especially critical since its importance only recently has become recognized, and development of the areas continues at an ever-increasing rate. Monitoring the status of breeding sites is equally necessary.

**4. Population and Habitat Enhancement:** Sensitivity of piping plovers to any sort of human presence has become obvious. Biologists, as well as the general public, have to recognize that their interactions with piping plovers may seriously affect the birds' reproductive success or chances of returning in subsequent years. Future plans to band birds or carry out research projects will have to be considered carefully and initiated only if they involve investigation of a critical problem that needs resolution.

At many locations, piping plover breeding activity takes place on a limited portion of beach. Hence, restriction of human access to small sections of beach will improve piping plover reproductive success without significantly decreasing the recreational value of the area.

Acquisition and strict protection of areas where there are large concentrations of birds—for example, Bolivar, Texas, Big Quill Lake in Saskatchewan, and the Platte River in Nebraska—may be the most significant contribution biologists and conservationists can make to preserve piping plovers. Nomination of sites for inclusion in the Sister Reserve System would be a starting point to ensure future protection of historically important sites (Myers pers. comm. 1986).

The indirect effects of human disturbance may be more difficult to remedy than is recreational development, but require immediate attention. Man-induced increases of predators have become a major problem throughout the species' range. A long-term solution to the problem is not immediately obvious, but needs to be addressed. Perhaps the most difficult issue to resolve is the artificial manipulation of water levels. Artificially controlled high or low water levels have seriously affected reproductive success for piping plovers in Manitoba, Minnesota, and Nebraska and may decrease nesting habitat in North Dakota in the near future.

Development of artificial habitat in areas frequented by piping plovers may be used to increase current population levels or as a mitigative measure when development of an area is irreversible.

# REFERENCES

American Ornithologists' Union. 1986. Resolutions.
Amos, T. 1984. Personal Communication, March.

Beach, H. 1985. Personal Communication, August.

Bell, F.H. 1978. *The Piping Plover* (Charadrius melodus) in *Canada: A Status Report.* Report to COSEWIC. Ottawa, Canada.

Bent, A.C. 1929. "Life histories of North American shorebirds," *U.S. National Museum Bulletin* 146:236-246.

Cairns, W.E. and I.A. McLaren. 1980. "Status of the piping plover on the east coast of North America," *American Birds* 34:206-208.

Cairns, W.E. 1982. "Biology and behavior of breeding piping plovers," *Wilson Bulletin* 94:531-545.

Flemming, S.P. 1984. The Status and Responses of Piping Plovers (*Charadrius melodus* Ord) to Recreational Activity in Nova Scotia. Honors Thesis. Acadia University, Nova Scotia.

Haig, S.M. Personal Observation.

———. and L.W. Oring. 1985. "Distribution and status of the piping plover throughout the annual cycle," *Journal of Field Ornithology* 56:334-345.

———. 1985. *Status Report on the Piping Plover in Canada.* Report to Committee on the Status of Endangered Wildlife in Canada, Ottawa.

———. 1986. *1986 Status of the Piping Plover in Manitoba.* Report to Manitoba Department of Natural Resources.

———. 1987. Population, Biology, and Life History Patterns of the Piping Plover. Ph.D. dissertation. University of North Dakota.

———. and L.W. Oring. 1986. *Population Evaluation of Piping Plovers at Lake of the Woods, MN.* Report to Minnesota Department of Natural Resources.

———. "Status of the piping plover in Manitoba," in *Proceedings of Prairie Endangered Species Symposium.* Canadian Wildlife Service. Edmonton, Canada. In press.

———. 1986. *Ducks Unlimited Wood River Delta/Old Wives Lake Development: Piping Plover Assessment.* Report to Ducks Unlimited-Canada.

Harris, W., G. Wapple, R. Wapple, K. DeSmet and S. Lamont. 1985. Saskatchewan Piping Plovers-1984. *Prairie Environmental Services.* Saskatchewan, Canada.

Hjertaas, D. 1986. Personal Communication, July.

Hushagen, J. 1986. Personal Communication, July.

Johnson, C. 1987. Aspects of the Winter Ecology of the Piping Plover in Coastal Alabama. M.S. thesis. Auburn University.

Myers, J.P. 1986. Personal Communication, June.

Palmer, R.S. 1967. "Piping plover," in G. D. Stout ed., *The Shorebirds of North America.* Viking Press. New York.

Parks-Canada. 1985. *Piping Plover in Prince Edward Island National Park.* Pamphlet.

Prindiville, E.M. 1986. Habitat Selection and Productivity of Piping Plovers in Central North Dakota. M.S. Thesis. University of Missouri-Columbia.

Quinn, J. and R. Walden. 1966. "Notes on the incubation and rearing of the piping plover (*Charadrius melodus*)," *Aviculture Magazine* 72:145-146.

Ridgway, R. 1919. "*Charadrius melodus* Ord," in pp. 128-132, *The Birds of North and Middle America.* U.S. National Museum 8. Washington, D.C.

Ryan, M. 1986. Personal Communication, July.

Sidle, J. 1985. "Determination of Endangered and Threatened Status for the Piping Plover: Final Rule," *Federal Register* 50: 50726-50733.

Tate, J. 1981. "Blue list for 1981," *American Birds* 35:3-10.

Terwilliger, K. 1986. Personal Communication, July.

Tull, C.E. 1984. A Study of the Nesting Piping Plovers of Kouchibouguac National Park, New Brunswick. M.S. Thesis. University of New Brunswick.

Wiens, T.P. 1986. Nest-site Tenacity and Mate Retention in the Piping Plover (*Charadrius melodus*). M.S. Thesis. University of Minnesota-Duluth.

Wilcox, L. 1959. "A twenty year banding study on the piping plover," *Auk* 76:129-152.

Wilson, A. and C.L. Bonaparte. "Piping plover," in pp. 464-470, *The Natural History of the Birds of the United States.* Cassell, Petter and Galpin. New York.

*Susan M. Haig is currently the team leader for the U.S. Fish and Wildlife Service Great Lakes/Northern Great Plains Piping Plover Recovery Team, and is also a member of the Canadian Wildlife Service Piping Plover Recovery Team.*

*Lewis W. Oring, a professor at the University of North Dakota, conducts population studies and endocrinology research on shorebirds.*

Although viable black bear populations exist in 23 states and all Canadian provinces, some local U.S. populations, particularly in the Southeast, have been all but extirpated. *Leonard Lee Rue III*

# The Black Bear

## Michael Pelton
### University of Tennessee

## SPECIES DESCRIPTION AND NATURAL HISTORY

In the eastern part of their range, black bears (*Ursus americanus*) are predominantly a uniform black, but this changes to a variety of color phases in the West ranging from black to cinnamon to brown to blonde. Some individuals may have a white chest mark, varying from a few white hairs to a large distinctive V-shaped blaze.

Black bears generally reach full skeletal development by age four, but males may continue to grow in body mass for several more years. Adult females weigh from 90 to 180 pounds, while males range from 135 to 350 pounds. An occasional adult male will exceed 550 pounds. They range in length from three to six feet. Their short, heavy, muscular stature makes them well-adapted for negotiating thick understory vegetation and a generally forested habitat (Pelton 1982).

Black bears reach sexual maturity in three to five years, although the nutritional quality of the habitat can affect the age at first estrus (Rogers 1976). Breeding occurs in summer (mid-June to mid-August), and the breeding season is the only time adult males are tolerant of

Audubon Wildlife Report 1987

521

other individuals in the population. Exceptions may occur at sites of high food availability, such as garbage dumps, salmon streams, or campgrounds.

**Breeding**

Sexually mature males may breed with any number of receptive females during the breeding season. The fertilized egg does not implant in the uterus until November or early December (Wimsatt 1963), and young are born in winter dens in late January or early February (Wathen 1983). The short period of fetal development, about two months, results in the birth of very small altricial young no more than eight inches long. Litters typically include two young, but may be as high as five. Young stay with their mother through their first summer and go back into dens with the mother the next winter. The family finally separates in late spring or early summer, when the mother comes into estrus. Thus, breeding typically takes place every other year. However, numerous environmental factors may disrupt this cycle, such as poor food production or loss of litters to predation or malnutrition (Wathen 1983).

During their active period, which begins when they leave their winter dens between early April and mid May, black bears are interested primarily in obtaining food. They feed in early morning and evening, and rest during night and midday. However, the pattern may be disrupted during the breeding season (Garshelis and Pelton 1980). In addition, black bears may respond to human activities by becoming predominantly nocturnal or diurnal to avoid human contact. As fall approaches, their normally crepuscular activities become less evident as they begin to move extensively and forage almost continuously, taking advantage of whatever high-energy food resources are available. During this period they may gain as much as five to seven pounds of fat daily (Jonkel and Cowan 1971).

Although they are classified as carnivores and their dentition is adapted for an omnivorous diet, black bears feed primarily on vegetation, mostly berries and acorns (Eagle and Pelton 1980). Animal material consists primarily of colonial insects, such as yellow jackets and honeybees, or beetles and beetle larvae. An occasional small mammal, such as an armadillo or woodchuck, and even less commonly a large mammal, such as a white-tailed deer fawn, domestic pig, or sheep, makes up a very small part of the diet.

Home range sizes may vary from as small as a half square mile to more than 60 square miles (Alt *et al.* 1976, Amstrup and Beecham 1976, Lindzey and Meslow 1977, Garshelis and Pelton 1981). Females are typically more sedentary while males range widely, particularly during the breeding season. Extensive movements also are associated with foraging activities and with dispersal of younger animals in search of habitat where competition with older established animals is less intense (Rogers 1977).

The high mobility of black bears is a major contributor to mortality outside the legal hunting season. Their wide-ranging habits result in bears being shot in backyards, killed on highways, and illegally hunted. The availability of fall foods seems to play an important role in the movements and, therefore, the overall population dynamics of this species, affecting both natality and mortality (Pelton 1986).

## SIGNIFICANCE OF THE SPECIES

Black bears are among the most adaptable large carnivores in North America (Matson 1967). However, because the species does require some degree of isolation, remoteness, and relatively undisturbed habitat, several eastern national forests have chosen it as their management indicator species. In this role, black bears serve as environmental monitors of changes taking place on national forests as well as on other large tracts of land. Also, because the black bear is much more common than its close relatives, the polar and grizzly bears, meaningful scientific data about black bears are generated more easily. Thus, through technology transfer, much of the information acquired can be applied to the scarcer grizzly or polar bear and even to bear species in other parts of the world. As increasing environmental pressures affect the other bear species, the usefulness of black bears as models or surrogates will become more important.

Some 25,000 to 30,000 black bears are taken yearly in North America (Cowan 1972), representing a considerable expenditure of money by thousands of hunters. In addition, the sale of bear claws, hides, canine teeth, and gall bladders has enhanced the commercial value of the animals to the extent that illegal hunting has become a serious problem in some parts of the black bear range. Moreover, park and forest visitors observe black bears. Often, local communities have benefited greatly from tourists who want to see a wild bear or camp or hike in bear country. To many, the black bear is a symbol of the remaining wilderness in the eastern United States.

Black bears also can have significant negative impacts. They often come in conflict with people and their activities, particularly where food or garbage is involved (Tate and Pelton 1980). If a bear robs picnic tables and garbage cans, becomes aggressive toward people (Tate and Pelton 1980), destroys beehives (Brady and Maehr 1982), damages commercially valuable trees (Poelker and Hartwell 1973), or kills an occasional sheep, steps often must be taken to remove it from the area. This can be a costly and perennial operation, particularly where black bears are abundant (Harms 1980). Thus, the bear sometimes is relegated to pest status or hunting seasons and bag limits are liberalized.

## HISTORICAL PERSPECTIVE

Black bears ranged over most of forested North America. They were and still are the most widely distributed member of the bear family on this continent (Hall 1981). During pre-Columbian times, native Indians used black bears for a variety of purposes, and the species was held in high esteem by most Indian tribes. Because of the relatively low population densities, Indians had little effect on the habitat or the bears. However, as white settlers cleared forests for agriculture and livestock, the eastern landscape changed dramatically. As more people populated the fertile valleys, bears were forced into the less accessible reaches of their habitat. Black bear skins and meat were a source of food and income for these early settlers. In addition, conflicts arose between settlers and bears as the adaptable black bear quickly raided livestock and crops. These conflicts led to extensive bear hunting, forcing the animal even further into less accessible areas.

For some 200 years, the species' eastern range was altered drastically and the bear virtually extirpated from large areas. However, two relatively recent events took place that contributed to the bear's present distribution in parts of its eastern range: reversion of abandoned farmland to forest, and the establishment of a vast network of state or federally owned forests, parks, and wildlife refuges. The latter development guaranteed some permanence and stability of forest habitat. Low human populations in much of the bear's northern and western range have left large blocks of its historical range intact. Extensive coniferous forests across Canada still support black bear populations as they did during pre-Columbian times.

## CURRENT TRENDS

Viable populations of black bears exist in 23 states and in all the Canadian provinces and territories (Cowan 1972). Although, human population pressures and extensive clearing of forests extirpated black bears in several mid-western and eastern states, the species is more adaptable than either the grizzly or polar bear and has persisted even in some areas that have incredible human population pressures. Viable populations in the Catskill Mountains of New York and Pocono Mountains of Pennsylvania attest to the species' ability to survive despite human activities and developments (Clarke 1974, Alt and Carr 1984).

Although more than 200,000 black bears presently inhabit the lower 48 states, they are barely surviving in some areas. Whether the scattered pockets of publicly owned refugia in the Southeast are large enough to sustain viable bear numbers is unknown. Population geneticists predict that without help, many of these populations are doomed. Without exchange of genetic materials among bear populations, some populations will inbreed into oblivion. The picture is brighter outside the Southeast. In most of its range, the species is given game status, and, consequently, population trends are watched more carefully and periodic research is conducted to address future needs. In many parts of its range, the species enjoys stable or even increasing numbers (Burk 1979).

## MANAGEMENT

Management strategies for black bears vary from total protection of isolated populations in some areas of the Southeast to almost year-round hunting seasons in areas of the Northwest and Canada, where there are large, heavily forested areas with sparse human populations (Burk 1979). Hunter-take trends and research results determine the extent to which resource agencies manipulate bag limits and the timing and length of the season. For example, recent research has revealed that female bears usually den earlier than males. Thus, by scheduling the hunting season later in the fall, some states have been able to skew the sex ratio of bears killed in favor of productive females, giving them more protection (Rieffenberger 1980). Where bears are abundant, fall and spring hunting may be permitted, with or without dogs, and baiting and trapping may be legal. Bag limits usually exceed more than one bear per person per season (Burk 1979). Occasionally, closing the hunting season for one or more years is warranted (Conley 1979).

The development of a better aging technique has allowed resource agencies to assess black bear population status more accurately. Although age structure alone is not a reliable indicator of population health, linking ages to the natality and mortality rates of a population produces a relatively accurate indicator of population status. Where populations are too low to generate such information or when no reliable hunting data are available, resource agencies have a particularly difficult job accurately assessing populations (Pelton 1983). They then must rely on other indirect indicators. Currently, several agencies are assessing the usefulness of bait stations as an indirect means of determining population status (Johnson 1985). Unfortunately, the most vulnerable populations are also the most difficult to monitor.

Regardless of their population status in a given area, black bears occasionally come in contact with people and their garbage, food, crops, or livestock. Under these circumstances, the problem bear is then either killed or captured and transplanted. Neither solution is always acceptable or satisfactory. Recent research in the use of aversive stimuli may offer a viable third alternative.

Completely separating people from bears is difficult, but it is the only alternative that offers a total solution to the problem. If people expect to coexist with black bears, they must learn to accept a certain level of occasional inconvenience and allow the responsible resource agencies greater latitude in taking measures to deal with individual problem bears.

## PROGNOSIS

Three sometimes insidious problems will affect the black bear significantly in parts of its future range: increasing human population pressures resulting in further loss or degradation of existing bear habitat; increasing efficiency of bear hunters through the use of CB radios, all terrain vehicles, and radio-collared hunting dogs; and increased economic incentives to kill bears legally or illegally for their claws, hides, and gall bladders (Pelton 1986).

However, as long as relatively large undisturbed tracts of forested land exist in North America, black bears will continue to survive. The permanence of state, federal, and provincial parks, refuges, and forest ensures the bear's future. However, on private lands, where extensive land clearing and settlement occurs in high-growth areas, the prognosis is bleak. Without islands of public lands in such areas, black bears will disappear. In the Southeast, the species already has retreated to such islands. Eventually, this fragmentation may lead to total extirpation on some of these sites. Where human population numbers have stabilized or even decreased, as in some areas of the Northeast, black bears have responded by returning to areas that have been reforested. This species has been remarkably resilient in the face of tremendous human pressures, and there is no reason to think that it will not be so in the future if given some degree of human tolerance and acceptance.

# RECOMMENDATIONS

Responsible agencies should continue to work toward better ways of assessing population status. Hunter-take data alone are inadequate. Two or more independent estimates of population status should be used. The smaller the population, the more critical the need for an accurate count.

Knowledge of seasonal habitat requirements also is important so that land-management plans can address adequately the species' food and space requirements. In some areas, too many open roads lead to unacceptably high mortality rates. Thus, land managers, planners, and other developers should be aware of the potential consequences of future developments on public lands. As populations become vulnerable as a result of increased access, potentially damaging hunting practices should be monitored closely and regulated. Marketing of bear parts and incentives for doing so should be curtailed to prevent excessive take.

The availability of fall food seems to be a major limiting factor for this species throughout its range, whether it is oak acorns, beechnuts, blueberries, or abandoned apple orchards. Therefore, agencies responsible for bear-habitat management should consider carefully such factors as the effects various timber-harvest strategies have on the short-term and long-term availability of fall foods.

Dealing with problem bears is still an area for further research. Developing mutually acceptable ways to separate bears and people is critical.

The species should be more fully recognized for its value as an environmental monitor and an important component of North American forests, and not just as an economic or huntable product of the forest.

# REFERENCES

Alt, G.L., F.W. Alt and J.S. Lindzey. 1976. "Home range and activity patterns of black bears in northeastern Pennsylvania," *Transactions of the Northeast Section of the Wildlife Society* 33:45-56.

Alt, G.L. and P.C. Carr. 1984. "Pennsylvania status report," *in* pp. 27-29, D.S. Maehr and J.R. Brady eds., *Proceedings of the Seventh Eastern Workshop on Black Bear Management and Research.*

Amstrup, S.C. and J. Beecham. 1976. "Activity patterns of radio collared black bears in Idaho," *Journal of Wildlife Management* 40:340-348.

Brady, J.R. and D.S. Maehr. 1982. "A new method for dealing with apiary-raiding black bears," *Proceedings of the Annual Conference of the Southeast Fish and Wildlife Agencies* 36:571-577.

Burk, D. (ed.) 1979. "The black bear in modern North America," *Proceedings of the Workshop on the Management Biology of North American Black Bear.* The Boone and Crockett Club and The Amwell Press. Clinton, New Jersey. 299 pp.

Clarke, S.H. 1974. "New York status report," pp. 21-23, *in* M.R. Pelton and R.H. Conley eds., *Proceedings of the Second Eastern Workshop on Black Bear Management and Research.*

Conley, R.H. 1979. "Report from Tennessee," pp. 97-102, *in* D. Burk ed., *The Black Bear in Modern North America.* The Boone and Crockett Club and The Amwell Press. Clinton, New Jersey. 299 pp.

Cowan, I. McT. 1972. "The status and conservation of bears *(Ursidae)* of the world," *International Conference on Bear Research and Management* 2:342-367.

Eagle, T.C. and M.R. Pelton. 1980. "Seasonal nutrition of black bears in the Great Smoky Mountains National Park," *International Conference on Bear Research and Management* 5:94-101.

Garshelis, D.L. and M.R. Pelton. 1980. "Activity of black bears in the Great Smoky Mountains National Park," *Journal of Mammalogy* 61:8-19.

_____. 1981. "Movements of black bears in the Great Smoky Mountains National Parks," *Journal of Wildlife Management* 45:912-925.

Hall, E.R. 1981. *The Mammals of North America. 2nd edition.* John Wiley and Sons. New York. 1181 pp.

Harms, D. 1980. "Black bear management in Yosemite National Park," *International Conference on Bear Research and Management* 4:205-212.

Jonkel, C.J. and Cowan, I.M. 1971. "The black bear in the spruce-fir forest," *Wildlife Monograph* 27:1–57.

Johnson, K.G. 1985. *Annual Black Bear Bait Station Report.* Department of Forestry, Wildlife, and Fisheries, University of Tennessee. Knoxville, Tennessee. 48 pp.

Lindzey, F.G. and E.C. Meslow. 1977. "Home range and habitat use by black bears in southwestern Washington," *Journal of Wildlife Management* 41:413-425.

Matson, J.R. 1967. *The Adaptable Black Bear.* Dorrance and Company. Philadelphia, Pennsylvania. 147 pp.

Pelton, M.R. 1982. "Black bear," pp. 504-514, *in* J.A. Chapman and G.A. Feldhamer eds., *Wild Mammals of North America.* The Johns Hopkins University Press. Baltimore and London. 1147 pp.

_____. (ed.) 1983. "The tri-state black bear study report," *Tennessee Wildlife Resources Agency Technical Report* 83-9. 286 pp.

_____. 1986. "Habitat needs of black bears in the East," *in* D.L. Kulhavy and R.N. Conner eds., *Wilderness and Natural Areas in the Eastern United States: A Management Challenge.* Center for Applied Studies, School of Forestry, Stephen F. Austin State University. Nacogdoches, Texas. 416 pp.

Poelker, R.J. and H.D. Hartwell. 1973. "Black bear of Washington," *Washington State Game Department Biology Bulletin* 18. 180 pp.

Rieffenberger, J. 1980. "Status report of West Virginia black bears," pp. 54-55, *in* J.M. Collins and A.E. Ammons eds., *Proceedings of the Fifth Eastern Black Bear Workshop.*

Rogers, L.L. 1976. "Effects of mast and berry crop failures on survival, growth, and reproductive success of black bears," *Transactions of the North American Wildlife and Natural Resources Conference* 41:432-438.

_____. 1977. Movements and social relationships of black bears in northeastern Minnesota. Ph.D Dissertation. University of Minnesota. St. Paul, Minnesota. 194 pp.

Tate, J. and M.R. Pelton. 1983. "Human-bear interactions in the Great Smoky Mountains National Park," *International Conference on Bear Research and Management* 5:312-321.

Wathen, Wm. G. 1983. Reproductive biology and denning ecology of black bears in the Great Smoky Mountains. MS Thesis. University of Tennessee. Knoxville, Tennessee. 135 pp.

Wimsatt, W.A. 1963. "Delayed implantation in the Ursidae, with particular reference to the black bear," pp. 49-76, *in* A.C. Ender ed., *Delayed Implantation.* University of Chicago Press. Chicago, Illinois. 316 pp.

*Michael Pelton, a professor of wildlife science at the University of Tennessee, currently is coordinating a research project on brown bears in the Cantabrian Mountains of northern Spain.*

Although limited to only nine populations, all in North Carolina, the rough-leaved loosestrife faces a promising future because of increased federal and state attention. *Vonda Franz/North Carolina Plant Conservation Program*

# The Rough-Leaved Loosestrife

Nora Murdock

*U.S. Fish and Wildlife Service*

## SPECIES DESCRIPTION AND NATURAL HISTORY

The rough-leaved loosestrife (*Lysimachia asperulaefolia*) is a perennial herb endemic to the coastal plain and sandhills of North and South Carolina. The slender upright stems grow from an underground stem, called a rhizome, and reach heights of one to two feet. Whorls, usually of three to four leaves, encircle the stem at intervals beneath the showy yellow flowers. Flowering occurs from mid-May through June, with fruits present from July through October (Kral 1983, Radford *et al.* 1968). The rough-leaved loosestrife is distinguished easily from the only other similar southeastern species, *L. loomisii* Torrey, which has broader, glandular leaves and much larger flowers (Kral 1983). The rough-leaved loosestrife generally occurs in the ecotones or edges between longleaf-pine uplands and pond-pine pocosins (areas of dense shrub and vine growth usually on peaty, poorly drained soil) on moist to seasonally saturated sands, and on shallow organic soils overlying sand (Barry 1980). The plant also has been found on deep peat in the low shrub community of large Carolina bays. The grass-shrub ecotone where the rough-leaved loosestrife is found is fire-maintained, as are the adjacent plant communities, including longleaf pine-scrub

Audubon Wildlife Report 1987

531

oak, savannah, and flatwoods. Suppression of naturally occurring fire in these ecotones results in shrubs increasing in density and height and expanding until they eliminate the open edges required by the loosestrife. Although the species once was native to South Carolina, it is believed extirpated from that state (Rayner 1985) and is restricted to nine populations in seven North Carolina counties (Carter 1985).

## SIGNIFICANCE OF THE SPECIES

Perhaps because of its rarity and relative obscurity, the rough-leaved loosestrife is not a significant component of the commercial trade in native plants. However, other species of this genus are sold commercially as ornamentals, and this species, with its showy flowers, has potential for horticultural use. Other species of the genus also have produced extracts used to manufacture insecticides (U.S. Department of Agriculture 1975). Although no economic value is known for this particular loosestrife species, its rarity probably has ensured its exclusion from tests for commercially valuable chemicals.

The rough-leaved loosestrife, whose biology only recently has been studied in detail, shares its habitat with a number of other plants and animals, many of them also rare or endangered, that have evolved as fire-dependent organisms. Continued study of this species should reveal important details about the relationship between naturally occurring fire and the survival of this ecosystem as a whole.

## HISTORICAL PERSPECTIVE

The rough-leaved loosestrife was described as a new species by Jean Louis Marie Poiret in 1814. The material upon which he based his description was collected in North Carolina, but was attributed mistakenly to an Egyptian collection (Ray 1956). Although intensive searches have been conducted in numerous areas of suitable habitat, only 19 populations have been reported. Since discovery of the species, 53 percent of the known populations have been extirpated, largely because of drainage and conversion of the habitat for silviculture and agriculture. Residential and industrial development has eliminated some habitat directly and altered water regimes in adjacent areas to the point that the species can no longer survive. Fire suppression, as mentioned earlier, is a serious problem. Of the 10 extirpated populations, four were eliminated by drainage and subsequent conversion to pine plantation or other intensive silvicultural practices, three disappeared because of fire suppression, two were eliminated by residential or industrial development, and one was lost when the area was drained and converted to agricultural use. At least seven of the remaining nine populations are threatened by habitat alteration. Populations on military installations are potentially threatened by mechanized military training activities. Although this has not been a documented problem for the species so far, some of the small, fragile pocosins inhabited by the plant could be destroyed easily by heavy tracked vehicles such as tanks. Nonetheless, in areas where they have not survived on adjacent privately owned land, populations may persist on military bases because of periodic fires incidental to military training and the Defense Department's prescribed burning programs.

In 1983, a 200-acre tract of the Croatan National Forest, including part of one of the remaining populations of the rough-leaved loosestrife, was designated for a county landfill site. Some of the plants that existed on the edge of the proposed landfill were removed from the area. A 1986 field survey of the transplant sites indicated that none of the transplanted individuals survived. Fortunately, construction of the landfill fell short of encompassing the remainder of this population, and the surviving plants appear to be doing well.

## CURRENT TRENDS

The rough-leaved loosestrife was proposed as an endangered species by the U.S. Fish and Wildlife Service (FWS) on April 10, 1986 under the authority of the Endangered Species Act (U.S. Fish and Wildlife Service 1986) and is expected to be listed officially by the spring of 1987. The act protects listed plants by prohibiting their removal from federal lands and by the prohibition of sale, import, export, or transport in interstate or foreign commerce. The species is listed by North Carolina as endangered and by South Carolina as endangered and "of national concern." However, only North Carolina offers legal protection for state-listed plants. In North Carolina this protection (North Carolina General Statutes §106-202.12 to 106-202.19 [Cun. Supp. 1985]) prohibits intrastate trade without a permit and bans the taking of plants without the written permission of landowners and a state permit. North Carolina also provides for monitoring and management of state-listed species. However, state prohibitions against taking are difficult to enforce and do not cover adverse alterations of habitat, such as disruption of drainage patterns and water tables or exclusion of fire.

Many of the remaining populations are small in number of individual stems and in terms of area covered by the plants. In addition, the rhizomatous nature of the species suggests that many fewer individual plants exist than stem counts would indicate, with as many as 50 or more stems arising from a single rhizome or plant (Sutter 1985). Therefore, genetic variability within populations is relatively low, making it more important to maintain as much habitat and as many of the remaining colonies as possible. In addition, intensive studies have revealed that for unknown reasons turnover in individual stems is high from year to year. For example, of 50 individuals marked in 1983 and subsequently monitored, only eight remained by 1985 (Sutter 1985). Although the species seems to have high seed viability and good seed set, in 1985 less than three percent of the plants in all populations flowered (Carter 1985, Moore 1985, Sutter 1985, Moloney 1985).

Much remains unknown about the demographics and reproductive requirements of the rough-leaved loosestrife. However, the current distribution of this species is ample evidence of its dependence on fire. Of the nine remaining populations, seven are completely on publicly owned lands or lands owned by The Nature Conservancy and are managed with prescribed fire or exposed to naturally occurring periodic fires. The other two sites are partially in private ownership and are either exposed to periodic fire or are adjacent to areas burned regularly. Populations in areas that have not been burned recently tend to be feeble and reproduce poorly (Moore 1985, Carter 1985).

Only two of the remaining populations are considered relatively secure. One of these, which also is one of the most vigorous populations, is owned by The Nature Conservancy, which actively manages the site with prescribed fire. The second population occupies land belonging to a private landowner who intends to manage the area in ways compatible with the survival of this species.

The remaining seven populations are all potentially subject to some form of threat, including silvicultural site preparation, fire exclusion, rotation burning that exceeds three years between fires, timber-harvesting activities, drainage, development, and, possibly, mechanized military training activities. Although several of the public agencies that manage the land upon which this species occurs have expressed willingness to manage for perpetuation of the species, its survival and recovery are not assured. Because the species must be exposed to periodic fire, and since wildfires rarely are allowed to burn, prescribed fire is critical to the species' survival. This means that sites where the plant occurs cannot simply be set aside and protected but require active management, which in turn requires the expenditure of increasingly limited public funds and resources.

## MANAGEMENT

Active management for the rough-leaved loosestrife at one of the remaining nine sites is ongoing and producing good results (Annand 1985). Populations on land administrated by the U.S. Forest Service and Department of Defense have benefited from ongoing programs of prescribed burning, and personnel with these agencies have indicated their willingness to cooperate in managing for the species, contingent upon available funding. The North Carolina Department of Agriculture's Plant Protection Program has initiated intensive studies of this species at one site and also has submitted a request for funds under Section 6 of the Endangered Species Act in order to continue and expand this work in 1987.

Once listed, the rough-leaved loosestrife also will receive the protection provided under Section 7 of the Endangered Species Act, which prohibits federal agencies from authorizing, funding, or carrying out actions likely to jeopardize the continued existence of endangered or threatened species. Since six of the remaining nine populations occur on federally owned lands, the consultation process called for in the law should resolve potential conflicts where federal actions may affect existing populations.

Much remains to be learned about the loosestrife's biology. However, recovery actions undoubtedly will include refinement of management methodology and development of techniques for transplanting individuals from thriving populations into secure areas of historic habitat.

## PROGNOSIS

Now that the federal listing process has drawn increased state and federal attention to this species and private landowners have expressed their willingness to participate in the active management required for the species' survival, the outlook for the future of the rough-leaved loosestrife is promising. Substantial work on protection of the species has been initiated by The Nature Conservancy and the North Carolina Plant Protection Program and is expected to be augmented in the near future by the efforts of personnel at the Fort Bragg and Sunny Point military reservations, the U.S. Forest Service, and the North Carolina Department of Natural Resources and Community Development, as well as by continuing FWS efforts.

## RECOMMENDATIONS

Further work is required before recommended actions can be organized into a recovery plan for this species. However, several actions required for the species' survival and recovery have been identified. These include regular prescribed burning, protection from drainage, and protection from activities resulting in large-scale soil disturbance where the plants occur. Ongoing and proposed studies of the loosestrife's population biology and ecology will provide data essential to the development of future recovery and management strategies. If suitable secure sites within the species' historic range are located, and if a successful transplantation technique can be developed, transplantation from large and vigorous populations may be used to further ensure the species' continued survival.

## REFERENCES

Annand, F. 1985. The Nature Conservancy, North Carolina office. Personal communication with the U.S. Fish and Wildlife Service.

Barry, J.M. 1980. *Natural Vegetation of South Carolina.* University of South Carolina Press. Columbia, South Carolina. 214 pp.

Carter, J.H., III. 1985. *Rough-leaved Loosestrife in North Carolina.* Status survey report submitted to North Carolina Department of Agriculture. 4 pp.

Kral, R. 1983. *A Report on Some Rare, Threatened, or Endangered Forest-related Vascular Plants of the South.* U.S. Forest Service Technical Publication R8-TP2. 1,305 pp.

Mathews, T.D., F.W. Stapor, Jr., C.R. Richter, J.W. Miglarese, M.D. McKenzie, and L.A. Barclay. (eds). 1980. *Ecological Characterization of the Sea Island Coastal Region of South Carolina and Georgia.* U.S. Fish and Wildlife Service, FWS/OBS-79/40. Volume 1. 212 pp.

Moloney, K. 1985. *Preliminary Report on the 1985 Census of* Lysimachia asperulaefolia *in the Green Swamp of North Carolina.* Report to the North Carolina Department of Agriculture. 15 pp.

Moore, J. 1985. North Carolina Natural Heritage Program. Personal communication with the U.S. Fish and Wildlife Service.

Radford, A.E., H.E. Ahles, and C.R. Bell. 1968. *Manual of the Vascular Flora of the Carolinas.* University of North Carolina Press. Chapel Hill, North Carolina. 1,183 pp.

Ray, J.D. 1956. "The genus *Lysimachia* in the New World," *Illustrated Biological Monographs* 24:1-68

Rayner, D.A. 1985. Letter to Robert Sutter, North Carolina Department of Agriculture, regarding the status of *Lysimachia asperulaefolia* in South Carolina.

Sutter, R. 1985. North Carolina Department of Agriculture Plant Conservation Program. Personal communication with the U.S. Fish and Wildlife Service.

U.S. Department of Agriculture, Agriculture Research Service. 1975. *Insecticides from Plants; a Review of the Literature, 1954-1971.* Agricultural Handbook Number 461. 138 pp.

U.S. Fish and Wildlife Service. 1986. "Proposed endangered status for *Lysimachia asperulaefolia,*" *Federal Register* 51:12451-12455.

*Nora Murdock is a biologist for the U.S Fish and Wildlife Service Endangered Species Field Station in Asheville, North Carolina.*

Upper Silver King Creek, flowing beneath the mountains of Alpine County, California, and its tributaries, may hold the only remaining Paiute trout. Inset: A Paiute trout. *Ed Lorentzen*

# The Paiute Trout

## Bob Behnke
*Colorado State University*

## SPECIES DESCRIPTION AND NATURAL HISTORY

J. O. Snyder described the Paiute trout (*Salmo seleniris*) in 1933 based on specimens collected above Llewellyn Falls on Silver King Creek in the Lahontan basin of Alpine County, California. Subsequent study of Paiute trout specimens demonstrated that they are morphologically and electrophoretically identical to Lahontan cutthroat, *S. clarki henshawi*, except that *seleniris* specimens have no or very few spots on the body (Ryan and Nicola 1976, Behnke and Zarn 1976, Behnke 1960, Busack and Gall 1981). The Paiute trout is now recognized as a subspecies of cutthroat trout, *S.c. seleniris*, and presumably evolved from a population of Lahontan cutthroat trout that had been isolated in Silver King Creek for perhaps 5,000 to 8,000 years (Ryan and Nicola 1976, Behnke and Zarn 1976, Behnke 1960, Busack and Gall 1981, U.S. Fish and Wildlife Service 1985, Wong 1975).

### Range and Distribution

Paiute cutthroat trout presently are known from only a few small streams in California: Fly Valley, Four Mile Canyon, and Corral Valley creeks, all small tributaries to Silver King Creek; North Fork Cotton-wood Creek in Mono County; and Stairway Creek, Madera County. Paiute trout also may occur in Cabin Creek in Mono County and in the outlet of Fresno County's Sharktooth Lake. The last two localities require verification.

The type-locality habitat of Silver King Creek above Llewellyn Falls is about 8,000 to 8,300 feet in elevation. The creek's maximum summer temperature is about 65 degrees Fahrenheit. The stream is mainly shallow riffles with a scarcity of large pool habitat (Ashley 1970, Dunham 1968). The North Fork Cottonwood Creek is smaller and located at slightly higher elevations, but overall is not strikingly different from Silver King Creek (Schneegas and Pister 1965).

## Diet

Paiute trout, as all trout, are essentially opportunistic feeders. In their present habitats they subsist almost entirely on insects. They feed on aquatic larval stages throughout much of the year and also, during summer, on adult aquatic and terrestrial insects (Ryan and Nicola 1976, Behnke and Zarn 1976, U.S. Fish and Wildlife Service 1985, Wong 1975). In still-water environments they also consume crustaceans. The lack of any real differences in feeding preferences or niche differentiation from other trout species makes the Paiute trout unable to coexist with other trout.

Food requirements are not a limitation factor for the preservation of Paiute trout or for their successful establishment in a new environment.

## Home Range/Territory

Territoriality is typical of Paiute trout and of all species of stream trout. Any particular stream section, such as a pool-riffle sequence, will be inhabited by different size classes. Typically, the largest fish is dominant and uses the best resting and feeding habitats. Aggression is sometimes observed, but once a social hierarchy is established, agonistic encounters are rare (Wong 1975, Diana 1975).

Paiute trout generally are sedentary once a territorial residency has been established. They undertake no migrations. Spawning occurs in suitable gravel areas near the resident sites, typically within 100 feet (Diana 1975).

## Spawning

Reproductive-site requirements are similar to those of other trout species. Spawning occurs in gravel areas, typically in riffles and above or below pools where adequate gravel is available for nest construction.

Paiute trout usually are sexually mature at two years. Spawning occurs from May to July depending on water temperature. The female excavates a nest, called a redd, and spawns with a dominant male, but smaller, subdominant males also may participate in egg fertilization. The eggs incubate during the period of increasing water temperatures, from about 42 to 52 degrees Fahrenheit, for about 35 days before hatching. An eight-inch female will spawn about 250 to 400 eggs. Few fish survive to spawn again (Busack and Gall 1981).

After spawning, no care or protection is given to the redd and no care or protection is given to the young (Ryan and Nicola 1976, U.S. Fish and Wildlife Service 1985).

**Population Biology**

The main factor limiting population size is the limited range of present populations, which number 2,000 or fewer fish one year or more in age living in about 10 miles of small streams. The limited habitat also may reduce life span. Very few Paiute trout live more than three years. Populations are depressed by severe floods or droughts. Stream sections that pass through terrestrial habitat degraded by livestock grazing could support more Paiute trout if the surrounding habitat were improved (Ryan and Nicola 1976, Busack and Gall 1981, Dunham 1968).

## SIGNIFICANCE OF THE SPECIES

As the only North American trout species lacking spots on the body, *S.c. seleniris* serves as an example of a morphological pecularity evolved in isolation from its parent stock. Such species, if properly studied, can provide biologists with a better understanding of the evolutionary forces that shape all life.

## HISTORICAL PERSPECTIVE

Most of what is known about the original distribution of *S.c. seleniris* rests on the accounts of a stockman, Virgil Connell, who pastured sheep in the Silver King Creek drainage from about 1890 to the 1940s (Ryan and Nicola 1976). Connell stated that when he first came to Silver King Creek, the headwaters above Llewellyn Falls were barren of fish. Paiute trout occurred at that time only in Silver King Creek below Llewellyn Falls and in Coyote Valley and Corral Valley creeks, tributaries to lower Silver King Creek. Because a barrier falls blocks access to Coyote Valley and Corral Valley creeks, Connell believed these creeks also were once barren of fish but had been stocked with Paiute trout from Silver King Creek by Canadian loggers working in the area in the 1860s.

A shepherd working for Connell stocked Paiute trout above Llewellyn Falls in 1912 to establish a new population in upper Fish Valley. Connell observed hybrid Paiute trout-rainbow trout below Llewellyn Falls in 1924.

Paiute trout from Silver King, Coyote Valley, and Corral Valley creeks were transplanted into Mono County's North Fork Cottonwood in 1946 by the California Department of Fish and Game (Ryan and Nicola 1976). In 1947, the fish and game department made another transplant from Corral and Coyote Valley creeks into Fly Valley Creek, a tributary to upper Silver King Creek barren of fish at the time (Ryan and Nicola 1976).

In 1968, Paiute trout from North Fork Cottonwood Creek were transplanted into Sharktooth Lake, a headwater tributary to the San Joaquin River drainage in Fresno County, and into Cabin Creek in the Long Valley basin of the Death Valley system in Mono County (Ryan and Nicola 1976). In 1975, no Paiute trout were found in Sharktooth Lake, but some were observed in an outlet stream. Their present status there is unknown (Ryan and Nicola 1976). Paiute trout became established in Cabin Creek, but their purity is not known. Sometime prior to 1965, rainbow trout were introduced illegally into the North Fork Cottonwood Creek above the barrier falls, and they hybridized with the Paiute trout (Wong 1975).

Similarly, brook trout (*Salvelinus fontinalis*) invaded Delaney Creek and eliminated Paiute trout introduced there in 1966. In 1972, however, some of the Paiute trout from Delaney Creek were transplanted into Stairway Creek, a headwater tributary to the San Joaquin River. A population has been established in Stairway Creek and is recognized by the U.S. Fish and Wildlife (FWS) as a pure population of *S.c. seleniris* (U.S. Fish and Wildlife Service 1985).

In 1970, the lower half of North Fork Cottonwood Creek was treated with rotenone to eliminate hybrids (Wong 1975). The Paiute trout in this creek are recognized by FWS (U.S. Fish and Wildlife Service 1985). However, the population in the lower section of this stream appears to retain a few rainbow trout genes, which can be detected by electrophoresis of proteins even though no physical evidence of hybridization shows (Busack and Gall 1981).

Paiute trout in Silver King Creek above Llewellyn Falls became hybridized with rainbow trout inadvertently stocked by the California Department of Fish and Game in 1949. A mistaken aerial plant of Lahontan cutthroat trout also was made by the Fish and Game Department into Whitecliff Lake, a tributary to upper Silver King

Creek in 1955. A hybrid influence rapidly spread through the Paiute trout population there, except for the populations isolated by barrier falls in Fly Valley and Four Mile Canyon creeks (U.S. Fish and Wildlife Service 1985, Ryan and Nicola 1976). In 1964, upper Silver King Creek was treated with rotenone in an attempt to eliminate hybrids, and its waters were stocked with pure Paiute trout from Four Mile Canyon and Fly Valley creeks. The treatment was not successful, and hybrids were again found in 1968. Silver King Creek was again treated with rotenone in 1976, but this too failed to eliminate hybrids (U.S. Fish and Wildlife Service 1985). Presently, only Fly Valley Creek and Four Mile Canyon Creek are believed to contain *S.c. seleniris* in the upper Silver King drainage.

Corral Valley and Coyote Valley creeks in 1964 also were found to have Paiute trout-rainbow trout hybrids (U.S. Fish and Wildlife Service 1985, Ryan and Nicola 1976). These streams were treated with rotenone in 1964 and stocked with pure Paiute trout from Fly Valley and Four Mile Canyon creeks. The 1964 treatment failed, and these streams were treated again in 1977 and restocked with fish from the same source creeks (U.S. Fish and Wildlife Service 1985). Coyote Valley Creek trout are again hybridized, but to date, the fish in Corral Valley Creek appear to be pure *S.c. seleniris* (U.S. Fish and Wildlife Service 1985).

## CURRENT TRENDS

The present presumed pure populations recognized by FWS (U.S. Fish and Wildlife Service 1985) are limited to about 10 miles of small stream habitat in Fly Valley and Four Mile Canyon creeks, Corral Creek in the Silver King drainage, North Fork Cottonwood Creek, and Stairway Creek. The population in the lower half of North Fork Cottonwood Creek, although phenotypically Paiute trout, probably retains some rainbow trout genes as a residue from incomplete eradication of hybrids in 1970 (Busack and Gall 1981). In 1983, Paiute cutthroat trout were stocked into Heenan Lake as a brood stock for future propagation.

There is no question that the cause of the near demise of Paiute trout was due to the stocking of rainbow trout in the Silver King Creek drainage. Recovery efforts have been hampered by the lack of suitable barren waters for transplants and by the difficulties of obtaining the complete hybrid eradication necessary to reestablish populations in the Silver King drainage or to establish new populations elsewhere.

Other impacts that, although they have not threatened extinction, have acted to limit abundance include livestock grazing, which caused habitat degradation; overfishing and poaching, because Paiute trout are highly vulnerable to angling; and beaver activity. Beaver are not native to the east side of the Sierra's but were introduced and became established in the Silver King drainage and North Fork Cottonwood Creek. The heavier activity of damming and destruction of vegetation has caused severe erosion problems probably augmented by domestic livestock grazing (U.S. Fish and Wildlife Service 1985).

## MANAGEMENT

The main thrust of a management program has been to maintain and expand pure populations by fish eradication treatments and transplants. In 1986, the U.S. Forest Service initiated and revised livestock-grazing management strategy for Silver King Creek, and a cooperative venture between the U.S. Forest Service, California Department of Fish and Game, and Trout Unlimited resulted in livestock exclosure fencing and habitat-improvement work on Silver King Creek.

## PROGNOSIS

Future threats to Paiute trout will always include the possibility of nonnative trout introductions that will eliminate Paiute trout through hybridization or competition. All present Paiute habitats are on national forest lands that allow for revised grazing management to protect habitat, but habitat degradation from livestock is likely to remain a problem (U.S. Fish and Wildlife Service 1985). Small-scale hydropower development must be considered as a possible, but probably remote, threat. The protected status of *S.c. seleniris* should spare it the inroads of hydropower development (U.S. Fish and Wildlife Service 1985).

A point to be emphasized is that Paiute trout do not require any unique habitat. They can thrive in essentially any habitat in which other species of trout or subspecies of cutthroat trout can thrive. The only limitation is that Paiute trout cannot coexist in habitat occupied by other trout species.

## RECOMMENDATIONS

The following measures should be taken:

1. continue transplants to new waters;
2. improve livestock-grazing management where streams are affected;

3. continue habitat-improvement and erosion-control work;
4. chemically treat Silver King Creek when hybrids increase to 50 percent of the population.

## REFERENCES

Ashley, R.R. 1970. *Habitat Management Plan—Paiute Trout.* U.S. Forest Service. Toiyable National Forest. Reno, Nevada. 19 pp.

Behnke, R.J. 1960. Taxonomy of the cutthroat trout of the Great Basin with notes on the rainbow series. M.A. Thesis. University of California at Berkeley. 98 pp.

_____. and M. Zarn. 1976. *Biology and Management of Threatened and Endangered Western Trouts.* General Technical Report RM-28. U.S. Department of Agriculture Forest Service. 45 pp.

_____. 1985. Unpublished data. Fishery and Wildlife Biology, Colorado State University. Fort Collins, Colorado.

Busack, C.A. and G.A.E. Gall. 1981. "Introspective hybridization in population of Paiute cutthroat trout (*Salmo clarki seleniris*)," *Canadian Journal of Fisheries and Aquatic Sciences* 38:939-951.

Diana, J.S. 1975. The movement and distribution of Paiute trout, *Salmo clarki seleniris*, in the North Fork of Cottonwood Creek, Mono County, White Mountains, California. M.A. Thesis. California State University.

Dunham, D.K. 1968. *Preliminary Survey Analysis of Silver King Creek Habitat Above Llewellyn Falls, Alpine County, California.* U.S. Forest Service. Toiyable National Forest. Reno, Nevada. 10 pp.

Ryan, J.H. and S.J. Nicola. 1976. "Status of the Paiute Cutthroat Trout, *Salmo clarki seleniris*, in California." California Department of Fish and Game, Inland Fisheries Administration Report 76-3. 56 pp.

Schneegas, F.R. and F.P. Pister. 1965. *Paiute Trout Habitat Management Plan.* U.S. Forest Service. Inyo National Forest. Bishop, California. 46 pp.

Snyder, J.O. 1933. "Description of *Salmo seleniris* a new California trout," *Proceedings of the California Academy of Sciences* 20:471-472.

U.S. Fish and Wildlife Service. 1985. *Paiute Cutthroat Trout Recovery Plan.* U.S. Fish and Wildlife Service. Portland, Oregon. 68 pp.

Wong, D.M. 1975. Aspects of the life history of the Paiute cutthroat trout, *Salmo clarki seleniris*, in North Fork Cottonwood Creek, Mono County, California. M.A. Thesis. California State University. Long Beach, California. 178 pp.

*Bob Behnke is professor of fisheries biology at Colorado State University.*

# Part Four

# Appendices

# APPENDIX A

# Forest Service Directory

## WASHINGTON HEADQUARTERS

*Mailing Address:*
Forest Service-USDA
P.O. Box 2417
Washington, D.C. 20013

*General Information:*
(202) 655-4000
Public Inquiries
(202) 447-3957

| Title | Name | Phone |
|---|---|---|
| Chief | F. Dale Robertson | 202 447-6661 |
| Associate Chief | George M. Leonard | 202 447-7491 |

### National Forest System

| | | |
|---|---|---|
| Deputy Chief | J. Lamar Beasley | 202 447-3523 |
| Director, Engineering | Sterling Wilcox | 202 235-8035 |
| Director, Lands | Richard D. Hall | 202 235-8212 |
| Director, Land Management Planning | Everett L. Towle | 202 447-6697 |
| Director, Minerals and Geology Mgmt. | Buster LaMoure | 202 235-8105 |
| Director, Range Management | Robert M. Williamson | 202 235-8139 |
| Director, Recreation Management | Roy W. Feuchter | 202 447-3706 |
| Director, Timber Management | Dave Hessell | 202 447-6893 |
| Director, Watershed and Air Management | David G. Unger | 202 235-8096 |
| Director, Wildlife and Fisheries | Robert D. Nelson | 202 235-8015 |

### State and Private Forestry

| | | |
|---|---|---|
| Deputy Chief | Allan J. West | 202 447-6657 |
| Director, Fire and Aviation Management | Lawrence A. Amicarella | 202 235-8039 |
| Director, Cooperative Forestry | Tony Dorrell | 202 235-2212 |
| Director, Forest Pest Management | Vacant | 202 235-1560 |

### Research

| | | |
|---|---|---|
| Deputy Chief | John Ohman | 202 447-6665 |
| Director, Forest Environmental Research | Ronald D. Lindmark | 202 235-1071 |

549

| Title | Name | Phone |
|---|---|---|
| Director, Forest Fire and Atmospheric Sciences Research | William Sommers | 202 235-8195 |
| Director, Forest Insect and Disease Research | James Stewart | 202 235-8065 |
| Director, Forest Products and Harvesting Research | Stanley O. Bean, Jr. | 202 235-1203 |
| Director, Forest Resources Economics Research | H. Fred Kuiser, Jr. | 202 447-2747 |
| Director, International Forestry | David A. Harcharik | 202 235-2743 |
| Director, Timber Management Research | Stanley L. Krugman | 202 235-8200 |

### Programs and Legislation

| | | |
|---|---|---|
| Deputy Chief | Jeff M. Sirmon | 202 447-6663 |
| Director, Environmental Coordination | David E. Ketcham | 202 447-4708 |
| Director, Legislative Affairs | Roger Leonard | 202 447-4708 |
| Director, Policy Analysis | Christopher Risbrudt | 202 447-2775 |
| Director, Program Development and Budget | John A. Leasure | 202 447-6987 |
| Director, Resources Program and Assessment | Thomas E. Hamilton | 202 382-8235 |

### Administration

| | | |
|---|---|---|
| Deputy Chief | William Rice | 202 447-6707 |

### Office of General Council—USDA

| | | |
|---|---|---|
| Assistant General Council, Natural Resources Division | Clarence W. Brizee | 202 447-7121 |

# REGIONAL HEADQUARTERS AND NATIONAL FORESTS

### Region 1—Northern Region

Federal Building      406 329-3011
P.O. Box 7669
Missoula, MT 59807

| | |
|---|---|
| Regional Forester | James C. Overbay |
| Director, Wildlife and Fisheries | Kirk Horn |

### Region 2—Rocky Mountain

11177 West 8th Ave.      303 236-3711
P.O. Box 25127
Lakewood, CO 80225

| | |
|---|---|
| Regional Forester | Gary Cargill |
| Director, Range, Wildlife Fisheries and Ecology | Glen Hetzel |

| Title | Name | Phone |
|---|---|---|

### Region 3—Southwestern

Federal Building
517 Gold Ave., SW
Albuquerque, NM 87102 — 505 842-2401

| Regional Forester | Sotero Muniz | |
| Director, Wildlife Management | William D. Zeedyk | |

### Region 4—Intermountain

Federal Building
324 25th Street
Odgen, UT 84401 — 801 625-5412

| Regional Forester | J.S. Tixier | |
| Director, Wildlife Management | William R. Burbridge | |

### Region 5—Pacific Southwest

630 Sansome Street
San Francisco, CA 94111 — 415 556-4310

| Regional Forester | Zane G. Smith, Jr. | |
| Director, Fisheries and Wildlife | | |
| Management | Randall Long | |

### Region 6—Pacific Northwest

319 S.W. Pine St.
P.O. Box 3623
Portland, OR 97208 — 503 221-3625

| Regional Forester | James Torrence | |
| Director, Fish and Wildlife | Hugh Black, Jr. | |

### Region 8—Southern

1720 Peachtree Rd, N.W.
Atlanta, GA 30367 — 404 347-4177

| Regional Forester | John E. Alcock | |
| Director, Fisheries, | | |
| Wildlife, and Range | Jerry P. McIlwain | |

### Region 9—Eastern

310 West Wisconsin Ave.
Milwaukee, WI 53203 — 414 291-3693

| Regional Forester | Floyd J. Marita | |
| Director, Range, Wildlife, and | | |
| Landscape Management | Bruce Hronek | |

### Region 10—Alaska

Federal Office Building
P.O. Box 1628
Juneau, AK 99802 — 907 586-7263

| Regional Forester | Michael A. Barton | |
| Director, Wildlife and Fisheries | Philip J. Janik | |

## Forest and Range Experiment Stations

Intermountain Station
Laurence E. Lassen, Director
502 25th Street
Ogden, UT 84401
(801) 625-5412

Northeastern Station
Denver P. Burns, Director
370 Reed Road
Broomall, PA 19008
(215) 461-3006

Pacific Southwest Station
Roger R. Bay, Director
1960 Addison Street
Box 245
Berkeley, CA 94701
(415) 486-3291

Southeastern Station
Jerry Cisco, Director
200 Weaver Blvd
Asheville, NC 28804
(704) 259-6758

Forest Products Laboratory
John Erickson
Gifford Pinchot Drive
Box 5130
Madison, WI 53705
(608) 264-5600

State and Private Forestry Offices
are located in the Regional
Headquarters, except for the Eastern
Region, where it is at:

Northeastern Area
Thomas Schenarts, Director
370 Reed Road
Broomall, PA 19008
(215) 461-3125

North Central Station
Robert A. Hann, Director
1992 Folwell Ave.
St. Paul, MN 56108
(612) 642-5207

Pacific Northwest Station
Robert L. Ethington, Director
P.O. Box 3890
Portland, OR 97208
(503) 294-2052

Rocky Mountain Station
Charles M. Loveless, Director
240 W. Prospect
Fort Collins, CO 80526
(303) 221-4390

Southern Station
Thomas H. Ellis, Director
T-10210, U.S. Postal Service Bldg.
701 Loyola Ave.
New Orleans, LA 70113
(504) 589-6787

---

## APPENDIX B

# U.S. Fish and Wildlife Service Directory

---

## WASHINGTON HEADQUARTERS

Mailing Address:
Fish and Wildlife Service
Department of the Interior
18th and C Streets, NW
Washington, D.C. 20240

The Fish and Wildlife Service Washington headquarters is being reorganized as this volume goes to press. Thus, only top-level positions are listed here and even these could change. Call the appropriate assistant director or the office of Public Affairs for specific program directors and phone numbers.

| Title | Name | Phone |
|---|---|---|
| Director | Frank Dunkle | 202-343-4717 |
| Deputy Director | Steve Robinson | 202-343-4545 |
| Assistant Director, Internal Affairs | Sam Marler | 202-343-2500 |
| Chief, Legislative Services | Vacant | 202-343-5403 |
| Chief, International Affairs | Lawrence Mason | 202-343-5188 |
| Chief, Public Affairs | Phil Million | 202-343-5634 |
| Assistant Director, Refuges and Wildlife | James Gritman (acting) | 202-343-5333 |
| (This was called formerly Wildlife Resources. It includes most refuge operations and management, migratory-bird management, realty, and law enforcement.) | | |
| Assistant Director, Fish and Wildlife Enhancement | Ronald Lambertson | 202-343-4646 |
| (This includes activities previously covered under Habitat Resources and Federal Assistance, such as endangered species, federal aid to states, ecological services, resource contaminants, environmental coordination, and the wildlife permit office.) | | |
| Assistant Director, Fisheries | Joseph H. Kutkuhn | 202-343-6394 |
| Assistant Director, Research and Development | Harold J. O'Connor | 202-343-4767 |
| Assistant Director, Policy, Budgeting, and Administration | Joe Doddridge | 202-343-4888 |

553

| Title | Name | Phone |
| --- | --- | --- |

# FISH AND WILDLIFE SERVICE—REGIONAL OFFICES

## Region 1: *California, Hawaii, Idaho, Nevada, Oregon, Washington, Pacific Trust Territories.*

Fish and Wildlife Service
Lloyd 500 Building, Suite 1692
500 NE Multnomah Street
Portland, Or 97232

| Title | Name | Phone |
| --- | --- | --- |
| Regional Director | Rolf L. Wallenstrom | 503-231-6118 |
| Assistant Regional Director, Refuges and Wildlife | Lawrence W. Debates | 503-231-6214 |
| Assistant Regional Director, Fisheries | Erwin W. Steuke | 503-231-5967 |
| Assistant Regional Director, Fish and Wildlife Enhancement | David F. Riley | 503-231-6159 |
| Deputy Assistant Regional Director Fish and Wildlife Enhancement (Federal aid contact) | William F. Shake | 503-231-6159 |
| Chief, Div. of Endangered Species | Wayne White | 503-231-6131 |
| Wetlands Coordinator | Dennis Peters | 503-231-6154 |
| Assistant Regional Director, Law Enforcement | David L. McMullen | 503-231-6125 |
| Assistant Regional Director, Public Affairs | William Meyer | 503-231-6121 |

## Region 2: *Arizona, New Mexico, Oklahoma, Texas.*

Fish and Wildlife Service
P.O. Box 1306
Albuquerque, NM 87103

| Title | Name | Phone |
| --- | --- | --- |
| Regional Director | Michael J. Spear | 505-766-2321 |
| Assistant Regional Director, Refuges and Wildlife | W. Ellis Klett | 505-766-1829 |
| Assistant Regional Director, Fisheries and Federal Assistance | Conrad A. Fjetland | 505-766-2323 |
| Chief, Div. of Federal Aid | Donald G. Kuntzelman | 505-766-2321 |
| Assistant Regional Director, Fish and Wildlife Enhancement | James A. Young | 505-766-2324 |
| Chief, Div. of Endangered Species | James Johnson | 505-766-2323 |
| Wetlands Coordinator | Warren Hagenbuck | 505-766-2914 |
| Assistant Regional Director, Law Enforcement | John E. Cross | 505-766-2091 |
| Assistant Regional Director, Public Affairs | Thomas Smylie | 505-766-3940 |

| Title | Name | Phone |
|-------|------|-------|

## Region 3: *Iowa, Illinois, Indiana, Michigan, Minnesota, Missouri, Ohio, Wisconsin.*

Fish and Wildlife Service
Bishop Henry Whipple Building
Fort Snelling Twin Cities, MN 55111

| Title | Name | Phone |
|-------|------|-------|
| Regional Director | Harvey K. Nelson | 612-725-3563 |
| Assistant Regional Director, Refuges and Wildlife | John Eadie | 612-725-3507 |
| Assistant Regional Director, Fisheries and Federal Assistance | John S. Popowski | 612-725-3505 |
| Chief, Div. of Federal Aid | Joseph W. Artmann | 612-725-3596 |
| Assistant Regional Director, Fish and Wildlife Enhancement | Gerald Lowry | 612-725-3510 |
| Chief, Div. of Endangered Species | James Engel | 612-725-3276 |
| Wetlands Coordinator | Ronald Erickson | 612-725-3593 |
| Assistant Regional Director, Law Enforcment | Larry Hood | 612-725-3530 |
| Assistant Regional Director, Public Affairs | James Ross | 612-725-3520 |

## Region 4: *Alabama, Arkansas, Florida, Georgia, Kentucky, Louisiana, Mississippi, North Carolina, South Carolina, Tennessee, Puerto Rico, Virgin Islands.*

Fish and Wildlife Service
R.B. Russell Building
75 Spring Street, SW
Atlanta, GA 30303

| Title | Name | Phone |
|-------|------|-------|
| Regional Director | James W. Pulliam, Jr. | 404-331-3588 |
| Assistant Regional Director, Refuges and Wildlife | Harold W. Benson | 404-331-3538 |
| Assistant Regional Director, Fisheries | Frank R. Richardson | 404-331-3576 |
| Assistant Regional Director, Fish and Wildlife Enhancement | Warren T. Olds, Jr. | 404-331-6343 |
| Chief, Div. of Federal Aid | Robert L. Barber | 404-331-3580 |
| Chief, Div. of Endangered Species | Marshall P. Jones | 404-331-3583 |
| Wetlands Coordinator | John Hefner | 404-331-6343 |
| Assistant Regional Director, Law Enforcement | Dan M. Searcy | 404-331-5872 |
| Assistant Regional Director, Public Affairs | Donald Pfitzer | 404-331-3594 |

| Title | Name | Phone |
|-------|------|-------|

### Region 5: Connecticut, Delaware, Maine, Maryland, Massachusetts, New Hampshire, New Jersey, New York, Pennsylvania, Rhode Island, Vermont, Virginia, West Virginia.

| | | |
|-------|------|-------|
| Fish and Wildlife Service<br>One Gateway Center, Suite 700<br>Newton Corner, MA 01258 | | 617-965-5100 |
| Regional Director | Howard N. Larsen | x200 |
| Assistant Regional Director, Refuges and Wildlife | Donald Young | x222 |
| Assistant Regional Director, Fisheries and Federal Assistance | James E. Weaver | x208 |
| Chief, Div. of Federal Aid | William T. Hesselton | x212 |
| Assistant Regional Director, Fish and Wildlife Enhancement | Donald W. Woodard | x217 |
| Chief, Div. of Endangered Species | Paul Nickerson | x316 |
| Wetlands Coordinator | Ralph Tiner | x379 |
| Assistant Regional Director, Law Enforcement | Eugene Hester | x254 |
| Assistant Regional Director, Public Affairs | Inez Conner | x206 |

### Region 6: Colorado, Kansas, Montana, Nebraska, North Dakota, South Dakota, Utah, Wyoming.

| | | |
|-------|------|-------|
| Fish and Wildlife Service<br>P.O. Box 25486<br>Denver Federal Center<br>Denver, CO 80225 | | |
| Regional Director | Galen L. Buterbaugh | 303-236-7920 |
| Assistant Regional Director, Refuges and Wildlife | Nelson B. Kverno | 303-236-8145 |
| Assistant Regional Director, Fisheries and Federal Aid | Vacant | 303-236-8154 |
| Chief, Div. of Federal Aid | Jerry J. Blackard | 303-236-7392 |
| Assistant Regional Director, Fish and Wildlife Enhancement | William E. Marten (acting) | 303-236-8189 |
| Chief, Div. of Endangered Species | Barry Mulder | 303-236-7398 |
| Wetlands Coordinator | Charles Elliot | 303-236-8180 |
| Assistant Regional Director, Law Enforcement | Terry L. Grosz | 303-236-7540 |
| Assistant Regional Director, Public Affairs | Jack Hallowell (acting) | 303-236-7904 |

| Title | Name | Phone |
|-------|------|-------|

### Region 7: Alaska.

Fish and Wildlife Service
1011 E. Tudor Road
Anchorage, AK 99503

| Title | Name | Phone |
|-------|------|-------|
| Regional Director | Robert E. Gilmore | 907-786-3542 |
| Assistant Regional Director, Refuges and Wildlife | John P. Rogers | 907-786-3538 |
| Assistant Regional Director, Fisheries and Federal Assistance | Jon M. Nelson | 907-786-3539 |
| Chief, Branch of Federal Aid | William H. Martin | 907-786-3542 |
| Assistant Regional Director, Fish and Wildlife Enhancement | Robert D. Jacobsen | 907-786-3522 |
| Chief, Branch of Ecological Services and Endangered Species | Dennis Money | 907-786-3435 |
| Wetlands Coordinator | John Hall | 907-786-3403 |
| Assistant Regional Director, Law Enforcement | Vacant | 907-786-3311 |
| Assistant Regional Director, Public Affairs | George Sura | 907-786-3486 |

# APPENDIX C

# National Park Service Directory

◇
_____

## WASHINGTON HEADQUARTERS

National Park Service
Interior Building
Washington, D.C. 20240
General Information:
202 343-4747

| Title | Name | Phone |
| --- | --- | --- |
| Director | Wm. Penn Mott | 202 343-4621 |
| Deputy Director | Denis Galvin | 202 343-5081 |
| Special Asst. for | | |
| Policy Development | Vacant | 202 343-7456 |
| Public Affairs | George J. Berklacy | 202 343-6843 |
| Leg. & Congressional | Rob Wallace | 202 343-5883 |
| Equal Opport. Officer | Marshall Brookes | 202 343-6738 |
| Minority Businesses | Barbara Guillard-Payn | 202 343-3884 |

### Associate Directors:

| | | |
| --- | --- | --- |
| Natural Resources | Richard Briceland | 202 343-5193 |
| Park Operations | Stanley Albright | 202 343-5651 |
| Cultural Resources | Jerry Rogers | 202 343-7625 |
| Planning and | | |
| Development | James Stewart (acting) | 202 343-1264 |
| Administration | Edward Davis | 202 343-6741 |

### Natural Resources Division:

| | | |
| --- | --- | --- |
| Air Quality | Molly Ross | 202 343-4911 |
| Special Science | | |
| Projects | Al Greene | 202 343-8114 |
| Energy, Mining, & | | |
| Minerals | Carol McCoy | 202 343-4650 |
| Biological Resources | John Dennis | 202 343-8128 |
| Water Resources | Tom Lucke | 202 221-5341 |

# REGIONAL OFFICES

### North Atlantic Regional Office
National Park Service
15 State Street
Boston, MA 02109
(617) 565-8800

Regional Director: Hobart Cabler, Jr.
Chief Scientist: Michael Soukup
Natural Resource Contacts:
Nora Mitchell
Len Bobinchock

The region includes Connecticut, Maine, Massachusetts, New Hampshire, New Jersey, New York, Rhode Island, and Vermont.

### Mid-Atlantic Regional Office
National Park Service
143 South Third Street
Philadelphia, PA 19106
(215) 597-7013

Regional Director: James Coleman
Chief Scientist: John Karish
Natural Resource Contact:
William Supernaugh

The region includes Delaware, Maryland, Pennsylvania, Virginia, and West Virginia.

### National Capital Region
National Park Service
1100 Ohio Drive, SW
Washington, D.C. 20242
(202) 426-6612

Regional Director: Manus J.
Fish, Jr.
Chief Scientist: William Anderson
Natural Resource Contact:
Stan Locke

The National Capital Region covers parks in the metropolitan area of Washington, D.C. and certain field areas in Maryland, Virginia, and West Virginia.

### Southeast Regional Office
National Park Service
75 Spring SW. Street
Atlanta, GA 30303
(404) 331-5185

Regional Director: Robert Baker
Chief Scientist: Dominic Dottavio
Resource Specialist Contact:
Bill Sturgeon

The region includes Alabama, Georgia, Kentucky, Mississippi, North Carolina, South Carolina, Tennessee, Puerto Rico, and the Virgin Islands.

### Midwest Regional Office
National Park Service
1709 Jackson Street
Omaha, NE 68102
(402) 221-3431

Regional Director: Charles
Odegaard
Chief Scientist: Michael Ruggiero
Natural Resource Contact:
Ben Holmes

The region includes Illinois, Indiana, Iowa, Kansas, Minnesota, Michigan, Missouri, Nebraska, Ohio, and Wisconsin.

### Rocky Mountain Regional Office
National Park Service
655 Parfet Street
Denver, CO 80225
(303) 236-8700

Regional Director: Lorraine
Mincemeyer
Chief Scientist: Dan Huff
Natural Resource Contact:
Cecil Lewis

The region includes Colorado, Montana, North Dakota, South Dakota, Utah, and Wyoming.

## Southwest Regional Office

National Park Service
Old Santa Fe Trail
P.O. Box 728
Santa Fe, NM 87501
(505) 988-6388

Regional Director: John E. Cook
Chief Scientist: Milford Fletcher
Natural Resource Contact:
Milford Fletcher

The region includes part of Arizona, Arkansas, Louisiana, New Mexico, Oklahoma, and Texas.

## Western Regional Office

National Park Service
450 Golden Gate Avenue
P.O. Box 36063
San Francisco, CA 94102
(415) 556-4196

Regional Director: Howard
 Chapman
Chief Scientist: Bruce Kilgore
Natural Resource Contact:
Bruce Kilgore

The region includes part of Arizona, California, Hawaii, and Nevada.

## Pacific Northwest Regional Office

National Park Service
83 South King Street
Suite 212
Seattle, WA 98104
(206) 442-5565

Regional Director: William Briggle
 (acting)
Chief Scientist: James Larson
Natural Resource Contact: Ed Menning, Janet Edwards

The region includes Idaho, Oregon, and Washington.

## Alaska Regional Office

National Park Service
2525 Gambell Street, Room 107
Anchorage, AK 99503
(907) 271-2690

Regional Director: Boyd Evison
Chief Scientist: Al Lovass
Natural Resource Contact:
Al Lovass

The region includes Alaska.

# Bureau of Land Management Directory

## WASHINGTON HEADQUARTERS

Bureau of Land Management
U.S. Department of the Interior
Washington, D.C. 20240

Robert Burford, Director
Bureau of Land Management
202-343-3801

Henry R. Smith, Assistant Director
Land and Renewable Resources
202-343-4896

David Almand, Chief
Division of Wildlife and
Fisheries
202-653-9202

## STATE OFFICE DIRECTORS AND BIOLOGISTS

### Alaska
Mike Penfold, State Director
*Craig Altop, State Office Biologist
Bureau of Land Management
701 C Street
Anchorage, AK 99513
Commercial: (907) 271-5555

### Arizona
Dean Bibles, State Director
Bureau of Land Management
3707 North 7th Street
Phoenix, AZ 85011
Com: (602) 241-5504

### California
Ed Hastey, State Director
Mike Ferguson, State Office Bio.
*Butch Olendorff
Bureau of Land Management
Federal Office Building
2800 Cottage Way
Sacramento, CA 95825
Com: (916) 378-4725

561

### Colorado

Neil Morck, State Director
*Lee Upham, State Office Bio.
Bureau of Land Management
2020 Arapahoe Street
Denver, CO 80205
Com: (303) 236-1700

### Denver Service Ctr.

*Allen Cooperrider, Svc. Ctr. Bio.
Bureau of Land Management
Denver Service Center
Bldg. 50, Denver Federal Ctr.
Denver, CO 80225
Com: (303) 236-0161

### Eastern States Office

Curtis Jones, Director
*Tom Hewett, State Office Biologist
Bureau of Land Managment
Eastern States Office
350 South Pickett Street
Alexandria, VA 22304
Com: (703) 274-0190

### Idaho

Del Vail, State Director
*Allen Thomas, State Office Biologist
Roger Rosentretter, State Office
 Biologist
Bureau of Land Management
3380 Americana Terrace
Boise, ID 83706
Com: (208) 334-1771

### Montana (MT, SD, ND)

Dean Stepanek, State Director
Ray Hoem, State Office Bio.
*Dan Hinckley
Bureau of Land Management
222 North 32nd Street
Billings, MT 59107
Commercial: (406) 657-6561

### Nevada

Ed Spang, State Director
David Goicoechea, State Off.
 Biologist
*Osborne Casey
Bureau of Land Management
300 Booth St./Rm. 3038
Reno, NV 89520
Com: (702) 784-5311

### New Mexico (NM, OK, TX)

Larry Woodard, State
Director
*Brian Mills, Off. Bio.
Bureau of Land Management
Montoya Federal Bldg.
South Federal Place
Santa Fe, NM 87501
Com: (505) 988-6316

### Oregon (OR, WA)

Charles Luscher, State Dir.
Art Oakley, State Office Bio.
*Bill Nietro
Bureau of Land Management
825 NE. Multnomah Street
Portland, OR 97208
Comm: (503) 231-6274

### Utah

Roland Robison, State
Director
*Jerry Farringer, State Off. Bio.
Bureau of Land Management
324 South State Street
Salt Lake City, UT 84111
Com: (801) 524-5311

### Wyoming (WY, KS, NE)

Hillary Oden, State Director
*Dave Roberts, State Off. Bio.
Bureau of Land Management
2515 Warren Avenue
Cheyenne, WY 82003
Com: (307) 772-2111

*Biologist for Endangered Species

# APPENDIX E

# Wetlands Management Directory

## ENVIRONMENTAL PROTECTION AGENCY

Headquarters
U.S. Environmental Protection Agency
401 M St., SW.
Washington, D.C. 20360

Lee Thomas, Administrator
(202) 382-4700

Larry Jensen
Assistant Administrator for Water
(202) 382-5700

Rebecca Hanmer, Deputy Assistant
Administrator for Water
(202) 382-5707

John Meagher, Acting Director
Office of Wetlands Protection
(202) 382-5043

## REGIONAL OFFICES

### Region I
Michael Deland, Administrator
John F. Kennedy Federal Bldg.,
Room 2203
Boston, MA 02203
(617) 565-3400

### Region II
Christopher J. Daggett,
Administrator,
26 Federal Plaza
Room 1009
New York, NY 10007
(212) 264-2525

### Region III
James M. Seif, Administrator
Curtis Building
6th and Walnut Streets
Philadelphia, PA 19106
(215) 597-9815

### Region IV
Jack Ravan, Administrator
345 Courtland St., NE
Atlanta, GA 30308
(404) 881-4727

**Region V**
Valdas V. Adamkus,
Administrator
230 S. Dearborn
Chicago, IL 60604
(312) 353-2000

**Region VI**
Robert E. Layton, Jr.,
Administrator
First International Bldg.
1201 S. Elm Street
Dallas, TX 75270
(214) 767-2600

**Region VII**
Morris Kay, Administrator
1735 Baltimore Street
Kansas City, MO 64108
(913) 236-2800

**Region VIII**
John Welles, Administrator
Lincoln Tower Bldg., Room 900
1860 Lincoln Street
Denver, CO 80203
(303) 293-1603

**Region IX**
Judith E. Ayers, Administrator
215 Freemont Street
San Francisco, CA 94105
(415) 974-8153

**Region X**
Robie G. Russell, Administrator
1200 Sixth Avenue
Seattle, WA 98101
(206) 442-5810

# ARMY CORPS OF ENGINEERS

Headquarters
Army Corps of Engineers
Office of the Chief of Engineers
Pulaski Bldg.
20 Massachusetts Avenue, NW
Washington, D.C. 20314

Robert K. Dawson
Assistant Secretary of the Army
for Civil Works
(202) 697-3365

Lieutenant General E.R. Heiberg III
Chief, Corps of Engineers,
(CECG/DAEN-ZA)
(202) 272-0000

Major General H.J. Hatch
Director of Civil Works (DAEN-CWZ)
(202) 272-0099

Bernard N. Goode
Chief, Regulatory Branch
(DAEN-CWO-N)
(202) 272-0199

## Offices

Lower Mississippi Valley Division
P.O. Box 80
Vicksburg, MS 39180
(601) 634-5818

Missouri River Division
P.O. Box 103 Downtown Station
Omaha, NE 68101
(402) 221-7290

New England Division
424 Trapelo Road
Waltham, MA 02254
(617) 647-8338
(No district offices)

North Atlantic Division
90 Church Street
New York, NY 10077
(212) 264-7535

North Central Division
536 S. Clark Street
Chicago, IL 60605-1592
(312) 353-6379

North Pacific Division
P.O. Box 2870
Portland, OR 97208
(503) 221-3780

Ohio River Division
P.O. Box 1159
Cincinnati, OH 45201-1159
(513) 684-3972

South Atlantic Division
510 Title Building
30 Pryor St., SW.
Atlanta, GA 30303
(404) 331-6744

South Pacific Division
630 Sansome Street, Room 1216
San Francisco, CA 94111
(415) 556-2648

Southwestern Division
1114 Commerce Street
Dallas, TX 75242
(214) 767-2432

# NATIONAL MARINE FISHERIES SERVICE HEADQUARTERS
(See NMFS listings in Appendix F. Habitat Conservation Division)

## *NORTHEAST REGION*
(includes area from Maine to North Carolina)

*Main Offices*
(ME, NH, MA, RI)
Thomas E. Bigford, Branch Chief
Fish Pier
Gloucester, MA 01930
(617) 281-3600

Naragansett Laboratory
Tracy McKenzie, Biologist
South Ferry Road
Naragansett, RI 02882

*Field Offices*
(NY, CT)
Milford Laboratory
Michael Ludwig, Asst. Branch Chief
Rogers Avenue
Milford, CT 06460
(203) 783-4228

(NJ)
Sandy Hook Laboratory
Stanley W. Gorski, Asst. Branch Chief
P.O. Box 428
Highlands, NJ 07732
(201) 342-8237

(MD, VA, PA, DE)
Oxford Laboratory
Edward W. Christoffers, Asst.
Branch Chief
Railroad Avenue
Oxford, MD 21654
(301) 226-5771

Woods Hole Laboratory
Bruce Higgins, Asst. Branch
Chief
Water Street
Woods Hole, MA 02543
(617) 548-5123

## *SOUTHEAST REGION*
(included area from North Carolina to Mexico)

*Regional Offices*
Richard J. Hoogland, Asst. Regional Director
9450 Koger Blvd.
St. Petersburg, FL 33702
(813) 893-3503

*Field Offices*
(NC, SC, GA)
Pivers Island
Randall Cheek, Area Supervisor
P.O. Box 570
Beaufort, NC 28516
(919) 728-5090

(FL, AL, MS, VI, PR)
Edwin Keppner, Area Supervisor
3500 Dellwood Beach Rd.
Panana City, FL 32407
(904) 234-5061

(LA, TX)
Donald Moore, Area Supervisor
4700 Avenue U
Galveston, TX 77550
(409)-766-3699

## SOUTHWEST REGION

(California and U.S. Pacific Islands)

*Regional Office*
James J. Slawson, Branch Chief
300 South Ferry Street
Terminal Island, CA 90731
(213) 548-2518

(HI and West Pacific)
John J. Naughton, Biologist
2570 Dole Street
P.O. Box 3830
Honolulu, HI 96812
(808) 955-8831

*Field Offices*
(Northern California)
James R. Bybee, Biologist
777 Sonoma Avenue
Santa Rosa, CA 95404
(707)-525-4275

## NORTHWEST REGION

(Oregon, Washington, and Idaho)

*Portland Office*
(OR, ID)
Dale Evans, Division Chief
Merrit E. Tuttle, Branch Chief
847 N.E. 19th Avenue. #350
Portland, OR 97232-2279
(503) 230-5400

*Field Office*
(Washington)
Alan B. Groves, Biologist
7600 Sand Point Way, NE
BIN: C15700
Seattle, WA 98115
(206) 526-6172

## *ALASKA REGION*

*Regional Office*
(Southern Alaska)
Theodore F. Meyers, Division Chief
P.O. Box 1668
Juneau, AK 99802
(907) 586-7235

*Anchorage Field Office*
(Northern Alaska)
Ronald J. Morris, Supervisor
Federal Bldg. & U.S. Court House
701 C St., Box 43
Anchorage, AK 99513
(907) 271-5006

# APPENDIX F

# National Marine Fisheries Service Directory

## WASHINGTON HEADQUARTERS

Department of Commerce
National Oceanic and Atmospheric Administration
National Marine Fisheries Service
1825 Connecticut Avenue, NW
Washington, DC 20235

| | | |
|---|---|---|
| Assistant Administrator For Fisheries | William E. Evans | 202-673-5450 |
| Chief, Management and Budget | Samuel W. McKeen | 202-673-5455 |
| Chief, Constituent Affairs | John Dunnigan (acting) | 202-673-5429 |
| Chief, Policy and Planning | John T. Everett | 202-673-5464 |
| Deputy Assistant Adminstrator for Fisheries Resources Management | Carmen J. Blondin | 202-673-5260 |
| Director, Office of Fisheries Management | Richard B. Roe | 202-673-5263 |
| Director, Office of Industry Services | Carmen J. Blondin (acting) | 202-673-5260 |
| Director, Office of International Fisheries | Henry R. Beasley | 202-673-5279 |
| Director, Office of Protected Species and Habitat Conservation | Nancy Foster | 202-673-5348 |
| Chief, Protected Species Division | R.B. Brumsted | 202-673-5349 |
| Chief, Habitat Conservation Division | Kenneth R. Roberts | 202-673-5353 |
| Director, Office of Enforcement | Morris M. Pallozzi | 202-673-5295 |

# REGIONAL OFFICES

Richard Schaefer
Director, Northeast Region (ME, NH, MA, CT, RI, NY, NJ, DE, MA, VA, WV, PA, VT, OH, IN, IL, MI, WI, MN)
National Marine Fisheries Service
14 Elm Street, Federal Buildling
Gloucester, MA 01930
(617) 281-3600

Jack T. Brauner
Director, Southeast Region (NC, SC, GA, FL, AL, MS, LA, TX, OK, NE, NM, KS, IA, MO, AR, TN, KY)
National Marine Fisheries Service
9450 Koger Boulevard
St. Petersburg, FL 33702
(813) 893-3141

Roland A. Schmitten
Director, Northwest Region (OR, WA, ID, MT, ND, SD, CO, WY, UT)
National Marine Fisheries Service
7600 Sand Point Way, NE.
BIN C15700
Seattle, WA 98115-0070
(206) 526-6150

E. Charles Fullerton
Director, Southwest Region (CA, NV, AZ, HI)
National Marine Fisheries Service
300 S. Ferry Street
Terminal Island, CA 90731
(213) 548-2575

Robert W. McVey
Director, Alaska Region
National Marine Fisheries Service
P.O. Box 1668
Juneau, AK 99802
(907) 586-7221

## APPENDIX G

# Budget Information Contacts on Federal Fish and Wildlife Programs

| Title | Name | Phone |
|---|---|---|
| **Army Corps of Engineers (Wetlands 404 Program)** | | |
| Chief, Programs Division Office of the Corps of Engineers | Don B. Cluff | 202 272-0191 |
| **Bureau of Land Management** | | |
| Chief, Office of Budget | Roger L. Hildeberdel | 202 343-8571 |
| Budget Analyst, Resource Programs | Phil Morland | 202 343-8571 |
| **Environmental Protection Agency (Wetlands/404 Program)** | | |
| Director, Budget Office | Alvin Pesachowitz | 202 475-8340 |
| Budget Analyst, 404 Program | James F. Horn (acting) | 202 382-4170 |
| **Fish and Wildlife Service** | | |
| Deputy Assistant Director, Policy, Budget, and Administration | Edwin A. Verburg | 202 343-4329 |
| Chief, Budget Division | James C. Leupold | 202 343-2444 |
| **Forest Service** | | |
| Director, Program Development and Budget | John A. Leasure | 202 447-6987 |
| Leader, Program, Planning, and Development Team | Cindy King-Lucus (acting) | 202 382-9125 |
| **Marine Mammal Commission** | | |
| Executive Director | John R. Twiss, Jr. | 202 653-6237 |

| Title | Name | Phone |
|-------|------|-------|

## National Marine Fisheries Service

Budget Analyst, Office of Policy and
  Planning      Donald A. Wickham      202 673-5464

## National Park Service

Chief, Budget Division      C. Bruce Sheaffer      202 343-4566
Supervisory Budget Analyst      Rory D. Westberg      202 343-8746

# APPENDIX H

# Congressional Contacts and Addresses

### Bill Status

To determine the status of legislation in the House or Senate, call the Bill Status Office at (202) 225-1772

### Copies of Legislation and Reports

To obtain copies of bills, committee reports, or public laws, write the congressional document office. All requests should list documents in numerical order, lowest to highest, and must include a self-addressed mailing label. You may obtain one free copy each of up to six different documents per request.

Senate Document Room (202) 224-7860
B04, Hart Building
Washington, D.C. 20510

## CONGRESSIONAL COMMITTEES

To obtain detailed information about pending wildlife legislation or congressional oversight activity contact the appropriate House or Senate Committee.

### HOUSE OF REPRESENTATIVES

#### *Committee on Agriculture,* Rm. 1301, Longworth House

Office Bldg., Washington, D.C. 20515 (202, 225-2171)
Chairman: E (Kika) de la Garza (TX)

Concerned with adulteration of seeds, insect pests, and protection of birds and animals in forest reserves; agriculture generally; agricultural and industrial chemistry; agricultural colleges and experiment stations; agricultural economics and research; agricultural education extension services; agricultural production and marketing and stabilization of prices of agricultural products; animal industry and diseases of animals;

crop insurance and soil conservation; dairy industry; entomology and plant quarantine; extension of farm credit and farm security; forestry in general, and forest reserves other than those created from the public domain; human nutrition and home economics; inspection of livestock and meat products; plant industry, soils, and agricultural engineering; rural electrification; commodities exchanges and rural development.

## Committee on Appropriations, Rm H-218, Capitol Bldg., Washington, D.C. 20515 (202, 225-2771)

Chairman: Jamie L. Whitten (MS)

Concerned with appropriation of the revenue for the support of the government, recissions of appropriations contained in appropriation acts, and transfers of unexpended balances.

## Committee on Interior and Insular Affairs, Rm. 1324, Longworth House Office Bldg., Washington, D.C. 20515 (202, 225-2761)

Chairman: Morris K. Udall (AZ)

Concerned with forest reserves and national parks created from the public domain; forfeiture of land grant and alien ownership, including alien ownership of mineral lands; geological survey; interstate compacts relating to apportionment of waters for irrigation purposes; irrigation and reclamation, including water supply for reclamation projects, and easements of public lands for irrigation projects, and acquisition of private lands when necessary to complete irrigation projects; measures relation to the care and management of Indians, including the care and allotment of Indian lands and general and special measures relating to claims which are paid out of Indian funds; measures relating generally to the insular possessions of the U.S., except matters affecting their revenue and appropriations; military parks and battlefields; national cemeteries administered by the secretary of the Interior, and parks within the District of Columbia; mineral land laws and claims and entries thereunder; mineral resources of the public lands; mining interests generally; mining schools and experimental stations; petroleum conservation on the public lands and conservation of the radium supply in the U.S.; preservation of prehistoric ruins and objects of interest on the public domain; public lands generally, including entry, easements, and grazing thereon; relations of the U.S. with the Indians and the Indian tribes; regulation of the domestic nuclear energy industry, including regulation of research and development reactors and nuclear regulatory research. Also special oversight functions with respect to all programs affecting Indians and non-military nuclear energy and research and development including the disposal of nuclear waste.

## Committee on Merchant Marine and Fisheries, Rm. 1334, Longworth House Office Bldg., Washington, D.C. 20515 (202, 225-4047)

Chairman: Walter B. Jones (NC)

Concerned with merchant marine generally; oceanography and marine affairs, including coastal zone management; Coast Guard, including lifesaving service, light-houses, lightships, and ocean derelicts; fisheries and wildlife, including research, restoration, refuges, and conservation; measures relating to the regulation of common carriers by water (except matters subject to the jurisdiction of the Interstate Commerce Commission) and to the inspection of merchant marine vessels, lights and signals, lifesaving equipment, and fire protection on such vessels; Merchant Marine officers and seaman; navigation and the laws relating thereto, including pilotage, Panama Canal and the maintenance and operation of the Panama Canal consistent with the treaty with Panama and the implementation legislation enacted pursuant to such treaty; and interoceanic canals generally; primary oversight jurisdiction over the Outer Continental Shelf Lands Act and legislative jurisdiction over any proposed amendments. Registering and licensing of vessels and small boats; rules and international arrangements to prevent collisions at sea; United States Coast Guard and Merchant Marine Academies, and State Maritime Academies; international fishing agreements.

## SENATE

### Committee on Agriculture, Nutrition and Forestry, Rm 328-A, Russell Bldg., Washington, D.C. 20510 (202, 224-2035)

Chairman: Patrick Leahy (VT)

Concerned with agriculture and agricultural commodities; inspection of livestock, meat and agricultural products; animal industry and diseases of animals; pests and pesticides; agriculutural extension services and experiment station; forestry, forest reserves and wilderness areas other than those created from the public domain; agricultural economics and research; human nutrition; home economics; extension of farm credit and farm security; rural development, rural electrification and watersheds; agricultural production and marketing and stabilization of prices of agricultural products; crop insurance and soil conservation; school nutrition programs; food stamp programs; food from fresh waters; plant industry, soils, and agricultural engineering; the committee also studies and reviews, on a comprehensive basis, matters relating to food, nutrition and hunger, both in the U.S. and in foreign countries, and rural affairs and reports on them from time to time.

### Committee on Appropriations, S-128, The Capitol, Washington, D.C. 20510 (202, 224-3471)

Chairman: John Stennis (MS)

Concerned with all proposed legislation, messages, petitions, memorials, and other matters relating to appropriation of the revenue for the support of the government.

### Committee on Commerce, Science and Transportation, US Senate, SD-508, Washington, D.C. 20510 (202, 224-5115)

Chairman: Ernest Hollings

Concerned with interstate commerce; transportation; regulation of interstate common carriers, including railroads, buses, trucks, vessels, pipelines and civil aviation; merchant marine and navigation; marine and ocean navigation, safety and transportation, including navigational aspects of deepwater ports; Coast Guard; inland waterways, except construction; communications; regulation of consumer products and services, except for credit, financial services and housing; the Panama Canal, except for maintenance, operation, administration, sanitation and government, and interoceanic canals generally; standards and measurements; highway safety; science, engineering and technology research and development and policy; nonmilitary aeronautical and space sciences; transportation and commerce aspects of Outer Continental Shelf lands; marine fisheries; coastal zone management; oceans, weather and atmospheric activities; sports.

## Committee on Energy and Natural Resources, Rm. SD-358, Dirksen Bldg., Washington, D.C. 20510 (202, 224-4971)

Chairman: J. Bennett Johnston (LA)

Jurisdiction: Coal production, distribution utilization; energy policy, regulation, conservation, and research; hydroelectric power; irrigation and reclamation; national parks; wilderness areas; historical sites; public lands and forest; oil and gas production and distribution; mining, mineral lands, mining claims; solar energy systems; extraction of minerals from oceans and Outer Continental Shelf lands.

## Committee on Environment and Public Works, Rm. SD-410, Dirksen Bldg., Washington, D.C. 20510 (202, 224-6176)

Chairman: Quentin Burdick (ND)

Jurisdiction: all proposed legislation, messages, petitions, memorials, and other matters relating to the following subjects; environmental policy; environmental research and development; ocean dumping; fisheries and wildlife; environmental aspects of Outer Continental Shelf lands; solid waste disposal and recycling; environmental effects of toxic substances, other than pesticides; water resources; flood control and improvements of rivers and harbors, including environmental aspects of deepwater ports; public works, bridges, and dams; water pollution; air pollution; noise pollution; nonmilitary environmental regulation and control of nuclear energy; regional economic development; construction and maintenance of highways; public buildlings and improved grounds of the United States generally, including Federal buildings in the District of Columbia. The committee also studies and reviews, on a comprehensive basis, matters relating to environmental protection and resource utilization and conservation, and report on them from time to time.

# APPENDIX I

# The Federal Endangered and Threatened Species List

**Title 50—Wildlife and Fisheries**

**PART 17—ENDANGERED AND THREATENED WILDLIFE AND PLANTS**

`  ·    ·    ·    ·    ·  `

**Subpart B—Lists**

Source: 48 FR 34182, July 27, 1983, unless otherwise noted.

**§ 17.11  Endangered and threatened wildlife.**

(a) The list in this section contains the names of all species of wildlife which have been determined by the Services to be Endangered or Threatened. It also contains the names of species of wildlife treated as Endangered or Threatened because they are sufficiently similar in appearance to Endangered or Threatened species (see § 17.50 *et seq.*).

(b) The columns entitled "Common Name," "Scientific Name," and "Vertebrate Population Where Endangered or Threatened" define the species of wildlife within the meaning of the Act. Thus, differently classified geographic populations of the same vertebrate subspecies or species shall be identified by their differing geographic boundaries, even though the other two columns are identical. The term "Entire" means that all populations throughout the present range of a vertebrate species are listed. Although common names are included, they cannot be relied upon for identification of any specimen, since they may vary greatly in local usage. The Services shall use the most recently accepted scientific name. In cases in which confusion might arise, a synonym(s) will be provided in parentheses. The Services shall rely to the extent practicable on the *International Code of Zoological Nomenclature.*

(c) In the "Status" column the following symbols are used: "E" for Endangered, "T" for Threatened, and "E [or T] (S/A)" for similarity of appearance species.

(d) The other data in the list are nonregulatory in nature and are provided for the information of the reader. In the annual revision and compilation of this Title, the following information may be amended without public notice: the spelling of species' names, historical range, footnotes, references to certain other applicable portions of this Title, synonyms, and more current names. In any of these revised entries, neither the species, as defined in paragraph (b) of this section, nor its status may be changed without following the procedures of Part 424 of this Title.

(e) The "Historic Range" indicates the known general distribution of the species or subspecies as reported in the current scientific literature. The present distribution may be greatly reduced from this historic range. This column does not imply any limitation on the application of the prohibitions in the Act or implementing rules. Such prohibitions apply to all individuals of the species, wherever found.

(f)(1) A footnote to the **Federal Register** publication(s) listing or reclassifying a species is indicated under the column "When Listed." Footnote numbers to §§ 17.11 and 17.12 are in the same numerical sequence, since plants and animals may be listed in the same **Federal Register** document. That document, at least since 1973, includes a statement indicating the basis for the listing, as well as the effective date(s) of said listing.

(2) The "Special Rules" and "Critical Habitat" columns provide a cross reference to other sections in Parts 17, 222, 226, or 227. The "Special Rules" column will also be used to cite the special rules that describe experimental populations and determine if they are essential or nonessential. Separate listing will be made for experimental populations, and the status column will include the following symbols: "XE" for an essential experimental population and "XN" for a nonessential

experimental population. The term "NA" (not applicable) appearing in either of these two columns indicates that there are no special rules and/or critical habitat for that particular species. However, all other appropriate rules in Parts 17, 217–227, and 402 still apply to that species. In addition, there may be other rules in this Title that relate to such wildlife, e.g., port-of-entry requirements. It is not intended that the references in the "Special Rules" column list all the regulations of the two Services which might apply to the species or to the regulations of other Federal agencies or State or local governments.

(g) The listing of a particular taxon includes all lower taxonomic units. For example, the genus *Hylobates* (gibbons) is listed as Endangered throughout its entire range (China, India, and SE Asia); consequently, all species, subspecies, and populations of that genus are considered listed as Endangered for the purposes of the Act. In 1978 (43 FR 6230–6233) the species *Haliaeetus leucocephalus* (bald eagle) was listed as Threatened in "USA (WA, OR, MN, WI, MI)" rather than its entire population; thus, all individuals of the bald eagle found in those five States are considered listed as Threatened for the purposes of the Act.

(h) The "List of Endangered and Threatened Wildlife" is provided below:

**EDITORIAL NOTE:** This is a compilation and special reprint of 50 CFR 17.11 and 17.12 and is current as of the date shown on the cover. Minor changes and corrections to the October 1, 1985, compilation of 50 CFR have been incorporated in this printing, as well as all published final rules that have subsequent appeared in the **Federal Register**. Otherwise no entry in these lists has been significantly affected. This list has been prepared by the staff of the Office of Endangered Species, U.S. Fish and Wildlife Service, Washington, D.C. 20240. Readers are requested to advise the Service of any errors in this list. Copies are available from the Publication Unit, U.S. Fish and Wildlife Service, Washington, D.C. 20240.

| Species — Common name | Species — Scientific name | Historic range | Vertebrate population where endangered or threatened | Status | When listed | Critical habitat | Special rules |
|---|---|---|---|---|---|---|---|
| **MAMMALS** | | | | | | | |
| Anoa, lowland | *Bubalus depressicornis (=B. anoa depressicornis)* | Indonesia | Entire | E | 3 | NA | NA |
| Anoa, mountain | *Bubalus quarlesi (=B. anoa quarlesi)* | Indonesia | do | E | 15 | NA | NA |
| Antelope, giant sable | *Hippotragus niger variani* | Angola | do | E | 15 | NA | NA |
| Argali | *Ovis ammon hodgsoni* | China (Tibet, Himalayas) | do | E | 15 | NA | NA |
| Armadillo, giant | *Priodontes maximus (=giganteus)* | Venezuela and Guyana to Argentina | do | E | 15 | NA | NA |
| Armadillo, pink fairy | *Chlamyphorus truncatus* | Argentina | do | E | 3 | NA | NA |
| Ass, African wild | *Equus asinus (=africanus)* | Somalia, Sudan, Ethiopia | do | E | 3 | NA | NA |
| Ass, Asian wild (=kulan, onager) | *Equus hemionus* | Southwestern and Central Asia | do | E | 3 | NA | NA |
| Avahi | *Avahi (=Lichanotus) laniger (=entire genus)* | Malagasy Republic (=Madagascar) | do | E | 3 | NA | NA |
| Aye-Aye | *Daubentonia madagascariensis* | Malagasy Republic (=Madagascar) | do | E | 3 | NA | NA |
| Babirusa | *Babyrousa babyrussa* | Indonesia | do | E | 15 | NA | NA |
| Baboon, gelada | *Theropithecus gelada* | Ethiopia | do | T | 16 | NA | 17.40(c) |
| Bandicoot, barred | *Perameles bougainville* | Australia | do | E | 4 | NA | NA |
| Bandicoot, desert | *Perameles eremiana* | do | do | E | 6 | NA | NA |
| Bandicoot, lesser rabbit | *Macrotis leucura* | do | do | E | 4 | NA | NA |
| Bandicoot, pig-footed | *Chaeropus ecaudatus* | do | do | E | 4 | NA | NA |
| Bandicoot, rabbit | *Macrotis lagotis* | do | do | E | 4 | NA | NA |
| Banteng | *Bos javanicus (=banteng)* | Southeast Asia | do | E | 3 | NA | NA |
| Bat, Bulmer's fruit (flying fox) | *Aproteles bulmerae* | Papua New Guinea | do | E | 139 | NA | NA |
| Bat, bumblebee | *Craseonycteris thonglongyai* | Thailand | do | E | 139 | NA | NA |
| Bat, gray | *Myotis grisescens* | Central and Southeastern U.S.A. | do | E | 13 | NA | NA |
| Bat, Hawaiian hoary | *Lasiurus cinereus semotus* | U.S.A. (HI) | do | E | 2 | NA | NA |
| Bat, Indiana | *Myotis sodalis* | Eastern and Midwestern U.S.A. | do | E | 1 | 17.95(a) | NA |
| Bat, little Mariana fruit | *Pteropus tokudae* | Western Pacific Ocean: U.S.A. (Guam) | do | E | 156 | NA | NA |
| Bat, Mariana fruit | *Pteropus mariannus mariannus* | Western Pacific Ocean: U.S.A. (Guam, Rota, Tinian, Saipan, Aguigan). | Guam. | E | 156 | NA | NA |
| Bat, Ozark big-eared | *Plecotus townsendii ingens* | U.S.A. (MO, OK, AR) | do | E | 85 | NA | NA |
| Bat, Rodrigues fruit (flying fox) | *Pteropus rodricensis* | Indian Ocean: Rodrigues Island. | do | E | 139 | NA | NA |
| Bat, Singapore roundleaf horseshoe | *Hipposideros ridleyi* | Malaysia | do | E | 139 | NA | NA |
| Bat, Virginia big-eared | *Plecotus townsendii virginianus* | U.S.A. (KY, WV, VA) | do | E | 85 | 17.95(a) | NA |
| Bear, brown | *Ursus arctos pruinosus* | China (Tibet) | do | E | 15 | NA | NA |
| Bear, brown | *Ursus arctos arctos* | Palearctic | Italy. | E | 15 | NA | NA |
| Bear, brown or grizzly | *Ursus arctos (=U.a. horribilis)* | Holarctic | U.S.A.—48 conterminous States. | T | 1, 2, 9 | NA | 17.40(b) |
| Bear, brown or grizzly | *Ursus arctos (=U.a. nelsoni)* | Holarctic | Mexico. | E | 3 | NA | NA |
| Beaver | *Castor fiber birulai* | Mongolia | Entire | E | 15 | NA | NA |
| Bison, wood | *Bison bison athabascae* | Canada, Northwestern U.S.A. | Canada. | E | 3 | NA | NA |
| Bobcat | *Felis rufus escuinapae* | Central Mexico | Entire | E | 15 | NA | NA |
| Bontebok (antelope) | *Damaliscus dorcas dorcas* | South Africa | do | E | 15 | NA | NA |
| Camel, Bactrian | *Camelus bactrianus (=ferus)* | Mongolia, China. | do | E | 15 | NA | NA |

| Species | | Historic range | Vertebrate population where endangered or threatened | Status | When listed | Critical habitat | Special rules |
|---|---|---|---|---|---|---|---|
| Common name | Scientific name | | | | | | |
| Caribou, woodland | Rangifer tarandus caribou | Canada, U.S.A. (AK, ID, ME, MI, MN, MT, NH, VT, WA, WI). | Canada (that part of S.E. Brit. Col. bounded by the Can.-USA border, Columbia R., Kootenay R., Kootenay L., and Kootenai R.), U.S.A. (ID, WA). | E | 128E, 136E, 143 | NA | NA |
| Cat, Andean | Felis jacobita | Chile, Peru, Bolivia, Argentina | Entire | E | 15 | NA | NA |
| Cat, black-footed | Felis nigripes | Southern Africa | do | E | 15 | NA | NA |
| Cat, flat-headed | Felis planiceps | Malaysia, Indonesia | do | E | 15 | NA | NA |
| Cat, Iriomote | Felis (Mayailurus) iriomotensis | Japan (Iriomote Island, Ryuku Islands) | do | E | 50 | NA | NA |
| Cat, leopard | Felis bengalensis bengalensis | India, Southeast Asia | do | E | 15 | NA | NA |
| Cat, marbled | Felis marmorata | Nepal, Southeast Asia, Indonesia | do | E | 15 | NA | NA |
| Cat, Pakistan sand | Felis margarita scheffeli | Pakistan | do | E | 139 | NA | NA |
| Cat, Temminck's (= golden cat) | Felis temmincki | Nepal, China, Southeast Asia, Indonesia (Sumatra). | do | E | 15 | NA | NA |
| Cat, tiger | Felis tigrinus | Costa Rica to northern Argentina | do | E | 5 | NA | NA |
| Chamois, Apennine | Rupicapra rupicapra ornata | Italy | do | E | 15 | NA | NA |
| Cheetah | Acinonyx jubatus | Africa to India | do | T | 3, 5 | NA | NA |
| Chimpanzee | Pan troglodytes | West and Central Africa | do | E | 16 | NA | 17.40(c) |
| Chimpanzee, pygmy | Pan paniscus | Zaire | do | T | 16 | NA | 17.40(c) |
| Chinchilla | Chinchilla brevicaudata boliviana | Bolivia | do | E | 15 | NA | NA |
| Civet, Malabar large-spotted | Viverra megaspila civettina | India | do | E | 50 | NA | NA |
| Cochito (= Gulf of California harbor porpoise). | Phocoena sinus | Mexico (Gulf of California) | do | E | 169 | NA | NA |
| Colobus, Preuss's red | Colobus badius preussi | Cameroon | do | E | 139 | NA | NA |
| Cougar, eastern | Felis concolor cougar | Eastern North America | do | E | 6 | NA | NA |
| Deer, Bactrian | Cervus elaphus bactrianus | U.S.S.R., Afghanistan | do | E | 50 | NA | NA |
| Deer, Bawean | Axis (=Cervus) porcinus kuhli | Indonesia | do | E | 3 | NA | NA |
| Deer, Barbary | Cervus elaphus barbarus | Morocco, Tunisia, Algeria | do | E | 50 | NA | NA |
| Deer, Cedros Island mule | Odocoileus hemionus cedrosensis | Mexico (Cedros Island) | do | E | 10 | NA | NA |
| Deer, Columbian white-tailed | Odocoileus virginianus leucurus | U.S.A. (WA, OR) | do | E | 1 | NA | NA |
| Deer, Corsican red | Cervus elaphus corsicanus | Corsica, Sardinia | do | E | 50 | NA | NA |
| Deer, Eld's brow-antlered | Cervus eldi | India to Southeast Asia | do | E | 3 | NA | NA |
| Deer, Formosan sika | Cervus nippon taiouanus | Taiwan | do | E | 50 | NA | NA |
| Deer, hog | Axis (=Cervus) porcinus annamiticus | Thailand, Indochina | do | E | 15 | NA | NA |
| Deer, key | Odocoileus virginianus clavium | U.S.A. (FL) | do | E | 1 | NA | NA |
| Deer, marsh | Blastocerus dichotomus | Argentina, Uruguay, Paraguay, Bolivia, Brazil. | do | E | 3 | NA | NA |
| Deer, McNeill's | Cervus elaphus macneilli | China (Sinkiang, Tibet) | do | E | 3 | NA | NA |
| Deer, musk | Moschus spp. (all species) | Central and East Asia | Afghanistan, Bhutan, Burma, China (Tibet, Yunnan), India, Nepal, Pakistan, Sikkim. | E | 15 | NA | NA |
| Deer, North China sika | Cervus nippon mandarinus | China (Shantung and Chihli Provinces). | Entire | E | 50 | NA | NA |
| Deer, pampas | Ozotoceros bezoarticus | Brazil, Argentina, Uruguay, Bolivia, Paraguay. | do | E | 15 | NA | NA |

| Species | | Historic range | Vertebrate population where endangered or threatened | Status | When listed | Critical habitat | Special rules |
|---|---|---|---|---|---|---|---|
| Common name | Scientific name | | | | | | |
| Deer, Persian fallow | *Dama dama mesopotamica* | Iraq, Iran | do | E | 3 | NA | NA |
| Deer, Philippine | *Axis (= Cervus) porcinus calamianensis* | Philippines (Calamian Islands) | do | E | 15 | NA | NA |
| Deer, Ryukyu sika | *Cervus nippon keramae* | Japan (Ryukyu Islands) | do | E | 50 | NA | NA |
| Deer, Shansi sika | *Cervus nippon grassianus* | China (Shansi Province) | do | E | 50 | NA | NA |
| Deer, South China sika | *Cervus nippon kopschi* | Southern China | do | E | 50 | NA | NA |
| Deer, swamp (= barasingha) | *Cervus duvauceli* | India, Nepal | do | E | 3 | NA | NA |
| Deer, Yarkand | *Cervus elaphus yarkandensis* | China (Sinkiang) | do | E | 50 | NA | NA |
| Dhole (= Asiatic wild dog) | *Cuon alpinus* | U.S.S.R., Korea, China, India, Southeast Asia. | do | E | 3 | NA | NA |
| Dibbler | *Antechinus apicalis* | Australia | do | E | 4 | NA | NA |
| Dog, African wild | *Lycaon pictus* | Sub-Saharan Africa | do | E | 139 | NA | NA |
| Drill | *Papio leucophaeus* | Equatorial West Africa | do | E | 16 | NA | NA |
| Dugong | *Dugong dugon* | East Africa to southern Japan, including U.S.A. (Trust Territories). | do | E | 4 | NA | NA |
| Duiker, Jentink's | *Cephalophus jentinki* | Sierra Leone, Liberia, Ivory Coast | do | E | 50 | NA | NA |
| Eland, Western giant | *Taurotragus derbianus derbianus* | Senegal to Ivory Coast | do | E | 50 | NA | NA |
| Elephant, African | *Loxodonta africana* | Africa | do | T | 40 | NA | 17.40(e) |
| Elephant, Asian | *Elephas maximus* | South-central and Southeast Asia | do | E | 15 | NA | NA |
| Ferret, black-footed | *Mustela nigripes* | Western U.S.A., Western Canada | do | E | 1,3 | NA | NA |
| Fox, Northern swift | *Vulpes velox hebes* | U.S.A. (northern plains), Canada | Canada | E | 3 | NA | NA |
| Fox, San Joaquin kit | *Vulpes macrotis mutica* | U.S.A. (CA) | Entire | E | 1 | NA | NA |
| Fox, Simien | *Canis (Simenia) simensis* | Ethiopia | do | E | 50 | NA | NA |
| Gazelle, Clark's (= Dibatag) | *Ammodorcas clarkei* | Somalia, Ethiopia | do | E | 3 | NA | NA |
| Gazelle, Cuvier's | *Gazella cuvieri* | Morocco, Algeria, Tunisia | do | E | 3 | NA | NA |
| Gazelle, Mhorr | *Gazella dama mhorr* | Morocco | do | E | 3 | NA | NA |
| Gazelle, Moroccan (= Dorcas) | *Gazella dorcas massaesyla* | Morocco, Algeria, Tunisia | do | E | 3 | NA | NA |
| Gazelle, Rio de Oro Dama | *Gazella dama lozanoi* | Western Sahara | do | E | 3 | NA | NA |
| Gazelle, Arabian | *Gazella gazella* | Arabian Peninsula, Palestine, Sinai. | do | E | 50 | NA | NA |
| Gazelle, sand | *Gazella subgutturosa marica* | Israel, Iraq, Jordan, Syria, Arabian Peninsula. | do | E | 50 | NA | NA |
| Gazelle, Saudi Arabian | *Gazella dorcas saudiya* | Somalia. | do | E | 50 | NA | NA |
| Gazelle, Pelzeln's | *Gazella dorcas pelzelni* | Somalia. | do | E | 50 | NA | NA |
| Gazelle, slender-horned (= Rhim) | *Gazella leptoceros* | Sudan, Egypt, Algeria, Libya | do | E | 3 | NA | NA |
| Gibbons | *Hylobates spp. (including Nomascus)* | China, India, Southeast Asia | do | E | 3, 15 | NA | NA |
| Goat, wild (= Chiltan markhor) | *Capra aegagrus (= falconeri chiltanensis)* | Southwestern Asia | Chiltan Range of west-central Pakistan. | E | 15 | NA | NA |
| Goral | *Nemorhaedus goral* | East Asia | Entire | E | 15 | NA | NA |
| Gorilla | *Gorilla gorilla* | Central and Western Africa | do | E | 3 | NA | NA |
| Hare, hispid | *Caprolagus hispidus* | India, Nepal, Bhutan | do | E | 15 | NA | NA |
| Hartebeest, Swayne's | *Alcelaphus buselaphus swaynei* | Ethiopia, Somalia | do | E | 50 | NA | NA |
| Hartebeest, Tora | *Alcelaphus buselaphus tora* | Ethiopia, Sudan, Egypt | do | E | 50 | NA | NA |
| Hog, pygmy | *Sus salvanius* | India, Nepal, Bhutan, Sikkim | do | E | 3 | NA | NA |
| Horse, Przewalski's | *Equus przewalskii* | Mongolia, China | do | E | 15 | NA | NA |
| Huemul, North Andean | *Hippocamelus antisensis* | Ecuador, Peru, Chile, Bolivia, Argentina. | do | E | 15 | NA | NA |
| Huemul, South Andean | *Hippocamelus bisulcus* | Chile, Argentina | do | E | 15 | NA | NA |
| Hyena, Barbary | *Hyaena hyaena barbara* | Morocco, Algeria, Tunisia | do | E | 3 | NA | NA |
| Hyena, brown | *Hyaena brunnea* | Southern Africa | do | E | 3 | NA | NA |
| Ibex, Pyrenean | *Capra pyrenaica pyrenaica* | Spain | do | E | 3 | NA | NA |
| Ibex, Walia | *Capra walie* | Ethiopia | do | E | 3 | NA | NA |
| Impala, black-faced | *Aepyceros melampus petersi* | Namibia, Angola | do | E | 3 | NA | NA |
| Indri | *Indri indri (= entire genus)* | Malagasy Republic (= Madagascar) | do | E | 3 | NA | NA |
| Jaguar | *Panthera onca* | U.S.A. (TX, NM, AZ), C. and S. America. | Mexico southward. | E | 5 | NA | NA |

| Species | | Historic range | Vertebrate population where endangered or threatened | Status | When listed | Critical habitat | Special rules |
|---|---|---|---|---|---|---|---|
| Common name | Scientific name | | | | | | |
| Jaguarundi | *Felis yagouaroundi cacomitli* | U.S.A. (TX), Mexico | Entire | E | 15 | NA | NA |
| Jaguarundi | *Felis yagouaroundi fossata* | Mexico, Nicaragua | do | E | 15 | NA | NA |
| Jaguarundi | *Felis yagouaroundi panamensis* | Nicaragua, Costa Rica, Panama | do | E | 15 | NA | NA |
| Jaguarundi | *Felis yagouaroundi tolteca* | U.S.A. (AZ), Mexico | do | E | 15 | NA | NA |
| Kangaroo, eastern gray | *Macropus giganteus* (all subspecies except *tasmaniensis*) | Australia | do | T | 7 | NA | 17.40(a) |
| Kangaroo, red | *Macropus (Megaleia) rufus* | do | do | T | 7 | NA | 17.40(a) |
| Kangaroo, Tasmanian forester | *Macropus giganteus tasmaniensis* | Australia (Tasmania) | do | E | 6 | NA | NA |
| Kangaroo, western gray | *Macropus fuliginosus* | Australia | do | T | 7 | NA | 17.40(a) |
| Kouprey | *Bos sauveli* | Vietnam, Laos, Cambodia, Thailand | do | E | 3 | NA | NA |
| Langur, capped | *Presbytis pileata* | India, Burma, Bangladesh | do | E | 15 | NA | NA |
| Langur, entellus | *Presbytis entellus* | China (Tibet), India, Pakistan, Kashmir, Sri Lanka, Sikkim, Bangladesh. | do | E | 15 | NA | NA |
| Langur, Douc | *Pygathrix nemaeus* | Cambodia, Laos, Vietnam | do | E | 3 | NA | NA |
| Langur, Francois' | *Presbytis francoisi* | China (Kwangsi), Indochina. | do | E | 16 | NA | NA |
| Langur, golden | *Presbytis geei* | India (Assam), Bhutan. | do | E | 15 | NA | NA |
| Langur, long-tailed | *Presbytis potenziani* | Indonesia | do | T | 16 | NA | 17.40(c) |
| Langur, Pagi Island | *Nasalis (Simias) concolor* | do | do | E | 3 | NA | NA |
| Langur, purple-faced | *Presbytis senex* | Sri Lanka (=Ceylon) | do | T | 16 | NA | 17.40(c) |
| Langur, Tonkin snub-nosed | *Pygathrix (Rhinopithecus) avunculus* | Vietnam | do | E | 16 | NA | 17.40(c) |
| Lechwe, red | *Kobus leche* | Southern Africa | do | T | 3, 15, 106 | NA | NA |
| Lemurs | Lemuridae (incl. Cheirogaleidae, Lepiemuridae); all members of genera *Lemur, Phaner, Hapalemur, Lepilemur, Microcebus, Allocebus, Cheirogaleus, Varecia.* | Malagasy Republic (=Madagascar) | do | E | 3, 15 | NA | NA |
| Leopard | *Panthera pardus* | Africa, Asia | Wherever found, except where it is listed as Threatened as set forth below. | E | 3, 5, 114 | NA | NA |
| Do | do | do | In Africa, in the wild, south of, and including, the following countries: Gabon, Congo, Zaire, Uganda, Kenya. | T | 3, 5, 114 | NA | 17.40(f) |
| Leopard, clouded | *Neofelis nebulosa* | Southeast and south-central Asia, Taiwan. | Entire | E | 3, 15 | NA | NA |
| Leopard, snow | *Panthera uncia* | Central Asia | do | E | 5 | NA | NA |
| Linsang, spotted | *Prionodon pardicolor* | Nepal, Assam, Vietnam, Cambodia, Laos, Burma. | do | E | 15 | NA | NA |
| Lion, Asiatic | *Panthera leo persica* | Turkey to India. | do | E | 3 | NA | NA |
| Loris, lesser slow | *Nycticebus pygmaeus* | Indochina | do | T | 16 | NA | 17.40(c) |
| Lynx, Spanish | *Felis (=Lynx) pardina* | Spain, Portugal | do | E | 3 | NA | NA |
| Macaque, Formosan rock | *Macaca cyclopis* | Taiwan | do | T | 16 | NA | 17.40(c) |
| Macaque, Japanese | *Macaca fuscata* | Japan (Shikoku, Kyushu and Honshu Islands). | do | T | 16 | NA | 17.40(c) |
| Macaque, lion-tailed | *Macaca silenus* | India | do | E | 3 | NA | NA |
| Macaque, stump-tailed | *Macaca arctoides* | India (Assam) to southern China. | do | T | 16 | NA | 17.40(c) |

| Common name | Scientific name | Historic range | Vertebrate population where endangered or threatened | Status | When listed | Critical habitat | Special rules |
|---|---|---|---|---|---|---|---|
| Macaque, Toque | *Macaca sinica* | Sri Lanka (=Ceylon) | do | T | 16 | NA | 17.40(c) |
| Manatee, Amazonian | *Trichechus inunguis* | South America (Amazon River Basin) | do | E | 3 | NA | NA |
| Manatee, West African | *Trichechus senegalensis* | West Coast of Africa from Senegal River to Cuanza River | do | T | 52 | NA | NA |
| Manatee, West Indian (Florida) | *Trichechus manatus* | U.S.A. (southeastern), Caribbean Sea, South America | do | E | 1, 3 | 17.95(a) | NA |
| Mandrill | *Papio sphinx* | Equatorial West Africa | do | E | 16 | NA | NA |
| Mangabey, Tana River | *Cercocebus galeritus* | Kenya | do | E | 3 | NA | NA |
| Mangabey, white-collared | *Cercocebus torquatus* | Senegal to Ghana; Nigeria to Gabon | do | E | 16 | NA | NA |
| Margay | *Felis wiedii* | U.S.A. (TX), C. and S. America | Mexico southward | E | 5 | NA | NA |
| Markhor, Kabul | *Capra falconeri megaceros* | Afghanistan, Pakistan | Entire | E | 15 | NA | NA |
| Markhor, straight-horned | *Capra falconeri jerdoni* | do | do | E | 15 | NA | NA |
| Marmoset, buff-headed | *Callithrix flaviceps* | Brazil | do | E | 139 | NA | NA |
| Marmoset, cotton-top | *Saguinus oedipus* | Costa Rica to Colombia | do | E | 16 | NA | NA |
| Marmoset, Goeldi's | *Callimico goeldii* | Brazil, Colombia, Ecuador, Peru, Bolivia | do | E | 3 | NA | NA |
| Marmot, Vancouver Island | *Marmota vancouverensis* | Canada (Vancouver Island) | do | E | 139 | NA | NA |
| Marsupial, eastern jerboa | *Antechinomys laniger* | Australia | do | E | 4 | NA | NA |
| Marsupial-mouse, large desert | *Sminthopsis psammophila* | do | do | E | 4 | NA | NA |
| Marsupial-mouse, long-tailed | *Sminthopsis longicaudata* | do | do | E | 4 | NA | NA |
| Marten, Formosan yellow-throated | *Martes flavigula chrysospila* | Taiwan | do | E | 3 | NA | NA |
| Monkey, black colobus | *Colobus satanas* | Equatorial Guinea, People's Republic of Congo, Cameroon, Gabon | do | E | 16 | NA | NA |
| Monkey, black howler | *Alouatta pigra* | Mexico, Guatemala, Belize | do | T | 16 | NA | 17.40(c) |
| Monkey, Diana | *Cercopithecus diana* | Coastal West Africa | do | E | 16 | NA | NA |
| Monkey, howler | *Alouatta palliata* (=villosa) | Mexico to South America | do | E | 15 | NA | NA |
| Monkey, L'hoest's | *Cercopithecus lhoesti* | Upper Eastern Congo Basin, Cameroon | do | E | 16 | NA | NA |
| Monkey, Preuss' red colobus | *Colobus badius preussi* | Cameroon | do | E | 139 | NA | NA |
| Monkey, proboscis | *Nasalis larvatus* | Borneo | do | E | 15 | NA | NA |
| Monkey, red-backed squirrel | *Saimiri oerstedii* | Costa Rica, Panama | do | E | 3 | NA | NA |
| Monkey, red-bellied | *Cercopithecus erythrogaster* | Western Nigeria | do | E | 16 | NA | NA |
| Monkey, red-eared nose-spotted | *Cercopithecus erythrotis* | Nigeria, Cameroon, Fernando Po | do | E | 16 | NA | NA |
| Monkey, spider | *Ateles geoffroy frontatus* | Costa Rica, Nicaragua | do | E | 3 | NA | NA |
| Monkey, spider | *Ateles geoffroy panamensis* | Costa Rica, Panama | do | E | 3 | NA | NA |
| Monkey, Tana River red colobus | *Colobus rufomitratus* (=badius) *rufomitratus* | Kenya | do | E | 3, 16 | NA | NA |
| Monkey, woolly spider | *Brachyteles arachnoides* | Brazil | do | E | 3 | NA | NA |
| Monkey, yellow-tailed woolly | *Lagothrix flavicauda* | Andes of northern Peru | do | E | 16 | NA | NA |
| Monkey, Zanzibar red colobus | *Colobus kirki* | Tanzania | do | E | 3 | NA | NA |
| Mouse, Alabama beach | *Peromyscus polionotus ammobates* | U.S.A. (AL) | do | E | 183 | 17.95(a) | NA |
| Mouse, Australian native | *Zyzomys* (=Notomys) *pedunculatus* | Australia | do | E | 15 | NA | NA |
| Mouse, Australian native | *Notomys aquilo* | do | do | E | 15 | NA | NA |
| Mouse, Choctawhatchee beach | *Peromyscus polionotus allophrys* | U.S.A. (FL) | do | E | 183 | 17.95(a) | NA |
| Mouse, Field's | *Pseudomys fieldi* | Australia | do | E | 4 | NA | NA |
| Mouse, Gould's | *Pseudomys gouldii* | do | do | E | 6 | NA | NA |
| Mouse, Key Largo cotton | *Peromyscus gossypinus allapaticola* | U.S.A. (FL) | do | E | 131E, 160 | NA | NA |
| Mouse, New Holland | *Pseudomys novaehollandiae* | Australia | do | E | 4 | NA | NA |
| Mouse, Perdido Key beach | *Peromyscus polionotus trissyllepsis* | U.S.A. (AL, FL) | do | E | 183 | 17.95(a) | NA |
| Mouse, salt marsh harvest | *Reithrodontomys raviventris* | U.S.A. (CA) | do | E | 2 | NA | NA |
| Mouse, Shark Bay | *Pseudomys praeconis* | Australia | do | E | 4 | NA | NA |
| Mouse, Shortridge's | *Pseudomys shortridgei* | do | do | E | 4 | NA | NA |
| Mouse, Smoky | *Pseudomys fumeus* | do | do | E | 4 | NA | NA |
| Mouse, western | *Pseudomys occidentalis* | do | do | E | 4 | NA | NA |

| Common name | Scientific name | Historic range | Vertebrate population where endangered or threatened | Status | When listed | Critical habitat | Special rules |
|---|---|---|---|---|---|---|---|
| Muntjac, Fea's | Muntiacus feae | Northern Thailand, Burma | do | E | 50 | NA | NA |
| Native-cat, eastern | Dasyurus viverrinus | Australia | do | E | 6 | NA | NA |
| Numbat | Myrmecobius fasciatus | do | do | E | 4, 6 | NA | NA |
| Ocelot | Felis pardalis | U.S.A. (AZ, TX) to C. and S. America | do | E | 5, 119 | NA | NA |
| Orangutan | Pongo pygmaeus | Borneo, Sumatra | do | E | 3 | NA | NA |
| Oryx, Arabian | Oryx leucoryx | Arabian Peninsula | do | E | 3 | NA | NA |
| Otter, Cameroon clawless | Aonyx (Paraonyx) congica microdon | Cameroon, Nigeria | do | E | 3 | NA | NA |
| Otter, giant | Pteronura brasiliensis | South America | do | E | 3 | NA | NA |
| Otter, long-tailed | Lutra longicaudis (incl. platensis) | do | do | E | 3, 15 | NA | NA |
| Otter, marine | Lutra felina | Peru south to Straits of Magellan | do | E | 15 | NA | NA |
| Otter, southern river | Lutra provocax | Chile, Argentina | do | E | 15 | NA | NA |
| Otter, southern sea | Enhydra lutris nereis | West coast U.S.A. (WA, OR, CA) south to Mexico (Baja California) | do | T | 21 | NA | NA |
| Panda, giant | Ailuropoda melanoleuca | People's Republic of China | do | E | 139 | NA | NA |
| Pangolin (= scaly anteater) | Manis temminicki | Africa | do | E | 15 | NA | NA |
| Panther, Florida | Felis concolor coryi | U.S.A. (LA and AR east to SC and FL) | do | E | 1 | NA | NA |
| Planigale, little | Planigale ingrami subtilissima (formerly P. subtilissima) | Australia | do | E | 4 | NA | NA |
| Planigale, southern | Planigale tenuirostris | do | do | E | 4 | NA | NA |
| Porcupine, thin-spined | Chaetomys subspinosus | Brazil | do | E | 3 | NA | NA |
| Possum, mountain pygmy | Burramys parvus | Australia | do | E | 4 | NA | NA |
| Possum, scaly-tailed | Wyulda squamicaudata | do | do | E | 3 | NA | 17.40(g) |
| Prairie dog, Mexican | Cynomys mexicanus | Mexico | do | E | 3 | NA | NA |
| Prairie dog, Utah | Cynomys parvidens | U.S.A. (UT) | do | T | 6, 149 | NA | NA |
| Pronghorn, peninsular | Antilocapra americana peninsularis | Mexico (Baja California) | do | E | 10 | NA | NA |
| Pronghorn, Sonoran | Antilocapra americana sonoriensis | U.S.A. (AZ), Mexico | do | E | 1, 3 | NA | NA |
| Pudu | Pudu pudu | Southern South America | do | E | 15 | NA | NA |
| Puma, Costa Rican | Felis concolor costaricensis | Nicaragua, Panama, Costa Rica | do | E | 15 | NA | NA |
| Quokka | Setonix brachyurus | Australia | do | E | 6 | NA | NA |
| Rabbit, Ryukyu | Pentalagus furnessi | Japan (Ryukyu Islands) | do | E | 50 | NA | NA |
| Rabbit, volcano | Romerolagus diazi | Mexico | do | E | 3 | NA | NA |
| Rat, false water | Xeromys myoides | Australia | do | E | 4 | NA | NA |
| Rat, Fresno kangaroo | Dipodomys nitratoides exilis | U.S.A. (CA) | do | E | 170 | 17.95(a) | NA |
| Rat, Morro Bay kangaroo | Dipodomys heermann morroensis | do | do | E | 2 | 17.95(a) | NA |
| Rat, stick-nest | Leporillus conditor | Australia | do | E | 6 | NA | NA |
| Rat-kangaroo, brush-tailed | Bettongia penicillata | do | do | E | 4 | NA | NA |
| Rat-kangaroo, Gaimard's | Bettongia gaimardi | do | do | E | 6 | NA | NA |
| Rat-kangaroo, Lesuer's | Bettongia lesueur | do | do | E | 4 | NA | NA |
| Rat-kangaroo, plain | Caloprymnus campestris | do | do | E | 4 | NA | NA |
| Rat-kangaroo, Queensland | Bettongia tropica | do | do | E | 4 | NA | NA |
| Rhinoceros, black | Diceros bicornis | Sub-Saharan Africa | do | E | 97 | NA | NA |
| Rhinoceros, great Indian | Rhinoceros unicornis | India, Nepal | do | E | 4 | NA | NA |
| Rhinoceros, Javan | Rhinoceros sondaicus | Indonesia, Indochina, Burma, Thailand, Sikkim, Bangladesh, Malaysia | do | E | 3 | NA | NA |
| Rhinoceros, northern white | Ceratotherium simum cottoni | Zaire, Sudan, Uganda, Central African Republic | do | E | 3 | NA | NA |
| Rhinoceros, Sumatran | Dicerorhinus (=Didermoceros) sumatrensis | Bangladesh to Vietnam to Indonesia (Borneo) | do | E | 3 | NA | NA |
| Saiga, Mongolian (antelope) | Saiga tatarica mongolica | Mongolia | do | E | 15 | NA | NA |
| Saki, white-nosed | Chiropotes albinasus | Brazil | do | E | 3 | NA | NA |
| Seal, Caribbean monk | Monachus tropicalis | Caribbean Sea, Gulf of Mexico | do | E | 1, 2, 45 | NA | NA |
| Seal, Guadalupe fur | Arctocephalus townsendi | U.S.A. (Farallon Islands, CA) south to Mexico (Islas Revillagigedo) | do | T | 212 | NA | 227.11 |

| Common name | Scientific name | Historic range | Vertebrate population where endangered or threatened | Status | When listed | Critical habitat | Special rules |
|---|---|---|---|---|---|---|---|
| Seal, Hawaiian monk. | *Monachus schauinslandi* | Hawaiian Archipelago. | do. | E | 18 | NA | NA |
| Seal, Mediterranean monk. | *Monachus monachus* | Mediterranean, Northwest African Coast and Black Sea. | do. | E | 3 | NA | NA |
| Seledang (= Gaur). | *Bos gaurus* | Bangladesh, Southeast Asia, India. | do. | E | 3 | NA | NA |
| Serow, Sumatran. | *Capricornis sumatraensis* | Sumatra. | do. | E | 15 | NA | NA |
| Serval, Barbary. | *Felis serval constantina* | Algeria. | do. | E | 3 | NA | NA |
| Shapo. | *Ovis vignei vignei* | Kashmir. | do. | E | 15 | NA | NA |
| Shou. | *Cervus elaphus wallichi* | Tibet, Bhutan. | do. | E | 3 | NA | NA |
| Siamang. | *Symphalangus syndactylus* | Malaysia, Indonesia. | do. | E | 15 | NA | NA |
| Sifakas. | *Propithecus* spp. (all species) | Malagasy Republic (=Madagascar). | do. | E | 4 | NA | NA |
| Sloth, Brazilian three-toed. | *Bradypus torquatus* | Brazil. | do. | E | 3, 4 | NA | NA |
| Solenodon, Cuban. | *Solenodon (Atopogale) cubanus* | Cuba. | do. | E | 3 | NA | NA |
| Solenodon, Haitian. | *Solenodon paradoxus* | Dominican Republic, Haiti. | do. | E | 3 | NA | NA |
| Squirrel, Carolina northern flying | *Glaucomys sabrinus coloratus* | U.S.A. (NC, TN). | do. | E | 189 | NA | NA |
| Squirrel, Delmarva Peninsula fox | *Sciurus niger cinereus* | U.S.A. (Delmarva Peninsula to south-east PA). | Entire, except U.S.A. Sussex Co., DE. | E | 1, 161, 168 | NA | NA |
| Do. | do. | do. | U.S.A. (DE—Sussex County). | XN | 161 | NA | 17.84(a) |
| Squirrel, Virginia northern flying | *Glaucomys sabrinus fuscus* | U.S.A. (VA, WV). | Entire. | E | 189 | NA | NA |
| Stag, Barbary | *Cervus elaphus barbarus* | Tunisia, Algeria. | do. | E | 3 | NA | NA |
| Stag, Kashmir | *Cervus elaphus hanglu* | Kashmir. | do. | E | 3 | NA | NA |
| Suni, Zanzibar | *Neotragus (Nesotragus) moschatus moschatus* | Zanzibar (and nearby islands). | do. | E | 50 | NA | NA |
| Tahr, Arabian | *Hemitragus jayakari* | Oman. | do. | E | 50 | NA | NA |
| Tamaraw | *Bubalus mindorensis* | Philippines. | do. | E | 4 | NA | NA |
| Tamarin, golden-rumped (=golden-headed Tamarin; =golden-lion Marmoset). | *Leontopithecus* ( =*Leontideus*) spp. (all species). | Brazil. | do. | E | 3 | NA | NA |
| Tamarin, pied. | *Saguinus bicolor.* | Northern Brazil. | do. | E | 16 | NA | NA |
| Tamarin, white-footed. | *Saguinus leucopus.* | Northern Colombia. | do. | T | 16 | NA | NA |
| Tapir, Asian. | *Tapirus indicus.* | Burma, Laos, Cambodia, Vietnam, Malaysia, Indonesia, Thailand. | do. | E | 15 | NA | 17.40(c) |
| Tapir, Brazilian. | *Tapirus terrestris.* | Colombia and Venezuela south to Paraguay and Argentina. | do. | E | 3 | NA | NA |
| Tapir, Central American. | *Tapirus bairdii.* | Southern Mexico to Colombia and Ecuador. | do. | E | 3 | NA | NA |
| Tapir, mountain. | *Tapirus pinchaque.* | Colombia, Ecuador and possibly Peru and Venezuela. | do. | E | 3 | NA | NA |
| Tarsier, Philippine. | *Tarsius syrichta.* | Philippines. | do. | E | 3 | NA | NA |
| Tiger. | *Panthera tigris.* | Temperate and Tropical Asia. | do. | E | 16 | NA | 17.40(c) |
| Tiger, Tasmanian (= Thylacine). | *Thylacinus cynocephalus* | Australia. | do. | E | 3, 5 | NA | NA |
| Uakari (all species). | *Cacajao* spp. (all species). | Peru, Brazil, Ecuador, Colombia, Venezuela. | do. | E | 3 | NA | NA |
| Urial. | *Ovis musimon* ( =*orientalis*) *ophion* | Cyprus | do. | T | 16 | NA | 17.40(c) |
| Vicuna. | *Vicugna vicugna* | South America (Andes) | do. | E | 166 | 17.95(a) | NA |
| Vole, Amargosa. | *Microtus californicus scirpensis* | U.S.A. (CA). | do. | E | 15 | NA | NA |
| Wallaby, banded hare. | *Lagostrophus fasciatus* | Australia. | do. | E | 4 | NA | NA |
| Wallaby, brindled nail-tailed. | *Onychogalea fraenata* | do. | do. | E | 4 | NA | NA |
| Wallaby, crescent nail-tailed. | *Onychogalea lunata* | do. | do. | E | 4 | NA | NA |
| Wallaby, Parma. | *Macropus parma* | do. | do. | E | 4 | NA | NA |
| Wallaby, Western hare. | *Lagorchestes hirsutus* | do. | do. | E | 4 | NA | NA |
| Wallaby, yellow-footed rock. | *Petrogale xanthopus* | do. | do. | E | 6 | NA | NA |
| Whale, blue. | *Balaenoptera musculus* | Oceanic | do. | E | 3 | NA | NA |

| Species | | Historic range | Vertebrate population where endangered or threatened | Status | When listed | Critical habitat | Special rules |
|---|---|---|---|---|---|---|---|
| Common name | Scientific name | | | | | | |
| Whale, bowhead | *Balaena mysticetus* | Oceanic (north latitudes only) | do | E | 3 | NA | NA |
| Whale, finback | *Balaenoptera physalus* | Oceanic | do | E | 3 | NA | NA |
| Whale, gray | *Eschrichtius robustus* | North Pacific Ocean: coastal and Bering Sea | do | E | 3 | NA | NA |
| Whale, humpback | *Megaptera novaeangliae* | Oceanic | do | E | 3 | NA | NA |
| Whale, right | *Balaena glacialis* | do | do | E | 3 | NA | NA |
| Whale, Sei | *Balaenoptera borealis* | do | do | E | 3 | NA | NA |
| Whale, sperm | *Physeter catodon* | do | do | E | 3 | NA | NA |
| Wolf, gray | *Canis lupus* | Holarctic | U.S.A. (48 conterminous States, except MN, Mexico. | E | 1, 6, 13, 15, 35 | 17.95(a) | 17.40(d) |
| Do | do | do | U.S.A. (MN) | T | 35 | 17.95(a) | 17.40(d) |
| Wolf, maned | *Chrysocyon brachyurus* | Argentina, Bolivia, Brazil, Paraguay, Uruguay | Entire | E | 4 | NA | NA |
| Wolf, red | *Canis rufus* | U.S.A. (southeastern U.S.A. west to central TX) | do | E | 1 | NA | NA |
| Wombat, hairy-nosed (=Barnard's and Queensland hairy-nosed) | *Lasiorhinus krefftii* (formerly *L. barnardi* and *L. gillespiei*) | Australia | do | E | 4, 6 | NA | NA |
| Woodrat, Key Largo | *Neotoma floridana smalli* | U.S.A. (FL) | do | E | 131E, 160 | NA | NA |
| Yak, wild | *Bos grunniens* | China (Tibet), India | do | E | 3 | NA | NA |
| Zebra, Grevy's | *Equus grevyi* | Kenya, Ethiopia, Somalia | do | T | 54 | NA | NA |
| Zebra, Hartmann's mountain | *Equus zebra hartmannae* | Namibia, Angola | do | T | 54, 111 | NA | NA |
| Zebra, mountain | *Equus zebra zebra* | South Africa | do | E | 15, 111 | NA | NA |
| **BIRDS** | | | | | | | |
| Akepa, Hawaii (honeycreeper) | *Loxops coccineus coccineus* | U.S.A. (HI) | do | E | 2 | NA | NA |
| Akepa, Maui (honeycreeper) | *Loxops coccineus ochraceus* | do | do | E | 2 | NA | NA |
| Akialoa, Kauai (honeycreeper) | *Hemignathus procerus* | do | do | E | 1 | NA | NA |
| Akiapolaau (honeycreeper) | *Hemignathus munroi* ( =*wilsoni*) | do | do | E | 1 | NA | NA |
| Albatross, short-tailed | *Diomedea albatrus* | North Pacific Ocean: Japan, U.S.S.R., U.S.A. (AK, CA, HI, OR, WA) | Entire, except U.S.A. | E | 3 | NA | NA |
| Blackbird, yellow-shouldered | *Agelaius xanthomus* | U.S.A. (PR) | Entire | E | 17 | 17.95(b) | NA |
| Bobwhite, masked (quail) | *Colinus virginianus ridgwayi* | U.S.A. (AZ), Mexico (Sonora) | do | E | 1, 3 | NA | NA |
| Booby, Abbott's | *Sula abbotti* | Indian Ocean: Christmas Island | do | E | 15 | NA | NA |
| Bristlebird, western | *Dasyornis brachypterus longirostris* | Australia | do | E | 3 | NA | NA |
| Bristlebird, western rufous | *Dasyornis broadbenti littoralis* | do | do | E | 15 | NA | NA |
| Broadbill, Guam | *Myiagra freycineti* | Western Pacific Ocean: U.S.A. (Guam) | do | E | 156 | NA | NA |
| Bulbul, Mauritius olivaceous | *Hypsipetes borbonicus olivaceus* | Indian Ocean: Mauritius | do | E | 3 | NA | NA |
| Bullfinch, Sao Miguel (finch) | *Pyrrhula pyrrhula murina* | Eastern Atlantic Ocean: Azores | do | E | 3 | NA | NA |
| Bushwren, New Zealand | *Xenicus longipes* | New Zealand | do | E | 3 | NA | NA |
| Bustard, great Indian | *Choriotis nigriceps* | India, Pakistan | do | E | 3 | NA | NA |
| Cahow (=Bermuda Petrel) | *Pterodroma cahow* | North Atlantic Ocean: Bermuda | do | E | 3 | NA | NA |
| Condor, Andean | *Vultur gryphus* | Colombia to Chile and Argentina | do | E | 4 | NA | NA |
| Condor, California | *Gymnogyps californianus* | U.S.A. (OR, CA), Mexico (Baja California) | do | E | 1 | 17.95(b) | NA |
| Coot, Hawaiian (=alae keo keo) | *Fulica americana alai* | U.S.A. (HI) | do | E | 2 | NA | NA |
| Cotinga, banded | *Cotinga maculata* | Brazil | do | E | 15 | NA | NA |
| Cotinga, white-winged | *Xipholena atropurpurea* | do | do | E | 15 | NA | NA |
| Crane, black-necked | *Grus nigricollis* | China (Tibet) | do | E | 15 | NA | NA |
| Crane, Cuba sandhill | *Grus canadensis nesiotes* | West Indies: Cuba | do | E | 15 | NA | NA |
| Crane, hooded | *Grus monacha* | Japan, U.S.S.R. | do | E | 4 | NA | NA |

| Species — Common name | Species — Scientific name | Historic range | Vertebrate population where endangered or threatened | Status | When listed | Critical habitat | Special rules |
|---|---|---|---|---|---|---|---|
| Crane, Japanese | *Grus japonensis* | China, Japan, Korea, U.S.S.R | do. | E | 3 | NA | NA |
| Crane, Mississippi sandhill | *Grus canadensis pulla* | U.S.A. (MS) | do. | E | 6 | 17.95(b) | NA |
| Crane, Siberian white | *Grus leucogeranus* | U.S.S.R. (Siberia) to India, including Iran and China. | do. | E | 4 | NA | NA |
| Crane, white-naped | *Grus vipio* | Mongolia. | do. | E | 15 | NA | NA |
| Crane, whooping | *Grus americana* | Canada, U.S.A. (Rocky Mountains east to Carolinas), Mexico. | do. | E | 1, 3 | 17.95(b) | NA |
| Creeper, Hawaii | *Oreomystis* (=*Loxops*) *mana* | U.S.A. (HI) | do. | E | 10 | NA | NA |
| Creeper, Molokai (=kakawahie) | *Paroreomyza* (=*Oreomystis*, =*Loxops*) *flammea.* | do. | do. | E | 2 | NA | NA |
| Creeper, Oahu (=alauwahio) | *Paroreomyza* (=*Oreomystis*, =*Loxops*) *maculata.* | do. | do. | E | 2 | NA | NA |
| Crow, Hawaiian (='alala) | *Corvus hawaiiensis* (=*tropicus*). | do. | do. | E | 1 | NA | NA |
| Crow, Mariana | *Corvus kubaryi.* | Western Pacific Ocean: U.S.A. (Guam, Rota). | do. | E | 156 | NA | NA |
| Cuckoo-shrike, Mauritius | *Coquus* (=*Coracina*) *typicus.* | Indian Ocean: Mauritius. | do. | E | 3 | NA | NA |
| Cuckoo-shrike, Reunion | *Coquus* (=*Coracina*) *newtoni.* | Indian Ocean: Reunion. | do. | E | 3 | NA | NA |
| Curassow, razor-billed | *Mitu* (=*Crax*) *mitu mitu.* | Brazil (Eastern). | do. | E | 15 | NA | NA |
| Curassow, red-billed | *Crax blumenbachii.* | Brazil. | do. | E | 4 | NA | NA |
| Curassow, Trinidad white-headed | *Pipile pipile pipile.* | West Indies: Trinidad. | do. | E | 3 | NA | NA |
| Curlew, Eskimo | *Numenius borealis* | Alaska and northern Canada to Argentina. | do. | E | 1, 3 | NA | NA |
| Dove, cloven-feathered | *Drepanoptila holosericea* | Southwest Pacific Ocean: New Caledonia. | do. | E | 3 | NA | NA |
| Duck, Grenada gray-fronted | *Leptotila rufaxilla wellsi* | West Indies: Grenada. | do. | E | 3 | NA | NA |
| Duck, Hawaiian (=koloa) | *Anas wyvilliana* | U.S.A. (HI) | do. | E | 1 | NA | NA |
| Duck, Laysan | *Anas laysanensis* | do. | do. | E | 1 | NA | NA |
| Duck, pink-headed | *Rhodonessa caryophyllacea* | India. | do. | E | 15 | NA | NA |
| Duck, white-winged wood | *Carina scutulata* | India, Malaysia, Indonesia, Thailand. | do. | E | 3 | NA | NA |
| Eagle, Greenland white-tailed | *Haliaeetus albicilla groenlandicus* | Greenland and adjacent Atlantic islands. | do. | E | 15 | NA | NA |
| Eagle, harpy | *Harpia harpyja* | Mexico south to Argentina. | do. | E | 15 | NA | NA |
| Eagle, Philippine (=monkey-eating) | *Pithecophaga jefferyi* | Philippines | do. | E | 3 | NA | NA |
| Eagle, bald | *Haliaeetus leucocephalus* | North America south to northern Mexico. | U.S.A. (conterminous States, except WA, OR, MN, WI, MI). | E | 1, 34 | NA | NA |
| Do. | do. | do. | U.S.A. (WA, OR, MN, WI, MI). | T | 34 | NA | 17.41(a) |
| Eagle, Spanish imperial | *Aquila heliaca adalberti* | Spain, Morocco, Algeria. | do. | E | 3 | NA | NA |
| Egret, Chinese | *Egretta eulophotes* | China, Korea. | Entire. | E | 3 | NA | NA |
| Falcon, American peregrine | *Falco peregrinus anatum* | Nests from central Alaska across north-central Canada to central Mexico, winters south to South America. | do. | E | 2, 3, 145 | 17.95(b) | NA |
| Falcon, Arctic peregrine | *Falco peregrinus tundrius* | Nests from northern Alaska to Greenland; winters south to Central and South America. | do. | T | 2, 3, 145 | NA | NA |
| Falcon, Eurasian peregrine | *Falco peregrinus peregrinus* | Europe, Eurasia south to Africa and Mideast. | do. | E | 15 | NA | NA |
| Falcon, peregrine | *Falco peregrinus* | Worldwide, except Antarctica and most Pacific Islands. | Wherever found in wild in the conterminous 48 States. | E(S/A) | 145 | NA | NA |

| Species | | Historic range | Vertebrate population where endangered or threatened | Status | When listed | Critical habitat | Special rules |
|---|---|---|---|---|---|---|---|
| Common name | Scientific name | | | | | | |
| Finch, Laysan (honeycreeper) | Telespyza (= Psittirostra) cantans | U.S.A. (HI) | Entire | E | 1 | NA | NA |
| Finch, Nihoa (honeycreeper) | Telespyza (= Psittirostra) ultima | ...do | ...do | E | 1 | NA | NA |
| Flycatcher, Euler's | Empidonax euleri johnstonei | West Indies: Grenada | ...do | E | 3 | NA | NA |
| Flycatcher, Seychelles paradise | Terpsiphone corvina | Indian Ocean: Seychelles | ...do | E | 3 | NA | NA |
| Flycatcher, Tahiti | Pomarea nigra | South Pacific Ocean: Tahiti | ...do | E | 3 | NA | NA |
| Fody, Seychelles (weaver-finch) | Foudia sechellarum | Indian Ocean: Seychelles | ...do | E | 3 | NA | NA |
| Frigatebird, Andrew's | Fregata andrewsi | East Indian Ocean | ...do | E | 15 | NA | NA |
| Goose, Aleutian Canada | Branta canadensis leucopareia | U.S.A. (AK, CA, OR, WA), Japan | ...do | E | 1,3 | NA | NA |
| Goose, Hawaiian (=nene) | Nesochen (=Branta) sandvicensis | U.S.A. (HI) | ...do | E | 1 | NA | NA |
| Goshawk, Christmas Island | Accipiter fasciatus natalis | Indian Ocean: Christmas Island | ...do | E | 3 | NA | NA |
| Grackle, slender-billed | Quiscalus (=Cassidix) palustris | Mexico | ...do | E | 3 | NA | NA |
| Grasswren, Eyrean (flycatcher) | Amytornis goyderi | Australia | ...do | E | 3 | NA | NA |
| Grebe, Atitlan | Podilymbus gigas | Guatemala | ...do | E | 3 | NA | NA |
| Greenshank, Nordmann's | Tringa guttifer | U.S.S.R., Japan, south to Malaya, Borneo. | ...do | E | 15 | NA | NA |
| Guan, horned | Oreophasis derbianus | Guatemala, Mexico | ...do | E | 3 | NA | NA |
| Gull, Audouin's | Larus audouinii | Mediterranean Sea | ...do | E | 3 | NA | NA |
| Gull, relict | Larus relictus | India, China | ...do | E | 15 | NA | NA |
| Hawk, Anjouan Island sparrow | Accipiter francesii pusillus | Indian Ocean: Comoro Islands | ...do | E | 3 | NA | NA |
| Hawk, Galapagos | Buteo galapagoensis | Ecuador (Galapagos Islands) | ...do | E | 3 | NA | NA |
| Hawk, Hawaiian (=io) | Buteo solitarius | U.S.A. (HI) | ...do | E | 1 | NA | NA |
| Hermit, hook-billed (hummingbird) | Glaucis (=Ramphodon) dohrnii | Brazil | ...do | E | 15 | NA | NA |
| Honeycreeper, crested (=akohekohe) | Palmeria dolei | U.S.A. (HI) | ...do | E | 1 | NA | NA |
| Hornbill, helmeted | Rhinoplax vigil | Thailand, Malaysia | ...do | E | 15 | NA | NA |
| Honeyeater, helmeted | Meliphaga cassidix | Australia | ...do | E | 4 | NA | NA |
| Ibis, Japanese crested | Nipponia nippon | China, Japan, U.S.S.R., Korea | ...do | E | 3 | NA | NA |
| Kagu | Rhynochetos jubatus | South Pacific Ocean: New Caledonia | ...do | E | 3 | NA | NA |
| Kakapo (=owl-parrot) | Strigops habroptilus | New Zealand | ...do | E | 3 | NA | NA |
| Kestrel, Mauritius | Falco punctatus | Indian Ocean: Mauritius | ...do | E | 3 | NA | NA |
| Kestrel, Seychelles | Falco araea | Indian Ocean: Seychelles Islands | ...do | E | 3 | NA | NA |
| Kingfisher, Guam Micronesian | Halcyon cinnamomina cinnamomina | Western Pacific Ocean: U.S.A. (Guam) | ...do | E | 156 | NA | NA |
| Kite, Cuba hook-billed | Chondrohierax uncinatus wilsonii | West Indies: Cuba | ...do | E | 3 | NA | NA |
| Kite, Grenada hook-billed | Chondrohierax uncinatus mirus | West Indies: Grenada | ...do | E | 3 | NA | NA |
| Kite, Everglade snail | Rostrhamus sociabilis plumbeus | U.S.A. (FL) | ...do | E | 1 | 17.95(b) | NA |
| Kokako (wattlebird) | Callaeas cinerea | New Zealand | ...do | E | 3 | NA | NA |
| Macaw, glaucous | Anodorhynchus glaucus | Paraguay, Uruguay, Brazil | ...do | E | 15 | NA | NA |
| Macaw, indigo | Anodorhynchus leari | Brazil | ...do | E | 15 | NA | NA |
| Macaw, little blue | Cyanopsitta spixii | ...do | ...do | E | 15 | NA | NA |
| Magpie-robin, Seychelles (thrush) | Copsychus sechellarum | Indian Ocean: Seychelles Islands | ...do | E | 3 | NA | NA |
| Malkoha, red-faced (cuckoo) | Phaenicophaeus pyrrhocephalus | Sri Lanka (=Ceylon) | ...do | E | 3 | NA | NA |
| Mallard, Mariana | Anas oustaleti | West Pacific Ocean: U.S.A. (Guam, Mariana Islands). | ...do | E | 23 | NA | NA |
| Megapode, Micronesian (=La Perouse's) | Megapodius laperouse | West Pacific Ocean: U.S.A. (Palau Island, Mariana Islands). | ...do | E | 3 | NA | NA |
| Megapode, Maleo | Macrocephalon maleo | Indonesia (Celebes) | ...do | E | 3 | NA | NA |
| Millerbird, Nihoa (old world warbler) | Acrocephalus familiaris kingi | U.S.A. (HI) | ...do | E | 1 | NA | NA |
| Monarch, Tinian (old world flycatcher) | Monarcha takatsukasae | Western Pacific Ocean: U.S.A. (Mariana Islands). | ...do | E | 3 | NA | NA |
| Moorhen (=gallinule), Hawaiian common. | Gallinula chloropus sandvicensis | U.S.A. (HI) | ...do | E | 1 | NA | NA |
| Moorhen (=gallinule), Mariana common | Gallinula chloropus guami | Western Pacific Ocean: U.S.A. (Guam, Tinian, Saipan, Pagan). | ...do | E | 156 | NA | NA |
| Nightjar (=whip-poor-will), Puerto Rico. | Caprimulgus noctitherus | U.S.A. (PR) | ...do | E | 6 | NA | NA |

| Species | | Historic range | Vertebrate population where endangered or threatened | Sta-tus | When listed | Critical habitat | Special rules |
|---|---|---|---|---|---|---|---|
| Common name | Scientific name | | | | | | |
| Nukupu'u (honeycreeper) | Hemignathus lucidus | U.S.A. (HI) | do. | E | 1, 2 | NA | NA |
| 'O'o, Kauai (='O'o 'A'a) (honeyeater) | Moho braccatus | do. | do. | E | 1 | NA | NA |
| Ostrich, Arabian | Struthio camelus syriacus | Jordan, Saudi Arabia | do. | E | 3 | NA | NA |
| Ostrich, West African | Struthio camelus spatzi | Spanish Sahara | do. | E | 3 | NA | NA |
| 'O'u (honeycreeper) | Psittirostra psittacea | U.S.A. (HI) | do. | E | 1 | NA | NA |
| Owl, Anjouan scops | Otus rutilus capnodes | Indian Ocean: Comoro Island | do. | E | 3 | NA | NA |
| Owl, giant scops | Otus gurneyi | Philippines: Marinduque and Mindanao Island. | do. | E | 15 | NA | NA |
| Owl, Seychelles | Otus insularis | Indian Ocean: Seychelles Islands | do. | E | 3 | NA | NA |
| Owlet, Morden's (=Sokoke) | Otus ireneae | Kenya | do. | E | 3 | NA | NA |
| Palila (honeycreeper) | Loxioides (=Psittirostra) bailleui | U.S.A. (HI) | do. | E | 1 | 17.95(b) | NA |
| Parakeet, Forbes' | Cyanoramphus auriceps forbesi | New Zealand | do. | E | 3, 15 | NA | NA |
| Parakeet, golden | Aratinga guarouba | Brazil | do. | E | 4 | NA | NA |
| Parakeet, golden-shouldered (=hooded). | Psephotus chrysopterygius | Australia | do. | E | 3 | NA | NA |
| Parakeet, Mauritius | Psittacula echo | Indian Ocean: Mauritius. | do. | E | 3 | NA | NA |
| Parakeet, ochre-marked | Pyrrhura cruentata | Brazil | do. | E | 3 | NA | NA |
| Parakeet, orange-bellied | Neophema chrysogaster | Australia | do. | E | 4 | NA | NA |
| Parakeet, paradise (=beautiful) | Psephotus pulcherrimus | do. | do. | E | 4 | NA | NA |
| Parakeet, scarlet-chested (=splendid) | Neophema splendida | do. | do. | E | 4 | NA | NA |
| Parakeet, turquoise | Neophema pulchella | do. | do. | E | 3 | NA | NA |
| Parrot, Australian | Geopsittacus occidentalis | do. | do. | E | 3 | NA | NA |
| Parrot, Bahaman or Cuban | Amazona leucocephala | West Indies: Cuba, Bahamas, Caymans | do. | E | 3, 15 | NA | NA |
| Parrot, ground | Pezoporus wallicus | Australia | do. | E | 6 | NA | NA |
| Parrot, imperial | Amazona imperialis | West Indies: Dominica | do. | E | 3 | NA | NA |
| Parrot, Puerto Rican | Amazona vittata | U.S.A. (PR) | do. | E | 1 | NA | NA |
| Parrot, red-browed | Amazona rhodocorytha | Brazil | do. | E | 3 | NA | NA |
| Parrot, red-capped | Pionopsitta pileata | do. | do. | E | 15 | NA | NA |
| Parrot, red-necked | Amazona arausiaca | West Indies: Dominica | do. | E | 50 | NA | NA |
| Parrot, red-spectacled | Amazona pretrei pretrei | Brazil, Argentina | do. | E | 15 | NA | NA |
| Parrot, St. Lucia | Amazona versicolor | West Indies: St. Lucia. | do. | E | 3 | NA | NA |
| Parrot, St. Vincent | Amazona guildingii | West Indies: St. Vincent. | do. | E | 3 | NA | NA |
| Parrot, thick-billed | Rhynchopsitta pachyrhyncha | Mexico, U.S.A. (AZ, NM) | Mexico. | E | 3 | NA | NA |
| Parrot, vinaceous-breasted | Amazona vinacea | Brazil | do. | E | 15 | NA | NA |
| Parrotbill, Maui (honeycreeper) | Pseudonestor xanthophrys | U.S.A. (HI) | Entire. | E | 1 | NA | NA |
| Pelican, brown | Pelecanus occidentalis | U.S.A. (Carolinas to TX, CA), West Indies, C. and S. America: Coastal. | Entire, except U.S. Atlantic coast, FL, AL. | E | 2, 3, 171 | NA | NA |
| Penguin, Galapagos | Spheniscus mendiculus | Ecuador (Galapagos Islands) | Entire | E | 3 | NA | NA |
| Petrel, Hawaiian dark-rumped | Pterodroma phaeopygia sandwichensis | U.S.A. (HI) | do. | E | 2, 4, 1 | NA | NA |
| Pheasant, bar-tailed | Syrmaticus humiae | Burma, China, India | do. | E | 3 | NA | NA |
| Pheasant, Blyth's tragopan | Tragopan blythii | Burma, China, India | do. | E | 3 | NA | NA |
| Pheasant, brown eared | Crossoptilon mantchuricum | China | do. | E | 3 | NA | NA |
| Pheasant, Cabot's tragopan | Tragopan caboti | do. | do. | E | 3 | NA | NA |
| Pheasant, Chinese monal | Lophophorus lhuysii | China | do. | E | 3 | NA | NA |
| Pheasant, Edward's | Lophura edwardsi | Vietnam | do. | E | 3 | NA | NA |
| Pheasant, Elliot's | Syrmaticus ellioti | China | do. | E | 3 | NA | NA |
| Pheasant, imperial | Lophura imperialis | Vietnam | do. | E | 15 | NA | NA |
| Pheasant, Mikado | Syrmaticus mikado | Taiwan | do. | E | 3 | NA | NA |
| Pheasant, Palawan peacock | Polyplectron emphanum | Philippines | do. | E | 3 | NA | NA |
| Pheasant, Sclater's monal | Lophophorus sclateri | Burma, China, India | do. | E | 3 | NA | NA |
| Pheasant, Swinhoe's | Lophura swinhoii | Taiwan | do. | E | 3 | NA | NA |
| Pheasant, western tragopan | Tragopan melanocephalus | India, Pakistan | do. | E | 3 | NA | NA |

| Species | | Historic range | Vertebrate population where endangered or threatened | Status | When listed | Critical habitat | Special rules |
|---|---|---|---|---|---|---|---|
| Common name | Scientific name | | | | | | |
| Pheasant, white eared | Crossoptilon crossoptilon | China (Tibet), India | do | E | 4 | NA | NA |
| Pigeon, Azores wood | Columba palumbus azorica | East Atlantic Ocean: Azores | do | E | 3 | NA | NA |
| Pigeon, Chatham Island | Hemiphaga novaeseelandiae chathamensis | New Zealand | do | E | 3 | NA | NA |
| Pigeon, Mindoro zone-tailed | Ducula mindorensis | Philippines | do | E | 15 | NA | NA |
| Pigeon, Puerto Rican plain | Columba inornata wetmorei | U.S.A. (PR) | do | E | 2 | NA | NA |
| Piping-guan, black-fronted | Pipile jacutinga | Argentina | do | E | 15 | NA | NA |
| Pitta, Koch's | Pitta kochi | Philippines | do | E | 15 | NA | NA |
| Plover, New Zealand shore | Thinornis novaeseelandiae | New Zealand | do | E | 3 | NA | NA |
| Plover, piping | Charadrius melodus | U.S.A. (Great Lakes, northern Great Plains, Atlantic and Gulf Coasts, PR, VI), Canada, Mexico, Bahamas, West Indies. | Great Lakes watershed in States of IL, IN, MI, MN, NY, OH, PA, and WI and Province of Ontario. | E | 211 | NA | NA |
| Do | do | do | Entire, except those areas where listed as endangered above. | T | 211 | NA | NA |
| Po'ouli (honeycreeper) | Melamprosops phaeosoma | U.S.A. (HI) | do | E | 10 | NA | NA |
| Prairie-chicken, Attwater's greater | Tympanuchus cupido attwateri | U.S.A. (TX) | do | E | 1 | NA | NA |
| Quail, Merriam's Montezuma | Cyrtonyx montezumae merriami | Mexico (Vera Cruz) | do | E | 15 | NA | NA |
| Quetzel, resplendent | Pharomachrus mocinno | Mexico to Panama | do | E | 15 | NA | NA |
| Rail, Aukland Island | Rallus pectoralis muelleri | New Zealand | do | E | 3 | NA | NA |
| Rail, California clapper | Rallus longirostris obsoletus | U.S.A. (CA) | do | E | 2 | NA | NA |
| Rail, Guam | Rallus owstoni | Western Pacific Ocean: U.S.A. (Guam) | do | E | 146E, 156 | NA | NA |
| Rail, light-footed clapper | Rallus longirostris levipes | U.S.A. (CA), Mexico (Baja California) | do | E | 2 | NA | NA |
| Rail, Lord Howe wood | Tricholimnas sylvestris | Australia (Lord Howe Island) | do | E | 15 | NA | NA |
| Rail, Yuma clapper | Rallus longirostris yumanensis | Mexico, U.S.A. (AZ, CA) | do | E | 1 | NA | NA |
| Rhea, Darwin's | Pterocnemia pennata | Argentina, Bolivia, Peru, Uruguay | do | E | 3 | NA | NA |
| Robin, Chatham Island | Petroica traversi | New Zealand | do | E | 3 | NA | NA |
| Robin, scarlet-breasted (flycatcher) | Petroica multicolor multicolor | Australia (Norfolk Island) | do | E | 3 | NA | NA |
| Rockfowl, grey-necked | Picathartes oreas | Cameroon, Gabon | do | E | 3 | NA | NA |
| Rockfowl, white-necked | Picathartes gymnocephalus | Africa: Togo to Sierra Leone | do | E | 3 | NA | NA |
| Roller, long-tailed ground | Uratelornis chimaera | Malagasy Republic (=Madagascar) | do | E | 3 | NA | NA |
| Scrub-bird, noisy | Atrichornis clamosus | Australia | do | E | 3 | NA | NA |
| Shama, Cebu black (thrush) | Copsychus niger cebuensis | Philippines | do | E | 10 | NA | NA |
| Shearwater, Newell's Townsend's (formerly Manx) (="A'o) | Puffinus auricularis (formerly puffinus) newelli | U.S.A. (HI) | do | T | 10 | NA | NA |
| Shrike, San Clemente loggerhead | Lanius ludovicianus mearnsi | U.S.A. (CA) | do | E | 26 | NA | NA |
| Siskin, red | Carduelis (=Spinus) cucullata | South America | do | E | 15 | NA | NA |
| Sparrow, Cape Sable seaside | Ammodramus (=Ammospiza) maritimus mirabilis | U.S.A. (FL) | do | E | 1 | 17.95(b) | NA |
| Sparrow, dusky seaside | Ammodramus (=Ammospiza) maritimus nigrescens | do | do | E | 1 | 17.95(b) | NA |
| Sparrow, San Clemente sage | Amphispiza belli clementeae | U.S.A. (CA) | do | T | 26 | NA | NA |
| Starling, Ponape mountain | Aplonis pelzelni | West Pacific Ocean: U.S.A. (Caroline Islands) | do | E | 3 | NA | NA |
| Starling, Rothschild's (myna) | Leucopsar rothschildi | Indonesia (Bali) | do | E | 3 | NA | NA |
| Stilt, Hawaiian (="Ae'o) | Himantopus himantopus knudseni | U.S.A. (HI) | do | E | 2 | NA | NA |

| Species — Common name | Species — Scientific name | Historic range | Vertebrate population where endangered or threatened | Status | When listed | Critical habitat | Special rules |
|---|---|---|---|---|---|---|---|
| Stork, oriental white | Ciconia ciconia boyciana | China, Japan, Korea, U.S.S.R. | do | E | 3 | NA | NA |
| Stork, wood | Mycteria americana | U.S.A., (CA, AZ, TX, to Carolinas), Mexico, Central and South America. | U.S.A. (AL, FL, GA, SC). | E | 142 | NA | NA |
| Swiftlet, Vanikoro | Aerodramus (=Collocalia) vanikorensis bartschi. | Western Pacific Ocean: U.S.A. (Guam, Rota, Tinian, Saipan, Aggiuan). | Entire. | E | 156 | NA | NA |
| Teal, Campbell Island flightless | Anas aucklandica nesiotis | New Zealand (Campbell Island) | do | E | 15 | NA | NA |
| Tern, California least | Sterna antillarum (=albifrons) browni | Mexico, U.S.A. (CA) | do | E | 2, 3 | NA | NA |
| Tern, least | Sterna antillarum | U.S.A. (Atlantic and Gulf coasts, Miss. R. Basin, CA), Gr. and Lesser Antilles, Bahamas, Mexico; winters C. America, northern S. America. | U.S.A. [AR, CO, IA, IL, IN, KS, KY, LA (Miss. R. and tribs. N of Baton Rouge), MS (Miss. R.), MO, MT, NE, NM, ND, OK, SD, TN, TX (Except within 50 miles of coast)]. | E | 182 | | |
| Thrasher, white-breasted | Ramphocinclus brachyurus | West Indies: St. Lucia, Martinique | Entire | E | 3 | NA | NA |
| Thrush, large Kauai | Myadestes (=Phaeornis) myadestinus | U.S.A. (HI) | do | E | 2 | NA | NA |
| Thrush, Molokai (=oloma o) | Myadestes (=Phaeornis) lanaiensis (=obscurus) rutha. | do | do | E | 2 | NA | NA |
| Thrush, New Zealand (wattlebird) | Turnagra capensis | New Zealand | do | E | 3 | NA | NA |
| Thrush, small Kauai (=puaiohi) | Myadestes (=Phaeornis) palmeri | U.S.A. (HI) | do | E | 1 | NA | NA |
| Tinamou, solitary | Tinamus solitarius | Brazil, Paraguay, Argentina | do | E | 15 | NA | NA |
| Trembler, Martinique (thrasher) | Cinclocerthia ruficauda gutturalis | West Indies: Martinique | do | E | 3 | NA | NA |
| Wanderer, plain (collared-hemipode) | Pedionomous torquatus | Australia | do | E | 6 | NA | NA |
| Warbler (wood) Bachman's | Vermivora bachmani | U.S.A.(Southeastern), Cuba. | do | E | 1, 3 | NA | NA |
| Warbler (wood), Barbados yellow | Dendroica petechia petechia | West Indies: Barbados. | do | E | 3 | NA | NA |
| Warbler (wood), Kirtland's | Dendroica kirtlandi | U.S.A. (principally MI), Canada, West Indies: Bahama Islands. | do | E | 1, 3 | NA | NA |
| Warbler (willow), nightingale reed | Acrocephalus luscinia | Western Pacific Ocean. | U.S.A. (Mariana Islands). | E | 3, 4 | NA | NA |
| Warbler (willow), Rodrigues | Bebrornis rodericanus | Mauritius (Rodrigues Islands) | Entire | E | 3 | NA | NA |
| Warbler (willow), Semper's | Leucopeza semperi | West Indies: St. Lucia | do | E | 3 | NA | NA |
| Warbler (willow), Seychelles | Bebrornis sechellensis | Indian Ocean: Seychelles Island | do | E | 3 | NA | NA |
| Whipbird, Western | Psophodes nigrogularis | Australia | do | E | 15 | NA | NA |
| White-eye, bridled | Zosterops conspicillata conspicillata | Western Pacific Ocean: U.S.A. (Guam) | do | E | 156 | NA | NA |
| White-eye, Norfolk Island | Zosterops albogularis | Indian Ocean: Norfolk Islands | do | E | 15 | NA | NA |
| White-eye, Ponape greater | Rukia longirostra (=sanfordi) | West Pacific Ocean: U.S.A. (Caroline Islands). | do | E | 3 | NA | NA |
| White-eye, Seychelles | Zosterops modesta | Indian Ocean: Seychelles | do | E | 3 | NA | NA |
| Woodpecker, imperial | Campephilus imperialis | Mexico | do | E | 3 | NA | NA |
| Woodpecker, ivory-billed | Campephilus principalis | U.S.A. (southcentral and southeastern), Cuba. | do | E | 1, 3 | NA | NA |
| Woodpecker, red-cockaded | Picoides (=Dendrocopos) borealis. | U.S.A. (southcentral and southeastern) | do | E | 2 | NA | NA |
| Woodpecker, Tristam's | Dryocopus javensis richardsi | Korea | do | E | 3 | NA | NA |
| Wren, Guadeloupe house | Troglodytes aedon guadeloupensis | West Indies: Guadeloupe. | do | E | 3 | NA | NA |
| Wren, St. Lucia house | Troglodytes aedon mesoleucus | West Indies: St. Lucia. | do | E | 3 | NA | NA |

| Species | | Historic range | Vertebrate population where endangered or threatened | Sta-tus | When listed | Critical habitat | Special rules |
|---|---|---|---|---|---|---|---|
| Common name | Scientific name | | | | | | |
| **REPTILES** | | | | | | | |
| Alligator, American | *Alligator mississippiensis* | Southeastern U.S.A. | Wherever found in wild except those areas where listed as threatened as set forth below. | E | 1, 11, 51, 60, 113, 134 | NA | NA |
| Do | do | | U.S.A. (FL and certain areas of GA and SC, as set forth in 17.42(a)(1)). | T | 20, 47, 51, 60, 134 | NA | 17.42(a) |
| Do | do | | U.S.A. (LA and TX). | T(S/A) | 11, 47, 51, 60, 113, 134 | NA | 17.42(a) |
| Do | do | | In captivity wherever found. | T(S/A) | 11, 47,51 | NA | 17.42(a) |
| Alligator, Chinese | *Alligator sinensis* | China | Entire | E | 15 | NA | NA |
| Anole, Culebra Island giant | *Anolis roosevelti* | U.S.A. (PR: Culebra Island) | do | E | 25 | 17.95(c) | NA |
| Boa, Jamaican | *Epicrates subflavus* | Jamaica | do | E | 3 | NA | NA |
| Boa, Mona | *Epicrates monensis monensis* | U.S.A. (PR) | do | T | 33 | 17.95(c) | NA |
| Boa, Puerto Rico | *Epicrates monensis* | do | do | E | 2 | NA | NA |
| Boa, Round Island [no common name] | *Casarea dussumieri* | Indian Ocean: Mauritius | do | E | 88 | NA | NA |
| Boa, Round Island [no common name] | *Bolyeria multocarinata* | do | do | E | 88 | NA | NA |
| Boa, Virgin Islands tree | *Epicrates monensis granti* | U.S. and British Virgin Islands | do | E | 2, 86 | NA | NA |
| Caiman, Apaporis River | *Caiman crocodilus apaporiensis* | Colombia | do | E | 15 | NA | NA |
| Caiman, black | *Melanosuchus niger* | Amazon basin | do | E | 15 | NA | NA |
| Caiman, broad-snouted | *Caiman latirostris* | Brazil, Argentina, Paraguay, Uruguay | do | E | 15 | NA | NA |
| Caiman, Yacare | *Caiman crocodilus yacare* | Bolivia, Argentina, Peru, Brazil | do | E | 3 | NA | NA |
| Chuckwalla, San Esteban Island | *Sauromalus varius* | Mexico | do | E | 88 | NA | NA |
| Crocodile, African dwarf | *Osteolaemus tetraspis tetraspis* | West Africa | do | E | 15 | NA | NA |
| Crocodile, African slender-snouted | *Crocodylus cataphractus* | Western and central Africa | do | E | 5 | NA | NA |
| Crocodile, American | *Crocodylus acutus* | U.S.A. (FL), Mexico, South America, Central America, Caribbean. | do | E | 10, 87 | 17.95(c) | NA |
| Crocodile, Ceylon mugger | *Crocodylus palustris kimbula* | Sri Lanka | do | E | 15 | NA | NA |
| Crocodile, Congo dwarf | *Osteolaemus tetraspis osborni* | Congo River drainage | do | E | 15 | NA | NA |
| Crocodile, Cuban | *Crocodylus rhombifer* | Cuba | do | E | 3 | NA | NA |
| Crocodile, Morelet's | *Crocodylus moreletii* | Mexico, Belize, Guatemala | do | E | 3 | NA | NA |
| Crocodile, mugger | *Crocodylus palustris palustris* | India, Pakistan, Iran, Bangladesh | do | E | 15 | NA | NA |
| Crocodile, Nile | *Crocodylus niloticus* | Africa | do | E | 3 | NA | NA |
| Crocodile, Orinoco | *Crocodylus intermedius* | South America. Orinoco River Basin. | do | E | 3 | NA | NA |
| Crocodile, Philippine | *Crocodylus novaeguineae mindorensis* | Philippine Islands | do | E | 15 | NA | NA |
| Crocodile, saltwater (=estuarine) | *Crocodylus porosus* | Southeast Asia, Australia, Papua-New Guinea, Pacific Islands. | Entire, except Papua-New Guinea | E | 87 | NA | NA |
| Crocodile, Siamese | *Crocodylus siamensis* | Southeast Asia, Malay Peninsula. | Entire | E | 15 | NA | NA |
| Gavial (=gharial) | *Gavialis gangeticus* | Pakistan, Burma, Bangladesh, India, Nepal. | do | E | 3, 15 | NA | NA |
| Gecko, day | *Phelsuma edwardnewtoni* | Indian Ocean: Mauritius. | do | E | 3 | NA | NA |
| Gecko, Monito | *Sphaerodactylus micropithecus* | U.S.A. (PR) | do | E | 125 | 17.95(c) | NA |
| Gecko, Round Island day | *Phelsuma guentheri* | Indian Ocean: Mauritius. | do | E | 3 | NA | NA |
| Gecko, Serpent Island | *Cyrtodactylus serpensinsula* | do | do | T | 129 | NA | NA |

| Species | | Historic range | Vertebrate population where endangered or threatened | Sta-tus | When listed | Critical habitat | Special rules |
|---|---|---|---|---|---|---|---|
| Common name | Scientific name | | | | | | |
| Iguana, Acklins ground | *Cyclura rileyi nuchalis* | West Indies: Bahamas | do | T | 129 | NA | NA |
| Iguana, Allen's Cay | *Cyclura cychlura inornata* | do | do | T | 129 | NA | NA |
| Iguana, Andros Island ground | *Cyclura cychlura cychlura* | do | do | T | 129 | NA | NA |
| Iguana, Anegada ground | *Cyclura pinguis* | West Indies: British Virgin Islands (Anegada Islands) | do | E | 3 | NA | NA |
| Iguana, Barrington land | *Conolophus pallidus* | Ecuador (Galapagos Islands) | do | E | 3 | NA | NA |
| Iguana, Cayman Brac ground | *Cyclura nubila caymanensis* | West Indies: Cayman Islands | do | T | 129 | NA | NA |
| Iguana, Cuban ground | *Cyclura nubila nubila* | Cuba | Entire (excluding population introduced in Puerto Rico). | T | 129 | NA | NA |
| Iguana, Exuma Island | *Cyclura cychlura figginsi* | West Indies: Bahamas | Entire | T | 129 | NA | NA |
| Iguana, Fiji banded | *Brachylophus fasciatus* | Pacific: Fiji, Tonga | do | E | 88 | NA | NA |
| Iguana, Fiji crested | *Brachylophus vitiensis* | Pacific: Fiji | do | E | 88 | NA | NA |
| Iguana, Grand Cayman ground | *Cyclura nubila lewisi* | West Indies: Cayman Islands | do | E | 129 | NA | NA |
| Iguana, Jamaican | *Cyclura collei* | West Indies: Jamaica | do | E | 129 | NA | NA |
| Iguana, Mayaguana | *Cyclura carinata bartschi* | West Indies: Bahamas | do | T | 129 | NA | NA |
| Iguana, Mona ground | *Cyclura stejnegeri* | U.S.A. (PR: Mona Island) | do | T | 33 | 17.95(c) | NA |
| Iguana, Turks and Caicos | *Cyclura carinata carinata* | West Indies: Turks and Caicos Islands | do | T | 129 | NA | NA |
| Iguana, Watling Island ground | *Cyclura rileyi rileyi* | West Indies: Bahamas | do | E | 129 | NA | NA |
| Iguana, White Cay ground | *Cyclura rileyi cristata* | do | do | T | 129 | NA | NA |
| Lizard, blunt-nosed leopard | *Gambelia (= Crotaphytus) silus* | U.S.A. (CA) | do | E | 1 | NA | NA |
| Lizard, Coachella Valley fringe-toed | *Uma inornata* | do | do | T | 105 | 17.95(c) | NA |
| Lizard, Hierro giant | *Gallotia simonyi simonyi* | Spain (Canary Islands) | do | E | 144 | NA | NA |
| Lizard, Ibiza wall | *Podarcis pityusensis* | Spain (Balearic Islands) | do | T | 144 | NA | NA |
| Lizard, Island night | *Xantusia (= Klauberina) riversiana* | U.S.A. (CA) | do | T | 26 | NA | NA |
| Lizard, St. Croix ground | *Ameiva polops* | U.S.A. (VI) | do | E | 24 | 17.95(c) | NA |
| Monitor, Bengal | *Varanus bengalensis* | Iran, Iraq, India, Sri Lanka, Malaysia, Afghanistan, Burma, Vietnam, Thailand | do | E | 15 | NA | NA |
| Monitor, desert | *Varanus griseus* | North Africa to Neareast, Caspian Sea through U.S.S.R. to Pakistan, Northwest India. | do | E | 15 | NA | NA |
| Monitor, Komodo Island | *Varanus komodoensis* | Indonesia (Komodo, Rintja, Padar, and western Flores Island). | do | E | 15 | NA | NA |
| Monitor, yellow | *Varanus flavescens* | West Pakistan through India to Bangladesh. | do | E | 15 | NA | NA |
| Python, Indian | *Python molurus molurus* | Sri Lanka and India | do | E | 15 | NA | NA |
| Rattlesnake, Aruba Island | *Crotalus unicolor* | Aruba Island (Netherland Antilles) | do | T | 129 | NA | NA |
| Rattlesnake, New Mexican ridge-nosed | *Crotalus willardi obscurus* | U.S.A. (NM), Mexico | do | T | 43 | 17.95(c) | NA |
| Skink, Round Island | *Leiolopisma telfairi* | Indian Ocean: Mauritius | do | T | 129 | NA | NA |
| Snake, Atlantic salt marsh | *Nerodia fasciata taeniata* | U.S.A. (FL) | do | T | 30 | NA | NA |
| Snake, eastern indigo | *Drymarchon corais couperi* | U.S.A. (AL, FL, GA, MS, SC) | do | T | 32 | NA | NA |
| Snake, San Francisco garter | *Thamnophis sirtalis tetrataenia* | U.S.A. (CA) | do | E | 1 | NA | NA |
| Tartaruga | *Podocnemis expansa* | South America: Orinoco and Amazon River basins. | do | E | 3 | NA | NA |
| Terrapin, river (= Tuntong) | *Batagur baska* | Malaysia, Bangladesh, Burma, India, Indonesia. | do | E | 3 | NA | NA |
| Tomistoma | *Tomistoma schlegelii* | Malaysia, Indonesia | do | E | 15 | NA | NA |
| Tortoise, angulated | *Geochelone yniphora* | Malagasy Republic (= Madagascar) | do | E | 15 | NA | NA |
| Tortoise, Bolson | *Gopherus flavomarginatus* | Mexico | do | E | 46 | NA | NA |
| Tortoise, desert | *Scaptochelys (= Gopherus) agassizii* | U.S.A. (UT, AZ, CA, NV); Mexico | Beaver Dam Slope, Utah. | T | 103 | 17.95(c) | NA |

| Species | | Historic range | Vertebrate population where endangered or threatened | Status | When listed | Critical habitat | Special rules |
|---|---|---|---|---|---|---|---|
| Common name | Scientific name | | | | | | |
| Tortoise, Galapagos | *Geochelone elephantopus* | Ecuador (Galapagos Islands) | Entire | E | 3 | NA | NA |
| Tortoise, radiated | *Geochelone (= Testudo) radiata* | Malagasy Republic (= Madagascar) | do | E | 3 | NA | NA |
| Tracaja | *Podocnemis unifilis* | South America: Orinoco and Amazon River basins. | do | E | 3 | NA | NA |
| Tuatara | *Sphenodon punctatus* | New Zealand | do | E | 3 | NA | NA |
| Turtle, aquatic box | *Terrapene coahuila* | Mexico | do | E | 6 | NA | NA |
| Turtle, black softshell | *Trionyx nigricans* | Bangladesh | do | E | 15 | NA | NA |
| Turtle, Burmese peacock | *Morenia ocellata* | Burma | do | E | 15 | NA | NA |
| Turtle, Central American river | *Dermatemys mawii* | Mexico, Belize, Guatemala | do | E | 129 | NA | NA |
| Turtle, Cuatro Cienegas softshell | *Trionyx ater* | Mexico | do | E | 15 | NA | NA |
| Turtle, geometric | *Psammobates geometricus* (= *Geochelone geometrica*). | South Africa | do | E | 15 | NA | NA |
| Turtle, green sea | *Chelonia mydas* | Circumglobal in tropical and temperate seas and oceans. | Wherever found except where listed as endangered below | T | 2, 42 | NA | 17.42(b) and Parts 220 and 227. |
| Do | do | do | Breeding colony populations in Fl. and on Pacific coast of Mexico. | E | 2, 42 | NA | NA |
| Turtle, hawksbill sea (= carey) | *Eretmochelys imbricata* | Tropical seas | Entire | E | 3 | 17.95(c) | NA |
| Turtle, Indian sawback | *Kachuga tecta tecta* | India | do | E | 15 | NA | NA |
| Turtle, Indian softshell | *Trionyx gangeticus* | Pakistan, India | do | E | 15 | NA | NA |
| Turtle, Kemp's (= Atlantic) Ridley sea | *Lepidochelys kempi* | Tropical and temperate seas in Atlantic Basin. | do | E | 4 | NA | NA |
| Turtle, leatherback sea | *Dermochelys coriacea* | Tropical, temperate, and subpolar seas | do | E | 3 | 17.95(c), 226.71 | NA |
| Turtle, loggerhead sea | *Caretta caretta* | Circumglobal in tropical and temperate seas and oceans. | do | T | 42 | NA | 17.42(b) and Parts 220 and 227. |
| Turtle, Olive (Pacific) Ridley sea | *Lepidochelys olivacea* | Tropical and temperate seas in Pacific Basin. | Wherever found except where listed as endangered below. | T | 42 | NA | 17.42(b) and Parts 220 and 227. |
| Do | do | do | Breeding colony populations on Pacific coast of Mexico. | E | 42 | NA | NA |
| Turtle, peacock softshell | *Trionyx hurum* | India, Bangladesh | Entire | E | 15 | NA | NA |
| Turtle, Plymouth red-bellied | *Pseudemys* (=*Chrysemys*) *rubriventris bangsi.* | U.S.A. (MA) | do | E | 90 | 17.95(c) | NA |
| Turtle, short-necked or western swamp | *Pseudemydura umbrina* | Australia | do | E | 3 | NA | NA |
| Turtle, spotted pond | *Geoclemys* (= *Damonia*) *hamiltonii* | North India, Pakistan | do | E | 15 | NA | NA |
| Turtle, three-keeled Asian | *Melanochelys* (= *Geoemyda, Nicoria*) *tricarinata* | Central India to Bangladesh and Burma | do | E | 15 | NA | NA |
| Viper, Lar Valley | *Vipera latifii* | Iran | do | E | 129 | NA | NA |
| **AMPHIBIANS** | | | | | | | |
| Coqui, golden | *Eleutherodactylus jasperi* | U.S.A. (PR) | do | T | 29 | 17.95(d) | NA |

| Common name | Scientific name | Historic range | Vertebrate population where endangered or threatened | Status | When listed | Critical habitat | Special rules |
|---|---|---|---|---|---|---|---|
| **Species** | | | | | | | |
| Frog, Israel painted | Discoglossus nigriventer | Israel | do. | E | 3 | NA | NA |
| Frog, Panamanian golden | Atelopus varius zeteki | Panama | do. | E | 15 | NA | NA |
| Frog, Stephen Island | Leiopelma hamiltoni | New Zealand | do. | E | 3 | NA | NA |
| Salamander, Chinese giant | Andrias davidianus davidianus | Western China | do. | E | 15 | NA | NA |
| Salamander, desert slender | Batrachoseps aridus | U.S.A. (CA) | do. | E | 6 | NA | NA |
| Salamander, Japanese giant | Andrias davidianus japonicus | Japan | do. | E | 15 | NA | NA |
| Salamander, Red Hills | Phaeognathus hubrichti | U.S.A. (AL) | do. | T | 19 | NA | NA |
| Salamander, San Marcos | Eurycea nana | U.S.A. (TX) | do. | T | 98 | 17.95(d) | 17.43(a) |
| Salamander, Santa Cruz long-toed | Ambystoma macrodactylum croceum | U.S.A. (CA) | do. | E | 1 | NA | NA |
| Salamander, Texas blind | Typhlomolge rathbuni | U.S.A. (TX) | do. | E | 1 | NA | NA |
| Toad, African viviparous | Nectophrynoides spp. | Tanzania, Guinea, Ivory Coast, Cameroon, Liberia, Ethiopia. | do. | E | 15 | NA | NA |
| Toad, Cameroon | Bufo superciliaris | Equatorial Africa. | do. | E | 15 | NA | NA |
| Toad, Houston | Bufo houstonensis | U.S.A. (TX) | do. | E | 2 | 17.95(d) | NA |
| Toad, Monte Verde | Bufo periglenes | Costa Rica | do. | E | 15 | NA | NA |
| Toad, Wyoming | Bufo hemiophrys baxteri | U.S.A. (WY) | do. | E | 1,8 | NA | NA |
| **FISHES** | | | | | | | |
| Ala Balik (trout) | Salmo platycephalus | Turkey | Entire | E | 3 | NA | NA |
| Ayumodoki (loach) | Hymenophysa (= Botia) curta | Japan | do. | E | 3 | NA | NA |
| Blindcat, Mexican (catfish) | Prietella phreatophila | Mexico | do. | E | 3 | NA | NA |
| Bonytoungue, Asian | Scleropages formosus | Thailand, Indonesia, Malaysia. | do. | E | 15 | NA | NA |
| Catfish [no common name] | Pangasius sanitwongsei | Thailand | do. | E | 3 | NA | NA |
| Catfish, giant | Pangasianodon gigas | do. | do. | E | 3 | NA | NA |
| Catfish, Yaqui | Ictalurus pricei | U.S.A. (AZ), Mexico | do. | T | 157 | 17.95(e) | 17.44(g) |
| Cavefish, Alabama | Speoplatyrhinus poulsoni | U.S.A. (AL) | do. | E | 28 | 17.95(e) | NA |
| Cavefish, Ozark | Amblyopsis rosae | U.S.A. (AR, MO, OK) | do. | T | 164 | NA | NA |
| Chub, bonytail | Gila elegans | U.S.A. (AZ, CA, CO, NV, UT, WY) | do. | E | 92 | NA | NA |
| Chub, Borax Lake | Gila boraxobius | U.S.A. (OR) | do. | E | 124 | 17.95(e) | NA |
| Chub, Chihuahua | Gila nigrescens | U.S.A. (NM), Mexico (Chihuahua) | do. | T | 132 | NA | 17.44(g) |
| Chub, humpback | Gila cypha | U.S.A. (AZ, CO, UT, WY) | do. | E | 1 | NA | NA |
| Chub, Hutton tui | Gila bicolor ssp. | U.S.A. (OR) | do. | T | 174 | NA | 17.44(j) |
| Chub, Mohave tui | Gila bicolor mohavensis | U.S.A. (CA) | do. | E | 2 | NA | NA |
| Chub, Owens tui | Gila bicolor snyderi | do. | do. | E | 195 | 17.95(e) | NA |
| Chub, Pahranagat roundtail | Gila robusta jordani | U.S.A. (NV) | do. | E | 2 | NA | NA |
| Chub, slender | Hybopsis cahni | U.S.A. (TN, VA) | do. | T | 28 | 17.95(e) | 17.44(c) |
| Chub, spotfin | Hybopsis monacha | U.S.A. (AL, GA, NC, TN, VA) | do. | T | 28 | 17.95(e) | 17.44(c) |
| Chub, Yaqui | Gila purpurea | U.S.A. (AZ), Mexico | do. | E | 157 | 17.95(e) | NA |
| Cicek (minnow) | Acanthorutilus handlirschi | Turkey | do. | E | 3 | NA | NA |
| Cui-ui | Chasmistes cujus | U.S.A. (NV) | do. | E | 117E, 127E | NA | NA |
| Dace, Ash Meadows speckled | Rhinichthys osculus nevadensis | do. | do. | E | 130 | 17.95(e) | NA |
| Dace, desert | Eremichthys acros | do. | do. | T | 210 | 17.95(e) | 17.44(m) |
| Dace, Foskett speckled | Rhinichthys osculus ssp. | U.S.A. (OR) | do. | T | 174 | NA | 17.44(j) |
| Dace, Kendall Warm Springs | Rhinichthys osculus thermalis | U.S.A. (WY) | do. | E | 2 | NA | NA |
| Dace, Moapa | Moapa coriacea | U.S.A. (NV) | do. | E | 1 | NA | NA |
| Darter, amber | Percina antesella | U.S.A. (GA, TN) | do. | E | 196 | 17.95(e) | 17.44(b) |
| Darter, bayou | Etheostoma rubrum | U.S.A. (MS) | do. | T | 10 | NA | NA |
| Darter, fountain | Etheostoma fonticola | U.S.A. (TX) | do. | E | 2 | 17.95(e) | NA |
| Darter, leopard | Percina pantherina | U.S.A. (AR, OK) | do. | T | 31 | 17.95(e) | 17.44(d) |
| Darter, Maryland | Etheostoma sellare | U.S.A. (MD) | do. | E | 1 | NA | NA |
| Darter, Niangua | Etheostoma nianguae | U.S.A. (MO) | do. | T | 185 | 17.95(e) | 17.44(k) |

| Common name | Scientific name | Historic range | Vertebrate population where endangered or threatened | Status | When listed | Critical habitat | Special rules |
|---|---|---|---|---|---|---|---|
| Darter, Okaloosa | *Etheostoma okaloosae* | U.S.A. (FL) | do | E | 6 | NA | NA |
| Darter, slackwater | *Etheostoma boschungi* | U.S.A. (AL, TN) | do | T | 28 | 17.95(e) | 17.44(c) |
| Darter, snail | *Percina tanasi* | U.S.A. (AL, GA, TN) | do | T | 12,150 | NA | NA |
| Darter, watercress | *Etheostoma nuchale* | U.S.A. (AL) | do | E | 2 | NA | NA |
| Gambusia, Big Bend | *Gambusia gaigei* | U.S.A. (TX) | do | E | 1 | NA | NA |
| Gambusia, Clear Creek | *Gambusia heterochir* | do | do | E | 1 | NA | NA |
| Gambusia, Amistad | *Gambusia amistadensis* | do | do | E | 93 | NA | NA |
| Gambusia, Pecos | *Gambusia nobilis* | U.S.A. (NM, TX) | do | E | 2 | NA | NA |
| Gambusia, San Marcos | *Gambusia georgei* | U.S.A. (TX) | do | E | 98 | 17.95(e) | NA |
| Killifish, Pahrump | *Empetrichthys latos* | U.S.A. (NV) | do | E | 1 | NA | NA |
| Logperch, Conasauga | *Percina jenkinsi* | U.S.A. (GA, TN) | do | E | 196 | 17.95(e) | NA |
| Madtom, Scioto | *Noturus trautmani* | U.S.A. (OH) | do | E | 10 | NA | NA |
| Madtom, Smoky | *Noturus baileyi* | U.S.A. (TN) | do | E | 163 | 17.95(e) | NA |
| Madtom, yellowfin | *Noturus flavipinnis* | U.S.A. (GA, TN, VA) | do | T | 28 | 17.95(e) | 17.44(c) |
| Nekogigi (catfish) | *Coreobagrus ichikawai* | Japan | do | E | 3 | NA | NA |
| Puplish, Ash Meadows Amargosa | *Cyprinodon nevadensis mionectes* | U.S.A. (NV) | do | E | 117E, 127E, 130 | 17.95(e) | NA |
| Puplish, Comanche Springs | *Cyprinodon elegans* | U.S.A. (TX) | do | E | 1 | NA | NA |
| Puplish, Devils Hole | *Cyprinodon diabolis* | U.S.A. (NV) | do | E | 1 | NA | NA |
| Puplish, Leon Springs | *Cyprinodon bovinus* | U.S.A. (TX) | do | E | 102 | 17.95(e) | NA |
| Puplish, Owens | *Cyprinodon radiosus* | U.S.A. (CA) | do | E | 1 | NA | NA |
| Puplish, Warm Springs | *Cyprinodon nevadensis pectoralis* | U.S.A. (NV) | do | E | 2 | NA | NA |
| Shiner, beautiful | *Notropis formosus* | U.S.A. (AZ, NM), Mexico | do | T | 157 | 17.95(e) | 17.44(g) |
| Spinedace, Big Spring | *Lepidomeda mollispinis pratensis* | U.S.A. (NV) | do | T | 173 | 17.95(e) | 17.44(i) |
| Spinedace, White River | *Lepidomeda albivallis* | do | do | E | 203 | 17.95(e) | NA |
| Springfish, Hiko White River | *Crenichthys baileyi grandis* | do | do | E | 206 | 17.95(e) | NA |
| Springfish, White River | *Crenichthys baileyi baileyi* | do | do | E | 206 | 17.95(e) | NA |
| Squawfish, Colorado | *Ptychocheilus lucius* | U.S.A. (AZ, CA, CO, NM, NV, UT, WY), Mexico. | Entire, except Salt and Verde R. drainages, AZ | E | 1, 193 | NA | NA |
| Do | do | do | Salt and Verde R. drainages, AZ. | XN | 193 | NA | 17.84(b) |
| Stickleback, unarmored threespine | *Gasterosteus aculeatus williamsoni* | U.S.A. (CA) | do | E | 2 | NA | NA |
| Sturgeon, shortnose | *Acipenser brevirostrum* | U.S.A. and Canada (Atlantic Coast) | do | E | 1 | NA | NA |
| Sucker, Modoc | *Catostomus microps* | U.S.A. (CA) | do | E | 184 | 17.95(e) | NA |
| Sucker, Warner | *Catostomus warnerensis* | U.S.A. (OR) | do | T | 205 | 17.95(e) | 17.44(l) |
| Tango, Miyako (Tokyo bittering) | *Tanakia tanago* | Japan | do | E | 3 | NA | NA |
| Temolek, Ikan (minnow) | *Probarbus jullieni* | Thailand, Cambodia, Vietnam, Malaysia, Laos. | do | E | 15 | NA | NA |
| Topminnow, Gila | *Poeciliopsis occidentalis* | U.S.A. (AZ, NM), Mexico | do | E | 1 | NA | NA |
| Totoaba (seatrout or weakfish) | *Cynoscion macdonaldi* | Mexico (Gulf of California) | do | E | 45 | NA | NA |
| Trout, Apache | *Salmo apache* | U.S.A. (AZ) | do | T | 1, 8 | NA | 17.44(a) |
| Trout, Gila | *Salmo gilae* | U.S.A. (AZ, NM) | do | E | 1 | NA | NA |
| Trout, greenback cutthroat | *Salmo clarki stomias* | U.S.A. (CO) | do | T | 1, 38 | NA | 17.44(f) |
| Trout, Lahontan cutthroat | *Salmo clarki henshawi* | U.S.A. (CA, NV) | do | T | 2, 8 | NA | 17.44(i) |
| Trout, Little Kern golden | *Salmo aguabonita whitei* | U.S.A. (CA) | do | T | 37 | 17.95(e) | 17.44(e) |
| Trout, Paiute cutthroat | *Salmo clarki seleniris* | do | do | T | 1, 8 | NA | 17.44(a) |
| Woundfin | *Plagopterus argentissimus* | U.S.A. (AZ, NV, UT) | Entire, except Gila R. drainage, AZ, NM. | E | 2, 193 | NA | NA |

| | Species | | Historic range | Vertebrate population where endangered or threatened | Status | When listed | Critical habitat | Special rules |
|---|---|---|---|---|---|---|---|---|
| Common name | Scientific name | | | | | | | |
| Woundfin | Plagopterus argentissimus | | U.S.A. (AZ, NV, UT) | Gila R. drainage AZ, NM. | XN | 193 | NA | 17.84(b) |
| **SNAILS** | | | | | | | | |
| Snail, Chittenango ovate amber | Succinea chittenangoensis | | U.S.A. (NY) | NA. | T | 41 | NA | NA |
| Snail, flat-spired three-toothed | Tricodopsis platysayoides | | U.S.A. (WV) | NA. | T | 41 | NA | NA |
| Snail, Iowa Pleistocene | Discus macclintocki | | U.S.A. (IA) | NA. | E | 41 | NA | NA |
| Snail, Manus Island tree | Papustyla pulcherrima | | Pacific Ocean: Admiralty Is. (Manus Is.) | NA. | T | 3 | NA | NA |
| Snail, noonday | Mesodon clarki nantahala | | U.S.A. (NC) | NA. | T | 41 | NA | NA |
| Snail, Oahu tree | Achatinella spp. (all species) | | U.S.A. (HI) | NA. | E | 108, 112 | NA | NA |
| Snail, painted snake coiled forest | Anguispira picta | | U.S.A. (TN) | NA. | T | 41 | NA | NA |
| Snail, Stock Island | Orthalicus reses | | U.S.A. (FL) | NA. | T | 41 | NA | NA |
| Snail, Virginia fringed mountain | Polygyriscus virginianus | | U.S.A. (VA) | NA. | E | 41 | NA | NA |
| **CLAMS** | | | | | | | | |
| Pearly mussel, Alabama lamp | Lampsilis virescens | | U.S.A. (AL, TN) | NA. | E | 15 | NA | NA |
| Pearly mussel, Appalachian monkeyface | Quadrula sparsa | | U.S.A. (TN, VA) | NA. | E | 15 | NA | NA |
| Pearly mussel, birdwing | Conradilla caelata | | ....do | NA. | E | 15 | NA | NA |
| Pearly mussel, Cumberland bean | Villosa (= Micromya) trabalis | | U.S.A. (KY, TN) | NA. | E | 15 | NA | NA |
| Pearly mussel, Cumberland monkeyface | Quadrula intermedia | | U.S.A. (AL, TN, VA) | NA. | E | 15 | NA | NA |
| Pearly mussel, Curtis' | Epioblasma (= Dysnomia) florentina curtisi. | | U.S.A. (MO) | NA. | E | 15 | NA | NA |
| Pearly mussel, dromedary | Dromus dromas | | U.S.A. (TN, VA) | NA. | E | 15 | NA | NA |
| Pearly mussel, green-blossom | Epioblasma (= Dysnomia) torulosa gubernaculum. | | ....do | NA. | E | 15 | NA | NA |
| Pearly mussel, Higgins' eye | Lampsilis higginsi | | U.S.A. (IL, IA, MN, MO, NE, WI). | NA. | E | 15 | NA | NA |
| Pearly mussel, Nicklin's | Megalonaias nicklineana | | Mexico | NA. | E | 15 | NA | NA |
| Pearly mussel, orange-footed | Plethobasus cooperianus | | U.S.A. (AL, IN, IA, KY, OH, PA, TN) | NA. | E | 15 | NA | NA |
| Pearly mussel, pale lilliput | Toxolasma (= Carunculina) cylindrellus | | U.S.A. (AL, TN) | NA. | E | 15 | NA | NA |
| Pearly mussel, pink mucket | Lampsilis orbiculata | | U.S.A. (AL, IL, IN, KY, MO, OH, PA, TN, WV). | NA. | E | 15 | NA | NA |
| Pearly mussel, Tampico | Cyrtonaias tampicoensis tecomatensis | | Mexico | NA. | E | 15 | NA | NA |
| Pearly mussel, tubercled-blossom | Epioblasma (= Dysnomia) torulosa torulosa. | | U.S.A. (IL, IN, KY, TN, WV). | NA. | E | 15 | NA | NA |
| Pearly mussel, turgid-blossom | Epioblasma (= Dysnomia) turgidula | | U.S.A. (AL, TN). | NA. | E | 15 | NA | NA |
| Pearly mussel, white cat's paw | Epioblasma (= Dysnomia) sulcata delicata. | | U.S.A. (IN, MI, OH). | NA. | E | 15 | NA | NA |
| Pearly mussel, white wartyback | Plethobasus cicatricosus | | U.S.A. (AL, IN, TN). | NA. | E | 15 | NA | NA |
| Pearly mussel, yellow-blossom | Epioblasma (= Dysnomia) florentina florentina. | | U.S.A. (AL, TN). | NA. | E | 15 | NA | NA |
| Pigtoe, fine-rayed | Fusconaia cuneolus | | U.S.A. (AL, TN, VA). | NA. | E | 15 | NA | NA |
| Pigtoe, rough | Pleurobema plenum | | U.S.A. (IN, KY, TN, VA). | NA. | E | 15 | NA | NA |
| Pigtoe, shiny | Fusconaia edgariana | | U.S.A. (AL, TN, VA). | NA. | E | 15 | NA | NA |
| Pocketbook, fat | Potamilus (= Proptera) capax. | | U.S.A. (AR, IN, MO, OH). | NA. | E | 15 | NA | NA |
| Riffle shell, tan | Epioblasma walkeri | | U.S.A. (KY, TN, VA). | NA. | E | 27 | NA | NA |
| Spiny mussel, Tar River | Elliptio (= Canthyria) steinstansana | | U.S.A. (NC). | NA. | E | 188 | NA | NA |
| **CRUSTACEANS** | | | | | | | | |
| Amphipod, Hay's Spring | Stygobromus hayi | | U.S.A. (DC). | NA. | E | 115 | NA | NA |
| Isopod, Madison Cave | Antrolana lira | | U.S.A. (VA). | NA. | T | 123 | NA | 17.46(a) |
| Isopod, Socorro | Thermosphaeroma (= Exosphaeroma) thermophilus. | | U.S.A. (NM). | NA. | E | 36 | NA | NA |
| Shrimp, Kentucky cave | Palaemonias ganteri | | U.S.A. (KY) | NA. | E | 135 | 17.95(h) | NA |

| Species | | Historic range | Vertebrate population where endangered or threatened | Status | When listed | Critical habitat | Special rules |
|---|---|---|---|---|---|---|---|
| Common name | Scientific name | | | | | | |
| **INSECTS** | | | | | | | |
| Beetle, delta green ground | *Elaphrus viridis* | U.S.A. (CA) | NA | T | 100 | 17.95(i) | NA |
| Beetle, valley elderberry longhorn | *Desmocerus californicus dimorphus* | do | NA | T | 99 | 17.95(i) | NA |
| Butterfly, El Segundo blue | *Euphilotes (=Shijimiaeoides) battoides allyni* | do | NA | E | 14 | NA | NA |
| Butterfly, Lange's metalmark | *Apodemia mormo langei* | do | NA | E | 14 | NA | NA |
| Butterfly, lotis blue | *Lycaeides argyrognomon lotis* | do | NA | E | 14 | NA | NA |
| Butterfly, mission blue | *Icaricia icarioides missionensis* | do | NA | E | 14 | NA | NA |
| Butterfly, Oregon silverspot | *Speyeria zerene hippolyta* | U.S.A. (OR, WA) | NA | T | 95 | 17.95(i) | NA |
| Butterfly, Palos Verdes blue | *Glaucopsyche lygdamus palosverdesensis* | U.S.A. (CA) | NA | E | 96 | 17.95(i) | NA |
| Butterfly, San Bruno elfin | *Callophrys mossii bayensis* | do | NA | E | 14 | NA | NA |
| Butterfly, Schaus swallowtail | *Heraclides (Papilio) aristodemus ponceanus.* | U.S.A. (FL) | NA | E | 13,159 | NA | NA |
| Butterfly, Smith's blue | *Euphilotes (=Shijimiaeoides) enoptes smithi.* | U.S.A. (CA) | NA | E | 14 | NA | NA |
| Moth, Kern primrose sphinx | *Euproserpinus euterpe* | do | NA | T | 91 | NA | NA |
| Naucorid, Ash Meadows | *Ambrysus amargosus* | U.S.A. (NV) | NA | T | 181 | 17.95(i) | NA |

EDITORIAL NOTE: For "When listed" citations, see list following; for symbols in "When listed" see below:
#—Indicates FR where species was delisted; relisting of the species is indicated by subsequent number(s).
E—Indicates Emergency rule publication (see FR document for effective dates); subsequent number(s) indicate FR final rule, if applicable under "when listed."

1—32 FR 4001; March 11, 1967.
2—35 FR 16047; October 13, 1970.
3—35 FR 8495; June 2, 1970.
4—35 FR 18320; December 2, 1970.
5—37 FR 6476; March 30, 1972.
6—38 FR 14678; June 4, 1973.
7—39 FR 44991; December 30, 1974.
8—40 FR 29864; July 16, 1975.
9—40 FR 31736; July 28, 1975.
10—40 FR 44151; September 25, 1975.
11—40 FR 44418; September 26, 1975.
12—40 FR 47506; October 9, 1975.
13—41 FR 17740; April 28, 1976.
14—41 FR 22044; June 1, 1976.
15—41 FR 24064; June 14, 1976.
16—41 FR 45993; October 19, 1976.
17—41 FR 51021; November 19, 1976.
18—41 FR 51612; November 23, 1976.
19—41 FR 53034; December 3, 1976.
20—42 FR 2076; January 10, 1977.
21—42 FR 2968; January 14, 1977.
23—42 FR 28137; June 2, 1977.
24—42 FR 28545; June 3, 1977.
25—42 FR 37373; July 21, 1977.
26—42 FR 40685; August 11, 1977.
27—42 FR 42353; August 23, 1977.
28—42 FR 45528; September 9, 1977.
29—42 FR 58755; November 11, 1977.
30—42 FR 60745; November 29, 1977.
31—43 FR 3715; January 27, 1978.
32—43 FR 4028; January 31, 1978.
33—43 FR 4621; February 3, 1978.
34—43 FR 6233; February 14, 1978.
35—43 FR 9612; March 9, 1978.
36—43 FR 12691; March 27, 1978.
37—43 FR 15429; April 13, 1978.
38—43 FR 16345; April 18, 1978.
40—43 FR 20504; May 12, 1978.
41—43 FR 28932; July 3, 1978.
42—43 FR 32808; July 28, 1978.
43—43 FR 34479; August 4, 1978.
45—44 FR 21289; April 10, 1979.
46—44 FR 23064; April 17, 1979.
48—44 FR 29480; May 21, 1979.
50—44 FR 37126; June 25, 1979.
51—44 FR 37132; June 25, 1979.
52—44 FR 42911; July 20, 1979.
54—44 FR 49220; August 21, 1979.
55—44 FR 54007; September 17, 1979.
60—44 FR 59084; October 12, 1979.
85—44 FR 69208; November 30, 1979.
86—44 FR 70677; December 7, 1979.
87—44 FR 75076; December 18, 1979.
88—45 FR 18010; March 20, 1980.
90—45 FR 21833; April 2, 1980.
91—45 FR 24090; April 8, 1980.
92—45 FR 27713; April 23, 1980.
93—45 FR 28722; April 30, 1980.
94—45 FR 35821; May 28, 1980.
95—45 FR 44935; July 2, 1980.
96—45 FR 44939; July 2, 1980.
97—45 FR 47352; July 14, 1980.
98—45 FR 47355; July 14, 1980.
99—45 FR 52803; August 8, 1980.
100—45 FR 52807; August 8, 1980.
102—45 FR 54678; August 15, 1980.
103—45 FR 55654; August 20, 1980.
105—45 FR 63812; September 25, 1980.
106—45 FR 65132; October 1, 1980.
108—46 FR 3178; January 13, 1981.
111—46 FR 11665; February 10, 1981.
112—46 FR 40025; August 6, 1981.
113—46 FR 40664; August 10, 1981.
114—47 FR 4204; January 28, 1982.
115—47 FR 5425; February 5, 1982.
117—47 FR 19995; May 10, 1982.
119—47 FR 31670; July 21, 1982.
123—47 FR 43701; October 4, 1982.
124—47 FR 43962; October 5, 1982.
125—47 FR 46093; October 15, 1982.
127—48 FR 612; January 5, 1983.
128—48 FR 1726; January 14, 1983.
129—48 FR 28464; June 22, 1983.
130—48 FR 40184; September 2, 1983.
131—48 FR 43043; September 21, 1983.
132—48 FR 46057; October 11, 1983.

134—48 FR 46336; October 12, 1983.
135—48 FR 46341; October 12, 1983.
136—48 FR 49249; October 25, 1983.
137—49 FR 1058; January 9, 1984.
138—49 FR 1994; January 17, 1984.
139—49 FR 2783; January 23, 1984.
142—49 FR 7335; February 28, 1984.
143—49 FR 7394; February 29, 1984.
144—49 FR 7398; February 29, 1984.
145—49 FR 10526; March 20, 1984.
146—49 FR 14356; April 11, 1984.
149—49 FR 22334; May 29, 1984.
150—49 FR 27514; July 5, 1984.
156—49 FR 33885; August 27, 1984.
157—49 FR 34494; August 31, 1984.
159—49 FR 34504; August 31, 1984.
160—49 FR 34510; August 31, 1984.
161—49 FR 35954; September 13, 1984.
163—49 FR 43069; October 26, 1984.
164—49 FR 43969; November 1, 1984.
166—49 FR 45163; November 15, 1984.
168—49 FR 49639; December 21, 1984.
169—50 FR 1056; January 9, 1985.
170—50 FR 4226; January 30, 1985.
171—50 FR 4945; February 4, 1985.
173—50 FR 12302; March 28, 1985.
174—50 FR 12305; March 28, 1985.
181—50 FR 20785; May 20, 1985.
182—50 FR 21792; May 28, 1985.
183—50 FR 23884; June 6, 1985.
184—50 FR 24530; June 11, 1985.
185—50 FR 24653; June 12, 1985.
186—50 FR 25678; June 20, 1985.
188—50 FR 26575; June 27, 1985.
189—50 FR 27002; July 1, 1985.
193—50 FR 30194; July 24, 1985.
195—50 FR 31596; August 5, 1985.
196—50 FR 31603; August 5, 1985.
203—50 FR 37198; September 12, 1985.
205—50 FR 39117; September 27, 1985.
206—50 FR 39123; September 27, 1985.
210—50 FR 50308; December 10, 1985.
211—50 FR 50733; December 11, 1985.
212—50 FR 51252; December 16, 1985.
[48 FR 34182, July 27, 1983; 48 FR 34961, Aug. 2, 1983, as amended at 48 FR 39943, Sept. 2, 1983; 48 FR 46337, Oct. 12, 1983; 48 FR 52743, Nov. 22, 1983; 49 FR 1058, Jan. 9, 1984; 49 FR 33892, Aug. 27, 1984]

**Editorial Note:** For additional **Federal Register** citations affecting the table in § 17.11(h), see the listing which follows the table.

## § 17.12 Endangered and threatened plants.

(a) The list in this section contains the names of all species of plants which have been determined by the Services to be Endangered or Threatened. It also contains the names of species of plants treated as Endangered or Threatened because they are sufficiently similar in appearance to Endangered or Threatened species (see § 17.50 *et seq.*).

(b) The columns entitled "Scientific Name" and "Common Name" define the species of plant within the meaning of the Act. Although common names are included, they cannot be relied upon for identification of any specimen, since they may vary greatly in local usage. The Services shall use the most recently accepted scientific name. In cases in which confusion might arise, a synonym(s) will be provided in parentheses. The Services shall rely to the extent practicable on the *International Code of Botanical Nomenclature*.

(c) In the "Status" column the following symbols are used: "E" for Endangered, "T" for Threatened, and "E

[or T] (S/A)" for similarity of appearance species.

(d) The other data in the list are nonregulatory in nature and are provided for the information of the reader. In the annual revision and compilation of this Title, the following information may be amended without public notice: the spelling of species' names, historical range, footnotes, references to certain other applicable portions of this Title, synonyms, and more current names. In any of these revised entries, the status, as defined in paragraph (b) of this section, nor its status may be changed without following the procedures of Part 424 of this Title.

(e) The "Historic Range" indicates the known general distribution of the species or subspecies as reported in the current scientific literature. The present distribution may be greatly reduced from this historic range. This column does not imply any limitation on the application of the prohibitions in the Act or implementing rules. Such prohibitions apply to all individuals of the plant species, wherever found.

(f)(1) A footnote to the **Federal Register** publication(s) listing or reclassifying a species is indicated under the column "When Listed." Footnote numbers to §§ 17.11 and 17.12 are in the same numerical sequence, since plants and animals may be listed in the same **Federal Register** document. That document, at least since 1973, includes a statement indicating the basis for the listing, as well as the effective date(s) of said listing.

(2) The "Special Rules" and "Critical Habitat" columns provide a cross reference to other sections in Parts 17, 222, 226, or 227. The "Special Rules" column will also be used to cite the special rules which describe experimental populations and determine if they are essential or nonessential. Separate listings will be made for experimental populations, and the status column will include the following symbols: "XE" for an essential experimental population and "XN" for a nonessential experimental population. The term "NA" (not applicable) appearing in either of these two columns indicates that there are no special rules and/or critical habitat for that particular species. However, all other appropriate rules in Parts 17, 217–227, and 402 still apply to that species. In addition, there may be other rules in this Title that relate to such plants, e.g., port-of-entry requirements. It is not intended that the references in the "Special Rules" column list all the regulations of the two Services which might apply to the species or to the regulations of other Federal agencies or State or local governments.

(g) The listing of a particular taxon includes all lower taxonomic units [see § 17.11(g) for examples].

(h) The "List of Endangered and Threatened Plants" is provided below:

| Species | | Historic range | Sta-tus | When listed | Critical habitat | Special rules |
|---|---|---|---|---|---|---|
| Scientific name | Common name | | | | | |
| Agavaceae—Agave family: | | | | | | |
| Agave arizonica | Arizona agave | U.S.A. (AZ) | E | 147 | NA | NA |
| Alismataceae—Water-plantain family: | | | | | | |
| Sagittaria fasciculata | Bunched arrowhead | U.S.A. (NC, SC) | E | 53 | NA | NA |
| Apiaceae—Parsley family: | | | | | | |
| Eryngium constancei | Loch Lomond coyote-thistle | U.S.A. (CA) | E | 194E | NA | NA |
| Asteraceae—Aster family: | | | | | | |
| Bidens cuneata | Cuneate bidens | U.S.A. (HI) | E | 141 | NA | NA |
| Dyssodia tephroleuca | Ashy dogweed | U.S.A. (TX) | E | 152 | NA | NA |
| Echinacea tennesseensis | Tennessee purple coneflower | U.S.A. (TN) | E | 49 | NA | NA |
| Enceliopsis nudicaulis var. corrugata | Ash Meadows sunray | U.S.A. (NV) | T | 181 | 17.96(a) | NA |
| Erigeron maguirei var. maguirei | Maguire daisy | U.S.A. (UT) | E | 202 | NA | NA |
| Erigeron rhizomatus | Rhizome fleabane | U.S.A. (NM) | T | 177 | NA | NA |
| Grindelia fraxinopratensis | Ash Meadows gumplant | U.S.A. (CA, NV) | T | 181 | 17.96(a) | NA |
| Lipochaeta venosa | None | U.S.A. (HI) | E | 73 | NA | NA |
| Pityopsis ruthii (=Heterotheca ruthii, =Chrysopsis ruthii) | Ruth's golden aster | U.S.A. (TN) | E | 191 | NA | NA |
| Senecio franciscanus | San Francisco Peaks groundsel | U.S.A. (AZ) | T | 137 | 17.96(a) | NA |
| Solidago shortii | Short's goldenrod | U.S.A. (KY) | E | 201 | NA | NA |
| Solidago spithamaea | Blue Ridge goldenrod | U.S.A. (NC, TN) | T | 175 | NA | NA |
| Stephanomeria malheurensis | Malheur wire-lettuce | U.S.A. (OR) | E | 126 | 17.96(a) | NA |
| Townsendia aprica | Last Chance townsendia | U.S.A. (UT) | T | 200 | NA | NA |
| Berberidaceae—Barberry family: | | | | | | |
| Mahonia sonnei (=Berberis s.) | Truckee barberry | U.S.A. (CA) | E | 76 | NA | NA |
| Betulaceae—Birch family: | | | | | | |
| Betula uber | Virginia round-leaf birch | U.S.A. (VA) | E | 39 | NA | NA |
| Boraginaceae—Borage family: | | | | | | |
| Amsinckia grandiflora | Large-flowered fiddleneck | U.S.A. (CA) | E | 179 | 17.96(a) | NA |
| Brassicaceae—Mustard family: | | | | | | |
| Arabis mcdonaldiana | McDonald's rock-cress | U.S.A. (CA) | E | 44 | NA | NA |
| Erysimum capitatum var. angustatum | Contra Costa wallflower | do | E | 39 | 17.96(a) | NA |
| Thelypodium stenopetalum | Slender-petaled mustard | do | E | 158 | NA | NA |
| Buxaceae—Boxwood family: | | | | | | |
| Buxus vahlii | Vahl's boxwood | U.S.A. (PR) | E | 197 | NA | NA |
| Cactaceae—Cactus family: | | | | | | |
| Ancistrocactus tobuschii (=Echinocactus t., Mammillaria t.) | Tobusch fishhook cactus | U.S.A. (TX) | E | 80 | NA | NA |
| Cereus eriophorus var. fragrans | Fragrant prickly-apple | U.S.A. (FL) | E | 208 | NA | NA |
| Cereus robinii | Key tree-cactus | U.S.A. (FL), Cuba | E | 153 | NA | NA |
| Coryphantha minima (=C. nellieae, Escobaria n., Mammillaria n.) | Nellie cory cactus | U.S.A. (TX) | E | 81 | NA | NA |
| Coryphantha ramillosa | Bunched cory cactus | U.S.A. (TX), Mexico (Coahuila) | T | 77 | NA | NA |
| Coryphantha sneedii var. leei (=Escobaria l., Mammillaria l.) | Lee pincushion cactus | U.S.A. (NM) | T | 61 | NA | NA |
| Coryphantha sneedii var. sneedii (=Escobaria s., Mammillaria s.) | Sneed pincushion cactus | U.S.A. (TX, NM) | E | 82 | NA | NA |
| Echinocactus horizonthalonius var. nicholii | Nichol's Turk's head cactus | U.S.A. (AZ) | E | 71 | NA | NA |
| Echinocereus engelmannii var. purpureus | Purple-spined hedgehog cactus | U.S.A. (UT) | E | 58 | NA | NA |
| Echinocereus fendleri var. kuenzleri (=E. kuenzleri, E. hempelii of authors, not Fobe) | Kuenzler hedgehog cactus | U.S.A. (NM) | E | 70 | NA | NA |
| Echinocereus lloydii (=E. roetteri var. l.) | Lloyd's hedgehog cactus | U.S.A. (TX) | E | 67 | NA | NA |

| Species — Scientific name | Common name | Historic range | Status | When listed | Critical habitat | Special rules |
|---|---|---|---|---|---|---|
| *Echinocereus reichenbachii var. albertii (=E. melanocentrus)* | Black lace cactus | ...........do............ | E | 68 | NA | NA |
| *Echinocereus triglochidiatus var. arizonicus (=E. arizonicus)* | Arizona hedgehog cactus | U.S.A. (AZ) | E | 62 | NA | NA |
| *Echinocereus triglochidiatus var. inermis (=E. coccineus var. i., E. phoeniceus var. i.)* | Spineless hedgehog cactus | U.S.A. (CO, UT) | E | 83 | NA | NA |
| *Echinocereus viridiflorus var. davisii (=E. davisii)* | Davis green pitaya | U.S.A. (TX) | E | 81 | NA | NA |
| *Neolloydia mariposensis (=Echinocactus m., Echinomastus m.)* | Lloyd's Mariposa cactus | U.S.A. (TX), Mexico (Coahuila) | T | 77 | NA | NA |
| *Pediocactus bradyi (=Toumeya b.)* | Brady pincushion cactus | U.S.A. (AZ) | E | 63 | NA | NA |
| *Pediocactus knowltonii (=P. bradyi var. k. Toumeya k.)* | Knowlton cactus | U.S.A. (NM, CO) | E | 72 | NA | NA |
| *Pediocactus peeblesianus var. peeblesianus (=Echinocactus p., Navajoa p., Toumeya p., Utahia p.)* | Peebles Navajo cactus | U.S.A. (AZ) | E | 69 | NA | NA |
| *Pediocactus sileri (=Echinocactus s., Utahia s.)* | Siler pincushion cactus | U.S.A. (AZ, UT) | E | 64 | NA | NA |
| *Sclerocactus glaucus (=Echinocactus g., E. subglaucus, E. whipplei var. g., Pediocactus g., S. franklinii, S. whipplei var. g.)* | Uinta Basin hookless cactus | U.S.A. (CO, UT) | T | 59 | NA | NA |
| *Sclerocactus mesae-verdae (=Coloradoa m., Echinocactus m., Pediocactus m.)* | Mesa Verde cactus | U.S.A. (CO, NM) | T | 75 | NA | NA |
| *Sclerocactus wrightiae (=Pediocactus w.)* | Wright fishhook cactus | U.S.A. (UT) | E | 58 | NA | NA |
| Caryophyllaceae—Pink family: | | | | | | |
| *Schiedea adamantis* | Diamond Head schiedea | U.S.A. (HI) | E | 141 | NA | NA |
| Chenopodiaceae—Goosefoot family: | | | | | | |
| *Nitrophila mohavensis* | Amargosa nitrewort | U.S.A. (CA) | E | 181 | 17.96(a) | NA |
| Cistaceae—Rockrose family: | | | | | | |
| *Hudsonia montana* | Mountain golden heather | U.S.A. (NC) | T | 107 | 17.96(a) | NA |
| Crassulaceae—Stonecrop family: | | | | | | |
| *Dudleya traskiae* | Santa Barbara Island liveforever | U.S.A. (CA) | E | 39 | NA | NA |
| Cupressaceae—Cypress family: | | | | | | |
| *Fitzroya cupressoides* | Chilean false larch (=alerce) | Chile, Argentina | T | 79 | NA | NA |
| Cyperaceae—Sedge family: | | | | | | |
| *Carex specuicola* | None | U.S.A. (AZ) | T | 178 | 17.96(a) | NA |
| Ericaceae—Heath family: | | | | | | |
| *Arctostaphylos pungens var. ravenii (=A. hookeri ssp. ravenii)* | Presidio (=Raven's) manzanita | U.S.A. (CA) | E | 65 | NA | NA |
| *Rhododendron chapmanii* | Chapman rhododendron | U.S.A. (FL) | E | 47 | NA | NA |
| Euphorbiaceae—Spurge family: | | | | | | |
| *Euphorbia (=Chamaesyce) deltoidea ssp. deltoidea* | Spurge | U.S.A. (FL) | E | 192 | NA | NA |
| *Euphorbia (=Chamaesyce) garberi* | None | ...........do............ | T | 192 | NA | NA |
| *Euphorbia skottsbergii var. kalaeloana* | Ewa Plains 'akoko | U.S.A. (HI) | E | 120 | NA | NA |
| *Jatropha costaricensis* | Costa Rican jatropha | Costa Rica | E | 154 | NA | NA |
| Fabaceae—Pea family: | | | | | | |
| *Amorpha crenulata* | Crenulate lead-plant | U.S.A. (FL) | E | 192 | NA | NA |
| *Astragalus humillimus* | Mancos milk-vetch | U.S.A. (CO, NM) | E | 187 | NA | NA |
| *Astragalus perianus* | Rydberg milk-vetch | U.S.A. (UT) | T | 39 | NA | NA |
| *Astragalus phoenix* | Ash Meadows milk-vetch | U.S.A. (NV) | T | 181 | 17.96(a) | NA |
| *Baptisia arachnifera* | Hairy rattleweed | U.S.A. (GA) | E | 39 | NA | NA |
| *Galactia smallii* | Small's milkpea | U.S.A. (FL) | E | 192 | NA | NA |
| *Hoffmannseggia tenella* | Slender rush-pea | U.S.A. (TX) | E | 207 | NA | NA |
| *Lotus dendroideus ssp. traskiae (=L. scoparius ssp. t.)* | San Clemente Island broom | U.S.A. (CA) | E | 26 | NA | NA |

| Species | | Historic range | Status | When listed | Critical habitat | Special rules |
|---|---|---|---|---|---|---|
| Scientific name | Common name | | | | | |
| *Vicia menziesii* | Hawaiian vetch | U.S.A. (HI) | E | 39 | NA | NA |
| **Frankeniaceae—Frankenia family:** | | | | | | |
| *Frankenia johnstonii* | Johnston's frankenia | U.S.A. (TX), Mexico (Nuevo Leon). | E | 155 | NA | NA |
| **Gentianaceae—Gentian family:** | | | | | | |
| *Centaurium namophilum* | Spring-loving centaury | U.S.A. (CA, NV) | T | 181 | 17.96(a) | NA |
| **Hydrophyllaceae—Waterleaf family:** | | | | | | |
| *Phacelia argillacea* | Clay phacelia | U.S.A. (UT) | E | 44 | NA | NA |
| *Phacelia formosula* | North Park phacelia | U.S.A. (CO) | E | 121 | NA | NA |
| **Lamiaceae—Mint family:** | | | | | | |
| *Acanthomintha obovata* ssp. *duttonii* | San Mateo thornmint | U.S.A. (CA) | E | 204 | NA | NA |
| *Dicerandra cornutissima* | Longspurred mint | U.S.A. (FL) | E | 209 | NA | NA |
| *Dicerandra frutescens* | Scrub mint | ......do | E | 209 | NA | NA |
| *Dicerandra immaculata* | .......do | ......do | E | 180 | NA | NA |
| *Haplostachys haplostachya* var. *angustifolia* | None | U.S.A. (HI) | E | 73 | NA | NA |
| *Hedeoma apiculatum* | McKittrick pennyroyal | U.S.A. (TX, NM) | T | 118 | 17.96(a) | NA |
| *Hedeoma todsenii* | Todsen's pennyroyal | U.S.A. (NM) | E | 112 | 17.96(a) | NA |
| *Pogogyne abramsii* | San Diego mesa mint | U.S.A. (CA) | E | 110, 112 | 44 | NA | NA |
| *Stenogyne angustifolia* var. *angustifolia* | None | U.S.A. (HI) | E | 73 | NA | NA |
| **Liliaceae—Lily family:** | | | | | | |
| *Harperocallis flava* | Harper's beauty | U.S.A. (FL) | E | 57 | NA | NA |
| *Trillium persistens* | Persistent trillium | U.S.A. (GA, SC) | E | 39 | NA | NA |
| **Loasaceae—Loasa family:** | | | | | | |
| *Mentzelia leucophylla* | Ash Meadows blazing star | U.S.A. (NV) | T | 181 | 17.96(a) | NA |
| **Malvaceae—Mallow family:** | | | | | | |
| *Callirhoe scabriuscula* | Texas poppy-mallow | U.S.A. (TX) | E | 109, 112 | NA | NA |
| *Kokia cookei* | Cooke's kokio | U.S.A. (HI) | E | 74 | NA | NA |
| *Kokia drynarioides* | Koki'o (= hau-hele'ula or Hawaii tree cotton) | ......do | E | 167 | 17.96(a) | NA |
| *Malacothamnus clementinus* | San Clemente Island bush-mallow | U.S.A. (CA) | E | 26 | NA | NA |
| *Sidalcea pedata* | Pedate checker-mallow | ......do | E | 158 | NA | NA |
| **Nyctaginaceae—Four-o'clock family:** | | | | | | |
| *Mirabilis macfarlanei* | MacFarlane's four-o'clock | U.S.A. (ID, OR) | E | 66 | NA | NA |
| **Onagraceae—Evening-primrose family:** | | | | | | |
| *Camissonia benitensis* | San Benito evening-primrose | U.S.A. (CA) | T | 172 | NA | NA |
| *Oenothera avita* ssp. *eurekensis* | Eureka Valley evening-primrose | ......do | E | 39 | NA | NA |
| *Oenothera deltoides* ssp. *howellii* | Antioch Dunes evening-primrose | ......do | E | 39 | 17.96(a) | NA |
| **Orchidaceae—Orchid family:** | | | | | | |
| *Isotria medeoloides* | Small whorled pogonia | U.S.A. (CT, IL, MA, MD, ME, MI, MO, NC, NH, NJ, NY, PA, RI, SC, VA, VT), Canada (Ont.). | E | 122 | NA | NA |
| *Spiranthes parksii* | Navasota ladies'-tresses | U.S.A. (TX) | E | 116 | NA | NA |
| **Papaveraceae—Poppy family:** | | | | | | |
| *Arctomecon humilis* | Dwarf bear-poppy | U.S.A. (UT) | E | 78 | NA | NA |

| Species — Scientific name | Common name | Historic range | Status | When listed | Critical habitat | Special rules |
|---|---|---|---|---|---|---|
| Pinaceae—Pine family: | | | | | | |
| *Abies guatemalensis* | Guatemalan fir (= pinabete) | Mexico, Guatemala, Honduras, El Salvador. | T | 84 | NA | NA |
| Poaceae—Grass family: | | | | | | |
| *Tuctoria mucronata* ( = *Orcuttia m.* ) | Solano grass | U.S.A. (CA) | E | 44 | NA | NA |
| *Panicum carteri* | Carter's panicgrass | U.S.A. (HI) | E | 133 | 17.96(a) | NA |
| *Swallenia alexandrae* | Eureka Dune grass | U.S.A. (CA) | E | 39 | NA | NA |
| *Zizania texana* | Texas wild-rice | U.S.A. (TX) | E | 39 | 17.96(a) | NA |
| Polygalaceae—Milkwort family: | | | | | | |
| *Polygala smallii* | Tiny polygala | U.S.A. (FL) | E | 192 | NA | NA |
| Polygonaceae—Buckwheat family: | | | | | | |
| *Eriogonum gypsophilum* | Gypsum wild-buckwheat | U.S.A. (NM) | T | 110, 112 | 17.96(a) | NA |
| *Eriogonum pelinophilum* | Clay-loving wild-buckwheat | U.S.A. (CO) | E | 151 | 17.96(a) | NA |
| Primulaceae—Primrose family: | | | | | | |
| *Primula maguirei* | Maguire primrose | U.S.A. (UT) | T | 199 | NA | NA |
| Ranunculaceae—Buttercup family: | | | | | | |
| *Aconitum noveboracense* | Northern wild monkshood | U.S.A. (IA, NY, OH, WI). | T | 39 | NA | NA |
| *Delphinium kinkiense* | San Clemente Island larkspur | U.S.A. (CA) | E | 26 | NA | NA |
| Rhamnaceae—Buckhorn family: | | | | | | |
| *Gouania hillebrandii* | None | U.S.A. (HI) | E | 165 | 17.96(a) | NA |
| Rosaceae—Rose family: | | | | | | |
| *Cowania subintegra* | Arizona cliffrose | U.S.A. (AZ) | E | 148 | NA | NA |
| *Ivesia eremica* | Ash Meadows ivesia | U.S.A. (NV) | T | 181 | 17.96(a) | NA |
| *Potentilla robbinsiana* | Robbins' cinquefoil | U.S.A. (NH, VT) | E | 104 | 17.96(a) | NA |
| Rubiaceae—Coffee family: | | | | | | |
| *Gardenia brighamii* | Na'u (Hawaiian gardenia) | U.S.A. (HI) | E | 198 | NA | NA |
| Rutaceae—Citrus family: | | | | | | |
| *Zanthoxylum thomasianum* | Prickly-ash | U.S.A. (PR, VI) | E | 213 | NA | NA |
| Sarraceniaceae—Pitcher plant family: | | | | | | |
| *Sarracenia oreophila* | Green pitcher plant | U.S.A. (AL, GA, TN) | E | 56, 89 | NA | NA |
| Saxifragaceae—Saxifrage family: | | | | | | |
| *Ribes echinellum* | Miccosukee gooseberry | U.S.A. (FL, SC) | T | 190 | NA | NA |
| Scrophulariaceae—Snapdragon family: | | | | | | |
| *Castilleja grisea* | San Clemente Island Indian paintbrush | U.S.A. (CA) | E | 26 | NA | NA |
| *Cordylanthus maritimus* ssp. *maritimus* | Salt marsh bird's-beak | U.S.A. (CA), Mexico (Baja California). | E | 44 | NA | NA |
| *Pedicularis furbishiae* | Furbish lousewort | U.S.A. (ME), Canada (New Brunswick). | E | 39 | NA | NA |
| Solanaceae—Nightshade family: | | | | | | |
| *Goetzea elegans* | Beautiful goetzea, matabuey | U.S.A. (PR) | E | 176 | NA | NA |
| Styracaceae—Styrax family: | | | | | | |
| *Styrax texana* | Texas snowbells | U.S.A. (TX) | E | 162 | NA | NA |

| Species | | Historic range | Sta-tus | When listed | Critical habitat | Special rules |
|---|---|---|---|---|---|---|
| Scientific name | Common name | | | | | |
| Taxaceae—Yew family: | | | | | | |
| *Torreya taxifolia* | Florida torreya | U.S.A. (FL, GA) | E | 140 | NA | NA |

E—Indicates Emergency rule publication (see FR document for effective dates); subsequent number(s) indicate FR final rule, if applicable under "when listed."

EDITORIAL NOTE: For "When listed" citations, see list following; for symbols in "When listed" see below:

26—42 FR 40685; August 11, 1977.
39—43 FR 17916; April 26, 1978.
44—43 FR 44812; September 28, 1978.
47—44 FR 24250; April 24, 1979.
49—44 FR 32605; June 6, 1979.
53—44 FR 43701; July 25, 1979.
56—44 FR 54923; September 21, 1979.
57—44 FR 58863; October 2, 1979.
58—44 FR 58868; October 11, 1979.
59—44 FR 58870; October 11, 1979.
61—44 FR 61556; October 25, 1979.
62—44 FR 61558; October 25, 1979.
63—44 FR 61786; October 26, 1979.
64—44 FR 61788; October 26, 1979
65—44 FR 61911; October 26, 1979.
66—44 FR 61913; October 26, 1979.
67—44 FR 61916; October 26, 1979.
68—44 FR 61920; October 26, 1979.
69—44 FR 61924; October 26, 1979.
70—44 FR 61927; October 26, 1979.
71—44 FR 61929; October 26, 1979.
72—44 FR 62246; October 26, 1979.
73—44 FR 62469; October 30, 1979.
74—44 FR 62471; October 30, 1979.
75—44 FR 62474; October 30, 1979.
76—44 FR 64247; November 6, 1979.
77—44 FR 64250; November 6, 1979.
78—44 FR 64252; November 6, 1979.
79—44 FR 64733; November 7, 1979.
80—44 FR 64738; November 7, 1979.
81—44 FR 64740; November 7, 1979.
82—44 FR 64743; November 7, 1979.
83—44 FR 64746; November 7, 1979.
84—44 FR 65005; November 8, 1979.
89—45 FR 18929; March 24, 1980.
104—45 FR 61944; September 17, 1980.
107—45 FR 69360; October 20, 1980.
109—46 FR 3184; January 13, 1981.
110—46 FR 5730; January 19, 1981.
112—46 FR 40025; August 6, 1981.
116—47 FR 19539; May 6, 1982.
118—47 FR 30440; July 13, 1982.
120—47 FR 36846; August 24, 1982.
121—47 FR 38540; September 1, 1982.
122—47 FR 38927; September 10, 1982.
126—47 FR 50885; November 10, 1982.
133—48 FR 46331; October 12, 1983.
137—48 FR 52747; November 22, 1983.
140—49 FR 2786; January 23, 1984.
141—49 FR 6102; February 17, 1984.
147—49 FR 21058; May 18, 1984.
148—49 FR 22329; May 29, 1984.
151—49 FR 28565; July 13, 1984.
152—49 FR 29234; July 19, 1984.
153—49 FR 29237; July 19, 1984.
154—49 FR 30201; July 27, 1984.
155—49 FR 31421; Aug. 7, 1984.
158—49 FR 34500; Aug. 31, 1984.
162—49 FR 40038; October 12, 1984.
165—49 FR 44756; November 9, 1984.

167—49 FR 47400; December 4, 1984.
168—49 FR 49639; December 21, 1984.
172—50 FR 5758; February 12, 1985.
175—50 FR 12309; March 28, 1985.
176—50 FR 15567; April 19, 1985.
177—50 FR 16682; April 26, 1985.
178—50 FR 19373; May 8, 1985.
179—50 FR 19377; May 8, 1985.
180—50 FR 20214; May 15, 1985.
181—50 FR 20786; May 20, 1985.
187—50 FR 26572; June 27, 1985.
190—50 FR 29341; July 18, 1985.
191—50 FR 29344; July 18, 1985.
192—50 FR 29349; July 18, 1985.
194—50 FR 31190; August 1, 1985.
197—50 FR 32575; August 13, 1985.
198—50 FR 33731; August 21, 1985.
199—50 FR 33734; August 21, 1985.
200—50 FR 33737; August 21, 1985.
201—50 FR 36089; September 5, 1985.
202—50 FR 36091; September 5, 1985.
204—50 FR 37863; September 18, 1985.
207—50 FR 45618; November 1, 1985.
208—50 FR 45621; November 1, 1985.
209—50 FR 45624; November 1, 1985.
213—50 FR 51870; December 20, 1985.
[48 FR 34182, July 27, 1983; 48 FR 34961, Aug. 2, 1983, as amended at 49 FR 33893, Aug. 27, 1984]

**Editorial Note:** For additional **Federal Register** citations affecting the table in § 17.12(h), see the listing which follows the table.

## SPECIES REMOVED FROM THE ENDANGERED AND THREATENED LISTS

The following list of wildlife removed from the list at § 17.11 is provided for informational purposes only and is not codified in the Code of Federal Regulations. Only species completely removed from the list are included below. In cases where only a portion of the vertebrate species is delisted, the entry remains in § 17.11 in the modified form with the citation to the **Federal Register** indicted under "When listed."

The Service's listing regulations at 50 CFR 424.11(c) and (d) are as follows:

(c) A species shall be listed or reclassified if the Secretary determines, on the basis of the best scientific and commercial data available after conducting a review of the species'

status, that the species is endangered or threatened because of any one or a combination of the following factors:

(1) The present or threatened destruction, modification, or curtailment of its habitat or range;

(2) Overutilization for commercial, recreational, scientific, or educational purposes;

(3) Disease or predation;

(4) The inadequacy of existing regulatory mechanisms; or

(5) Other natural or manmade factors affecting its continued existence.

(d) The factors considered in delisting a species are those in paragraph (c) of this section as they relate to the definitions of endangered and threatened species. Such removal must be supported by the best scientific and commercial data available to the Secretary after conducting a review of the status of the species. A species may be delisted only if such data substantiate that it is neither endangered nor threatened for one or more of the following reasons:

(1) *Extinction.* Unless all individuals of the listed species had been previously identified and located, and were later found to be extirpated from their previous range, a sufficient period of time must be allowed before delisting to indicate clearly that the species is extinct.

(2) *Recovery.* The principal goal of the U.S. Fish and Wildlife Service and the National Marine Fisheries Services is to return listed species to a point at which protection under the Act is no longer required. A species may be delisted on the basis of recovery only if the best scientific and commercial data available indicate that it is no longer endangered or threatened.

(3) *Original data for classification in error.* Subsequent investigations may show that the best scientific or commercial data available when the species was listed, or the interpretation of such data, were in error.

| Species | | Historic range | Former vertebrate population where endangered or threatened | Former status | Delisted | |
|---|---|---|---|---|---|---|
| Common name | Scientific name | | | | Citation | Reason |
| Duck, Mexican | *Anas "diazi"* | U.S.A. (AZ, NM, TX) to central Mexico. | U.S. only | E | 43 FR 32258–61; January 25, 1978. | Original data in error. |
| Pupfish, Tecopa | *Cyprinodon nevadensis calidae.* | U.S.A. (CA). | Entire | E | 47 FR 2317–19; January 15, 1982. | Extinct. |
| Cisco, longjaw | *Coregonus alpenae* | U.S.A. and Canada (Lakes Michigan, Huron, Erie). | do | E | 48 FR 39941–43; September 2, 1983. | Extinct. |
| Pike, blue | *Stizostedion vitreum glaucum.* | U.S.A. and Canada (Lakes Erie, Ontario). | do | E | do | Extinct. |
| Sparrow, Santa Barbara song | *Melospiza melodia graminea* | U.S.A. (CA). | do | E | 48 FR 46336–37; October 12, 1983. | Extinct. |
| Treefog, Pine Barrens | *Hyla andersoni.* | U.S.A. (FL, AL, NC, SC, NJ). | Florida | E | 48 FR 52740–43; November 22, 1983. | Original data in error. |
| Pearly mussel, Sampson's | *Epioblasma ( =Dysnomia) sampsoni.* | U.S.A. (IL, IN). | NA | E | 49 FR 1057–58; January 9, 1984. | Extinct. |
| Turtle, Indian flap-shelled | *Lissemys punctata punctata* | India, Pakistan, Bangladesh | Entire | E | 49 FR 7394–98; February 29, 1984. | Original data in error. |
| Butterfly, Bahama swallowtail | *Heraclides ( =Papilio) andraemon bonhotei.* | U.S.A. (FL), Bahamas | NA | T | 49 FR 34501–34504; August 31, 1984. | Original data in error. |
| Dove, Palau | *Gallicolumba canifrons* | W. Pacific: U.S.A. (Palau Islands). | Entire | E | 50 FR 37192–37194; September 12, 1985. | Recovered. |
| Fantail, Palau (Old World flycatcher). | *Rhipidura lepida.* | do | do | E | do | Recovered. |
| Owl, Palau | *Pyroglaux ( = Otus) podargina* | do | do | E | do | Recovered. |

# The National Wildlife Refuge System Directory

◇

*Refuges are arranged by states. Add "National Wildlife Refuge" to the name of each refuge unless otherwise designated. The abbreviation "WMD" refers to Wetland Management District; "WPA" refers to Waterfowl Production Area. Refuges administered from headquarters on another refuge are indented under the refuge responsible for their administration. See last page for Regional Office information.*

| REFUGE | MANAGER | ADDRESS | PHONE |
|---|---|---|---|
| **ALABAMA** | | | |
| BON SECOUR | Jerome T. Carroll | P.O. Box 1650, Gulf Shores, AL 36542 | (205-690-2181) |
| CHOCTAW | Cecil E. McMullan | Box 808, 2704 Westside College Ave., Jackson, AL 36545 | (205-246-3583) |
| EUFAULA | Donald E. Temple | Route 2, Box 97-B, Eufaula, AL 36027 | (205-687-4065) |
| WHEELER | Thomas Z. Atkeson | Box 1643, Decatur, AL 35602 | (205-353-7243) |
|   BLOWING WIND CAVE   FERN CAVE   WATERCRESS DARTER | | | |
| **ALASKA** | | | |
| ALASKA MARITIME | John L. Martin | 202 West Pioneer Ave., Homer, AK 99603 | (907-235-6546) |
|   ALASKA PENINSULA UNIT   BERING SEA UNIT   CHUKCHI SEA UNIT   GULF OF ALASKA UNIT | | | |
|   ALEUTIAN ISLANDS UNIT | C. Fred Zeillemaker | P.O. Box 5251, Naval Air Station Adak FPO Seattle, WA 98791 | (907-592-2406) |
| ALASKA PENINSULA | Vacant | P.O. Box 277, King Salmon, AK 99613 | (907-246-3339) |
| ARCTIC | Glen W. Elison | Box 20, 101-12th Avenue, Fairbanks, AK 99701 | (907-456-0250) |
| BECHAROF | Vacant | P.O. Box 277, King Salmon, AK 99613 | (907-246-3339) |
| INNOKO | Phillip J. Feiger | General Delivery, McGrath, AK 99627 | (907-542-3251) |
| IZEMBEK | John E. Sarvis | Pouch #2, Cold Bay, AK 99571 | (907-532-2445) |
| KANUTI | Ervin McIntosh | Box 20, 101-12th Avenue, Fairbanks, AK 99701 | (907-456-0329) |
| KENAI | Robert L. Delaney | P.O. Box 2139, Soldotna, AK 99669 | (907-262-7021) |
| KODIAK | Jay Bellinger | P.O. Box 825, Kodiak, AK 99615 | (907-487-2600) |
| KOYUKUK | Mike Nunn | P.O. Box 287, Galena, AK 99741 | (907-656-1231) |
| NOWITNA | James Fisher | P.O. Box 287, Galena, AK 99741 | (907-656-1231) |

| | | | |
|---|---|---|---|
| **SELAWIK** | Kent Hall | P.O. Box 270, Kotzebue, AK 99752 | (907-442-3799) |
| **TOGIAK** | Dave Fisher | P.O. Box 10201, Dillingham, AK 99576 | (907-842-1063) |
| **YUKON DELTA** | Ron Perry | P.O. Box 346, Bethel, AK 99559 | (907-543-3151) |
| **YUKON FLATS** | Lou Swenson | P.O. Box 101, 12th Avenue, Fairbanks, AK 99701 | (907-456-0250) |

## ARIZONA

| | | | |
|---|---|---|---|
| **BUENOS AIRES** | Wayne A. Schifflett | Box 109, Sasabe, AZ 85633 | (602-629-5120) |
| **CABEZA PRIETA** | Linda Hagen | Box 418, Ajo, AZ 85321 | (602-387-6483) |
| **CIBOLA** | Wesley V. Martin | Box AP, Blythe, CA 92225 | (602-857-3253) |
| **HAVASU** | Jim Good | Box A, Needles, CA 92363 | (619-326-3853) |
| **IMPERIAL** | Arnold W. Nidecker III | Box 72217, Martinez Lake, AZ 85365 | (602-783-3371) |
| **KOFA** | Milton K. Haderlie | Box 6290, Yuma, AZ 85364 | (602-783-7861) |
| **SAN BERNARDINO** | Benjamin Robertson | RR 1, Box 228R, Douglas, AZ 85607 | (602-364-2104) |

## ARKANSAS

| | | | |
|---|---|---|---|
| **BIG LAKE** | Donald J. Kosin | Box 67, Manila, AR 72442 | (501-564-2429) |
| **FELSENTHAL** | Robert J. Bridges | Box 279, Crossett, AR 71635 | (501-364-3167) |
| **HOLLA BEND** | Martin D. Perry | Box 1043, 115 S. Denver Street, Russellville, AR 72801 | (501-968-2800) |
| **WAPANOCCA** | Michael Riley | Box 279, Turrell, AR 72384 | (501-343-2595) |
| **WHITE RIVER** | Marvin T. Hurdle | Box 308, 321 W. 7th Street, De Witt, AR 72042 | (501-946-1468) |

## CALIFORNIA

**CIBOLA** (see AZ)

**HAVASU** (see AZ)

**IMPERIAL** (see AZ)

| | | | |
|---|---|---|---|
| **KERN** | Thomas J. Charmley | Box 219, Delano, CA 93216-0219 | (805-725-2767) |
| BITTER CREEK    BLUE RIDGE    HOPPER MOUNTAIN    PIXLEY    SEAL BEACH | | | (805-725-5284) |
| **KLAMATH BASIN REFUGES** | Robert C. Fields | Route 1, Box 74, Tulelake, CA 96134 | (916-667-2231) |
| BEAR VALLEY (OR)    CLEAR LAKE    KLAMATH FOREST (OR)    LOWER KLAMATH (OR & CA)    TULE LAKE    UPPER KLAMATH (OR) | | | |
| **MODOC** | Edward C. Bloom | Box 1610, Alturas, CA 96101 | (916-233-3572) |
| **SACRAMENTO** | Edward J. Collins | Route 1, Box 311, Willows, CA 95988 | (916-934-2801) |
| BUTTE SINK    COLUSA    DELEVAN    SUTTER | | | |
| **SALTON SEA** TIJUANA SLOUGH | Gary Kramer | Box 120, Calipatria, CA 92233 | (619-348-5278) |
| **SAN FRANCISCO BAY** | Roger D. Johnson | Box 524, Newark, CA 94560 | (415-792-0222) |
| ANTIOCH DUNES    CASTLE ROCK    ELLICOTT SLOUGH    FARALLON    HUMBOLDT BAY    SALINAS LAGOON    SAN PABLO BAY | | | |
| **SAN LUIS** GRASSLANDS    KESTERSON    MERCED | Gary R. Zahm | Box 2176, Los Banos, CA 93635 | (209-826-3508) |

## COLORADO

| | | | |
|---|---|---|---|
| **ALAMOSA/MONTE VISTA** | Melvin T. Nail | Box 1148, Alamosa, CO 81101 | (303-589-4021) |

| ARAPAHO | Eugene C. Patten | Box 457, Walden, CO 80480 | (303-723-4717) |
| BAMFORTH (WY)    HUTTON LAKE (WY)    PATHFINDER (WY) | | | |

| BROWNS PARK (see UT) | James A. Creasey | 1318 Highway 318, Maybell, CO 81640 | (303-365-3613) |

## CONNECTICUT

CONNECTICUT COASTAL (see RI)

SALT MEADOW (see RI)

## DELAWARE

| BOMBAY HOOK | Paul D. Daly | Route 1, Box 147, Smyrna, DE 19977 | (302-653-9345) |
| PRIME HOOK | George F. O'Shea | Route 1, Box 195, Milton, DE 19968 | (302-684-8419) |

## FLORIDA

| CHASSAHOWITZKA | Glenn A. Carowan, Jr. | Route 2, Box 44, Homosassa, FL 32646 | (904-382-2201) |
| CEDAR KEYS    CRYSTAL RIVER    EGMONT KEY    LOWER SUWANNEE    PASSAGE KEY    PINELLAS | | | |

| J.N. "DING" DARLING | Albert R. Hight | One Wildlife Drive, Sanibel, FL 33957 | (813-472-1100) |
| CALOOSAHATCHEE    ISLAND BAY    MATLACHA PASS    PINE ISLAND | | | |

| LAKE WOODRUFF | Leon I. Rhodes | Box 488, DeLeon Springs, FL 32028 | (904-985-4673) |

| MERRITT ISLAND | Stephen R. Vehrs | Box 6504, Titusville, FL 32780 | (305-867-4820) |
| PELICAN ISLAND    ST. JOHNS | | | |

| NATIONAL KEY DEER | Deborah G. Holle | Box 510, Big Pine Key, FL 33043 | (305-872-2239) |
| CROCODILE LAKE    GREAT WHITE HERON    KEY WEST | | | |

| ST. MARKS | Joe D. White | Box 68, St. Marks, FL 32355 | (904-925-6121) |

| ST. VINCENT | Jerry L. Holloman | Box 447, Apalachicola, FL 32320 | (904-653-8808) |

| LOXAHATCHEE | Burkett S. Neely, Jr. | Route 1, Box 278, Boynton Beach, FL 33437 | (305-732-3684) |
| HOBE SOUND | | | |

## GEORGIA

EUFAULA (see AL)

| GEORGIA COASTAL COMPLEX | John P. Davis | Box 8487, Savannah, GA 31412 | (912-944-4415) |
| BLACKBEARD ISLAND    HARRIS NECK    PINCKNEY ISLAND (SC)    SAVANNAH TYBEE    WASSAW    WOLF ISLAND | | | |

| OKEFENOKEE | John D. Schroer | Rte. 2, Box 338, Folkston, GA 31537 | (912-496-7366) |

| PIEDMONT | Ronnie L. Shell | Round Oak, GA 31038 | (912-986-5441) |

## HAWAII

| HAWAIIAN AND PACIFIC ISLANDS COMPLEX | Jerry Leinecke | P.O. Box 50167, 300 Ala Moana Blvd., Honolulu, HI 96850 | (808-546-5608) |
| REMOTE ISLAND REFUGES | Richard C. Wass | (see above) | |
| BAKER ISLAND    HAWAIIAN ISLANDS    HOWLAND ISLAND | | JARVIS ISLAND    JOHNSTON ATOLL    ROSE ATOLL | |
| WETLANDS REFUGES | James Krakowski | (see above) | |
| JAMES C. CAMPBELL    KAKAHAIA    PEARL HARBOR | | | |
| KILAUEA POINT WILDLIFE ADMINISTRATIVE SITE | | Box 87, Kilauea, Kauai, HI 96754 | (808-828-1413) |
| HANALEI    HULEIA | | | |

## IDAHO

| DEER FLAT | James R. Messerli | Box 448, Nampa, ID 83651 | (208-467-9278) |

| KOOTENAI | Larry D. Napier | Star Route 1, Box 160, Bonners Ferry, ID 83805 | (208-267-3888) |
|---|---|---|---|
| SOUTHEAST IDAHO REFUGE COMPLEX | Charles S. Peck, Jr. | Federal Bldg., Rm. 142, 250 S. 4th Ave., Pocatello, ID 83201 | (208-236-6833) |
| BEAR LAKE | Gerald L. Deutscher | 370 Webster, Box 9, Montpelier, ID 83254 | (208-847-1757) |
| CAMAS | Jack L. Richardson | HC 69 Box 1700, Hamer, ID 83245 | (208-662-5423) |
| GRAYS LAKE | Eugene C. Barney | HC 70 Box 4090, Wayan, ID 83285 | (208-574-2178) |
| MINIDOKA | John D. Hill | Route 4, P.O. Box 290, Rupert, ID 83550 | (208-436-3589) |

## ILLINOIS

| CHAUTAUQUA MEREDOSIA | Thomas S. Sanford | Route 2, Havana, IL 62644 | (309-535-2290) |
|---|---|---|---|
| CRAB ORCHARD | Wayne D. Adams | Box J, Carterville, IL 62918 | (618-997-3344) |
| MARK TWAIN | Robert H. Stratton, Jr. | 311 North 5th St., Suite 100, Great River Plaza, Quincy, IL 62301 | (217-224-8580) |
| CALHOUN DISTRICT CLARENCE CANNON (see MO) LOUISA DISTRICT (see IA) | George N. Peyton | Box 142, Brussels, IL 62013 | (618-883-2524) |

UPPER MISSISSIPPI RIVER NATIONAL WILDLIFE AND FISH REFUGE (see MN)

| SAVANNA DISTRICT | Larry A. Wargowski | Post Office Bldg., Box 250, Savanna, IL 61074 | (815-273-2732) |
|---|---|---|---|

## INDIANA

| MUSCATATUCK | Leland E. Herzberger | Route 7, Box 189A, Seymour, IN 47274 | (812-522-4352) |
|---|---|---|---|

## IOWA

| DE SOTO | George E. Gage | Route 1, Box 114, Missouri Valley, IA 51555 | (712-642-4121) |
|---|---|---|---|
| MARK TWAIN (see IL.) LOUISA DISTRICT | Wayne Stanley | Route 1, Wapello, IA 52653 | (319-523-6982) |
| UNION SLOUGH | John Guthrie | Route 1, Box 52, Titonka, IA 50480 | (515-928-2523) |

UPPER MISSISSIPPI RIVER WILDLIFE AND FISH REFUGE (see MN)

| MCGREGOR DISTRICT | John R. Lyons | McGregor, IA (see Upper Mississippi River Complex, MN) | |
|---|---|---|---|

## KANSAS

| FLINT HILLS | William Wilson | Box 128, Hartford, KS 66854 | (316-392-5553) |
|---|---|---|---|
| KIRWIN | Lee Wright | Kirwin, KS 67644 | (913-543-6673) |
| QUIVIRA | James McCollum | Rt. 3, Box 48A, Stafford, KS 67578 | (316-486-2393) |

## LOUISIANA

| BOGUE CHITTO BRETON    DELTA | Stephen K. Joyner | 1010 Gause Blvd., Bldg. 936, Slidell, LA 70458 | (504-643-5817) |
|---|---|---|---|
| CATAHOULA | Patrick D. Hagan | P.O. Drawer LL, Jena, LA 71342 | (318-992-5261) |
| D'ARBONNE UPPER OUACHITA | Lee R. Fulton | Box 3065, Monroe, LA 71201 | (318-325-1735) |
| LACASSINE SHELL KEYS | Bobby W. Brown | Route 1, Box 186, Lake Arthur, LA 70549 | (318-774-2750) |
| SABINE | John R. Walther | MRH 107, Hackberry, LA 70645 | (318-762-4620) |

## MAINE

| MOOSEHORN CARLTON POND WPA    CROSS ISLAND    FRANKLIN ISLAND | Douglas M. Mullen | Box X, Calais, ME 04619    PETIT MANAN    SEAL ISLAND | (207-454-3521) |
|---|---|---|---|

POND ISLAND (see MA)

RACHEL CARSON (see MA)

## MARYLAND

| | | | |
|---|---|---|---|
| BLACKWATER<br>  MARTIN   SUSQUEHANNA | Don R. Perkuchin | Route 1, Box 121, Cambridge, MD 21613 | (301-228-2677)<br>(301-228-2692) |
| CHINCOTEAGUE (see VA) | | | |
| EASTERN NECK | Harold C. Olsen | Route 2, Box 225, Rock Hall, MD 21661 | (301-639-7056) |
| PATUXENT | David L. Trauger | Laurel, MD 20708 | (301-498-0214) |

## MASSACHUSETTS

| | | | |
|---|---|---|---|
| GREAT MEADOWS<br>  JOHN HAY (NH)   OXBOW   WAPACK (NH) | Lloyd Culp | Weir Hill Road, Sudbury, MA 01776 | (617-443-4661) |
| PARKER RIVER<br>  MASSASOIT   MONOMOY   NANTUCKET<br>  POND ISLAND (ME)   THACHER ISLAND | John L. Fillio | Northern Blvd., Plum Island, Newburyport,<br>MA 01950 | (617-465-5753) |
| RACHEL CARSON | Maurice Mills, Jr. | Route 2, Box 98, Wells, ME 04090 | (207-646-9226) |

## MICHIGAN

| | | | |
|---|---|---|---|
| SENEY<br>  HARBOR ISLAND   HURON | Donald Frickie | Seney, MI 49883 | (906-586-9851) |
| SHIAWASSEE<br>  MICHIGAN ISLANDS   WYANDOTTE | Joe W. Hardy | 6975 Mower Road, Route 1, Saginaw, MI 48601 | (517-777-5930) |

## MINNESOTA

| | | | |
|---|---|---|---|
| AGASSIZ | Joseph Kotok | Middle River, MN 56737 | (218-449-4115) |
| BIG STONE | James Heinecke | 25 NW 2nd St., Ortonville, MN 56278 | (612-839-3700) |
| MINNESOTA VALLEY | Edward S. Crozier | 4101 E. 78th Street, Bloomington, MN 55420 | (612-854-5900) |
| MINNESOTA WETLANDS<br>COMPLEX | Norrel F. Wallace | Route 1, Box 76, Fergus Falls, MN 56537 | (218-739-2291) |
|   MORRIS WMD | Alfred Radtke | Route 1, Box 208, Mill Dam Road, Morris, MN 56267 | (612-589-1001) |
|   DETROIT LAKES WMD | Howard A. Lipke | Route 3, Box 47D, Detroit Lakes, MN 56501 | (218-847-4431) |
|   FERGUS FALLS WMD | Rollin Siegfried | Route 1, Box 76, Fergus Falls, MN 56537 | (218-739-2291) |
|   LITCHFIELD WMD | Matthias A. Kerschbaum | 305 North Sibley, Litchfield, MN 55355 | (612-693-2849) |
| RICE LAKE<br>  MILLE LACS   SANDSTONE | David E. Heffernan | Route 2, McGregor, MN 55760 | (218-768-2402) |
| SHERBURNE | Ronald V. Papike | Route 2, Zimmerman, MN 55398 | (612-389-3323) |
| TAMARAC | Omer N. Swenson | Rural Route, Rochert, MN 56578 | (218-847-2641) |
| UPPER MISSISSIPPI RIVER<br>COMPLEX | Richard Berry | 51 East 4th Street, Winona, MN 55987 | (507-452-4232) |
|   LA CROSSE DISTRICT (WI)   MCGREGOR DISTRICT (IA)   SAVANNA DISTRICT (IL)   TREMPEALEAU (WI) | | | |
|   UPPER MISSISSIPPI RIVER<br>  NATIONAL WILDLIFE AND FISH REFUGE | Robert L. Howard | 51 East 4th Street, Winona, MN 55987 | (507-452-4232) |
|   WINONA DISTRICT | Robert Bartels | 51 East 4th Street, Winona, MN 55987 | (507-454-7351) |

## MISSISSIPPI

| | | | |
|---|---|---|---|
| HILLSIDE<br>  MATHEWS BRAKE   MORGAN BRAKE   PANTHER SWAMP | Vacant | Box 107, Yazoo City, MS 39194 | (601-746-8511) |
| MISSISSIPPI SANDHILL CRANE | George L. Chandler, Jr. | Box 699, Gautier, MS 39553 | (601-497-6322) |
| NOXUBEE | Jimmie L. Tisdale | Route 1, Box 142, Brooksville, MS 39739 | (601-323-5548) |

## NEVADA

| | | | |
|---|---|---|---|
| **DESERT NATIONAL WILDLIFE RANGE** | Robert G. Yoder | 1500 North Decatur Blvd., Las Vegas, NV 89108 | (702-646-3401) |
| AMARGOSA PUPFISH STATION    ASH MEADOWS    MOAPA VALLEY    PAHRANAGAT | | | |
| **RUBY LAKE** | Jerry Wilson | Ruby Valley, NV 89833 | (702-779-2237) |
| **SHELDON** (see OR) | | | |
| **STILLWATER** | Morris C. LeFever | Box 1236, 1510 Rio Vista Road, Fallon, NV 89406 | (702-423-5128) |
| ANAHO ISLAND    FALLON | | | |

## NEW HAMPSHIRE

| | | | |
|---|---|---|---|
| **JOHN HAY** (see MA) | | | |
| **WAPACK** (see MA) | | | |

## NEW JERSEY

| | | | |
|---|---|---|---|
| **EDWIN B. FORSYTHE** | David L. Beall | Great Creek Road, Box 72, Oceanville, NJ 08231 | (609-652-1665) |
| BRIGANTINE DIVISION | Paul D. Caldwell | (see above) | |
| BARNEGAT DIVISION | Harold Laskowski | 700 West Bay Avenue, P.O. Box 544, Barnegat, NJ 08005 | (609-698-1387) |
| **GREAT SWAMP** | William Koch | Pleasant Plains Road, RD 1, Box 152, Basking Ridge, NJ 07920 | (201-647-1222) |
| **KILLCOHOOK** (see PA) | | | |
| **SUPAWNA MEADOWS** (see PA) | | | |

## NEW MEXICO

| | | | |
|---|---|---|---|
| **BITTER LAKE** | LeMoyne B. Marlatt | Box 7, Roswell, NM 88201 | (505-622-6755) |
| **BOSQUE DEL APACHE** | William H. Hutchinson | Box 1246, Socorro, NM 87801 | (505-835-1828) |
| SAN ANDRES | John R. Munoz | Box 756, Las Cruces, NM 88001 | (505-835-1828) |
| SEVILLETA | Theodore M. Stans | General Delivery, San Acacia, NM 87831 | (505-864-4021) |
| **GRULLA** (see TX) | | | |
| **LAS VEGAS** | Stephen S. Berlinger | Route 1, Box 399, Las Vegas, NM 87701 | (505-425-3581) |
| **MAXWELL** | Jon M. Brock | Box 276, Maxwell, NM 87728 | (505-375-2331) |

## NEW YORK

| | | | |
|---|---|---|---|
| **IROQUOIS** | Edwin H. Chandler | P.O. Box 517, Casey Road, Alabama, NY 14003 | (716-948-9154) |
| **MONTEZUMA** | Grady E. Hocutt | 3395 Route 5/20 East, Seneca Falls, NY 13148 | (315-568-5987) |
| **TENSAS RIVER** | Ray Aycock | Merchant's National Bank Bldg., 820 S. St., Vicksburg, MS 39180 | (601-634-7257) |
| **YAZOO** | Tim Wilkins | Route 1, Box 286, Hollandale, MS 38748 | (601-839-2638) |

## MISSOURI

| | | | |
|---|---|---|---|
| **CLARENCE CANNON** (Under MARK TWAIN - See IL) | Ross Adams | Box 88, Annada, MO 63330 | (314-847-2333) |
| **MINGO** | Gerald L. Clawson | Route 1, Box 103, Puxico, MO 63960 | (314-222-3589) |
| **SQUAW CREEK** | Berlin A. Heck | Box 101, Mound City, MO 64470 | (816-442-3187) |

| | | | |
|---|---|---|---|
| SWAN LAKE | John Toll | Box 68, Sumner, MO 64681 | (816-856-3323) |

## MONTANA

| | | | |
|---|---|---|---|
| BENTON LAKE | Robert L. Pearson | Box 450, Black Eagle, MT 59414 | (406-727-7400) |
| BOWDOIN | Gene Sipe | Box J, Malta, MT 59538 | (406-654-2863) |
| BLACK COULEE    CREEDMAN COULEE    HEWITT LAKE    LAKE THIBADEAU | | | |
| CHARLES M. RUSSELL | Ralph F. Fries | Box 110, Lewistown, MT 59457 | (406-538-8706) |
| HAILSTONE    HALFBREED LAKE    MASON    NICHOLS COULEE    UL BEND    WAR HORSE | | | |
| FORT PECK WILDLIFE STATION | Vacant | Box 166, Fort Peck, MT 59223 | (406-526-3464) |
| JORDAN WILDLIFE STATION | David F. Bennett | Box 63, Jordan, MT 59337 | (406-557-6145) |
| SAND CREEK WILDLIFE STATION | Vacant | River Route, Roy, MT 59471 | (406-464-5181) |
| LEE METCALF | Robert C. Twist | Box 257, Stevensville, MT 59870 | (406-777-5552) |
| MEDICINE LAKE | Eugene Stroops | Medicine Lake, MT 59247 | (406-789-2305) |
| LAMESTEER | | | |
| NATIONAL BISON RANGE | John M. Malcolm | Moiese, MT 59824 | (406-644-2211) |
| NINE-PIPE    PABLO | | | |
| NORTHWEST MONTANA WMD | Raymond L. Washtak | 780 Creston Hatchery Road, Kalispell, MT 59901 | (406-755-7870) |
| SWAN RIVER | | | (406-755-9311) |
| RED ROCK LAKES | Barry Reiswig | Monida Star Route, Box 15, Lima, MT 59739 | (406-276-3347) |

## NEBRASKA

| | | | |
|---|---|---|---|
| CRESCENT LAKE | Kevin J. Brennan | HC 68, Box 21, Ellsworth, NE 69340 | (308-762-4893) |
| NORTH PLATTE | | | |
| DESOTO (see IA) | | | |
| FORT NIOBRARA/VALENTINE | Robert M. Ellis | Hidden Timber Route, Valentine, NE 69201 | (402-376-3789) |
| VALENTINE | Leonard L. McDaniel | | |
| RAINWATER BASIN WMD | Alan K. Trout | Box 1786, Kearney, NE 68847 | (308-236-5015) |
| WERTHEIM | Roger Spaulding | P.O. Box 21, Shirley, NY 11967 | (516-286-0485) |
| AMAGANSETT    CONSCIENCE POINT    LIDO BEACH    OYSTER BAY    SEATUCK    TARGET ROCK | | | |
| ELIZABETH A MORTON | John Phillips | RD Box 359, Noyac Road, Sag Harbor, NY 11963 | (516-725-2270) |

## NORTH CAROLINA

| | | | |
|---|---|---|---|
| ALLIGATOR RIVER | John T. Taylor | Manteo, NC 27954 | |
| CURRITUCK | | | |
| GREAT DISMAL SWAMP (see VA) | | | |
| MACKAY ISLAND (see VA) | | | |
| MATTAMUSKEET | Larry R. Ditto | Route 1, Box N-2, Swanquarter, NC 27885 | (919-926-4021) |
| CEDAR ISLAND    PUNGO    SWANQUARTER | | | |
| PEA ISLAND | Mervin A. Dunaway | Box 150, Rodanthe, NC 27968 | (919-987-2394) |
| PEE DEE | M. Bruce Blihovde | Box 780, Wadesboro, NC 28170 | (704-694-4424) |

## NORTH DAKOTA

| | | | |
|---|---|---|---|
| ARROWWOOD | John R. Foster | Rural Route 1, Pingree, ND 58476 | (701-285-3341) |
| CHASE LAKE    SLADE | | | |
| LONG LAKE | Michael McEnroe | Moffit, ND 58560 | (701-387-4397) |
| VALLEY CITY WMD | Lloyd A. Jones | Rural Route 1, Valley City, ND 58072 | (701-845-3466) |

| AUDUBON | Ronald D. Shupe | Rural Route 1, Coleharbor, ND 58531 | (701-442-5474) |
|---|---|---|---|
| DES LACS | Delano Pierce | Box 578, Kenmare, ND 58746 | (701-385-4046) |
| LAKE ZAHL | | | |
| CROSBY WMD | Thad L. Fuller | Box 148, Crosby, ND 58730 | (701-965-6488) |
| LAKE ILO | Richard Potter | Dunn Center, ND 58626 | (701-548-4467) |
| LOSTWOOD | Karen A. Smith | Rural Route 2, Kenmare, ND 58746 | (701-848-2722) |
| DEVILS LAKE WMD | David E. Janes | Box 908, Devils Lake, ND 58301 | (701-662-8611) |
| LAKE ALICE    SULLYS HILL NATIONAL GAME PRESERVE | | | |
| J. CLARK SALYER | Darrold Walls | Upham, ND 58789 | (701-768-2548) |
| KULM WMD | Larry West | Box E, Kulm, ND 58456 | (701-647-2866) |
| TEWAUKON | David G. Potter | Rural Route 1, Cayuga, ND 58013 | (701-724-3598) |
| UPPER SOURIS | Maurice B. Wright | Rural Route 1, Foxholm, ND 58738 | (701-468-5467) |

## OHIO

| OTTAWA | Michael Tansy | 14000 W. State Route 2, Oak Harbor, OH 43449 | (419-898-0014) |
|---|---|---|---|
| CEDAR POINT    WEST SISTER ISLAND | | | |

## OKLAHOMA

| SALT PLAINS | Ronald S. Sullivan | Route 1, Box 76, Jet, OK 73749 | (405-626-4794) |
|---|---|---|---|
| SEQUOYAH | John R. Akin | Route 1, Box 18A, Vian, OK 74962 | (918-773-5251) |
| TISHOMINGO | Larry M. Ivy | Route 1, Box 151, Tishomingo, OK 73460 | (405-371-2402) |
| WASHITA | Kenneth O. Butts | Route 1, Box 68, Butler, OK 73625 | (405-473-2205) |
| OPTIMA | | | |
| WICHITA MOUNTAINS WILDLIFE REFUGE | Robert A. Karges | Route 1, Box 448, Indiahoma, OK 73552 | (405-429-3221) |

## OREGON

**COLUMBIAN WHITE-TAILED DEER** (see WA)

**KLAMATH FOREST AND UPPER KLAMATH** (see CA)

**LEWIS AND CLARK** (see WA)

| MALHEUR | George Constantino | P.O. Box 113, Burns, OR 97720 | (503-493-2323) |
|---|---|---|---|
| SHELDON/HART MOUNTAIN COMPLEX | Marvin R. Kaschke | P.O. Box 111, Room 308, U.S. Post Office Building, Lakeview, OR 97630 | (503-947-3315) |
| SHELDON | Joseph Welch | (see above) | (503-947-3316) |
| HART MOUNTAIN | Rodney A. Blacker | (see above) | (503-947-3315) |
| UMATILLA | Laurence N. Dean | P.O. Box 239, Umatilla, OR 97882 | (503-922-3232) |
| COLD SPRINGS    MCKAY CREEK | | | |
| MCNARY | Lawrence Dudley | Box 308, Burbank, WA 99323 | (509-547-4942) |
| TOPPENIS | George J. Fenn | Route 1, Box 1300, Toppenish, WA 98948 | (509-865-2405) |
| WESTERN OREGON REFUGE COMPLEX | Palmer Sekora | Route 2, Box 208, Corvallis, OR 97333 | (503-757-7236) |
| WILLIAM L. FINLEY | Daniel L. Boone | Route 2, Box 208, Corvallis, OR 97333 | (503-757-7236) |
| CAPE MEARES    OREGON ISLANDS    THREE ARCH ROCKS | | | |
| ANKENY | Clifford L. Himmel | 2301 Wintel Road South, Jefferson, OR 97352 | (503-327-2444) |
| BASKETT SLOUGH | Ralph Lettenmaier | 10995 Highway 22, Dallas, OR 97338 | (503-623-2749) |

## PENNSYLVANIA

| ERIE | Thomas Mountain | RD 1, Wood Duck Lane, Guy Mills, PA 16327 | (814-789-3585) |
|---|---|---|---|

| TINICUM NATIONAL ENVIRONMENTAL CENTER | Richard F. Nugent | Suite 104, Scott Plaza 2, Philadelphia, PA 19113 | (215-521-0662) |
|---|---|---|---|
| KILLCOHOOK (NJ)   SUPAWNA MEADOWS (NJ) | | | |

## PUERTO RICO

| CARIBBEAN ISLANDS | Sean B. Furniss | Box 510, Carr. 301, KM 5.4, Boqueron, PR 00622 | (809-851-3637) |
|---|---|---|---|
| BUCK ISLAND (VIRGIN ISLANDS)   CABO ROJO   CULEBRA   DESECHEO   GREEN CAY (VIRGIN ISLANDS) | | | |

## RHODE ISLAND

| NINIGRET | Charles Blair | Box 307, Charlestown, RI 02813 | (401-364-3106) |
|---|---|---|---|
| BLOCK ISLAND   CONNECTICUT COASTAL (CT)   SACHUEST POINT   SALT MEADOW (CT)   TRUSTOM POND | | | |

## SOUTH CAROLINA

| CAPE ROMAIN | George R. Garris | 390 Bulls Island Rd., Awendaw, SC 29429 | (803-928-3368) |
|---|---|---|---|
| CAROLINA SANDHILLS | Ron Snyder | Route 2, Box 130, McBee, SC 29101 | (803-335-8401) |
| PINCKNEY ISLAND (see GA) | | | |
| SANTEE | Glenn W. Bond, Jr. | Route 2, Box 66, Summerton, SC 29148 | (803-478-2217) |

## SOUTH DAKOTA

| LACREEK | Rolf H. Kraft | Star Route 3, Box 14, Martin, SD 57551 | (605-685-6508) |
|---|---|---|---|
| LAKE ANDES | Harry T. Stone | RR #1, Box 77, Lake Andes, SD 57356 | (605-487-7603) |
| KARL E. MUNDT | | | |
| MADISON WMD | David L. Gilbert | Box 48, Madison, SD 57042 | (605-256-2974) |
| SAND LAKE | Sammy J. Waldstein | Rural Route 1, Columbia, SD 57433 | (605-885-6320) |
| POCASSE | | | |
| WAUBAY | John W. Koerner | Rural Route 1, Box 79, Waubay, SD 57273 | (605-947-4695) |

## TENNESSEE

| CROSS CREEKS | Vicki C. Grafe | Route 1, Box 229, Dover, TN 37058 | (615-232-7477) |
|---|---|---|---|
| HATCHIE | Marvin L. Nichols | Box 187, Brownsville, TN 38012 | (901-772-0501) |
| LOWER HATCHIE | | | |
| REELFOOT | Wendell E. Crews | Rt. 2, Hwy. 157, Union City, TN 38261 | (901-538-2481) |
| LAKE ISOM | | | |
| TENNESSEE | Carrell L. Ryan | Box 849, Paris, TN 38242 | (907-642-2091) |

## TEXAS

| ANAHUAC | Russel W. Clapper | Box 278, Anahuac, TX 77514 | (409-267-3337) |
|---|---|---|---|
| MCFADDIN/TEXAS POINT | Wayne J. King | Box 278, Anahuac, TX 77514 | (409-971-2909) |
| ARANSAS | E. Frank Johnson | Box 100, Austwell, TX 77950 | (512-286-3559) |
| MATAGORDA | | | |
| ATTWATER PRAIRIE CHICKEN | Tom Prusa | Box 518, Eagle Lake, TX 77434 | (409-234-3021) |
| BRAZORIA | Ronald G. Bisbee | Box 1088, Angleton, TX 77515 | (409-849-6062) |
| BIG BOGGY    MOODY | | | |
| SAN BERNARD | Dave Stanbrough | Box 1088 Angleton, TX 77515 | (409-964-3639) |
| HAGERMAN | James M. Williams | Route 3, Box 123, Sherman, TX 75090 | (214-786-2826) |

| LAGUNA ATASCOSA | Gary N. Burke | Box 450, Rio Hondo, TX 78583 | (512-748-3607) |
|---|---|---|---|
| MULESHOE | Rodney F. Krey | Box 549, Muleshoe, TX 79347 | (806-946-3341) |
|   GRULLA (NM) | | | |
|   BUFFALO LAKE | Johnny H. Beall | Box 228, Umbarger, TX 79091 | (806-499-3382) |
| SANTA ANA | Nita M. Fuller | Route 1, Box 202A, Alamo, TX 78516 | (512-787-3079) |
|   LOWER RIO GRANDE VALLEY | Robert W. Shumacher | Route 1, Box 202A, Alamo, TX 78516 | (512-787-3079) |

## UTAH

| BEAR RIVER MIGRATORY BIRD REFUGE | Peter Smith | Box 459, Brigham City, UT 84302 | (801-723-7707) |
|---|---|---|---|
| FISH SPRINGS | Charles Darling | P.O. Box 568, Dugway, UT 84022 | (801-522-5353) |
| OURAY | Keith S. Hansen | 447 East Main Street, Suite 4, Vernal, UT 84078 | (801-789-0351) |

## VERMONT

| MISSISQUOI | Robert A. Zelley | RFD 2, Swanton, VT 05488 | (802-868-4781) |
|---|---|---|---|

## VIRGINIA

| BACK BAY | Ralph M. Keel, Jr. | 287 Pembroke Office Park, Pembroke #2, Suite 218, Virginia Beach, VA 23462 | (804-490-0505) |
|---|---|---|---|
|   PLUM TREE ISLAND | | | |
| CAPE CHARLES | Sherman W. Stairs | RFD 1, Box 122B, Cape Charles, VA 23310 | (804-331-2760) |
|   FISHERMAN ISLAND | | | |
| CHINCOTEAGUE | Dennis Holland | Box 62, Chincoteague, VA 23336 | (804-336-6122) |
|   WALLOPS ISLAND | | | (804-336-5600) |
| GREAT DISMAL SWAMP | James Oland | 3216 Desert Road, P.O. Box 349, Suffolk, VA 23434 | (804-986-3705) |
|   NANSEMOND | | | |
| MACKAY ISLAND (NC) | William H. Hegge | P.O. Box 31, Knotts Island, NC 27950 | (919-429-3100) |
| MASON NECK | Thomas Stewart | 14416 Jefferson Davis Highway, Suite 20A, Woodbridge, VA 22191 | (703-690-1297) |
|   FEATHERSTONE   MARUMSCO | | | |
| PRESQUILE | Barry Brady | Box 620, Hopewell, VA 23860 | (804-458-7541) |

## WASHINGTON

| COLUMBIA | David E. Goeke | 44 S. 8th Avenue, P.O. Drawer F, Othello, WA 99344 | (509-488-2668) |
|---|---|---|---|
|   SADDLE MOUNTAIN | | | |
| LOWER COLUMBIA RIVER COMPLEX | John W. Kincheloe | 1309 NE 134th St., Room C, Vancouver, WA 98685 | (206-696-7796) |
|   PIERCE RANCH | | | |
|   CONBOY LAKE | Harold E. Cole, Jr. | P.O. Box 5, Glenwood, WA 98619 | (509-364-3410) |
|   RIDGEFIELD | Bruce Wiseman | P.O. Box 457, Ridgefield, WA 98642 | (206-887-3883) |
|   WILLAPA | James A. Hidy | Ilwaco, WA 98624 | (206-484-3482) |
|     COPALIS  FLATTERY ROCKS | QUILLAYUTE NEEDLES | WASHINGTON ISLANDS | |
|   COLUMBIAN WHITE-TAILED DEER | Gary A. Hagedorn | P.O. Box 566C, Cathlamet, WA 98612 | (206-795-3915) |
|     LEWIS AND CLARK (OR) | | | |

MCNARY (see OR)

TOPPENISH (see OR)

| NISQUALLY | Willard B. Hesselbart | 100 Brown Farm Road, Olympia, WA 98506 | (206-753-9467) |
|---|---|---|---|
|   SAN JUAN ISLANDS   PROTECTION ISLAND | | | |
|   DUNGENESS | Vernon K. Wray | 2109 Old Olympic Highway, Sequim, WA 98382 | (206-683-7040) |
| TURNBULL | Donald M. White | Route 3, Box 385, Cheney, WA 99004 | (509-235-4723) |

UMATILLA (see OR)

## WISCONSIN

| | | | |
|---|---|---|---|
| **HORICON**<br>    FOX RIVER    GRAVEL ISLAND    **GREEN BAY** | James Lennartson | Route 2, Mayville, WI 53050 | (414-387-2658) |
| **NECEDAH** | James M. Carroll, Jr. | Star Route West, Box 386, Necedah, WI 54646 | (608-565-2551) |
| **UPPER MISSISSIPPI RIVER NATIONAL WILDLIFE AND FISH REFUGE** (see MN) | | | |
|     LA CROSSE DISTRICT | Vacant | Room 208, P.O. Building, Box 415, La Crosse, WI 54601 | (608-783-6451) |
|     TREMPEALEAU | Robert L. Drieslein | Route 1, Trempealeau, WI 54661 | (608-539-2311) |
| **WISCONSIN WMD** | Eldon McLaury | 6006 Schroeder Road, Madison, WI 53711 | (608-264-5469) |

## WYOMING

| | | | |
|---|---|---|---|
| **BAMFORTH** (see CO) | | | |
| **HUTTON LAKE** (see CO) | | | |
| **NATIONAL ELK REFUGE** | John E. Wilbrecht | Box C, Jackson, WY 83001 | (307-733-9212) |
| **PATHFINDER** (see CO) | | | |
| **SEEDSKADEE** | Joe B. Rodriquez, Jr. | P.O. Box 67, Green River, WY 82935 | (307-875-2187) |

## REGIONAL OFFICES

| | | | |
|---|---|---|---|
| **REGION 1** | Richard J. Myshak,<br>*Regional Director* | Lloyd 500 Building, Suite 1692,<br>500 NE Multnomah Street, Portland, OR 97232 | (503-231-6118) |
| **REGION 2** | Michael J. Spear,<br>*Regional Director* | Box 1306, Albuquerque,<br>NM 87103 | (505-766-2321) |
| **REGION 3** | Harvey K. Nelson,<br>*Regional Director* | Federal Building, Fort Snelling,<br>Twin Cities, MN 55111 | (612-725-3563) |
| **REGION 4** | James W. Pulliam, Jr.,<br>*Regional Director* | Richard B. Russell Federal Bldg.,<br>75 Spring Street, SW, Atlanta, GA 30303 | (404-221-3588) |
| **REGION 5** | Howard N. Larsen,<br>*Regional Director* | One Gateway Center, Suite 700,<br>Newton Corner, MA 02158 | (617-965-5100) |
| **REGION 6** | Galen A. Buterbaugh,<br>*Regional Director* | 134 Union Blvd., Lakewood, CO<br>Box 25486, Denver Federal Center, Denver, CO 80225 | (303-236-7920) |
| **REGION 7** | Robert E. Gilmore,<br>*Regional Director* | 1011 E. Tudor Road,<br>Anchorage, AK 99503 | (907-786-3542) |

## WASHINGTON OFFICE

| | | | |
|---|---|---|---|
| **DIRECTOR** | Vacant | Interior Building, 18th & C Sts. NW,<br>Washington, DC 20240 | (202-343-4717) |
| **DEPUTY DIRECTOR** | F. Eugene Hester | (see above) | (202-343-4545) |
| **ASSOCIATE DIRECTOR,**<br>    Wildlife Resources | Ronald E. Lambertson | (see above) | (202-343-5333) |
| **DEPUTY ASSOCIATE DIRECTOR,**<br>    National Wildlife Refuge System | Walter O. Steglitz | (see above) | (202-343-5333 |
| **CHIEF, DIVISION OF REFUGE MANAGEMENT** | James F. Gillett | (see above) | (202-343-4311) |

# Land and Water Conservation Fund: Appropriations by Agency, 1981–1987

## FISCAL YEAR 1981

### National Park Service

| | |
|---|---:|
| Deficiences and Relocation | $ 2,500,000 |
| Inholdings | 1,000,000 |
| Preauthorization | 300,000 |
| Appalachian National Scenic Trail | 6,500,000 |
| Big Cypress National Preserve | 5,171,000 |
| Big Thicket National Preserve | 5,000,000 |
| Buffalo National River | 1,526,500 |
| C & O Canal National Historical Park | 500,000 |
| Cuyahoga Valley National Recreation Area | 5,000,000 |
| Delaware Water Gap National Recreation area | 1,000,000 |
| Fire Island National Seashore | 500,000 |
| Jean Lafitte | 1,500,000 |
| Redwood National Park | 5,000,000 |
| St. Croix National Scenic Riverway | 500,000 |
| Santa Monica Mountains | 15,908,500 |
| Voyageurs National Park | 2,000,000 |
| New Jersey Pinelands | 2,950,000 |
| Administration | 5,623,000 |
| **Total** | **62,479,000** |

## Fish and Wildlife Service

Endangered Species Act:

| | |
|---|---|
| American Crocodile | $ 2,400,000 |
| Blunt-nosed Leopard Lizard | 2,149,000 |
| Key Deer | 1,000,000 |
| Moapa Dace | 889,000 |
| Plymouth Red-bellied Turtle | 220,000 |

Specially Legislated Areas:

| | |
|---|---|
| Bogue Chitto | 6,400,000 |
| Bon Secour | 5,862,000 |
| Great Dismal Swamp | 1,000,000 |

Fish and Wildlife Act of 1956:

| | |
|---|---|
| Rio Grande Valley | 459,000 |
| **Subtotal** | **21,520,000** |
| Recissions (includes recissions of some funds in some areas above) | −12,217,000 |
| **Total** | **9,303,000** |

## Forest Service

| | |
|---|---|
| Endangered Species | 330,000 |
| Mount Roger National Recreation Area | 500,000 |
| Sawtooth National Recreation Area | 3,936,000 |
| Spruce Knob-Seneca Rocks National Recreation Area | 250,000 |
| Boundary Waters Wilderness | 3,000,000 |
| Other Wilderness | 500,000 |

Recreation Composites:

| | |
|---|---|
| Huron Manistee National Forest | 13,500,000 |
| Nantahala National Forest | 13,400,000 |
| Appalachian Trail | 2,000,000 |
| Slippage | −1,000,000 |
| **Total** | **39,416,000** |

## Bureau of Land Management

| | |
|---|---|
| Bizz Johnson (Susan River) Trail | 435,000 |
| Rogue River Wild and Scenic River | 567,000 |
| **Total** | **1,002,000** |

# FISCAL YEAR 1982

## National Park Service

| | |
|---|---|
| Administrative Expenses | 8,617,000 |
| Deficiences | 1,000,000 |
| Inholdings | 1,000,000 |
| Allegheny Portage RR National Historic Site and Johnstown Flood National Monument | 500,000 |
| Appalachian National Scenic Trail | 2,800,000 |

| | |
|---|---:|
| Big Cypress National Preserve | $19,650,000 |
| Big Thicket National Preserve | 4,500,000 |
| Biscayne National Park | 2,000,000 |
| Buffalo National River | 2,200,000 |
| Cape Cod National River | 5,500,000 |
| Channel Islands National Park | 4,000,000 |
| Chattachoochee River National Recreation Area | 14,500,000 |
| Cumberland Island National Seashore | 11,000,000 |
| Cuyahoga Valley National Recreation Area | 5,000,000 |
| Delaware Water Gap National Recreation Area | 1,000,000 |
| Ebey's Landing National Historic River (?) | 2,100,000 |
| Fort Sumter National Monument | 383,000 |
| Golden Gate National Recreation Area | 10,000,000 |
| Indiana Dunes National Lakeshore | 2,400,000 |
| Jean Lafitte National Historic Park | 2,500,000 |
| Lassen Volcanic National Park | 5,500,000 |
| Lower St. Croix National Scenic River | 1,000,000 |
| New River Gorge National River | 2,000,000 |
| Redwood National Park—litigation support | 3,000,000 |
| St. Croix National Scenic River | 500,000 |
| San Antonion Missions National Historic Park | 1,400,000 |
| Santa Monica Mountains National Recreation Area | 5,000,000 |
| Upper Delaware Wild and Scenic River | 600,000 |
| Valley Forge National Historic Park | 4,000,000 |
| Virgin Islands National Park | 3,550,000 |
| New Jersey Pinelands | 5,881,000 |
| **Total** | **129,081,000** |

## Fish and Wildlife Service

| | |
|---|---:|
| Recreation Use Act of 1962: | |
|   Trustom Pond | 423,000 |
| Endangered Species Act: | |
|   California Condor | 1,151,000 |
|   Yaqui Tominnow | 816,000 |
| Specially Legislated Areas: | |
|   Bogue Chitto | 1,920,000 |
|   San Francisco Bay | 960,000 |
|   Bon Secour | 3,360,000 |
|   Tensas | 4,800,000 |
|   Alaska Maritime | 1,920,000 |
| Acquisition Management | 997,000 |
| Deficiences and Emergencies | 144,000 |
| **Total** | **16,491,000** |

## Forest Service

| | |
|---|---:|
| Appalachian Trail | 2,112,000 |
| Boundary Waters Wilderness | 2,371,000 |
| Lake Tahoe Basin | 6,700,000 |
| California condor habitat | 312,000 |
| Kirtland warbler habitat | 77,000 |

Wildlife Habitat Management:
  Allegheny National Forest    $    84,000
  Nicolet National Forest    196,000
Sawtooth National Recreation Area    3,830,000
Spruce Knob-Seneca Rocks National Recreation Area    1,248,000
Other high priority recreation areas    480,000
Middle Fork Salmon Wild and Scenic River    288,000
Eleven Point Wild and Scenic River    1,440,000
Other high priority wild and scenic river    480,000
Recreation Composites:
  Daniel Boone National Forest    288,000
  Nicolet National Forest    488,000
  Other high priority areas    1,507,000
Deficiences and Inholdings    441,000

**Total**    **22,334,000**

## Bureau of Land Management

King Range National Conservation Area    672,000
Pacific Crest Trail    125,000
Yaquina Head Outstanding Natural Area    2,620,000
Acquisition Management    295,000

**Total**    **3,712,000**

# FISCAL YEAR 1983

## National Park Service

Appalachian National Scenic Trail    10,000,000
Big Cypress National Park    500,000
Biscayne Bay National Park    4,000,000
Buffalo River    2,000,000
Cape Lookout National Seashore    2,000,000
Cuyahoga Valley National Recreation Area    6,000,000
Delaware Water Gap National Recreation Area    1,000,000
Golden Gate National Recreation Area    2,200,000
Great Smoky Mountains National Park    1,500,000
Gulf Islands    3,700,000
Indiana Dunes National Lakeshore    1,400,000
James A. Garfield National Historic Site    205,000
Jean Lafitte National Historic Park    2,500,000
Martin Luther King, Jr., National Historic Site    500,000
Olympic National Park    9,700,000
Voyageurs National Park    7,500,000
New Jersey Pinelands    5,000,000

**Total**    **67,505,000**

## Fish and Wildlife Service

| | |
|---|---:|
| Recreational Use Act of 1962: | |
|   Wertheim | $ 1,377,000 |
| Endangered Species Act: | |
|   American Crocodile | 2,766,000 |
|   Kirtland's Warbler | 500,000 |
|   Plymouth Red-bellied Turtle | 275,000 |
|   Manatee | 500,000 |
|   Bear Valley | 812,000 |
| Specially Legislated Areas: | |
|   Tensas | 5,200,000 |
|   Bogue Chitto | 1,000,000 |
|   Bon Secour | 3,500,000 |
|   Bandon Marsh | 270,000 |
|   Protection Island | 2,000,000 |
|   Alaska Maritime | 5,500,000 |
| Fish and Wildlife Act of 1956: | |
|   Rio Grande Valley | 1,000,000 |
|   Lower Suwannee | 1,500,000 |
|   Acquistion Management | 1,000,000 |
| **Total** | **27,200,000** |

## Forest Service

| | |
|---|---:|
| Deficiences | 722,000 |
| Inholdings and Composites | 1,742,000 |
| Appalachian Trail | 1,360,000 |
| Boundary Waters Wilderness | 3,000,000 |
| Cascade Head | 707,000 |
| Alpine Lakes | 26,464,000 |
| Lake Tahoe | 10,000,000 |
| Mt. Rogers National Recreation Area | 200,000 |
| Ausable River Huron-Manistee National Forest | 2,000,000 |
| Three Sisters Wilderness | 2,000,000 |
| Sawtooth National Recreation Area | 8,700,000 |
| Cranberry Wilderness | 2,200,000 |
| **Total** | **59,077,000** |

## Bureau of Land Management

| | |
|---|---:|
| Bogue River Wild Scenic River | 161,000 |
| Acquisition Management | 150,000 |
| **Total** | **311,000** |

# FISCAL YEAR 1984

## National Park Service

| | |
|---|---:|
| Appalachian National Scenic Trail | 15,500,000 |
| Big Cypress National Preserve | 7,000,000 |
| Buffalo National River | 1,000,000 |
| Cape Lookout National Seashore | 4,000,000 |
| Chaco Culture National Historic Park | 500,000 |

| | |
|---|---:|
| Chatahoochee River National Recreation Area | $ 1,000,000 |
| Congaree Swamp National Monument | 25,000,000 |
| Coronado National Monument | 1,000,000 |
| Cuyahoga Valley National Recreation Area | 2,500,000 |
| Franklin D. Roosevelt National Historic Site | 400,000 |
| Golden Gate National Recreation Area | 2,200,000 |
| Indiana Dunes National Lakeshore | 1,500,000 |
| Jean Lafitte National Historic Park | 3,000,000 |
| Lower St. Crois Wild and Scenic River | 1,500,000 |
| Manassas National Historic Park | 3,000,000 |
| Monocacy National Battlefield | 3,000,000 |
| New River Gorge National River | 1,000,000 |
| Obed Wild and Scenic River | 1,000,000 |
| Olympic National Park | 2,000,000 |
| Point Reyes National Seashore | 1,000,000 |
| Redwood National Park | 2,000,000 |
| San Antonio Missions National Historic Site | 1,000,000 |
| Santa Monica Mountains National Recreation Area | 15,000,000 |
| Saratoga National Historic Park | 500,000 |
| Sleeping Bear Dunes National Lakeshore | 12,000,000 |
| Upper Delaware National Scenic River | 600,000 |
| Upper St. Croix Wild and Scenic River | 500,000 |
| Voyageurs National Park | 4,000,000 |
| Women's Rights National Historic Park | 500,000 |
| Deficiences | 1,500,000 |
| New Jersey Pinelands | 6,150,000 |
| Administration | 7,800,000 |
| **Total** | **128,650,000** |

## Fish and Wildlife Service:

| | |
|---|---:|
| Endangered Species Act: | |
| Masked Bobwhite Quail | 5,000,000 |
| California Condor | 5,000,000 |
| American Crocodile | 5,000,000 |
| National Key Deer | 2,000,000 |
| Hawaiian Forest Birds | 4,500,000 |
| Kirtland's Warbler | 1,000,000 |
| Mississippi Sandhill Crane | 2,000,000 |
| Bear Valley | 400,000 |
| Leatherback Sea Turtle | 2,500,000 |
| Specially Legislated Areas: | |
| Bon Secour | 2,500,000 |
| Bogue Chitto | 1,000,000 |
| Minnesota Valley | 1,000,000 |
| Great Dismal Swamp | 2,500,000 |
| Protection Island | 2,000,000 |
| Fish and Wildlife Act of 1956: | |
| Lower Suwannee | 2,000,000 |
| Rio Grande Valley | 1,500,000 |

| | |
|---|---:|
| Acquisition Management | $  1,500,000 |
| Transfer to BLM | −6,000,000 |
| **Total** | **46,297,000** |

## Forest Service

| | |
|---|---:|
| Boundary Waters Wilderness | 3,000,000 |
| Cascade Head | 800,000 |
| Eleven Point Wild and Scenic River | 600,000 |
| Flathead Wild And Scenic River | 600,000 |
| Kirtland's Warbler | 800,000 |
| Lake Tahoe | 19,500,000 |
| Rogue Wild and Scenic River | 1,000,000 |
| Sawtooth National Recreation Area | 2,500,000 |
| Spruce Knob-Seneca Rocks | 800,000 |
| Walkinshaw Wetlands | 352,000 |
| High-priority Recreation Composites | 2,000,000 |
| California Condor habitat | 800,000 |
| Daniel Boon National Forest, Red River Gorge | 600,000 |
| Nonongahela National Forest | 1,200,000 |
| Columbia River Gorge | 1,500,000 |
| **Total** | **36,052,000** |

## Bureau of Land Management

| | |
|---|---:|
| Bizz Johnson (Susan River) Trail | 100,000 |
| Perins Peak Habitat Management Area | 426,000 |
| Rio Grande River | 300,000 |
| Pacific Crest Trail | 100,000 |
| Rogue River Wild and Scenic River | 335,000 |
| Acquisition Management | 130,000 |
| **Total** | **1,391,000** |

# FISCAL YEAR 1985

## National Park Service

| | |
|---|---:|
| Alaska areas | 490,000 |
| Antietem National Battlefield | 490,000 |
| Big Cypress National Preserve | 1,960,000 |
| Biscayne National Park | 980,000 |
| Chaco Culture National Historic Park | 980,000 |
| Channel Islands National Park | 20,700,000 |
| Chattachoochee River National Recreation Area | 4,980,000 |
| C & O Canal | 490,000 |
| Cuyahoga River National Recreation Area | 1,960,000 |
| Delaware Water Gap National Recreation Area | 1,764,000 |

| | |
|---|---:|
| Fort Frederica | $ 294,000 |
| Franklin D. Roosevelt National Historic Site | 265,000 |
| Golden Gate National Recreation Area | 980,000 |
| Gunnison National Monument | 1,274,000 |
| Indiana Dunes National Lakeshore | 1,348,000 |
| Jean Lafitte National Lakeshore | 3,000,000 |
| Lower St. Crois | 490,000 |
| Manasses National Battlefield Park | 2,940,000 |
| Martin Luther King, Jr., National Historic Site | 490,000 |
| Monocacy National Battlefield | 1,470,000 |
| New River Gorge National River | 3,920,000 |
| Obed Wild and Scenic River | 490,000 |
| Petersburg | 1,519,000 |
| Point Reyes National Seashore | 2,450,000 |
| Rocky Mountain National Park | 980,000 |
| Santa Monica Mountains National Recreation Area | 8,001,000 |
| Saratoga National Historic Park | 196,000 |
| St. Croix Wild and Scenic River | 980,000 |
| Salinas | 490,000 |
| Theodore Roosevelt National Historic Site | 245,000 |
| Valley Forge | 1,470,000 |
| Voyageurs National Park | 980,000 |
| War in the Pacific | 1,176,000 |
| Deficiences and relocation | 1,715,000 |
| Inholdings | 4,900,000 |
| Administration | 6,885,000 |
| **Total** | **95,682,000** |

## Fish and Wildlife Service

| | |
|---|---:|
| Recreational Use Act of 1962: | |
|   Karl Mundt | 294,000 |
|   Kofa | 343,000 |
|   Parker River | 392,000 |
|   Trustom Pond | 637,000 |
| Endangered Species Act: | |
|   Ash Meadow | 588,000 |
|   Masked Bobwhite Quail | 3,920,000 |
|   California Condor | 3,920,000 |
|   American Crocodile | 4,900,000 |
|   National Key Deer | 2,450,000 |
|   Hawaiian Forest Birds | 4,410,000 |
|   Kirtland's Warbler | 935,000 |
|   Bear Valley | 784,000 |
|   Clear Creek Gambusia | 20,000 |
|   Coachella Valley | 4,900,000 |
|   Florida Panther | 3,920,000 |
|   Moapa Dace | 784,000 |
|   Ozark Big-eared Bat | 98,000 |
|   Parhrummp Killifish | 176,000 |
| Specially Legislated: | |
|   Bon Secour | 2,940,000 |
|   Bogue Chitto | 1,940,000 |

| | |
|---|---|
| Connecticut Coastal | $ 1,470,000 |
| Great Dismal Swamp | 1,470,000 |
| Fish and Wildlife Act of 1956: | |
| Lower Suwannee | 3,381,000 |
| Rio Grande Valley | 7,350,000 |
| Banks Lake | 596,000 |
| Cartegena/Torteguero | 4,900,000 |
| Currituck | 3,430,000 |
| Acquisition Management | 1,470,000 |
| **Total** | **63,218,000** |

## Forest Service

| | |
|---|---|
| Flathead Wild and Scenic River | 981,000 |
| White River National Forest | 981,000 |
| Santa Fe National Forest | 981,000 |
| Salmon Wild and Scenic River | 1,469,000 |
| Sawtooth National Recreation Area | 3,920,000 |
| Toiyabe National Forest | 3,920,000 |
| Lake Tahoe Basin | 16,802,000 |
| Endangered Species habitat, CA | 1,570,000 |
| Cascade Head | 759,000 |
| Mt. St. Helens National Volcanic Monument | 350,000 |
| Nantahala National Forest | 1,225,000 |
| Pisgah National Forest | 366,000 |
| Allegheny National Forest | 1,962,000 |
| Green Mountain National Forest | 3,331,000 |
| Monongahela National Forest | 440,000 |
| Spruce Knob-Seneca Rocks National Recreation Area | 981,000 |
| Wayne National Forest | 1,177,000 |
| White Mountain National Forest | 3,920,000 |
| Appalachian Trail | 981,000 |
| Cash Equalization | 1,038,000 |
| **Total** | **47,109,000** |

## Bureau of Land Management

| | |
|---|---|
| King range National Conservation Area | 980,000 |
| Rio Grande Wild and Scenic River | 147,000 |
| Upper Missouri Wild and Scenic River | 294,000 |
| Upper Sacramento River | 980,000 |
| Acquisition Management | 294,000 |
| **Total** | **2,695,000** |

## National Park Service

| | |
|---|---|
| Emergencies, hardships, deficiencies, and relocation | 2,378,000 |
| Inholdings | 2,854,000 |
| Appalachian Trail | 6,659,000 |
| Big Cypress National Preserve | 1,903,000 |

| | |
|---|---:|
| Big Thicket National Preserve | $ 1,903,000 |
| Cuyahoga Valley National Recreation Area | 4,281,000 |
| Delaware Water Gap National Recreation Area | 3,329,000 |
| Golden Gate National Recreation Area | 1,903,000 |
| Lake Clark National Park and Preserve | 1,427,000 |
| New River Gorge National River | 285,000 |
| North Cascades National Park | 951,000 |
| Olympic National Park | 951,000 |
| Point Reyes National Seashore | 951,000 |
| Salinas National Monument | 571,000 |
| San Antonio Missions National Historic Park | 1,903,000 |
| Santa Monica Mountains National Recreation Area | 7,610,000 |
| Sleeping Bear Dunes National Lakeshore | 1,427,000 |
| Administration | 4,756,000 |
| **Total** | **45,993,000** |

## Fish and Wildlife Service

| | |
|---|---:|
| Endangered Species Act: | |
| Coachella Valley | 4,970,000 |
| Crocodile Lake | 1,491,000 |
| Fakahatchee Strand | 2,982,000 |
| National Key Deer | 1,988,000 |
| Upper Nakalau Forest | 5,964,000 |
| Specifically Legislated: | |
| Bon Secour | 994,000 |
| Connecticut Coastal | 1,024,000 |
| Minnesota Valley | 1,988,000 |
| Fish and Wildlife Act of 1956: | |
| Lower River Grande | 4,970,000 |
| Lower Suwannee | 2,485,000 |
| Steigerwald Lake | 596,000 |
| Recreational Use Act of 1962: | |
| Cape Charles | 2,624,000 |
| Great Swamp | 994,000 |
| National Elk | 1,392,000 |
| Willapa | 3,380,000 |
| Inholdings | 994,000 |
| Acquisition Management | 1,590,000 |
| **Total** | **40,426,000** |

## Forest Service

| | |
|---|---:|
| Appalachian Trail | 665,700 |
| Columbia Gorge | 1,141,200 |
| Green Mountain National Forest | 6,371,700 |
| Huron National Forest | 760,800 |
| Lake Tahoe | 2,853,000 |
| Nantahala National Forest | 951,000 |
| Sawtooth National Recreation Area | 1,902,000 |
| Wayne National Forest | 1,902,000 |

| | |
|---|---:|
| Wilderness Inholdings | $ 2,377,500 |
| Endangered Species Habitat | 951,000 |
| Edwards Investment | 3,708,000 |
| Acquisition Management | 100 |
| **Total** | **23,584,900** |

## Bureau of Land Management

| | |
|---|---:|
| King Range National Conservation Area | 475,000 |
| Steens Mountain National Recreation Area | 999,000 |
| Wilderness Inholdings | 475,000 |
| Acquisition Management | 289,000 |
| **Total** | **2,188,000** |

## FISCAL YEAR 1987*

### National Park Service

| | |
|---|---:|
| Acquisition Management | 5,000,000 |
| Hardships, inholdings and emergencies | 5,000,000 |
| Acadia National Park | 3,500,000 |
| Apostle Islands National Lakeshore | 300,000 |
| Appalachian Trail | 7,000,000 |
| Big Cypress National Preserve | 2,000,000 |
| Big Thicket National Preserve | 4,000,000 |
| Cuyahoga Valley National Recreation Area | 4,500,000 |
| Delaware Water Gap National Recreation Area | 2,000,000 |
| Gates of the Arctic National Park | 175,000 |
| Golden Gate National Recreation Area | 2,000,000 |
| Haleakala National Park | 1,000,000 |
| Indiana Dunes National Lakeshore | 1,000,000 |
| Lake Clark National Park and Preserve | 1,675,000 |
| Lowell National Historic Park | 800,000 |
| Mound City Group | 1,000,000 |
| New River Gorge National River | 1,000,000 |
| North Cascades National Park | 6,500,000 |
| Olympic National Park | 2,000,000 |
| San Antonio Mission National Historic Park | 500,000 |
| Santa Monica Mountains National Recreation Area | 6,000,000 |
| Sequoia-Kings Canyon National Park | 1,100,000 |
| Wind Cave National Park | 200,000 |
| **Total** | **52,250,000** |

### Fish and Wildlife Service

| | |
|---|---:|
| Inholdings | 1,000,000 |
| Acquisition management | 1,750,000 |

* As of November 1, 1986. Does not include supplementals or recissions.

| | |
|---|---:|
| Alligator River | $ 650,000 |
| Aransas | 3,000,000 |
| Ash Meadows | 500,000 |
| Bayou Savage | 3,000,000 |
| Bogue Chitto | 1,000,000 |
| Bon Secour | 500,000 |
| Connecticut Coastal | 600,000 |
| Eastern Shore | 375,000 |
| Finnegan Cut | 1,100,000 |
| Florida Panther | 3,000,000 |
| Great Dismal Swamp | 750,000 |
| Hakalau Forest | 3,000,000 |
| Kirtlands Warbler | 300,000 |
| Lower Rio Grande | 6,000,000 |
| Lower Suwannee | 1,500,000 |
| Minnesota Valley | 1,500,000 |
| National Key Deer | 2,000,000 |
| Rachel Carson | 900,000 |
| Red Rocks Lake | 2,000,000 |
| Sacramento | 2,200,000 |
| San Francisco Bay | 1,500,000 |
| Tensas River | 1,000,000 |
| Willapa | 3,300,000 |
| **Total** | **42,425,000** |

## Forest Service

| | |
|---|---:|
| Acquisition management | 3,206,000 |
| Appalachian Trail | 1,500,000 |
| AuSable-Manistee Rivers | 6,000,000 |
| Columbia River Gorge | 4,650,000 |
| Jefferson National Forest | 280,000 |
| Lake Tahoe | 7,000,000 |
| Mono Lake-Inyo National Forest | 400,000 |
| Mount Rogers National Recreation Area | 1,000,000 |
| Ottawa National Forest | 3,000,000 |
| Pisgah National Forest | 900,000 |
| Wasatch National Forest/Little Cottonwood Canyon | 2,500,000 |
| Wayne National Forest | 2,000,000 |
| Endangered Species Habitat | 2,000,000 |
| Inholdings and recreation composites | 5,000,000 |
| **Total** | **52,236,000** |

## Bureau of Land Management

| | |
|---|---:|
| Acquisition Management | 300,000 |
| El Malpais Natural Area | 250,000 |
| Gila Lower Box Area of Critical Concern | 250,000 |
| King Range Conservation Area | 1,000,000 |
| Owyhee National Wild River | 700,000 |
| Red Rock Recreation Area | 3,000,000 |

| | |
|---|---:|
| Steens Mountain Recreation Area | $   225,000 |
| Upper Missouri Wild and Scenic River | 500,000 |
| Inholdings, including designated wilderness areas | 500,000 |
| **Subtotal** | **6,525,000** |
| Recission: cash equalization for Navajo- Hopi land exchanges | −3,200,000 |
| Portion funded from unobligated balances from the Rogue Wild and Scenic River | −305,000 |
| **Total** | **3,020,000** |

# APPENDIX L

# The National Forest Plan Status Report and Appeals

## (Current as of January 1987)

Source: The Wilderness Society

## PART 1. THE NATIONAL FOREST PLAN STATUS REPORT

| Forest Service Regions | Draft Plan Issued | Final Plan Issued, or Date Due | Adm. Appeal |
|---|---|---|---|
| **Region 1. Northern** | | | |
| Beaverhead | Yes | Yes | Yes |
| Bitterroot | Yes | No − 2/87 | — |
| Clearwater | Yes | No − 6/87 | — |
| Custer | Yes | No − 1/87 | — |
| Deerlodge | Yes | No − 2/87 | — |
| Flathead | Yes | Yes | Yes |
| Gallatin | Yes | No − 2/87 | — |
| Helena | Yes | Yes | Yes |
| Idaho Panhandle | Yes | No − 5/87 | — |
| Kootenai | Yes | No − 2/87 | — |
| Lewis and Clark | Yes | Yes | Yes |
| Lolo | Yes | Yes | Yes |
| Nezperce | Yes | No − 5/87 | — |
| Subtotal | 13 | 5 | 5 |

| Forest Service Regions | Draft Plan Issued | Final Plan Issued, or Date Due | Adm. Appeal |
|---|---|---|---|

### Region 2. Rocky Mountains

| | | | |
|---|---|---|---|
| Arapaho-Roosevelt | Yes | Yes | Yes |
| Bighorn | Yes | Yes | Yes |
| Black Hills | Yes | Yes | Yes |
| GMUG | Yes | Yes | Yes |
| Medicine Bow | Yes | Yes | Yes |
| Nebraska | Yes | Yes | Yes |
| Pike-San Isabel | Yes | Yes | Yes |
| Rio Grande | Yes | Yes | Yes |
| Routt | Yes | Yes | Yes |
| San Juan | Yes | Yes | Yes |
| Shoshone | Yes | Yes | Yes |
| White River | Yes | Yes | Yes |
| Subtotal | 12 | 12 | 12 |

### Region 3. Southwestern

| | | | |
|---|---|---|---|
| Apache–Sitgreaves | Yes | No–3/87 | — |
| Carson | Yes | Yes | Yes |
| Cibola | Yes | Yes | Yes |
| Coconino | Yes | No–1/87 | — |
| Coronado | Yes | Yes | Yes |
| Gila | Yes | Yes | — |
| Kaibab | Yes | No–7/87 | — |
| Lincoln | Yes | Yes | Yes |
| Prescott | Yes | No–2/87 | — |
| Santa Fe | Yes | No–4/87 | — |
| Tonto | Yes | Yes | Yes |
| Subtotal | 11 | 6 | 5 |

### Region 4. Intermountain

| | | | |
|---|---|---|---|
| Ashley | Yes | Yes | Yes |
| Boise | No | No–3/88 | — |
| Bridger-Teton | Yes | No–11/87 | — |
| Caribou | Yes | Yes | Yes |
| Challis | Yes | No–3/87 | — |
| Dixie | Yes | Yes | Yes |
| Fishlake | Yes | Yes | Yes |
| Humboldt | Yes | Yes | Yes |
| Manti-LaSal | Yes | Yes | Yes |
| Payette | Yes | No–3/87 | — |
| Salmon | Yes | No–3/87 | — |
| Sawtooth | Yes | No–3/87 | — |
| Targhee | Yes | Yes | Yes |
| Toiyabe | Yes | Yes | Yes |
| Uinta | Yes | Yes | — |
| Wasatch-Cache | Yes | Yes | — |
| Subtotal | 15 | 10 | 8 |

| Forest Service Regions | Draft Plan Issued | Final Plan Issued, or Date Due | Adm. Appeal |
|---|---|---|---|
| **Region 5. Pacific Southwest** | | | |
| Angeles | Yes | No−4/87 | − |
| Cleveland | Yes | Yes | Yes |
| Eldorado | Yes | No−8/87 | − |
| Inyo | Yes | No−10/87 | − |
| Klamath | No | No−10/88 | − |
| Lake Tahoe Basin | Yes | No−6/87 | − |
| Lassen | Yes | No−6/87 | − |
| Los Padres | Yes | No−6/87 | − |
| Mendocino | Yes | No−9/87 | − |
| Modoc | No | No−1/88 | − |
| Plumas | Yes | No−6/87 | − |
| San Bernardino | Yes | No−6/87 | − |
| Sequoia | Yes | No−6/87 | − |
| Shasta-Trinity | Yes | No−9/87 | − |
| Sierra | Yes | No−9/87 | − |
| Six Rivers | No | No−10/87 | − |
| Stanislaus | Yes | No−6/87 | − |
| Tahoe | Yes | No−1/88 | − |
| Subtotal | 15 | 1 | 1 |
| **Region 6. Pacific Northwest** | | | |
| Colville | No | No−3/88 | − |
| Deschutes | Yes | No−4/87 | − |
| Fremont | No | No−3/88 | − |
| Gifford Pinchot | No | No−3/88 | − |
| Malheur | No | No−3/88 | − |
| Mt. Baker-Snoqualmie | No | No−3/88 | − |
| Mt. Hood | No | No−9/87 | − |
| Ochoco | No | No−8/87 | − |
| Okanogan | Yes | No−3/87 | − |
| Olympic | Yes | No−2/88 | − |
| Rogue River | No | No−3/88 | − |
| Siskiyou | No | No−2/88 | − |
| Siuslaw | Yes | No−3/88 | − |
| Umatilla | No | No−3/88 | − |
| Umpqua | No | No−3/88 | − |
| Wallowa-Whitman | Yes | No−4/87 | − |
| Wenatchee | Yes | No−5/87 | − |
| Willamette | No | No−3/88 | − |
| Winema | No | No−3/88 | − |
| Subtotal | 7 | 0 | 0 |

| Forest Service Regions | Draft Plan Issued | Final Plan Issued, or Date Due | Adm. Appeal |
|---|---|---|---|
| **Region 8. Southern** | | | |
| Alabama | Yes | Yes | Yes |
| Caribbean | Yes | Yes | Yes |
| Chattahoochee-Oconee | Yes | Yes | Yes |
| Cherokee | Yes | Yes | Yes |
| Croatan-Uwharrie | Yes | Yes | Yes |
| Daniel Boone | Yes | Yes | Yes |
| Florida | Yes | Yes | — |
| Francis Marion | Yes | Yes | Yes |
| George Washington | Yes | Yes | Yes |
| Jefferson | Yes | Yes | Yes |
| Kisatchie | Yes | Yes | Yes |
| Mississippi | Yes | Yes | Yes |
| Nantahala-Pisgah | Yes | No — 2/87 | — |
| Ouachita | Yes | Yes | Yes |
| Ozark-St. Francis | Yes | Yes | Yes |
| Sumter | Yes | Yes | Yes |
| Texas | Yes | No — 2/87 | — |
| Subtotal | 15 | 13 | 13 |
| **Region 9. Eastern** | | | |
| Allegheny | Yes | Yes | Yes |
| Chequamegon | Yes | Yes | Yes |
| Chippewa | Yes | Yes | Yes |
| Green Mountain | Yes | Yes | Yes |
| Hiawatha | Yes | No — 1/87 | Yes |
| Hoosier | Yes | Yes | — |
| Huron-Manistee | Yes | Yes | Yes |
| Mark Twain | Yes | Yes | Yes |
| Monongahela | Yes | Yes | Yes |
| Nicolet | Yes | Yes | Yes |
| Ottawa | Yes | Yes | Yes |
| Shawnee | Yes | Yes | Yes |
| Superior | Yes | Yes | Yes |
| Wayne | Yes | Yes | — |
| White Mountain | Yes | Yes | Yes |
| Subtotal | 15 | 13 | 13 |
| **Region 10. Alaska** | | | |
| Chugach | Yes | Yes | Yes |
| Tongass | No | No — /79 | — |
| Subtotal | 1 | 1 | 1 |
| **Total** | **106** | **63** | **59** |

## PART 2. APPEALS ON NATIONAL FOREST PLANS

### Region 1. Northern

| Forest | Lead Conservation Appellant | Issues Raised in Appeal | Co-Appellants | Other Appeal(s) on Conservation Grounds | Opposing Appeal(s) |
|--------|------------------------------|--------------------------|----------------|------------------------------------------|---------------------|
| Beaverhead | National Wildlife Federation; Contact(s): Tom France, N. Rockies Natural Resource Center, 240 N. Higgins, Missoula, MT 59801 (406) 721-6705; Peter Coppelman, The Wilderness Society, 1400 Eye St., NW, Washington, DC 20005, (202) 842-3400 | • Roadless Area Management (Wilderness Recommendations, RAREII study)<br>• Road Construction<br>• Watershed Protection (Riparian)<br>• Fisheries<br>• Oil and Gas Leasing<br>• Economic Suitability (Below-cost Timber Sales)<br>• Wildlife | Sierra Club; Beaverhead Forest Concerned Citizens; Skyline, Anaconda, Jefferson Valley Sportsmen; MT Wilderness Assn.; and others. | Group of West Big Hole Ranchers | Inland Forest Resource Council; Montana Mining Assn. |
| Flathead | Resources Unlimited Contact: Rosalind Yanishevsky, Whale Buttes Rd., Palebridge, MT (406) 752-2620. | • Old Growth<br>• Watershed Protection (Riparian)<br>• Wildlife<br>• Fisheries<br>• Economic Suitability (Below-cost Timber Sales)<br>• Recreation | Five Valleys Audubon Society—There are 37 Conservationist appeals and two opposing appeals by industry of the final plan for the Flathead. | | |

| | | | | |
|---|---|---|---|---|
| Helena | Helena Forest Coalition Contacts: Ken Knudson, 8 South Benton, Helena, MT 59601 (406) 442-2617; John Gatchell, Montana Wilderness Assn., Box 635, Helena, MT 59624 (406) 443-7350 | • Wildlife<br>• Roadless Area Management (Wilderness Recommendation, RAREII Study)<br>• Road Construction<br>• Clearcutting<br>• Oil and Gas Leasing<br>• Off-Road Vehicles<br>• Timber Harvest Levels | Montana Wilderness Assn. | |
| Lewis and Clark | Montana Wilderness Assn. Contacts: John Gatchell, Box 635, Helena, MT 59624 (406) 4437350 | • Oil and Gas Leasing<br>• Wildlife<br>• Roadless Area Management (Wilderness Recommendations, RAREII study)<br>• Watershed Protection (Riparian)<br>• Economic Suitability (Below-cost Timber Sales)<br>• Physically Unsuitable Timber Lands | Sierra Club, The Wilderness Society, Resources Limited, Billings Rod and Gun Club, Southeastern Montana Sportsmen's Assn., *et al.* | John Swanson, Montana Wildlands Coalition, A Group to Preserve Indian Rights, American Rivers Conservation Council. | City of Judith Gap, Intermountain Forest Industry Assn., Western Environmental Trades Assn. |

| Forest | Lead Conservation Appellant | Issues Raised in Appeal | Co-Appellants | Other Appeal(s) on Conservation Grounds | Opposing Appeal(s) |
|---|---|---|---|---|---|
| Lolo | Montana Wilderness Assn. Contact: John Gatchell, Box 635, Helena, MT 59624 (406) 443-7350 | • Wildlife<br>• Roadless Area Management (Wilderness Recommendations, RAREII Study)<br>• Economic Suitability (Below-cost Timber Sales)<br>• Fisheries<br>• Watershed Protection (Riparian) | | | |

### Region 2. Rocky Mountains

| Forest | Lead Conservation Appellant | Issues Raised in Appeal | Co-Appellants | Other Appeal(s) on Conservation Grounds | Opposing Appeal(s) |
|---|---|---|---|---|---|
| Arapaho-Roosevelt | Colorado Mountain Club Contact: Ann Vickery, 5255 Pennsylvania Boulder, CO 80303 (303) 499-3001 | • Economic Suitability<br>• NEPA (Violations)<br>• Biological Diversity | | | |

| | | | | | |
|---|---|---|---|---|---|
| Bighorn | Sierra Club–Wyoming Chapter Contacts: Larry Mehlhaff, 23 N. Scott, Sheridan, WY 82801 (307) 672-0425; Doug Honnold Sierra, Club Legal Defense Fund, 1600 Broadway, Suite 1600 Denver, CO 80202 (303) 863-9898 | • NEPA (Violations)<br>• Community Stability<br>• Roadless Area Management (Wilderness Recommendations, RAREII Study)<br>• Clearcutting<br>• Economic Suitability (Below-cost Timber Sales)<br>• Timber Harvest Levels<br>• Road Construction | Willow Park Reservoir Company, Rock Creek and Piney Reservoir and Ditch Company, Bighorn Forest Users Coalition. | | Wyoming Sawmills, Inc. |
| Black Hills | National Wildlife Federation Contact: Tom Lustig, Rocky Mountain Natural Resource Clinic, University of Colorado Law School, Campus Box 401, Boulder, CO 80309 (303) 492-6557 | Minerals/Mining | | | |
| GMUG (Grand Mesa, Uncompahgre, Gunnison National Forests) | Natural Resources Defense Council Contact: Kaid Benfield, 1350 New York Ave., NW Suite 300, Washington, DC 20005 (202) 783-7800 | • Economic Suitability (Below-cost Timber Sales)<br>• Physically Unsuitable Timber Lands NEPA (Violations) | High Country Citizens Alliance, The Wilderness Society, National Audubon Society, CO Wildlife Federation | Colorado Dept. of Natural Resources | National Forest Products Assn. |

| Forest | Lead Conservation Appellant | Issues Raised in Appeal | Co-Appellants | Other Appeal(s) on Conservation Grounds | Opposing Appeal(s) |
|---|---|---|---|---|---|
| Medicine Bow | Sierra Club–Snowy Range Chap. Contact: Jeff Foster, 514 Russell, Laramie, WY 82070 (307) 742-9600. | • Economic Suitability<br>• NEPA (Violations)<br>• Watershed Protection (Riparian)<br>• Monitoring and Mitigation Problems | | | |
| Nebraska | Assn. of Natural Grasslands – Appeal Suspended. | | | | |
| Rio Grande | Colorado Mountain Club Contacts: Rocky Smith, 1030 Pearl Street, No. 9, Denver, CO 80203 (303) 861-2001; Ann Vickery, 5255 Pennsylvania, Boulder, CO 80303 (303) 499-3000. | • Monitoring and Mitigation Problems | | | |
| Routt | Troublesome RARE III Contacts: Al and Richard Wahl, 4505 Eldridge Road, Golden, CO 80401 (307) 279-3884. | • Economic Suitability (Below-cost Timber Sales) | | Service Creek Protection Assn., Rabbit Ears Audubon Society. | |

| Forest | Contact | Issues | Organizations | Other |
|---|---|---|---|---|
| San Juan | Natural Resources Defense Council Contact: Kaid Benfield, 1350 New York Ave., NW, Suite 300, Washington, DC 20005 (202) 783-7800. | • Physically Unsuitable Timber Lands • Economic Suitability (Below-cost Timber Sales) • NEPA (Violations) | CO Mountain Club, CO Open Space Council, San Juan Audubon Society, The Wilderness Society, CO Wildlife Federation, Public Land Institute. National Audubon Society. | Colorado Dept. of Natural Resources |
| Shoshone | Greater Yellowstone Coalition Contacts: Louisa Wilcox, Box 1874, Bozeman, MT 59705 (406) 586-1593; Mathew M. Reid, Wyoming Wildlife Federation, P.O. Box 106, Cheyenne, WY 82003 (307) 637-5433. | • Biological Diversity • Timber Harvest Levels • Oil and Gas Leasing • Roadless Area Management Recommendations, (RAREII Study) • Budget for the Plan • Monitoring and Mitigation Problems • NEPA (Violations) | The Wilderness Society, National Audubon Society, Dubois Wildlife Federation, County Resource Council, and others. | Rocky Mountain Oil and Gas Company. |
| White River | Colorado Mountain Club Contacts: Rocky Smith, 1030 Pearl Street No. 9, Denver, CO 80203 (303) 861-2001; Ann Vickery, 5255 Pennsylvania, Boulder, CO 80303 (303) 499-3001. | • Roadless Area Management (Wilderness Recommendations, RAREII Study) | Aspen Wilderness | Sierra Club |

## Region 3. Southwestern

| Forest | Lead Conservation Appellant | Issues Raised in Appeal | Co-Appellants | Other Appeal(s) on Conservation Grounds | Opposing Appeal(s) |
|---|---|---|---|---|---|
| Carson | John Swanson, Minneapolis, MN | • Roadless Area Management (Wilderness Recommendation, RAREII Study). | | | |
| Cibola | John Summers, 305 Solana, NE Albuquerque, NM (505) 881-0944. | • Recreation<br>• Fisheries<br>• Watershed Protection (Riparian)<br>• Cultural/Archaeological Resources<br>• Budget for the Plan | National Wildlife Federation, Sierra Club, Sandoval Environmental Action Commission, Los Huertas Ditch Association, others. | John Swanson | |
| Lincoln | Sierra Club | | The Wilderness Society | John Swanson | Two appeals by ORV clubs; an unidentified logging company; an unidentified individual (grazer?). |
| Coronado | John Swanson, Minneapolis, MN | • Roadless Area Management (Wilderness Recommendations, RAREII Study). | | | |

| | | | |
|---|---|---|---|
| Tonto | John Swanson (Appeal dismissed) Minneapolis, MN | • Roadless Area Management (Wilderness Recommendations, RAREII Study). | |

## *Region 4. Intermountain*

| | | | |
|---|---|---|---|
| Ashley | John Swanson, Minneapolis, MN | • Roadless Area Management (Wilderness Recommendations, RAREII Study). | |
| Caribou | Idaho Natural Resources Legal Contact: Ed Stockley, P.O. Box 1946, Boise ID 83701 (208) 343-8978. | • Economic Suitability (Below-cost Timber Sales) • Timber Harvest Levels • Roadless Area Management (Wilderness Recommendations, RAREII Study). | Idaho Conservation League, Sierra Club. |
| | | | Intermountain Forest Industry Assn. |
| Dixie | Utah Wilderness Assn. Contact: Dick Carter, Salt Lake City, UT 84111 (801) 245-6747; Gary Macfarlane, 455 East 400 South, B-40 Salt Lake City, UT 84111 (801) 359-1327. | • Timber Harvest Levels • Off-Road Vehicles | The Wilderness Society |
| | | | John Swanson |

| Forest | Lead Conservation Appellant | Issues Raised in Appeal | Co-Appellants | Other Appeal(s) on Conservation Grounds | Opposing Appeal(s) |
|---|---|---|---|---|---|
| Fishlake | John Swanson, Minneapolis, MN | • Roadless Area Management (Wilderness Recommendations, RAREII Study). | | Utah Congressional Delegation. | Utah Wilderness Assn. |
| Humboldt | Sierra Club Contact: Sally Kabisch, Northern California Office, 5428 College Ave., Oakland, CA 94618 (415) 654-7847. | • Roadless Area Management (Wilderness Recommendations, RAREII Study) • Grazing | The Wilderness Society | John Buckley, John Swanson, American Rivers Conservation Council. | |
| Manti-Sal | Utah Wilderness Assn. Contact: Dick Carter, 455 East 400 S., B-40, Salt Lake City, UT 84111 (801) 359-1337. | • Roadless Area Management (Wilderness Recommencations, RAREII Study) • Minerals/Mining • Grazing | | John Swanson, Sierra Club, Seven Rivers Chapter. | |
| Targhee | Edward Loosli | • Wildlife | | Sierra Club—on behalf of Forest Service | Idaho Public Land Use Committee. |
| Toiybe | Sierra Club Contact: Sally Kabisch, Northern California Office, 5428 College Ave., Oakland, CA 94618 (415) 654-7847. | • Roadless Area Management (Wilderness Recommendation, RAREII Study) | Friends of Nevada Wilderness, The Wilderness Society | | |

## Region 5. *Pacific Southwest*

| | | | |
|---|---|---|---|
| Cleveland | Sierra Club-San Diego Chapter | • Roadless Area Management (Wilderness Recommendations, RAREII Study) | Wildlife Society–So. California Chap.; Steve Loe; Three other individuals filed appeals. |

## Region 8. *Southern*

| | | | |
|---|---|---|---|
| Alabama | Alabama Audubon Society Contact: David Carr, Esq. (Legal Counsel) Southern Env. Law Center, 201 West Main, Suite 104, Charlottesville, VA 22901 (804) 977-4090. | • Roadless Area Management (Wilderness Recommendations, RAREII Study) | The Wilderness Society, Birmingham Audubon Society, Sierra Club/Alabama Chapter, Alabama Conservancy. |
| Caribbean | National Wildlife Federation, 1412 16th St., NW Washington, DC 20036 (202) 637-3724. | • Biological Diversity<br>• Timber Harvest Levels<br>• Wildlife<br>• Recreation<br>• Watershed Protection (Riparian) | Sierra Club, The Wilderness Society, Puerto Rican Natural History Society, Borinquen Audubon Society, Conservation Trust, others. |

| Forest | Lead Conservation Appellant | Issues Raised in Appeal | Co-Appellants | Other Appeal(s) on Conservation Grounds | Opposing Appeal(s) |
|---|---|---|---|---|---|
| Chattahoochee-Oconee | Sierra Club-Georgia Chapter Contact: Chuck McGrady, 2546 Hawthorne Place, Atlanta, GA 30345 (404) 391-8423. | • NEPA (Violations)<br>• Physically Unsuitable Timber Lands<br>• Economic Suitability (Below-cost Timber Sales)<br>• Infestation<br>• Roadless Area Management (Wilderness Recommendations, RAREII Study). | GA Botanical Society, GA Trout Unlimited, Atlanta Audubon Society, GA Conservancy, Friends of the Mountains, The Wilderness Society | | |
| Cherokee | The Wilderness Society Contacts: Ron Tipton, 1819 Peachtree Rd., NE Suite 210, Atlanta GA 30309 (404) 355-1783; Peter Kirby, The Wilderness Society, 1400 Eye Street, NW Washington, DC (202) 842-3400. | • Clearcutting<br>• Timber Harvest Levels<br>• Roadless Area Management (Wilderness Recommendations, RAREII Study)<br>• Economic Suitability (Below-cost Timber Sales)<br>• Wildlife<br>• Fisheries<br>• Biological Diversity | TN Audubon Council, TN Citizens for Wilderness Planning, Great Smoky Mountains Hiking Club, Sierra Club/TN Chapter. | Common Sense | |

| | | | | |
|---|---|---|---|---|
| Croatan-Ywharrie | American Rivers Conservation Council Contacts: Chris Brown, 801 Pennsylvania Ave., SE Suite 303, Washington, DC 20003 (202) 547-6900; Bob Dreher, Esq. Sierra Club Legal Defense Fund, 1516 P Street, NW, Suite 300, Washington, DC 20005 (202) 667-4500. | • Wild and Scenic Rivers | | |
| Florida | National Wildlife Federation, 1412 Sixteenth St., NW, Washington, DC 20036 (202) 637-3724. | • Wildlife<br>• Roadless Area Management (Wilderness Recommendations, RAREII Study)<br>• Grazing<br>• Clearcutting<br>• Fisheries<br>• Watershed Protection (Riparian)<br>• Type Conversion | Florida Wildlife Federation, Florida Audubon Society, Coastal Plains Institute, The Wilderness Society, National Audubon Society. | Florida Forestry Assn. |
| Francis Marion | Santee Preservation Society Contact: Theodore Rosegarten, P.O. Box 397, McClellanville, SC. 29458 | • Wildlife<br>• Type Conversion<br>• Biological Diversity | | |

| Forest | Lead Conservation Appellant | Issues Raised in Appeal | Co-Appellants | Other Appeal(s) on Conservation Grounds | Opposing Appeal(s) |
|---|---|---|---|---|---|
| George Washington | Virginia Wilderness Committee Contacts: Ernie Dickerman, Route 1, Box 156, Swoope, VA 24479 (703) 337-8000; Bob Dreher, Sierra Club Legal Defense Fund, 1516 P Street, NW Suite 300, Washington, DC 20005 (202) 667-4500. | • Road Construction<br>• Type Conversion<br>• Timber Harvest Levels<br>• Clearcutting<br>• Recreation<br>• Wildlife<br>• Economic Suitability (Below-cost Timber Sales) | Sierra Club, Defenders of Wildlife, Natural Resources Defense Council, The Wilderness Society. | John Swanson, American Rivers Conservation Council, West Virginia Dept./Natural Resources, Appalachian Trail Conference. | 10 appeals by Loggers/Timber Companies |
| Jefferson | Citizens Task Force Contacts: Jim Loesel, 2753 Tanglewood SW, Roanoke, VA 24018 (703) 774-6690; Rick Middleton, Esq., & David Carr, Esq., Southern Env. Law Ctr., 201 W. Main, Suite 104, Charlottesville, VA 22901 (804) 977-4090. | • NEPA (Violations)<br>• Wildlife<br>• Roadless Area Management (Wilderness Recommendations, RAREII Study)<br>• Clearcutting<br>• Physically Unsuitable Timber Lands<br>• Economic Suitability (Below-cost Timber Sales)<br>• Fisheries | Conservation Council of VA Foundation, Citizens Environmental Council, Craig Wildlife Association, Old Dominion Sportsmen's Association, etc. | | Off-Road Vehicle Users-appeal suspended |
| Kisatchie | Keep Kisatchie Coalition Contact: Pat Sewell, 815 Market Place, Shreveport, LA 71101 | • Timber Harvest<br>• Wildlife<br>• Recreation<br>• Clearcutting | | | |

| | Contacts | Issues | Organizations | People |
|---|---|---|---|---|
| Mississippi | Sierra Club, Mississippi Chap. Contacts: Tom Pullen, Box 1655, Vicksburg, MS 39180 (601) 634-5851; Tom Hudson, P.O. Box 4335, Jackson, MS 39216 | • NEPA (Violations)<br>• Roadless Area Management (Wilderness Recommendations, RAREII Study)<br>• Road Construction<br>• Off-Road Vehicles<br>• Clearcutting<br>• Pesticides<br>• Recreation | | |
| Ouachita | Oklahoma Wilderness Coalition Contacts: Mark Derichsweiler, 312 Keith, Norman, OK 73069 (405) 271-7325; Lu Willis, Esq., Suite 101, 4000 Classen Ctr., Oklahoma City, OK 73118 (405) 528-0191. | • NEPA (Violations)<br>• Economic Suitability [Below-cost Timber Sales]<br>• Physically Unsuitable Timber Lands<br>• Clearcutting<br>• Biological Diversity<br>• Road Construction<br>• Type Conversion | Sierra Club-AR Chap., OK Wildlife Federation, The Wilderness Society, AR Conservation Coalition, OK Scenic Rivers Assn. | John Swanson, Jerry Williams, *et al.*, AR Conservation Coalition, David Thompson |
| Ozark–St. Francis | Newton County Wildlife Assn. Contacts: Barry Weaver, P.O. Box 501, Jasper, AR 72641 (501) 446-2194; Tom McKinny, Forest Chair Sierra Club, AR Chapter, Jasper, AR (501) 442-4044. | • Type Conversion<br>• NEPA (Violations)<br>• Wildlife<br>• Road Construction<br>• Clearcutting<br>• Fisheries<br>• Watershed Protection (Riparian) | Sierra Club-AR Chap., The Wilderness Society. | John Swanson American Rivers Conservation Council. |

| Forest | Lead Conservation Appellant | Issues Raised in Appeal | Co-Appellants | Other Appeal(s) on Conservation Grounds | Opposing Appeal(s) |
|--------|------------------------------|--------------------------|----------------|------------------------------------------|---------------------|
| Sumter | National Wild Turkey Federation Contact: Wild Turkey Bldg., P.O. Box 530, Edgefield, SC 29824 (803) 637-3106. | • Wildlife<br>• Road Construction<br>• Biological Diversity<br>• Physically Unsuitable Timber Lands | | SC Wildlife and Marine Resources Dept. | |

## Region 9. Eastern

| Forest | Lead Conservation Appellant | Issues Raised in Appeal | Co-Appellants | Other Appeal(s) on Conservation Grounds | Opposing Appeal(s) |
|--------|------------------------------|--------------------------|----------------|------------------------------------------|---------------------|
| Allegheny | John Swanson, Minneapolis, MN | • Roadless Area Management (Wilderness Recommendations, RAREII Study) | | | |
| Chequamegon | Sierra Club-John Muir Chapter Contacts: George Hall, 2724 Regent St., Madison, WI 53705 (608) 266-3751; Walter Kuhlman, Esq., P.O. Box 927, Madison, WI 53701 (608) 257-9521. | • Economic Suitability (Below-cost Timber Sales)<br>• Biological Diversity<br>• Wildlife<br>• Road Construction | Wisconsin Forest Conservation Task Force | John Swanson, The Wilderness Society, Wisconsin Audubon Society, et al., State of Wisconsin | MI/WI Timber Producers |

| | | | |
|---|---|---|---|
| Chippewa | American Rivers Conservation Council Contact: Chris Brown, 801 Pennsylvania Ave., SE, Suite 300, Washington, DC 20003 (202) 547-6900; Bob Dreher, Esq. Sierra Club Legal Defense Fund, 1516 P St., NW Suite 300, Washington, DC 20005 (202) 667-4500. | • Wild and Scenic Rivers | John Swanon |
| Hiawatha | The Wilderness Society Contact: Michael Kellert, 1800 Hatcher St., Ann Arbor, MI 48109. | • Roadless Area Management (Wilderness Recommendations, RAREII Study) • Timber Harvest Levels • Economic Suitability (Below-cost Timber Sales) • Wildlife • Biological Diversity • Wild and Scenic Rivers • Semi-Primitive Recreation | Sierra Club, Detroit Audubon Society, Upper Peninsula Environmental Coalition, Les Cheneaus Islands Assn. | John Swanson | MI/WI Timber Products Assn., Two individual appellants. |

| Forest | Lead Conservation Appellant | Issues Raised in Appeal | Co-Appellants | Other Appeal(s) on Conservation Grounds | Opposing Appeal(s) |
|---|---|---|---|---|---|
| Hoosier | Hoosier Environmental Council Contact: Jeff St. Clair, RR #3, Box 516B, Nashville, TN 47448 (812) 988-6958; Eric Jorgensen, Sierra Club Legal Defense Fund, 1516 P St., NW Suite 300, Washington, DC 20005 (202) 667-4500. | • Timber Harvest Levels<br>• Oil and Gas Leasing<br>• Road Construction<br>• Wildlife<br>• Semi-Primitive<br>• Research Natural Areas | Sierra Club, Izaak Walton League, National Audubon Society-Sassafras chap., others. | | |
| Huron–Manistee | Sierra Club-Mackinac Chap. Contacts: Mike Kellert, 1800 Hatcher St., Ann Arbor, MI 48103 (313) 668-0365; Linda Berker, Esq., 8415 Davison Road, Suite A, Davison, MI 48423 (313) 653-8242. | • Wildlife<br>• Roadless Area Management (Wilderness Recommendations, RAREII Study)<br>• Timber Harvest Levels<br>• Semi-Primitive Recreation<br>• Oil and Gas Leasing | The Wilderness Society, Detroit Audubon Society, West MI Environmental Action Council, Hamlin Lake Assn., Defenders of Wildlife. | John Swanson; American Rivers Conservation | MI Multiple-Use Coalition, Several Off-Road Vehicle Enthusiasts. |
| Mark Twain | Mark Twain Forest Planning Task Force Contact: John Karel, 29 Bearfield Road, Columbia, MO 65201 (314) 449-5029; Mark Kaiser, 4000 Hyde Park #98, Columbia, MO 65201 (314) 875-5399. | • Timber Harvest<br>• Road Construction<br>• Wildlife<br>• Minerals/Mining<br>• Wild and Scenic Rivers | | American Rivers Conservation Council, John Swanson. | |

| | | | | |
|---|---|---|---|---|
| Monongahela | David Powell, Washington, DC (202) 828-2406. | • Timber Harvest Levels<br>• Road Construction<br>• Wildlife | John Swanson WV Wild Turkey Federation, Ruffed Grouse Society/Natl Capitol Chap., Hillard Dolin, American Rivers Conservation Council. | Slavin Hollows Hunting Group |
| Nicolet | Sierra Club-John Muir Chap. Contacts: George Hall, 2427 Regent St., Madison, WI (608) 266-3751; Walter Kuhlman, Esq., P.O. Box 927, Madison, WI 53701 (608) 257-9521. | • Biological Diversity<br>• Road Construction<br>• Wildlife<br>• Economic Suitability (Below-cost Timber Sales) | Wisconsin Forest Conservation Task Force | John Swanson, The Wilderness Society, WI Audubon Society, *et al.* State of Wisconsin | MI/WI Timber Producers Carl Fate |
| Ottawa | Sierra Club/ Mackinac Chap. Contact: Ann Woiwode, 115 West Alleghan, Suite 330, Lansing, MI 48933 | • Roadless Area Management (Wilderness Recommendations, RAREII Study)<br>• Timber Harvest Levels<br>• Economic Suitability (Below-cost Timber Sales)<br>• Road Construction<br>• Wildlife<br>• Recreation | The Wilderness Society, others. | John Swanson | Operation Action – U.P. Ontonagan County Econ. Development Corp. MI Multiple-Use MI/WI Timber Producers Assn., Long Year Office, A local land owner. |

| Forest | Lead Conservation Appellant | Issues Raised in Appeal | Co-Appellants | Other Appeal(s) on Conservation Grounds | Opposing Appeal(s) |
|---|---|---|---|---|---|
| Shawnee | Sierra Club-Great Lakes Chap. Contact: Jim Bensman, 301-F Big Arch, Godfrey, IL 62035 (618) 466-7143. | | Assn./Concerned Environmentalists, Friends of the Earth, International Wildlife Coalition, IL South Proj., McHenry County Defenders, Wilderness Society. | John Swanson | |
| Superior | Friends of the Boundary Waters Contacts: Kevin Proescholdt, 1313 5th St., SE Minneapolis, MN 55414 (612) 379-3835; Brian O'Neill, Esq., 2300 Multifoods Tower, Minneapolis, MN 55402 (612) 371-5379. | • Road Construction<br>• Wildlife<br>• Economic Suitability (Below-cost Timber Sales)<br>• Roadless Area Management (Wilderness Recommendations, RAREII Study)<br>• Wild and Scenic Rivers | Sierra Club, The Wilderness Society, Defenders of Wildlife | American Rivers Conservation Council | |

| | | | | |
|---|---|---|---|---|
| White Mountains | Conservation Law Foundation Contact: Doug Foy, 3 Joy St., Boston, MA 01208 (617) 742-2540; Sarah Muyskens, The Wilderness Society, NE Reg. Office, 20 Park Plaza, Suite 536, Boston, MA 02116 (617) 350-8866. | • Roadless Area Management (Wilderness Recommendations, RAREII Study) • Wildlife • Wild and Scenic Rivers • Watershed Protection (Riparian) • Economic Suitability (Below-cost Timber Sales) • Timber Harvest Levels • Recreation | The Wilderness Society, Sierra Club, National Audubon Society, Defenders of Wildlife. | New Hampshire Timberland Owners Assn. |

### Region 10. Alaska

| | | | | |
|---|---|---|---|---|
| Chugach | Sierra Club Legal Defense Fund Contact: Laurie Adams & Steve Kallick, 419 6th St., Suite 321, Juneau, AK 99801 (907) 586-2751. | • Timber Harvest • Roadless Area Management (Wilderness Recommendations, RAREII Study) • Economic Suitability (Below-cost Timber Sales) | The Wilderness Society, Sierra Club, National Audubon Society, 13 other groups. | |

# APPENDIX M

# Budget Histories of Agencies with Fish and Wildlife Habitat Management Responsibilities: FWS, BLM, USFS, NPS, NMFS

## INTRODUCTION

All data in the charts below were supplied by the budget offices of the individual agencies. Budget figures for 1980 through 1986 are "actual" appropriations, including supplemental and rescinded funds. Appropriations for 1987 include only the initial appropriations made by Congress in October 1986 in the Continuing Appropriations and Drug Supplemental Bill, P.L. 99–500, and do not include supplementals and recissions. Full-time equivalents (FTEs) or work years for 1980 through 1985 reflect actual FTEs reported for each activity by agency personnel. FTEs for 1986 are estimates only. Estimated FTEs for 1987 are not available.

Calculations to convert current dollars into 1982 constant dollars were made using Gross National Product implicit price deflators reported in the February 1986 issue of *Survey of Current Business* for fiscal years 1980 through 1985. Gross National Product implicit price deflators for the first three quarters of fiscal year 1986 were taken from the September 1986 issue of *Survey of Current Business*, and the price deflator for the last quarter of fiscal year 1986 was obtained from the Bureau of Economic Analysis, Department of Commerce, in November 1986. Conversion of 1987 appropriations into 1982 dollars is based on projections from the Congressional Budget Office as of November 1986, which projected an implicit price deflator of 2.9 for fiscal year 1987.

652

NATIONAL PARK SERVICE BUDGET HISTORY, 1982-87[1,2]

(in 000s of dollars)

| | 1982 Actual | 1983 Actual | 1984 Actual | 1985 Actual | 1986 Actual | 1987 President's Request | 1987 Appropriations |
|---|---|---|---|---|---|---|---|
| **OPERATION OF THE NATIONAL PARK SERVICE** | | | | | | | |
| **Park Management** | | | | | | | |
| Management of Park Areas | 60,123 | 59,410 | 63,100 | 62,680 | 58,878 | 62,498 | 62,705 |
| 82$ | 60,123 | 57,057 | 58,235 | 55,854 | 51,094 | 52,705 | 52,879 |
| Concessions Management | 2,449 | 2,736 | 3,539 | 3,500 | 3,395 | 3,548 | 3,548 |
| 82$ | 2,449 | 2,628 | 3,266 | 3,119 | 2,946 | 2,992 | 2,992 |
| Interpretation & Visitor Services | 58,966 | 62,887 | 68,643 | 63,839 | 62,312 | 57,413 | 68,054 |
| 82$ | 58,966 | 60,397 | 63,351 | 56,887 | 54,074 | 48,416 | 57,390 |
| Visitor Protection & Safety | 63,742 | 70,117 | 72,012 | 78,982 | 78,498 | 76,361 | 86,807 |
| 82$ | 63,742 | 67,340 | 66,460 | 70,381 | 68,121 | 64,395 | 73,204 |
| Maintenance | 210,444 | 249,915 | 234,942 | 235,900 | 228,788 | 233,826 | 243,360 |
| 82$ | 210,444 | 240,018 | 216,828 | 210,210 | 198,542 | 197,185 | 205,225 |
| **Resources Management:** | | | | | | | |
| Cultural Resources Management | 31,442 | 41,955 | 41,913 | 44,945 | 41,125 | 38,640 | 44,083 |
| 82$ | 31,442 | 40,294 | 38,682 | 40,050 | 35,688 | 32,585 | 37,175 |
| Natural Resources Management | 39,213 | 48,270 | 52,211 | 51,089 | 53,603 | 47,797 | 56,825 |
| 82$ | 39,213 | 46,359 | 48,186 | 45,525 | 46,517 | 40,307 | 47,921 |
| Subtotal: Resources Management | 70,655 | 90,225 | 94,124 | 96,034 | 94,728 | 86,437 | 100,908 |
| 82$ | 70,655 | 86,652 | 86,867 | 85,576 | 82,205 | 72,892 | 85,096 |

| | 1982 Actual | 1983 Actual | 1984 Actual | 1985 Actual | 1986 Actual | 1987 President's Request | 1987 Appropriations |
|---|---|---|---|---|---|---|---|
| Information Publications........ | 2,660 | 3,026 | 2,940 | 2,850 | 2,766 | -- | 3,400 |
| 82$............ | 2,660 | 2,906 | 2,713 | 2,540 | 2,400 | -- | 2,867 |
| International Park Affairs...... | 526 | 628 | 401 | 518 | 758 | 423 | 771 |
| 82$............ | 526 | 603 | 370 | 462 | 658 | 357 | 650 |
| Volunteers-in-Parks............ | 244 | 479 | 500 | 490 | 466 | -- | 500 |
| 82$............ | 244 | 460 | 461 | 437 | 404 | -- | 422 |
| Youth Conservation Corps[3]..... | [1,000] | 3,300 | [3,300] | [3,332] | [3,139] | -- | [1,000] |
| 82$............ | [1,000] | 3,169 | [3,046] | [2,969] | [2,724] | -- | [ 843] |
| Enhanced Park Operations[4]..... | -- | -- | -- | -- | -- | -- | 15,000 |
| 82$............ | -- | -- | -- | -- | -- | -- | 12,650 |
| Subtotal: Park Management...... | 469,809 | 542,723 | 540,201 | 544,793 | 530,596 | 520,506 | 585,053 |
| 82$............ | 469,809 | 521,231 | 498,552 | 485,465 | 460,451 | 438,943 | 493,375 |
| Forest Fire Suppression........ | 3,352 | 1,200 | 3,800 | 5,076 | 10,619 | 1,319 | 1,319 |
| 82$............ | 3,352 | 1,152 | 3,507 | 4,523 | 9,215 | 1,112 | 1,112 |
| **Park Recreation & Wilderness Planning** | | | | | | | |
| Water Resources Studies........ | 1,464 | 1,566 | 1,944 | 1,908 | 1,827 | 2,909 | 2,909 |
| 82$............ | 1,464 | 1,504 | 1,794 | 1,700 | 1,585 | 2,453 | 2,453 |
| General Management Plans....... | 2,273 | 2,221 | 2,922 | 2,360 | 2,232 | 2,332 | 2,332 |
| 82$............ | 2,273 | 2,133 | 2,697 | 2,103 | 1,763 | 1,967 | 1,967 |
| Rivers and Trails Studies...... | 899 | -- | -- | -- | -- | -- | |
| 82$............ | 899 | -- | -- | -- | -- | -- | |

| | | | | | | | |
|---|---|---|---|---|---|---|---|
| Subtotal: Park Recreation and Wilderness Planning | 4,636 | 3,787 | 4,866 | 4,268 | 4,059 | 5,241 | 5,241 |
| 82$ | 4,636 | 3,637 | 4,491 | 3,803 | 3,522 | 4,420 | 4,420 |
| Statutory or Contractual Aid for Other Activities | 1,954 | 2,507 | 2,570 | 3,866 | 3,326 | 1,816 | 11,488[5] |
| 82$ | 1,954 | 2,408 | 2,372 | 3,445 | 2,886 | 1,531 | 9,688 |
| General Administration | 41,777 | 55,062 | 65,133 | 68,815 | 62,034 | 67,600 | 69,670 |
| 82$ | 41,777 | 52,853 | 60,130 | 61,321 | 53,833 | 57,007 | 58,753 |
| TOTAL: OPERATION OF THE NPS | 521,528 | 605,279 | 616,570 | 626,818 | 610,634 | 596,482 | 672,771[6] |
| 82$ | 521,528 | 581,310 | 569,032 | 558,558 | 529,908 | 503,013 | 567,348 |
| OPERATION OF THE NPS - FEE SYSTEM[4] | -- | -- | -- | -- | -- | 59,000 | -- |
| 83$ | -- | -- | -- | -- | -- | 49,755 | -- |
| NATIONAL RECREATION AND PRESERVATION: | | | | | | | |
| Recreation Programs | 2,602 | 1,437 | 682 | 625 | 600 | 284 | 600 |
| 82$ | 2,602 | 1,380 | 629 | 557 | 521 | 239 | 506 |
| Natural Programs | 1,170 | 1,693 | 1,694 | 1,712 | 1,582 | 541 | 1,582 |
| 82$ | 1,170 | 1,626 | 1,563 | 1,526 | 1,373 | 456 | 1,334 |
| National Register | 5,934 | 4,513 | 5,611 | 6,667 | 6,549 | 6,843 | 6,584 |
| 82$ | 5,934 | 4,334 | 5,178 | 5,941 | 5,683 | 5,771 | 5,552 |
| Environmental & Compliance Review | 597 | 386 | 390 | 392 | 383 | 400 | 383 |
| 82$ | 597 | 371 | 360 | 349 | 332 | 337 | 323 |
| Grant Administration | 2,304 | 2,026 | 2,000 | 1,715 | 1,441 | 1,479 | 1,479 |
| 82$ | 2,304 | 1,946 | 1,846 | 1,528 | 1,250 | 1,247 | 1,247 |

| | 1982 Actual | 1983 Actual | 1984 Actual | 1985 Actual | 1986 Actual | 1987 President's Request | 1987 Appropriations |
|---|---|---|---|---|---|---|---|
| TOTAL: NATIONAL RECREATION AND PRESERVATION........... | 12,607 | 10,055 | 10,377 | 11,111 | 10,555 | 9,547 | 10,628 |
| 82$ | 12,607 | 9,657 | 9,577 | 9,901 | 9,160 | 8,051 | 8,963 |
| URBAN PARK AND RECREATION FUND........... | 7,680 | 40,000 | 6,700 | -- | -- | -- | -- |
| 82$ | 7,680 | 38,416 | 6,183 | -- | -- | -- | -- |
| HISTORIC PRESERVATION FUND........... | 25,740 | 51,000 | 27,500 | 25,480 | 23,729 | -- | 24,250 |
| 82$ | 25,740 | 48,980 | 25,380 | 22,705 | 20,592 | -- | 20,450 |
| VISITOR FACILITIES FUND[7]........... | -- | -- | 5,800 | 5,880 | [8,086] | [8,500] | [8,500] |
| 82$ | -- | -- | 5,353 | 5,240 | [7,017] | [7,168] | [7,168] |
| CONSTRUCTION........... | 95,852 | 160,096 | 66,690 | 101,545 | 112,408 | 29,114 | 88,095 |
| 82$ | 95,852 | 153,756 | 61,548 | 90,487 | 97,548 | 24,552 | 74,291 |
| CONSTRUCTION - HIGHWAY TRUST FUND[8]........... | -- | -- | [14,000] | [28,000] | [9,857] | -- | [12,500] |
| 82$ | -- | -- | [1,292] | [24,951] | [8,554] | -- | [10,541] |
| LAND ACQUISITION AND STATE ASSISTANCE - LWCF ASSISTANCE TO STATES........... | 4,381 | 115,000 | 75,000 | 73,482 | 47,663 | 2,270 | 34,970 |
| 82$ | 4,381 | 110,446 | 69,218 | 65,480 | 41,362 | 1,914 | 29,490 |
| Park Acquisitions........... | 129,081 | 121,505 | 128,650 | 95,682 | 46,041 | 13,000 | 52,250 |
| 82$ | 129,081 | 116,693 | 118,731 | 85,262 | 39,954 | 10,963 | 44,062 |
| TOTAL: LAND ACQUISITION AND STATE ASSISTANCE........... | 133,462 | 236,505 | 203,650 | 169,164 | 93,604 | 15,270 | 87,220 |
| 82$ | 133,462 | 227,139 | 187,949 | 150,742 | 81,230 | 12,877 | 73,553 |

| | | | | | | | |
|---|---|---|---|---|---|---|---|
| MISCELLANEOUS OTHER PROJECTS.............. | 4,212 | 4,336 | 4,542 | 4,847 | 4,875 | 4,771 | 5,096 |
| 82$.............. | 4,212 | 4,164 | 4,192 | 4,319 | 4,231 | 4,023 | 4,297 |
| TOTAL: NPS APPROPRIATIONS.............. | 800,781 | 1,107,271 | 955,829 | 972,845 | 855,805 | 714,184 | 889,060 |
| 82$.............. | 800,781 | 1,063,423 | 882,135 | 866,902 | 742,668 | 602,271 | 749,744 |
| MISCELLANEOUS PERMANENT Appropriations & Trust Funds.............. | 1,574 | 2,875 | 7,561 | 20,982 | 24,060 | 20,091 | 20,091 |
| 82$.............. | 1,574 | 2,761 | 6,978 | 18,697 | 20,879 | 16,943 | 16,943 |
| TOTAL: NPS .............. | 802,355 | 1,110,146 | 963,390 | 993,827 | 879,865 | 734,275 | 909,151 |
| 82$.............. | 802,355 | 1,066,184 | 889,113 | 885,599 | 737,513 | 619,214 | 766,687 |

1. Budget figures for years prior to 1982 are not shown because comparison between current budgets and years prior to 1982 is difficult for various reasons. For example, some programs now funded under the Park Service were funded then under the Heritage Conservation and Recreation Service.

2. The NPS budget chart does not include FTEs because NPS has no system for tracking actual FTEs in various programs. FTEs reported by NPS in annual budget documents are simply estimates based on the assumption that part allocation of employee time does not vary substantially from year to year.

3. Brackets indicate this amount is to be spent on YCC "within available funds" appropriated to other accounts.

4. For 1987, the administration requested $59 million in appropriations from user fees expected to result from proposed recreation-fee increases, with appropriations to be used to fund the fee-collection program and to offset some base costs of the Operation of the National Park System (ONPS) and $14.207 million to be used to "enhance" park operations. Congress rejected this funding approach and appropriated funds to cover base programs through the ONPS account, but retained the concept of a generic "enhance park operations" item, funded in ONPS at $15 million.

5. Includes $8 million for the Steamtown Historic Site appropriated under the Steamtown Historic Site Act of 1986.

6. Represents funds available in ONPS, including $657.613 million in appropriations plus $15.158 million from an unappropriated balance in Planning, Development, and Operation of Recreation Facilities.

7. In 1986 and 1987, Congress transferred dollars from the Visitor Facilities Fund, comprised of concessioner franchise fees, to Construction. Construction totals reflect this transfer.

8. These funds are appropriated from the Highway Trust Fund for the relocation of a highway that runs through the Cumberland Gap National Historic Park. Funding is used by the Federal Highway Administration to liquidate contract authority and is not added into NPS appropriations.

NATIONAL MARINE FISHERIES SERVICE BUDGET HISTORY, 1982-87[1]

(in 000s of dollars)

| | 1982 Actual | 1983 Actual | 1984 Actual | 1985 Actual | 1986 Actual | 1987 President's Request | 1987 Appropriations |
|---|---|---|---|---|---|---|---|
| **MARINE FISHERY RESOURCE PROGRAMS** | | | | | | | |
| *Information Collection and Analysis* | | | | | | | |
| Resource Information.............. | 40,316 | 43,931 | 45,549 | 54,505 | 64,854 | 47,807 | 72,583 |
| 82$........[2]................ | 40,316 | 42,196 | 42,037 | 48,569 | 56,280 | 36,099 | 61,209 |
| Workyears...................... | 893 | 884 | 851 | 887 | 963 | 823 | - |
| Fishery Industry Information.......... | 8,801 | 9,435 | 8,932 | 9,419 | 8,462 | 5,927 | 8,847 |
| 82$........................... | 8,801 | 9,062 | 8,243 | 8,393 | 7,343 | 4,998 | 7,461 |
| Workyears...................... | 202 | 137 | 109 | 117 | 120 | 100 | - |
| Information Analysis & Dissemination.. | 21,437 | 17,859 | 17,831 | 18,509 | 17,219 | 16,691 | 17,470 |
| 82$........................... | 21,437 | 17,154 | 16,456 | 16,493 | 14,923 | 14,076 | 14,732 |
| Workyears...................... | 450 | 351 | 326 | 328 | 317 | 249 | - |
| Subtotal, Information Collection.... | 70,554 | 71,225 | 72,312 | 82,433 | 90,535 | 65,425 | 98,900 |
| 82$........................... | 70,554 | 68,412 | 66,737 | 73,466 | 78,566 | 55,173 | 83,402 |
| Workyears...................... | 1,545 | 1,372 | 1,286 | 1,332 | 1,400 | 1,172 | - |
| *Conservation & Management Operations* | | | | | | | |
| Fishery Management Programs........ | 28,655 | 30,965 | 34,204 | 29,632 | 25,886 | 13,834 | 26,297 |
| 82$........................... | 28,655 | 29,712 | 31,567 | 26,405 | 22,464 | 11,666 | 22,176 |
| Workyears...................... | 286 | 239 | 219 | 215 | 230 | 228 | - |
| Protected Species Management | 7,650 | 30,149[3] | 7,053 | 4,635 | 3,433 | 3,718 | 3,622 |
| 82$........................... | 7,650 | 28,958 | 6,509 | 4,130 | 2,979 | 3,135 | 3,054 |
| Workyears...................... | 124 | 169 | 68 | 63 | 66 | 66 | - |
| Habitat Conservation.............. | 4,958 | 4,763 | 4,550 | 5,399 | 5,329 | 3,059 | 5,265 |
| 82$........................... | 4,958 | 4,575 | 4,199 | 4,811 | 4,625 | 2,580 | 4,440 |
| Workyears...................... | 139 | 93 | 89 | 87 | 92 | 78 | - |
| Enforcement & Surveillance......... | 9,569 | 7,755 | 7,629 | 7,337 | 7,632 | 7,689 | 8,000 |
| 82$........................... | 9,569 | 7,449 | 7,041 | 6,538 | 6,623 | 6,484 | 6,746 |
| Workyears...................... | 228 | 135 | 131 | 136 | 141 | 137 | - |

| | | | | | | | |
|---|---|---|---|---|---|---|---|
| **Subtotal, Conservation & Management Operations** | 50,832 | 73,632 | 53,446 | 47,003 | 42,280 | 28,300 | 43,184 |
| 82$ | 50,832 | 70,724 | 49,325 | 41,884 | 36,691 | 23,865 | 36,417 |
| Workyears | 777 | 636 | 507 | 501 | 529 | 509 | – |
| **State & Industry Programs** | | | | | | | |
| Grants to States | 7,375 | 7,000 | 9,700 | 8,000 | 10,047 | – | 9,000 |
| 82$ | 7,375 | 6,724 | 8,952 | 7,129 | 8,719 | – | 7,590 |
| Workyears | – | – | – | – | – | – | – |
| Fisheries Development Programs | –[4] | 10,341 | 11,261 | 13,550 | 11,919 | 2,964 | 11,012 |
| 82$ | – | 9,933 | 10,393 | 12,074 | 10,343 | 2,500 | 9,286 |
| Workyears | – | 214 | 235 | 215 | 245 | 99 | – |
| Financial Services Program Administration | 399 | 541 | 508 | 374 | 628 | – | – |
| 82$ | 399 | 520 | 469 | 333 | 545 | – | – |
| Workyears | 13 | 14 | 13 | 18 | 25 | – | – |
| **Subtotal, State & Industry Assistance** | 7,774 | 17,882 | 21,469 | 21,924 | 22,594 | 2,964 | 20,012 |
| 82$ | 7,774 | 17,176 | 19,814 | 19,536 | 19,607 | 2,500 | 16,876 |
| Workyears | 13 | 228 | 248 | 234 | 270 | 99 | – |
| **TOTAL, MARINE FISHERY RESOURCES** | 129,160[4] | 162,739 | 147,217 | 151,360 | 155,409 | 96,689 | 162,096 |
| 82$ | 129,160 | 156,311 | 135,867 | 134,877 | 134,864 | 81,538 | 136,696 |
| Workyears | 2,335 | 2,336 | 2,041 | 2,067 | 2,199 | 1,780 | – |

1. Prior to 1982, NMFS used a different budget structure. Budget categories in these years are not comparable with current categories and thus are not shown.

2. NMFS measures work effort in work years, which is essentially the same as FTEs.

3. 1983 appropriations for Protected Species Management include a one-time payment of more than $20 million to Pribilovians in Alaska.

4. In 1982, Fisheries Development Programs were funded elsewhere in the NOAA budget. Exact figures for this program in 1982 are not available, but NMFS budget staff say it probably was funded at close to current levels, bringing the 1982 total NMFS budget to about $150 million.

BUREAU OF LAND MANAGEMENT BUDGET HISTORY, 1980-87

(in 000s of dollars)

| | 1980[1,2,3] Actual | 1981[1,2,3] Actual | 1982[1] Actual | 1983[4] Actual | 1984[4] Actual | 1985 Actual | 1986 Actual | 1987 President's Request | 1987 Appropriations |
|---|---|---|---|---|---|---|---|---|---|
| **MANAGEMENT OF LANDS AND RESOURCES** | | | | | | | | | |
| **Onshore Energy & Minerals Management** | | | | | | | | | |
| **Energy Resources** | | | | | | | | | |
| Oil and Gas Leasing.............. | 7,475 | 14,444 | 17,859 | 28,666 | 40,492 | 42,804 | 42,630 | 46,519 | 46,019 |
| 82$.............................. | 8,821 | 15,507 | 17,859 | 27,531 | 37,370 | 38,143 | 36,994 | 39,229 | 38,808 |
| FTEs............................. | – | – | 564 | 792 | 1,110 | 1,134 | 1,210 | 1,188 | – |
| Coal Leasing..................... | 17,400 | 24,414 | 17,947 | 20,259 | 17,420 | 17,962 | 18,506 | 13,695 | 13,695 |
| 82$.............................. | 20,534 | 26,211 | 17,947 | 19,457 | 16,077 | 16,006 | 16,060 | 11,549 | 11,549 |
| FTEs............................. | – | – | 294 | 313 | 331 | 285 | 320 | 280 | – |
| Geothermal Leasing............... | 1,480 | 2,091 | 2,305 | 2,760 | 2,957 | 3,227 | 2,639 | 2,475 | 2,475 |
| 82$.............................. | 1,747 | 2,245 | 2,305 | 2,651 | 2,729 | 2,876 | 2,290 | 2,087 | 2,087 |
| FTEs............................. | – | – | 60 | 62 | 72 | 72 | 61 | 55 | – |
| Oil Shale/Tar Sands.............. | 420 | 4,452 | 3,675 | 4,118 | 2,148 | 2,172 | 2,008 | – | – |
| 82$.............................. | 496 | 4,780 | 3,675 | 3,955 | 1,982 | 1,935 | 1,743 | – | – |
| FTEs............................. | – | – | 62 | 73 | 47 | 37 | 35 | – | – |
| Subtotal: Energy Resources...... | 26,775 | 45,401 | 41,786 | 55,803 | 63,017 | 66,165 | 65,783 | 62,689 | 62,189 |
| 82$.............................. | 31,597 | 48,743 | 41,786 | 53,593 | 58,158 | 58,960 | 57,086 | 52,866 | 52,444 |
| FTEs............................. | – | – | 980 | 1,240 | 1,560 | 1,528 | 1,626 | 1,523 | – |
| **Non-energy Minerals** | | | | | | | | | |
| Mineral Material Sales........... | 1,585 | 1,884 | 1,818 | 2,072 | 2,353 | 2,131 | 2,090 | 2,184 | 2,184 |
| 82$.............................. | 1,870 | 2,023 | 1,818 | 1,990 | 2,172 | 1,899 | 1,813 | 1,842 | 1,842 |
| FTEs............................. | – | – | 50 | 51 | 59 | 54 | 54 | 54 | – |
| Mining Law Administration........ | 3,274 | 4,244 | 6,365 | 6,559 | 7,302 | 7,920 | 7,801 | 8,210 | 9,010 |
| 82$.............................. | 3,864 | 4,556 | 6,365 | 6,299 | 6,739 | 7,058 | 6,770 | 6,923 | 7,598 |
| FTEs............................. | – | – | 209 | 196 | 211 | 210 | 215 | 217 | – |

| | | | | | | | | | |
|---|---|---|---|---|---|---|---|---|---|
| **Mineral Leasing** | 1,366 | 1,497 | 1,588 | 3,324 | 3,834 | 4,041 | 4,027 | 3,868 | 3,868 |
| 82$ | 1,612 | 1,607 | 1,588 | 3,192 | 3,538 | 3,601 | 3,495 | 3,262 | 3,262 |
| FTEs | – | – | 31 | 70 | 79 | 79 | 85 | 78 | – |
| **Uranium Operations** | – | – | – | – | 622 | 617 | 594 | 621 | 621 |
| 82$ | – | – | – | – | 574 | 550 | 515 | 524 | 524 |
| FTEs | – | – | – | – | 12 | 12 | 12 | 12 | – |
| **Subtotal: Non-Energy Minerals** | 6,225 | 7,625 | 9,771 | 11,955 | 14,111 | 14,709 | 14,512 | 14,883 | 15,683 |
| 82$ | 7,346 | 8,186 | 9,771 | 11,482 | 13,023 | 13,107 | 12,594 | 12,551 | 13,225 |
| FTEs | – | – | 290 | 317 | 361 | 355 | 366 | 361 | – |
| **Subtotal: Energy & Minerals Management** | 33,000 | 53,026 | 51,557 | 67,758 | 77,128 | 80,874 | 80,295 | 77,572 | 77,872 |
| 82$ | 38,943 | 56,929 | 51,557 | 65,075 | 71,181 | 72,067 | 69,680 | 65,416 | 65,669 |
| FTEs | – | – | 1,270 | 1,557 | 1,921 | 1,883 | 1,992 | 1,884 | – |
| **Land and Realty Management** | | | | | | | | | |
| **Realty Operations** | 22,590 | 25,511 | 27,016 | 32,553 | 38,075 | 37,800 | 36,340 | 35,222 | 38,472 |
| 82$ | 26,658 | 27,389 | 27,016 | 31,264 | 35,139 | 33,684 | 31,536 | 29,703 | 32,443 |
| FTEs | – | – | 878 | 948 | 982 | 970 | 1,005 | 985 | – |
| **Withdrawal Processing & Review** | 1,993 | 2,731 | 4,088 | 4,079 | 3,529 | 4,034 | 3,583 | 3,732 | 3,732 |
| 82$ | 2,352 | 2,932 | 4,088 | 3,917 | 3,257 | 3,595 | 3,109 | 3,147 | 3,147 |
| FTEs | – | – | 111 | 99 | 87 | 100 | 93 | 93 | – |
| **Subtotal: Lands & Realty Management** | 24,583 | 28,242 | 31,104 | 36,632 | 41,604 | 41,834 | 39,923 | 38,954 | 42,204 |
| 82$ | 29,010 | 30,321 | 31,104 | 35,181 | 38,396 | 37,278 | 34,645 | 32,850 | 35,591 |
| FTEs | – | – | 989 | 1,047 | 1,069 | 1,070 | 1,098 | 1,078 | – |
| **Renewable Resource Management** | | | | | | | | | |
| **Forest Management** | | | | | | | | | |
| **Public Domain** | 5,672 | 6,601 | 6,100 | 4,770 | 5,186 | 6,835 | 6,521 | 5,106 | 6,106 |
| 82$ | 6,694 | 7,087 | 6,100 | 4,581 | 4,786 | 6,091 | 5,659 | 4,306 | 5,149 |
| FTEs | – | – | 221 | 138 | 135 | 152 | 150 | 127 | – |
| **Western Oregon** | 1,141 | 792 | 2,163 | 936 | 939 | 920 | 875 | – | 914 |
| 82$ | 1,346 | 850 | 2,163 | 899 | 867 | 820 | 759 | – | 771 |
| FTEs | – | – | – | – | – | – | – | – | – |

| | 1980[1,2,3] Actual | 1981[1,2,3] Actual | 1982[1] Actual | 1983[4] Actual | 1984[4] Actual | 1985 Actual | 1986 Actual | 1987 President's Request | 1987 Appropriations |
|---|---|---|---|---|---|---|---|---|---|
| Subtotal: Forest Management | 6,813 | 7,393 | 8,263 | 5,706 | 6,125 | 7,755 | 7,396 | 5,106 | 7,020 |
| 82$ | 8,040 | 7,937 | 8,263 | 5,480 | 5,653 | 6,910 | 6,418 | 4,306 | 5,920 |
| FTEs | – | – | 221 | 138 | 135 | 152 | 150 | 127 | – |
| **Range Management** | | | | | | | | | |
| Wild Horse & Burro Management | 4,582 | 5,704 | 5,418 | 4,877 | 5,766 | 17,039 | 16,234 | 15,200 | 17,777 |
| 82$ | 5,407 | 6,124 | 5,418 | 4,684 | 5,321 | 15,183 | 14,088 | 12,818 | 14,991 |
| FTEs | – | – | 96 | 88 | 98 | 148 | 130 | 125 | – |
| Grazing Management | 28,663 | 36,110 | 36,138 | 34,754 | 32,138 | 30,969 | 29,319 | 30,860 | 36,360[5] |
| 82$ | 33,825 | 38,768 | 36,138 | 33,378 | 29,660 | 27,596 | 25,443 | 26,024 | 30,662 |
| FTEs | – | – | 994 | 927 | 857 | 798 | 775 | 780 | – |
| Subtotal: Range Management | 33,245 | 41,814 | 41,556 | 39,631 | 37,904 | 48,008 | 45,553 | 46,060 | 54,137 |
| 82$ | 39,232 | 44,892 | 41,556 | 38,062 | 34,982 | 42,780 | 39,531 | 38,842 | 45,654 |
| FTEs | – | – | 1,090 | 1,015 | 955 | 946 | 905 | 905 | – |
| **Soil, Water, and Air Management** | | | | | | | | | |
| Soil, Water and Air Management | 13,816 | 18,037 | 17,042 | 16,346 | 15,972 | 15,185 | 13,981 | 12,687 | 13,337 |
| 82$ | 16,304 | 19,365 | 17,042 | 15,699 | 14,741 | 13,531 | 12,133 | 10,699 | 11,247 |
| Hazardous Waste Management[6] | – | – | – | 600 | 600 | 1,274 | 1,705 | 1,782 | 1,782 |
| 82$ | – | – | – | 576 | 554 | 1,135 | 1,480 | 1,503 | 1,503 |
| Subtotal: Soil, Water, and Air | 13,816 | 18,037 | 17,042 | 16,946 | 16,572 | 16,459 | 15,686 | 14,469 | 15,119 |
| 82$ | 16,304 | 19,365 | 17,042 | 16,275 | 15,294 | 14,667 | 13,612 | 12,202 | 12,750 |
| FTEs | – | – | 310 | 307 | 306 | 308 | 290 | 278 | – |
| Wildlife Habitat Management | 12,554 | 16,017 | 14,918 | 15,150 | 13,604 | 15,833 | 15,364 | 13,801 | 16,111 |
| 82$ | 14,815 | 17,196 | 14,918 | 14,550 | 12,555 | 14,109 | 13,333 | 11,638 | 13,586 |
| FTEs | – | – | 360 | 340 | 312 | 328 | 320 | 300 | – |

| | | | | | | | | | |
|---|---|---|---|---|---|---|---|---|---|
| [Threatened & Endangered Species[7]] [82$]........ | [3,932] [3,316] | [2,932] [2,413] | [3,827] [3,321] | [3,966] [3,534] | [2,650] [2,446] | [1,650] [1,585] | NA | NA | NA |
| **Recreation Management** | | | | | | | | | |
| Cultural Resources.... 82$..... FTEs..... | 6,618 / 5,581 / – | 5,078 / 4,282 / 120 | 5,783 / 5,018 / 125 | 5,279 / 4,704 / 119 | 4,843 / 4,470 / 116. | 4,566 / 4,385 / 117 | 4,510 / 4,510 / 102 | 3,402 / 3,652 / – | 2,192 / 2,587 / – |
| Wilderness Management.... 82$..... FTEs..... | 7,254 / 6,117 / – | 7,254 / 6,117 / 150 | 6,967 / 6,046 / 150 | 6,419 / 5,720 / 150 | 7,020 / 6,479 / 174 | 12,179 / 11,697 / 176 | 13,970 / 13,970 / 197 | 10,317 / 11,076 / – | 7,677 / 9,060 / – |
| Recreation Resources Management 82$..... FTEs..... | 9,092 / 7,667 / – | 7,198 / 6,070 / 180 | 7,727 / 6,705 / 190 | 6,750 / 6,015 / 160 | 6,633 / 6,122 / 169 | 6,489 / 6,232 / 170 | 5,688 / 5,688 / 165 | 6,011 / 6,453 / – | 6,101 / 7,200 / – |
| Subtotal: Recreation Management 82$..... FTEs..... | 22,964 / 19,366 / – | 19,530 / 16,470 / 450 | 20,477 / 17,770 / 465 | 18,448 / 16,439 / 429 | 18,496 / 17,070 / 459 | 23,234 / 22,314 / 463 | 24,168 / 24,168 / 464 | 19,730 / 21,182 / – | 15,970 / 18,846 / – |
| Fire Management..... 82$..... FTEs..... | 8,847 / 7,461 / – | 8,847 / 7,461 / 145 | 8,444 / 7,328 / 140 | 7,390 / 6,585 / 136 | 7,666 / 7,075 / 153 | 9,334 / 8,964 / 145 | 7,231 / 7,231 / 152 | 7,519 / 8,072 / – | 6,797 / 8,021 / – |
| Subtotal: Renewable Resource Management..... 82$..... FTEs..... | 124,198 / 104,736 / – | 107,813 / 90,919 / 2,205 | 112,920 / 97,992 / 2,270 | 113,893 / 101,490 / 2,299 | 100,367 / 92,629 / 2,320 | 110,001 / 105,645 / 2,408 | 113,198 / 113,198 / 2,597 | 110,510 / 118,644 / – | 89,195 / 105,259 / – |
| **Planning and Data Management** | | | | | | | | | |
| Planning..... 82$..... FTEs..... | 9,525 / 8,032 / – | 9,525 / 8,032 / 217 | 9,047 / 7,851 / 215 | 9,124 / 8,130 / 215 | 8,921 / 8,233 / 227 | 8,704 / 8,359 / 226 | 8,661 / 8,661 / 233 | 12,289 / 13,193 / – | 9,665 / 11,406 / – |
| Data Management..... 82$..... FTEs..... | 14,888 / 12,555 / – | 14,888 / 12,555 / 235 | 13,106 / 11,373 / 220 | 13,613 / 12,131 / 218 | 14,376 / 13,268 / 230 | 12,932 / 12,420 / 200 | 12,012 / 12,012 / 210 | 15,767 / 16,927 / – | 12,103 / 14,283 / – |

| | 1980[1,2,3] Actual | 1981[1,2,3] Actual | 1982[1] Actual | 1983[4] Actual | 1984[4] Actual | 1985 Actual | 1986 Actual | 1987 President's Request | 1987 Appropriations |
|---|---|---|---|---|---|---|---|---|---|
| **Subtotal: Planning & Data Management** | 21,768 | 28,056 | 20,673 | 21,636 | 23,297 | 22,737 | 22,153 | 24,413 | 24,413 |
| 82$ | 25,688 | 30,121 | 20,673 | 20,779 | 21,501 | 20,261 | 19,224 | 20,587 | 20,587 |
| FTEs | - | - | 443 | 426 | 457 | 433 | 435 | 452 | - |
| **Cadastral Survey** | 18,454 | 19,193 | 19,637 | 21,594 | 23,873 | 24,676 | 25,605 | 22,691 | 26,681 |
| 82$ | 21,778 | 20,606 | 19,637 | 20,739 | 22,032 | 21,989 | 22,220 | 19,135 | 22,500 |
| FTEs | 444 | - | 444 | 476 | 468 | 425 | 430 | 421 | - |
| **Fire Control[8]** | 49,750 | 49,750 | 59,560 | 42,910 | 54,931 | 74,101 | 3,901 | 4,076 | 87,076 |
| 82$ | 58,710 | 53,412 | 59,560 | 41,211 | 50,696 | 66,031 | 3,885 | 3,437 | 73,431 |
| FTEs | - | - | 837 | 870 | 842 | 991 | 868 | 868 | - |
| **Technical Services** | 11,476 | 12,119 | 11,137 | 12,953 | 12,975 | 14,202 | 14,814 | 15,065 | 16,065 |
| 82$ | 13,543 | 13,011 | 11,137 | 12,440 | 11,975 | 12,655 | 12,856 | 12,704 | 13,548 |
| FTEs | - | - | 196 | 222 | 231 | 236 | 232 | 229 | - |
| **General Administration** | 75,268 | 76,142 | 77,180 | 75,865 | 82,352 | 83,136 | 79,528 | 85,101 | 85,101 |
| 82$ | 88,824 | 81,746 | 77,180 | 72,861 | 76,003 | 74,082 | 69,014 | 71,766 | 71,766 |
| FTEs | - | - | 1,277 | 1,227 | 1,291 | 1,207 | 1,195 | 1,149 | - |
| **TOTAL MANAGEMENT OF LANDS & RESOURCES** | 323,494 | 377,038 | 384,026 | 389,349 | 416,527 | 455,453 | 379,139 | 375,685 | 483,610 |
| 82$ | 381,755 | 404,788 | 384,026 | 373,931 | 384,413 | 405,854 | 329,017 | 316,815 | 407,828 |
| FTEs | - | - | 8,117 | 8,233 | 8,599 | 8,544 | 8,520 | 8,286 | - |
| **CONSTRUCTION AND ACCESS** | 5,284 | 3,682 | 2,627 | 2,243 | 3,070 | 2,028 | 1,335 | 1,200 | 2,800 |
| 82$ | 6,236 | 3,953 | 2,627 | 2,154 | 2,833 | 1,807 | 1,159 | 1,012 | 2,361 |
| FTEs | - | - | 78 | 47 | 33 | 25 | 25 | 25 | - |
| **PAYMENTS IN LIEU OF TAXES** | 108,000 | 103,000 | 95,520 | 96,230 | 105,000 | 102,900 | 99,882 | 105,000 | 105,000 |
| 82$ | 127,451 | 110,581 | 95,520 | 92,419 | 96,905 | 91,694 | 86,678 | 88,547 | 88,547 |
| FTEs | - | 1 | 1 | 1 | 1 | 1 | 1 | 1 | - |
| **LAND ACQUISITION[9]** | [2,750] | [1,002] | 3,712 | 311 | 6,201 | 4,695 | 2,188 | - | 3,020 |
| 82$ | [3,245] | [1,076] | 3,712 | 299 | 5,723 | 4,184 | 1,899 | - | 2,547 |
| FTEs | [-] | [-] | 10 | 7 | 6 | 12 | 7 | 4 | - |

| | | | | | | | | | |
|---|---|---|---|---|---|---|---|---|---|
| **O & C GRANT LANDS** | 54,524 | 51,160 | 53,379 | 56,939 | 48,536 | 57,620 | 50,721 | 43,361 | 43,687 |
| 82$ | 45,980 | 43,143 | 46,322 | 50,738 | 44,794 | 55,338 | 50,721 | 46,552 | 51,555 |
| FTEs | – | 988 | 998 | 995 | 1,021 | 1,053 | 1,089 | – | – |
| **SPECIAL ACQUISITION-CRANBERRY** | – | – | – | 14,700 | – | – | – | – | – |
| 82$ | – | – | – | 13,099 | – | – | – | – | – |
| FTEs | – | – | – | – | – | – | – | – | – |
| **RANGE IMPROVEMENT FUND** | 9,253 | 8,506 | 9,570 | 10,000 | 10,000 | 11,200 | 13,500 | 13,117 | 10,620 |
| 82$ | 7,803 | 7,173 | 8,305 | 8,911 | 9,229 | 10,756 | 13,500 | 14,082 | 12,533 |
| FTEs | – | 114 | 119 | 114 | 133 | 145 | 151 | – | – |
| **SERVICE CHARGES, DEPOSITS, & FORFEITURES** | 5,195 | 5,195 | 4,247 | 5,230 | 3,860 | 5,357 | 6,341 | 5,823 | 6,922 |
| 82$ | 4,381 | 4,381 | 3,686 | 4,660 | 3,562 | 5,145 | 6,341 | 6,252 | 8,169 |
| FTEs | – | 57 | 57 | 57 | 54 | 68 | 109 | – | – |
| **MISCELLANEOUS TRUST FUNDS** | 100 | 100 | 100 | 100 | 700 | 700 | 700 | 1,068 | 1,183 |
| 82$ | 084 | 084 | 087 | 089 | 646 | 672 | 700 | 1,147 | 1,396 |
| FTEs | – | – | 0 | 0 | 17 | 16 | 14 | – | – |
| **RECREATION DEVELOPMENT & OPERATIONS OF FACILITIES** | – | – | – | – | – | – | – | – | 300 |
| 82$ | – | – | – | – | – | – | – | – | 354 |
| FTEs | – | – | – | – | – | – | – | – | – |
| **TOTAL APPROPRIATIONS** | 663,502 | 546,846 | 549,840 | 652,045 | 593,894 | 563,010 | 557,147 | 547,089 | 499,490 |
| 82$ | 559,531 | 461,155 | 477,151 | 581,037 | 548,105 | 540,715 | 557,147 | 587,355 | 589,448 |
| FTEs | – | 9,475 | 9,727 | 9,748 | 9,864 | 9,570 | 9,537 | – | – |
| **PERMANENT & TRUST FUNDS[10]** | 53,323 | 53,323 | 13,663[9] | 147,660 | 66,197 | 584,412 | 635,538 | 440,066 | 373,959 |
| 82$ | 44,967 | 44,967 | 11,857 | 131,580 | 61,093 | 561,269 | 635,538 | 472,455 | 441,309 |
| FTEs | – | 127 | 127 | 125 | 93 | 70 | 5 | – | – |
| **OTHER FTEs** | – | 193 | 203 | 223 | 317 | 305 | 253 | – | – |

| | 1980[1,2,3] Actual | 1981[1,2,3] Actual | 1982[1] Actual | 1983[4] Actual | 1984[4] Actual | 1985 Actual | 1986 Actual | 1987 President's Request | 1987 Appropriations |
|---|---|---|---|---|---|---|---|---|---|
| TOTAL: BLM.............. | 873,449 | 987,155 | 1,192,685 | 1,147,422 | 660,091 | 799,705 | 563,503 | 600,169[11] | 716,825 |
| 825.................. | 1,030,757 | 1,059,810 | 1,192,685 | 1,101,984 | 609,198 | 712,617 | 489,008 | 506,123 | 604,499 |
| FTEs................. | – | – | 9,795 | 9,945 | 10,274 | 10,096 | 10,057 | 9,795 | – |

1. Funds appropriated to BLM in 1980, 1981, and 1982 for outer-continental-shelf oil and gas leasing are omitted for purposes of comparison. O.C.S. responsibilities were transferred to the Minerals Management Service in 1983.

2. Prior to 1982, BLM included General Administration costs in funding for each program. Appropriations in 1981 and 1982 have been adjusted to remove General Administration costs for purposes of comparison.

3. BLM did not measure staff levels in FTEs prior to 1982.

4. BLM assumed additional minerals responsibilities in mid-1983 in a merger with the Minerals Management Service. Much of the increase in the Energy and Minerals Management budget in 1983 and 1984 is due to this shift in responsibilities.

5. Five million dollars of the increase in grazing management is for a grasshopper eradication program never before funded in this category.

6. The hazardous-waste-management program does not actually appear as a separate line item in the budget but is funded with funds appropriated to the Soil, Water, and Air Management subactivity. The amount allocated internally by BLM to the program is shown here. In 1987, Congress for the first time earmarked a specific amount -- $1.782 million -- for the hazardous-waste program.

7. This shows the amount of wildlife-habitat-management funding allocated internally by BLM to threatened and endangered species. Prior to 1983, BLM did not track this funding separately.

8. Prior to 1987, BLM paid most firefighting costs by borrowing funds from other agencies. To cover the amount spent, Congress would appropriate funds in a supplemental appropriations bill the following year, after which BLM would reimburse the other agencies for the borrowed funds. BLM estimated that firefighting costs for 1986 were $86 million, which would bring the total 1986 appropriations to $635.840 million. In 1987, however, Congress for the first time appropriated funds for firefighting up front.

9. Prior to 1982, land-acquisition funds were appropriated to the Heritage Conservation and Recreation Service. Amounts shown here are for comparison.

10. Permanent and trust funds consist of payments to states for their share of receipts from development activities on federal lands. Prior to 1984, this included payments to states for their share of offshore leasing royalties, a function assumed by the Minerals Management Service in 1984. In 1985, BLM made an early payment to Oregon and California Grant Land counties of their 1986 share of receipts, causing 1985 budget authority to be unusually high and 1986 to be unusually low.

11. The administration also requested $3.4 million and a reduction of 37 FTEs to begin interchanging BLM and Forest Service lands in an effort to improve management efficiency. Congress did not approve the interchange and rejected the funding changes, as it has for the past several years.

FOREST SERVICE BUDGET HISTORY, 1980 – 87

(in 000s of dollars)

| | 1980[1] Actual | 1981[1] Actual | 1982[1] Actual | 1983[1] Actual | 1984[1] Actual | 1985 Actual | 1986 Actual | 1987 President's Request | 1987 Appropriations |
|---|---|---|---|---|---|---|---|---|---|
| **FOREST RESEARCH** | | | | | | | | | |
| Wildlife, Range, & Fish Habitat.. | 7,513 | 8,395 | 9,334 | 8,706 | 9,163 | 9,108 | 9,072 | 9,291 | 11,491 |
| $000s | 8,866 | 9,013 | 9,334 | 8,361 | 8,457 | 8,116 | 7,873 | 7,835 | 9,690 |
| FTEs | 191 | 218 | 217 | 194 | 198 | 191 | 195 | 193 | – |
| Special Project, Competitive Grants | – | – | – | – | – | 7,840 | 6,507 | – | 6,000 |
| $000s | – | – | – | – | – | 6,986 | 5,647 | – | 5,060 |
| FTEs | – | – | – | – | – | – | – | – | – |
| Other Research | 88,404 | 100,058 | 102,811 | 98,966 | 100,240 | 104,718 | 104,548 | 102,190 | 111,391 |
| $000s | 104,326 | 107,422 | 102,811 | 95,047 | 95,511 | 93,314 | 90,727 | 86,177 | 93,936 |
| FTEs | 2,220 | 2,402 | 2,393 | 2,221 | 2,193 | 2,210 | 2,221 | 2,120 | – |
| TOTAL: FOREST RESEARCH | 95,917 | 108,453 | 112,145 | 107,672 | 109,403 | 121,666 | 120,127 | 111,481 | 128,882 |
| $000s | 113,192 | 116,435 | 112,145 | 103,408 | 100,968 | 108,417 | 104,246 | 94,012 | 108,686 |
| FTEs | 2,411 | 2,620 | 2,610 | 2,415 | 2,391 | 2,401 | 2,416 | 2,313 | – |
| **STATE AND PRIVATE FORESTRY** | | | | | | | | | |
| Forest Management and Utilization | 20,123 | 23,450 | 22,522 | 17,080 | 10,713 | 10,756 | 9,518 | | 9,925 |
| $000s | 23,747 | 25,176 | 22,522 | 16,404 | 9,887 | 9,585 | 8,260 | | 8,370 |
| FTEs | 178 | 180 | 237 | 158 | 107 | 98 | 97 | | – |
| Other Programs | 50,732 | 47,717 | 43,033 | 45,755 | 50,040 | 47,536 | 45,803 | 24,871 | 49,021 |
| $000s | 59,869 | 51,229 | 43,033 | 43,943 | 46,182 | 42,359 | 39,748 | 20,974 | 41,339 |
| FTEs | 578 | 454 | 451 | 480 | 473 | 488 | 455 | 433 | – |
| TOTAL: STATE AND PRIVATE FORESTRY.. | 70,855 | 71,167 | 65,555 | 62,835 | 60,753 | 58,292 | 55,321 | 24,871 | 58,946 |
| $000s | 83,616 | 76,405 | 65,555 | 60,347 | 56,069 | 51,944 | 48,008 | 20,974 | 49,709 |
| FTEs | 756 | 634 | 688 | 638 | 580 | 586 | 552 | 433 | – |

| | 1980[1] Actual | 1981[1] Actual | 1982[1] Actual | 1983[1] Actual | 1984 Actual | 1985 Actual | 1986 Actual | 1987 President's Request | 1987 Appropriations |
|---|---|---|---|---|---|---|---|---|---|
| **NATIONAL FOREST SYSTEM** | | | | | | | | | |
| Minerals Area Management | 12,213 | 15,175 | 18,691 | 22,598 | 25,670 | 26,572 | 27,164 | 26,025 | 26,319 |
| 82$ | 14,413 | 16,292 | 18,691 | 21,703 | 23,691 | 23,678 | 23,573 | 21,947 | 22,195 |
| FTEs | 320 | 517 | 579 | 630 | 659 | 643 | 663 | 634 | – |
| Real Estate Management | 18,071 | 20,547 | 20,636 | 19,935 | 18,709 | 20,836 | 19,978 | 19,845 | 19,845 |
| 82$ | 21,326 | 22,060 | 20,636 | 19,146 | 17,227 | 18,567 | 17,337 | 16,735 | 16,735 |
| FTEs | 545 | 717 | 658 | 527 | 469 | 477 | 473 | 461 | – |
| Land Line Location | 16,959 | 25,341 | 25,011 | 25,034 | 29,448 | 29,090 | 27,399 | 23,011 | 26,363 |
| 82$ | 20,013 | 27,206 | 25,011 | 24,043 | 27,178 | 25,922 | 23,777 | 19,405 | 22,232 |
| FTEs | 493 | 596 | 545 | 581 | 583 | 568 | 560 | 495 | – |
| Maintenance of Facilities | 9,989 | 11,523 | 11,833 | 21,710 | 14,070 | 14,792 | 14,124 | 14,735 | 14,735 |
| 82$ | 11,788 | 12,371 | 11,833 | 20,850 | 12,985 | 13,181 | 12,257 | 12,426 | 12,426 |
| FTEs | 220 | 292 | 275 | 318 | 308 | 297 | 296 | 296 | – |
| Forest Fire Protection | 124,779 | 141,092 | 142,235 | 153,889 | 156,734 | 156,591 | 151,669 | 147,225 | 154,796 |
| 82$ | 147,252 | 151,476 | 142,235 | 147,795 | 144,650 | 139,538 | 131,618 | 124,155 | 130,539 |
| FTEs | 5,173 | 4,773 | 4,488 | 4,600 | 4,305 | 4,072 | 4,090 | 3,906 | – |
| Forest Fire Fighting | 92,275 | 104,275 | 69,004 | 1,000 | 35,301 | 62,227 | 166,652 | 1,000 | 125,000 |
| 82$ | 108,894 | 111,950 | 69,004 | 960 | 32,579 | 55,450 | 144,621 | 84 | 105,413 |
| FTEs | – | – | – | – | – | – | – | – | – |
| Cooperative Law Enforcement | 3,576 | 4,411 | 3,734 | 5,174 | 5,175 | 7,212 | 6,659 | 2,450 | 6,660 |
| 82$ | 4,220 | 4,736 | 3,734 | 4,969 | 4,776 | 6,427 | 5,779 | 2,066 | 5,616 |
| FTEs | 23 | 33 | 12 | 12 | 11 | 14 | 14 | 14 | – |
| Forest Road Maintenance | 56,446 | 62,473 | 65,286 | 73,666 | 64,650 | 65,406 | 61,856 | 49,270 | 61,770 |
| 82$ | 66,612 | 67,071 | 65,286 | 70,749 | 59,665 | 58,283 | 53,679 | 41,550 | 52,091 |
| FTEs | 1,885 | 1,625 | 1,205 | 1,403 | 1,283 | 1,194 | 1,185 | 1,040 | – |
| Forest Trail Maintenance | 9,109 | 11,226 | 11,312 | 13,988 | 9,267 | 9,256 | 9,537 | 8,365 | 11,000 |
| 82$ | 16,750 | 12,052 | 11,312 | 13,343 | 8,553 | 8,248 | 8,276 | 7,054 | 9,276 |
| FTEs | 529 | 442 | 360 | 400 | 344 | 272 | 290 | 260 | – |
| Timber Sales Administration & Management | 137,428 | 155,485 | 159,836 | 162,125 | 187,547 | 194,702 | 174,007 | 171,092 | 184,139 |
| 82$ | 162,179 | 166,929 | 159,836 | 155,705 | 173,087 | 173,499 | 151,003 | 144,282 | 155,284 |
| FTEs | 6,042 | 5,646 | 5,621 | 5,108 | 5,617 | 5,478 | 5,300 | 5,135 | – |

| | | | | | | | | | |
|---|---|---|---|---|---|---|---|---|---|
| Reforestation & Stand Improvement² | 78,819 | 82,911 | 95,611 | 57,963 | 19,651 | 67,259 | 95,128 | 57,948 | 58,893 |
| 82$ | 93,014 | 89,013 | 95,611 | 55,668 | 18,136 | 59,934 | 82,552 | 48,868 | 49,664 |
| FTEs | 2,625 | 2,309 | 2,400 | 953 | 392 | 1,153 | 1,974 | 580 | - |
| **Recreation Use** | | | | | | | | | |
| Recreation Management | 73,305 | 77,934 | 78,804 | 85,905 | 84,747 | 84,741 | 82,216 | 33,742 | 90,824 |
| 82$ | 86,507 | 83,670 | 78,804 | 82,503 | 78,213 | 75,513 | 71,347 | 28,455 | 76,592 |
| FTEs | - | - | - | - | - | 2,131 | 2,153 | 848 | - |
| Wilderness Management | 4,247 | 5,494 | 6,093 | 6,703 | 6,798 | 7,746 | 7,520 | 8,030 | 10,030 |
| 82$ | 5,012 | 5,898 | 6,093 | 6,438 | 6,274 | 6,902 | 6,526 | 6,772 | 8,458 |
| FTEs | - | - | - | - | - | 222 | 222 | 225 | - |
| Cultural Resource Management | 4,235 | 5,936 | 6,283 | 7,166 | 9,374 | 9,570 | 9,281 | 9,368 | 9,368 |
| 82$ | 4,998 | 6,373 | 6,283 | 6,882 | 8,651 | 8,528 | 8,054 | 7,900 | 7,900 |
| FTEs | - | - | - | - | - | 250 | 250 | 244 | - |
| Subtotal: Recreation Use | 81,784 | 89,363 | 91,180 | 99,774 | 100,919 | 102,057 | 99,017 | 51,140 | 110,222 |
| 82$ | 96,513 | 95,940 | 91,180 | 95,823 | 93,138 | 90,943 | 85,927 | 43,126 | 92,950 |
| FTEs | 3,078 | 3,155 | 2,772 | 2,923 | 2,708 | 2,603 | 2,625 | 1,317 | - |
| **Wildlife and Fish Habitat Management** | | | | | | | | | |
| Administration & Coordination | 14,838 | 14,903 | 18,369 | 18,487 | 22,055 | 22,371 | 22,698 | 23,360 | 25,272 |
| 82$ | 17,503 | 16,000 | 18,369 | 17,755 | 20,355 | 19,935 | 19,697 | 19,699 | 21,312 |
| FTEs | - | - | - | - | - | 551 | 585 | 582 | - |
| Wildlife Habitat Improvement | 14,865 | 15,728 | 7,410 | 7,310 | 5,693 | 6,300 | 6,440 | 4,980 | 6,480 |
| 82$ | 17,542 | 16,886 | 7,410 | 7,020 | 5,254 | 5,614 | 5,589 | 4,200 | 5,465 |
| FTEs | - | - | - | - | - | 152 | 162 | 129 | - |
| Resident Fish Habitat Improvement³ | - | - | 6,078 | 6,246 | 2,047 | 1,748 | 1,886 | 1,370 | 1,370 |
| 82$ | - | - | 6,078 | 5,999 | 1,889 | 1,558 | 1,637 | 1,155 | 1,155 |
| FTEs | - | - | - | - | - | 35 | 40 | 30 | - |
| Threatened & Endangered Species Habitat Improvement | 865 | 911 | 1,279 | 1,306 | 2,432 | 2,464 | 2,368 | 1,235 | 3,505 |
| 82$ | 1,021 | 978 | 1,279 | 1,254 | 2,244 | 2,196 | 2,055 | 1,041 | 2,956 |
| FTEs | - | - | - | - | - | 44 | 44 | 27 | - |

| | 1980 Actual[1] | 1981 Actual[1] | 1982 Actual[1] | 1983 Actual[1] | 1984 Actual | 1985 Actual | 1986 Actual | 1987 President's Request | 1987 Appropriations |
|---|---|---|---|---|---|---|---|---|---|
| **Anadromous Fish Habitat** | | | | | | | | | |
| Improvement | -- | -- | -- | -- | 3,133 | 3,843 | 3,695 | 2,835 | 4,535 |
| 82$ | -- | -- | -- | -- | 2,891 | 3,424 | 3,207 | 2,391 | 3,824 |
| FTEs | -- | -- | -- | -- | - | 56 | 56 | 45 | - |
| **Subtotal: Wildlife & Fish Habitat** | 30,563 | 31,542 | 33,136 | 33,349 | 35,360 | 36,726 | 37,087 | 33,780 | 41,537 |
| 82$ | 36,067 | 33,863 | 33,136 | 32,038 | 32,634 | 32,727 | 32,184 | 28,487 | 35,028 |
| FTEs | 1,039 | 1,105 | 941 | 893 | 877 | 838 | 887 | 813 | - |
| **Range Management** | | | | | | | | | |
| Grazing Program | 24,716 | 21,455 | 23,458 | 23,787 | 24,232 | 24,691 | 23,231 | 25,595 | 24,355 |
| 82$ | 29,167 | 23,034 | 23,458 | 22,845 | 22,364 | 22,002 | 20,160 | 21,584 | 20,539 |
| FTEs | - | - | - | - | - | 626 | 615 | 632 | - |
| Range Improvements | 2,711 | 2,619 | 2,761 | 2,250 | 2,323 | 2,320 | 2,092 | 769 | 769 |
| 82$ | 3,199 | 2,812 | 2,761 | 2,161 | 2,144 | 2,067 | 1,815 | 648 | 648 |
| FTEs | - | - | - | - | - | 41 | 38 | 16 | - |
| Wild Horses and Burros | 415 | 284 | 315 | 584 | 293 | 176 | 262 | 275 | 275 |
| 82$ | 490 | 305 | 315 | 561 | 270 | 157 | 227 | 232 | 232 |
| FTEs | - | - | - | - | - | 3 | 4 | 4 | - |
| Noxious Weed Control | - | 1,209 | 753 | 410 | 419 | 983 | 1,309 | 1,180 | 1,400 |
| 82$ | - | 1,298 | 753 | 394 | 387 | 876 | 1,136 | 995 | 1,960 |
| FTEs | - | - | - | - | - | 17 | 21 | 19 | - |
| **Subtotal: Range Management** | 27,842 | 25,566 | 27,287 | 27,031 | 27,267 | 28,120 | 26,894 | 27,819 | 26,799 |
| 82$ | 32,856 | 27,448 | 27,287 | 25,961 | 25,164 | 25,058 | 23,339 | 23,460 | 22,600 |
| FTEs | 958 | 931 | 836 | 719 | 710 | 687 | 678 | 671 | - |
| **Soil, Water, and Air Management** | | | | | | | | | |
| Administration | 14,805 | 15,505 | 19,550 | 18,708 | 20,881 | 22,044 | 21,237 | 22,797 | 24,030 |
| 82$ | 17,471 | 16,646 | 19,550 | 17,967 | 19,271 | 19,643 | 18,429 | 19,225 | 20,264 |
| FTEs | - | - | - | - | - | 520 | 520 | 527 | - |
| Improvements | 8,287 | 5,020 | 1,800 | 2,355 | 2,409 | 3,105 | 2,988 | 1,225 | 3,125 |
| 82$ | 9,779 | 5,389 | 1,800 | 2,262 | 2,223 | 2,767 | 2,593 | 1,033 | 2,635 |
| FTEs | - | - | - | - | - | 52 | 52 | 27 | - |

| | | | | | | | | | |
|---|---|---|---|---|---|---|---|---|---|
| Soil and Water Inventories..... | 6,065 | 4,765 | 6,299 | 6,659 | 6,666 | 7,650 | 10,665 | 10,033 | 14,132 |
| 82$..... | 5,115 | 4,018 | 5,466 | 5,934 | 6,152 | 7,347 | 10,665 | 10,771 | 16,677 |
| FTEs..... | - | 87 | 106 | 108 | - | - | - | - | - |
| Subtotal: Soil, Water, & Air. | 33,220 | 28,787 | 30,524 | 31,808 | 29,956 | 28,713 | 32,015 | 30,558 | 37,225 |
| 82$..... | 28,014 | 24,276 | 26,489 | 28,344 | 27,646 | 27,576 | 32,015 | 32,807 | 43,929 |
| FTEs..... | - | 641 | 678 | 680 | 715 | 713 | 861 | 948 | 1,079 |
| General Administration..... | 256,996 | 256,996 | 251,229 | 258,844 | 259,865 | 260,915 | 242,290 | 267,097 | 254,812 |
| 82$..... | 216,725 | 216,725 | 218,017 | 230,656 | 239,829 | 250,583 | 242,290 | 286,755 | 300,704 |
| FTEs..... | - | 5,358 | 5,472 | 5,722 | 5,938 | 6,099 | 6,226 | 6,978 | 7,072 |
| Youth Conservation Corps..... | - | - | - | - | - | 3,400 | - | - | 52,624 |
| 82$..... | - | - | - | - | - | 3,265 | - | - | 62,102 |
| FTEs..... | - | - | - | - | - | - | - | - | - |
| USFS/BLM Interchange..... | - | 5 | - | - | - | - | - | - | - |
| TOTAL: NATIONAL FOREST SYSTEM..... | 1,158,294 | 894,488 | 1,198,924 | 1,111,548 | 1,019,589 | 1,010,264 | 1,049,097 | 1,078,585 | 1,044,514 |
| 82$..... | 976,789 | 750,105 | 1,040,426 | 990,500 | 940,979 | 970,276 | 1,049,097 | 1,157,969 | 1,232,631 |
| FTEs..... | - | 21,621 | 25,185 | 24,698 | 24,919 | 25,916 | 27,779 | 30,067 | 31,551 |
| MOUNT ST. HELENS..... | - | - | - | - | - | - | - | 36,049 | 25,000 |
| 82$..... | - | - | - | - | - | - | - | 38,702 | 29,503 |
| FTEs..... | | | | | | | | 122 | 121 |
| CONSTRUCTION | | | | | | | | | |
| Facilities..... | 25,332 | 11,736 | 26,853 | 27,862 | 23,867 | 51,461 | 17,853 | 19,481 | 23,195 |
| 82$..... | 21,362 | 9,898 | 23,303 | 24,828 | 22,027 | 49,423 | 17,853 | 20,915 | 27,372 |
| FTEs..... | - | 129 | 179 | 182 | 193 | 177 | 214 | 146 | 182 |
| Forest Roads..... | 228,803 | 178,485 | 180,935 | 228,914 | 222,675 | 245,169 | 236,204 | 224,760 | 214,419 |
| 82$..... | 192,950 | 150,516 | 157,015 | 203,985 | 205,507 | 235,460 | 236,204 | 241,302 | 253,036 |
| FTEs..... | - | 3,410 | 3,500 | 3,711 | 4,178 | 4,394 | 5,157 | 5,160 | 4,807 |
| Trails..... | 7,301 | 4,976 | 6,866 | 7,093 | 5,182 | 4,936 | 4,638 | 3,443 | 6,594 |
| 82$..... | 6,157 | 4,196 | 5,958 | 6,321 | 4,782 | 4,741 | 4,038 | 3,696 | 7,782 |
| FTEs..... | - | 140 | 176 | 178 | 98 | 90 | 91 | 103 | 230 |
| Chugach Natives..... | - | - | - | - | - | 9,000 | 3,000 | - | - |
| 82$..... | - | - | - | - | - | 8,644 | 3,000 | - | - |
| FTEs..... | - | - | - | - | - | - | - | - | - |

| | 1980[1] Actual | 1981[1] Actual | 1982[1] Actual | 1983[1] Actual | 1984[1] Actual | 1985[1] Actual | 1986 Actual | 1987 President's Request | 1987 Appropriations |
|---|---|---|---|---|---|---|---|---|---|
| TOTAL: CONSTRUCTION | 244,268 | 247,684 | 261,095 | 310,566 | 251,724 | 263,869 | 214,654 | 195,197 | 261,436 |
| $'s | 288,190 | 265,914 | 261,095 | 298,266 | 232,316 | 231,134 | 186,277 | 164,610 | 220,469 |
| FTEs | 5,219 | 5,409 | 5,462 | 4,661 | 4,469 | 4,071 | 3,853 | 3,679 | – |
| LAND ACQUISITION – LWCF | 24,391 | 41,930 | 26,262 | 63,077 | 40,025 | 50,535 | 31,356 | 3,206 | 52,236 |
| $'s | 28,784 | 45,016 | 26,262 | 60,579 | 36,985 | 45,032 | 27,211 | 2,704 | 44,051 |
| FTEs | 310 | 106 | 85 | 98 | 87 | 79 | 77 | 70 | – |
| ACQUISITION OF LANDS – SPECIAL ACTS | 325 | 754 | 724 | 753 | 780 | 706 | 744 | 966 | 966 |
| $'s | 384 | 809 | 724 | 723 | 720 | 629 | 617 | 815 | 815 |
| FTEs | – | – | 2 | 2 | 2 | 1 | 1 | 1 | – |
| ACQUISITION TO COMPLETE EXCHANGES | 284 | 532 | 151 | 109 | 380 | 92 | 20 | 895 | 895 |
| $'s | 335 | 571 | 151 | 105 | 351 | 82 | 17 | 755 | 755 |
| FTEs | – | – | – | – | – | – | – | – | – |
| APPROPRIATED TRUST FUNDS | – | 90 | 86 | 90 | 06 | 35 | 85 | 90 | 90 |
| $'s | – | 97 | 86 | 86 | 06 | 31 | 74 | 76 | 76 |
| FTEs | – | – | – | – | – | – | – | – | – |
| RANGE BETTERMENT FUND | 5,633 | 6,940 | 6,583 | 5,378 | 4,028 | 3,966 | 3,798 | 3,800 | 3,800 |
| $'s | 6,648 | 7,451 | 6,583 | 5,165 | 3,717 | 3,534 | 3,296 | 3,205 | 3,205 |
| FTEs | 129 | 104 | 156 | 121 | 75 | 64 | 62 | 62 | – |
| CONSTRUCTION & OPERATION OF REC. FACILITIES | 3,728 | – | – | – | – | – | – | – | – |
| FTEs | 129 | – | – | – | – | – | – | – | – |
| OPERATION & MAINTENANCE OF REC. FACILITIES[4] | – | – | – | – | – | – | – | 52,000 | 0 |
| $'s | – | – | – | – | – | – | – | 1,307 | 0 |
| FTEs | – | – | – | – | – | – | – | – | – |
| TOTAL: APPROPRIATED FUNDS | 1,514,855 | 1,592,184 | 1,521,698 | 1,560,744 | 1,486,738 | 1,610,709 | 1,625,029 | 1,286,994 | 1,665,545 |
| $'s | 1,787,680 | 1,709,369 | 1,521,698 | 1,498,939 | 1,372,111 | 1,435,303 | 1,410,200 | 1,085,322 | 1,404,554 |
| FTEs | 40,626 | 39,062 | 36,782 | 33,851 | 32,523 | 31,900 | 32,148 | 29,486 | – |

## PERMANENT APPROPRIATIONS

| | | | | | | | | | |
|---|---|---|---|---|---|---|---|---|---|
| Working Funds | 108,091 | 125,817 | 122,020 | 153,162 | 178,823 | 157,934 | 155,192 | 135,397 | 140,684 |
| 82$ | 127,558 | 135,077 | 122,020 | 147,097 | 165,036 | 140,735 | 134,676 | 114,180 | 118,639 |
| FTEs | 2,466 | 1,887 | 2,300 | 1,883 | 1,992 | 1,991 | 2,333 | 2,219 | – |
| Payments to States & Counties | 280,295 | 241,218 | 243,434 | 143,657 | 203,331 | 235,700 | 228,644 | 84,890 | 289,916 |
| 82$ | 330,776 | 258,972 | 243,434 | 137,968 | 187,654 | 210,032 | 198,417 | 71,588 | 244,486 |
| FTEs | – | – | – | – | – | – | – | – | – |
| TOTAL: PERMANENT APPROPRIATIONS | 388,386 | 367,035 | 365,454 | 296,819 | 382,154 | 393,634 | 383,836 | 220,287 | 430,600 |
| 82$ | 458,334 | 394,049 | 365,454 | 285,065 | 352,690 | 350,767 | 333,093 | 185,768 | 363,125 |
| FTEs | 2,466 | 1,887 | 2,300 | 1,883 | 1,992 | 1,991 | 2,333 | 2,219 | – |
| TRUST FUNDS/COOPERATIVE WORK | 146,561 | 153,465 | 103,800 | 169,937 | 231,103 | 234,625 | 155,091 | 197,616 | 197,616 |
| 82$ | 172,957 | 164,760 | 103,800 | 163,207 | 213,285 | 209,074 | 134,588 | 166,650 | 166,650 |
| FTEs | 2,950 | 2,025 | 2,500 | 2,648 | 2,622 | 2,592 | 2,601 | 3,128 | – |
| REFORESTATION TRUST FUND | – | – | 1,098 | 104,000 | 65,931 | 37,405 | – | 30,000 | 30,000 |
| 82$ | – | – | 1,098 | 99,882 | 60,848 | 33,332 | – | 25,299 | 25,299 |
| FTEs | – | – | – | 1,909 | 1,635 | 821 | – | 600 | – |
| TRANSFER ACCOUNTS | | | | | | | | | |
| FTEs | 4,186 | 2,450 | 1,402 | 1,559 | 1,362 | 1,218 | 1,964 | 1,322 | – |
| TOTAL: FOREST SERVICE | 2,049,002 | 2,112,684 | 1,992,050 | 2,131,500 | 2,165,926 | 2,268,483 | 2,163,956 | 1,734,897 | 2,323,761 |
| 82$ | 2,418,971 | 2,268,178 | 1,992,050 | 2,047,093 | 1,998,933 | 2,021,445 | 1,877,881 | 1,463,039 | 1,959,628 |
| FTEs | 50,228 | 45,424 | 42,984 | 41,850 | 40,134 | 38,524 | 39,046 | 36,755 | – |

1.  The Forest Service considers FTEs at the subactivity level to be unreliable prior to 1985, and they are not listed here.

2.  1986 reforestation appropriations include a transfer of $30 million from the reforestation trust fund.

3.  Resident-fish-habitat improvement is included in wildlife-habitat improvement in 1980 and 1981.

4.  This $52 million in the president's 1987 budget request was expected to result from increased recreation-user fees proposed in legislation by the administration. Combined with the $51 million in appropriations requested under the recreation-use activity, the president's budget would have provided a total of $103 million for recreation. Congress did not approve the fee-increase legislation and instead appropriated all recreation funds, $110.2 million, under recreation use.

# Index

Abalone fishery, 461
Acadia National Park, 298
Accelerated Refuge Maintenance and
    Management program, 256
    funding of, 326
Acid rain, 248
ADC, *see* Animal damage control
    program
African Development Bank, 313–317
*Aix sponsa, see* Wood duck
Alabama flattened musk turtle, 156
Alaska
    Bureau of Land Management, 9, 10, 54
    national wildlife refuges, 253–255
    planning and wilderness, 253, 254
Alaska Game Law of 1925, 103, 104
Alaska Lands Act, Tongass National
    Forest, 274, 277
Alaska National Interest Lands
    Conservation Act, 253
    Bureau of Land Management lands, 54
    Tongass National Forest, 274
Alaskan geese, subsistence hunting, 103,
    104
Alaskan sea otter, 457
Alligator River National Wildlife Refuge,
    155
Aluminum, in fish, 115
*American Cetacean Society v. Baldridge*,
    165, 174
American Fisheries Society, fisheries
    management study, 109, 110
American Ornithological Union, 270
American Ornithologists' Union
    piping plover conservation, 515
    red-cockaded woodpecker, report, 485
American Recreation Coalition, 77
American Society for Testing and
    Materials, 233, 234
American wigeon, 90, 93, 95

Anadromous fish, *see also* specific
    species
    Columbia river basin, 111
    funding
        Fish and Wildlife Service, 323, 325,
            330
        grants, 123, 124
    jurisdiction over, 108
    Klamath River, 122, 123
    research, appropriations, 351
    restoration, Olympic National Park,
        299
Anadromous Fish Conservation Act
    grant-in-aid program, 123, 124
    reauthorization, 144
Anadromous-fish initiative, Forest
    Service, 279, 280
Andrews, Mark, 182
Animal Damage Control Act of 1931,
    224, 230
Animal damage control program
    animal rights issue, 234, 235
    budget for, 224
    cost effectiveness of, 223
    coyote control, 223, 228–232
    extension education, 225–228
    future directions of, 224
    inhumane means, 223, 224
    in Kansas, 230, 231
    killing of nontarget species, 234
    legal developments, 236
    legislative developments, 235, 236
    loss data, 234
    national advisory committee, 226
    predator control, 228–232
    preventive control, 227, 230, 231
    research, 233, 234
    transfer from Interior to Agriculture,
        224–228, 235
Animal rights, 234, 235

675

Antarctic Marine Living Resources
Program, 351
Apalachicola National Forest, 283
APHIS, *see* Department of Agriculture,
Animal and Plant Health Inspection
Service
Aquaculture, 110
Aquatic-resource education program, 72
Aquatic Resources Trust Fund, 72, 75
Arctic goose, 97
Arctic National Wildlife Refuge, 243,
254, 255
Areas of critical environmental concern
definition of, 50
designation of, 50, 52, 53
management of, 50
nomination of, 50
Army Corps of Engineers
budget for, 208, 216
information contact, 570
capability study, 215
Clean Water Act, Section 404,
184–188, 192, 193
directory, 564, 565
planning regulation on environmental
resources, 204, 205
treatment of recommendations on
permit applications, 188–191
water projects, 202
Ash Meadows National Wildlife Refuge,
hunting, 250
Asian Development Bank, 313–317
Atlantic States Marine Fisheries
Commission, striped bass
conservation, 116–118
Atlantic Striped Bass Conservation Act,
107
amendments, 116–118
reauthorization, 144
Atlantic Tunas Convention Act, 144
Attleboro mall, 185, 186
Environmental Protection Agency
disagreement, 187, 188
404(b)(1) guidelines, 196
mitigation, 186, 187
practicable alternatives, 187


Bailey, Theodore N., 419
Bait station, 231
Bald eagle
Indian hunting rights, 158
lead poisoning, 86, 159

Pittston oil refinery, 148
restoration, 299
Bald Eagle Protection Act, 158
Bateman, Herbert, 253
Bayou Sauvage Urban National Wildlife
Refuge, 261
Bean, Michael J., 78
Bentsen, Lloyd, 156
*Bersani v. U.S. EPA*, 196
Big Cypress National Preserve, 257–259
Big-game population, 25
Bighorn sheep, 3
challenge grant, 29, 342
Desert National Wildlife Refuge, 260,
261
restoration, 298, 299
Bill Status Office, 572
Biological diversity, tropical rainforest,
317, 318
Biological Diversity Workshop, 295,
296
BIOSCI, 296
Bison
conflict with, 300
running buffalo clover, 441
Black bear, 520–529
active period of, 522
aging technique, 525
breeding of, 521–523
current trends regarding, 524, 525
diet of, 521, 527
habitat requirements of, 527
historical perspective on, 524
home range, size of, 521, 522
and humans
conflict with, 523, 524, 526
response to, 522, 525
hunting of, 523–526
as indicator species, 523
management of, 525, 526
mobility of, 523
population assessment of, 525–527
recommendations regarding, 527
removal of, 524, 527
in Shenandoah National Park, 301
species
description of, 521–523
significance of, 523, 524
Black duck
habitat protection, 97
kill level, 92
population of, 90, 91
Black fly, nuisance control program, 304

Black-footed ferret, 447–455
   activity of, 448, 449
   breeding of, 449
   canine distemper in, 450, 451, 454
   captive breeding of, 451, 453, 454
   captive population of, 150, 154, 156,
      452
   compound 1080 and, 232
   current trends regarding, 451, 452
   diet of, 448
   distribution of, 447, 448
   as endangered species, 450, 451, 453
   funding for research on, 454
   genetic fitness of, 449, 453, 454
   historical perspective on, 450, 451
   known population of, 448, 451
   longevity of, 449, 450
   management of, 452, 453
   physical description of, 447
   and prairie dog, coexistence with, 448,
      450–454
   prognosis for, 453
   recommendations regarding, 453, 454
   reward for, 453
   species
      description of, 447–450
      significance of, 450
   sylvatic plague and, 450
   in winter, 448, 449
Blackbird, toxicant, 233
BLM, *see* Bureau of Land Management
Blue crab, 130
Blue-winged teal, 90, 93, 95
Boating, recreational facilities, 72
Boating Safety Account, 72
Bobcat, 398–409
   adaptation of to humans, 401, 406
   breeding of, 400
   and coyotes, 400, 403, 404
   current trends regarding, 404
   diet of, 402
   as ecological indicator, 403
   as endangered species, 404
   habitat of, 401, 402
   historical perspective on, 403, 404
   management of, 404–406
   mortality factors of, 400
   pelt, value of, 403, 404
   physical characteristics of, 399, 400
   population, estimate of, 405
   prognosis for, 406, 407
   protection of by CITES, 404, 405
   range of, 399

   recommendations regarding, 407
   reintroduction of, 406, 407
   similarity of to lynx, 400, 412
   social organization and territoriality
      of, 400, 401
   species
      description of, 399–402
      significance of, 402, 403
   trapping and hunting of, 400, 404–407
*Bob Marshall Alliance v. Watt*, 160
Bony tail chub, 152
Bosco, Douglas, 122
Bosque del Apache National Wildlife
      Refuge, hunting, 250, 251
Botswana, World Bank involvement in,
      313, 316
Brant, 96
Brazil, World Bank involvement in, 313,
      316
Breaux, John, 102, 118, 124, 125, 138
Bureau of Land Management
   accounting method, 17
   agency structure and function, 12, 13
   in Alaska, 9, 10, 54
   allotment management plan, 24
   appropriations, 1986, 16
   areas of critical environmental
      concern, 50–53
   biologists, 561, 562
   botanists, 28, 342
   budget, 14, 321, 322, 339–345
      current level, 15–17
      cuts, 8, 9, 18, 19
      energy and minerals management,
         340, 344, 345
      grazing management program, 37
      history, 660–666
      information contacts, 570
      land acquisition, 341, 344
      Land and Water Conservation Fund,
         appropriations, 616, 618, 619,
         621, 623, 625–627
      range management and
         improvements, 341, 343, 344
      recreation management, 341, 343,
         344
      soil, water, and air management,
         341, 343, 344
      total, 339–341
      trends, 17–21
      wildlife habitat management, 341,
         342, 344
   commercial forest, 11

Bureau of Land Management (cont.)
   criticism of, 4, 7, 8, 50
   directory, 561, 562
   Division of Rangeland Resources, 31
   energy and minerals management, 13,
      14
      appropriations, 15, 16, 21
   energy and mining law administration,
      11
   grazing management, 31–41
   history
      current, 8, 9
      internal, 7, 8
   instant study area, 54
   land
      amount of, 3
      location of, 4, 5
      poor condition of, 5, 6, 15, 29
      type of, 5
   Land Acquisition, 17
   land base, 9–11
   land use planning, 21–24
   management framework plan, 21
   Management of Lands and Resources
      account, 15, 16, 18
   mineral resources, jurisdiction, 3
   natural areas, 51
   organizational shift, 46
   organizations and responsibilities of,
      9–21
   overview of, 3–9
   personnel, 339
      current level, 15–17
      grazing management program, 37
      hydrologists, 43–45
      professionals and specialists,
         decline in, 20, 21
      trends, 17–21
   public land, in Western states, 10, 11
   Range Improvement Fund, 17, 38, 39,
      41, 42
   rangeland, 11
   Range Management, 15–17
   range politics, 6, 7
   Renewable Resources Management,
      15, 16
   research, 13
   resource management plan, 22–24
   responsibilities of, 339
   soil scientists, 43, 44
   soil survey, 43
   Soil, Water, and Air Branch, 42–49
   special management areas, 50–56
   spotted owl management, 272, 273
   state office directors, 561, 562
   Washington headquarters, 561
   water rights, 46, 47
      non-reserved, 48
      reserved, 47, 48
   watershed-condition analysis, 45
   watershed management, 44–46
   wilderness, 53–57
   wild horses and burros, 13, 15, 17, 35
   wildlife and fish habitat management,
      24–30
      appropriations, 17
   wildlife-related scientists, 28
Bureau of Reclamation
   cost-sharing, 208
   funds, 216, 217
   goal, 205, 211
   Newlands Project, 428, 429, 431,
      433–435
   water-diversion project, first, 218, 219
   water projects, 202
   water-supply contract, 209
Burford, Robert, 8, 35
Burro
   management, 13, 15, 17, 35, 343
   removal program, 300
Byron, Beverly, 260

Cabeza Prieta National Wildlife Refuge,
   260, 261
California Department of Fish and Game,
   sea otter management, 467–470
California Desert Conservation Area, 4
California–Nevada interstate water
   compact, 157, 218, 219
California sea otter, see Southern sea
   otter
Calio study, 133–136
Canada
   migratory bird treaty, 83, 93–98
   Pacific Salmon Treaty, 110–112
   piping plover recovery plan, 515
   U.S. government funding, 98
Canada goose, 82, 96
Canine distemper, 450, 451, 454
Canvasback, 90, 92, 95
Capital gains, elimination of preferential
   rate, 184
Captive Breeding Specialist Group, 453
Caribbean National Forest and the
   Puerto Rican parrot, 283, 284
Caribou, woodland, transplant program,
   284, 285

Carlsbad Caverns, 300
Carter, Jimmy, 208
Center for Environmental Education, 140
Central Valley, California, 201, 202
  irrigation projects, 219
*Cervis elaphus, see* Elk
Chafee, John, 102, 118
Channelization of streams, 394, 396
*Charadrius melodus, see* Piping plover
Charles M. Russell National Wildlife Refuge, 251
Charles River Project, 207
*Chasmistes cujus, see* Cui-ui
Child Survival Act, Title III, 317
Chincoteague National Wildlife Refuge, 238, 252, 253
Chlordane, in fish, 114, 115
CITES, *see* Convention on International Trade in Endangered Species of Wild Flora and Fauna
Clean Air Act, Class I parks, 295
Clean Water Act, 204
  efficacy of, 116
  and Magnuson Fishery Conservation and Management Act, 143
  Section 404
    administrative penalties, 193
    environmental guidelines disputed, 184–188
    404(b)(1) guidelines, 196
    isolated wetlands, jurisdiction of, 195, 196
    key contacts, 563–567
    pending issues, 192, 913
    slowing wetland loss, 180
    solid waste regulation, 192
    taking decision overturned, 193–195
    water dependency test, 185, 186
Cliff Dam, 208
Coachella Valley fringe-toed lizard, 153
Coal leasing program, 13, 14
Colorado River squawfish, 152
Columbia River, fishing rights, 126
Columbia River Basin, anadromous fish stock, 111
Commerce Clause of the Constitution, 195
Commercial Fisheries Research and Development Act, 143
Committee on Agriculture, 572, 573
Committee on Agriculture, Nutrition, and Forestry, 574

Committee on Appropriations
  House of Representatives, 573
  Senate, 574
Committee on Commerce, Science, and Transportation, 574
Committee on Energy and Natural Resources, 575
Committee on Environmental and Public Works, 575
Committee on Interior and Insular Affairs, 573
Committee on Merchant Marine and Fisheries, 573, 574
COMMON, 296, 297
Compound 1080, 222, 231, 232
Conable, Barber, 313
Concho water snake, 156, 157
Condor, captive breeding program, 147, 150, 154, 156, 160
Congressional contacts and addresses, 572–575
Congressional document office, 572
Connell, Virgil, 541, 542
Conrad, David, 121
*Contaminant Issues of Concern, National Wildlife Refuges,* 243–247
Convention on International Trade in Endangered Species of Wild Fauna and Flora, 307
  annual report, 309, 310
  European Economic Community membership amendment, 309, 310
  infractions proposal, 310
  purpose and effectiveness, 308
  Singapore, wildlife import ban, 310, 311
  spotted cat protection, 404, 405
Cooper Ornithological Society, 270
Coordinated Operating Agreement on State Water Project and Central Valley Project, 219
Cotton mouse, Key Largo, 153
Cox, Dr. Christine Schonewald, 295
Coyote
  and bobcats, 400, 403, 404
  control of, 223
    compound 1080, 222, 231, 232
    cooperative agreement, 228
    eradication, 230
    Kansas animal damage control program, 230, 231
    lethal method, 228–232
    nonlethal method, 230–232

Coyote (*cont.*)
  philosophical debate, 228–230
  population recovery, 229
  public opposition, 229, 230
Crab Orchard refuge, 244, 246, 247
Croatan National Forest, 533
Crocodile, American, 153
Cui-ui, 219, 424–436
  current trends regarding, 430, 431
  as endangered species, 432
  hatchery rearing of, 432
  life cycle of, 426
  management of, 432, 433
  Paiute Tribe and, 426–429, 432–435
  prognosis for, 433–435
  recommendations regarding, 435
  recovery plan for, 432
  research program on, 433
  spawning of, 424–433
  species
    description of, 425, 426
    significance of, 426, 427
  and water quality, 435
Current Federal Aid Research System,
    74, 75
Cutthroat trout, 219, *see also* Lahontan
    cutthroat trout

Dam, new, 121
D'Arbonne National Wildlife Refuge,
    251, 252, 262
David Koch Cui-ui Hatchery, 432
Dawson, Robert, 209
DDT, in fish, 114, 115
Death Valley, burro removal program,
    300
Deer Creek dam and reservoir, 214
*Defenders of Wildlife, Sierra Club, and
    Friends of Animals and their
    Environment v. Administrator,
    Environmental Protection Agency,
    and Secretary, U.S. Department of
    the Interior,* 236
Deficit Reduction Act of 1984, 72
Denver Wildlife Research Center, 233
Department of Agriculture, Animal and
    Plant Health Inspection Service,
    animal damage control program,
    224–228, 235
Department of Commerce, marine
    mammal responsibility, 163
Department of the Interior, marine
    mammal responsibility, 163, 164

Derby Dam, 428, 432, 434
Desertification, 5, 31
Desert National Wildlife Refuge, 260,
    261
Devil's Hole pupfish, 151
Dingell–Johnson Act, 61
  anadromous-fish work, 124
  appropriations, 329
  Arizona, 72
  fish- and wildlife-resource
      management plan, 69–71
  fish restoration, 324
  Florida, 72
  funds
    increase in, 72
    use of, 62, 72, 73
  sport fish, use for, 62, 72
Dinosaur National Monument, 297, 298
Diving ducks, contaminants, 248
Division of Plant Protection and
    Quarantine, 225
Drift-net fisheries, north Pacific, 144, 145
Driftnets, 172
Duck, *see also* Black duck
  breeding population, 89–91, 95
  fall-flight, 91
  hunting restriction, 89, 91, 92
  number killed, 89
  population increase, 88, 89
Duck stamp
  price, 259
  receipts, 327, 328, 330
  use of, 98, 99, 193
Ducks Unlimited
  funding challenge, 97
  migratory bird habitat, 85
  piping plover, 515

Eastern elk, 494, 500
Electric Consumers Protection Act of
    1986, 118–122
Elk, 494–507
  adult males, decline in, 503
  antlers of, 496
  breeding of, 496, 497
  bugling of, 497
  control of numbers of, 503
  current trends regarding, 502
  diet of, 497
  habitat requirements of, 499, 502
  historical perspective on, 500, 501
  hunting of, 500, 503–505
  management of, 502, 503

movements of, 497–499
population of, 501
private landowners' tolerance for, 503, 505
prognosis for, 504
recommendations regarding, 504, 505
restoration of, 299
species
    description of, 494–499
    significance of, 499, 500
    winter range of, 25, 301, 497, 498, 502, 503
    yearling, as breeder, 496, 497
Elwha Restoration Steering Committee, 299
Emergency Striped Bass Study, 118
Emergency Wetlands Resources Act, 98–100, 193, 259
Endangered and threatened species list, federal, 576–603
Endangered species, *see also* specific species
international trade, regulation, 308–311
protection, 26, 27
Endangered Species Act, 203, 204
fish, federal authority over, 107, 108
incidental taking of endangered species, 152, 153, 157, 373
marine mammals, 164, 173
population estimate, 405
provision added in 1982, 152–154
reauthorization, 156, 157
sea otter translocation amendment, 469
Section 7
    actions hurting recovery, 149, 150
    cumulative effects, consideration of, 150
    geographical scope, 149
    new regulations, 148–150
wetland protection, 180
Endangered species biologist, training, 486
Endangered species information tracking system, 285
Endangered-species initiative, Forest Service, 279
Endangered species program
comprehensive conservation planning, new approach, 151
critical habitat, 147
legal developments, 158–160
legislation, 156, 157
new regulations to implement Section 7, 148–150
protected species list, 147
recovery plan, 147, 148
    implementation of, 151–154
    species reintroduction, 154–156
Engle Act, 260
*Enhydra lutris nereis, see* Southern sea otter
Environmental Protection Agency
budget information contacts, 570
directory, 563, 564
pesticide registration, 230
regional offices, 563, 564
Section 404 of the Clean Water Act, 184–188, 192, 193
Environmental zone, 102
Erosion
prevention, 45
in West, 42
European Economic Community
CITES membership, 309, 310
trade in CITES Appendix I species, 311
*Evolution of National Wildlife Law, The,* 78
Excise tax
federal grants-in-aid, 323
for funding nongame conservation projects, 76–78

Farm Bill, 1985, 123
Farm-drainage pollution, 212, 213
Federal Aid in Fish Restoration Act, *see* Dingell–Johnson Act
Federal Aid in Wildlife Restoration Act *see* Pittman–Robertson Act
Federal Aid in Wildlife Restoration Program, 62, 63
Federal Energy Regulatory Commission
comprehensive planning, 119
dispute-resolution procedure, 120
fish and wildlife mitigation, 119, 120
hydroelectric facility licensing, 112, 113, 118–122
Umpqua Basin, 128
Federal grant
fund distribution and use, 68
incompatible use of areas acquired with, 73, 74
state planning efforts, status of, 68–71
for state wildlife conservation, 61–79

Federal Insecticide, Fungicide, and
    Rodenticide Act, reauthorization,
    235, 236
Federal Land Policy and Management
    Act, 4, 8, 21, 22, 39–41, 50, 53, 56
Federal Power Act
    comprehensive planning, 122
    fishery protection, 118, 119
*Felis lynx*, see Lynx
*Felis pardina*, see Lynx, Spanish
*Felis rufus*, see Bobcat
Finfish, incidental capture of, 139, 140
Fire dependence
    red-cockaded woodpecker, 478–493
    rough-leaved loosestrife, 531–536
Firefighting
    Bureau of Land Management, 339,
        340
    Forest Service, 332, 333
First National Wilderness Management
    Workshop, Steering Committee,
    293
Fish, *see also* Anadromous fish; specific
        species
    hatchery system, 124, 125
    imported and exported, 142
    inland, 107
    ocean, 108
    propagation, 108
    sport, Dingell–Johnson act, 62, 72
    stocks overfished or overcapitalized,
        134
Fish and wildlife agency budgets,
        321–354
Fish and Wildlife Conservation Act,
    *see* Forsythe–Chafee Act
Fish and Wildlife Coordination Act
    amendment, 100–102, 125, 193
    hydroelectric facilities, 121
    mitigation measures, 203, 204
Fish and wildlife habitat management,
    *see also* specific agency
    budget histories, 652–673
    Forest Service, 278–280
Fish and Wildlife Improvement Act of
    1978, 104
Fish and wildlife mitigation, 119, 120,
    124, 125
Fish and wildlife program, budget
    information contacts, 570, 571
Fish and Wildlife Reference Service, 74,
    75
Fish and Wildlife Service
    budget, 321–331

Construction and Anadromous Fish,
        323, 325, 330
    endangered species, 323, 325, 326,
        329, 330
    fish and wildlife restoration, 323,
        331
    fishery resources, 323, 325–327, 329
    habitat resources, 323–326
    information contacts, 570
    land acquisition, 323–325, 327, 328,
        330, 331
    total, 323, 324
    wildlife resources, 323, 325–328
    directory, 553–557
    Division of Federal Aid, 61, 73, 74
    Division of Migratory Bird
        Management, 84
    Division of Refuge Management, 84
    endangered species management, 147
    federal-aid budget, 61, 62
    federal-aid program
        legal developments, 78
        legislation, 75–78
        monitoring, 73, 74
        role in, 63, 68
        staff cut, 75, 76
    federal grants-in-aid, 322, 323, 324
    inland fisheries management, 108
    international wildlife conservation,
        307
    Land and Water Conservation Fund,
        appropriations, 616, 617,
        619–626
    marine mammal protection, 164
    migratory birds, principal offices
        responsible for, 84
    mutual agreement, 68
    personnel, 322
    regional offices, 554–557
    research coordination, 74, 75
    resource management, funds for, 322,
        323
    responsibilities, 322
    sea otter management, 467–470
    Washington headquarters, 553
Fish consumption, toxic contamination,
        115
Fishermen, commercial, 141
Fisherman's Protective Act, Pelly
        Amendment, 165–167, 174
Fishery, *see also* Inland fisheries; Marine
        fisheries
    excessive catch capacity, 135
    foreign, porpoise capture, 171, 172

management needs, 72
management plan, 132, 143
marine mammal conflicts, 170–173
optimum yield, 132, 133
trends
  domestic commercial, 140, 141
  foreign, 142
  recreational, 141, 142
Fishery advisory council, 122, 123
Fishery conservation act, 134–136, 138
amendment, 143
funding, 143
Fishery Conservation and Management
  Act of 1976, 107
Fishery conservation zone, 132
Fishery Management Council, Gulf of
  Mexico, 137, 138
Fishing
foreign, 132, 140, 142
recreational, 60
national park, 300
Flood control, 255, 256
Florida national forests and biological
  diversity, 281, 283
Florida panther
protection of, 302
reintroduction of, opposition to, 154
wildlife refuge, 257–259
*Florida Rock Industries, Inc. v. United
  States*, 193–195
Food Security Act of 1985, swampbuster
  provision, 181–183
Foreign Assistance Act of 1961,
  amendment, 317, 318
Foreign-assistance appropriations bill,
  315
Forest and Rangeland Renewable
  Resources Planning Act of 1974,
  278
Forest management
all age, 486
even age, 485
rotation age, 485, 486
Forest Road Program, 338, 339
Forest Service, *see also* National Forest
  System
below-cost timber sale, 285, 286
budget, 321, 322, 331–339
  history, 667–673
  information contacts, 570
  land acquisition, 332, 334, 337, 338
  range management and
    improvement, 332, 334, 336,
    337
recreation use, 332, 337
road construction, 338, 339
soil, water, and air management,
  332, 334, 336, 337
timber program, 332–334, 337–339
total, 332–334
wildlife and fish habitat
  management, 332, 334–337
wildlife and fish research, 332, 334,
  336, 337
Caribbean National Forest and the
  Puerto Rican parrot, 283, 284
challenge grant program, 335
directory, 549–552
endangered species information
  tracking system, 285
firefighting, 332, 333
fisheries management, 108
Florida national forests and biological
  diversity, 281, 283
forest and range experiment stations,
  552
forest plan, 10- to 15-year, 266, 267
habitat in system, 265
Land and Water Conservation Fund,
  appropriations, 616–619, 621,
  623–626
land-use plan, 504, 505
legal developments, 287, 288
Paiute trout management, 544
personnel, 331
pine beetle suppression and the red-
  cockaded woodpecker, 287, 288
red-cockaded woodpecker habitat
  management, 485
regional headquarters, 550, 551
resource-allocation plan, 504, 505
Resources Planning Act program,
  1985, 277–281
responsibilities, 331
road construction, 280, 286
spotted owl/old-growth management,
  267–273
Tongass National Forest, 273–277
Washington headquarters, 549, 550
wilderness legislation, 286, 287
woodland caribou, 284, 285
Forsythe–Chafee Act, 61
appropriations, 62, 69
conservation plan, 69
funding study, 76–78
reauthorization legislation, 76–78
Friends of the Earth, 121
*Friends of the Earth v. Hintz*, 197, 198

Fur Seal Act of 1966, 170
Fur seal population, 170
FWS, *see* Fish and Wildlife Service

Gadwall, 93, 95
Game animals, Pittman–Robertson Act, 62, 63
Garrison Diversion Unit, redesign, 208, 216–218
Garrison Diversion Unit Reformulation Act of 1986, 216
General Land office, 7
Gill and trammel-set net, southern sea otter drowning, 466, 470–472
Gill nets, 172, 173
Glacier National Park, 290
*Global 2000* study, 308
Goose, population status and goals, 96
Gorton, Slade, 143
Graham, Bob, 153
Grand Teton National Park, 301
Granite Reef Aqueduct, 211
Grasshopper control, 343
Grays Harbor, 197
Grazing
    allotment management plan, 33
    coexistence with fish and wildlife, 32
    cooperative management agreement program, 37
    environmental impact statement, 33
        Reno resource area, 36
    inventory data, use of, 34, 35
    management objectives, 35
    monitoring, 36
    in national park, 301
    and Paiute trout, 543, 544
    permit, 31
        allocation of, 6
        plans and adjustments, 32–36
    reduction in, 32
        progress toward, 36, 37
    in riparian area, 30, 31
    water use, 48, 49
    in wildlife refuge, 251
Grazing advisory board, 40–42
Grazing fees, 336
    controversy, 38, 39
    formula, 39, 40
    permit value, 38
    range improvement fund, contribution to, 38, 39, 41, 42
Grazing management, 31–41
    funding, 343, 344

Grazing Service, 6, 7, 38
Greenbelt, importance, 394, 396
*Greenpeace International, Inc. v. Baldridge*, 175
Green-winged teal, 92, 95
Grizzly bear, management concern, 156
Guadalupe Mountains National Park, 300
Guam rail, 150, 154
Gulf Islands National Seashore, 299
Gypsy moth, 301

Halibut fishery, nearshore commercial set-net, 461, 462
Hawaiian Monk Seal, critical habitat, 175
Hazardous-waste management, funding, 343
Heflin, Howell, 156
Hester, Eugene, 77
Historic Preservation Fund, 346
Hodel, Donald, 56
Horses and burros, wild, 12, 13, 15, 17, 35, 300, 343
Hot-spot strategy, 86
House of Representatives, committees, 572–574
House Subcommittee on Fisheries and Wildlife Conservation and the Environment, 138
Hovanitz, William, 374
H.R. 1027, 156
H.R. 1406, 77
H.R. 1790, 260
H.R. 2704, 100–102, 125, 193
H.R. 3113, 219
H.R. 3167, 124, 125
H.R. 3358, 118
H.R. 4531, 173
H.R. 4568, 319
H.R. 4681, 318, 319
H.R. 4960, 138
*Humane Society v. Hodel, The*, 249, 261, 262
Humpback chub, 152
Hunting, *see also* Trapping; Whaling
    Alaskan geese, 103, 104
    black bear, 523–526
    bobcat, 400, 404–407
    duck, 89, 91, 92
    elk, 500, 503–505
    National Wildlife Refuge System, 249–251, 262

subsistence, 103, 104, 168, 170
wood duck, 390–393, 395, 396
Hydroelectric facilities
  and fish, 118–122
  fishery recommendations, 127, 128
  salmon, damage to, 111–113
Hydrologists, 43–45


Iceland, whaling, 167, 174
Increment borer, 264
Indian fishery rights, 125–127
Information system, National Park
  Service, 296, 297
Inland fisheries management
  federal, 107–128
  Indian, 107, 110, 125–127
  legal developments, 125–128
  legislation, 116–125
  problems with, 109, 110
  state, 107, 109, 110, 126
Inorganic metals, in fish, 115
Integrated Pest Management Decision
  Tree Module, 296, 297
Inter-American Development Bank,
  313–317
Inter-American Tropical Tuna
  Commission, 171
Interim Convention for the Conservation
  of Northern Pacific Fur Seals, 168
Interior Department, international
  authority, 319
Interjurisdictional Fisheries Act, 143, 144
International Association of Fish and
  Wildlife Agencies, 87
International Convention for the
  Regulation of Whaling, 166
International Fur Seal Treaty, sea otter
  protection, 463
International Whaling Commission,
  164–168, 307
  quotas, 174
  Scientific Committee, 166
International wildlife conservation
  agencies, 307, 308
  assessment, 308
  CITES, 308–311
  Interior Department international
    authority, 319
  legislation, 317–319
  multilateral development institutions,
    308, 311–317
  trade in endangered plants and
    animals, regulation, 308–311

tropical rainforest, 308, 311, 312
  and biological diversity, 317, 318
  unsound natural-resources
    exploitation, 318, 319
Interstate 10, redesign of, 148
Investment tax credit, elimination of,
  184
Inyo National Forest, 298, 299


Jaguar hide, 306
Jantzen, Robert, 77
Japan
  fish catch and import, 142
  whaling, 165, 168, 174
*Jones v. Gordon*, 175


Kasten, Robert, 314
Kelp, and southern sea otter, 458, 460,
  461
Kemp's ridley sea turtle, 139
Kenai National Wildlife Refuge, 244, 245,
  247
Kesterson National Wildlife Refuge,
  pollution, 115, 212, 213, 243, 244
Kingsley Dam hydropower plant, 214
Kisatchie Wilderness Area, 486
Kissimmee River, restoration, 207
Klamath River fishery restoration, 122,
  123
Knutson–Vandenberg Act, 336
Kraft Slough, wildlife refuge, 218


Lacey Act, 125, 126
Laguna Atascosa refuge, 245, 247
Lahontan cutthroat trout
  similarity to Paiute trout, 539
  water rights, 157, 430
Land and Water Conservation Fund
  appropriations by area, 615–627
  land acquisition, 257, 258
    Bureau of Land Management, 344,
      349
    Fish and Wildlife Service, 323–325,
      330, 331, 349
    Forest Service, 332, 337, 338, 349
    National Park Service, 346, 348,
      349
Land and Water Conservation Fund Act
  of 1965, *see also* Emergency
  Wetlands Resources Act
  amendment, 98–100

Land-managing agency budgets, comparison, 15
Laxalt, Paul, 157, 219
Lead poisoning, 86–88
in refuge system, 249, 251
Lead shot, nationwide phase-out, 86–88
Least Bell's vireo, 153
Leghold trap ban, 232, 235
Legislation, copies of, 572
Leopold Report, 295
Lesser sandhill crane, 213
Lewis and Clark National Forest, oil and gas leases, 160
Little green heron, 178
Livestock industries, political power of, 6, 7, 33, 40
Livestock protection collar, 231
Lock and Dam 26, 206
Loggerhead sea turtle, 139
Longleaf-pine forest, 283
Lower Rio Grande Valley refuge, 247
Lower Snake River Compensation Plan, 329
Lynx, 410–422
CITES, Appendix II, 417, 418, 420
current trends regarding, 416, 417
density of, 412
diet of, 413
as endangered species, 417, 419
habitat of, 412, 413
historical perspective on, 415, 416
as indicator species, 415
management of, 417–419
monitoring of, 418
pelt, value of, 414, 418
physical characteristics of, 411, 412
population cycle of, 414, 415
prey, effect of on, 414, 415
prognosis for, 418, 419
range of, 412, 413
recommendations regarding, 419, 420
reproduction of, 413
research on, 420
similarity of to bobcat, 400, 412
and snowshoe hare population, 412–414, 419
Spanish, 411–413, 417
species
description of, 411–414
significance of, 414, 415
trapping of, 416–420
*Lysimachia asperulaefolia, see* Rough-leaved loosestrife

McClure, James, 260, 284, 286
Magnuson Fishery Conservation and Management Act
American Fisheries Society study, 109, 110
first decade of, 131
fisheries-management decision, 132
foreign fishing, 132, 140
National Oceanic and Atmospheric Administration study, 109
Packwood–Magnuson Amendment, 165, 166, 174
reauthorization, 142–144
Malheur National Wildlife Refuge, flood control, 255, 256
Mallard, 90, 92, 95–97
Management indicator species, 268, 269, 373, 403, 415, 483, 499, 512, 523
Manatee, tagging, 162
Manitoban elk, 494, 500, 501
Marble Bluff Dam and Fish Facility, 430–433
Marine fisheries management, *see also* National Marine Fisheries Service
Calio study, 133–136
conservation and allocation decisions, 133–135
federal, 131–145
fishery trends
domestic commercial, 140, 141
foreign, 142
recreational, 141, 142
Gulf and south Atlantic shrimp, 139, 140
highly migratory species, 135, 136
interjurisdictional management, 135
legislation, 142–145
limited entry, 135
redfish, 136–139
review of, 133–136
Marine Mammal Commission, 164
budget information contact, 570
Marine mammal protection
agencies responsible for, 163, 164
commercial whaling, 164–168
fishery conflicts, 170–173
legal developments, 174, 175
legislation, 173
moratorium, 163, 165, 168, 174
northern fur seal hunt, 168–170
Marine Mammal Protection Act, 163, 164, 168
incidental taking of marine mammals, 173

porpoise, capture of, 170–173
southern sea otter, 463
walrus, 363, 366
Marine mammals, *see also* specific
     species
incidental taking of, 157
Marine Protection, Research, and
     Sanctuaries Act of 1972, 164
Martin, Glen, 229
Massachusetts Fisheries and Wildlife
     Division, 207
Melcher, John, 286
Merchant Marine and Fisheries
     Committee, House, 123, 125
Merriam elk, 494, 500
*Michael J. Caire, M.D., et al. v. Lee J*
     *Fulton,* 251, 262
Migratory bird, *see also* specific species
breeding bird survey, 85
Canada, treaty with regarding, 83,
     93–98
classification of, 85
duck, population increase of, 88–92
Emergency Wetlands Resources Act,
     98–100
Fish and Wildlife Coordination Act
     Amendments, 100–102
flyway council, 84, 85
lead shot, nationwide phase-out,
     86–88
legal developments, 103, 104
legislation, 98–102
North American Waterfowl
     Management Plan, 93–98
private, nonprofit organization, 85
protection and management of,
     83–105
tax code changes, 102
threatened or endangered, 85
Migratory Bird Conservation Fund, 99
funding, 327, 328
land acquisition, 257, 259
Migratory Bird Treaty Act
hunting restrictions, 103
piping plover, 513
wood duck, 392
Military Lands Withdrawal Act of 1985,
     260, 261
Minerals Management Service, 7, 21
sea otter research program, 468
Mineral resource, regulatory authority,
     252
Mission blue butterfly, 370–378
breeding of, 371, 372

current trends regarding, 374, 375
food plants and, 372
historical perspective on, 374
incidental take of, 373, 375
as indicator, 373
life cycle of, 372
management of, 375–377
patrolling in, 372
prognosis for, 377
Quarry Products, Inc., and, 376, 377
range of, 372
recommendations regarding, 377, 378
recovery plan for, 375
San Bruno Mountain and, 152,
     372–377
species
     description of, 371–374
     significance of, 373, 374
Mono Lake, 220
Mott, William, Jr., 291–296
Mountain goat management, 300
Mountain lion, 300, 301
Mrazek, Robert, 277
*Mustela nigripes, see* Black-footed
     ferret

Narmada Valley Dam Project, 316
Narrows Dam, 214
National Aquaculture Act, 123
National Audubon Society, 85
*National Audubon Society v. Hester,*
     159, 160
*National Audubon Society v. Superior*
     *Court of Alpine County,* 220
National Contaminant Biomonitoring
     Program, 114
National Environmental Policy Act, 204
environmental impact statement, 150
wetlands protection, 180, 192
National Fish and Seafood Promotion
     Council, 143
National Fish Hatchery System, 124, 125
National Forest Management Act, 266,
     267
National Forest Plan status report,
     628–651
National Forest System, *see also* Forest
     Service
demands on, 266
diversity requirement, 266, 267
function of, 267
funding, 331, 332, 337, 338
grazing, 336

National Forest System (*cont.*)
  resources, 265
  timber harvest, 266
National Marine Fisheries Service, 108,
    *see also* Marine fisheries
    management
  budget, 321, 322, 349–354
    conservation and management
        operations, 350, 352, 353
    history, 658, 659
    information collection and analysis,
        350–353
    information contact, 571
    state and industry programs, 350,
        352–354
    total, 351
  directory, 565–569
  endangered species management, 147
  international wildlife conservation,
      307
  key 404 contact, 565–567
  marine mammal protection, 164
  personnel, 350
  regional offices, 569
  responsibilities, 349
  role of, 132
  Washington headquarters, 568
  wetland permit recommendations,
      studies on, 188–191
National Oceanic and Atmospheric
    Administration
  fisheries management study, 109
  marine fisheries management, 134
National Park Service
  appropriations, 295
  biological diversity, 295, 296
  budget, 321, 322, 345–349
    history, 653–657
    information contacts, 571
    Land and Water Conservation Fund,
        346, 348, 349
    park management and natural
        resources, 346–348
    total, 346, 347
  commercial fishing, 304
  conflicts with neighbors, 300, 301
  control of exotics, 299, 300
  Director Mott's 12-point plan, 292–296
  directory, 558–560
  entrance fee, 347, 348
  expert policy-review panel, 295
  fisheries management, 108
  information system, 296, 297
  insect control, 304

international wildlife conservation,
    307
Land and Water Conservation Fund,
    appropriations, 615–625
legal developments, 303, 304
legislative developments, 302, 303
management area, 291
management mandate, 291, 292
natural-resources management, 292
personnel, 345
rare and endangered species programs,
    301, 302
regional offices, 559, 560
resident superintendent, 292
responsibilities, 345
restoration of species, 298, 299
trapping, 303, 304
usable resource inventory, 294, 295
Washington headquarters, 558
Water Resources Unit, 298
water rights, 297, 298
wilderness management, improving,
    293, 294
and wildlife, 291–305
National Park Organic Act mandate, 298
National Park Service Organic Act of
    1916, 303
National Park System, 345
National Research Council workshop, 34
*National Resources Defense Council v.
    Hodel*, 40
*National Rifle Association et al v.
    Arnett*, 303, 304
National Wetlands Inventory, 98, 100
  status, 191
National Wilderness Preservation
    System, 266
National Wilderness System, 50
National Wildlife Federation, steel-shot
    zone, 86
*National Wildlife Federation v. Hanson*,
    197
*National Wildlife Federation v. Hodel*,
    CIVS-86-194-EJG, 88, 158, 159
*National Wildlife Federation v. Hodel*,
    23 ERC 1089, 87
National Wildlife Refuge System
  accomplishments, 240
  acreage, 240
  Alaska issues, 253–255
  budget, 256
    contamination cleanup, 248
  compatibility issues, 248–253
  directory, 604–614

easement regulations, revision, 259
environmental impact statement, 257
funding, 322, 325
hunting, fishing, and trapping,
    249–251, 262
land acquisition, 257, 258
land exchange, 257–259
legal developments, 261, 262
legislation, 259–261
line of authority, 240–242
livestock grazing, 251
mission statement, 239
oil and gas drilling, 251, 252, 254,
    255, 262
ongoing work, 243
operations and maintenance, 256, 257
public use, 252, 253
staffing, 256, 257
use, maximizing, 239, 240
water quality/toxic contamination,
    243–248
National Wildlife Refuge System
    Administration Act, 240, 248
Natural-resources exploitation as a
    form of unfair trade practice, 318,
    319
Nature Conservancy
    piping plover, 515
    rough-leaved loosestrife, 535
    wetland acquisition, 85
Navajo–Hopi land exchange, 344
Newlands Project, 428, 429, 431,
    433–435
NMFS, *see* National Marine Fisheries
    Service
Nongame Act, *see* Forsythe–Chafee Act
Nongame animals, Pittman–Robertson
    Act, 62
Nongame conservation projects, funding,
    76–78
Nonmigratory bird protection, 83
North American Waterfowl Management
    Plan, 93, 94
    funding, 97, 98
    habitat protection, 94–97
    implementation, 97
North Atlantic Salmon Conservation
    Organization, 113
North Carolina Plant Protection
    Program, 535
North Cascades Complex, 300
Northern fur seal hunt, 168–170
Northern pintail, 90, 92, 95–97
Northern shoveler, 93, 95

Northern Pacific Fisheries Act, 1982
    amendments, 172
Norway, whaling, 166, 174
Noxubee National Wildlife Refuge, 482,
    487
NP FLORA, 296

Pacific Northwest Electric Power
    Planning and Conservation Act, 204
Pacific Salmon Commission, 112
Pacific Salmon Treaty, 110–112
Paiute Tribe
    and cui-ui, 426–429, 432–435
    Kuyuidokado band, 426, 427
Paiute trout, 538–545
    current trends regarding, 543, 544
    diet of, 540
    habitat requirements of, 544
    historical perspective on, 541–543
    hybridization of, 542–545
    and livestock grazing, 543, 544
    management of, 544
    population biology of, 541
    prognosis for, 544
    range and distribution of, 539, 540
    recommendations regarding, 544,
        545
    similarity of to Lahontan cutthroat
        trout, 539
    spawning of, 540, 541
    species
        description of, 539–541
        significance of, 541
    territory of, 540
    transplantation of, 542–544
*Palila v. Hawaii Department of Land
    and Natural Resources*, 159
PCBs, in fish, 115
Peregrine falcon, reintroduction of, 25,
    298
PESTS, 296
*Picoides borealis, see* Red-cockaded
    woodpecker
Pine beetle, southern
    management of, 486
    suppression of and the red-cockaded
        woodpecker, 287, 288
Pine Ridge National Recreation Area,
    286
Piping plover, 508–519
    black breast band in, 509
    breeding of, 511, 517
    census of, 513–516

Piping plover (*cont.*)
  current trends regarding, 513, 514, 516
  diet of, 512
  endangered status of, 515
  habitat needs and status of, 517
  historical perspective on, 512, 513
  human disturbance, effect of on, 517
  international conservation of, 515
  life history parameters of, 516
  management of, 515
  migration of, 512
  population and habitat enhancement
    of, 517
  prognosis for, 515, 516
  range of, 510, 511
  recommendations regarding, 516, 517
  recovery program for, 301
  species
    description of, 509–512
    significance of, 512
Pittman–Robertson Act, 61
  achievements, 63–67
    biological, 63, 68
  appropriations, 329
  expenditures, 69
  fiftieth anniversary, 62, 63
  fish and wildlife-resource management
    plan, 69–71
  game animals, use for, 62, 63
  lands acquired in fee title fiscal years
    1938–1984, 64, 65
  nongame animals, use for, 62
  wildlife management areas and
    refuges, 66, 67
Pittston oil refinery, 148
P.L. 98–269, 72
P.L. 99–198, 123
P.L. 99–375, 78
P.L. 99–490, 286
P.L. 99–495, 118, 119
P.L. 99–504, 286
P.L. 99–529, 317
P.L. 99–552, 122
P.L. 99–555, 286
P.L. 99–584, 286
P.L. 99–591, 295
P.L. 99–625, 157
P.L. 99–645, 98–100
P.L. 99–659, 124, 142–144, 157
P.L. 99–662, 193
Plants, rare, 27
Platte River, protection of, 213, 214
*Plebejus icarioides missionensis, see*
  Mission blue butterfly

Polonoroeste Project, 316
Pond 12, 195, 196
Porpoise
  capture of in tuna nets, 170–172
  Dall, incidental drowning, 172
*Potential Funding Sources to Implement*
  *the Fish and Wildlife Conservation*
  *Act of 1980*, 76
Prairie Bend project, 214
Prairie dog, coexistence of with black-
  footed ferret, 448, 450–454
Presidential Task Force on Regulatory
  Relief, 185
Proxmire, William, 286
Prudhomme, Paul, 137
Public Rangelands Improvement Act
  grazing fee formula, 39, 40
  range improvement fund, 343
Public trust doctrine, 220
Public Utilities Regulatory Policies Act
  fishery protection, 118, 120–122
  moratorium, 121
Public Water Reserve No. 107, 47
Puerto Rican parrot, 283, 284
Purse seining
  porpoise capture, 170, 171
  redfish, 138, 139
Pyramid construction company, 185–188,
  196
Pyramid Lake, 424–436
  water projects, 219


Quarry Products, Inc., 376


Range Betterment Fund, 336
Range improvement fund
  appropriations, 343
  and grazing fees, 38, 39
  use of, 41
Range Program Summary, 35
Reclamation Act of 1902, 202, 208
Recreational use, promotion, 61
Red-cockaded woodpecker, 478–493
  biological problems of, 484
  cavity abandonment by, 481
  cavity excavation by, 480, 481
  cavity transfer by, 481
  census of, 488, 489
  clan social system of, 481, 482
  colony of, 481, 482, 489
  current trends regarding, 487, 488
  decline of, cause, 484

distribution of, 479, 480, 484
economic problems regarding, 485,
    486
education problems regarding, 486
endangered status of, 479, 484, 485
fire, importance of to, 479, 480, 483
foraging ecology of, 482, 483
forest plan for, Florida, 281, 283
habitat of, 480
    corridor of on interstate highway
        rights-of-way, 490
historical perspective on, 484–487
home range, need of for large, 483
management of, 488, 489
need of for nearby colonies, 482
new colony initiation of, 482
oil and gas drilling on D'Arbonne
    National Wildlife Refuge and,
    251, 252
pine beetle suppression and, 287, 288
political problems regarding, 484,
    485
problems regarding, 484–487
prognosis for, 489, 490
recommendations regarding, 490, 491
recovery plan for, 485, 490
relocation of, 490, 491
resin well and, 481
scaling technique and, 483
species
    description of, 479–483
    significance of, 483, 484
    survival needs of, 480
Red-Cockaded Woodpecker Recovery
    Team, 485
Red drum, *see* Redfish
Red heart fungus, 481
Red wolf
    captive population of, 150, 154
    reintroduction, controversy regarding,
        155
Redfish
    commercial catch of, 136–138
    fishery management plan for, 137, 138
    recreational catch of, 138, 139
Redhead, 95
Redwood Expansion Act of 1978, 303,
    304
Reforestation Trust Fund, 333
Reports, copies of, 572
Resin well, 481
Resource management plan, 22
    amendment, 23
    fish and wildlife, state, 69–71

monitoring, 23
planning process, 22, 23
public comment period, 22, 23
quality of, 24
rate of preparation of, 23, 24
Resources Planning Act program
    criticism of, 277, 278
    fish and wildlife habitat management,
        278–280
    funding, 333
    goals, 282
    high-bound program, 278–280
    low-bound program, 278–280
    significance and outlook, 280, 281
    timber and roads, 280
    update, 1985, 277–281
Rhizobial competition, 441
Right whale, Pittston oil refinery, 148
Riparian area management, 29–31
    range improvement fund, 41
Road construction
    Forest Service, 286
    funding, 338, 339
    Resources Planning Act program,
        1985, 280
    riparian habitat, effect on, 29
Rocky Mountain elk, *see* Elk
Rocky Mountain National Park, 301
Rocky Mountain wolf, reintroduction
    controversy regarding, 155, 156
Roosevelt elk, *see* Elk
Ross' goose, 96
Rough-leaved loosestrife, 530–536
    current trends regarding, 533, 534
    as endangered species, 533, 535
    fire dependence of, 531–536
    habitat of, 531
    historical perspective on, 532, 533
    management of, 535
    prognosis for, 535
    protection of, 533, 535
    recommendations regarding, 535, 536
    recovery plan for, 535, 536
    remaining populations of, 534
    species
        description of, 531, 532
        significance of, 532
    transplantation of, 533
Running buffalo clover, 438–445
    and bison, 441
    cultivation of, 442, 443
    current trends regarding, 442, 443
    disappearance of, cause of, 441, 443
    as endangered species, 440, 442

Running buffalo clover (*cont.*)
  historical perspective on, 440, 441
  interaction of with white clover, 441,
    443
  management of, 442, 443
  prognosis for, 443, 444
  protection of, 443
  recommendations regarding, 444
  reintroduction of, 443
  rhizobial competition of with other
    species, 441, 443
  species
    description of, 439, 440
    significance of, 440
Russell, Dick, 117


S. 725, 156, 157
S. 740, 98–100
S. 991, 173
S. 1813, 118
S. 1839, 102
S. 2347, 157
S. 2412, 260
S. 2457, 157, 218, 219
S. 2611, 144, 145
Sagebrush Rebellion, 7, 8, 34, 37
*Salmo clarki henshawi, see* Lahontan
  cutthroat trout
*Salmo seleniris, see* Paiute trout
Salmon
  Atlantic, restoration of, 112–114
  catch, Canadian and Greenland
    fishermen, 113, 114
  catch level, 112
  Chinook, Klamath River, 122
  Columbia River Basin, 111
  illegal fishing, 114
  Pacific
    interception, 111
    treaty, 110–112
  restoration, 111–114
San Bruno Mountain, mission blue
  butterfly, 152, 372–377
San Bruno Mountain Habitat
  Conservation Plan, 375, 376
San Francisco Bay, 213, 248
San Luis Drain, 212
San Pedro Riparian Area, 25
  appropriations, 343
Sandhill crane, 148, 320
Savannah River Plant, 482, 485–487, 489
Scaup, 90, 93, 95

Sea turtle, incidental capture of, 139, 140
Sea urchin, predation of by sea otter, 460
Sea World, whaling permit overturned,
    174, 175
Secretary of Commerce, fishery
    management by, 132, 137, 138
Seiberling, John, 277, 318, 319
Selenium
  in fish, 115
  Kesterson National Wildlife Refuge,
    212, 213, 243
  toxic effects, 247
Seminole Reservoir, 214
Semi-postal stamp, 76–78
Senate committees, 574, 575
Sequoia National Park, 299
Sewalls Falls dam, 113
Sheep industry, political power of, 230
Shellfishing industry, and southern sea
    otter, 461, 471
Shenandoah National Park, black
    bear, 301
Shrimp, Gulf and south Atlantic, 139,
    140
*Sierra Club v. Block*
  pine beetle suppression, 287
  water rights, 220, 297
*Sierra Club and the Wilderness Society
  v. Block*, 287, 288
Sierra Nevada Bighorn Sheep Recovery
    and Conservation Plan, 298, 299
Sierra Pacific Power Company, 434
Silver King Creek, 539–545
Simpson, Alan, 156
Singapore, wildlife import ban, 310, 311
Single-lethal-dose bait, 231, 232
Sister Reserve System, 517
Sitka black-tailed deer, Tongass National
    Forest, 275
Small Reclamation Projects Act of 1956,
    reauthorization, 219
Snake River Birds of Prey Natural Area, 4
Snow goose, 96
Snowshoe hare, and lynx population,
    412–414, 419
Society for Range Management, 34
Sodium monofluoroacetate, *see*
    Compound 1080
Soil Conservation Service, water projects,
    202
Soil scientists, 43, 44
Soils management, 43, 44
Southern pine forest, red-cockaded
    woodpecker, 478–493

Southern sea otter, 456–477
  census of, 463, 465
  commercial exploitation of, 463
  contemporary problems regarding,
    463–467
  diet of, 460
  distribution and abundance of, 462, 463
  drowning of in gill nets, 172, 173, 466,
    470–472
  economic importance of, 461, 462
  as endangered species, 462, 463
  environmental impact statement
    regarding, 469
  fairway system of travel lanes, effect
    of on, 468, 469
  foraging behavior of, 459, 460
  fur of, 458, 459
  historical perspective on, 462–467
  illegal shooting of, 467, 472
  interaction of with marine
    communities, 460, 461
  and kelp, 458, 460, 461
  legal status of, 463
  management of, 467–470
  Minerals Management Service and,
    468
  morphology of, 458
  and nearshore commercial set-net
    halibut fishery, 461, 462
  oil spill, risk to from, 462, 463,
    466–469, 471, 472
  physiology of, 458, 459
  population growth rate of, 463, 465
  prognosis for, 471
  range of
    historic and current, 457, 458
    rate of expansion of, 463, 464
  recommendations regarding, 471, 472
  recovery plan for, 464, 467, 468
  reintroduction controversy regarding,
    154, 155
  reproduction of, 459
  sea urchin predation by, 460
  shark attack on, 467
  shellfishing industry, impact of on,
    461, 471
  species
    description of, 457–460
    significance of, 460–462
  status review, 1984, 464, 466
  tourist industry and, 462
  translocation of, 157, 173, 469–471
  zonal management program for, 471,
    472

South Korea, whaling, 167, 174
Soviet Union
  walrus hunting, 361, 363, 365, 366
  whaling, 166
Species conservation, Fish and Wildlife
  Service, 63, 68
Sport Fish Restoration Account, 72
Spotted owl, 11
  Alternative F, 271
  Audubon's independent panel of
    scientists, 270
  Bureau of Land Management
    management, 272
  Congressional action on, 272, 273
  Forest Service guidelines regarding,
    270–272
  funding for, 335, 336
  habitat available for, 267, 271
  information on, lack of, 269, 270
  as management indicator species, 268,
    269
  management plan for, 270
  outlook for, 273
  population of, 267, 268
  threatened or endangered species,
    listing of, 273
Stacy Dam and Reservoir, 157
Stafford, Robert, 205
Stampede Dam and Reservoir,
  429–435
State Fishing and Boating Statistics,
  Projected Plans for Wallop-Breaux
  Funds, 73
*Steamboaters v. The Federal Energy
  Regulatory Commission, The,* 127,
  128
Steelhead trout, 122
Steel-shot zone, 86–88
Stevens, Ted, 143, 144
Stevens amendment, 86
Stillwater National Wildlife Management
  Area, 245, 247
Striped bass
  commercial catch of, 116
  conservation of, 116–118
  female fish, catch restriction, 117,
    118
  Hudson River, 127
  minimum-length catch requirement
    for, 117
  recreational catch of, 117
Striped Bass Emergency Council, 117
Strychnine, 236
Studds, Gerry, 118

Subsistence hunting
  Alaskan geese, 103, 104
  seals, 170
  whales, 168
Suisun Marsh, 219
Superfund, 116
Surplus-crop penalty, 210, 218
Swampbuster provision,
  commencement of wetland
    conversion, 182, 183
  definition of converted wetland, 183
Sybille Wildlife Research Unit, black-
  footed ferret, 451–454
Sylvatic plague, 450
Symms, Steven, 156

Tall Timbers Research Station, 487
Tauzin, Billy, 137
Tax code change, 102
Tax Reform Act of 1986, 102
  wetland protection, 181, 183, 184
Taylor Grazing Act, 5, 6, 33
Tellico Dam, 148
Ten Thousand Island National Wildlife
  Refuge, 257–259
Tennessee–Tombigbee Waterway, 200,
  206
Tennessee Valley Authority, water
  projects, 202
Terr Onne Corporation, 251, 252, 262
TEX, 296
Theodore Roosevelt National Park, 299
Timber harvest
  Bureau of Land Management, 272
  Caribbean National Forest, 283, 284
  National Forest System, 266
  old-growth, and spotted owl, 267–273
Timber management, Tongass National
  Forest, 273–277
Timber program, Forest Service budget,
  332–334, 337–339
Timber sale
  below-cost, 285, 286
  Resources Planning Act, 1985, 280
Tongass National Forest, timber
  management, 273–277
Tongass Supply Fund, 274, 276, 277
Topa-Topa, 147
Toxaphene, in fish, 115
Toxic collar, 231, 232
Toxic contamination
  and fish, 114–116
  national wildlife refuges, 243–248

Toxic Substances Control Act, 116
*Track 12, Inc., v. District Engineer*, 197
Trapping, *see also* Hunting
  lynx, 416–420
  in national parks, 303, 304
Trawling Efficiency Device, 139, 140
Treasury Department, multilateral
  development banks, influence on,
    313–317
*Trifolium stoloniferum*, see Running
  buffalo clover
Tropical rainforest
  biological diversity of, 317, 318
  destruction of, 308, 311, 312
Truckee Meadows, 429, 431, 433
Truckee River, 427–435
Tule elk, 494, 499–501
Tuna
  fishery conservation act, 135, 136
  fishing, capture of porpoises, 170–172
  Mexican, embargo, 172
Two Forks Dam and Reservoir, 214

Udall, Morris K., 255, 277
University of Idaho Wilderness Center,
  294
Upland-game-bird habitat, 25
Upper Mississippi Management Act of
  1986, 215
Upper Mississippi River System
  contaminant study, 248
  water project mitigation, 205, 206
Upper Ouachita National Wildlife
  Refuge, 262
*Ursus americanus*, *see* Black bear
*U.S. v. Akers*, 197
*U.S. v. Denver*, 297, 298
*U.S. v. Dion*, 158
*U.S. v. Moore et al.*, 304
*U.S. v. Oregon*, 126
*U.S. v. Riverside Bauview Homes*, 194
*U.S. v. Sohappy*, 125, 126
*U.S. v. Washington* (759 F.2nd 1353), 126
*U.S. v. Washington* (761 F.2nd 1404), 126
U.S. Agency for International
  Development funds, 318
U.S. Commissioner of Fish and Fisheries,
  107
U.S. Fish and Wildlife Service, *see* Fish
  and Wildlife Service
U.S. Forest Service, *see* Forest Service
U.S. Geological Survey, 54
Utah Wilderness Coalition, 54

Valley Forge National Historic Park, 301
Vertebrate Control Agents task force, 233

Wade, Dr. Dale A., 226
Wallop-Breaux Fund, *see* Aquatic
    Resources Trust Fund
Walrus, 357–368
    annual take, 363
    Atlantic, 357
    computer modeling and, 365
    diet of, 360
    distribution of, 359
    historical perspective on, 361
    hunting of, 361–364
    Laptev, 357
    management of, 363, 364
        with Soviet Union, 365, 366
    migration of, 359
    monitoring of, 363–365
    offshore oil drilling, effect of on, 365
    Pacific, 357–368
    physical characteristics of, 358, 359
    population of, density-dependent
        change, 362
    productivity of, 362, 363
    prognosis for, 364
    recommendations regarding, 364–366
    reproduction of, 359, 360
    species
        description of, 357–360
        significance of, 360, 361
    tusks of, 358, 360
Water clarity and quality, measurement
    of, 106
Water diversion, from Western rivers,
    150
Water flow, critical, protection, 152
Waterfowl habitat
    boreal forest, 94
    prairie, 94, 95, 97
Water projects
    adverse environmental effects of, 201,
        202
    agency roles in, 203
    appropriations limit to, 218
    conservation and, 210–212
    cost sharing of, 207–209, 215
    deauthorization of, 215
    economics of, 207–210
    federal agencies responsible for, 202
    funding of, 208, 215–217
    harbor-deepening, 215
    inland waterways, 215

legal developments, 220
legislative developments, 214–219
long-term offsite impact of, 212, 213
mitigation of, 203–207, 215, 218
moratorium on, *de facto*, 208
new habitat creation by, 202
public trust doctrine and, 220
spending for, 202, 203
state and private construction, 209
urban water development, 210
Western landscape, 201
Western water rights, 210–212
and wildlife, 201–221
Water quality, national wildlife refuges,
    243–248
Water Resources Development Act of
    1986, 205, 206, 214–216
Water Resources Policy Act of 1985, 193
Water rights
    appropriation system, 46, 47
    federal, 297
    National Park Service, 297, 298
    non-reserved, 48
    policy change, 49
    prior appropriation doctrine, 211, 297
    Pyramid Lake Paiute Tribe, 428, 429,
        434, 435
    reserved, 47, 48
    Western, 210–212
Watershed management, 44–46
Watershed Protection and Flood
    Prevention Act of 1954, 202
Water use
    inventory, 46
    for stock, 48, 49
Watt, James, 35, 55
Western Governors Association, 211
Westway highway project, 127
Wetlands
    acquisition of, 98, 99
    agricultural conversion of, 180–184,
        197
    artifically created, 197
    assessment of, methodology for, 191
    conversion potential of in critical
        problem areas, 182
    ecological function of, 179
    inventory of, 98, 100
    isolated, jurisdiction over, 195, 196
    loss of, rate of, 180
    Mississippi alluvial plain, 98, 100
    mitigation of
        Attleboro mall, 186, 187
        compliance with, 190

Wetlands (*cont.*)
  outdoor recreation and, 99
  ownership of, 180
  prairie-pothole region, 98, 100
  priority conservation plan for, 99
  protection of, 95–97
  regulation of, 180
  species occurring in, 179
Wetlands Loan Act
  appropriations, 323, 325, 327, 328,
    330, 331
  extension of, 193, 259
  migratory bird habitat, 99
Wetlands protection programs
  legal developments, 193–198
  legislation, 193
  National Wetlands Inventory, 191
  permit recommendations, studies,
    188–191
  removing federal incentives for
    wetlands destruction, 180–184
  Section 404 permit program,
    environmental guidelines
    disputed, 184–188
  solid waste regulation, 192
  up-front planning, 191, 192
Wetlands Trust, establishment, 217
Whale status chart, 169
Whaling
  commercial, 164–168
  Japanese, 165, 168
  Norwegian, 166
  prognosis, 167, 168
  sanctions, discretionary nature of,
    174
  with scientific research permits, 166,
    167
  Sea World permit overturned, 174, 175
  Soviet, 166
  subsistence, 168
White-fronted goose, 96
White-tailed deer, 302
Whooping crane, snow geese hunting,
    250, 251
Wild and Scenic Rivers Act, 204
Wild and Scenic Rivers System, 50
Wilderness
  coordinators, 294
  human-caused change indicators, 294
  legislation, 286, 287
  management, 56
  study, 53–56
    area management, 56, 57
  water rights, 47

Wilderness Act
  Bureau of Land Management, 56
  timber harvest, 266, 287
  wetland protection, 180
Wilderness management, National Park
    Service, 293, 294
Wilderness Management and Policy, Task
    Force, 293, 294
Wilderness Society, forest management
    reform, 274
Wildlife agency, state, federal aid, 62
Wildlife and fish habitat management
  budget, 27
  contribution, private, 28
  endangered and threatened species
    protection, 26, 27
  habitat management, 26
  projects, 25
  riparian area management, 28–30
  staffing, 27, 28
  volunteers, 28
  wildlife data and expertise, 25, 26
Wildlife conservation, federal grants,
    61–79
Wildlife Conservation Fund of America,
    The, 1980, 62
Wildlife education, 486
Wildlife habitat, protected with federal
    assistance, 63–67
Wildlife management area, federal aid
    grant, 66, 67
Wildlife planning, 69–71
Wildlife refuge, *see also* National
    Wildlife Refuge System
  federal aid grant, 66, 67
Wind Cave National Monument,
    299
Winnemucca lake, 427, 429
*Winters v. the United States*, 435
Wood duck, 380–397
  breeding of, 383–387
  clutch size of, 385
  current trends of, 393, 394
  diet of, 389, 390
  dump nesting of, 385
  egg laying of, 384, 385
  flapper stage of, 387
  flocking of, 388, 389
  habitat of, 394–396
  historical perspective on, 391–393
  hunting of, 390–393, 395, 396
  incubation of, 385, 386
  management of, 394, 395
  migration of, 389

molt of leading into eclipse plumage, 387, 388
  as national symbol, 390
  nest house of, 383, 386, 393, 396
  nesting success of, 386
  nesting time of, 383, 384
  physical characteristics of, 381, 382
  prognosis for, 395, 396
  range of, 382, 383
  recommendations regarding, 396
  research on, 393, 394
  roosting behavior of, 388
  species
    description of, 381–390
    significance of, 390, 391
  survival study on, 394
  young, 386, 387
Woodrat, Key Largo, 153
Working Group on Mulilateral Assistance, 313

World Bank, 308, 312–317
  demonstration against, 316
  lending in 1985, 314
  Office of Environmental and Scientific Affairs, 314
  U.S. voting power in, 315, 316
World Conservation Strategy, 318
Wyoming Game and Fish Department, Sybille Wildlife Research Unit, 451–454
*Wyoming v. Nebraska*, 220

Yazoo pumping station, 208, 209
Yellowleg, 238
Yellowstone National Park
  bison, 300
  Fishing Bridge area, 302
  wolf reintroduction, 301
Yosemite National Park, bighorn sheep, 298, 299
Yukon-Kuskokwim Delta, 103, 104